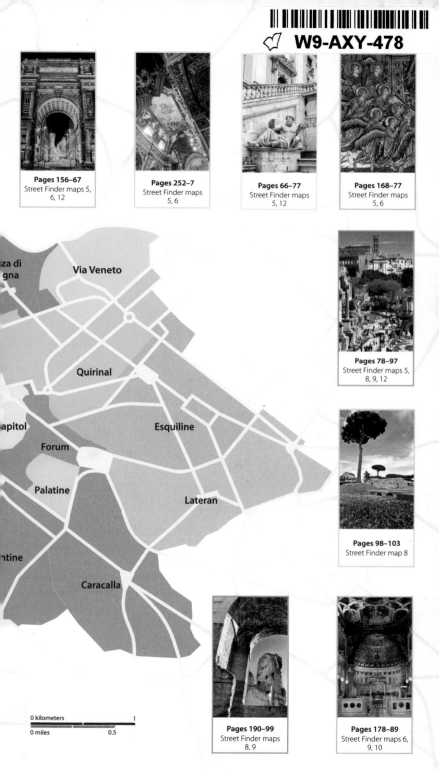

W9-AXY-478

Pages 156–67
Street Finder maps 5, 6, 12

Pages 252–7
Street Finder maps 5, 6

Pages 66–77
Street Finder maps 5, 12

Pages 168–77
Street Finder maps 5, 6

Pages 78–97
Street Finder maps 5, 8, 9, 12

Pages 98–103
Street Finder map 8

Pages 190–99
Street Finder maps 8, 9

Pages 178–89
Street Finder maps 6, 9, 10

za di
gna

Via Veneto

Quirinal

apitol

Forum

Esquiline

Palatine

Lateran

ntine

Caracalla

0 kilometers 1

0 miles 0.5

EYEWITNESS TRAVEL

ROME

EYEWITNESS TRAVEL

ROME

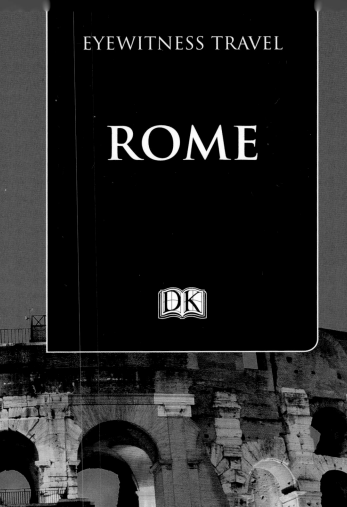

LONDON, NEW YORK,
MELBOURNE, MUNICH AND DELHI
www.dk.com

Project Editor Fiona Wild
Art Editor Annette Jacobs
Editors Ferdie McDonald, Mark Ronan, Anna Streiffert
Designer Lisa Kosky
Design Assistant Marisa Renzullo
Picture Research Catherine O'Rourke
Research in Rome Sam Cole
DTP Editor Siri Lowe

Main Contributors
Olivia Ercoli, Ros Belford, Roberta Mitchell

Photographers
John Heseltine, Mike Dunning, Kim Sayer

Illustrators
Studio Illibill, Kevin Jones Associates, Martin Woodward, Robbie Polley

This book was produced with the assistance of
Websters International Publishers.

Printed and bound by
South China Printing Co. Ltd., China

First American edition 1993
13 14 15 16 10 9 8 7 6 5 4 3 2 1

Published in the United States by DK Publishing,
375 Hudson Street, New York, New York 10014

Reprinted with revisions
2001, 2002, 2003, 2004, 2005, 2006, 2007, 2008, 2009,
2010, 2011, 2012, 2013

Copyright 1993, 2013 © Dorling Kindersley Limited, London
A Penguin Company

Published in Great Britain by Dorling Kindersley Limited.
A catalog record for this book is available from the Library of Congress.
ISSN: 1542-1554
ISBN: 978-1-46540-053-6

Floors are referred to throughout in accordance with American usage;
ie the "first floor" is the floor at ground level.

MIX
Paper from
responsible sources
FSC™ C018179

The information in this
DK Eyewitness Travel Guide is checked annually.
Every effort has been made to ensure that this book is as up- to-date as possible at
the time of going to press. Some details, however, such as telephone numbers,
opening hours, prices, gallery hanging arrangements and travel information, are
liable to change. The publishers cannot accept responsibility for any consequences
arising from the use of this book, nor for any material on third party websites, and
cannot guarantee that any website address in this book will be a suitable source of
travel information. We value the views and suggestions of our readers very highly.
Please write to: Publisher, DK Eyewitness Travel Guides, Dorling Kindersley, 80
Strand, London WC2R 0RL, UK, or email: travelguides@dk.com.

Front cover main image: Colosseum, Rome

◀ The Colosseum by night

Contents

Colosseum

Introducing Rome

Moses by Michelangelo in
San Pietro in Vincoli

Fresco in Villa Farnesina

Rome Area by Area

The Tempietto

Arch of Titus

Travelers' Needs

Mosaic in Santa Prassede

Survival Guide

Outdoor café in Santa Maria in Trastevere

The basilica of St. Peter's in Vatican City

HOW TO USE THIS GUIDE

This Eyewitness Travel Guide helps you get the most from your stay in Rome with the minimum of practical difficulty. The opening section, *Introducing Rome*, locates the city geographically, sets modern Rome in its historical context, and explains how Roman life changes through the year. *Rome at a Glance* is an overview of the city's attractions. The main sightseeing section, *Rome Area by Area,* starts on page 64. It describes all the important sights with maps, photographs, and detailed illustrations. In addition, nine planned walks take you to parts of Rome you might otherwise miss.

Carefully researched tips for hotels, shops and markets, restaurants and cafés, sports and entertainment are found in *Travelers' Needs*, and the *Survival Guide* has advice on everything from mailing a letter to catching the Metro.

Finding Your Way Around the Sightseeing Section

Each of the sixteen sightseeing areas in the city is color-coded for easy reference. Every chapter opens with an introduction to the part of Rome it covers, describing its history and character, followed by a Street-by-Street map illustrating the heart of the area. Finding your way around each chapter is made simple by the numbering system used throughout. The most important sights are covered in detail in two or more full pages.

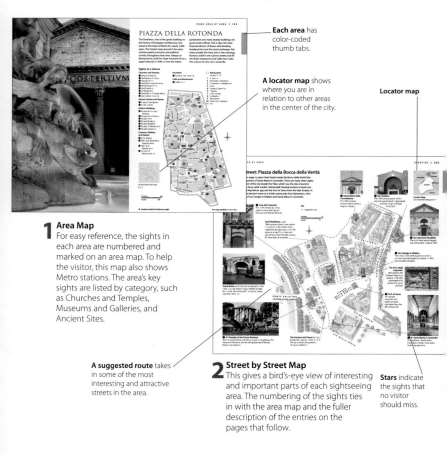

Each area has color-coded thumb tabs.

A locator map shows where you are in relation to other areas in the center of the city.

Locator map

1 Area Map
For easy reference, the sights in each area are numbered and marked on an area map. To help the visitor, this map also shows Metro stations. The area's key sights are listed by category, such as Churches and Temples, Museums and Galleries, and Ancient Sites.

A suggested route takes in some of the most interesting and attractive streets in the area.

2 Street by Street Map
This gives a bird's-eye view of interesting and important parts of each sightseeing area. The numbering of the sights ties in with the area map and the fuller description of the entries on the pages that follow.

Stars indicate the sights that no visitor should miss.

Rome Area Map

The colored areas shown on this map (see inside front cover) are the sixteen main sightseeing areas of Rome – each covered in a full chapter in Rome Area by Area (pp64–257). They are highlighted on other maps throughout the book. In Rome at a Glance (pp44–59), for example, they help locate the top sights. They are also used to help you find the locations of the nine guided walks (p275).

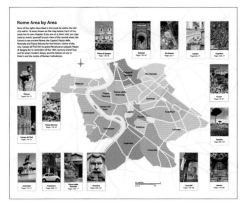

Numbers refer to each sight's location on the area map and its place in the chapter.

Practical information provides everything you need to know to visit each sight. Map references pinpoint the sight's location on the Street Finder map (see pp388–411).

The facade of each major sight is shown to help you spot it quickly.

The visitors' checklist gives all the practical information needed to plan your visit.

3 Detailed information

All the important sights in Rome are described individually. They are listed in order following the numbering on the area map at the start of the section. Practical information includes a map reference, opening hours, and telephone numbers. The key to the symbols is on the back flap.

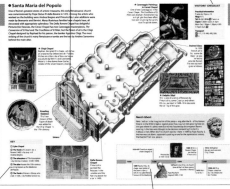

Numbered circles point out major features of the sight has listed in key.

4 Rome's major sights

Historic buildings are dissected to reveal their interiors; museums and galleries have color-coded floorplans to help you find the most important exhibits.

A timeline charts the key events in the history of the building.

INTRODUCING ROME

GREAT DAYS IN ROME

Rome is a city packed with treasures and wonderful things to see and do. Its history can be traced in the crumbling columns of the ancient empire, the medieval alleys, Renaissance palaces, Baroque fountains, and elegant piazzas. Whether here for several days or just wanting a flavor of this great city, you need to make the most of your time. Over the following pages, you'll find itineraries for some of the best of Rome's attractions, arranged first by theme, and then by length of stay. Price guides on pages 10–11, include travel, food and admission for two adults, while family prices are for two adults and two children.

Teatro di Marcello and the trio of standing columns

Ancient Rome

Two adults
allow at least €150

- **Explore the Republic**
- **Lunch in medieval ambience**
- **Absorb Imperial grandeur**
- **See how the Caesars lived**

Morning
Cram highlights of the 1,000-year history of ancient Rome's Republic and Empire into one very full day. Start at its heart, the **Roman Forum** (see pp78–93), then spend an hour or so perusing some of its treasures inside the **Capitoline Museums** (see pp70–3). Stroll over to Largo della Torre Argentina to gaze upon the remains of three Republican-era temples and the crumbling brick steps of the 55 BC Baths of Pompey, where Julius Caesar was murdered, ending the Republican era. The Baths of Pompey complex included a theater that has now vanished, but some of its vaults survive in the foundations of the Campo de' Fiori area's medieval buildings – including the basement rooms of **Ristorante Da Pancrazio** (see p312), which serves excellent pasta.

Afternoon
Return to the core of ancient Rome past the Teatro di Marcello – model for the Colosseum – and the two tiny **Temples of the Forum Boarium** (see p205) in Piazza della Bocca della Verità. Go up Via del Velabro and skirt around the edge of the Forum. Head to the dank **Mamertine Prison** (see p93) to see where enemies of Rome were held and executed. Next, explore the ruins of Rome's Imperial era – the **Market and Forum of Trajan** (see pp90–91), and look down on the **Forums of Caesar**, **Augustus**, and **Nerva** (see pp92–3). At the end, you can admire the **Colosseum** (see pp94–5), built over Nero's former artificial lake. Stroll up the Via Sacra to roam the **Palatine Hill** (see pp99–103; entry for this and the Colosseum is included on the Forum ticket), peppered with original palatial homes.

Christian Rome

Two adults allow €140

- The Vatican Museums
- Picnic on the Piazza
- Mosaics and a Mithraic temple
- Holy (dinner) orders

Morning
Exploring the **Vatican Museums** (see pp232–45) can easily occupy a full morning. When you're hungry, leave the museum and walk four streets up Via Tunisi to shop for goodies at the outdoor market on Via Andrea Doria. Take them back to picnic on Piazza San Pietro.

Afternoon
Pop into **St. Peter's Basilica** (see pp228–31) to marvel at this capital of Christendom, then admire the glittering mosaics of **Santa Maria Maggiore** (see pp174–5). Afterward, visit **San Clemente** (see pp188–9), a gorgeous 12th-century church built atop a 4th-century one, which stands on an ancient Mithraic temple. You will find important works by Raphael, Bernini, Caravaggio, and Bramante in the church of **Santa Maria del Popolo** (see pp140–41).

Detail of the mosaics in Santa Maria Maggiore

Dolce & Gabbana store window in Piazza di Spagna

Enjoy the evening *passeggiata* (Rome's see-and-be-seen stroll along the Via del Corso) with a drink at one of the busy cafés flanking the piazza. Finish off by eating in a hearty trattoria **Al Duello** *(see p311)*, or the sophisticated seafood restaurant **La Pallacorda** *(see p313)*.

Art and Shopping

Two adults
allow at least €30

- **Fountains and piazzas**
- **National Gallery treasures**
- **Temples and boutiques**
- **Spanish Steps and the Trevi Fountain**

Morning
Start at the fruit and flower market of **Campo de' Fiori** *(see pp145–55)*, located around a statue of Giordano Bruno, who was burned at the stake in the Middle Ages. **Piazza Navona** *(see p118–29)*, with its Baroque fountains and excellent cafés, owes its oval shape to the ancient stadium beneath (a fragment is visible at its north end). Visit the collections of the National Gallery in the **Palazzo Altemps** *(see p129)*. Peek into the church of **San Luigi dei Francesi** *(see p124)* for the early Caravaggios, then duck into Corso del Rinascimento 40 to see the hidden fantasy facade on **Sant'Ivo alla Sapienza** *(see p124)*. Do not miss Rome's **Pantheon** *(see pp114–15)*, an ancient temple (now church), and **Santa Maria sopra Minerva** *(see p112)*, for its art. Try the cappuccinos at **Caffè Sant'Eustachio** *(see p322)*.

Afternoon
Cross the Via del Corso, and enjoy an afternoon's shopping in the chic boutiques of **Via Condotti** *(see p135)* and its tributaries fanning out from the base of the **Spanish Steps** *(see pp136–7)*. To end the day, treat yourself to some of Rome's best ice cream at **San Crispino** *(see p322)*, and wander over to the nearby **Trevi Fountain** *(see p161)* before it melts.

A Family Day

Family of 4 allow at least €200

- **Cycle in Villa Borghese park**
- **See puppets, creatures, and creepy crypts**
- **Cross the Tiber for medieval alleys and panoramic views**

Morning
Rent bikes in **Villa Borghese** park *(see pp260–61)* where, as well as exploring, you can visit the Etruscan Museum in **Villa Giulia** *(see pp264–5)* or the excellent **Galleria Borghese** *(see pp262–3; book ahead)*. If the kids need less art and more fun, take in Rome's zoo, the **Bioparco** *(see p261)*. If it's a Sunday, stop at **Pincio Gardens** *(see pp138–9)* for an open-air carousel and the San Carlino, one of Rome's few remaining puppet theaters, which puts on *Pulcinella* shows from 11am.

Afternoon
Return the bikes and stroll past the top of the **Spanish Steps** *(see pp136–7)* down Via Gregoriana, looking for the Palazzetto Zuccari at number 28, whose windows and doors are shaped into hideous creatures. Below Via Veneto's **Santa Maria della Concezione** *(see p256)* lies the creepy Capuchin Crypts, which are covered in mosaics made from the bones of monks. (Cappuccino coffee was named after the color of these friars' robes.)

At Piazza della Bocca della Verità, on the porch of **Santa Maria in Cosmedin** *(see p204)*, sits the Mouth of Truth, an ancient drain cover carved as a monstrous face. The story goes that if you tell a lie with your fingers in the mouth, it will bite them off. Head across the river to **Trastevere** *(see pp209–15)*, an area of twisting medieval alleys. Climb **Janiculum Hill** *(see pp217–19)* to enjoy the sweeping views of the city. Descend to Trastevere for a pizza at **Pizzeria Ivo** *(see p320)*.

View of Via Condotti from the top of the Spanish Steps

2 days in Rome

- Marvel at the treasures in the Vatican Museums
- See the sites of the ancient city, from the Colosseum to the Palatine
- Watch the world go by from the Spanish Steps

Day 1
Morning Buy tickets online to avoid the lines at the **Vatican Museums** (pp232–45), the largest art collection in the world. Admire Michelangelo's masterpieces in the **Sistine Chapel** (pp242–5), then head to the vast, ornate basilica, **St. Peter's** (pp228–31).

Afternoon Cross the river via the Ponte Vittorio Emmanuel II to the heart of the historic downtown. A brisk walk takes in all the major sights, from the Baroque splendor of **Piazza Navona** (p122) to the architectural marvel of the ancient **Pantheon** (pp114–15). Be sure to also visit the **Trevi Fountain** (p161) and the **Spanish Steps** (pp136–7).

Day 2
Morning Take a trip to the **Colosseum** (pp94–7), Rome's spectacular amphitheater, then take a stroll through the **Forum** (pp80–89), once the beating heart of the Empire. One ticket (buy at the entrance to the Forum) grants access to both

sites, as well as the **Palatine** (pp100–103), where Rome's emperors had their palaces. Don't miss the beautiful 2,000-year-old frescoes in the **House of Livia** (p103).

Afternoon Take the glass elevator to the top of the **Victor Emmanuel Monument** (p76) for some of the best views in town. From here, an easy walk will lead you via the ancient **Portico of Octavia** (p154) to **Campo de' Fiori** (p148) for some people-watching. Cross **Ponte Sisto** (p212) to the picturesque neighborhood of **Trastevere** (pp208–215) for dinner and a pleasant evening stroll.

3 days in Rome

- Be awed by the magificent interiors of the Pantheon
- Admire the art collection of the Borghese family
- Make a wish and throw a coin in the Trevi Fountain

Day 1
Morning A lifetime is not enough to see everything in the **Vatican Museums** (pp232–45), so focus on highlights such as awe-inspiring ancient sculpture the *Laocoön* (p237), and the Renaissance treasures in the **Raphael Rooms** (pp240–41). Finish your visit with the magnificent **Sistine Chapel** (pp242–45) and the grand basilica of **St. Peter's** (pp228–31).

Baroque Trevi Fountain, one of the most familiar sights of Rome

Afternoon A short walk from the Vatican is the imposing **Castel Sant'Angelo** (pp250–51). Cross Ponte Sant'Angelo to browse the antique shops lining **Via dei Coronari** (p128), then continue on to Rome's loveliest square, **Piazza Navona** (p122). Visit the **Pantheon** (pp114–15) for stunning architecture, before moving on to **Sant'Ignazio di Loyola** (p108) to see the *trompe l'oeil* paintings housed within.

Day 2
Morning Relive Rome's glorious past by roaming through the ancient paths, grandiose arches, and solitary columns of the **Forum** (pp80–89). Explore the **Palatine** (pp100–103), and if you have time, climb the terraces of the **Colosseum** (pp94–7).

Afternoon See layers of history at **San Clemente** (pp188–9), then walk across the **Circus Maximus** (p207) to the beautifully simple church **Santa Maria in Cosmedin** (p204). Bustling **Campo de' Fiori** (p148) and lively **Trastevere** (pp208–215) are a pleasant stroll away.

Day 3
Morning Reserve in advance to visit the magnificent **Museo e Galleria Borghese** (pp262–3), with its masterpieces by Bernini. Afterward, make your way to **Piazza del Popolo** (p139) with its towering obelisk and fantastic churches. Join the crowds on the **Spanish Steps** (pp136–7), then throw a coin in the **Trevi Fountain** (p161).

The Colosseum, where deadly gladiatorial combat and wild animal fights were once staged

Afternoon Stroll to the Capitol to visit the world's first public museum, **Palazzo Nuovo**, *(pp70–71)* for Greek and Roman sculpture, and the **Palazzo dei Conservatori** *(pp72–3)* for paintings by great artists such as Titian, Veronese, Rubens, and Caravaggio. Stop off at the nearby **Victor Emmanuel Monument** *(p76)* for some truly magnificent views of the city.

Santa Maria in Trastevere, with its 12th-century apse mosaic of the Coronation of the Virgin

5 days in Rome

- **View Michelangelo's stunning *Pietà* in St. Peter's**
- **Bike along the monument-lined Via Appia Antica**
- **Delight in Tivoli's ancient and Renaissance villas**

Day 1

Morning Walk in the footsteps of popes through the art-filled **Vatican Museums** *(pp232–45)* to the **Sistine Chapel** *(pp242–5)*. Take in the wonders of **St. Peter's** *(pp228–31)*, with Michelangelo's famous sculpture *Pietà*, his soaring dome, and Bernini's bronze masterpiece *baldacchino*. Take a tour of the Necropolis where St. Peter is buried.

Afternoon Visit the ancient, medieval, and Renaissance site of **Castel Sant'Angelo** *(pp250–51)*, before crossing the river to the French national church **San Luigi dei Francesi** *(p124)*, where three Caravaggio masterworks are on display.

Day 2

Morning Take the elevator to the top of the **Victor Emmanuel Monument** *(p76)* for wonderful views, and to check out the layout of the ruins of the **Forum** *(pp80–89)*, the **Palatine** *(pp100–103)*, and the **Colosseum** *(pp94–7)*. Then head down to see the ancient remains of these amazing historic sites close up.

Afternoon Marvel at the sheer enormity of the **Circus Maximus** *(p207)*. Just around the corner, find the Bocca della Verità in **Santa Maria in**

Cosmedin *(p204)*, and visit the well-preserved **Temples of the Forum Boarium** *(p205)*. Explore the much-recycled **Theater of Marcellus** *(p153)* and finish with a visit to the **Ghetto and Synagogue** *(p154)*. Look for a hidden gem, **Fontana delle Tartarughe** *(p152)*, nearby.

Day 3

Morning Stroll through leafy **Villa Borghese** *(p260)* to work up an appetite for the glorious art at the **Museo e Galleria Borghese** *(pp262–3)*. Check out the panoramic view from the **Pincio Gardens** *(p138)* before winding down to **Piazza del Popolo** *(p139)*. Explore the square's famous church, **Santa Maria del Popolo** *(pp140–41)*, with works by Caravaggio and Raphael. The elegant Rococo **Spanish Steps** *(pp136–7)* are just around the corner.

Afternoon Treat yourself to ice cream en route to the iconic **Trevi Fountain** *(p161)*. Continue your walk at a leisurely pace to the **Pantheon** *(pp114–15)* to explore its airy interiors. Next, visit the historic square **Campo de' Fiori** *(p148)* and walk over **Ponte Sisto** *(p212)* to gaze at medieval mosaics in **Santa Maria in Trastevere** *(p214–15)*.

Day 4

Morning Visit the lowest level of **San Clemente** *(pp188–9)*, where the ancient rites of Mithraism were practiced. Not far away, the **Baths of Caracalla** *(p199)* give an idea of ancient Roman bathing facilities.

Afternoon Ride a bike or take a walk along the **Via Appia Antica** *(p267)*, with sights along the way including the **Tomb of Cecilia Metella** *(p268)* and lots of spine-chilling catacombs.

Day 5

Morning Take a trip out of the city and explore the historic hill town of **Tivoli** *(p270)* and the surrounding area. Be sure to visit Renaissance **Villa d'Este** *(p270)*, with its world-famous gardens bursting with fountains and water features, sculptures and manicured hedges.

Afternoon

Wander the sprawling ruins of **Hadrian's Villa** *(p271)*, 4 miles (6 km) southwest of Tivoli, the emperor's 2nd-century AD summer retreat. It boasts pools, theaters, baths, libraries, and gymnasiums. The grounds of the villa are great for a picnic.

Corinthian columns of the Temple of Castor and Pollux, rebuilt in AD 6, in the Forum

Putting Rome on the Map

Since its foundation over 2,760 years ago on seven hills near the banks of the Tiber River, Rome has grown into a city of 3 million people covering 580 square miles (1,500 sq km) of central Italy. Within this area is the independent Vatican City State. Rome was made capital of the newly united Italy in 1870. It is about 17 miles (28 km) from the sea and has good rail and road links to nearby historic Italian towns and cities.

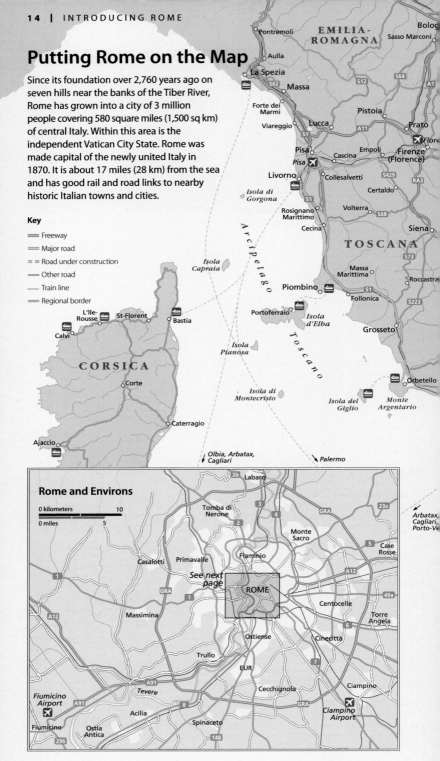

Key

- Freeway
- Major road
- Road under construction
- Other road
- Train line
- Regional border

Rome and Environs

0 kilometers 10
0 miles 5

For additional map symbols see back flap

Central Rome

This book divides central Rome into 16 areas and has further sections for sights on the outskirts of the city, including some day trips, as well as some suggested walks. Each of the main areas has its own chapter and contains a selection of sights that convey some of its history and distinctive character. The Forum will give you a glimpse of ancient Rome, while the Capitol, Piazza della Rotonda, and Piazza Navona represent the historic center. If you are interested in Renaissance palaces, make a point of visiting the fine examples in Campo de' Fiori. In Piazza di Spagna, you can find designer shops and hints of the Grand Tour, with its array of Renaissance, and Baroque art. A stop at the Vatican will reveal the impressive St. Peter's at the heart of Roman Catholicism.

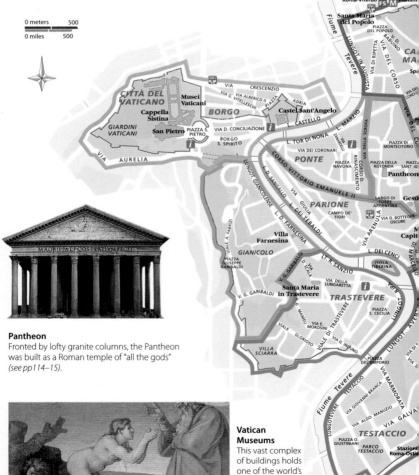

0 meters 500
0 miles 500

Pantheon
Fronted by lofty granite columns, the Pantheon was built as a Roman temple of "all the gods" (*see pp114–15*).

Vatican Museums
This vast complex of buildings holds one of the world's greatest collections of Classical and Renaissance art (*see pp232–45*).

Key to Symbols *see back flap*

Colosseum
One of Rome's most famous landmarks, the Colosseum *(see pp94–7)* was the venue for gladiatorial and animal fights. These provided a gory spectacle for Rome's citizens, up to 55,000 of whom would cram into the amphitheater at one time.

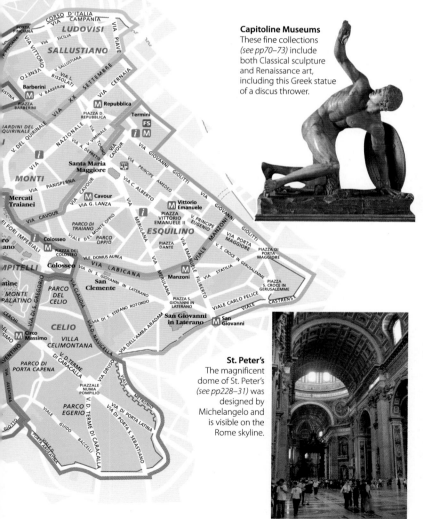

Capitoline Museums
These fine collections *(see pp70–73)* include both Classical sculpture and Renaissance art, including this Greek statue of a discus thrower.

St. Peter's
The magnificent dome of St. Peter's *(see pp228–31)* was designed by Michelangelo and is visible on the Rome skyline.

THE HISTORY OF ROME

One of the most ancient cities in Europe, Rome was founded over 2,760 years ago. Since then it has been continuously inhabited, and, as the headquarters first of the Roman Empire and then of the Catholic Church, it has had an immense impact on the world. Many European languages are based on Latin; many political and legal systems follow the ancient Roman model; and buildings all around the world utilize styles and techniques perfected in ancient Rome. The city itself retains layers of buildings spanning over two millennia. Not surprisingly, all this history can seem a little overwhelming.

Rome began as an Iron Age hut village, founded in the mid-8th century BC. In 616, the Romans' sophisticated Etruscan neighbors seized power, but were ousted in 509, when Rome became a Republic. It conquered most of the rest of Italy, then turned its attentions overseas, and by the 1st century BC ruled Spain, North Africa, and Greece. The expansion of the Empire provided opportunities for power-hungry individuals, and the clashing of egos led to the collapse of democracy. Julius Caesar ruled for a time as dictator, and his nephew Octavian became Rome's first emperor, assuming the title Augustus. During the reign of Augustus, Christ was born, and though Christians were persecuted until the 4th century AD, the new religion took hold and Rome became its main center.

Even though it was the seat of the papacy, during the Middle Ages Rome went into decline. The city recovered spectacularly in the mid-15th century, and for over 200 years was embellished by the greatest artists of the Renaissance and the Baroque. Finally, in 1870, Rome became the capital of the newly unified Italy.

15th-century map of Rome
from the north

◀ Detail from 2nd-century AD Roman mosaic from the Temple of Fortune in Palestrina

Rome's Early Development

According to the historian Livy, Romulus founded Rome in 753 BC. Some time later, realizing his tribe was short of females, he invited the neighboring Sabines to a festival, and orchestrated the mass abduction of their women. Although Livy's account is pure legend, there is evidence that Rome was founded around the middle of the 8th century BC, and that the Romans and Sabines united shortly afterward. Historical evidence also gives some support to Livy's claim that after Romulus's death, Rome was ruled by a series of kings, and that in the 7th century BC it was conquered by the Etruscans and ruled by the Tarquin family. Last of the dynasty was Tarquinius Superbus (Tarquin the Proud). His despotic rule led to the expulsion of the Etruscans and the founding of a Republic run by two annually elected consuls. The uprising was led by Lucius Junius Brutus, the model of the stern, patriotic Roman Republican.

Extent of the City
☐ 750BC   ▨ Today

Ceremonial trumpets

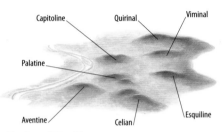

Capitoline   Quirinal   Viminal
Palatine
Aventine   Celian   Esquiline

The Seven Hills of Rome
By the 8th century BC, shepherds and farmers lived on four of Rome's seven hills. As the population grew, huts were built in the marshy valley later occupied by the Forum.

Iron Age Hut
Early settlers lived in wattle-and-daub huts. Traces of their foundations have been found on the Palatine.

Augur, digging foundation

Temple of Jupiter
This Renaissance painting by Perin del Vaga shows Tarquinius Superbus founding the Temple of Jupiter on the Capitol, the sacred citadel of Rome.

Etruscan jug (7th century BC)

750 BC Tarpeia betrays city to the Sabines

700 BC Approximate beginning of Etruscan period

800 BC

750

700

650

753 BC Legendary founding of Rome by Romulus, first of seven kings

715–713 BC King Numa Pompilius establishes 12-month calendar

659 BC Romans destroy rival city, Alba Longa

Romulus and Remus

The Legend of the She-Wolf
The evil king of Alba threw his baby nephews, Romulus and Remus, into the Tiber, but they were washed ashore and nursed by a she-wolf.

Apollo of Veio
Etruscan culture and religion were influenced by the Greeks. This 5th- or 6th-century statue of the Greek god Apollo comes from Veio and is in the Villa Giulia museum (see pp264–5).

Raven, guardian of the citadel

King Tarquin, holding stone worshipped as a thunderbolt

The Legend of Aeneas
Some Roman legends make the Trojan hero Aeneas the grandfather of Romulus and Remus.

Where to see Etruscan Rome

The Cloaca Maxima sewer still functions, but there are few other traces of Etruscan Rome. Most finds come from Etruscan sites outside Rome, like Tarquinia, with its tomb paintings of sumptuous banquets (see p273), but there are major collections in the Villa Giulia (pp264–5) and Vatican Museums (p236). The most famous object, however, is a bronze statue of the legendary she-wolf in the Capitoline Museums (p73). The Antiquarium Forense (p89) displays objects from the necropolis that once occupied the site of the Roman Forum.

Funeral urns shaped like huts were used for cremation from the mid-8th century BC.

Etruscan jewelry, like this 7th-century BC gold filigree brooch, was used for cremation. Treasures of this kind have given the Etruscans a reputation for luxurious living.

600 BC Possible date of construction of Cloaca Maxima sewer

565 BC Traditional date of the Servian Wall around Rome's seven hills

534 BC King Servius murdered

510 BC Temple of Jupiter consecrated on the Capitoline hill

Statue of Jupiter

600   **550**   **500**

578 BC Servius Tullius Etruscan king

16 BC Tarquinius Priscus, first Etruscan king. Forum and Circus Maximus established

509 BC L. J. Brutus expels Etruscans from Rome and founds the Republic

L. J. Brutus

507 BC War against Etruscans. Horatius defends wooden bridge across Tiber

Kings, Consuls, and Emperors

Rome had over 250 rulers in the 1,200 years between its foundation by Romulus and AD 476, when the last emperor was deposed by the German warrior Odoacer. Romulus was the first of seven kings, overthrown in 509 BC when Rome became a Republic. Authority was held by two annually elected consuls, but provision was made for the appointment of a dictator in times of crisis. In 494 BC, the office of Tribune was set up to protect the plebeians from injustice at the hands of their patrician rulers. Roman democracy, however, was always cosmetic. It was discarded completely in 27 BC, when absolute power was placed in the hands of the emperor.

Romulus, his twin Remus, and the she-wolf who nursed them

205 BC Scipio Africanus

218 BC Quintus Fabius Maximus

456 BC Lucius Quintus Cincinnatus

***c.* 753–715 BC** Romulus

800 BC	700	600	500	400	300
SEVEN KINGS			REPUBLIC		
800 BC	700	600	500	400	300

***c.* 715–673 BC** Numa Pompilius

396 BC Marcus Furius Camillus

***c.* 673–641 BC** Tullus Hostilius

***c.* 509 BC** Lucius Junius Brutus and Horatius Pulvillus

***c.* 641–616** BC Ancus Marcius

***c.* 534–509 BC** Tarquinius Superbus

***c.* 579–534 BC** Servius Tullius

616–579 BC Tarquinius Priscus

Tarquinius Priscus consulting an augur

Julius Caesar, whose rise to power marked the end of the Roman Republic

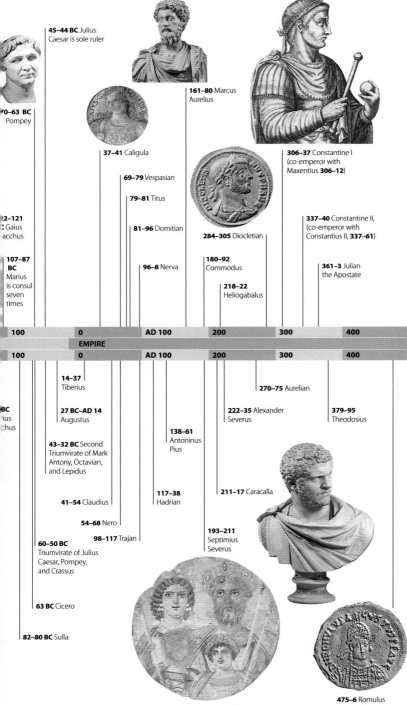

45–44 BC Julius Caesar is sole ruler

70–63 BC Pompey

161–80 Marcus Aurelius

37–41 Caligula

306–37 Constantine I (co-emperor with Maxentius **306–12**)

69–79 Vespasian

79–81 Titus

337–40 Constantine II, (co-emperor with Constantius II, **337–61**)

81–96 Domitian

284–305 Diocletian

122–121 BC Gaius Gracchus

107–87 BC Marius is consul seven times

180–92 Commodus

96–8 Nerva

218–22 Heliogabalus

361–3 Julian the Apostate

| 100 | 0 | AD 100 | 200 | 300 | 400 |

EMPIRE

| 100 | 0 | AD 100 | 200 | 300 | 400 |

14–37 Tiberius

270–75 Aurelian

...BC ...ius ...chus

27 BC–AD 14 Augustus

222–35 Alexander Severus

379–95 Theodosius

43–32 BC Second Triumvirate of Mark Antony, Octavian, and Lepidus

138–61 Antoninus Pius

41–54 Claudius

54–68 Nero

117–38 Hadrian

211–17 Caracalla

98–117 Trajan

193–211 Septimius Severus

60–50 BC Triumvirate of Julius Caesar, Pompey, and Crassus

63 BC Cicero

82–80 BC Sulla

Septimius Severus and family

475–6 Romulus Augustulus

The Roman Republic

By the mid-2nd century BC, Rome controlled the western Mediterranean, policing and defending it with massive armies. The troops had more loyalty to the generals than to distant politicians, giving men like Marius, Sulla, Pompey, and Caesar the muscle to seize political power. Meanwhile, peasants, whose land had been destroyed during the invasion of Hannibal in 219 BC, had flooded into Rome. They were followed by slaves and freedmen from conquered lands such as Greece, swelling the population to half a million. There was plenty of work for immigrants, constructing roads, aqueducts, markets, and temples, financed by taxes on Rome's expanding trade.

Extent of the City

☐ 400 BC   ◼ Today

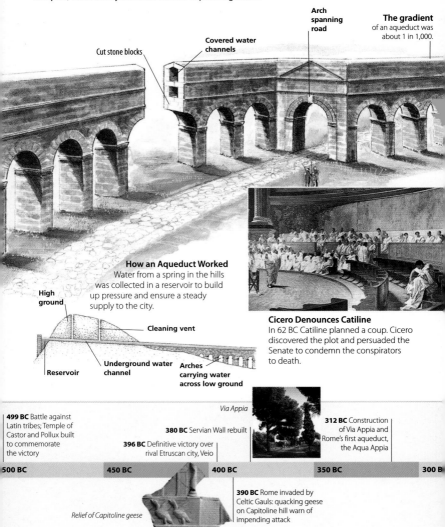

Arch spanning road

The gradient of an aqueduct was about 1 in 1,000.

Covered water channels

Cut stone blocks

How an Aqueduct Worked
Water from a spring in the hills was collected in a reservoir to build up pressure and ensure a steady supply to the city.

High ground

Cleaning vent

Reservoir

Underground water channel

Arches carrying water across low ground

Cicero Denounces Catiline
In 62 BC Catiline planned a coup. Cicero discovered the plot and persuaded the Senate to condemn the conspirators to death.

Via Appia

499 BC Battle against Latin tribes; Temple of Castor and Pollux built to commemorate the victory

380 BC Servian Wall rebuilt

396 BC Definitive victory over rival Etruscan city, Veio

312 BC Construction of Via Appia and Rome's first aqueduct, the Aqua Appia

| 500 BC | 450 BC | 400 BC | 350 BC | 300 B |

Relief of Capitoline geese

390 BC Rome invaded by Celtic Gauls: quacking geese on Capitoline hill warn of impending attack

Roman Street
In the 1st century BC, most buildings in Rome were made from brick and concrete. Only a few public buildings used marble.

Where to see Republican Rome

This fresco depicting a gang of slaves building a wall can be seen at the Museo Nazionale Romano *(see p165)*.

Aqueduct (2nd Century BC)
Rome owed much of its prosperity to its skilled civil engineers. When the city's wells were no longer sufficient, aqueducts were built to bring water from surrounding hills. Some aqueducts were more than 50 miles (80 km) long.

Arches for maintaining a constant gradient over low-lying land

Temple of Juno
The ruins of this 197 BC temple are embedded in the church of San Nicola in Carcere *(see p153)*. Romans consulted their gods before all important ventures.

The Temple of Saturn, first built in 497 BC, now consists of eight majestic columns overlooking the Forum at the end of the Via Sacra *(see p85)*.

Rome's loveliest Republican buildings are the two Temples of the Forum Boarium *(see p205)*. Four more temples can be seen in the Area Sacra of Largo Argentina *(p152)*. Most monuments from this period, however, lie underground. Only a few, like the Tomb of the Scipios *(p197)*, have been excavated. One of the bridges leading to Tiber Island *(p155)*, the Ponte Fabricio, dates from the 1st century BC and is still used by pedestrians.

Scipio Africanus
In 202 BC the Roman general Scipio defeated Hannibal. Rome replaced Carthage as master of the Mediterranean.

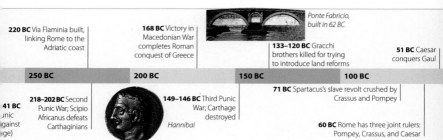

220 BC Via Flaminia built, linking Rome to the Adriatic coast

168 BC Victory in Macedonian War completes Roman conquest of Greece

Ponte Fabricio, built in 62 BC

133–120 BC Gracchi brothers killed for trying to introduce land reforms

51 BC Caesar conquers Gaul

250 BC   **200 BC**   **150 BC**   **100 BC**

...41 BC ...unic ...against ...ge)

218–202 BC Second Punic War; Scipio Africanus defeats Carthaginians

149–146 BC Third Punic War; Carthage destroyed

Hannibal

71 BC Spartacus's slave revolt crushed by Crassus and Pompey

60 BC Rome has three joint rulers: Pompey, Crassus, and Caesar

Imperial Rome

In 44 BC Caesar became dictator for life, only to be assassinated a month later. The result was 17 years of civil war, which ended only in 27 BC when Augustus became Rome's first emperor. The Empire expanded in fits and starts, but by the late 3rd century was so huge that Diocletian decided to share it between four emperors. Thanks to trade and taxes from its vast domains, Rome was the most magnificent city in the world, studded with the lavish buildings of emperors eager to advertise their civic munificence and military triumphs.

Extent of the City
☐ AD 250   ■ Today

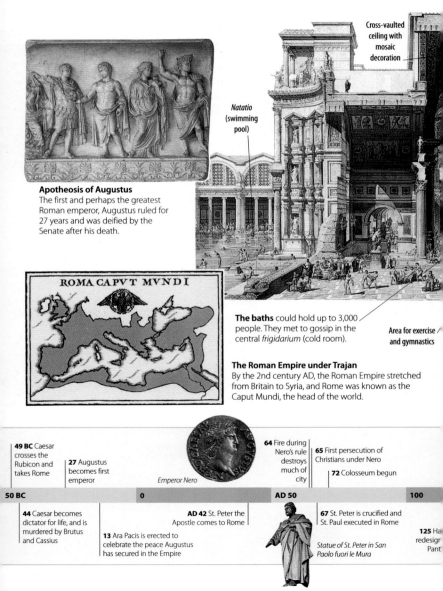

Cross-vaulted ceiling with mosaic decoration

Natatio (swimming pool)

Apotheosis of Augustus
The first and perhaps the greatest Roman emperor, Augustus ruled for 27 years and was deified by the Senate after his death.

ROMA CAPVT MVNDI

The baths could hold up to 3,000 people. They met to gossip in the central *frigidarium* (cold room).

Area for exercise and gymnastics

The Roman Empire under Trajan
By the 2nd century AD, the Roman Empire stretched from Britain to Syria, and Rome was known as the Caput Mundi, the head of the world.

---

49 BC Caesar crosses the Rubicon and takes Rome

27 Augustus becomes first emperor

Emperor Nero

64 Fire during Nero's rule destroys much of city

65 First persecution of Christians under Nero

72 Colosseum begun

| 50 BC | 0 | AD 50 | 100 |

44 Caesar becomes dictator for life, and is murdered by Brutus and Cassius

AD 42 St. Peter the Apostle comes to Rome

13 Ara Pacis is erected to celebrate the peace Augustus has secured in the Empire

Statue of St. Peter in San Paolo fuori le Mura

67 St. Peter is crucified and St. Paul executed in Rome

125 Ha redesign Pant

Roman Revelry
Banquets could last for up to 10 hours, with numerous courses, between which guests would retire to a small room to relax.

Where to see Imperial Rome

There are relics of Imperial Rome throughout the central city, some hidden below churches and palazzi, others, like the Forum (*see pp78–89*), the Palatine (*pp99–103*) and the Imperial Fora (*pp90–3*), fully excavated. The magnificence of the era, however, is best conveyed by the Pantheon (*pp114–15*) and the Colosseum (*pp94–7*).

Baths of Diocletian (AD 298)

Rome's public baths were not just places to keep clean. They also had bars, libraries, barber shops, brothels, and sports facilities.

The Arch of Titus (*p89*), erected in the Forum in AD 81, commemorates Emperor Titus's sack of Jerusalem in AD 70.

Tepidarium (warm room)

A relief of Mithras, a popular Persian god (3rd century AD), can be seen beneath the church of San Clemente (*pp188–9*).

Virgil (70–19 BC)
Virgil was Rome's greatest epic poet. His most famous work is the *Aeneid*, the story of the Trojan hero Aeneas's journey to the future site of Rome.

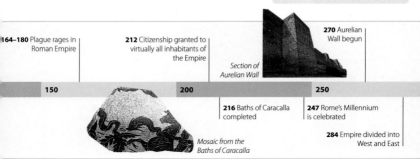

164–180 Plague rages in Roman Empire

212 Citizenship granted to virtually all inhabitants of the Empire

Section of Aurelian Wall

270 Aurelian Wall begun

150

200

250

216 Baths of Caracalla completed

247 Rome's Millennium is celebrated

284 Empire divided into West and East

Mosaic from the Baths of Caracalla

Early Christian Rome

In the 1st century AD, during the reign of Tiberius, a rebellious pacifist was crucified in a distant corner of the Empire. This was nothing unusual, but within a few years Jesus Christ and his teachings became notorious in Rome, his followers were perceived as a threat to public order, and many were executed. This was no deterrent, and the new religion spread through all levels of Roman society. When the Apostles Peter and Paul arrived in Rome, there was already a small Christian community, and in spite of continued persecution by the state, Christianity flourished. In AD 313 the Emperor Constantine issued an edict granting freedom of worship to Christians, and soon after founded a shrine on the site of St. Peter's tomb. This secured Rome's position as a center of Christianity, but in the 5th century the political importance of Rome declined and the city fell to Goths and other invaders.

Extent of the City
☐ AD 395   ▩ Today

St. Paul

Youthful, beardless representation of Christ

Santo Stefano Rotondo
This 17th-century engraving shows how a Roman temple *(top)* might have been transformed *(above)* into the 5th-century round church of Santo Stefano *(see p187).*

Classical-style border decorated with fruit

4th-Century Mosaic, Santa Costanza

Beautiful mosaics, often with palm trees and other oriental motifs suggesting Jerusalem, helped spread the message of early Christianity.

The Good Shepherd
The pagan image of a shepherd sacrificing a lamb became a Christian symbol.

c. **320** Building of first St. Peter's

356 Legendary founding of Santa Maria Maggiore

Gold solidus of Theodosius

410 Rome sacked by Alaric's Goths

455 Rome sacked again by Vandals

300   **350**   **400**   **450**

312 Control of Empire won by Constantine after battle at Milvian Bridge

Battle of the Milvian Bridge

380 Emperor Theodosius makes Christianity the official religion of the Roman Empire

395 Division of the Empire between Ravenna and Constantinople

422 Founding of Santa Sabina

Epigraph of Peter and Paul
This is one of hundreds of early Christian graffiti housed in the Lapidary Gallery of the Vatican (see p239).

Crucifixion, Santa Sabina
This 5th-century panel on the door of Santa Sabina (see p206) is one of the earliest known representations of the Crucifixion. Interestingly, Christ's cross is not actually shown.

St. Peter receiving peace from the Savior

Lambs symbolizing the Christian flock

Constantine's Cross
Constantine's vision of the True Cross during the Battle of the Milvian Bridge made him convert to Christianity.

Where to see Early Christian Rome

There are traces of early Christianity all over Rome. Many ancient churches were built over early Christian meeting places and sites of martyrdoms: among them San Clemente (see pp188–9), Santa Pudenziana (p173), and Santa Cecilia (p213). Outside the walls of the old city are miles of underground catacombs (pp267–8), many decorated with Christian frescoes, while the Vatican's Pio-Christian Museum (p238) has the best collection of early Christian art.

This figurine, carved out of bone, is embedded in the rock of the Catacombs of San Panfilo, just off the Via Salaria (see p56).

The Cross of Justin, in the Treasury of St. Peter's (p230), was given to Rome by the Emperor Justin II in AD 578.

A Byzantine image of St. Paul

496 Anastasius II is first pope to assume title Pontifex Maximus

475 Fall of Western Roman Empire; Byzantium becomes seat of Empire

500

550

590–604 Pope Gregory the Great strengthens the papacy

600

609 Pantheon is consecrated as a Christian church

630 Sant'Agnese fuori le Mura is built in Roman Byzantine style

The Papacy

The Pope is considered Christ's representative on earth, claiming his authority from St. Peter, the first Bishop of Rome. Though some popes have been great thinkers and reformers, the role has rarely been purely spiritual. In the Middle Ages, many popes were involved in power struggles with the Holy Roman Emperor. Renaissance popes like Julius II and Leo X, the patrons of Raphael and Michelangelo, lived as luxuriously as any secular prince. The popes listed here include all those who exercised significant political or religious influence, up as far as the end of the Counter-Reformation, when the power of the papacy began to wane.

St. Ludovic Kneels before Boniface *VIII* by Simone Martini

314–35 St. Sylvester I

590–604 St. Gregory the Great

Gregory the Great leading a procession to end the plague

955–64 John XII

222–30 St. Urban I

1227–41 Gregory IX

217–22 St. Callixtus I

496–8 Anastasius II

931–5 John XI

1216–27 Honorius III Savelli

891–6 Formosus

0   200   400   600   800   1000   120

PAPACY BASED IN ROME

0   200   400   600   800   1000   120

336 Mark

579–90 Pelagius II

1032–44, 1047–8 Benedict IX

352–66 Liberius

1073–85 St. Gregory VII

c. **88–97** St. Clement

608–15 St. Boniface IV

1099–1118 Paschal II

c. **42–67** St. Peter

731–41 St. Gregory III

1130–43 Innocent II

772–95 Adrian I

1154–9 Adrian IV

847–55 St. Leo IV

817–24 St. Paschal I

1198–1216 Innocent III

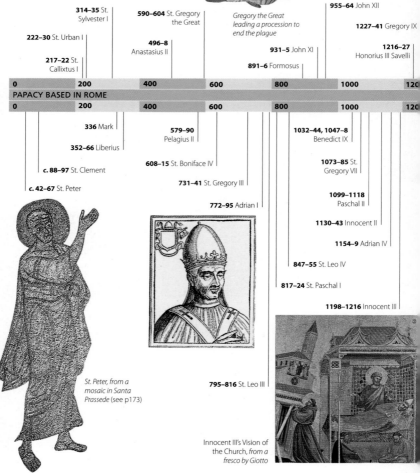

St. Peter, from a mosaic in Santa Prassede (see p173)

795–816 St. Leo III

Innocent III's Vision of the Church, *from a fresco by Giotto*

Portrait of Gregory XIII
by Lavinia Fontana

1560–65 Pius IV Medici

1555–9 Paul IV

1523–34
Clement VII Medici

1513–21 Leo X Medici

1492–1503
Alexander
VI Borgia

1484–92 Innocent
VIII Cybo

1471–84 Sixtus IV della Rovere

1464–71 Paul II Barbo

1458–64 Pius II
Piccolomini

1294–1303
Boniface VIII

1572–84 Gregory XIII Boncompagni

1670–76 Clement X Altieri

1667–9 Clement IX

1655–67 Alexander VII
Chigi

1605 Leo XI
Medici

1700–21 Clement XI

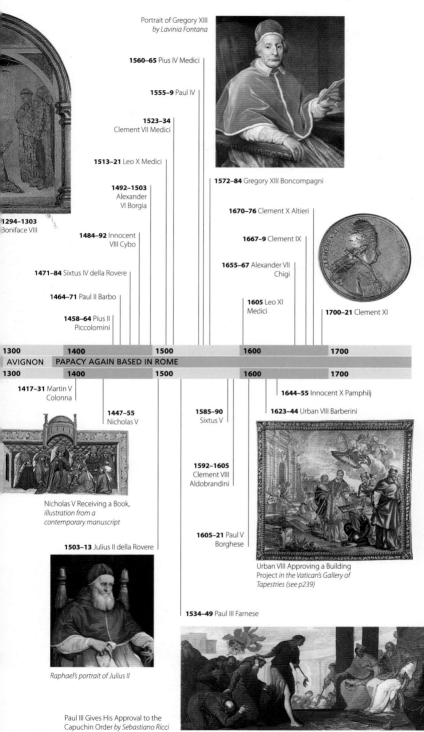

1300	1400	1500	1600	1700
AVIGNON	PAPACY AGAIN BASED IN ROME			
1300	1400	1500	1600	1700

1417–31 Martin V
Colonna

1447–55
Nicholas V

1585–90
Sixtus V

1592–1605
Clement VIII
Aldobrandini

1605–21 Paul V
Borghese

1644–55 Innocent X Pamphilj

1623–44 Urban VIII Barberini

1503–13 Julius II della Rovere

1534–49 Paul III Farnese

Nicholas V Receiving a Book,
*illustration from a
contemporary manuscript*

Raphael's portrait of Julius II

Urban VIII Approving a Building
Project *in the Vatican's Gallery of
Tapestries (see p239)*

Paul III Gives His Approval to the
Capuchin Order *by Sebastiano Ricci*

Medieval Rome

Supplanted by Constantinople as capital of the Empire in the 4th century, Rome was reduced to a few thousand inhabitants by the early Middle Ages, its power just a memory. In the 8th and 9th centuries, the growing importance of the papacy revived the city and made it once more a center of power. But continual conflicts between the pope and the Holy Roman Emperor soon weakened the papacy. The 10th, 11th, and 12th centuries were among the bleakest in Roman history: violent invaders left Rome poverty-stricken, and the constantly warring local barons tore apart what remained of the city. Despite this, the first Holy Year was declared in 1300 and thousands of pilgrims arrived in Rome. But by 1309 the papacy was forced to move to Avignon, leaving Rome to slide into further squalor and strife.

Extent of the City
☐ 1300   ▨ Today

San Giovanni in Laterano

Aurelian Wall

Charlemagne Crowned in St. Peter's
On Christmas Day in 800, Charlemagne was made "emperor of the Romans," ruler of a new Christian dominion to replace that of ancient Rome.

Trajan's Column

Column of Marcus Aurelius

Madonna and Child Mosaic
The Chapel of St. Zeno (817–24) in the church of Santa Prassede (see p173) has some of the best examples of Byzantine mosaics in Rome.

Medieval Plan of Rome
Maps like this one, illustrating the principal features of the city, were produced for pilgrims, the tourists of the Middle Ages.

725 King Ine of Wessex founds the first hostel for pilgrims in the Borgo

852 The Vatican is fortified with walls following a raid by Saracens

Emperor Otto I

961 King Otto the Great of Germany becomes first Holy Roman Emperor

700   **800**   **900**   **1000**

778 Charlemagne, King of the Franks, conquers Italy

800 Charlemagne crowned emperor in St. Peter's

880–932 Rome is ruled by two women, Theodora and then her daughter, Marozia

Stefaneschi Triptych (1315) Giotto and his pupils painted this triptych for Cardinal Stefaneschi as an altarpiece for St. Peter's. It is now in the Vatican Museums *(see p238)*.

Where to see Medieval Rome

Among the most interesting churches of the period are San Clemente, with a fine apse mosaic and Cosmati floor *(see pp188–9)*, Santa Maria in Trastevere *(pp214–15)* and Santa Maria sopra Minerva, Rome's only Gothic church *(p112)*. Santa Cecilia in Trastevere *(p213)* has a Cavallini fresco, and there is fine Cosmati work in Santa Maria in Cosmedin *(p204)*.

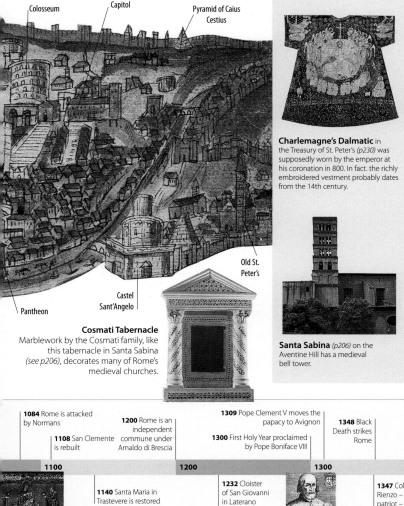

Colosseum Capitol Pyramid of Caius Cestius

Old St. Peter's

Castel Sant'Angelo

Pantheon

Cosmati Tabernacle Marblework by the Cosmati family, like this tabernacle in Santa Sabina *(see p206)*, decorates many of Rome's medieval churches.

Charlemagne's Dalmatic in the Treasury of St. Peter's *(p230)* was supposedly worn by the emperor at his coronation in 800. In fact. the richly embroidered vestment probably dates from the 14th century.

Santa Sabina *(p206)* on the Aventine Hill has a medieval bell tower.

1084 Rome is attacked by Normans

1108 San Clemente is rebuilt

1200 Rome is an independent commune under Arnaldo di Brescia

1309 Pope Clement V moves the papacy to Avignon

1300 First Holy Year proclaimed by Pope Boniface VIII

1348 Black Death strikes Rome

1100 **1200** **1300**

1140 Santa Maria in Trastevere is restored

Mosaic facade, Santa Maria in Trastevere (pp214–15)

1232 Cloister of San Giovanni in Laterano completed

Cola di Rienzo

1347 Cola di Rienzo – an Italian patriot – tries to restore the Roman Republic

Renaissance Rome

Pope Nicholas V came to the throne in 1447 determined to make Rome a city fit for the papacy. Among his successors, men like Julius II and Leo X eagerly followed his lead, and the city's appearance was transformed. The Classical ideals of the Renaissance inspired artists, architects and craftsmen, such as Michelangelo, Bramante, Raphael and Cellini, to build and decorate the churches and palaces of a newly confident Rome.

Extent of the City

☐ 1500   ☐ Today

Hemispherical dome

Balustrade of small columns

Classical colonnade of 16 Doric columns

School of Athens by Raphael
In this fresco *(see p241)* Raphael complimented many of his peers by representing them as ancient Greek philosophers. The building shown is based on a design by Bramante.

The Tempietto
The Tempietto (1502) at San Pietro in Montorio *(see p223)* was one of Bramante's first works in Rome. A simple, perfectly proportioned miniature Classical temple, it is a model of High Renaissance architecture.

Cosmati-style mosaic floor

Palazzo Caprini
Bramante's design had a strong influence on later Renaissance palazzi. Parts of the building survive in Palazzo dei Convertendi *(see p247)*.

1377 Papacy returns to Rome from Avignon under Pope Gregory XI

1409–15 Papacy moves to Pisa

1444 Birth of Bramante

1417 Pope Martin V ends the Great Schism in the papacy

1452 Demolition of old St. Peter's basilica begins

1350   **1400**   **1450**

1378–1417 The Great Schism, a division in the papacy in Avignon

Pope Martin V, reigned 1417–31

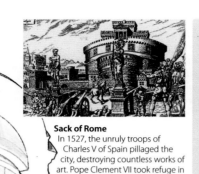

Sack of Rome
In 1527, the unruly troops of Charles V of Spain pillaged the city, destroying countless works of art. Pope Clement VII took refuge in Castel Sant'Angelo.

Pope Nicholas V
Nicholas ordered the demolition of the old St. Peter's.

Statue of St. Peter, believed to have been crucified on this site

Underground chapel

Where to see Renaissance Rome

The Campo de' Fiori area (see pp144–55) is full of grand Renaissance palazzi, especially along Via Giulia (pp278–9). Across the river stands the delightful Villa Farnesina (pp220–21). The most typical church of the period is Santa Maria del Popolo (pp140–41), and the best collection of Renaissance art is in the Vatican Museums (pp232–45). These include the Sistine Chapel (pp242–5) and the Raphael Rooms (pp240–41).

The Madonna di Foligno by Raphael (1511–12) is one of the fine Renaissance paintings in the Vatican Pinacoteca (p239).

The Pietà, commissioned for St. Peter's in 1501, was one of Michelangelo's first sculptures executed in Rome (p231).

1483 Birth of Raphael

1486 Building of Palazzo della Cancelleria

1519 Frescoes completed in Villa Farnesina

1527 Troops of Emperor Charles V sack Rome

Emperor Charles V

1500

irth of angelo

1508 Michelangelo begins painting the Sistine Chapel ceiling

1506 Pope Julius II orders start of work on new St. Peter's

1550

1547 Pope Paul III appoints Michelangelo architect of St. Peter's

Cumaean Sibyl, Sistine Chapel

Baroque Rome

By the 16th century, the Catholic Church had become immensely rich – one of the chief criticisms of the Protestant reformers. The display of grandeur and extravagance by the papal court contrasted sharply with the poverty of the people, and wealthy Roman society was characterized by sumptuous luxury and a ceaseless round of entertainment. To make the Catholic faith more appealing than Protestantism, scores of churches were built and monuments and fountains were erected to glorify the Holy See. The finest architects in the ornate, dramatic style of the Baroque were Bernini and Borromini.

Extent of the City
☐ 1645   ■ Today

Ceiling portraying heavenly scenes

Gian Lorenzo Bernini (1598–1680)
The favorite artist of the papacy, Bernini transformed Rome with his churches, palaces, statues, and fountains.

Monument to Pope Alexander VII
This Bernini tomb in St. Peter's (pp228–31) includes a skeleton brandishing an hourglass.

Tapestry of Pope Urban VIII
Bernini's most devoted patron, Pope Urban VIII Barberini (1623–44), is shown here receiving the homage of the nations.

Holy Family fresco

Pozzo Corridor
The use of perspective to create an illusion of depth and space was a favorite Baroque device. Andrea Pozzo painted this illusionistic corridor in the 1680s in the Rooms of St. Ignatius near the Gesù (see pp110–11).

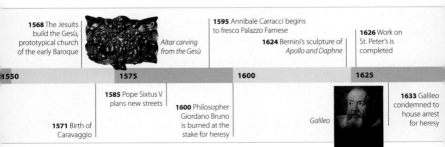

1568 The Jesuits build the Gesù, prototypical church of the early Baroque

Altar carving from the Gesù

1595 Annibale Carracci begins to fresco Palazzo Farnese

1624 Bernini's sculpture of *Apollo and Daphne*

1626 Work on St. Peter's is completed

1550   1575   1600   1625

1585 Pope Sixtus V plans new streets

1600 Philosopher Giordano Bruno is burned at the stake for heresy

1571 Birth of Caravaggio

Galileo

1633 Galileo condemned to house arrest for heresy

Illusionistic beams in ceiling

Chapel painted on flat slanting wall

Figures painted to be viewed from an angle

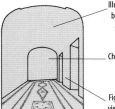

St. Ignatius, founder of the Jesuits

Queen Christina of Sweden
In a coup for Catholicism, Christina renounced Protestantism and abdicated her throne. In 1655 she moved to Rome, where she became the center of a lively literary and scientific circle.

Francesco Borromini (1599–1667)
In the many churches he built in Rome, Borromini made use of revolutionary geometric forms.

A marble rose marks the best place to stand to appreciate the illusion of space created by the artist.

San Carlo alle Quattro Fontane
One of Borromini's most influential designs was this tiny oval church (see p159) on the Quirinal hill.

Bernini designs ...h of Piazza ...na

Bernini's Fontana dei Fiumi in Piazza Navona

1694 Palazzo di Montecitorio is completed

1735 Spanish Steps are designed

1732 Work starts on the Trevi Fountain

1675	**1700**	**1725**

1657 Borromini completes Sant'Agnese in Agone

Bonnie Prince Charlie, pretender to the throne of England

1721 Bonnie Prince Charlie is born in Rome

1734 Clement XII makes Palazzo Nuovo world's first public museum

1656 Work starts on Bernini's colonnade for St. Peter's Square

Understanding Rome's Architecture

The architecture of Imperial Rome kept alive the Classical styles of ancient Greece, at the same time developing new, uniquely Roman forms based on the arch, the vault, and the dome. The next important period was the 12th century, when many Romanesque churches were built. The Renaissance saw a return to Classical ideals, inspired by the example of Florence, but in the 17th century Rome found a style of its own again in the flamboyance of the Baroque.

The entablature above these columns has both straight and arched sections (Hadrian's Villa).

Classical Rome

Most Roman buildings were of concrete faced with brick, but from the 1st century BC, the Romans started to imitate earlier Greek models, using marble to decorate temples and other public buildings.

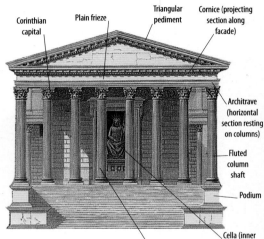

Corinthian capital

Plain frieze

Triangular pediment

Cornice (projecting section along facade)

Architrave (horizontal section resting on columns)

Fluted column shaft

Podium

Cella (inner sanctuary)

Colonnade enclosing portico

Roman temples were usually built on a raised dais or podium, to make them prominent. Many were fronted by a portico, a roofed porch with columns.

Caryatids were sculpted columns, usually in the form of a female figure. Roman caryatids, like this one in the Forum of Augustus, were often copied in detail from earlier Greek examples.

The orders of Classical architecture were building styles, each based on a different column design. The three major orders were borrowed by the Romans from the Greeks.

Doric order

Ionic order

Corinthian order

Aedicules were small shrines, framed by two pillars, usually containing a statue of a god.

Coffers were decorative sunken panels that reduced the weight of domed and vaulted ceilings.

Early Christian and Medieval Rome

The first Christian churches in Rome were based on the basilica: oblong, with three naves, each usually ending in an apse. From the 10th to the 13th centuries, most churches were built in the Romanesque style, which used the rounded arches of ancient Rome.

Basilicas in Rome have, in most cases, kept their original rectangular shape. The nave of San Giovanni in Laterano retains its 4th-century floorplan.

The triumphal arch divides the nave of a church from the apse. Here, in San Paolo fuori le Mura, it is decorated with mosaics.

Renaissance and Baroque Rome

Renaissance architecture (15th–16th centuries) drew its inspiration directly from Classical models. It revived the use of strict geometric proportions. The Baroque age (late 16th–17th centuries) broke many established rules, favoring grandiose decoration over pure Classical forms.

Putti were a popular decorative feature in the Baroque. A putto is a painting or a sculpture of a child like a Cupid or cherub.

A loggia is an open-sided gallery or arcade. It may be a separate structure or part of a building, as here at San Saba.

A tabernacle is used to house the Sacrament for the mass. This 13th-century Gothic wall tabernacle is in San Clemente.

A baldacchino is a canopy, supported on columns, rising over the main altar. This Baroque example is in St. Peter's.

Rusticated masonry decorates the exterior of many Renaissance palazzi. It consists of massive blocks divided by deep joints.

Cosmatesque Sculpture and Mosaics

The Cosmati family, active in Rome during the 12th and 13th centuries, have given their name to a particularly Roman style of decoration. They worked in marble, producing all kinds of fixtures for churches, including cloisters, episcopal thrones, tombs, pulpits, fonts, and candlesticks. These were often decorated with bands of colorful mosaic. They also left many fine floor mosaics, usually of white marble with an inlay of red and green porphyry. Ancient Roman columns were cut up to provide the materials. Several other families of stonemasons used a similar style, and their work is also described as Cosmatesque.

Cosmatesque floor, Santa Maria in Cosmedin

Rome During Unification

Under Napoleon, Italy had a brief taste of unity, but by 1815 it was once more divided into many small states and papal rule was restored in Rome. Over the next 50 years, patriots, led by Mazzini, Garibaldi, and others, struggled to create an independent, unified Italy. In 1848 Rome was briefly declared a Republic, but Garibaldi's forces were driven out by French troops. The French continued to protect the pope, while the rest of Italy was united as a kingdom under Vittorio Emanuele of Savoy. In 1870, troops stormed the city, and Rome became capital of Italy.

Extent of the City
☐ 1870   ▨ Today

Allegory of Italy's Liberty
This patriotic poster from 1890 shows the king, his chief minister Cavour, Garibaldi, and Mazzini. The woman in red represents Italy.

Porta Pia

Tricolored flag of the new Italian kingdom

Plumed hat of the Bersaglieri, crack troops from Savoy

Vittorio Emanuele II
Vittorio Emanuele of Savoy became the first King of Italy in 1861.

Royalists Storm Porta Pia
On September 20, 1870, troops of the kingdom of Italy put an end to the papal domination of Rome. They breached the city walls near Porta Pia; the pope retreated and Rome was made the Italian capital.

1751 Piranesi's *Views of Rome* revive interest in Classical ruins

1762 Trevi Fountain is completed

Napoleon Bonaparte

1799 Napoleon expelled from Italy by Austrians and Russians

1797 Napoleon captures Rome

1807 Birth of Garibaldi

1750

1775

1800

1792 Canova creates the Tomb of Pope Clement XIII, St. Peter's

1800–1 Napoleon Italy again

Piranesi etching of Trajan's Forum

Garibaldi and Rome

The charismatic leader Giuseppe Garibaldi had taken much of Italy from foreign rule by 1860. Rome still remained a crucial problem. Here he declares "O Roma o morte" (Rome or Death).

Villa Paolina

Giuseppe Verdi
(1813–1901)
Verdi, the opera composer, supported unification and in 1861 became a member of Italy's first national parliament.

Breach in Aurelian Wall

Victor Emmanuel Monument

A vast monument to Italy's first king *(see p76)* stands in Piazza Venezia.

· S·P·Q·R·
VRBE · ITALIAE · VINDICATA
INCOLIS · FELICITER · AVCTIS
GEMINOS · FORNICES · CONDIDIT

A Freed City

This marble plaque was set up at Porta Pia to commemorate the liberation of Rome.

Fountain in Piazza del Popolo

1816 Work begins on Piazza del Popolo

1848 Nationalist uprising in Rome. Pope flees and a Republic is formed

1849 Pope is restored to power, protected by a French garrison

1870 Royalist troops take Rome, completing the unification of Italy

1825

1850

1821 English poet Keats dies in Piazza di Spagna

1820 Revolts throughout Italy

Pope Pius IX

1860 Garibaldi and his 1,000 followers take Sicily and Naples

1861 Kingdom of Italy founded with capital in Turin

Modern Rome

The Fascist dictator Mussolini dreamed of recreating the immensity, order and power of the old Roman Empire: "Rome", he said, "must appear wonderful to the whole world". He began to build a grandiose new complex, EUR, in the suburbs, and razed 15 churches and many medieval houses to create space for wide new roads. Fortunately most of the old central has survived, leaving the city with one of Europe's most picturesque historic cores. To mark the Holy Year and the new millennium, many crumbling churches, buildings, and monuments were given a thorough facelift.

Extent of the City
☐ 1960s   ☐ Today

Mussolini's Plans for Rome
This propaganda poster reflects Mussolini's grandiose projects such as Via dei Fori Imperiali in the Forum area *(see p78)*, and EUR *(p268)*.

Pope Benedict XVI
The German cardinal Joseph Ratzinger became Pope Benedict XVI in 2005. He resigned in 2013, the first pope to do so in 600 years. The Pope exerts a tremendous influence on the lives of the world's Catholics.

Jubilee celebrations
Jubilee Years are usually celebrated every quarter of a century. Millions of Catholics visited Rome to celebrate the year 2000.

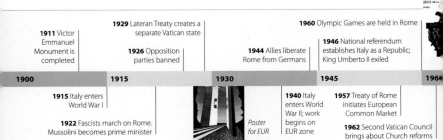

1911 Victor Emmanuel Monument is completed

1929 Lateran Treaty creates a separate Vatican state

1926 Opposition parties banned

1944 Allies liberate Rome from Germans

1960 Olympic Games are held in Rome

1946 National referendum establishes Italy as a Republic; King Umberto II exiled

1900   1915   1930   1945   196

1915 Italy enters World War I

1922 Fascists march on Rome. Mussolini becomes prime minister

Poster for EUR

1940 Italy enters World War II; work begins on EUR zone

1957 Treaty of Rome initiates European Common Market

1962 Second Vatican Council brings about Church reforms

Three Tenors Concert (1990)
Combining Italy's love for music and soccer, this opera recital at the Baths of Caracalla was broadcast live during the World Cup.

Poster for La Dolce Vita
In the 1950s and 1960s Rome was Europe's Hollywood. *Ben-Hur*, *Quo Vadis?* and *Cleopatra* were made at the Cinecittà studios, as well as Italian films like Fellini's *La Dolce Vita*.

Valentino Model
While not as important as Milan for fashion, Rome is still home to some of the industry's leading designers.

Downtown Traffic
Rome's streets are congested, and many buildings have been damaged by pollution. There are plans to close the historic downtown to traffic.

1978 Premier Aldo Moro kidnapped, then killed, by Red Brigades; Karol Wojtyla is elected Pope John Paul II

2004 EU constitution signed in Rome

2005 Pope John Paul II dies in Rome; he is succeeded by Benedict XVI

1990 Rome hosts soccer World Cup finals

2009 Rome hosts the World Swimming Championships

1975	1990	2005	2020

1981 Assassination attempt on Pope John Paul II in St Peter's Square

1993 Francesco Rutelli becomes Rome's first elected mayor

2000 Rome enters the 21st century with millions of pilgrims celebrating the Holy Year – the Jubilee

2013 Pope Benedict XVI resigns and Pope Francis is elected

2011 Rome celebrates 150 years of the Italian state

ROME AT A GLANCE

From its early days as a settlement of shepherds on the Palatine hill, Rome grew to rule a vast empire stretching from northern England to North Africa. Later, after the empire had collapsed, Rome became the center of the Christian world, and artists and architects flocked to work for the popes. The legacy of this history can be seen all over the city. The following pages are a time-saving summary of some of the best Rome has to offer. There are sections on churches, museums and galleries, fountains and obelisks, and celebrated artists and writers in Rome. Listed below are the top attractions that no visitor should miss.

Rome's Top Tourist Attractions

Capitoline Museums
See pp70–73.

Colosseum
See pp94–97.

Sistine Chapel
See pp242–245.

Spanish Steps
See p136.

Raphael Rooms
See pp242–243.

Trevi Fountain
See p159.

Castel Sant'Angelo
See pp250–251.

Pantheon
See pp114–115.

St. Peter's
See pp228–231.

Roman Forum
See pp80–89.

Piazza Navona
See p122.

◀ *The Last Judgment* by Michelangelo on the altar wall of the Sistine Chapel, Vatican

Rome's Best: Churches and Temples

As the center of Christianity, Rome has a vast wealth of beautiful and interesting churches. These range from magnificent great basilicas, built to assert the importance of the medieval and Renaissance Catholic church, to smaller, humbler buildings where the first Christians gathered, often in secret. Among the most fascinating early churches are those converted from ancient Roman temples. Additions to these over the years have resulted in some intriguing, many-layered buildings. A more detailed historical overview of Rome's churches is on pages 48–9.

Pantheon
This monumental 2,000-year-old building is one of the largest surviving temples of ancient Rome.

St. Peter's
At 450 ft (136 m) high, Michelangelo's dome is the tallest in the world. The artist died before seeing his work completed.

Vatican

Piaz
Spa

Piazza
della
Rotond

Piazza
Navona

Campo
de' Fiori

Janiculum

Trastevere

Aver

Santa Maria in Trastevere
Built over a very early Christian foundation, this church is famous for its ornate mosaics.

Santa Cecilia in Trastevere
This statue of Cecilia, showing her as she lay when her tomb was uncovered, was sculpted in 1599 by Stefano Maderno.

Santa Maria in Cosmedin
The decorations in this 6th-century church are 12th-century and earlier. A restored painting in the apse shows the Virgin, Child, and saints.

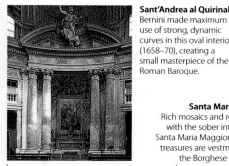

Sant'Andrea al Quirinale
Bernini made maximum use of strong, dynamic curves in this oval interior (1658–70), creating a small masterpiece of the Roman Baroque.

Santa Maria Maggiore
Rich mosaics and relics contrast with the sober interior form of Santa Maria Maggiore. Among its treasures are vestments bearing the Borghese coat of arms.

Santa Prassede
Magnificent Byzantine mosaics cover the walls and ceilings of this 9th-century church. This Christ with Angels is in the Chapel of St. Zeno.

Via Veneto

Quirinal

Esquiline

Lateran

Caracalla

0 meters 500
0 yards 500

Santa Croce in Gerusalemme
Saints adorn the facade of Santa Croce. Inside are relics of the Cross, brought from Jerusalem by St. Helena.

San Clemente
Different archaeological layers lie beneath the 12th-century church. This sarcophagus dates from the 4th century.

San Giovanni in Laterano
The original church was built by Constantine, the first Christian emperor. The Chapel of St. Venantius mosaics include the figure of St. Venantius himself.

Exploring Churches and Temples

There are more churches in Rome than there are days of the year, so you'll have to be selective. Catholic pilgrims have always been drawn to the seven major basilicas: **St. Peter's**, the heart of the Roman Catholic church, **San Giovanni in Laterano**, **San Paolo fuori le Mura**, **Santa Maria Maggiore**, **Santa Croce in Gerusalemme**, **San Lorenzo fuori le Mura**, and **San Sebastiano**. These have a wealth of relics, tombs, and magnificent works of art from many different periods. Smaller churches can be equally fascinating, especially those where the original character is preserved.

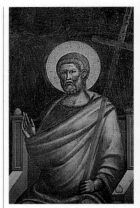

Ancient Temples

One pagan temple survives virtually unaltered since it was erected in the 2nd century AD. The **Pantheon**, "Temple of all the Gods," has a domed interior quite different in structure from any other church in Rome. It was reconsecrated as a Christian church in the 7th century.

Other Roman temples have been incorporated into Christian churches at various times. Two of these are in the Forum; **Santi Cosma e Damiano** was established in the Temple of Romulus in 526, while San Lorenzo in Miranda was built on to the ruins of the

The impressive domed interior of the Pantheon, which became a church in 609

Temple of Antoninus and Faustina in the 11th century. The Baroque facade, built in 1602, looms behind the columns of the temple.

Another church that clearly shows its ancient Roman origins is **Santa Costanza**, built as a mausoleum for Constantine's daughter. It is a round church with some splendid 4th-century mosaics.

Early Christian and Medieval Churches

Some early basilicas – the 5th-century **Santa Maria Maggiore** and **Santa Sabina**, for example – retain much of their original structure. Other, even earlier, churches such as the 4th-century **San Paolo fuori le Mura** and **San Giovanni in Laterano** still preserve their original basilica shape. San Paolo was rebuilt after a fire in 1823 destroyed the original building, and the San Giovanni of today dates from a 1646 reconstruction by Borromini. Both these churches still have their medieval cloisters.

Santa Maria in Trastevere and **Santa Cecilia in Trastevere**

13th-century fresco by Pietro Cavallini in Santa Cecilia

were built over houses where the earliest Christian communities met and worshipped in secret to avoid persecution. One church where the different layers of earlier structures can clearly be seen is **San Clemente**. At its lowest level, it has a Mithraic temple of the 3rd century AD. Other early churches include **Santa Maria in Cosmedin**, with its impressive Romanesque bell tower, and the fortified convent of **Santi Quattro Coronati**. Many Roman churches, most notably **Santa Prassede**, contain fine early Christian and medieval mosaics.

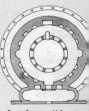
Cloister of San Giovanni in Laterano

Unusual Floor plans

The design of Rome's first churches was based on the ancient basilica, a rectangular building divided into three naves. Since then there have been many bold departures from this plan, including round churches, square churches based on the shape of the Greek cross, as in Bramante's plan for St. Peter's, and, in the Baroque period, even oval and hexagonal ones.

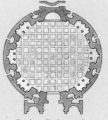
Pantheon (2nd century)

Santa Costanza (4th century)

Renaissance

The greatest undertaking of the Renaissance popes was the rebuilding of **St. Peter's**. Disagreements on the form it should take meant that, although work started in 1506, it was not completed until well into the 17th century. Fortunately, this did not prevent the building of Michelangelo's great dome. As well as working on St. Peter's, Michelangelo also provided the **Sistine Chapel** with its magnificent frescoes.

On a completely different scale, another key work of Renaissance architecture is Bramante's tiny **Tempietto** (1499) on the Janiculum. **Santa Maria della Pace** has a Bramante cloister, some frescoes by Raphael and a charming portico by Pietro da Cortona. Also of interest is Michelangelo's imaginative use of the great vaults of the Roman Baths of Diocletian in the church of **Santa Maria degli Angeli**.

There are other churches worth visiting for the sake of their outstanding paintings and sculptures. **Santa Maria del**

Popolo, for example, has two great paintings by Caravaggio, the Chigi Chapel designed by Raphael, and a series of 15th-century frescoes by Pinturicchio. **San Pietro in Vincoli**, besides having the chains with which St. Peter was bound in prison, also has Michelangelo's awe-inspiring statue of Moses, while **San Luigi dei Francesi** has three Caravaggios depicting St. Matthew and frescoes by Domenichino.

Interior of Rosati's dome in San Carlo ai Catinari (1620)

Baroque

The Counter-Reformation inspired the exuberant, lavish style of churches such as the **Gesù** and **Sant' Ignazio di Loyola**. The best-loved examples of Roman Baroque are the later works associated with Bernini, such as the great colonnade and baldacchino he built for **St. Peter's**. Of the smaller churches he designed, perhaps the finest is **Sant' Andrea al Quirinale**, while **Santa Maria della Vittoria** houses his truly astonishing Cornaro Chapel with its sculpture of the *Ecstasy of St. Teresa*. The late Baroque was not all Bernini, however. You should also look for churches such as **San Carlo ai Catinari** with its beautiful dome by Rosato Rosati

and the many churches by Bernini's rival, Borromini. **Sant'Agnese in Agone** and **San Carlo alle Quattro Fontane** are famed for the dramatic concave surfaces of their facades, while the complex structure of **Sant'Ivo alla Sapienza** makes it one of the miniature masterpieces of the Baroque.

Where to Find the Churches

Michelangelo's dramatic dome crowning the interior of St. Peter's

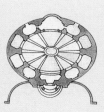

Bramante's St. Peter's (1503)

Sant'Andrea al Quirinale (1658)

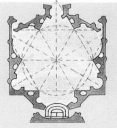

Sant'Ivo alla Sapienza (1642)

Rome's Best: Museums and Galleries

The museums of Rome are among the richest in the world; the Vatican alone contains incomparable collections of Egyptian, Etruscan, Greek, Roman, and early Christian artifacts, as well as frescoes by Michelangelo and Raphael, priceless manuscripts, and jewels. Excavations in the 19th century added treasures from ancient Rome, which are now on display in museums throughout the city. The finest Etruscan collections in the world can be enjoyed in the Villa Giulia. More details of Rome's museums and galleries are given on pages 52–5.

Villa Giulia
Etruscan treasures from Rome's early history are displayed in this beautiful Renaissance villa.

0 meters	500
0 yards	500

Vatican Museums
The galleries and long corridors hold priceless artifacts such as this 9th-century mosaic showing scenes from the life of Christ.

Vatican

Piazza
Navona

Piazza
Sp

Pia
de
Rot

Campo
de' Fior

Janiculum

Trastevere

Av

Galleria Spada
This collection's strength lies in its 17th- and 18th-century paintings. Earlier works include a *Visitation* by Andrea del Sarto (1486–1530).

Palazzo Corsini
Included here are works by Caravaggio, Rubens, and Van Dyck, as well as a painting of the Baroque sculptor Bernini – a rare portrait by Il Baciccia (1639–1709).

Galleria Doria Pamphilj
Most of the great names of the Renaissance are represented on this gallery's crowded walls. Titian (1485–1576) painted Salome early in his career.

Museo e Galleria Borghese

The ground-floor museum houses ancient Greek and Roman sculpture as well as early Bernini masterpieces such as his David (1619). Upstairs are paintings by Titian, Rubens, and other masters.

Palazzo Barberini

The works of art here date mainly from the 13th to the 16th centuries. This figure of Providence comes from Pietro da Cortona's *The Triumph of Divine Providence* (1633–9).

Via Veneto

Quirinal

Esquiline

Forum

Palatine

Lateran

Caracalla

Museo Nazionale Romano

This fresco, from Livia's Villa (1st century AD) outside Rome, is one of a huge collection of finds from archaeological sites throughout the city.

Palazzo Venezia

The highlights of Rome's most important museum of decorative arts are its Byzantine and medieval collections, including this Byzantine enamel of Christ dating from the 13th century.

Capitoline Museums: Palazzo dei Conservatori

Pietro da Cortona's *Rape of the Sabine Women* (1629) is one of many Baroque paintings in the picture gallery.

Capitoline Museums: Palazzo Nuovo

Among the sculptures is this head of Giulia Domna (wife of Septimius Severus) from the 2nd century AD.

Exploring Museums and Galleries

Rome's museums and galleries have two major strengths: Greek and Roman archaeological treasures, and paintings and sculptures of the Renaissance and the Baroque periods. The Vatican Museums have superb collections of both, as do, on a smaller scale, the Capitoline Museums. Fine paintings can also be found scattered throughout Rome in museums, galleries, and churches *(see pp48–9)*.

Centurion's breastplate, Museo della Civiltà Romana

5th-century BC Etruscan gold plate with inscription, Villa Giulia

Etruscan Artifacts

The Etruscans inhabited an area stretching from Florence to Rome from the 8th century BC, and ruled Rome from the late 7th century BC *(see pp20–21)*. It was the Etruscan custom to bury the dead along with their possessions, and as a result, Etruscan artifacts have been excavated from tombs all over central Italy. Three main collections can be seen in Rome. The **Villa Giulia** has been the home of the Museo Nazionale Etrusco since 1889. The villa, designed by Vignola for Pope Julius III for summer outings, is one of Rome's prettiest Renaissance buildings. Its gardens contain a reconstructed Etruscan temple. Not all objects here are Etruscan, however; some of the pottery,

figurines, and artifacts are relics of the Faliscans, Latins, and other tribes who inhabited central Italy before the Romans.

The Gregorian Etruscan Museum in the **Vatican Museums** was opened in 1837 to house Etruscan finds from tombs on Church-owned land. The Museo Barracco in the **Piccola Farnesina** has statues from the much older civilizations of ancient Egypt and Assyria.

Ancient Roman Art

The archaeological zone in Rome forms a huge open-air museum of evidence of ancient Roman life, while the porticoes and cloisters of the city's churches are filled with ancient sarcophagi and fragments of statuary. The largest important collection can be seen in the **Museo Nazionale Romano** at the Baths of Diocletian and the Palazzo Massimo. The museum's many ancient artifacts include, most notably, a sarcophagus from Livia's Villa at Prima Porta just north of Rome. Also on display are some wonderfully well-preserved mosaics. The museum's great collection of Roman statues is now housed in the **Palazzo Altemps**. The most important statues are in the **Vatican Museums**, which also have the best of the great Greek works, such as the *Laocoön*, brought to Rome around the 1st century AD. It had tremendous influence on the subsequent development of Roman art. Splendid copies of Greek originals can be seen in the **Capitoline Museums**.

In the Forum, occupying two floors of the church of Santa

Victory banner, Museo della Civiltà Romana

Francesca Romana, is the **Antiquarium Forense** with restored finds from the excavations. For those who enjoy history, the large-scale model at the **Museo della Civiltà Romana** in EUR gives an excellent idea of what ancient Rome looked like in the 4th century AD.

Muses in Raphael's *Parnassus* (1508–11), Vatican Museums

Art Galleries

In the past, many of Rome's great aristocratic families owned magnificent private collections of paintings and sculpture. Some of these are still housed in ancestral palazzi, which are open to the public. One is the **Galleria Doria Pamphilj**, which has the greatest concentration of paintings of any palazzo in Rome. It's well worth searching through the various rooms to find the pearls of the collection, which include works by Raphael, Filippo Lippi, Caravaggio, Titian, and Claude

Lorrain, and a portrait of Pope Innocent X Pamphilj by the Spanish artist Velázquez. The **Galleria Spada** collection, begun by Bernardino Spada in 1632, is still housed in the fine original gallery built for it. The paintings demonstrate 17th-century Roman taste and include works by Rubens, Guido Reni, Guercino, and Jan Brueghel the Elder. The **Galleria Colonna** contains a collection of art dating from the same period.

Other old family residences are now showcases for state art collections. The Galleria Nazionale d'Arte Antica is divided between **Palazzo Barberini** and **Palazzo Corsini**. Palazzo Barberini, built between 1625 and 1633 by Bernini and others for the Barberini family, houses paintings from the 13th to the 16th centuries. Pietro da Cortona painted the stunning *Triumph of Divine Providence* on the ceiling of the Grand Salon. Palazzo Corsini, on the south side of the Tiber, is famed for its collection of 16th–17th-century art. Another wonderful private

Hellenistic faun, Museo Borghese

collection was that of the Borghese family, also now managed by the state. The sculpture collection of the **Museo e Galleria Borghese** includes the amazing *Apollo and Daphne* by Bernini and the famous statue of Pauline Borghese by Canova. On the first floor is the picture collection with paintings by Titian, Correggio, and others.

The **Capitoline Museums** hold collections that were gifts of the popes to the people of Rome. The Pinacoteca (art gallery) in the **Palazzo dei Conservatori** contains works by Titian, Guercino, and Van Dyck. There is an art gallery at the **Vatican Museums**, but lovers of Renaissance art will head straight for the Sistine Chapel and the Raphael Rooms. Rome's main modern art collection is in the **Galleria Nazionale d'Arte Moderna**, though modern art is displayed in the Zaha Hadid–designed **MAXXI** museum.

Smaller Museums

The most important of the smaller collections is the beautifully laid out medieval museum in **Palazzo Venezia,** with exhibits ranging from ceramics to sculpture. Rome has a wealth of specialty museums like the **Museum of Musical Instruments**, the **Museo di Roma in Trastevere**, with tableaux showing life in Rome during the last century, and the **Burcardo Theater Museum**. For those with an interest in the English Romantic poets who lived in Rome in the 19th century, there is the **Keats-Shelley Memorial House**, a museum in the house where John Keats died. Focusing on the French Empire, the **Museo Napoleonico** has relics and paintings

Laocoön (1st century AD) in the Vatican's Pio-Clementine Museum

of Napoleon and members of his family, many of whom came to live in Rome.

The Deposition (1604) by Caravaggio, Vatican museums

Portrait of Pauline Borghese painted by Kinson (c. 1805), now in the Museo Napoleonico

Rome's Best: Fountains and Obelisks

Rome has some of the loveliest fountains in the world. Many of them are the work of the greatest Renaissance and Baroque sculptors. Some fountains are flamboyant displays, others restful trickles of water. Many are simply drinking fountains, while a few cascade from the sides of buildings. Obelisks date from far earlier in the city's history. Although some of them were commissioned by Roman emperors, many are even older and were brought to Rome by conquering armies. A more detailed overview of Rome's fountains and obelisks is on pages 56–7.

Piazza San Pietro
Twin fountains give life to the splendid monumental piazza of St. Peter's. Maderno designed the one on the Vatican side in 1614; the other was later built to match.

Piazza del Popolo
Nineteenth-century marble lions and fountains surround an ancient obelisk in the center of the piazza.

Vatican

Pia
S

**Piazza
Navona**

R

**Campo
de' Fiori**

Fontana dei Quattro Fiumi
The fountain of the four rivers is the work of Bernini. The four figures represent the Ganges, the Plate, the Danube, and the Nile.

Janiculum

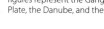

Trastevere

Obelisk of Santa
Maria sopra Minerva
The Egyptian obelisk, held up by Bernini's marble elephant, dates from the 6th century BC.

Fontana delle Tartarughe
One of Rome's more secret fountains, this jewel of Renaissance sculpture shows youths helping tortoises into a basin.

Fontana della Barcaccia
This elegant fountain of 1627 is probably the work of Pietro Bernini, father of the more famous Gian Lorenzo.

Trevi Fountain
The Trevi, inspired by Roman triumphal arches, was designed by Nicola Salvi in 1732. Tradition has it that a coin thrown into the water guarantees a visitor's return to Rome.

| 0 meters | 500 |
| 0 miles | 500 |

Via Veneto

Quirinal

Esquiline

Forum

Palatine

Lateran

Caracalla

ne

Fontana delle Naiadi
When this fountain was unveiled in 1901, the realistically sensual bronze nymphs caused a storm of protest.

Piazza della Bocca della Verità Fountain
In this 18th-century fountain, built by Carlo Bizzaccheri for Pope Clement XI, water spills over a craggy rock formation where two Tritons hold aloft a large shell.

Obelisk of Piazza San Giovanni in Laterano
The oldest obelisk in Rome dates from the 14th century BC. It came to Rome in AD 357, brought here on the orders of Constantine II.

Exploring Fountains and Obelisks

The popes who restored the ancient Roman aqueducts used to build fountains to commemorate their deeds of munificence. As a result, fountains of all sizes and shapes punctuate the city, drawing grateful crowds on hot summer days. Ancient obelisks provide powerful reminders of the debt Roman civilization owed to the Egyptians. Architects have learned to incorporate them into Roman piazzas in fascinating ways.

Fountains

The Trevi fountain is one of the most famous of all. It is a *mostra*, a monumental fountain built to mark the end of an aqueduct – in this case the Acqua Vergine, built by Marcus Agrippa in 19 BC, although the Trevi itself was only completed in 1762. Other *mostre* are the **Fontana dell'Acqua Paola**, built for Pope Paul V in 1612 on the Janiculum, and the **Moses Fountain**, commemorating the opening of the Acqua Felice by Pope Sixtus V in 1587.

Almost all Rome's famous piazzas have fountains. In **Piazza San Pietro** there is a matching pair of powerful fountains. Piazza Navona has Bernini's wonderful Baroque **Fontana dei Quattro Fiumi** (fountain of the four rivers) as its main attraction. The fountain's four figures each represent one of the principal rivers of the four continents then known. To the south of this is the smaller **Fontana del Moro** (the Moor), also by Bernini, showing an Ethiopian struggling with a dolphin. At the north end, Neptune wrestles with an octopus on a

19th-century fountain. In Piazza Barberini is the magnificent Bernini creation of 1642–3: the **Fontana del Tritone** with its sea god blowing through a shell.

More recently, large piazzas have been redesigned around fountains. Valadier's great design for **Piazza del Popolo** (1816–20) has marble lions and fountains surrounding the central obelisk plus two more fountains on the

Fountain of the four tiaras located behind St. Peter's

The Pantheon Fountain

east and west sides of the square. The early 20th century saw the opening of the **Fontana delle Naiadi** (nymphs) in Piazza della Repubblica; its earthy figures caused great scandal at the time. The highly original **Fountain of the Amphorae** (**map** 8 D2) was erected in Piazza dell'Emporio during the 1920s. The same designer, Pietro Lombardi, also created the **Fountain of the Four Tiaras** (**map** 3 C3) behind the colonnade of St. Peter's.

The city also has a number of smaller, and often very charming, fountains. At the foot of the Spanish Steps is the **Fontana della Barcaccia** (the leaking boat) of 1627; the **Fontana delle Tartarughe** (the tortoise fountain) has been in

Fontana dei Cavalli Marini

The Trevi Fountain

Appropriately for a fountain resembling a stage set, the theatrical Trevi has been the star of many movies set in Rome, including romantic films like *Three Coins in a Fountain* and *Roman Holiday*, but also *La Dolce Vita*, Fellini's satirical portrait of Rome in the 1950s. Whatever liberties Anita Ekberg took then, wading in the fountains of Rome is now forbidden, however tempting it could be in the summer heat.

Anita Ekberg in *La Dolce Vita* (1960)

the tiny Piazza Mattei since 1581, and by Santa Maria in Domnica is the **Fontana della Navicella** (little boat), created out of an ancient Roman sculpture in the 16th century. In the forecourt of **Santa Sabina** (**map** 8 D2) water gushes from a huge mask set in an ancient basin. The **Pantheon Fountain** (**map** 4 F4), from 1575, is by Jacopo della Porta. **Le Quattro Fontane** (four fountains) have stood at the Quirinal hill crossroads since 1593.

Fountains in parks and gardens include the **Galleon Fountain** (1620–21) at the Vatican, and the **Fontana dei Cavalli Marini** (seahorses), of 1791, at Villa Borghese. The somewhat decayed 16th-century terraced gardens of the **Villa d'Este**, with their display of over 500 fountains, are still worth a trip.

Piazza Navona with Fontana dei Quattro Fiumi, by Pannini (1691–1765)

The Ovato fountain at Villa d'Este

Obelisks

The most ancient and tallest of Rome's obelisks is the **Obelisk of Piazza di San Giovanni in Laterano**. Built of red granite, 100 ft (31 m) high, it came from the Temple of Amon at Thebes, erected in the 14th century BC. It was brought to Rome in AD 357 by the order of Constantine II and put up in the Circus Maximus. It was rediscovered in 1587, broken into three pieces, and reerected in the following year. Next in age is the obelisk in **Piazza del Popolo**, from the 13th or 12th century BC. It was brought to Rome in the time of Augustus and also erected in the Circus Maximus.

The slightly smaller **Obelisk of Piazza Montecitorio** was another of Augustus's trophies. The bronze ball and spike at the top recall its past use as a gnomon for a sundial of vast proportions. Other obelisks, such as the one at the top of the Spanish Steps, are Roman imitations of Egyptian originals. The **Obelisk of Piazza dell' Esquilino** and the one in **Piazza del Quirinale** (**map** 5 B4) first stood at the entrance to the Mausoleum of Augustus. When reerected, most obelisks were mounted on decorative bases, often with statues and fountains at their foot. Others became parts of sculptures. Bernini was the creator of the marble

Obelisk in Piazza del Popolo

elephant balancing the Egyptian **Obelisk of Santa Maria sopra Minerva** on its back, and the **Fontana dei Fiumi**, with an obelisk from the Circus of Maxentius. Another obelisk was added to the remodeled Pantheon Fountain in 1711. The obelisk in **Piazza San Pietro** is Egyptian but does not have the usual hieroglyphics.

Wall fountain at Villa d'Este

Artists and Writers Inspired by Rome

Artists and writers have been attracted to Rome since Classical times. Many came to work for the emperors; the poets Horace, Virgil, and Ovid, for example, all enjoyed the patronage of Emperor Augustus. Later on, especially in the Renaissance and Baroque periods, the greatest artists and architects came to Rome to compete for commissions from the popes. However, patronage was not the only magnet. Since the Renaissance, Rome's Classical past and its picturesque ruins have drawn artists, architects, and writers from all over Italy and abroad.

Diego Velázquez, one of many great 17th-century artists to visit Rome

Painters, Sculptors, and Architects

In the early 16th century, artists and architects were summoned from all parts of Italy to realize the grandiose building projects of the popes. From Urbino came Bramante (1444–1514) and Raphael (1483–1520); from Perugia, Perugino (1450–1523); from Florence, Michelangelo (1475–1564) and many others. They worked in the Vatican, on the new St. Peter's and the decoration of the Sistine Chapel. Artists were often well rewarded, but they also lived in dangerous times. Florentine sculptor and goldsmith Benvenuto Cellini (1500–71) helped defend Castel Sant' Angelo *(see pp250–51)* during the Sack of Rome (1527), but was later imprisoned there and made a dramatic escape. His memoirs tell the story.

Toward the end of the 16th century, Church patronage was generous to the Milanese-born Caravaggio (1571–1610) despite his violent character and unruly

Self-portrait by the 18th-century artist Angelica Kauffmann, *c.* 1770

life. The Carracci family from Bologna also flourished – especially brothers Annibale (1560–1609) and Agostino (1557–1602).

The work of Gian Lorenzo Bernini (1598–1680) can be seen all over Rome. He succeeded Carlo Maderno (1556–1629) as architect of St. Peter's, and created its great bronze baldacchino, the splendid colonnade *(see pp228–9)*, and numerous fountains, churches and sculptures. His rival for the title of leading architect of the Roman Baroque was Francesco Borromini (1599–1667), whose highly original genius can be appreciated in many Roman churches and palazzi.

In the 17th century it became more common for artists from outside Italy to come and work in Rome. Diego Velázquez (1599–1660), King Philip IV of Spain's court painter, came in 1628 to study the art treasures of the Vatican. Rubens (1577–

1640) came from Antwerp to study, and carried out various commissions. The French artists Nicolas Poussin (1594–1665) and Claude Lorrain (1600–82) lived here for many years.

The Classical revival of the 18th century attracted artists to Rome in unprecedented numbers. From Britain came the Scottish architect Robert Adam (1728–92) and the Swiss artist Angelica Kauffmann (1741–1807), who settled here and was buried with great honor in Sant'Andrea delle Fratte. After the excesses of the Baroque, sculpture also turned to the simplicity of Neo-Classicism. A leading exponent of this movement was Antonio Canova (1757–1821). Sculptors from all over Europe were influenced by him, including the Dane Bertel Thorvaldsen (1770–1844), who lived in Rome for many years.

Claude Lorrain's view of the Forum, painted in Rome in 1632

Writers

Dante (1262–1321) visited Rome during his exile from Florence and in the *Inferno* describes the great influx of pilgrims for the first Holy Year (1300). The poet Petrarch (1304–74), born in Arezzo, was crowned with laurels on the Capitol in 1341. The poet Torquato Tasso (1544–95), from Sorrento, was invited to receive a similar honor, but died soon after his arrival. He is buried in Sant'Onofrio *(see p223)* on the Janiculum. Two of the first writers from abroad to visit Rome were the French essayist Montaigne (1533–92) and English poet John Milton (1608–74). Then, by the early 18th century, writers seemed to flock to Rome.

Edward Gibbon (1737–94) was inspired to write *Decline and Fall of the Roman Empire* when he heard the monks singing the Angelus outside Santa Maria in Aracoeli *(see p75)*. German visitors included J. J. Winckelmann (1717–68), who wrote studies of ancient art, and poet J. W. von Goethe (1749–1832).

Torquato Tasso

In the Romantic period, Rome teemed with English writers: Keats, Shelley, and Byron, followed by the Brownings and Charles Dickens. Travel writers in the 19th century included Augustus Hare (1834–1903) and the German historian Ferdinand Gregorovius (1821–91). Much of *The Portrait of a Lady* by American Henry James (1843–1916) is set in Rome.

Modern life in Rome is brilliantly captured by the Roman writer Alberto Moravia (1907–90), whose residence is sometimes open to visitors (www.fondo albertomoravia.it).

Portrait of the poet John Keats painted by his friend Joseph Severn in 1819

Musicians

Giovanni Luigi da Palestrina (1525–94), from the town of that name, became choirmaster and organist to the Vatican and composed some of the greatest unaccompanied choral music ever written. In 1770 the 14-year-old Mozart heard Gregorio Allegri's unpublished *Miserere* in the Sistine Chapel and wrote it down from memory. Arcangelo Corelli (1653–1713), the great violinist and composer of the Baroque age, worked in Rome under the patronage of Cardinal Ottoboni. One of his first commissions was to provide a festival of music for Queen Christina of Sweden.

During the 19th century, the Prix de Rome brought many French musicians to study here at the Villa Medici *(see p137)*. Hector Berlioz (1803–69) owed the inspiration for his popular *Roman Carnival,* the overture to his opera *Benvenuto Cellini,* to his two-year stay in Rome. Georges Bizet (1838–75) and Claude Debussy (1862–1918) were also Prix de Rome winners. Franz Liszt (1811–86), after his 50th year, settled in Rome, took minor orders, and became known as Abbé Liszt. He wrote *Fountains of the Villa d'Este* while staying at the villa in Tivoli.

Giacomo Puccini

Twentieth-century musical associations with Rome include two popular works by Ottorino Respighi (1870–1936), *The Fountains of Rome* and *The Pines of Rome,* while Giacomo Puccini (1858–1924) used Roman settings when creating his dramatic, tragic opera *Tosca*.

Roman Cinema

The Cinecittà studios, built in 1937 just outside Rome, are most famous for the films made here in the 1940s – classics of Italian Neo-Realism such as Roberto Rossellini's *Roma Città Aperta* and Vittorio De Sica's *Sciuscià* and *Ladri di Biciclette*. The director most often linked with Roman cinema is Federico Fellini, through films like *La Dolce Vita* (1960) and *Roma* (1972). However, perhaps the most famous artist associated with Rome is the controversial writer-turned-film-maker Pier Paolo Pasolini (1922–75), widely known for his films *Teorema* (1968) and *Il Decamerone* (1971).

Since the 1950s, Rome and Cinecittà have also been much used for foreign films: from *Ben-Hur* and *Spartacus* in the 1950s through to *Gladiator* and Woody Allen's *To Rome with Love*.

Pier Paolo Pasolini

ROME THROUGH THE YEAR

The best times to visit Rome are spring and fall, when the weather is usually warm, and sometimes even hot enough to sunbathe and swim at the beaches and lakes outside the city. In the winter months, the weather tends to be gray and wet, while in high summer, most people (including Romans, who leave the city in droves) find the heat unbearable. Easter and Christmas are obviously very special in Rome, but there are other religious festivals worth seeing at other times of the year, as well as some enjoyable secular events like the Festa de' Noantri in Trastevere and the Flower Festival in Genzano. In villages outside Rome, local celebrations are held to welcome new crops such as strawberries and beans in the spring, and grapes and truffles in the fall.

Spring

Easter, falling in March or April, marks the official beginning of the tourist season in Rome. Catholics from all over the world flock into the city to make their pilgrimages to the main basilicas and to hear the Pope's Easter Sunday address outside St. Peter's, while the less devout come simply to take advantage of the mild weather. Meanwhile, Romans pile into their cars and head for the coast and country-side, so you can expect the roads, beaches, and restaurants of the Castelli Romani and Lake Bracciano to be busy.

Temperatures tend to be around 66°F (18°C), but can hit 82°F (28°C), so by mid-May it is usually possible to picnic or dine outside. However, there can still be sudden downpours and temperature swings, so do bring warm clothes and an umbrella.

Crowds gathering in St. Peter's Square at Easter

In April, tubs of colorful azaleas are set out on the Spanish Steps and along Via Veneto, and once the roses start to flower in the city's Rose Garden overlooking the Circus Maximus, it is opened to the public.

For two weeks from mid-May, Via dei Coronari is lit by candles, lined with plants, and hung with banners for the street's antique fair, while Via Margutta hosts an outdoor art show. In the first week of May the International Horse Show is held in the Villa Borghese. Also usually in May, many world-class tennis players flock to Rome to compete in the International Tennis Championships held annually at the Foro Italico.

Events

Festa di Santa Francesca Romana (*March 9*), Santa Francesca Romana. Blessing of the city's vehicles (*see p89*).
Festa di San Giuseppe (*19 March*), in the Trionfale area. St. Joseph's (and Father's) Day celebrated in the streets.
Rome Marathon (*late March*), through the city (*see p359*).
Festa della Primavera (*March/April*), Spanish Steps and Trinità dei Monti. Azaleas in the street and concerts.
Good Friday (*March/April*), Colosseum. Procession of the Cross at 9pm led by the Pope.
Easter Sunday (*March/April*), St. Peter's Square. Address made by the Pope (*see p229*).
Rome's Birthday (*April 21*), Piazza del Campidoglio and elsewhere.
Beni Culturali Week (*April*). Free entry to most galleries.
Art exhibition (*April/May*), Via Margutta (*see p345*).
International Horse Show (*early May*), Villa Borghese.
International Tennis Championships (*usually May*), Foro Italico (*see p358*).

International Horse Show in Villa Borghese in May

Average Daily Hours of Sunshine

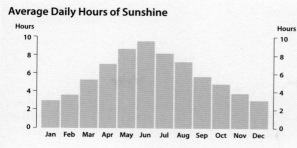

Hours

Jan	Feb	Mar	Apr	May	Jun	Jul	Aug	Sep	Oct	Nov	Dec

Sunshine Chart
Rome is famous for its light. June is the sunniest month, but it is also very dry, and without a shower or two, the heat can feel intense. In fall, Rome's southerly position means that the sun can still be enjoyably warm at midday.

Summer

In June, a season of concerts begins, with performances in some of the city's most beautiful palaces, churches. and courtyards. In July and August, opera and drama are staged at Ostia Antica *(see pp272–3)* and in various outdoor locations. During the summer there are also contemporary cultural events – film, music of all kinds, dance, and theater. On midsummer evenings there are stands and amusements on the Tiber embankments by Castel Sant'Angelo, while in the last two weeks of July, Trastevere becomes an open-air party as the Noantri festival is celebrated with trinket stands, dining in the street, and fireworks. The sales *(saldi)* begin in mid-July, and the Alta Moda Fashion Show is usually held mid- to late July at the Spanish Steps.

Many Romans leave the city at the end of June, when schools close, but since June and July are peak tourist months, hotels, cafés, restaurants, and all the main places of interest and

Flower-carpeted streets in Genzano

other attractions are packed. In August, when the temperature often soars to over 104°F (40°C), virtually all Romans flee the city for the seaside, meaning that many cafés, shops, and restaurants are closed for the entire month.

Events

Flower Festival *(June, the Sunday after Corpus Domini)*, Genzano, Castelli Romani, south of Rome. Streets are carpeted with flowers.
Festa di San Giovanni *(June 23–24)*, Piazza di Porta San Giovanni. Celebrated with meals of snails in tomato sauce, suckling pig, fair and fireworks display.
Festa di Santi Pietro e Paolo *(June 29)*, many churches. Celebrations mark the feast of saints Peter and Paul.

Tevere Expo *(end June–mid-July)*, along the Tiber. Crafts, food and wine, music, and fireworks *(see p345)*.
Festa de' Noantri *(last two weeks in July)*, the streets of Trastevere. Food and entertainment *(see p345 and p347)*.
Alta Moda Fashion Show *(usually mid- to late July)*, Spanish Steps *(see p345)*.
Estate Romana *(July/August)*, Villa Ada, Ostia Antica, in parks, by the Tiber. Opera, concerts, drama, dance, and film *(see p347)*.
Festa della Madonna della Neve *(August 5)*, Santa Maria Maggiore. Fourth-century snowfall reenacted with white flower petals *(see p174)*.
Ferragosto *(August 15)*, Santa Maria in Trastevere. Midsummer holiday; almost everything closes down. Celebrations are held for the Feast of the Assumption.

The heat of an August afternoon in front of St. Peter's

Display of Roberto Cavalli's fashion collection on the Spanish Steps

Average Monthly Rainfall

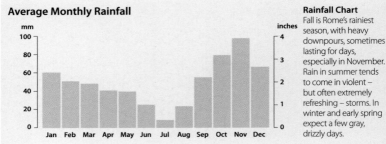

Rainfall Chart
Fall is Rome's rainiest season, with heavy downpours, sometimes lasting for days, especially in November. Rain in summer tends to come in violent – but often extremely refreshing – storms. In winter and early spring expect a few gray, drizzly days.

Fall

September and October are the best – and among the most popular – months to visit Rome. The fiery heat of July and August will have cooled a little, but midday can be very hot, and you can still eat and drink outside without feeling chilly until late at night. Visiting Rome in November is not recommended: it is the wettest month of the year and Roman rainstorms are often very strong and heavy.

At the beginning of October, an artisans' fair is held on Via dell'Orso and adjacent streets, while nearby the antiques galleries of Via dei Coronari hold an open house. There are also October antiques fairs in Orvieto and Perugia, two of the loveliest Umbrian hill towns, which are about an hour's drive north of Rome. In November, there's yet another prestigious antiques fair at the papal palace of Viterbo, 40 miles (65 km) north of Rome (see p273). Fall is the season of harvest festivals, so head out to the small towns around Rome to sample delicacies such as local cheeses, sausages, chestnuts, and mushrooms. Another reason for taking a trip out of Rome is the wine festival in Marino, in the Castelli Romani, south of the city. There are many opportunities to sample the wines of this region that was once the home to luxurious 16th- and 17th-century country residences but now is renowned particularly for its white wines.

Throughout the fall and winter in Rome, freshly roasted chestnuts can be bought from vendors on street corners, and occasionally there is a stand on Campo de' Fiori where you can sample *vino novello*, the new season's wine. On All Saints' and All Souls' Days, which fall on November 1 and 2, respectively, Romans make pilgrimages to place chrysanthemums on the tombs of relatives who are buried in the two main cemeteries of Prima Porta and Verano. On a much happier note, the classical concert and opera seasons begin again in October and November. Details of performances can be found in listings magazines such as *Trova-Roma* and *Roma c'è (see p346)*, in daily newspapers, such as *La Repubblica (see p375)*, and on posters around the city.

A roast chestnut stall in fall

Events

RomaEuropa *(fall)*. Films, dance, theater, and concerts around Rome (see p347).
La Notte Bianca *(September)*. Free entry to museums and galleries all night one Saturday.
Art fair *(September)*, Via Margutta *(see p345)*.
Crafts fair *(last week September/first week October)*, Via dell'Orso *(see p345)*.
International Festival of Cinema *(October)*. New screenings and stars aplenty *(see p352)*.
Marino Wine Festival *(first Sunday in October)*, Marino. Celebrations include tastings and street entertainment.
Antique Fair *(mid-October)*, Via dei Coronari *(see p345)*.
All Saints' and All Souls' Days *(November 1, 2)*, Prima Porta and Verano cemeteries. The Pope usually celebrates Mass in the Verano cemetery.
Festa di Santa Cecilia *(November 22)*, Santa Cecilia in Trastevere and Catacombs of San Callisto.

Fall in the Villa Doria Pamphilj park

Average Monthly Temperature

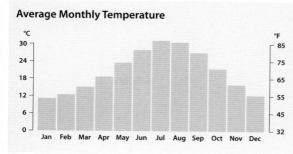

Temperature Chart
The chart shows the average minimum and maximum monthly temperatures. July and August can be unbearably hot, making sightseeing a chore. The fresher days of spring and fall are ideal to visit Rome, but there are some cloudy and rainy spells.

Winter

During the winter, Rome is bracingly chilly but the temperature rarely drops below freezing. Not all buildings are centrally heated, so if you are staying in a small hotel, bring warm clothes and request extra blankets as soon as you arrive, as they can be in short supply. Warm up in cafés with hot chocolate and cappuccino.

The Christmas season is great fun in Rome, especially if you have children. Manger scenes, *presepi*, are set up in many churches, piazzas, and public places, and from mid-December to Twelfth Night, Piazza Navona hosts a market where you can buy manger scenes, decorations, and toys. Unless you have friends in Rome, Christmas itself can be rather lonely, as it is very much a family event. On New Year's Eve, however, everyone is out on the street to drink sparkling wine and set off fireworks.

La Befana, on January 6, is a traditional holiday when a witch, called La Befana, delivers candy to children.

The Carnival season runs from late January to February, celebrated largely by children with costume parties and parades along Via Nazionale, Via

Market on Piazza Navona

Rome during one of its rare snowfalls

Cola di Rienzo, and the Pincio. Keep out of the way of teenagers with shaving-cream spray cans and water balloons.

Events

Festa della Madonna Immacolata *(December 8)*, Piazza di Spagna. In the Pope's presence, firemen climb up a ladder to place a wreath on the statue of the Virgin Mary.
Christmas Market *(mid-December– January 6)*, Piazza Navona. Christmas and children's market *(see p118)*.
Nativity scenes *(mid-December –mid-January)*, many churches. Life-size scene in St. Peter's Square, collection at Santi Cosma e Damiano.
Midnight Mass *(December 24)*, at most churches.
Christmas Day *(December 25)*, St. Peter's Square. Blessing by the Pope.
New Year's Eve *(December 31)*, all over city. Fireworks displays, furniture thrown out.
La Befana *(January 6)*, all over city. Parties for children.

Public Holidays

New Year's Day (Jan 1)
Epiphany (Jan 6)
Easter Monday Liberation Day (Apr 25)
Labor Day (May 1)
Republic Day (Jun 2)
SS Peter & Paul (Jun 29)
Ferragosto (Aug 15)
All Saints' Day (Nov 1)
Immaculate Conception (Dec 8)
Christmas Day (Dec 25)
Santo Stefano (Dec 26)

Via Condotti at Christmas

View of St. Peter's Basilica, Vatican ▶

CAPITOL

The temple of Jupiter on the Capitol, the southern summit of the Capitoline hill, was the center of the Roman world. Reached by a zigzag path up from the Forum, the temple was the scene of all the most sacred religious and political ceremonies. The hill and its temple came to symbolize Rome's authority as *caput mundi*, head of the world, and the Capitol gave its name to the seat of the US Congress. Throughout the city's history, the Capitol (Campidoglio) has remained the seat of municipal government. Today's city council, the Comune di Roma,

meets in the Renaissance splendor of Palazzo Senatorio. The Capitol also serves as Rome's Registry Office. Rome's position as a modern capital is forcefully expressed in the enormous Victor Emmanuel Monument, which unfortunately blots out the view of the Capitol from Piazza Venezia. The present arrangement on the hill dates from the 16th century, when Michelangelo created a beautiful piazza reached by a flight of steps, the Cordonata. Two of the buildings around the piazza now house the Capitoline Museums.

Sights at a Glance

Churches and Temples
7 Santa Maria in Aracoeli
8 Temple of Jupiter
12 San Marco

Museums and Galleries
1 Capitoline Museums: Palazzo Nuovo pp70–71
2 Capitoline Museums: Palazzo dei Conservatori pp72–3
11 Palazzo Venezia and Museum

Historic Buildings
5 Roman *Insula*

Historic Streets and Piazzas
3 Piazza del Campidoglio
4 Cordonata
6 Aracoeli Staircase

Ancient Sites
9 Carpeian Rock

Monuments
10 Victor Emmanuel Monument

0 meters 100
0 yards 100

See also Street Finder maps 5, 12

◀ The God of the Nile River in front of the Roman City Hall, Piazza del Campidoglio

For map symbols *see back flap*

Street by Street: The Capitol and Piazza Venezia

The Capitol, citadel of ancient Rome, is a must for every visitor. A broad flight of steps (the Cordonata) leads up to Michelangelo's spectacular Piazza del Campidoglio. This is flanked by the Palazzo Nuovo and Palazzo dei Conservatori, housing the Capitoline Museums with their fine collections of sculptures and paintings. The absence of cars makes the hill a welcome retreat from the squeal of brakes below, but you should brave the traffic to visit Palazzo Venezia and its museum.

⑩ Victor Emmanuel Monument
This huge white marble monument to Italy's first king was completed in 1911.

PIAZZA VENEZIA

PIAZZA VENEZIA

⑫ San Marco
The church of the Venetians in Rome has a fine 9th-century apse mosaic.

⑪ Palazzo Venezia
The museum's finest exhibits, such as this 13th-century gilded angel decorated with enamel, date from the late Middle Ages.

VIA DEL TEATRO DI MARCELLO

⑤ Roman *Insula*
This is a ruined apartment block dating from Imperial Rome.

④ Cordonata
Michelangelo's great staircase changed the orientation of the Capitol toward the west.

⑥ Aracoeli Staircase
When it was built in 1348, the staircase became a center for political debate.

Key

— Suggested route

| 0 meters | | 75 |
| 0 yards | | 75 |

② ★ Palazzo dei Conservatori
In this part of the Capitoline Museums, a fine series of reliefs from the Temple of Hadrian *(see p108)* is displayed in the courtyard.

❼ Santa Maria in Aracoeli
The treasures hidden behind the church's brick facade include this 15th-century fresco of the Funeral of St. Bernardino by Pinturicchio.

Locator Map
See Central Rome Map pp16–17

❶ ★ Palazzo Nuovo
This bust of Augustus in the Hall of the Emperors is one of many fine Classical sculptures in the Capitoline Museums.

VIA DI SAN PIETRO IN CARCERE

Palazzo Senatorio was used by the Roman Senate from about the 12th century. It now houses the offices of the mayor.

Palazzo dei Conservatori

❸ ★ Piazza del Campidoglio
Michelangelo designed both the geometric paving and the facades of the buildings.

VIA DEL TEMPIO DI GIOVE

❾ Tarpeian Rock
In ancient Rome, traitors were thrown to their death from this cliff on the Capitol.

❽ Temple of Jupiter
This artist's impression shows the gold and ivory statue of Jupiter that stood in the temple.

➊ Capitoline Museums: Palazzo Nuovo

A collection of Classical statues has been kept on the Capitoline hill since the Renaissance. The first group of bronze sculptures was given to the city by Pope Sixtus IV in 1471 and more additions were made by Pope Pius V in 1566. The Palazzo Nuovo was designed by Michelangelo as part of the renovation of the Piazza del Campidoglio, and after its completion in 1655, a number of the statues were transferred here. In 1734 Pope Clement XII Corsini decreed that the building be turned into the world's first public museum.

★ Capitoline Venus
This marble statue of Venus dating from around AD 100–150 is a Roman copy of the original carved in the 4th century BC by the Greek sculptor Praxiteles. The statue is prized for its striking beauty.

Museum Guide

The Palazzo Nuovo is devoted chiefly to sculpture, and most of its finest works, such as the Capitoline Venus, are Roman copies of Greek masterpieces. For visitors eager to identify the philosophers and poets of ancient Greece and the rulers of ancient Rome, there are collections of busts assembled in the 18th century. Admission price also includes entry to the Palazzo dei Conservatori opposite. A gallery below Piazza del Campidoglio links the two buildings.

Portrait of a Flavian Lady
The woman wears the fanciful and elaborate hairstyle popular among the female aristocracy of the 1st century AD.

First floor

47

46

48   49   50

Courtyard

Ground floor

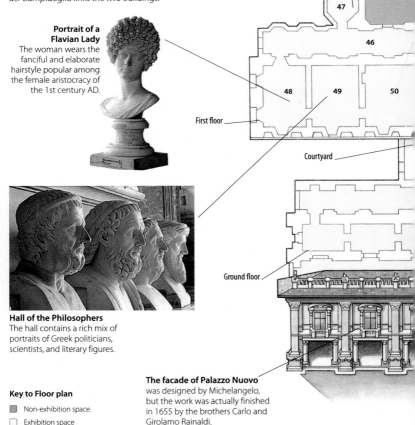

Hall of the Philosophers
The hall contains a rich mix of portraits of Greek politicians, scientists, and literary figures.

The facade of Palazzo Nuovo was designed by Michelangelo, but the work was actually finished in 1655 by the brothers Carlo and Girolamo Rainaldi.

Key to Floor plan

▪ Non-exhibition space

☐ Exhibition space

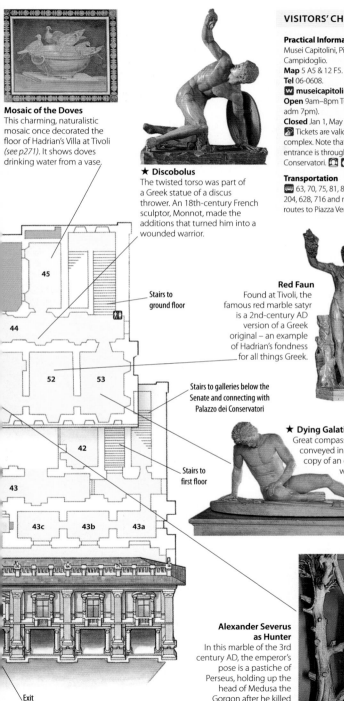

Mosaic of the Doves
This charming, naturalistic mosaic once decorated the floor of Hadrian's Villa at Tivoli *(see p271)*. It shows doves drinking water from a vase.

★ **Discobolus**
The twisted torso was part of a Greek statue of a discus thrower. An 18th-century French sculptor, Monnot, made the additions that turned him into a wounded warrior.

45

44

Stairs to ground floor

52   53

Stairs to galleries below the Senate and connecting with Palazzo dei Conservatori

42

Stairs to first floor

43

43c   43b   43a

Exit

VISITORS' CHECKLIST

Practical Information
Musei Capitolini, Piazza del Campidoglio.
Map 5 A5 & 12 F5.
Tel 06-0608.
🌐 **museicapitolini.org**
Open 9am–8pm Tue–Sun (last adm 7pm).
Closed Jan 1, May 1, Dec 25.
🎟 Tickets are valid for the whole complex. Note that the main entrance is through Palazzo dei Conservatori. 🔲 🎒 🖥 🏠 ♿

Transportation
🚌 63, 70, 75, 81, 87, 160, 170, 204, 628, 716 and many other routes to Piazza Venezia.

Red Faun
Found at Tivoli, the famous red marble satyr is a 2nd-century AD version of a Greek original – an example of Hadrian's fondness for all things Greek.

★ **Dying Galatian**
Great compassion is conveyed in this Roman copy of an original Greek work of the 3rd century BC.

Alexander Severus as Hunter
In this marble of the 3rd century AD, the emperor's pose is a pastiche of Perseus, holding up the head of Medusa the Gorgon after he killed her in her sleep.

❷ Capitoline Museums: Palazzo dei Conservatori

The Palazzo dei Conservatori was the seat of the city's magistrates during the late Middle Ages. Its frescoed halls are still used occasionally for political meetings, and the ground floor houses the municipal register office. The palazzo was built by Giacomo della Porta, who carried out Michelangelo's designs for the Piazza del Campidoglio in the mid-16th century. While much of the palazzo is dedicated to sculpture, the art galleries on the second floor hold works by Veronese, Guercino, Tintoretto, Rubens, Caravaggio, Van Dyck, and Titian.

Facade of Palazzo dei Conservatori
Work began on this Michelangelo design in 1563, the year before his death.

Museum Guide

The first-floor rooms have original 16th- and 17th-century decoration and Classical statues. The second-floor gallery holds paintings and a porcelain collection. Rooms 13 and 14 are used as temporary exhibition space.

Burial and Glory of St. Petronilla
This huge Baroque altarpiece was painted in 1622–23 by Guercino to hang in St. Peter's.

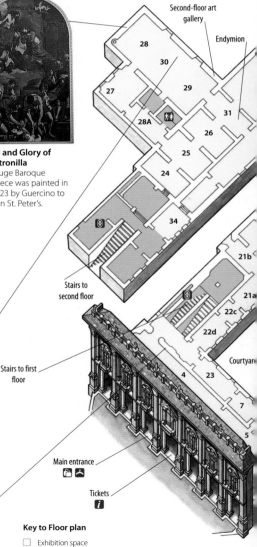

Second-floor art gallery

Endymion

28

30

27   29

31

28A

26

25

24   34

21b

21a

22c

22d

Courtyard

Stairs to second floor

Stairs to first floor   4   23

7

5

Main entrance

Tickets

★ St. John the Baptist
Painted in 1595–96, Caravaggio's sensual portrait of the young saint presents a highly unorthodox image of the forerunner of Christ.

The Horatii and Curatii
D'Arpino's fresco was painted in 1613 and depicts a duel taken from early Roman legend.

Key to Floor plan

☐ Exhibition space

▦ Non-exhibition space

Endymion
The youth doomed to sleep forever by the goddess Diana was painted by Pier Francesco Mola (1612–66), who studied under Cavalier d'Arpino.

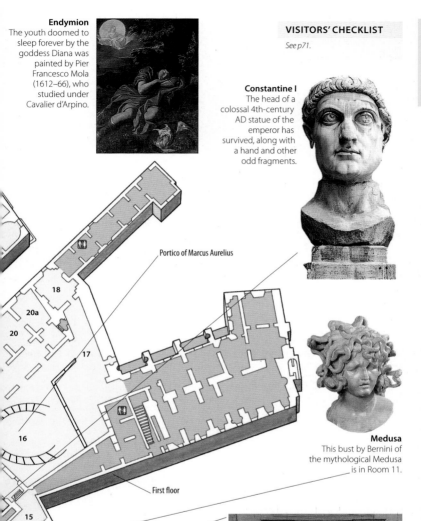

VISITORS' CHECKLIST
See p71.

Constantine I
The head of a colossal 4th-century AD statue of the emperor has survived, along with a hand and other odd fragments.

Portico of Marcus Aurelius

18

20a

20

17

16

First floor

15

14

13

12

Medusa
This bust by Bernini of the mythological Medusa is in Room 11.

★ **Spinario**
This is a charming bronze sculpture from the 1st century BC of a boy trying to remove a thorn from his foot.

★ **She-Wolf**
The Etruscan bronze of the wolf dates from the early 5th century BC. The legendary twins Romulus and Remus *(see pp20–21)* were probably added in the 15th century.

❸ Piazza del Campidoglio

Map 5 A5 & 12 F5. 🚌 40, 62, 63, 64, 95, 110, 170.

When Emperor Charles V visited Rome in 1536, Pope Paul III Farnese was so embarrassed by the muddy state of the Capitol that he asked Michelangelo to draw up plans for repaving the piazza, and for renovating the facades of the Palazzo dei Conservatori and Palazzo Senatorio.

Michelangelo proposed adding the Palazzo Nuovo to form a piazza in the shape of a trapezium, embellished with Classical sculptures chosen for their relevance to Rome. Building started in 1546 but progressed so slowly that Michelangelo only lived to oversee the double flight of steps at the entrance of Palazzo Senatorio. The piazza was completed in the 17th century, the design remaining largely faithful to the original. Pilasters two stories high and balustrades interspersed with statues link the buildings thematically. The piazza faces west toward St. Peter's, the Christian equivalent of the Capitol. At its center stands a replica of a statue of Marcus Aurelius. The original is in the Palazzo dei Conservatori (*see pp72–3*).

Statue of Marcus Aurelias on Piazza del Campidoglio

❹ Cordonata

Map 5 A5 & 12 F5. 🚌 40, 62, 63, 64, 95, 110, 170.

From Piazza Venezia, the Capitol is approached by a gently rising, subtly widening ramp – the Cordonata. At the foot is a pair of granite Egyptian lions, and on the left a 19th-century monument to Cola di Rienzo, close to where the dashing 14th-century tyrant was executed. The top of the ramp is guarded by Classical statues of the Dioscuri – Castor and Pollux.

❺ Roman *Insula*

Piazza d'Aracoeli. **Map** 5 A5 & 12 F4. **Tel** 06-0608. 🚌 40, 62, 63, 64, 95, 110, 170. **Open** by appt only: call first.

Two thousand years ago, the urban poor of Rome used to make their homes in *insulae* – apartment blocks. These were often badly maintained by landlords, and expensive to rent in a city where land costs were high. This 2nd-century AD tenement block, of barrel-vault construction, is the only survivor in Rome from that era. The fourth, fifth, and part of the sixth story remain above current ground level.

In the Middle Ages, a section of these upper stories was converted into a church; its bell tower and 14th-century Madonna in a niche are visible from the street.

During the Fascist years, the area was cleared, and three lower floors emerged. Some 380 people may have lived in the tenement, in the squalid conditions described by the 1st-century AD satirical writers Martial and Juvenal. The latter mentions that he had to climb 200 steps to reach his garret.

This *insula* may once have had more stories. The higher you lived, the more dismal the conditions, as the cramped spaces of the building's upper levels testify.

The Dioscuri twins looking onto the Cordonata leading up to the Piazza del Campidoglio

❻ Aracoeli Staircase

Piazza d'Aracoeli. **Map** 5 A5 & 12 F4.
🚌 40, 62, 63, 64, 95, 110, 170.

The Aracoeli Staircase numbers
124 marble steps (122 if you
start from the right) and was
completed in 1348, some say in
thanks for the passing of the
Black Death, but probably in
honor of the 1350 Holy Year.

The 14th-century tribune-
turned-tyrant Cola di Rienzo
used to harangue the masses
from the Aracoeli Staircase; in
the 17th century, foreigners
used to sleep on the steps, until
Prince Caffarelli, who lived on
the hill, scared them off by
rolling barrels filled with stones
down them.

Popular belief has it that by
climbing the steps on your
knees you can win the Italian
national lottery. From the top
there is a good view of Rome,
with the domes of Sant' Andrea
della Valle and St. Peter's slightly
to the right.

Aracoeli Staircase

❼ Santa Maria in Aracoeli

Piazza d'Aracoeli (entrances via
Aracoeli Staircase and door behind
Palazzo Nuovo). **Map** 5 A5 & 12 F4.
Tel 06-6976 38 39. 🚌 40, 62, 63, 64,
95, 110, 170. **Open** summer: 7:30am–
12:30pm, 3–6:30pm daily; winter:
7:30am–12:30pm, 2:30–5:30pm daily.

Dating from at least the 6th
century, the church of Santa
Maria in Aracoeli, or St. Mary of
the Altar in the Sky, stands on
the northern summit of the
Capitoline, on the site of the

Ceiling commemorating Battle of Lepanto in Santa Maria in Aracoeli

ancient temple to Juno. Its
22 columns were taken from
various ancient buildings; the
inscription on the third column
to the left tells us that it comes
"a cubiculo Augustorum" – from
the bedroom of the emperors.

The church of the Roman
senators and people, Santa
Maria in Aracoeli has been used
to celebrate many triumphs
over adversity. Its ceiling, with
naval motifs, commemorates
the Battle of Lepanto (1571), and
was built under Pope Gregory
XIII Boncompagni, whose family
crest, the dragon, can be seen
toward the altar end.

Many other Roman families
and individuals are honored by
memorials in the church. To the
right of the entrance door,
the tombstone of archdeacon
Giovanni Crivelli, rather than
being set into the floor of the
church, stands eternally at
attention, partly so that the
signature "Donatelli" (by
Donatello) can be read at
eye level.

The frescoes in the first
chapel on the right, painted
by Pinturicchio in the
1480s in the beautifully clear
style of the early Renaissance,
depict St. Bernardino of Siena.
On the left wall, the
perspective of *The Burial of
the Saint* slants to the right,
taking into account the
position of the viewer just
outside the chapel.

The church is most famous,
however, for an icon with
apparently miraculous powers,
the *Santo Bambino*, a
15th-century olive-wood figure
of the Christ Child that was
carved out of a tree from the
garden of Gethsemane. Its
powers are said to include
resurrecting the dead, and it is
sometimes summoned to the
bedsides of the gravely ill.
The original figure was stolen
in 1994 but has been replaced
by a replica.

At Christmas the Christ Child
takes its place in the center of a
picturesque crib (second chapel
to the left) but is usually to be
found in the sacristy, as is the
panel of the *Holy Family* from
the workshop of Giulio Romano.

The miraculous olive-wood Christ Child at
Santa Maria in Aracoeli

❽ Temple of Jupiter

Via del Tempio di Giove. **Map** 5 A5 & 12 F5. 🚍 40, 62, 63, 64, 95, 110, 170.

The temple of Jupiter, the most important in ancient Rome, was founded in honor of the arch-god around 509 BC on the southern summit of the Capitoline hill. From the few traces that remain, archaeologists have been able to reconstruct the rectangular, Greek appearance of the temple as it once stood. In places you can see remnants of its particularly Roman feature, the podium. Most of this lies beneath the Museo Nuovo wing of the Palazzo dei Conservatori (see pp72–3).

By walking around the site, from the podium's southwestern corner in Via del Tempio di Giove to its southeastern corner in Piazzale Caffarelli, you can see that the temple was about the same size as the Pantheon.

Ancient coin showing the Temple of Jupiter

❾ Tarpeian Rock

Via di Monte Caprino and Via del Tempio di Giove. **Map** 5 A5 & 12 F5. 🚍 40, 62, 63, 64, 95, 110, 170.

The southern tip of the Capitoline is called the Tarpeian Rock (Rupe Tarpea), after Tarpeia, the young daughter of Spurius Tarpeius, defender of the Capitol in the 8th-century BC Sabine War.

The Sabines, bent on vengeance for the rape of their women by Romulus and his

Sabine soldiers crushing the treacherous Tarpeia with their shields

men, bribed Tarpeia to let them up on to the Capitol. As the Augustan historian Livy records, the Sabines used to wear heavy gold bracelets and jeweled rings on their left hands, and Tarpeia's reward for her treachery was to be "what they wore on their shield-arms."

The Sabines kept to the letter of the bargain if not to its spirit; they repaid Tarpeia not with their jewelry but by crushing her to death between their shields. Tarpeia was possibly the only casualty of her act of treachery – as the invading warriors met the Roman defenders, the Sabine women leapt between the two opposing armies, forcing a reconciliation. Traitors and other condemned criminals were subsequently executed by being thrown over the sheer face of the rock.

The place has been considered dangerous and used to be fenced off, but restoration work is now under way.

❿ Victor Emmanuel Monument

Piazza Venezia. **Map** 5 A5 & 12 F4. **Tel** 06-678 0664. 🚍 40, 62, 63, 64, 95, 110, 170. **Open** 9:30am–6:30pm daily. 🖥

Known as Il Vittoriano, this monument was begun in 1885 and inaugurated in 1911 in honor of Victor Emmanuel II of Savoy, the first king of a unified Italy. The king is depicted here in a gilt bronze equestrian statue, oversized like the monument itself – the statue is 39 ft (12 m) long.

The edifice also contains a museum of the Risorgimento, the events that led to unification (see pp40–41). Built in white Brescian marble, the "wedding cake" (one of its many nicknames) will never mellow into the ocher tones of surrounding buildings. It is widely held to be the epitome of self-important, insensitive architecture, though the views it offers are spectacular. A glass elevator at the back of the building takes visitors to the very top.

Victor Emmanuel Monument in Piazza Venezia

⓫ Palazzo Venezia and Museum

Via del Plebiscito 118. **Map** 5 A4 & 12 E4. **Tel** 06-6999 4388. ▣ 40, 62, 63, 64, 95, 110, 170. **Open** 8:30am–7pm Tue–Sun (last adm: 30 min before closing). **Closed** Jan 1, May 1, Dec. 25. ▣▣ Temporary exhibitions.

The arched windows and doors of this Renaissance civic building are so harmonious that the facade was once attributed to the great Humanist architect Leon Battista Alberti (1404–72). It was more probably built by Giuliano da Maiano, who is known to have carved the fine doorway onto the piazza. Palazzo Venezia was built in 1455–64

Pope Paul II

for the Venetian cardinal Pietro Barbo, who later became Pope Paul II. It was at times a papal residence, but it also served as the Venetian Embassy to Rome before passing into French hands in 1797. Since 1916 it has belonged to the state; in the Fascist era, Mussolini used Palazzo Venezia as his headquarters and addressed crowds from the central balcony.

The interior is best seen by visiting the Museo del Palazzo Venezia, Rome's most under-rated museum. It holds first-class collections of early Renaissance paintings; painted wood sculptures and Renaissance chests from Italy; tapestries from all of Europe; majolica; silver; Neapolitan ceramic figurines; Renaissance bronzes; arms and armor; Baroque terra-cotta sculptures by Bernini, Algardi, and others; and 17th- and 18th-century Italian paintings. There is a marble screen from the Aracoeli convent, destroyed to make way for the Victor Emmanuel Monument, and a bust of Paul II, showing him to rank with Martin V and Leo X among the fattest-ever popes. The building also hosts major temporary exhibitions.

Palazzo Venezia with Mussolini's balcony in the center

⓬ San Marco

Piazza San Marco 48. **Map** 5 A4 & 12 F4. **Tel** 06-679 52 05. ▣ 40, 62, 63, 64, 95, 110, 170. **Open** 8:30am–noon, 4–6:30pm Tue–Sat, 9am–1pm, 4–8pm Sun. ✝

The church of San Marco was founded in 336 by Pope Mark, in honor of St. Mark the Evangelist. The Pope's relics lie under the altar. The church was restored by Pope Gregory IV in the 9th century – the magnificent apse mosaics date from this period.

Further major rebuilding took place in 1455–71, when Pope Paul II Barbo made San Marco the church of the Venetian community in Rome.

Coat of arms of Pope Paul II

The blue and gold coffered ceiling is decorated with Pope Paul's heraldic crest, the lion rampant, recalling the lion of St. Mark, the patron saint of Venice. The appearance of the rest of the interior, with its colonnades of Sicilian jasper, was largely the creation of Filippo Barigioni in the 1740s. Complemented by an interesting array of funerary monuments in the aisles, the style is typical of the late Roman Baroque.

Leon Battista Alberti, whose name is also mentioned tentatively in connection with Palazzo Venezia, may have been the architect of the elegant travertine arcade and loggia of the facade.

San Marco's apse mosaic of Christ, with Gregory IV on the far left

FORUM

The Forum was the center of political, commercial, and judicial life in ancient Rome. The largest buildings were the basilicas, where legal cases were heard. According to the playwright Plautus, the area teemed with "lawyers and litigants, bankers and brokers, shopkeepers and strumpets, good-for-nothings waiting for a tip from the rich."

As Rome's population boomed, the Forum became too small. In 46 BC Julius Caesar built a new one, setting a precedent that was followed by emperors from Augustus to Trajan. Emperors also erected triumphal arches to themselves, and just to the east Vespasian built the Colosseum, center of entertainment after the business of the day was done.

See also Street Finder maps 5, 8, 9, 12

Sights at a Glance

Churches and Temples
- **5** Temple of Saturn
- **8** Temple of Castor and Pollux
- **9** Temple of Vesta
- **11** Temple of Antoninus and Faustina
- **12** Temple of Romulus and Santi Cosma e Damiano
- **14** Santa Francesca Romana
- **17** Temple of Venus and Rome

Historic Buildings
- **1** Basilica Aemilia
- **2** Curia
- **7** Basilica Julia
- **10** House of the Vestal Virgins
- **13** Basilica of Constantine and Maxentius
- **18** *Trajan's Markets pp90–91*
- **20** Torre delle Milizie

- **21** Casa dei Cavalieri di Rodi
- **24** Mamertine Prison
- **27** *Colosseum pp94–7*

Museums
- **15** Antiquarium Forense

Arches and Columns
- **4** Arch of Septimius Severus
- **6** Column of Phocas
- **16** Arch of Titus
- **19** Trajan's Column
- **26** Arch of Constantine

Ancient Sites
- **3** Rostra
- **22** Forum of Augustus
- **23** Forum of Caesar
- **25** Forum of Nerva

☐ **Restaurants**
see pp310–11
1 Enoteca Provincia Romana

| 0 meters | 200 |
| 0 yards | 200 |

A Tour of the Roman Forum: West

To appreciate the layout of the Forum before visiting its confusing patchwork of ruined temples and basilicas, it is best to view the whole area from above, from the back of the Capitol. From there you can make out the Via Sacra (the Sacred Way), the route followed through the Forum by religious and triumphal processions toward the Capitol. Up until the 18th century, when archaeological excavations began, the Arch of Septimius Severus and the columns of the Temple of Saturn lay half-buried underground. Excavation of the Forum continues, and the ruins uncovered date from many different periods of Roman history.

The Temple of Vespasian was the point from where Piranesi made this 18th-century engraving of the Forum. Its three columns were then almost completely buried.

Temple of Concord

Portico of the Dii Consentes

❺ Temple of Saturn
The eight surviving columns of this temple stand close to the three columns of the Temple of Vespasian.

Arch of Septimius Severus

❸ Rostra
These are the ruins of the platform used for public oratory in the Forum.

❼ Basilica Julia
Named after Julius Caesar, who ordered its construction, the basilica housed important law courts.

❻ Column of Phocas
One of the very last monuments erected in the Forum, this single column dates from AD 608.

4 ★ Arch of Septimius Severus
A 19th-century engraving shows the arch after the Forum was first excavated.

Locator Map
See Central Rome Map pp16–17

Key

— Suggested route

| 0 meters | 75 |
| 0 yards | 75 |

Santi Luca e Martina was an early medieval church, but was rebuilt in 1635–64 by Pietro da Cortona.

The Forum included the area under Via dei Fori Imperiali. More parts have now been made public.

VIA DEI FORI IMPERIALI

VIA DELLA SALARA VECCHIA

DELLA CURIA

A SACRA

2 Curia
This 3rd-century rebuilding of the Curia was greatly restored in 1937.

1 Basilica Aemilia
This large meeting hall was razed to the ground in the 5th century AD.

Entrance to Forum

The Temple of Julius Caesar was erected in his memory by Augustus on the spot where Caesar's body was cremated after his assassination in 44 BC.

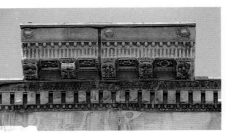

Julius Caesar

To Roman Forum: East
See pp82–3

8 Temple of Castor and Pollux
A temple to the twin brothers (of whom only Pollux was fathered by Jupiter) stood on this spot from the 5th century BC. This section of cornice and its supporting columns date from the rebuilding of AD 6.

A Tour of the Roman Forum: East

The eastern end of the Roman Forum is dominated by the massive barrel-vaulted ruins of the Basilica of Constantine. To picture the building as it was in the 4th century AD, you must imagine marble columns, floors, and statues, and glittering tiles of gilt bronze. The remains of the other important buildings are scant, though the garden and ponds in the center of the House of the Vestal Virgins make it a very attractive spot. The two churches in this part of the Forum cannot be reached from within the archaeological area, but are accessible from the road outside.

The Regia was the office of the Pontifex Maximus, the chief priest of ancient Rome.

To Forum entrance

VIA SACRA

⓫ Temple of Antoninus and Faustina
The portico of this temple, built in AD 141, has been incorporated in the church of San Lorenzo in Miranda.

An early Iron Age necropolis was found here in 1902. Finds from it, such as this burial urn, are on view in the Antiquarium.

❾ Temple of Vesta
Partly reconstructed, this tiny temple to the goddess of the hearth was one of ancient Rome's most sacred shrines.

❿ ★ House of the Vestal Virgins
The priestesses who tended the sacred flame in the Temple of Vesta lived here. The house was a large rectangular building around a central garden.

⓬ Temple of Romulus
This domed building from the 4th century AD has survived as part of the church of Santi Cosma e Damiano.

⓭ ★ Basilica of Constantine and Maxentius
The stark remains of the basilica's huge arches and ceilings give some idea of the original scale and grandeur of the Forum's public buildings.

Locator Map
See Central Rome Map pp16–17

⓮ Santa Francesca Romana
The church takes its name from a saint who cared for the Roman poor in the 15th century.

VIA DEI FORI IMPERIALI

⓯ Antiquarium Forense
A small museum houses archaeological finds made in the Forum. They include this frieze of *Aeneas and the Founding of Rome* from the Basilica Aemilia.

Colonnade surrounding Temple of Venus and Rome

VIA SACRA

⓱ Temple of Venus and Rome
These extensive ruins are of a magnificent temple, built here in AD 121 by the Emperor Hadrian, largely to his own design.

Ruined Baths

To the Palatine

⓰ Arch of Titus
This 19th-century reconstruction shows how the arch may have looked when it spanned the flagstone roadway of the Via Sacra.

Key

― Suggested route

0 meters   75
0 yards   75

❶ Basilica Aemilia

See Visitors' Checklist.

Originally this building was a rectangular colonnaded hall, with a multicolored marble floor and a bronze-tiled roof. It was built by the consuls Marcus Aemilius Lepidus and Marcus Fulvius Nobilor in 179 BC. The two consuls, who were elected annually, exercised supreme power over the Republic.

Basilicas in ancient Rome served no religious purpose; they were meeting halls for politicians, moneylenders, and *publicani* (businessmen contracted by the state to collect taxes). A consortium agreed to hand over a specified sum to the state, but its members were allowed to collect as much as they could and keep the difference. This is why tax collectors in the Bible were so loathed.

The basilica was rebuilt many times; it was finally burned down when the Visigoths sacked Rome in AD 410. Business seems to have continued until the last moment, for the pavement is splashed with tiny lumps of coins that melted in the fire.

Melted coins embedded in the floor of the Basilica Aemilia

The Curia, or the Court of Rome, as rebuilt by Diocletian in the 3rd century

❷ Curia

See Visitors' Checklist.

A modern restoration now stands over the ruins of the hall where Rome's Senate (chief council of state) used to meet. The first Curia stood on the site now occupied by the church of Santi Luca e Martina, but after the building was destroyed by fire in 52 BC, Julius Caesar built a new Curia at the edge of the Forum. This was restored by Domitian in AD 94 and, after another fire, rebuilt by Diocletian in the 3rd century. The building you see today is a 1937 restoration of Diocletian's Curia. Inside are two relief panels commissioned by Trajan to decorate the Rostra. One shows Trajan destroying records of unpaid taxes to free citizens from debt; in the other he sits on a throne receiving a mother and child.

❸ Rostra

See Visitors' Checklist.

Speeches were delivered from this dais, the most famous – thanks to Shakespeare – being Mark Antony's "Friends, Romans, Countrymen" oration after the assassination of Julius Caesar in 44 BC. Caesar himself had just reorganized the Forum, and this speech was made from the newly sited Rostra, where the ruins now stand. In the following year the head and hands of Cicero were put on display here after he had been put to death by the second Triumvirate (Augustus, Mark Antony, and Marcus Lepidus). Fulvia, Mark Antony's wife, stabbed the great orator's tongue with a hairpin. It was also here that Julia, Augustus's daughter, was said to have played the prostitute – one of many scandalous acts that led to her banishment.

The dais took its name from the ships' prows *(rostra)* with which it was decorated. Sheathed in iron (for ramming enemy vessels), these came from ships captured at the Battle of Antium in 338 BC.

❹ Arch of Septimius Severus

See Visitors' Checklist.

This triumphal arch, one of the most striking and best preserved monuments of the Forum, was erected in AD 203 to celebrate the tenth anniversary of the accession of

Honorary statue

Relief panel in balustrade, showing Trajan's acts of charity

Rostra
This reconstruction shows the platform for public speaking in the Forum, as it looked in Imperial times.

Prows of ships *(rostra)*

Septimius Severus. The relief panels – largely eroded – celebrate the emperor's victories in Parthia (modern-day Iraq and Iran) and Arabia. Originally, the inscription along the top of the arch was to Septimius and his two sons, Caracalla and Geta, but after Septimius died, Caracalla murdered Geta and had his brother's name removed. Even so, the holes into which the letters of his name were pegged are still visible.

During the Middle Ages, the central arch, half buried in earth and debris, was used to shelter a barber shop.

Triumphal arch of the Emperor Septimius Severus

❺ Temple of Saturn

See Visitors' Checklist.

The most prominent of the ruins in the fenced-off area between the Forum and the Capitoline Hill is the Temple of Saturn. It consists of a high platform, eight columns, and a section of entablature. There was a temple dedicated to Saturn here as early as 497 BC, but it had to be rebuilt many times, and the current remains date only from 42 BC.

Saturn was the mythical god-king of Italy, said to have presided over a prosperous and peaceful Golden Age from which slavery, private property, crime, and war were absent. As such, he appealed particularly to the lower and slave classes. Every year,

Ionic capitals on the surviving columns of the Temple of Saturn

between December 17 and December 23, Saturn's reign was remembered in a week of sacrifices and feasting, known as the Saturnalia.

As long as the revels lasted, the normal social order was turned upside down. Slaves were permitted to drink and dine with (and sometimes even be served by) their masters. Senators and other high-ranking Romans would abandon the aristocratic togas that they usually wore to distinguish themselves from the lower classes and wear more democratic, loose-fitting gowns. During the holidays, all the courts of law and schools in the city were closed. No prisoner could be punished, and no war could be declared.

People also celebrated the Saturnalia in their own homes: they exchanged gifts, in particular special wax dolls and wax tapers, and played light-hearted gambling games, the stakes usually being nuts, a symbol of fruitfulness. Much of the spirit and many of the rituals of the festival have been preserved in the Christian celebration of Christmas.

❻ Column of Phocas

See Visitors' Checklist.

This column, 44 ft (13.5 m) high, is one of the few to have remained upright since the day it was put up. Until 1816, when an inquisitive Englishwoman, Lady Elizabeth Foster, widow of the

fifth Duke of Devonshire, decided to excavate its pedestal, nobody knew what it was. It turned out to be the youngest of the Forum's monuments, erected in AD 608 in honor of the Byzantine emperor, Phocas, who had just paid a visit to Rome. The column may have been placed here as a mark of gratitude to Phocas for giving the Pantheon to the pope *(see pp114–15)*.

VISITORS' CHECKLIST

Practical Information
Entrance: Via della Salara Vecchia 5/6. **Map** 5 B5 & 8 F1. **Tel** 06-3996 7700. **Open** 8:30am–approx 1 hour before sunset daily (last adm: 1 hour before closing). **Closed** Jan 1, Dec 25. 🎫 (includes entry to Colosseum and Palatine).

Transportation
Ⓜ Colosseo. 🚌 75, 85, 87, 117, 175, 186, 810. 🚋 3 .

Slender, fluted Column of Phocas

Remains of the Basilica Julia, a Roman court of civil law

❼ Basilica Julia

See Visitors' Checklist, p85.

This immense basilica, which occupied the area between the temple of Saturn and the temple of Castor and Pollux, was begun by Julius Caesar in 54 BC and completed after his death by his great-nephew Augustus. It was damaged by fire almost immediately afterward in 9 BC, but was subsequently repaired and dedicated to the emperor's grandsons, Gaius and Lucius.

After numerous sackings and pilferings, only the steps, pavement, and column stumps remain. Nevertheless, the ground plan is fairly clear. The basilica had a central hall, measuring 260 ft by 59 ft (80 m by 18 m), surrounded by a double portico. The hall was on three floors, while the outer portico had only two.

The Basilica Julia was the seat of the *centumviri*, a body of 180 magistrates who tried civil law cases. They were split into four chambers of 45 men, and unless a case was particularly complicated, they would all sit separately.

The four courts were, however, divided only by screens or curtains, and the voices of lawyers and cheers and boos of spectators in the upper galleries echoed through the building. Lawyers hired crowds of spectators, who would applaud every time the lawyer who was paying them made a point and jeer at his opponents. The clappers and booers must have had a good deal of time on their hands: scratched into the steps are checkerboards where they played dice and other gambling games to while away the time between cases.

Corinthian columns of the Temple of Castor and Pollux

❽ Temple of Castor and Pollux

See Visitors' Checklist, p85.

The three slender fluted columns of this temple form one of the Forum's most beautiful ruins. The first temple here was probably dedicated in 484 BC in honor of the mythical twins and patrons of horsemanship Castor and Pollux. During the battle of Lake Regillus (499 BC) against the ousted Tarquin kings, the Roman dictator Postumius promised to build a temple to the twins if the Romans were victorious. Some said the twins appeared on the battlefield, helped theRomans to victory, and then materialized in the Forum – the temple marks the spot – to announce the news.

The temple, like most buildings in the Forum, was rebuilt many times. The three surviving columns date from the last occasion on which it was rebuilt – by the future Emperor Tiberius after a fire in AD 6. For a long period, the temple housed the city's office of weights and measures, and it was also used at times by a number of bankers.

❾ Temple of Vesta

See Visitors' Checklist, p85.

The Forum's most elegant temple, a circular building originally surrounded by a ring of 20 fine fluted columns, dates from the 4th century AD, though there had been a temple on the site for far longer. It was partially reconstructed in 1930.

The cult of the Vestals was one of the oldest in Rome, and centered on six Vestal Virgins, who were required to keep alight the sacred flame of Vesta, the goddess of the hearth.

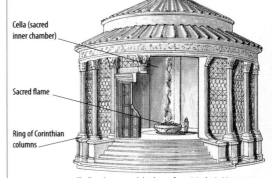
Cella (sacred inner chamber)

Sacred flame

Ring of Corinthian columns

The Temple preserved the shape of an original primitive structure made of wooden posts with a thatched roof.

This responsibility was originally entrusted to the daughters of the king, but it then passed to the Vestals, the only group of women priests in Rome. It was no easy task, as the flame was easily blown out. Any Vestal who allowed the flame to die was whipped by the high priest (Pontifex Maximus) and dismissed.

The girls, who had to belong to noble families, were selected when they were between 6 and 10 years old. They served for 30 years: the first ten were spent learning their duties, the next ten performing them and the final ten teaching novices. They enjoyed high status and financial security, but had to remain virgins. The penalty for transgressing was to be buried alive, although only ten Vestals are recorded as ever having suffered this fate. The men involved were whipped to death. When Vestals retired, they were free to live the rest of their lives as ordinary citizens. If they wished, they could marry, but few ever did.

Another of the Vestals' duties was to guard the Palladium, a sacred statue of the goddess Pallas Athenae. The irreverent Emperor Heliogabalus burgled the temple in the 3rd century AD. He thought he had succeeded in stealing the Palladium, but the Vestals had been warned of his intention and had replaced it with a replica.

Central courtyard of the House of the Vestal Virgins

❿ House of the Vestal Virgins

See Visitors' Checklist, p85.

Honorary statue of a Vestal Virgin

As soon as a girl became a Vestal, she came to live in the House of the Vestal Virgins. This was once an enormous complex with about 50 rooms on three stories. The only remains today are some of the rooms around the central courtyard. This space is perhaps the most evocative part of the Forum. Overlooking ponds of water lilies and goldfish is a row of eroded, and mostly headless, statues of senior Vestals, dating from the 3rd, and 4th centuries AD. The better-preserved examples are in the Museo Nazionale Romano *(see p165)*. On one of the pedestals the inscription has been removed because the disgraced Vestal in question may have been a certain Claudia, known to have betrayed the cult by converting to Christianity.

Though many of the rooms surrounding the courtyard are well preserved – some even retain flights of steps – entry is not allowed. If you peek into the series of rooms along the south side, however, you might be able to see the remains of a mill, used for grinding the grain with which the Vestals made a special sacrificial cake. The bakery was next door.

⓫ Temple of Antoninus and Faustina

See Visitors' Checklist, p85.

One of the Forum's oddest sights is the Baroque facade of the church of San Lorenzo in Miranda rising above the porch of a Roman temple. First dedicated in AD 141 by the Emperor Antoninus Pius to his late wife Faustina, the temple was rededicated to them both on the death of the emperor. In the 11th century it was converted into a church because it was believed that San Lorenzo (St. Lawrence) had been condemned to death there. The current church dates from 1601.

Temple of Antoninus and Faustina

Restored section of Temple of Vesta

⓬ Temple of Romulus and Santi Cosma e Damiano

See Visitors' Checklist, p85. Santi Cosma e Damiano: **Tel** 06-692 0441. **Open** 9am–1pm, 3–7pm daily. Crib: **Closed** Mon–Thu. Donation for crib. 🚹 ♿

No one is sure to whom the Temple of Romulus was dedicated, but it was probably to the son of Emperor Maxentius, and not to Rome's founder.

The temple is a circular brick building, topped by a cupola, with two rectangular side rooms and a concave porch. The heavy, dull bronze doors are original.

Since the 6th century the temple has acted as a vestibule to the church of Santi Cosma e Damiano, which itself occupies an ancient building – a hall in Vespasian's Forum of Peace. The entrance to the church is on Via dei Fori Imperiali. The beautiful carved figures of its 18th-century Neapolitan *presepio* (crib or Nativity scene) are on view, and the church has a vivid Byzantine apse mosaic with Christ pictured against orange clouds.

Roof of the Temple of Romulus

⓭ Basilica of Constantine and Maxentius

See Visitors' Checklist, p85.

The basilica's three vast, coffered barrel vaults are powerful relics of what was the largest building in the Forum. Work began in AD 308 under the Emperor Maxentius. When he was deposed by Constantine after the Battle of the Milvian Bridge in AD 312, work on the massive project continued under the new regime. The building, which, like other Roman basilicas, was used for the administration of justice and for carrying out business, is often referred to simply as the Basilica of Constantine.

The area covered by the basilica was roughly 330 ft by 215 ft (100 m by 65 m). It was originally designed to have a long nave and aisles running from east to west, but Constantine switched the axis around to create three short broad aisles with the main entrance in the center of the long south wall. The height of the building was 115 ft (35 m). In the apse at the western end, where it could be seen from all over the building, stood a 39-ft (12-m) statue of the emperor, made partly of wood and partly of marble. The giant head, hand, and foot are on display in the courtyard of the Palazzo dei Conservatori (*see pp72–3*). The roof of the basilica glittered with gilded tiles until the 7th century, when they were stripped off to cover the roof of the old St. Peter's.

The three barrel-vaulted aisles of the basilica were used as law courts.

The octagonal coffers in the vaulted ceiling were originally faced with marble.

The main entrance was added by Constantine in AD 313.

The roof was supported by eight massive Corinthian columns. One now stands in Piazza Santa Maria Maggiore (*see p175*).

⑭ Santa Francesca Romana

Piazza di Santa Francesca Romana.
Map 5 B5. **Tel** 06-679 5528. ⬚ 85, 87, 117, 175, 810. ⬚ 3. Ⓜ Colosseo.
Open 10:30am–noon, 4:30–6pm daily (times may vary). ⬚ ⬚

Every year on March 9, devout Roman drivers try to park as close as possible to this Baroque church with a Romanesque bell tower. The aim of their pilgrimage is to have their vehicles blessed by Santa Francesca Romana, the patron saint of motorists. During the 15th century, Francesca of Trastevere founded a society of pious women devoted to helping the less fortunate. After her canonization in 1608 the church, originally named Santa Maria Nova, was rededicated to Francesca.

The most curious sight inside the church is a flagstone with what are said to be the imprints of the knees of St. Peter and St. Paul. A magician, Simon Magus, decided to prove that his powers were superior to those of the Apostles by levitating above the Forum. As Simon was in mid-air, Peter and Paul fell to their knees and prayed fervently for God to humble him, and Simon immediately plummeted to his death.

Bell tower of Santa Francesca

Dedication to Titus and Vespasian on the Arch of Titus

⑮ Antiquarium Forense

See Visitors' Checklist, p85.

The former convent of Santa Francesca Romana is now occupied by the offices in charge of the excavations of the Forum and a small museum. The latter is currently being reorganized and the rooms are being restored. They contain Iron Age burial urns, graves, and their skeletal occupants, along with some ancient bric-a-brac exhumed from the Forum's drains. When the reorganization is complete, you should be able to see fragments of statues, capitals, friezes, and other architectural decoration taken from the Forum's buildings.

⑯ Arch of Titus

See Visitors' Checklist, p85.

This triumphal arch was erected in AD 81 by the Emperor Domitian in honor of the victories of his brother, Titus, and his father, Vespasian, in Judaea. In AD 66, the Jews, weary of being exploited by unscrupulous Roman officials, rebeled. A bitter war broke out; ending four years later in the fall of Jerusalem and the Jewish Diaspora.

Although the reliefs inside the arch are badly eroded, you can

Frieze of Aeneas in the Antiquarium Forense

make out a triumphant procession of Roman soldiers carrying off spoils from the Temple of Jerusalem. The booty includes the altar, silver trumpets, and a golden seven-branched candelabrum.

⑰ Temple of Venus and Rome

See Visitors' Checklist, p85.

The emperor Hadrian designed this temple to occupy what had been the vestibule to Nero's Domus Aurea (see p177). Many of the columns have been reerected, and though there is no access, there is a good view as you leave the Forum and from the upper tiers of the Colosseum. The temple, the largest in Rome, was dedicated to Roma, the personification of the city, and to Venus because she was the mother of Aeneas, father of Romulus and Remus. Each goddess had her own cella (shrine). When the architect Apollodorus pointed out that the seated statues in the niches were too big (had they tried to "stand," their heads would have hit the vaults), Hadrian had him put to death.

⑱ Trajan's Markets

Originally considered among the wonders of the Classical world, Trajan's Markets now show only a hint of their former splendor. Emperor Trajan and his architect, Apollodorus of Damascus, built this visionary new complex of 150 shops and offices (probably used for administering the corn dole) in the early 2nd century AD. It was the ancient Roman equivalent of the modern shopping center, selling everything from silks, and spices imported from the Middle East to fresh fish, fruit, and flowers.

The Markets Today
Above the facade stands the 13th-century Torre delle Milizie, built for defensive purposes.

Main Hall
Twelve shops were built on two floors, and the grain dole was shared out on the upper story. This was a free grain ration given to Roman men to prevent hunger.

KEY

① **Staircase**

② **Small semicircle of shops**

③ **Cross vaulting**

④ **Market shops** were built with arched entrances, with jambs and lintels creating rectangular portals and windows. A wooden mezzanine was used for storage.

⑤ **The terrace** over the archway spanning Via Biberatica has a good view of the Forum of Trajan below.

⑥ **Large hall with semidomed ceiling**

⑦ **Forum of Trajan**, built in front of the markets in AD 107–113, was flanked by the Basilica Ulpia. The basilica, measuring 558 ft by 197 ft (170 m by 60 m), was the largest in Rome. A small portion of the Forum has been excavated; unfortunately, however, the rest of it remains buried beneath modern Rome's busy city streets.

⑧ **Wall dividing market area from Forum of Trajan**

Trajan
The emperor was a benevolent ruler and a successful general.

Via Biberatica
The main street that runs through the market is named after the drinking inns that once lined it.

The Markets in the 16th Century
This fanciful fresco depicts a gladiatorial combat taking place in front of the partly buried remains of Trajan's Markets.

VISITORS' CHECKLIST

Practical Information
Mercati Traianei,
Via IV Novembre 94. **Map** 5 B4.
Tel 06-6992 3521.
Open 9am–7pm daily.
Last adm: 1 hour before closing.
Closed Jan 1, Dec 25. 🏛 ♿

Transportation
🚌 64, 70, 170 and many routes to
Piazza Venezia.

Upper Corridor
Shops on this upper level are thought to have sold wine and oil, since a number of storage jars were discovered here.

Market Shopping

Shops opened early, and closed about noon. The best ones were decorated with mosaics of the goods they sold. Almost all the shopping was done by men, though women visited the dressmaker and cobbler. The tradesmen were almost all male. In employment records for the period AD 117–193, the only female shop-keepers mentioned are three wool-sellers, two jewelers, a green-grocer, and a fishwife.

Fish mosaic

AD 100–112 Building of Trajan's Markets	**472** Invasion by Ricimer the Suevian. Some of his Germanic troops stationed here		**1200s** Torre delle Milizie built on top of the markets	**1572** Convent of Santa Caterina da Siena built over part of markets	**1924** Many medieval houses demolished
					1911–14 Convent demolished
AD 0	**AD 390**	**780**	**1170**	**1560**	
AD 117 Death of Trajan	**552** Byzantine takeover of Rome. Markets occupied and fortified by the army		**1300s** Annibaldi and Caetani families vie for control of the area	**1828** First tentative excavations, but value of site not recognized	
AD 98 Trajan succeeds Nerva as emperor				**1930–33** Markets finally excavated	

Detail of Trajan's Column

⑲ Trajan's Column

Via dei Fori Imperiali. **Map** 5 A4 & 12 F4. *See Visitors' Checklist for Trajan's Markets, p91.*

This elegant marble column was inaugurated by Trajan in AD 113, and celebrates his two campaigns in Dacia (Romania) in AD 101–3 and AD 107–8. The column, base, and pedestal are 131 ft (40 m) tall – precisely the same height as the spur of Quirinal Hill that was excavated to make room for Trajan's Forum.

Spiraling up the column are minutely detailed scenes from the campaigns, beginning with the Romans preparing for war and ending with the Dacians being ousted from their homeland. The column is pierced with small windows to illuminate its internal spiral staircase (closed to the public). If you wish to see the reliefs in detail, there is a complete set of casts in the Museo della Civiltà Romana in EUR *(see p268).*

When Trajan died in AD 117, his ashes, along with those of his wife Plotina, were placed in a golden urn in the column's hollow base. The column's survival was largely thanks to the intervention of Pope Gregory the Great (reigned 590–604). He was so moved by a relief showing Trajan helping a woman whose son had been killed that he begged God to release the emperor's soul from hell. God duly appeared to the pope to say that Trajan had been rescued, but asked him not to pray for the souls of any more pagans.

According to legend, when Trajan's ashes were exhumed, his skull and tongue were not only intact, but his tongue told of his release from hell. The land around the column was then declared sacred and the column itself was spared. The statue of Trajan remained on top of the column until 1587, when it was replaced with one of St. Peter.

⑳ Torre delle Milizie

Mercati Traianei, Via IV Novembre. **Map** 5 B4. **Tel** 06-679 0048. **Closed** to the public.

For centuries this massive brick tower was thought to have been the one in which Nero stood watching Rome burn, after he had set it alight to clear the city's slums. It is uncertain whether arson was among Nero's crimes, but it is certain that he did not watch the fire from this tower – it was built in the 13th century.

㉑ Casa dei Cavalieri di Rodi

Piazza del Grillo 1. **Map** 5 B5. **Tel** 06-0608. 🚌 85, 87, 117, 175, 186, 810. **Open** Tue am, Thu am (by appt only, well in advance).

Since the 12th century the crusading order, the Knights of St. John, also known as the Knights of Rhodes (Rodi) or Malta, have had their priorate in this medieval house above the Forum of Augustus. If you are lucky enough to get inside, ask to see the beautiful Cappella di San Giovanni (Chapel of St. John).

㉒ Forum of Augustus

Piazza del Grillo 1. **Map** 5 B5 & 12 F5. *See Trajan's Markets' Visitors' Checklist, p91.* **Tel** 06-0608. **Open** by appt.

The Forum of Augustus was built to celebrate Augustus's victory over Julius Caesar's assassins, Brutus and Cassius, at the Battle of Philippi in 41 BC. The temple in its center was dedicated to Mars the Avenger. The forum stretched from a high wall at the foot of the seedy Suburra quarter to the edge of the Forum of Caesar. At least half of it is now concealed below Mussolini's Via dei Fori Imperiali. The temple is easily identified, with its cracked steps and four Corinthian columns. Originally it had a statue of Mars that looked very much like Augustus. In case anyone failed to notice the resemblance, a giant statue of Augustus himself was placed against the Suburra wall.

㉓ Forum of Caesar

Via del Carcere Tulliano. **Map** 5 A5. **Tel** 06-0608. 🚌 85, 87, 175, 186, 810. 850. **Open** to research scholars by appt only.

The first of Rome's Imperial fora was built by Julius Caesar. He spent a fortune – most of it booty from his conquest of Gaul – buying up and demolishing houses on the site. Taking center stage was a temple dedicated in 46 BC to the goddess Venus Genetrix, from whom Caesar claimed descent. The temple contained statues of Caesar and Cleopatra as well as of Venus. All that remains of this temple to vanity is a platform

View of the Temple of Mars, Forum of Augustus

and three Corinthian columns. The forum was enclosed by a double colonnade that sheltered a row of shops, but this burned down in AD 80 and was rebuilt by Domitian, and Trajan also added the Basilica Argentaria and a heated public lavatory.

The forum is only open to the public by appointment, but parts are visible from above in Via dei Fori Imperiali.

17th-century view of the ruined Forum of Nerva

⑮ Forum of Nerva

Piazza del Grillo 1 (reached through Forum of Augustus). **Map** 5 B5. **Tel** 06-0608. 85, 87, 175, 186, 810. **Open** by appt only.

The Forum of Nerva was begun by his predecessor, Domitian, and completed in AD 97. Little more than a long corridor with a colonnade along the sides, and a Temple of Minerva at one end, it was also known as the Forum Transitorium because it lay between the Forum of Peace built by the Emperor Vespasian in AD 70 and the Forum of Augustus. Vespasian's forum is almost completely covered by Via dei Fori Imperiali, as is much

19th-century engraving of guards visiting prisoners in the Mamertine

⑭ Mamertine Prison

Clivo Argentario 1. **Map** 5 A5. **Tel** 06-6989 6380. 85, 87, 175, 186, 810. **Open** 9am–7pm daily (until 5pm in winter). every 20 minutes.

Below the 16th-century church of San Giuseppe dei Falegnami (St. Joseph of the Carpenters) is a dank dungeon in which, according to Christian legend, St. Peter was imprisoned. He is said to have caused a spring to bubble up into the cell and used the water to baptize his guards.

The prison, also known as Tullianum, was in an old cistern with access to the city's main sewer (the Cloaca Maxima). The lower cell was used for executions, and bodies were thrown into the sewer. Among the enemies of Rome executed here was the Gaulish leader Vercingetorix, defeated by Julius Caesar in 52 BC.

of the Forum of Nerva itself. Excavations have unearthed Renaissance shops, and taverns, but only part of the forum can be seen, including the base of the temple and two columns that were part of the original colonnade. These support a relief of Minerva above a frieze of young girls learning to sew, and weave.

⑯ Arch of Constantine

Between Via di San Gregorio and Piazza del Colosseo. **Map** 8 F1. 75, 85, 87, 175, 673, 810. 3. Colosseo.

This triumphal arch was dedicated in AD 315 to celebrate Constantine's victory three years before over his co-emperor, Maxentius. Constantine claimed he owed his victory to a vision of Christ, but there is nothing Christian about the arch – in fact, most of the medallions, reliefs, and statues were scavenged from earlier monuments. There are statues of Dacian prisoners taken from Trajan's Forum and reliefs of Marcus Aurelius, including one where he distributes bread to the poor. Inside the arch are reliefs of Trajan's victory over the Dacians. These were probably by the artist who worked on Trajan's Column.

Medallion on the Arch of Constantine

North side of the Arch of Constantine, facing the Colosseum

㉗ Colosseum

Rome's greatest amphitheater was commissioned by the Emperor Vespasian in AD 72 on the marshy site of a lake in the grounds of Nero's palace, the Domus Aurea (see p177). Deadly gladiatorial combats and wild animal fights were staged free of charge by the emperor and wealthy citizens for public viewing. The Colosseum was built to a practical design, with its 80 arched entrances allowing easy access for 55,000 spectators, but it is also a building of great beauty. The drawing here shows how it looked at the time of its opening in AD 80. It was one of several similar amphitheaters built in the Roman Empire, and some survive at El Djem in North Africa, Nîmes and Arles in France, and Verona in northern Italy. Despite being damaged over the years by neglect and theft, it remains a majestic sight.

KEY

① **The bollards** anchored the velarium.

② **The outer walls** are made of travertine. Stone plundered from the facade in the Renaissance was used to build several palaces, bridges, and parts of St. Peter's.

③ **The vomitorium** was the exit used from each numbered section.

④ **Brick** formed the inner walls.

⑤ **Entry routes** to take the spectators to their seats were reached by means of staircases to the various levels of the amphitheater.

⑥ **The podium** was a large terrace where the emperor and the wealthy upper classes had their seats.

⑦ **The velarium** was a huge awning that shaded spectators from the sun. Supported on poles attached to the upper story of the building, it was then hoisted into position with ropes anchored to bollards outside the stadium.

⑧ **Corinthian**

⑨ **Ionic columns**

⑩ **Doric columns**

⑪ **Arched entrances,** 80 in total, were all numbered to let in the vast crowds that attended the fights.

72 Emperor Vespasian begins work on the Colosseum			**1312** Emperor Henry VII gives Colosseum to the Senate and people of Rome
230 Colosseum restored by Alexander Severus	**248** Thousandth anniversary celebration of founding of Rome by Romulus and Remus	*A gladiator's shield*	
	442 Building damaged in an earthquake		
0	**400**	**800**	**1200**
81–96 Amphitheater completed in reign of Domitian	**523** Wild animal fights banned	**1200s** Frangipane family turns Colosseum into a fortress	
	404 Gladiatorial combats banned		
80 Vespasian's son, Titus, stages inaugural festival in the amphitheater. It lasts 100 days		**15th–16th centuries** Ruins used as quarry. Travertine blocks recycled by popes	

Internal Corridors
These were designed to allow the large and often unruly crowd to move freely and to be seated within 10 minutes of arriving at the Colosseum.

③

④

⑥

⑦

⑤

⑧

⑨

⑩

⑪

Colossus of Nero
The Colosseum may have acquired its name from this huge gilt bronze statue that stood near the amphitheater.

The Founder of the Colosseum
Vespasian was a professional soldier who became emperor in AD 69, founding the Flavian dynasty.

1870 All vegetation removed

1600

9 Colosseum dedicated to ssion of Jesus

1893–6
Structure below arena revealed

Flora of the Colosseum

By the 19th century the Colosseum was heavily overgrown. Different microclimates in various parts of the ruin had created an impressive variety of herbs, grasses, and wild flowers. Several botanists were inspired to study, and catalog them, and two books were published, one listing 420 different species.

Borage, an herb

How Fights Were Staged in the Arena

The emperors held shows here that often began with animals performing circus tricks. Then came the gladiators, who fought each other to the death. When one was killed, attendants dressed as Charon, the mythical ferryman of the dead, carried his body off on a stretcher, and sand was raked over the blood to prepare for the next bout. A badly wounded gladiator would surrender his fate to the crowd. The "thumbs up" sign from the emperor meant he could live, "thumbs down" that he died, and the victor became an instant hero. Animals were brought here from as far away as North Africa and the Middle East. The games held in AD 248 to mark the thousandth anniversary of Rome's founding saw the death of a host of lions, elephants, hippos, zebras, and elks.

Beneath the Arena
Late 19th-century excavations exposed the network of underground rooms where the animals were kept.

Interior of the Colosseum
The amphitheater was built in the form of an ellipse, with tiers of seats around a vast central arena.

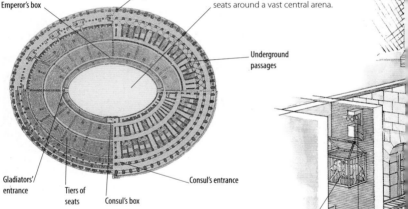

Emperor's entrance

Emperor's box

Underground passages

Gladiators' entrance

Tiers of seats

Consul's box

Consul's entrance

KEY

① **A complex** of rooms, passages, and elevators lies underneath the arena.

② **Metal fencing** kept animals penned in, while archers stood by just in case any escaped.

③ **Seating** was tiered, and different social classes were segregated.

④ **A winch** brought the animal cages up to arena level when they were due to fight.

⑤ **A ramp and trap door** alllowed the animal to reach the arena after walking along a corridor.

⑥ **Cages** were three-sided elevators that went up to the next level, where the animals were released.

Dramatic Entrances
Below the sand was a wooden floor through which animals, men, and scenery appeared in the arena.

Roman Gladiators
These were usually slaves, prisoners of war, or condemned criminals. Most were men, but there were a few female gladiators.

The Colosseum by Antonio Canaletto
This 18th-century view of the Colosseum shows the Meta Sudans fountain (now demolished). Water "sweated" from a metal ball on top of its brick cone.

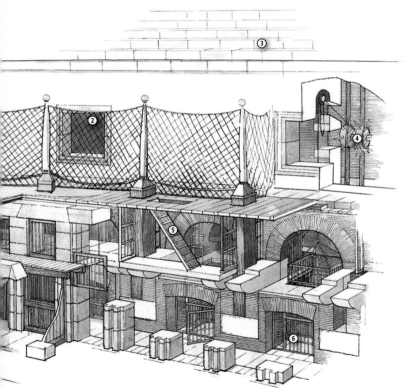

Sea Battles in the Arena

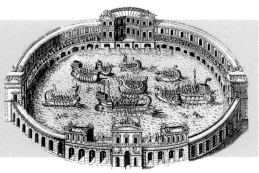

The historian Dion Cassius, writing in the 4th century AD, relates how, 150 years earlier, the Colosseum's arena was flooded to stage a mock sea battle. Scholars now believe that he was mistaken. The spectacle probably took place in the Naumachia of Augustus, a water-filled arena situated across the Tiber in Trastevere.

PALATINE

According to legend, Romulus and Remus were brought up here by a wolf in a cave. Traces of Iron Age huts, dating from the 9th century BC, have been found on the Palatine hill, providing archaeological support for the area's legendary links with the founding of Rome. The Palatine was a very desirable place to live, becoming home to some of the city's most famous inhabitants. The great orator Cicero had a house here, as did the lyric poet Catullus. Augustus was born on the hill and continued to live here in very modest circumstances even when he became emperor. The two buildings identified as the House of Augustus and the House of Livia, his wife, are among the best preserved. The first emperor's example of frugality was ignored by his successors, Tiberius, Caligula, and Domitian, who all built extravagant palaces here. The ruins of Tiberius's palace lie beneath the 16th-century Farnese Gardens. The most extensive ruins are those of the Domus Augustana and Domus Flavia, the two wings of Domitian's palace, and the later extension built by Septimius Severus.

Sights at a Glance

Temples
7 Temple of Cybele

Historic Buildings
1 Domus Flavia
3 Domus Augustana
5 House of Livia
6 House of Augustus

Ancient Sites
2 Cryptoporticus
4 Stadium
8 Huts of Romulus

Parks and Gardens
9 Farnese Gardens

See also Street Finder map 8

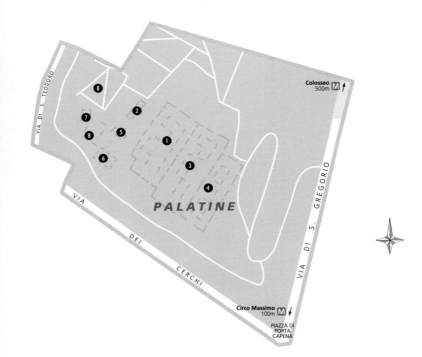

◀ Scenic view of umbrella pine trees on the Palatine Hill

For map symbols *see back flap*

A Tour of the Palatine

Shaded on its lower slopes with pines, and scattered in spring with wild flowers, the Palatine is the most pleasant and relaxing of the city's ancient sites. You can reach the hill by walking up from the Roman Forum *(see pp78–9)*. The area is dominated by the ruins of the Domus Flavia and the Domus Augustana, two parts of Domitian's huge palace built at the end of the 1st century AD. What you are able to see depends on where excavations are taking place at the time.

To Farnese Gardens *see p103*

7 Temple of Cybele
Also known as the Temple of the Magna Mater, this was the center of an important fertility cult.

8 Huts of Romulus
These are traces of a 9th-century BC village on the Palatine.

6 ★ House of Augustus
Splendid frescoes, painted in about 30 BC, can be seen in four rooms here.

5 ★ House of Livia
Many of the wall paintings have survived in the house where Augustus lived with his wife Livia.

| 0 meters | | 75 |
| 0 yards | | 75 |

Key

— Suggested route

1 ★ Domus Flavia
This oval fountain was designed to be seen from the dining hall of the palace.

3 Domus Augustana
The Roman emperors lived in this part of the palace, while the Domus Flavia was used for public functions.

2 Cryptoporticus
In this long underground tunnel, built by Nero, the stuccoes that decorated the walls and vault have been replaced with copies.

Locator Map
See Central Rome Map pp16–17

Octagonal fountain of the Domus Flavia

The Palatine Museum is inside a former convent, and houses artifacts from ancient Rome.

4 Stadium
Part of the Imperial palace, this enclosure may have been used by the emperors as a private garden.

Via San Gregorio entrance

The exedra of the Stadium may have housed a balcony for emperors to view races.

Baths of Septimius Severus

The Palace of Septimius Severus (reigned AD 193–211) was an extension of the Domus Augustana. It projected beyond the hillside, requiring enormous arched supports.

Substructure of palace

Marble pavement in the courtyard of the Domus Flavia

❶ Domus Flavia

See Visitors' Checklist.

In AD 81, Domitian, the third of the Flavian dynasty of emperors, decided to build a splendid new palace on the Palatine hill. But the western peak, the Germalus, was covered with houses and temples, while the eastern peak, the Palatium, was very steep. So the emperor's architect, Rabirius, flattened the Palatium and used the soil to fill in the cleft between the two peaks, burying (and preserving) a number of Republican-era houses.

The palace had two wings – one official (the Domus Flavia), the other private (the Domus Augustana). It was the main Imperial palace for 300 years. At the front of the Domus Flavia, the surviving stubs of columns and fragments of walls trace the shapes of three adjoining rooms. In the first of these, the Basilica, Domitian dispensed his personal brand of justice.

The central Aula Regia was a throne room decorated with 12 black basalt statues. The third room (now covered with corrugated plastic) was the Lararium, a shrine for the household gods known as Lares (usually the owner's ancestors). It may have been used for official ceremonies or by the palace guards.

Fearing assassination, Domitian had the walls of the courtyard covered with shiny marble slabs designed to act as mirrors so that he could see anyone lurking behind him. In the end, he was assassinated in his bedroom, possibly on the orders of his wife, Domitia. The courtyard is now a pleasant place to pause;

the flower beds in the center follow the maze pattern of a sunken fountain pool.

❷ Cryptoporticus

See Visitors' Checklist.

The Cryptoporticus, a series of underground corridors, was built by Nero to connect his Domus Aurea *(see p177)* with the palaces of earlier emperors on the Palatine. A further branch leading to the Palace of Domitian was added later. Its vaults are decorated with delicate stucco reliefs – copies of originals now kept in the Palatine's museum.

❸ Domus Augustana

See Visitors' Checklist.

This part of Domitian's palace was called the Domus Augustana because it was the private residence of the "august" emperors. On the upper level, a high brick wall remains, and you can make out the shape of its two courtyards. The far better-preserved lower level is closed to the public, though you can look down on its sunken courtyard with the geometric foundations of a fountain in its center. Sadly, you can't see the stairs linking the two levels (once lit by sunlight falling on a mirror-paved pool), nor the surrounding rooms, paved with colored marble.

❹ Stadium

See Visitors' Checklist.

The Stadium on the Palatine was laid out at the same time as the Palace of Domitian. It is not

clear whether it was a public stadium, a private track for exercising horses, or simply a large garden. The alcove in the eastern wall looks as though it may have held a box from which the emperor could have watched races. It is, however, known that the Stadium was used for foot races by the Ostrogothic king, Theodoric, in the 6th century – he added the small oval-shaped enclosure at the southern end of the site.

Stadium viewed from the south

❺ House of Livia

See Visitors' Checklist. If closed, apply to custodian.

This house dating from the 1st century BC is one of the best preserved on the Palatine. It was probably part of the house in which the Emperor Augustus and his wife Livia lived. Compared with later Imperial palaces, it is a relatively modest home. According to Suetonius, the biographer of Rome's early emperors, Augustus slept in

Remains of the Domus Augustana and the Palace of Septimius Severus

the same small bedroom for 40 years on a low bed that had "a very ordinary coverlet."

A flight of steps leads down to a mosaic-paved corridor into a courtyard. Its imitation-marble wall frescoes have been detached in order to preserve them, but they still hang in place. They are faded, but you can make out the veining patterns nonetheless. Off the courtyard are three small reception rooms. The frescoes in the central one include a faded scene of Hermes coming to the rescue of Zeus's beloved Io, who is guarded by the 100-eyed Argos. In the left-hand room are frescoed figures of griffins, and other beasts, while the decor in the right-hand room includes landscapes, and cityscapes.

Vaulted ceiling painting in the House of Augustus

Statue of the goddess Cybele

❻ House of Augustus

See Visitors' Checklist.

Painted in about 30 BC, the frescoes in the House of Augustus are among the most impressive existing examples of Roman wall paintings, similar in quality to those found in Pompeii and Herculaneum. In vivid shades of red, blue, and ocher, they include various *trompe l'oeil* effects, including a room with walls painted to resemble a stage with side doors, and a garden vista.

Although the frescoes are impressive, the house itself is modest. This is where Augustus (or Octavian, as he was then known) lived before assuming supreme power as Rome's first emperor. Only a few visitors are allowed in at any one time.

❼ Temple of Cybele

See Visitors' Checklist.

Other than a platform with a few column stumps and capitals, there is little to see of the Temple of Cybele, a popular fertility goddess imported to Rome from Asia. The priests of the cult castrated themselves in the belief that if they sacrificed their own fertility, they would guarantee that of the natural world. The annual festival of Cybele, in early spring, culminated with frenzied eunuch-priests slashing their bodies to offer up their blood to the goddess, and the ceremonial castration of novice priests.

❽ Huts of Romulus

See Visitors' Checklist.

According to legend, after killing his brother Remus, Romulus founded a village on the Palatine. In the 1940s a series of holes was found, and archaeologists deduced that these must originally have held the supporting poles of three Iron Age huts – the first foundations of Rome *(see pp20–21)*.

❾ Farnese Gardens

See Visitors' Checklist.

In the mid-1500s, Cardinal Alessandro Farnese, grandson of Pope Paul III, bought the ruins of Tiberius's palace on the Palatine. He filled in the ruined building and had the architect Vignola design a garden. The result was one of the first botanical gardens in Europe, its terraces linked by steps stretching from the House of Vestal Virgins in the Forum to the Palatine's Germalus peak. The gardeners introduced a number of plants to Italy and Europe, among them *Acacia farnesiana*. Farnese was at the center of a glittering set that included a number of courtesans, so the parties here are likely to have been somewhat unholy.

The area was dug up during the excavation of the Palatine and re-landscaped. The tree-lined avenues, rose gardens, and glorious views make it an ideal place to unwind.

VISITORS' CHECKLIST

Practical Information
Entrances & ticket kiosks: Via di San Gregorio 30. **Map** 8 E1–8 F1. **Tel** 06-3996 7700. **Open** 8:30am–approx 1 hour before sunset daily; last adm: 1 hour before closing. **Closed** Jan 1, Dec 25. 🎫 (includes entry to the Palatine Museum, the Forum & the Colosseum *see pp94–7*). 📷 🏛 📷

Transportation
🚌 75, 85, 87, 117, 175, 186, 810, 850 to Via dei Fori Imperiali. 🚊 3. Ⓜ Colosseo.

Farnese pavilions, relics of the age when the Palatine was a private garden

PIAZZA DELLA ROTONDA

The Pantheon, one of the great buildings in the history of European architecture, has stood at the heart of Rome for nearly 2,000 years. The historic area around it has seen uninterrupted economic and political activity throughout that time. Palazzo di Montecitorio, built for Pope Innocent XII as a papal tribunal in 1694, is now the Italian parliament, and many nearby buildings are government offices. This is also the main financial district of Rome, with banking headquarters and the stock exchange. Not many people live here, but in the evenings, Romans stroll in the narrow streets and fill the lively restaurants and cafés that make this a focus for the city's social life.

Sights at a Glance

Churches and Temples
1 Temple of Hadrian
3 Sant'Ignazio di Loyola
9 Gesù pp110–11
11 Santa Maria sopra Minerva
13 Pantheon pp114–15
14 Sant'Eustachio
15 La Maddalena
18 Santa Maria in Campo Marzio
20 San Lorenzo in Lucina

Historic Streets and Piazzas
2 Piazza di Sant'Ignazio
7 Via della Gatta

Historic Buildings
4 Palazzo del Collegio Romano
6 Palazzo Doria Pamphilj
8 Palazzo Altieri
17 Palazzo Baldassini
19 Palazzo Borghese
21 Palazzo di Montecitorio
24 Palazzo Capranica

Columns, Obelisks, and Statues
10 Vie' di Marmo
12 Obelisk of Santa Maria sopra Minerva
22 Obelisk of Montecitorio
23 Column of Marcus Aurelius

Fountains
5 Fontanella del Facchino

Cafés and Restaurants
16 Gaffè Giolitti

Restaurants
see pp311–15
1 Al Duello
2 Armando al Pantheon
3 Clemente alla Maddalena
4 Coso
5 Enoteca Capranica
6 Il Bacaro
7 La Pallacorda
8 La Rosetta
9 Maccheroni
10 Osteria del Sostegno
11 Vitti

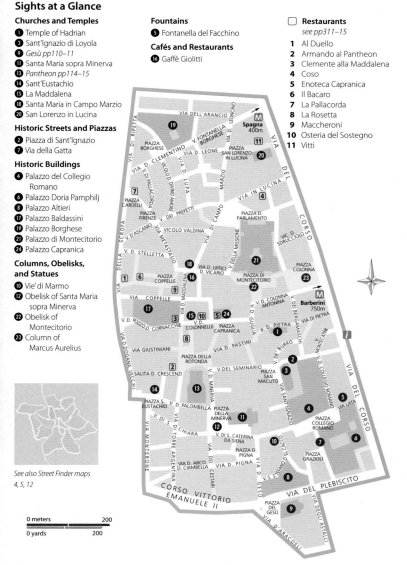

See also Street Finder maps 4, 5, 12

0 meters 200
0 yards 200

◀ Fountain outside the Pantheon at night

For map symbols see back flap

Street by Street: Piazza della Rotonda

If you wander through this area, sooner or later you will emerge into Piazza della Rotonda with its jumble of open-air café tables in front of the Pantheon. The refreshing splash of the fountain makes it a welcome resting place. In this warren of narrow streets, it can be hard to perceive just how close you are to some of Rome's finest sights. The magnificent art collection of Palazzo Doria Pamphilj and the Baroque splendor of the Gesù are just a few minutes' walk from the Pantheon. At night there is always a lively buzz of activity, as people dine in style or enjoy the coffee and ice cream for which the area is famous.

② Piazza di Sant'Ignazio
The square is a rare example of stylish domestic architecture from the early 18th century.

La Tazza d'Oro enjoys a reputation for the wonderful coffee consumed on its premises, as well as for its freshly ground coffee to take out. *(See p322.)*

① Temple of Hadrian
The columns of this Roman temple now form the facade of the stock exchange.

⑬ ★ Pantheon
The awe-inspiring interior of Rome's best-preserved ancient temple is only hinted at from the outside.

PIAZZA DI SANT'IGNAZIO

VIA DI SANT'IGNAZIO

VIA DEL SEMINARIO

PIAZZA DELLA ROTONDA

PIAZZA DELLA MINERVA

⑪ Santa Maria sopra Minerva
The rich decoration of Rome's only Gothic church was added in the 19th century.

⑫ Obelisk of Santa Maria sopra Minerva
In 1667 Bernini dreamed up the idea of mounting a recently discovered obelisk on the back of a marble elephant.

Locator Map
See Central Rome Map pp16–17)

❸ ★ Sant'Ignazio di Loyola
Andrea Pozzo painted this glorious Baroque ceiling (1685) to celebrate St. Ignatius and the Jesuit order.

❺ Fontanella del Facchino
The water in this small 16th-century fountain spurts from a barrel held by a porter.

❹ Palazzo del Collegio Romano
Up until 1870, the college educated many leading figures in the Catholic Church.

❻ ★ Palazzo Doria Pamphilj
Among the masterpieces in the art gallery of this magnificent family palazzo is this portrait of Pope Innocent X by Velázquez (1650).

❼ Via della Gatta
The street is named after the statue of a cat.

❽ Palazzo Altieri
This enormous 17th-century palazzo is decorated with the arms of Pope Clement X.

❾ ★ Gesù
The design of the first-ever Jesuit church had a great impact on religious architecture.

Key

— Suggested route

0 meters 75
0 yards 75

❿ Pie' di Marmo
This marble foot is a stray fragment from a gigantic Roman statue.

❶ Temple of Hadrian

La Borsa, Piazza di Pietra. **Map** 4 F3 & 12 E2. 117, 119, 492 and routes along Via del Corso or stopping at Piazza S. Silvestro. **Open** for exhibitions.

This temple honors the emperor Hadrian as a god, and was dedicated by his son, and successor Antoninus Pius in AD 145. The remains of the temple are visible on the southern side of Piazza di Pietra, incorporated into a 17th-century building. This was originally a papal customs house, completed by Carlo Fontana and his son in the 1690s. Today the building houses the Roman stock exchange (La Borsa).

Eleven marble Corinthian columns 49 ft (15 m) high stand on a base of *peperino*, a volcanic rock quarried from the Alban hills to the south of Rome. The columns decorated the northern flank of the temple enclosing its inner shrine, the *cella*. The *peperino* wall of the *cella* is still visible behind the columns, as is part of the coffered portico ceiling.

A number of reliefs from the temple, representing conquered Roman provinces, are now in the courtyard of the Palazzo dei Conservatori (*see pp72–3*). They reflect the mostly peaceful foreign policy of Hadrian's reign.

Remains of Hadrian's Temple

❷ Piazza di Sant'Ignazio

Map 4 F4 & 12 E3. 117, 119, 492 and routes along Via del Corso or stopping at Piazza S. Silvestro.

One of the major works of the Roman Rococo, the piazza (1727–8) is Filippo Raguzzini's

Illusionistic ceiling in the crossing of Sant'Ignazio

masterpiece. It offsets the imposing facade of the church of Sant'Ignazio with the intimacy of the houses belonging to the bourgeoisie. The theatrical setting, the curvilinear design, and the playful forms of its windows, balconies, and balusters mark the piazza as one of a highly distinct group of structures. Along with Palazzo Doria Pamphilj (1731), the facade of La Maddalena (1735), and the aristocratic Spanish Steps (1723), it belongs to the moment when Rome's bubbly Rococo triumphed over conservative Classicism.

❸ Sant'Ignazio di Loyola

Piazza di Sant'Ignazio. **Map** 4 F4 & 12 E3. **Tel** 06-679 4406. 117, 119, 492 and along Via del Corso. **Open** 7:30am–7pm daily (9am Sun).

The church was built by Pope Gregory XV in 1626 in honor of St. Ignatius of Loyola, founder of the Society of Jesus, and the man who most embodied the zeal of the Counter-Reformation.

Together with the Gesù (*see pp110–11*), Sant'Ignazio forms the center of the Jesuit area in Rome. Built in Baroque style, its vast interior, lined with

precious stones, marble, stucco, and gilt, creates a sense of theater. The church has a Latin-cross plan, with an apse and many side chapels. A cupola was planned but never built, so the space it would have filled was covered by a fake perspective painting. The piers built to uphold the cupola support the observatory of the Collegio Romano.

❹ Palazzo del Collegio Romano

Piazza del Collegio Romano. **Map** 5 A4 & 12 E3. 117, 119, 492 and along Via del Corso or stopping at Piazza Venezia. **Closed** to the public.

On the same block as the church of Sant'Ignazio is the palazzo used by Jesuits as a college where many future bishops, cardinals, and popes studied. The college was confiscated in 1870 and turned into an ordinary school. The portals bear the coat of arms of its founder, Pope Gregory XIII of Boncompagni (reigned 1572–85). The facade is also adorned with a bell, a clock, and two sundials. On the right is a tower built in 1787 as a meteorological observatory. Until 1925 its time signal regulated all the clocks within the city.

❺ Fontanella del Facchino

Via Lata. **Map** 5 A4 & 12 E3. 🚌 64, 81, 85, 117, 119, 492 and many other routes.

Il Facchino (the Porter), once in the Corso, now set in the wall of the Banco di Roma, was one of Rome's "talking statues" like Pasquino (see p126). Created around 1590, the fountain may have been based on a drawing by painter Jacopino del Conte. The statue of a man holding a barrel most likely represents a member of the Università degli Acquaroli (Fraternity of Water-carriers), though it is also said to be of Martin Luther, or of the porter Abbondio Rizzio, who died carrying a barrel.

The Facchino drinking fountain

❻ Palazzo Doria Pamphilj

Via del Corso 305. **Map** 5 A4 & 12 E3. **Tel** 06-679 7323. 🚌 64, 81, 85, 117, 119, 492 and many other routes. **Open** 10am–5pm daily. **Closed** Jan 1, Easter Sun, Dec 25. 🅿️ ♿ 📷 for private apartments. 🏠 🎦 🅿️ Concerts. 🆆 **doriapamphilj.it**

Palazzo Doria Pamphilj is a great island of stone in the heart of Rome, the oldest parts dating from 1435. Through the Corso entrance you can see the 16th-century porticoed courtyard with the coat of arms of the della Rovere family. The Aldobrandini were the next owners. Between 1601 and 1647 the mansion acquired a second courtyard and flanking wings at the expense of a public bath that stood nearby.

When the Pamphilj family took over, they completed the Piazza del Collegio Romano facade and the Via della Gatta

The facade of the Rococo palace building, Palazzo Doria Pamphilj

wing, a splendid chapel, and a theater inaugurated by Queen Christina of Sweden in 1684.

In the first half of the 1700s, Gabriele Valvassori created the gallery above the courtyard, and a new facade along the Corso, using the highly decorative style of the period known as the *barocchetto*, which now dominates the building. The stairways, and salons, the Mirror Gallery, and the picture gallery all radiate a sense of light and space.

The family collection in the Doria Pamphilj gallery has over 400 paintings dating from the 15th to the 18th centuries, including the famous portrait of Pope Innocent X Pamphilj by Velázquez. There are also works by Titian, Caravaggio, Lorenzo Lotto, and Guercino. The rooms in the private apartment still have many of their original furnishings, including splendid

Brussels and Gobelin tapestries. Occasionally, the gallery hosts concerts and evening visits of the collection.

❼ Via della Gatta

Map 5 A4 & 12 E3. 🚌 62, 63, 64, 70, 81, 87, 186, 492 & routes along Via del Plebiscito & Corso Vittorio Emanuele II.

This narrow street runs between the Palazzo Doria Pamphilj and the smaller Palazzo Grazioli. The ancient marble sculpture of a cat (gatta) that gives the street its name is on the first cornice on the corner of Palazzo Grazioli.

❽ Palazzo Altieri

Via del Gesù 93. **Map** 4 F4 & 12 E3. 🚌 46, 62, 63, 64, 70, 81, 87, 186, 492 and routes along Via del Plebiscito and Corso Vittorio Emanuele II. 🚋 8.

The Altieri family is first mentioned in Rome's history in the 9th century. This palazzo was built by the last male heirs, the brothers Cardinal Giambattista di Lorenzo Altieri and Cardinal Emilio Altieri, who later became Pope Clement X (reigned 1670–76). Many surrounding houses had to be demolished, but an old woman called Berta refused to leave, so her hovel was incorporated in the palazzo. Its windows are still visible on the west end of the building.

Caravaggio's *Rest during the Flight into Egypt* in Palazzo Doria Pamphilj

Gesù

Dating from between 1568 and 1584, the Gesù was the first Jesuit church to be built in Rome. Its design epitomizes Counter-Reformation Baroque architecture, and has been much imitated throughout the Catholic world. The layout proclaims the church's two major functions: a large nave with side pulpits for preaching to great crowds, and a main altar as the centerpiece for the celebration of the Mass. The illusionistic, decoration in the nave and dome was added a century later. Its message is clear, and confident: faithful Catholic worshippers will be joyfully uplifted into the heavens while Protestants, and other heretics are flung into the fires of Hell.

★ Chapel of Sant'Ignazio
Above its altar is a statue of the saint, framed by gilded lapis lazuli columns. The chapel was built in 1696–1700 by Andrea Pozzo, a Jesuit artist.

Triumph of Faith Over Idolatry
This vivid Baroque allegory sculpted by Théudon illustrates the great ambition of Jesuit theology.

St. Ignatius and the Jesuit Order

Spanish soldier Ignatius Loyola (1491–1556) joined the Church after being wounded in battle in 1521. He came to Rome in 1537 and founded the Jesuits, sending missionaries, and teachers all over the world to win souls for Catholicism.

Main entrance

Allegorical Figures
Antonio Raggi made these stuccoes, which were designed by Il Baciccia to complement the figures on his own nave frescoes.

KEY

① **The Chapel of St. Francis Xavier** is a memorial to the great missionary who died alone on an island off China in 1552.

Madonna della Strada
This 15th-century image, the Madonna of the Road, was originally displayed on the facade of Santa Maria della Strada, which once stood on this site.

VISITORS' CHECKLIST

Practical Information
Piazza del Gesù.
Map 4 F4 & 12 E4.
Tel 06- 697 001. **Open**
7am–12:30pm (7am–1pm Sun),
4–7:30pm daily. 🛗

Transportation
🚌 H, 46, 62, 64, 70, 81, 87, 186, 492, 628, 810 and other routes.
🚋 8.

★ Monument to San Roberto Bellarmino
Bernini captured the forceful personality of this anti-Protestant theologian, who died in 1621.

★ Nave Ceiling Decorations
The figures in Il Baciccia's astonishing fresco of the *Triumph of the Name of Jesus* spill out on to the coffered vaulting of the nave.

Cupola Frescoes
The cupola was completed by della Porta to Vignola's design. The frescoes, by Il Baciccia, feature Old Testament figures.

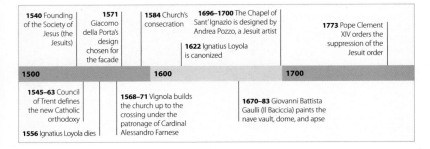

1500	1600	1700
1540 Founding of the Society of Jesus (the Jesuits)	**1584** Church's consecration	**1696–1700** The Chapel of Sant' Ignazio is designed by Andrea Pozzo, a Jesuit artist
1571 Giacomo della Porta's design chosen for the facade	**1622** Ignatius Loyola is canonized	**1773** Pope Clement XIV orders the suppression of the Jesuit order
1545–63 Council of Trent defines the new Catholic orthodoxy	**1568–71** Vignola builds the church up to the crossing under the patronage of Cardinal Alessandro Farnese	**1670–83** Giovanni Battista Gaulli (Il Baciccia) paints the nave vault, dome, and apse
1556 Ignatius Loyola dies		

Marble foot from a Roman statue

❿ Pie' di Marmo

Via Santo Stefano del Cacco. **Map** 4 F4 & 12 E3. 🚌 62, 63, 64, 70, 81, 87, 116, 186, 492 and other routes along Via del Corso, Via del Plebiscito, and Corso Vittorio Emanuele II.

It was popularly believed in the Middle Ages that half the population of ancient Rome was made up of bronze and marble statues. Fragments of these giants, usually gods or emperors, are scattered over the city. This piece, a marble foot *(pie' di marmo)*, comes from an area dedicated to the Egyptian gods Isis and Serapis and was probably part of a temple statue. Statues were painted and covered with jewels and clothes given by the faithful – a great fire risk with unattended burning tapers.

⓫ Santa Maria sopra Minerva

Piazza della Minerva 42. **Map** 4 F4 & 12 E3. **Tel** 06-679 3926. 🚌 116 and along Via del Corso, Via del Plebiscito, and Corso Vittorio Emanuele II. **Open** 7:30am–6:30pm Mon–Sat; 8am–1pm, 4–7pm Sun. Cloister: **Closed** for restoration – call for details. 🚹 🎵 Concerts.

Few other churches display such a complete and impressive record of Italian art. Dating from the 13th century, the Minerva is one of the few examples of Gothic architecture in Rome. It was the traditional stronghold of the Dominicans, whose anti-heretical zeal earned them the nickname of *Domini Canes* (the hounds of the Lord).

Built on ancient ruins, supposed to have been the Temple of Minerva, the simple T-shaped vaulted building acquired rich chapels and works of art by which its many patrons wished to be remembered. Note the Cosmatesque 13th-century tombs, and the exquisite works of 15th-century Tuscan and Venetian artists. Local talent of the period can be admired in Antoniazzo Romano's *Annunciation*, featuring Cardinal Juan de Torquemada, uncle of the infamous Spanish Inquisitor.

The more monumental style of the Roman Renaissance is well represented in the tombs of the 16th-century Medici popes, Leo X and his cousin Clement VII, and in the richly decorated Aldobrandini Chapel. Near the steps of the choir is the celebrated sculpture of the *Risen Christ*, started by Michelangelo but completed by Raffaele da Montelupo in 1521. There are also splendid works of art from the Baroque period, including a tomb, and a bust by Bernini.

The church is also visited because it contains the tombs of many famous Italians: St. Catherine of Siena, who died here in 1380; the Venetian sculptor Andrea Bregno (died 1506); the Humanist cardinal Pietro Bembo (died 1547); and Fra Angelico, the Dominican friar and painter, who died in Rome in 1455.

⓬ Obelisk of Santa Maria sopra Minerva

Piazza della Minerva. **Map** 4 F4 & 12 D3. 🚌 116 and routes along Via del Corso, and Corso Vittorio Emanuele II.

Originally meant to decorate Palazzo Barberini as a joke, this exotic elephant and obelisk sculpture is typical of Bernini's inexhaustible imagination. (The elephant was actually sculpted by Ercole Ferrata to Bernini's design.) When the ancient obelisk was found in the garden of the monastery of Santa Maria sopra Minerva, the friars wanted the monument erected in their piazza. The elephant was provided with its enormous saddle-cloth because of a friar's insistence that the gap under the animal's abdomen would undermine its stability. Bernini knew better: you need only look at the Fontana dei Quattro Fiumi *(see p122)* to appreciate his use of empty space. The elephant, an ancient symbol of intelligence and piety, was chosen as the embodiment of the virtues on which Christians should build true wisdom.

Bernini's Egyptian obelisk and marble elephant

Nave of Santa Maria sopra Minerva

⑬ Pantheon

See pp114–15.

⑭ Sant'Eustachio

Piazza Sant'Eustachio. **Map** 4 F4 & 12 D3. **Tel** 06-686 5334. 116, and routes along Corso Vittorio Emanuele II. **Open** 9am–noon, 4–7:30pm daily.

The origins of this church date to early Christian times, when it offered relief to the poor. In medieval times, many charitable brotherhoods elected Sant'Eustachio as their patron, and had chapels here.

The Romanesque bell tower is one of the few surviving remains of the medieval church, which was completely redecorated in the 17th and 18th centuries.

Nearby is the excellent Caffè Sant'Eustachio *(see p322).*

Bell tower of Sant'Eustachio

⑮ La Maddalena

Piazza della Maddalena. **Map** 4 F3 & 12 D2. **Tel** 06-899 281. 116, and many routes along Via del Corso, and Corso Vittorio Emanuele II. **Open** 8–11:45am, 5–8pm daily (from 9am Sat & Sun).

Situated in a small piazza near the Pantheon, the Maddalena's Rococo facade, built in 1735, epitomizes the love of light and movement of the late Baroque. Its curves are reminiscent of Borromini's San Carlo alle Quattro Fontane *(see p163)*. The facade has been lovingly restored, although diehard Neo-Classicists dismiss its painted stucco as "icing sugar."

The small size of the Maddalena did not deter the

The old-fashioned *salone* of the Caffè Giolitti

17th- and 18th-century decorators who filled the interior with ornaments from the floor to the top of the elegant cupola. The organ loft and choir are particularly powerful examples of the Baroque desire to fire the imagination of the faithful.

Many of the paintings, and sculptures adopt the Christian imagery of the Counter-Reformation. In the niches of the nave, the statues are personifications of virtues such as Humility and Simplicity. There are also scenes from the life of San Camillo, who died in the adjacent convent in 1614. The church belonged to his followers, the Camillians, a preaching order active in Rome's hospitals. Like the Jesuits, they commissioned powerful works of art to convey the force of their religious message.

La Maddalena's stuccoed facade

⑯ Caffè Giolitti

Via degli Uffici del Vicario 40. **Map** 4 F3 & 12 D2. **Tel** 06-699 1243. 116, and many routes along Via del Corso, and Corso Rinascimento. **Open** 7am–1am daily.

Founded in 1900, the Caffè Giolitti is the heir to the *Belle Époque* cafés that lined the nearby Via del Corso in Rome's first days as capital of the new Italian state. Its *salone* holds tourists in summer and Roman families on weekends, and on weekdays is frequented by local workers from a wide range of industries. Its ice cream is especially good.

⑰ Palazzo Baldassini

Via delle Coppelle 35. **Map** 4 F3 & 12 D2. 116, and many routes along Via del Corso, and Corso Rinascimento. **Closed** to the public.

Melchiorre Baldassini commissioned Antonio da Sangallo the Younger to build his home in Florentine Renaissance style in 1514–20. With its cornices marking the different floors and wrought-iron window grilles, this is one of the best examples of an early-16th-century Roman palazzo. It stands in the part of Rome still known as the Renaissance Quarter, which flourished around the long straight streets, such as Via di Ripetta and Via della Scrofa, built at the time of Pope Leo X (reigned 1513–21).

⓭ Pantheon

In the Middle Ages, the Pantheon, the Roman temple of "all the gods," became a church; in time, this magnificent building with its awe-inspiring domed interior became a symbol of Rome itself. The rectangular portico screens the vast hemispherical dome: only from inside can its true scale and beauty be appreciated. The rotunda's height and diameter are equal: 142 ft (43.3 m). The hole at the top of the dome, the *oculus*, provides the only light. We owe this marvel of Roman engineering to the emperor Hadrian, who designed it (AD 118–125) to replace an earlier temple built by Marcus Agrippa, son-in-law of Augustus. The shrines that now line the wall of the Pantheon range from the Tomb of Raphael to those of the kings of modern Italy.

★ Interior of the Dome
The dome was cast by pouring concrete mixed with tufa and pumice over a temporary wooden framework.

Floor Patterning
The marble floor, restored in 1873, preserves the original Roman design.

The portico, enclosed by granite columns

KEY

① **The immense portico** is built on the foundations of Agrippa's temple.

② **The walls of** the drum supporting the dome are 19 ft (6 m) thick.

③ **Oculus**

④ **Constructing the dome** from hollow decorative coffers reduced its weight.

Bell Towers
This 18th-century view by Bernardo Bellotto shows Bernini's much-ridiculed turrets, which were removed in 1883.

Raphael and La Fornarina

Raphael, at his own request, was buried here when he died in 1520. He had lived for years with his model, La Fornarina *(see p212)*, seen here in a painting by Giulio Romano, but she was excluded from the ceremony of his burial. On the right of his tomb is a memorial to his fiancée, Maria Bibbiena, niece of the artist's patron, Cardinal Dovizi di Bibbiena.

VISITORS' CHECKLIST

Practical Informationn
Piazza della Rotonda.
Map 4 F4 & 12 D3.
Tel 06-6830 0230.
Open 8.30am–7.30pm Mon–Sat, 9am–6pm Sun, 9am–1pm public hols.
Closed Jan 1, May 1, Dec 25.

Transportation
🚌 116 and routes along Via del Corso, Corso Vittorio Emanuele II & Corso del Rinascimento.

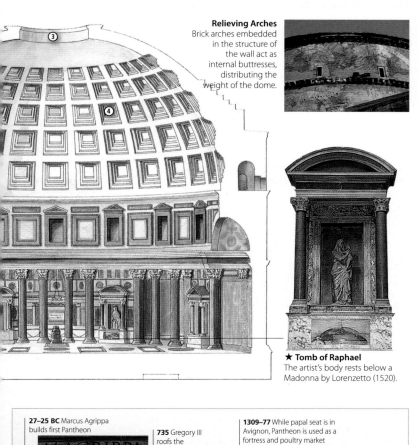

Relieving Arches
Brick arches embedded in the structure of the wall act as internal buttresses, distributing the weight of the dome.

★ **Tomb of Raphael**
The artist's body rests below a Madonna by Lorenzetto (1520).

27–25 BC Marcus Agrippa builds first Pantheon

Inscription on pediment

735 Gregory III roofs the Pantheon in lead

1309–77 While papal seat is in Avignon, Pantheon is used as a fortress and poultry market

| 50 BC | 0 | | AD 600 | 1200 | | 1800 |

118–25 Hadrian builds new Pantheon

609 Pope Boniface IV consecrates Pantheon as church of Santa Maria ad Martyres

663 Byzantine Emperor Constans II strips gilded tiles from the roof

1632 Urban VIII melts down bronze from portico for Bernini's baldacchino in St. Peter's

1888 Tomb of King Vittorio Emanuele II completed

Bernini's curving southern facade of Palazzo di Montecitorio

⑱ Santa Maria in Campo Marzio

Piazza di Campo Marzio 45. **Map** 4 F3 & 12 D2. **Tel** 06-679 4973. ▣ 116 and many routes on Via del Corso, and Corso Rinascimento. **Open** for services (10:30am Sun, and usually 4–7pm Mon–Fri).

Around the courtyard through which you enter the church, there are fascinating remnants of medieval houses. The church itself was rebuilt in 1685 by Antonio de Rossi, using a square Greek-cross plan with a cupola. Above the altar is a 12th-century painting of the Madonna, after which the church is named.

⑲ Palazzo Borghese

Largo della Fontanella di Borghese. **Map** 4 F3 & 12 D1. ▣ 81, 117, 492, 628. **Closed** to the public.

The palazzo was acquired in about 1605 by Cardinal Camillo Borghese, just before he became Pope Paul V. Flaminio Ponzio was hired to enlarge the building, and give it the grandeur appropriate to the residence of the pope's family. He added a wing overlooking Piazza Borghese, and the delightful porticoed courtyard inside. Subsequent enlargements included the building and decoration of a great *nymphaeum* known as the Bath of Venus. For more than two centuries this palazzo housed the Borghese family's renowned collection of paintings, which was bought by the Italian

state in 1902 and transferred to the Galleria Borghese *(see pp262–3)*.

Pope Paul V, who commissioned Palazzo Borghese for his family

⑳ San Lorenzo in Lucina

Via in Lucina 16A. **Map** 4 F3 & 12 E1. **Tel** 06-687 1494. ▣ 81, 117, 492, 628. **Open** 8am–8pm daily. ✝

The church is one of Rome's oldest Christian places of worship, and was probably built on a well sacred to Juno, protector of women. It was rebuilt during the 12th century, and today's external appearance is quite typical of the period, featuring a portico with reused Roman columns crowned by medieval capitals, a plain triangular pediment, and a Romanesque bell tower with colored marble inlay.
The interior was totally rebuilt in 1856–58. The old basilical plan was destroyed and the two side naves were replaced by Baroque

chapels. Do not miss the fine busts in the Fonseca Chapel, designed by Bernini, or the *Crucifixion* by Guido Reni above the main altar. There is also a 19th-century monument honoring French painter Nicolas Poussin, who died in Rome in 1655, and was buried in the church.

㉑ Palazzo di Montecitorio

Piazza di Montecitorio. **Map** 4 F3 & 12 E2. **Tel** 06-676 01. ▣ 116, and all routes along Via del Corso or stopping at Piazza S. Silvestro. **Open** 10am–3:30pm, usually 1st Sun each month (except Aug). Last adm: 3:30pm. ⓦ **camera.it**

The palazzo's first architect, Bernini, got the job after he presented a silver model of his design to the wife of his patron, Prince Ludovisi. The building was completed in 1694 by Carlo Fontana, and became the Papal Tribunal of Justice. In 1871 it was chosen to be Italy's new Chamber of Deputies, and by 1927 it had doubled in size with a second grand facade. The 630 members of parliament are elected by a majority system with proportional representation.

The church of San Lorenzo in Lucina

Emperor Augustus's obelisk

㉒ Obelisk of Montecitorio

Piazza di Montecitorio. **Map** 4 F3 & 12 E2. 116 and routes along Via del Corso or to Piazza S. Silvestro.

The measurement of time in ancient Rome was always a rather hit-or-miss affair: for many years, the Romans relied on an imported (and therefore inaccurate) sundial, a trophy from the conquest of Sicily. In 10 BC the Emperor Augustus laid out an enormous sundial in the Campus Martius. Its center was roughly in today's Piazza di San Lorenzo in Lucina. The shadow was cast by a huge granite obelisk that he had brought back from Heliopolis in Egypt. Unfortunately, this sundial too became inaccurate after 50 years, possibly due to the ground beneath it settling.

The obelisk was still in the piazza in the 9th century, but then disappeared until it was rediscovered lying under medieval houses in the reign of Pope Julius II (1503–13). The pope was intrigued, because Egyptian hieroglyphs were thought to hold the key to the wisdom of Adam before the Fall, but it was only under Pope Benedict XIV (reigned 1740–58) that the obelisk was finally unearthed. It was erected in its present location in 1792 by Pope Pius VI.

㉓ Column of Marcus Aurelius

Piazza Colonna. **Map** 5 A3 & 12 E2. 116 and routes along Via del Corso or to Piazza S. Silvestro.

Clearly an imitation of the Column of Trajan (see p92), this monument was erected after the death of Marcus Aurelius in AD 180 to commemorate his victories over the barbarian tribes of the Danube. The 80-year lapse between the two works produced a great artistic change: the wars of Marcus Aurelius are rendered with simplified pictures in stronger relief, sacrificing Classical proportions for the sake of clarity and immediacy. The spirit of the work is more akin to the 4th-century Arch of Constantine (see p93) than to Trajan's monument. Gone are the heroic qualities of the Roman soldiers, by now mostly barbarian mercenaries, and a sense of respect for the vanquished. A new emphasis on the supernatural points to the end of the Hellenistic tradition, and the beginning of Christianity.

Composed of 28 drums of marble, the column was restored in 1588 by Domenico Fontana on the orders of Pope Sixtus V. The emperor's statue on the summit was replaced by a bronze of St. Paul. The 20 spirals of the low relief chronicle the German war of AD 172–3, and (above) the Sarmatic war of AD 174–5. The column is almost 100 ft (30 m) high and 12 ft (3.7 m) in diameter. An internal spiral staircase leads to the top. The easiest way to appreciate the sculptural work, however, is to visit the Museo della Civiltà Romana in EUR (see p268) and study the casts of the reliefs.

Windows of Palazzo Capranica

㉔ Palazzo Capranica

Piazza Capranica. **Map** 4 F3 & 12 D2. 116, and routes along Via del Corso or to Piazza S. Silvestro.

One of Rome's small number of surviving 15th-century buildings, the palazzo was commissioned by Cardinal Domenico Capranica both as his family residence and as a college for higher education. Its fortress-like appearance is a patchwork of subsequent additions, not unusual in the late 15th century, when Rome was still hovering between medieval and Renaissance taste. The Gothic-looking windows on the right of the building show the cardinal's coat of arms, and the date 1451 is inscribed on the doorway underneath. The palazzo now houses a conference center.

Relief of the emperor's campaigns on the Column of Marcus Aurelius

PIAZZA NAVONA

The foundations of the buildings surrounding the elongated oval of Piazza Navona are the remains of the grandstands of the vast Stadium of Domitian. The piazza still provides a dramatic spectacle today with the obelisk of the Fontana dei Quattro Fiumi in front of the church of Sant' Agnese in Agone as its focal point. The predominant style of the area is Baroque, with many of the finest buildings dating from the reign of Innocent X Pamphilj (1644–55), patron of Bernini, and Borromini. Of special interest is the complex of the Chiesa Nuova, headquarters of the Filippini, the order founded by San Filippo Neri, the 16th-century "Apostle of Rome."

Sights at a Glance

Churches and Temples
4 Sant'Agnese in Agone
5 Santa Maria dell'Anima
6 Santa Maria della Pace
7 San Luigi dei Francesi
9 Sant'Ivo alla Sapienza
10 Sant'Andrea della Valle
15 Chiesa Nuova
16 Oratorio dei Filippini
20 San Salvatore in Lauro

Museums
12 Palazzo Braschi
21 Museo Napoleonico

Historic Buildings
3 Palazzo Pamphilj
8 Palazzo Madama
11 Palazzo Massimo
    alle Colonne
17 Torre dell'Orologio
18 Palazzo del Banco
    di Santo Spirito
23 Palazzo Altemps

Fountains and Statues
1 Fontana dei Quattro Fiumi
13 Pasquino

Historic Streets and Piazzas
2 Piazza Navona
14 Via del Governo Vecchio
19 Via dei Coronari

Restaurants
22 Rostaria dell'Orso

☐ **Restaurants**
see pp311–15

1 Baffetto
2 Capricci Siciliani
3 Casa Bleve
4 Cul de Sac
5 Enoteca Il Piccolo
6 Hostaria dell'Orso
7 Il Convivio-Troiani
8 Il Corallo
9 La Campana
10 Le Streghe

11 Montevecchio
12 Old Bear
13 Osteria del Gallo
14 Osteria del Pegno
15 Terra di Siena
16 The Library
17 Sangallo ai Coronari

See also Street Finder maps
4, 11, 12

◀ Detail from the Fontana dei Quattro Fiumi, Piazza Navona

For map symbols *see back flap*

Street by Street: Piazza Navona

No other piazza in Rome can rival the theatricality of Piazza Navona. Day or night, there is always something going on in the pedestrian area around its three flamboyant fountains. The Baroque is also represented in many of the area's churches. To discover an older Rome, walk along Via del Governo Vecchio to admire the façades of its Renaissance buildings, and browse in the fascinating antique shops.

⑯ Oratorio dei Filippini
The musical term oratorio comes from this place of informal worship.

⑰ Torre dell' Orologio
This clock tower by Borromini (1648) is part of the Convent of the Filippini.

VIA DEL CORALLO

VIA DEL GOVERNO VECCHIO

VIA DI PARIONE

⑮ Chiesa Nuova
This church was rebuilt in the late 16th century for the order founded by San Filippo Neri.

To Corso Vittorio Emanuele II

⑭ Via del Governo Vecchio
This street preserves a large number of fine Renaissance houses.

CORSO VITTORIO EMANUELE II

PIAZZA DI PASQU

⑬ Pasquino
Romans hung satirical verses and dialogues on this weather-beaten statue.

⑥ Santa Maria della Pace
This medallion shows Pope Sixtus IV who reigned 1471–84, and under whose orders the church was built.

❸ Palazzo Pamphilj
This grand town house was built for Pope Innocent X and his family in the mid-17th century.

PIAZZ DI SAN PANTALEO

⑪ Palazzo Massimo alle Colonne
The magnificent curving colonnade (1536) is by Baldassarre Peruzzi.

⑫ Palazzo Braschi
A late 18th-century building with a splendid balcony, the palazzo houses the Museo di Roma.

Key

— Suggested route

0 meters	75
0 yards	75

Locator Map
See Central Rome Map pp16–17

5 Santa Maria dell'Anima
For four centuries this has been the German church in Rome.

Santa Maria della Pace

4 Sant'Agnese in Agone
Borromini's startling concave facade (1657) dominates one side of Piazza Navona.

2 ★ Piazza Navona
This unique piazza owes its shape to a Roman racetrack, and its stunning decor to the genius of the Roman Baroque.

7 ★ San Luigi dei Francesi
An 18th-century statue of St. Louis stands in a niche in the facade.

8 Palazzo Madama
A spread-eagled stone lion skin decorates the central doorway of the palazzo, now the Italian Senate.

1 Fontana dei Quattro Fiumi
This fountain supporting an Egyptian obelisk was designed by Bernini.

The Fontana del Moro was remodeled in 1653 by Bernini, who designed the central sea god.

9 Sant'Ivo alla Sapienza
This tiny domed church is one of Borromini's most original creations. He worked on it between 1642 and 1650.

10 ★ Sant'Andrea della Valle
The church, with its grandiose facade by Carlo Rainaldi (1665), has gained fame outside Rome as the setting of the first act of Puccini's *Tosca*.

To Campo de' Fiori

❶ Fontana dei Quattro Fiumi

Piazza Navona. **Map** 4 E4 & 11 C3.
46, 62, 64, 70, 81, 87, 116, 492, 628.

Built for Pope Innocent X Pamphilj, this magnificent fountain in the center of Piazza Navona was unveiled in 1651. The pope's coat of arms, the dove, and the olive branch decorate the pyramid rock formation supporting the Roman obelisk, which once stood in the Circus of Maxentius on the Appian Way. Bernini designed the fountain, which was paid for by means of taxes on bread, and other staples. The great rivers – the Ganges, the Danube, the Nile, and the Plate – are represented by four giants. The Nile's veiled head symbolizes the river's unknown source, but there is also a legend that the veil conveys Bernini's dislike for the nearby Sant'Agnese in Agone, designed by his rival Borromini. Similarly, the athletic figure of the Plate, cringing with arm

Palazzo Pamphilj, the largest building in Piazza Navona

upraised, is supposed to express Bernini's fear that the church will collapse. However, these widely believed stories have no basis in fact: Bernini had completed the fountain before Borromini started work on the church.

❷ Piazza Navona

Map 4 E3 & 11 C2. 46, 62, 64, 70, 81, 87, 116, 492, 628.

Rome's most beautiful Baroque piazza follows the shape of Domitian's Stadium, which once stood on this site – some of its arches are still visible below the church of Sant'Agnese in Agone. The *agones* were athletic contests held in the 1st-century stadium, which could seat 33,000 people. The word "Navona" is thought to be a corruption of *in agone*. The piazza's unique appearance, and

atmosphere were created in the 17th century with the addition of the Fontana dei Quattro Fiumi. The other fountains date from the previous century but have been altered several times since. The basin of the Fontana di Nettuno, at the northern end, was built by Giacomo della Porta in 1576, while the statues of Neptune and the Nereids date from the 19th century. The Fontana del Moro, at the southern end, was also designed by della Porta, though Bernini altered it later, adding a statue of a Moor fighting a dolphin.

Up until the 19th century, Piazza Navona was flooded during August by plugging the fountain outlets. The rich would splash around in carriages, while street urchins paddled after them. Today, with its numerous shops, and cafés, the piazza is a favorite in all seasons. In summer it is busy with street entertainers, while in winter it fills with colorful stands selling toys, and sweets for the feast of the Befana.

Family dove and olive branch on facade of Palazzo Pamphilj

❸ Palazzo Pamphilj

Piazza Navona. **Map** 4 E4 & 11 C3.
46, 62, 64, 70, 81, 87, 116, 492, 628.
Closed to the public.

In 1644 Giovanni Battista Pamphilj became Pope Innocent X. During his 10-year reign, he heaped riches on his own family, especially his domineering sister-in-law, Olimpia Maidalchini. The "talking statue" Pasquino *(see p126)* gave her the nickname "Olim-Pia," Latin for "formerly virtuous." She lived in the grand Palazzo Pamphilj, which has frescoes by Pietro da Cortona, and a gallery by Borromini. The building is now the Brazilian embassy, and cultural center.

Symbolic figure of the Ganges River in the Fontana dei Quattro Fiumi

❹ Sant'Agnese in Agone

Piazza Navona. **Map** 4 E4 & 11 C3. **Tel** 06-6819 2134. 46, 62, 64, 70, 81, 87, 116, 492, 628. **Open** 9:30am–12:30pm, 4–7pm Tue–Sun.

This church is believed to have been founded on the site of the brothel where, in AD 304, the young St. Agnes was exposed naked to force her to renounce her faith. A marble relief in the crypt shows the miraculous growth of her hair, which fell around her body to protect her modesty. She was martyred on this site and is buried in the catacombs that bear her name along Via Nomentana *(see p266)*.

Today's church was commissioned by Pope Innocent X in 1652. The first architects were father and son Girolamo and Carlo Rainaldi, but they were replaced by Borromini in 1653. He stuck more or less to the Rainaldi plan except for the concave facade designed to emphasize the dome. A statue of St. Agnes on the facade is said to be reassuring the Fontana dei Quattro Fiumi's statue of the Plate River that the church is stable.

Carlo Saraceni's *Miracle of St. Benno and the Keys of Meissen Cathedral*

Statue of St. Agnes on facade of Sant' Agnese in Agone

Peruzzi in Santa Maria dell'Anima. It stands to the right of Giulio Romano's damaged altarpiece and is redolent of the pagan Renaissance spirit the pope had so condemned during his brief, rather gloomy reign, when patronage of the arts ground to a halt. Santa Maria dell'Anima is the German church in Rome, and some paintings, such as the *Miracle of St. Benno* by Carlo Saraceni (1618), illustrate events within the history of Germany.

❺ Santa Maria dell'Anima

Via Santa Maria dell'Anima 66. **Map** 4 E4 & 11 C2. **Tel** 06-682 8181. 46, 62, 64, 70, 81, 87, 116, 492, 628. **Open** 3–7pm daily (9am–1pm Thu–Tue).

Pope Adrian VI (reigned 1522–3), son of a shipbuilder from Utrecht, was the last non-Italian pope before John Paul II. He would have disapproved of his superb tomb by Baldassarre

❻ Santa Maria della Pace

Vicolo dell'Arco della Pace 5. **Map** 4 E3 & 11 C2. **Tel** 06-686 1156. 46, 62, 64, 70, 81, 87, 116, 492, 628. **Open** 9am–noon Mon, Wed, Sat. 2 steps. Exhibitions, concerts.

A drunken soldier allegedly pierced the breast of a painted Madonna on this site, causing it to bleed. Pope Sixtus IV della

Rovere (reigned 1471–84) placated the Virgin by ordering Baccio Pontelli to build her a church if she would bring the war with Turkey to an end. Peace was restored, and the church was named Santa Maria della Pace (St. Mary of Peace).

The cloister was added by Bramante in 1504. As in his famous Tempietto *(see p223)*, he scrupulously followed Classical rules of proportion, and achieved a monumental effect in a relatively small space. Pietro da Cortona may have had Bramante's Tempietto in mind when he added the church's charming semicircular portico in 1656. The interior, a short nave ending under an octagonal cupola, houses Raphael's famous frescoes of four *Sibyls*, and four *Prophets* by his pupil Timoteo Viti, painted for the banker Agostino Chigi in 1514. Baldassarre Peruzzi also did some work in the church (fresco in the first chapel on the left), as did the architect Antonio da Sangallo the Younger, who designed the second chapel on the right.

❼ San Luigi dei Francesi

Piazza di San Luigi dei Francesi 5. **Map**
4 F4 & 12 D2. **Tel** 06-688 271. 🚌 70,
81, 87, 116, 186, 492, 628. **Open**
10am–12:30pm, 3–7pm daily. **Closed**
Thu pm. 🚻 📷 📧

The French national church was
founded in 1518, but it took until
1589 to complete, with contribu-
tions by Giacomo della Porta
and Domenico Fontana. The
church serves as a last resting
place for many illustrious French
people, including Chateau-
briand's lover Pauline de
Beaumont.

Three Caravaggios hang in
the fifth chapel on the left, all
dedicated to St. Matthew.
Painted between 1597 and
1602, these were Caravaggio's
first great religious works: the
Calling of St. Matthew, the
Martyrdom of St. Matthew, and
St. Matthew and the Angel. The
first version of this last painting
was rejected because of its vivid
realism; never before
had a saint been
shown as a
tired old man
with dirty
feet. All three
works display a
highly dramatic
use of light.

St. Matthew and the Angel by Caravaggio, San Luigi dei Francesi

Shield linking symbols of France and
Rome on facade of San Luigi

❽ Palazzo Madama

Corso del Rinascimento. **Map** 4 F4 &
12 D3. **Tel** 06-6706 2430. 🚌 70, 81, 87,
116, 186, 492, 628. **Open** 10am–6pm
generally first Sat of month (exc Aug).
Tickets available from 8:30am on day
of visit. 🖥 **senato.it**

This 16th-century palazzo was
built for the Medici family. It was
the residence of Medici cousins
Giovanni and Giuliano, both
of whom became popes:
Giovanni as Leo X and Giuliano
as Clement VII. Caterina de'
Medici, Clement VII's niece,
also lived here before she was
married to Henry, son of King
Francis I of France, in 1533.

The palazzo takes its name
from Madama Margherita of
Austria, illegitimate daughter of
Emperor Charles V, who married
Alessandro de' Medici and, after
his death, Ottavio Farnese.
Thus part of the art collection
of the Florentine Medici family
was inherited by the Roman
Farnese family.

The spectacular facade was
built in the 17th century by
Paolo Maruccelli. He gave it
an ornate cornice and
whimsical decorative details
on the roof. Since 1871 the

Cornice of Palazzo Madama

palazzo has been the seat
of the upper house of the
Italian parliament.

❾ Sant'Ivo alla Sapienza

Corso del Rinascimento 40.
Map 4 F4 & 12 D3. **Tel** 06-361 2562.
🚌 40, 46, 64, 70, 81, 87, 116, 186, 492,
628. **Open** 9am–noon Sun. 🚻

The church's lantern is crowned
with a cross on top of a dramatic
twisted spiral – a highly
distinctive landmark from Rome's
roof terraces. No other Baroque
church is quite like this one,
made by Borromini. Based on a
ground design of astonishing
geometrical complexity, the
walls are a breathtaking
combination of concave and
convex surfaces. The church
stands in the small courtyard of
the Palazzo della Sapienza, seat
of the old University of Rome
from the 15th century until 1935.

Dome of Sant'Andrea della Valle

⑩ Sant'Andrea della Valle

Piazza Sant'Andrea della Valle. **Map** 4 E4 & 12 D4. **Tel** 06-686 1339. 🚌 H, 40, 46, 62, 64, 70, 81, 87, 116, 186, 492, 628. 🚋 8. **Open** 7:30am–noon, 4–7:15pm daily. 🕆

The church is the scene of the first act of Puccini's opera *Tosca*, though opera fans will not find the Attavanti chapel a poetic invention. The real church has much to recommend it – the impressive facade shows the flamboyant Baroque style at its best. Inside, a golden light filters through high windows, showing off the gilded interior. Here lie the two popes of the Sienese Piccolomini family: on the left of the central nave is the tomb of Pius II, the first Humanist pope (reigned 1458–64); Pope Pius III lies opposite – he reigned for less than a month in 1503.

The church is famous for its beautiful dome, the largest in Rome after St. Peter's. It was built by Carlo Maderno in 1622–5 and was painted with splendid frescoes by Domenichino and Giovanni Lanfranco. The latter's extravagant style, to be seen in the dome fresco *Glory of Paradise*, won him most of the commission, and the jealous Domenichino is said to have tried to kill his colleague. He failed, but Domenichino's jealousy was unnecessary, as shown by his two beautiful paintings of scenes from the

life of St. Andrew around the apse, and altar. In the Strozzi Chapel, built in the style of Michelangelo, the altar has copies of *Leah* and *Rachel* by Michelangelo in San Pietro in Vincoli *(see p172)*.

Roman column, Palazzo Massimo

⑪ Palazzo Massimo alle Colonne

Corso Vittorio Emanuele II 141. **Map** 4 F4 & 11 C3. 🚌 40, 46, 62, 64, 70, 81, 87, 116, 186, 492, 628. Chapel: **Open** 7am–noon Mar 16.

During the last two years of his life, Baldassarre Peruzzi built this palazzo for the Massimo family, whose home had been destroyed in the 1527 Sack of Rome. Peruzzi displayed great ingenuity in dealing with an awkwardly shaped site. The previous building had stood on the ruined Theater of Domitian, which created a curve in the great processional Via Papalis. Peruzzi's convex colonnaded facade follows the line of the street. His originality is also evident in the small square upper windows, the courtyard, and the stuccoed vestibule. The Piazza de' Massimi entrance has a Renaissance-style, frescoed facade. A single column from the theater has been set up in the piazza.

The Massimo family traced its origins to Quintus Fabius Maximus, conqueror of Hannibal in the 3rd

century BC, and their coat of arms is borne by an infant Hercules. Over the years the family produced many great Humanists, and in the 19th century, it was a Massimo who negotiated peace with Napoleon. On March 16 each year, the family chapel opens to the public to commemorate young Paolo Massimo's resurrection from the dead by San Filippo Neri in 1538.

⑫ Palazzo Braschi

Piazza San Pantaleo 10. **Map** 4 E4 & 11 C3. **Tel** 06-6710 8346. 🚌 40, 46, 62, 64, 70, 81, 87, 116, 186, 492, 628. **Open** 10am–8pm Tue–Sun (ticket office closes at 7pm). ♿ 🚻 🎧 📷 🖥

On one side of Piazza San Pantaleo is the last Roman palazzo to be built for the family of a pope. Palazzo Braschi was built in the late 18th century for Pope Pius VI Braschi's nephews by the architect Cosimo Morelli. He gave the building its imposing facade, which looks out on to the piazza.

The palazzo now houses the municipal Museo di Roma. It holds collections of pictures, drawings, and everyday objects illustrating life in Rome from medieval times to the 19th century.

Angel with raised wing by Ercole Ferrata, flanking the facade of Sant'Andrea della Valle

Pasquino, the most famous of Rome's satirical "talking statues"

⓫ Pasquino

Piazza di Pasquino. **Map** 4 E4 & 11 C3. 40, 46, 62, 64, 70, 81, 87, 116, 492, 628.

This rough chunk of marble is all that remains of a Hellenistic group, probably representing the incident in Homer's *Iliad* in which Menelaus shields the body of the slain Patroclus. For years it lay as a stepping stone in a muddy medieval street, until it was erected on this corner in 1501, near the shop of an outspoken cobbler named Pasquino. Freedom of speech was not encouraged in papal Rome, so the cobbler wrote out his satirical comments on current events and attached them to the statue.

Other Romans followed suit, hanging their maxims and verses on the statue by night to escape punishment. Despite the wrath of the authorities, the sayings of the "talking statue" (renamed Pasquino) were part of popular culture up until the 19th century. Other statues started to "talk" in the same vein; Pasquino used to conduct dialogues with the statue Marforio in Via del Campidoglio (now in the courtyard of Palazzo Nuovo, *see pp70–71*) and with the Babuino in Via del Babuino *(see p137)*. Pasquino still speaks on occasion, and Rome's English-language movie theater is named after him *(see p353)*.

⓮ Via del Governo Vecchio

Map 4 E4 & 11 B3. 40, 46, 62, 64.

The street takes its name from Palazzo del Governo Vecchio, the seat of papal government in the 17th and 18th centuries. Once part of the Via Papalis, which led from the Lateran to St. Peter's, the street is lined with 15th- and 16th-century houses and small workshops. Particularly interesting are those at No. 104 and No. 106. The small palazzo at No. 123 was once thought to have been the home of Bramante.

Opposite is Palazzo del Governo Vecchio. It is also known as Palazzo Nardini, from the name of its founder, which is inscribed on the first-floor windows, with the date 1477.

Via del Governo Vecchio

Facade of the Chiesa Nuova

⓯ Chiesa Nuova

Piazza della Chiesa Nuova. **Map** 4 E4 & 11 B3. **Tel** 06-687 52 89. 40, 46, 62, 64. **Open** 8am–noon (to 1pm Sun), 4:30–7pm daily.

San Filippo Neri (St. Philip Neri) is the most appealing of the Counter-Reformation saints. A highly unconventional reformer, he required his noble Roman followers to humble themselves in public. He made aristocratic young men parade through the streets of Rome in rags or even with a fox's tail tied behind them, and set noblemen to work as laborers building his church. With the help of Pope Gregory XIII, his church was built in place of an old medieval church, Santa Maria in Vallicella, and it has been known ever since as the Chiesa Nuova (new church).

Begun in 1575 by Matteo da Città di Castello and continued by Martino Longhi the Elder, it was consecrated in 1599 (although the facade, by Fausto Rughesi, was only finished in 1606). Against San Filippo's wishes, the interior was decorated after his death; Pietro da Cortona frescoed the nave, dome, and apse, taking nearly 20 years. There are also three paintings by Rubens: *Madonna and Angels* above the altar, *Saints Domitilla, Nereus and Achilleus* on the right of the altar, and *Saints Gregory, Maurus, and Papias* on the left. San Filippo is buried in his own chapel, to the left of the altar.

Borromini's facade of the Oratorio

⑯ Oratorio dei Filippini

Piazza della Chiesa Nuova. **Map** 4 E4 & 11 B3. **Tel** 06-6710 8100. 🚌 46, 62, 64. **Closed** for restoration.

With the adjoining church and convent, the oratory formed the center of Filippo Neri's religious order, which was founded in 1575. Its members are commonly known as Filippini. The musical term "oratorio" (a religious text sung by solo voices and chorus) derives from the services that

were held here. Filippo Neri came to Rome at age 18 to work as a tutor. The city was undergoing a period of religious strife and an economic slump after the Sack of Rome in 1527. There was also an outbreak of the plague. It was left to newcomers like Neri and Ignazio di Loyola to revive the spiritual life of the city.

Neri formed a brotherhood of laymen who worshipped together and helped pilgrims and the sick *(see Santissima Trinità dei Pellegrini p145)*. He founded the Oratory as a center for religious discourse. Its conspicuous curving brick facade was built by Borromini in 1637–43.

⑰ Torre dell' Orologio

Piazza dell'Orologio. **Map** 4 E4 & 11 B3. 🚌 40, 46, 62, 64.

Borromini built this clock tower to decorate one corner of the Convent of the Oratorians of San Filippo Neri in 1647–9. It is typical of Borromini in that the front and rear are concave and the sides convex. The mosaic of

the Madonna beneath the clock is by Pietro da Cortona, while on the corner of the building is a small tabernacle to the Madonna flanked by angels in the style of Bernini.

Pietro da Cortona (1596–1669)

⑱ Palazzo del Banco di Santo Spirito

Via del Banco di Santo Spirito. **Map** 4 D4 & 11 A2. 🚌 40, 46, 62, 64. **Open** normal banking hours.

Formerly the mint of papal Rome, this palazzo is often referred to as the Antica Zecca (old mint). The upper stories of the facade, built by Antonio da Sangallo the Younger in the 1520s, are in the shape of a Roman triumphal arch. Above it stand two Baroque statues symbolizing Charity, and Thrift, and in the center of the arch above the main entrance an inscription records the founding of the Banco di Santo Spirito by Pope Paul V Borghese in 1605.

Pope Paul was a very shrewd financier, and he encouraged Romans to deposit their money at the bank by offering the vast estates of the Hospital of Santo Spirito *(see p246)* as security. The system catered only to the rudimentary banking requirements of the population, but business was brisk as people deposited money here, safe in the knowledge that they could get it out simply by presenting a chit. The hospital coffers also gained from the system. The Banco di Santo Spirito still exists, but is now part of the Banca di Roma.

Facade of the Banco di Santo Spirito, built to resemble a Roman arch

Cloister, San Salvatore in Lauro

⓳ Via dei Coronari

Map 4 D3 & 11 B2. 🚌 40, 46, 62, 64, 70, 81, 87, 116, 186, 280, 492.

Large numbers of medieval pilgrims making their way to St. Peter's walked along this street to cross over the Tiber at Ponte Sant'Angelo. Of the businesses that sprang up to try to part the pilgrims from their money, the most enduring was the selling of rosaries, and the street is still named after the rosary sellers *(coronari)*. The street followed the course of the ancient Roman Via Recta (straight street), which originally ran from today's Piazza Colonna to the Tiber.

Making one's way through the vast throng of people in Via dei Coronari could be extremely hazardous. In the Holy Year of 1450, some 200 pilgrims died, crushed by the crowds or drowned in the Tiber. Following the tragedy, Pope Nicholas V demolished the Roman triumphal arch that stood at the entrance to Ponte Sant'Angelo. In the late 15th century, Pope Sixtus IV encouraged the building of private houses and palaces along the street.

Although the rosary sellers have been replaced by antique dealers, the street still has many original buildings from the 15th and 16th centuries. One of the earliest, at Nos. 156–7, is known as the House of Fiammetta, the mistress of Cesare Borgia.

⓴ San Salvatore in Lauro

Piazza San Salvatore in Lauro 15. **Map** 4 E3 & 11 B2. **Tel** 06-687 5187. 🚌 70, 81, 87, 116, 186, 280, 492. **Open** 9am–noon, 3–7pm daily. ✝

The church is named "in Lauro" after the laurel grove that grew here in ancient times. The church standing here today was constructed at the end of the 16th century by Ottaviano Mascherino. The bell tower and sacristy were 18th-century additions by Nicola Salvi, famous for the Trevi Fountain *(see p161)*.

The church contains the first great altarpiece by the 17th-century artist Pietro da Cortona, *The Birth of Jesus*, in the first chapel to the right.

The adjacent convent of San Giorgio, to the left, has a pretty

Facade of San Salvatore in Lauro

Renaissance cloister, a frescoed refectory, and the monument to Pope Eugenius IV (reigned 1431–47) moved here when the old St. Peter's was pulled down. An extravagant Venetian, Eugenius would willingly spend thousands of ducats on his gold tiara, but requested a "simple, lowly burial place" near his predecessor Pope Eugenius III. His portrait, painted by Salviati, hangs in the refectory.

In 1669 San Salvatore in Lauro became the seat of a pious association, the Confraternity of the Piceni, who were inhabitants of the Marche region. Fanatically loyal to the pope, the Piceni were traditionally employed as papal soldiers and tax collectors.

㉑ Museo Napoleonico

Piazza di Ponte Umberto 1. **Map** 4 E3 & 11 C1. **Tel** 06-6880 6286. 🚌 70, 81, 87, 116, 186, 280, 492. **Open** 10am–6pm Tue–Sun. **Closed** Jan 1, May 1, Dec 25. 🐾 🖼 📷 📷

This museum contains memorabilia and portraits of Napoleon Bonaparte and his family. Personal relics of Napoleon himself include an Indian shawl he wore during his exile on St. Helena.

After his death in 1821, the pope allowed many of Bonaparte's family to settle in Rome, including his mother, Letizia, who lived in Palazzo Misciattelli on Via del Corso, and his sister Pauline, who married the Roman Prince Camillo Borghese. The museum has a cast of her right breast, made by Canova in 1805 as a study for his statue of her as a reclining Venus, now in the Museo Borghese *(see p263)*. Portraits and personal effects of other members of the family are on display, including uniforms, court dresses, and a penny-farthing bicycle that belonged to Prince Eugène, the son of Emperor Napoleon III.

The last male of the Roman branch of the family was Napoleon Charles, portrayed in a late 19th-century painting by Guglielmo de Sanctis. The collection was assembled in 1927 by the Counts Primoli, the sons of Charles's sister, Carlotta Bonaparte.

The palace next door, in Via Zanardelli, houses the Racolta Praz, an impressive selection of over a thousand *objets d'art*, paintings, and pieces of furniture. Dating from the 17th and 18th centuries, they were collected by the art historian and literary critic Mario Praz.

Entrance to Museo Napoleonico

㉒ Hostaria dell'Orso

Via dei Soldati 25. **Map** 4 E3 & 11 C2. 70, 81, 87, 116, 186, 204, 280, 492, 628. **Open** 8pm–1am Mon–Sat.

This ancient inn *(see p314)* has a 15th-century portico and loggia built with columns from Roman ruins. Visitors to the inn included the 16th-century French writers Rabelais and Montaigne. Dante is also said to have stayed here.

㉓ Palazzo Altemps

Piazza Sant'Apollinare 46. **Map** 4 E3 & 11 C2. **Tel** 06-6872719. 70, 81, 87, 116, 280, 492, 628. **Open** 9am–7:45pm Tue–Sun (last adm: 1 hour before closing.) **Closed** Jan 1, Dec 25.

An extraordinary collection of Classical sculpture is housed in this branch of the Museo Nazionale Romano. Restored as a museum during the 1990s, the palazzo was originally built for Girolamo Riario, nephew of Pope Sixtus IV in 1480. The Riario coat of arms can still be seen in the janitor's room. In the popular uprising that followed the pope's death in 1484, the building was sacked, and Girolamo fled the city.

In 1568 the palazzo was bought by Cardinal Marco Sittico Altemps. His family was of German origin – the name is an Italianization of Hohenems – and influential in the church. The palazzo was renovated by Martino Longhi the Elder in the 1570s. He added the great belvedere, crowned with obelisks, and a marble unicorn.

The Altemps family were ostentatious collectors; the courtyard, and its staircase are lined with ancient sculptures. These form part of the museum's collection, together with the Ludovisi collection of ancient sculptures, which was previously housed in the Museo Nazionale Romano in the Baths of Diocletian *(see p161)*. Located on the ground floor is the Greek statue of Athena Parthenos and the

Side relief of the Ludovisi Throne, Palazzo Altemps

Dionysius group, a Roman copy of the Greek original. On the first floor, at the far end of the courtyard, visitors can admire the Painted Loggia, dating from 1595. The Ludovisi throne, a Greek original carved in the 5th century BC, is on the same floor. It is decorated with reliefs, one of which shows a young woman rising from the sea, thought to represent Aphrodite. In the room known as the Salone del Camino is the powerful statue *Galatian's Suicide*, a marble copy of a group originally made in bronze. Nearby is the Ludovisi Sarcophagus, dating from the 3rd century AD.

Galatian's Suicide in the Palazzo Altemps

PIAZZA DI SPAGNA

By the 16th century, the increase in numbers of visiting pilgrims and ecclesiastics was making life in Rome's already congested medieval center unbearable. A new triangle of roads was built, still in place today, to help channel pilgrims as quickly as possible from the city's north gate, the Porta del Popolo, to the Vatican. By the 18th century, hotels had sprung up all over the district. Today this attractive area offers much more: the superb works of Renaissance and Baroque art in Santa Maria del Popolo and Sant' Andrea delle Fratte, the magnificent reliefs of the restored Ara Pacis, art exhibitions in the Villa Medici, fine views of the city from the Spanish Steps, and the Pincio Gardens, and Rome's most famous shopping streets, centered on Via Condotti.

Sights at a Glance

Churches
- ❶ Sant'Andrea delle Fratte
- ❿ Trinità dei Monti
- ⓬ All Saints
- ⓮ Santa Maria dei Miracoli and Santa Maria in Montesanto
- ⓱ *Santa Maria del Popolo pp140–41*
- ㉑ San Rocco
- ㉒ Santi Ambrogio e Carlo al Corso

Museums and Galleries
- ❼ Keats-Shelley Memorial House
- ⓭ Casa di Goethe

Historic Buildings
- ❷ Palazzo di Propaganda Fide
- ⓫ Villa Medici

Arches, Gates, and Columns
- ❸ Colonna dell'Immacolata
- ⓰ Porta del Popolo

Historic Streets and Piazzas
- ❹ Via Condotti
- ❻ Piazza di Spagna
- ❾ Spanish Steps
- ⓰ Piazza del Popolo

Monuments and Tombs
- ⓳ Ara Pacis
- ⓴ Mausoleum of Augustus

Parks and Gardens
- ⓯ Pincio Gardens

Cafés and Restaurants
- ❺ Caffè Greco
- ❽ Babington's Tea Rooms

Restaurants
see pp315–17
1. Babette
2. Canova-Tadolini Museum Atelier
3. 'Gusto
4. Hamasei
5. Il Palazzetto
6. Imàgo
7. Le Jardin de Russie
8. Osteria Margutta
9. Rhome
10. Tati' al 28

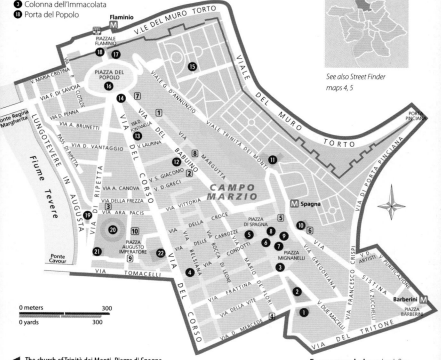

See also Street Finder maps 4, 5

◀ The church of Trinità dei Monti, Piazza di Spagna

For map symbols *see back flap*

Street by Street: Piazza di Spagna

The network of narrow streets between Piazza di Spagna, and Via del Corso is one of the liveliest areas in Rome, drawing throngs of tourists and Romans to its discreet and elegant shops. In the 18th century the area was full of hotels for frivolous English aristocrats doing the Grand Tour, but there were also artists, writers, and composers, who took the city's history and culture more seriously.

Spagna station

8 Babington's Tea Rooms
English tourists are catered for in the style of the 1890s.

6 ★ Piazza di Spagna
For almost three centuries, the square with its curious Barcaccia fountain in the center has been the chief meeting place for visitors to Rome.

PIAZZA DI SPAGNA

VIA VITTORIA

VIA DELLA CROCE

VIA BOCCA DI LEONE

VIA DELLA CARROZZE

5 Caffè Greco
Busts and portraits recall the café's former artistic patrons.

VIA DEL CORSO

Via delle Carrozze took its name from the carriages of wealthy tourists that used to line up here for repairs.

VIA DELLA CONDOTTI

VIA BORGONONA

VIA FRATT

4 Via Condotti
This shadowy, narrow street has the smartest shops in one of the smartest shopping areas in the world.

0 meters		75
0 yards		75

Bulgari sells very expensive jewelry behind an austere shopfront in Via Condotti.

Key

— Suggested route

M Metro station

⑨ ★ Spanish Steps
Even obscured by crowds, the steps are one of the glories of late Baroque Rome.

Locator Map
See Central Rome Map pp16–17

③ Colonna dell'Immacolata
A Roman column supports a statue of the Virgin Mary.

⑩ Trinità dei Monti
This 16th-century church has a spectacular setting, and some of the finest views in Rome.

① Sant'Andrea delle Fratte
Pasquale Marini painted *The Redemption* to decorate the interior of Borromini's high dome in 1691.

VIA DI PROPAGANDA

DELLA VITE

② Palazzo di Propaganda Fide
This facade (1665) was one of the last works of the great Francesco Borromini.

⑦ ★ Keats-Shelley Memorial House
The library is part of the small museum established in the house where the English poet Keats died in 1821.

❶ Sant'Andrea delle Fratte

Via Sant'Andrea delle Fratte 1. **Map** 5 A3. **Tel** 06-679 3191. 🚌 116, 117. Ⓜ Spagna. **Open** 6:30am –12:30pm, 4–7pm daily (4:30–7:30pm summer). ✝

When Sant'Andrea delle Fratte was built in the 12th century, this was the northernmost edge of Rome. Though the church is now firmly embedded in the city, its name (*fratte* means thickets) recalls its original setting.

The church was completely rebuilt in the 17th century, partly by Borromini. His bell tower and dome, best viewed from the higher ground farther up Via Capo le Case, are remarkable for the complex arrangement of concave and convex surfaces. The bell tower is particularly fanciful, with angel caryatids, flaming torches, and exaggerated scrolls like semi-folded hearts supporting a spiky crown.

In 1842, the Virgin Mary appeared in the church to a Jewish banker, who promptly converted to Christianity, and became a missionary. Inside, the chapel of the Miraculous Madonna is the first thing you notice. The church is better known, however, for the angels that Borromini's rival, Bernini, carved for the Ponte Sant'Angelo. Pope Clement IX declared them too lovely to be exposed to the weather, so they remained with Bernini's family until 1729, when they were moved to the church.

Angel by Bernini, Sant'Andrea delle Fratte

❷ Palazzo di Propaganda Fide

Via di Propaganda 1. **Map** 5 A2. **Tel** 06-6987 9299. **Fax** 06-6988 0246. 🚌 116, 117. Ⓜ Spagna. Museum: **Open** 2–6pm Mon, Wed, Fri.

The powerful Jesuit Congregation for the Propagation of the Faith was founded in 1622. Although Bernini had originally been commissioned to create their headquarters, Innocent X, who became pope in 1644, preferred the style of Borromini, who was asked to continue. His extraordinary west facade, completed in 1662, is striped with broad pilasters, between which the first-floor windows bend in, and the central bay bulges. A rigid band divides its floors, and the cornice above the convex central bay swerves inward. The more you look at it, the more restless it seems; a sign, perhaps, of the increasing unhappiness of the architect, who committed suicide in 1667. The building is now the Vatican's missionary museum.

Entrance to the Jesuit College

❸ Colonna dell'Immacolata

Piazza Mignanelli. **Map** 5 A2. 🚌 116, 117. Ⓜ Spagna.

Inaugurated in 1857, the column commemorates Pope Pius IX's proclamation of the doctrine of the Immaculate Conception, holding that the Virgin Mary was the only human being ever to have been born "without the stain of original sin." The column itself dates from ancient, pagan Rome but is crowned with a statue of the Virgin Mary.

On December 8, the Pope, assisted by firefighters, places a wreath around the head of the statue *(see p63)*.

Portrait of Pope Pius IX (reigned 1846–78)

❹ Via Condotti

Map 5 A2. 🚌 81, 116, 117, 119, 492, and many routes along via del Corso or stopping at Piazza S. Silvestro. Ⓜ Spagna. *See Shops and Markets pp325–37.*

Named after the conduits that carried water to the Baths of Agrippa near the Pantheon, Via Condotti is now home to the most traditional of Rome's designer clothes shops. Stores selling shoes and other leather goods are also well represented. The street is popular for early evening strolls, when elegant Italians mingle with tourists in shorts and walking shoes.

Slightly younger designers such as Laura Biagiotti and the Fendi sisters have shops on the parallel Via Borgognona, while Valentino and Giorgio Armani both have shops on Via Condotti itself. Valentino has a second branch on Via Bocca di Leone, which crosses Via Condotti just below Piazza di Spagna, and Versace also has a shop here. Giorgio Armani has a second store on nearby Via del Babuino, among the discreet art galleries, exclusive antique shops, and furnishing stores.

View along Via Condotti toward the Spanish Steps

❺ Caffè Greco

Via Condotti 86. **Map** 5 A2. **Tel** 06-67 91 700. 🚌 81, 116, 117, 119, 492. Ⓜ Spagna. **Open** 9am–8pm daily. **Closed** Jan 1, Aug 14 & 15. ♿

This café was opened by a Greek (hence *greco*) in 1760, and throughout the 18th century it was a favorite

Caffè Greco, over 240 years old

meeting place for foreign artists. Writers such as Keats, Byron, and Goethe and composers like Liszt, Wagner, and Bizet all breakfasted and drank here. So too did Casanova, and mad King Ludwig of Bavaria. Today, Italians stand in the crowded foyer to sip a quick espresso coffee, and foreigners sit in a cozy back room whose walls are studded with portraits of the café's illustrious customers.

Pope Urban VIII's arms, with the Barberini bees

❻ Piazza di Spagna

Map 5 A2. 🚌 116, 117, 119. Ⓜ Spagna.

Shaped like a crooked bow tie and surrounded by tall, shuttered houses painted in muted shades of ocher, cream, and russet, Piazza di Spagna (Spanish Square) is crowded all day and (in summer) most of the night. It is the most famous square in Rome, and has long been the haunt of foreign visitors and expatriates.

In the 17th century Spain's ambassador to the Holy See had his headquarters on the square, and the area around it was deemed to be Spanish territory. Foreigners who unwittingly trespassed were liable to be dragooned into the Spanish army. In the 18th and 19th centuries, Rome was almost as popular with visitors as it is today, and the square stood at the heart of the city's main hotel district. Some of the travelers came in search of knowledge and artistic inspiration, but most were more interested in gambling, collecting ancient statues, and conducting love affairs with Italian women.

Not surprisingly, the wealthy travelers attracted hordes of beggars, who were usually supplied with tear-jerking letters by scribes who worked in the square.

The Fontana della Barcaccia in the square is the least showy of Rome's Baroque fountains, and it is often completely screened from view by people resting on its rim. It was designed either by the famous Gian Lorenzo Bernini or by his father Pietro. Because the pressure from the aqueduct that feeds the fountain is extremely low, there are no spectacular cascades or spurts of water. Instead, Bernini constructed a leaking boat – *barcaccia* means useless, old boat – which lies half submerged in a shallow pool.

The bees and suns that decorate the Fontana della Barcaccia are taken from the family coat of arms of Pope Urban VIII Barberini, who commissioned the fountain.

The Fontana della Barcaccia at the foot of the Spanish Steps

Bust of Shelley by Moses Ezekiel

❼ Keats-Shelley Memorial House

Piazza di Spagna 26. **Map** 5 A2. **Tel** 06-678 4235. 🚌 116, 117, 119. Ⓜ Spagna. **Open** 10am–1pm, 2–6pm Mon–Fri; 11am–2pm, 3–6pm Sat. **Closed** Dec 8, Dec 24–Jan 1. 📷 📸 book in advance. 📱 w keats-shelley-house.org

In November 1820 the English poet John Keats came to stay with his friend, the painter Joseph Severn, in a dusty pink house, the Casina Rossa, on the corner of the Spanish Steps. Suffering from consumption, Keats had been sent to Rome by his doctor, in the hope that the mild, dry climate would help the young man's recovery. Depressed because of scathing criticism of his work and tormented by his love for a young girl named Fanny Brawne, Keats died the following February at age 25.

His death inspired fellow poet Percy Bysshe Shelley to write the poem *Mourn not for Adonais*. In July 1822 Shelley himself was drowned in a boating accident in the Gulf of La Spezia off the coast of Liguria. Keats, Shelley, and Severn are all buried in Rome's Protestant Cemetery (*see p207*).

In 1906 the house was bought by an Anglo-American association and preserved as a memorial and library in honor of English Romantic poets. The relics include a lock of Keats's hair, some fragments of Shelley's bones in a tiny urn, and a garish carnival mask picked up by Lord Byron as a souvenir of a trip to Venice. You can visit the room where Keats died, though all the original furniture was burned after his death, on papal orders.

❽ Babington's Tea Rooms

Piazza di Spagna 23. **Map** 5 A2. **Tel** 06-678 6027. 🚌 116, 117, 119. Ⓜ Spagna. **Open** 10am–9pm daily. **Closed** Dec 25. ♿

These august, old-fashioned tea rooms were opened in 1896 by two Englishwomen, Anna Maria and Isabel Cargill Babington, to serve homesick British tourists with scones, jam, and pots of Earl Grey tea. The food remains homey – shepherd's pie and chicken supreme for lunch, muffins and cinnamon toast for tea – although these days the menu offers pancakes with maple syrup for breakfast as well as the traditional bacon and eggs.

Purveyors of English breakfasts to homesick exiles since 1896

❾ Spanish Steps

Scalinata della Trinità dei Monti, Piazza di Spagna. **Map** 5 A2. 🚌 116, 117, 119. Ⓜ Spagna.

In the 17th century the French owners of Trinità dei Monti decided to link the church with Piazza di Spagna by building a magnificent new flight of steps. They also planned to place an equestrian statue of King Louis XIV at the top. Pope Alexander VII Chigi was not happy at the prospect of erecting a

The Spanish Steps in spring with azaleas in full bloom

statue of a French monarch in the papal city, and the arguments continued until the 1720s, when an Italian architect, Francesco de Sanctis, produced a design that satisfied both parties. The steps, completed in 1726, combine straight sections, curves, and terraces to create one of the city's most dramatic and distinctive landmarks.

When the Victorian novelist Charles Dickens visited Rome, he reported that the Spanish Steps were the meeting place for artists' models, who would dress in colorful traditional costumes, hoping to catch the attention of a wealthy artist. The steps are now a popular place to sit, write postcards, take photos, flirt, busk, or watch the passers-by, but eating here is not allowed.

19th-century engraving of the inner facade of the Villa Medici

A pupil of Michelangelo, Volterra had to paint clothes on the nudes in the *Last Judgment* in the Sistine Chapel in response to the objections of Pope Pius IV.

Michelangelo's influence is obvious in the powerfully muscled bodies shown in the *Deposition* (second chapel on the left). The circles of gesturing figures and dancing angels surrounding the Virgin Mary in the *Assumption* (third chapel on the right) have more in common with the graceful style of Raphael.

⓫ Villa Medici

Accademia di Francia a Roma, Viale Trinità dei Monti 1. **Map** 5 A2. **Tel** 06-676 1311. 🚌 117, 119. Ⓜ Spagna. **Open** for exhibitions, and concerts. Gardens: **Open** Tue–Sun (four to six guided visits daily; in English at noon). 🖼️ 📷 🅿️ 🌐 villamedici.it

Superbly positioned on the Pincio hill above Piazza di Spagna, this 16th-century villa has kept the name it assumed when Cardinal Ferdinando de' Medici bought it in 1576. From the terrace you can look across the city to Castel Sant'Angelo, from where Queen Christina of Sweden is said to have fired the large cannonball that now sits in the basin of the fountain.

The villa is home to the French Academy. This was founded by Louis XIV in 1666 to give a few select painters the chance to study in Rome. Nicolas Poussin

was one of the first advisers to the Academy, Ingres was a director and ex-students include Jean-Honoré Fragonard and François Boucher.

After 1803, when the French Academy moved to the Villa Medici, musicians were also admitted; both Berlioz and Debussy came to Rome as students of the Academy.

⓬ All Saints

Via del Babuino 153B. **Map** 4 F2. **Tel** 06-3600 1881. 🚌 117, 119. **Open** 8am–4pm daily. ✝️

In 1816 the Pope gave English residents, and visitors the right to hold Anglican services in Rome, but it wasn't until the early 1880s that they acquired a site to build their own church. The architect was G. E. Street, best known in Britain for his Neo-Gothic churches, and the London Law Courts. All Saints is also built in Victorian Neo-Gothic, and the interior, though splendidly decorated with different colored Italian marbles, has a very English air. Street also designed St. Paul's-within-the-Walls in Via Nazionale, whose interior is a jewel of British Pre-Raphaelite art.

The street on which All Saints stands got its name from the Fontana del Sileno, known as Babuino (baboon) due to the sad condition in which it was found.

Trinità dei Monti's bell towers

⓾ Trinità dei Monti

Piazza della Trinità dei Monti. **Map** 5 A2. **Tel** 06-679 4179. 🚌 116, 117, 119. Ⓜ Spagna. **Open** 9am–7pm Tue–Sun (closed 1–3pm Tue & Fri). ✝️

The views of Rome from the platform in front of the twin bell-towered facade of Trinità dei Monti are so beautiful that the church itself is often ignored. It is, however, unusual for Rome, for it was founded by the French in 1495, and although it was later badly damaged, there are still traces of attractive late Gothic latticework in the vaults of the transept. The interconnecting side chapels are decorated with Mannerist paintings, including two fine works by Daniele da Volterra.

Fontana del Sileno, on Via del Babuino since 1957

⑬ Casa di Goethe

Via del Corso 18. **Map** 4 F1. **Tel** 06-3265 0412. 🚌 117, 119, 490, 495, 628, 926. 🚋 2. Ⓜ Flaminio. **Open** 10am–6pm Tue–Sun. 📷 ♿ 🎁 📷 🆆 **casadigoethe.it**

The German poet, dramatist, and novelist Johann Wolfgang von Goethe (1749–1832) lived in this house from 1786 until 1788 and worked on a journal that eventually formed part of his travel book *The Italian Journey*. Rome's noisy street life irritated him, especially during Carnival time. He was a little perturbed by the number of murders in his neighborhood, but Rome energized him and his book became one of the most influential ever written about Italy.

⑭ Santa Maria dei Miracoli and Santa Maria in Montesanto

Piazza del Popolo. **Map** 4 F1. 🚌 117, 119, 490, 495, 628, 926. 🚋 2. Ⓜ Flaminio. Santa Maria dei Miracoli: **Tel** 06-361 0250. **Open** 6:30am–12:30pm, 4–7:30pm Mon–Sat; 8am–1pm, 5–7:30pm Sun & public hols. 🎁 ♿ Santa Maria in Montesanto: **Tel** 06-361 0594. **Open** 7–8am, 4:30–7:30pm Mon–Fri, 7–8am Sat, 11am–1pm Sun.

The two churches at the south end of Piazza del Popolo were designed by the architect Carlo Rainaldi (1611–91), proof that he could be as ingenious as his peers, Bernini and Borromini. To provide a focal point for the piazza, the churches had to appear symmetrical, but the site on the left was

Portrait of Goethe in the Roman countryside by Tischbein (1751–1821)

narrower. So Rainaldi gave Santa Maria dei Miracoli (on the right) a circular dome and Santa Maria in Montesanto an oval one to squeeze it into the narrower site, while keeping the sides of the supporting drums that face the piazza identical.

⑮ Pincio Gardens

Il Pincio. **Map** 4 F1. 🚌 117, 119, 490, 495, 628, 926. 🚋 2. Ⓜ Flaminio.

The Pincio Gardens lie above Piazza del Popolo on a hillside that has been so skillfully terraced, and richly planted with trees that, from below, the zig-zagging road climbing to the gardens is virtually invisible. In ancient Roman times, there were magnificent gardens on the Pincio hill, but the present gardens were designed in the early 19th century by Giuseppe Valadier (who also redesigned the Piazza del Popolo). The broad avenues, lined with umbrella pines, palm trees, and evergreen oaks,

The Pincio Gardens water clock

soon became a fashionable place to stroll, and even in the 20th century such diverse characters as Gandhi and Mussolini, Richard Strauss and King Farouk of Egypt patronized the Casina Valadier, an exclusive café, and restaurant in the grounds.

From the Pincio's main square, Piazzale Napoleone I, the panoramic views of Rome stretch from the Monte Mario to the Janiculum. For full effect, approach the gardens from the grounds of Villa Borghese *(see pp260–61)* above the Pincio, or along Viale della Trinità dei Monti. The panorama is particularly beautiful at sunset,

The twin churches of Santa Maria in Montesanto (left) and Santa Maria dei Miracoli in a 19th-century view of Piazza del Popolo the traditional time for tourists to take a stroll in the gardens.

One of the most striking features of the park itself is an Egyptian-style obelisk that Emperor Hadrian erected on the tomb of his favorite, the beautiful male slave Antinous. After the slave's premature death (according to some accounts, he died saving the emperor's life), Hadrian deified him.

The 19th-century water clock on Via dell'Orologio was designed by a Dominican monk. It was displayed at the Paris Exhibition of 1889.

The Casina Valadier restaurant in the Pincio Gardens

⓰ Piazza del Popolo

Map 4 F1. 🚌 117, 119, 490, 495, 926. 🚋 2. Ⓜ Flaminio.

A vast cobbled oval standing at the apex of the triangle of roads known as the Trident, Piazza del Popolo forms a grand symmetrical antechamber to the heart of Rome. Twin Neo-Classical facades stand on either side of the Porta del Popolo; an Egyptian obelisk rises in the center; and the matching domes and porticoes of Santa Maria dei Miracoli and Santa Maria in Montesanto flank the beginning of Via del Corso.

Although it is now one of the most unified squares in Rome, Piazza del Popolo evolved gradually over the centuries. In 1589 the great town-planning pope, Sixtus V, had the obelisk erected in the center by Domenico Fontana. Over 3,000

Traditional carnival band in Piazza del Popolo

years old, the obelisk was originally brought to Rome by Augustus to adorn the Circus Maximus after the conquest of Egypt. Almost a century later, Pope Alexander VII commissioned Carlo Rainaldi to build the twin Santa Marias.

In the 19th century the piazza was turned into a grandiose oval by Giuseppe Valadier, the designer of the Pincio Gardens. He also encased Santa Maria del Popolo in a Neo-Classical shell to make its south facade fit in better with the overall appearance of the piazza.

In contrast to the piazza's air of ordered rationalism, many of the events staged here were barbaric. In the 18th and 19th centuries, public executions were held in Piazza del Popolo, often as part of the celebration of Carnival. Condemned men were sometimes hammered to death by repeated blows to the temples. The last time a criminal was executed in this way was in 1826, even though the guillotine had by then been adopted as a more efficient means of execution.

The riderless horse races from the piazza down Via del Corso were scarcely more humane: the performance of the runners was enhanced by feeding the horses stimulants, wrapping them in nail-studded ropes, and letting off fireworks at their heels.

⓱ Santa Maria del Popolo

See pp140–41.

⓲ Porta del Popolo

Between Piazzale Flaminio and Piazza del Popolo. Map 4 F1. 🚌 117, 119, 490, 495, 926. 🚋 2. Ⓜ Flaminio.

The Via Flaminia, built in 220 BC to connect Rome with Italy's Adriatic coast, enters the city at Porta del Popolo, a grand 16th-century gate built on the orders of Pope Pius IV Medici. The architect, Nanni di Baccio Bigio, modeled it on a Roman triumphal arch. The outer face has statues of St. Peter and St. Paul on either side and a huge Medici coat of arms above.

A century later, Pope Alexander VII commissioned Bernini to decorate the inner face to celebrate the arrival in Rome of Queen Christina of Sweden. Lesser visitors were often held up while customs officers rifled through their luggage. The only way to speed things up was with a bribe.

Porta del Popolo's central arch

ⓘ Santa Maria del Popolo

One of Rome's greatest stores of artistic treasures, this early Renaissance church was commissioned by Pope Sixtus IV della Rovere in 1472. Among the artists who worked on the building were Andrea Bregno, and Pinturicchio. Later additions were made by Bramante and Bernini. Many illustrious families have chapels here, all decorated with appropriate splendor. The Della Rovere Chapel has delightful Pinturicchio frescoes, the Cerasi Chapel has two Caravaggio masterpieces, *The Conversion of St. Paul*, and *The Crucifixion of St. Peter*, but the finest of all is the Chigi Chapel designed by Raphael for his patron, the banker Agostino Chigi. The most striking of the church's many Renaissance tombs are the two by Andrea Sansovino behind the main altar.

★ Chigi Chapel
Raphael designed this chapel, which has an altarpiece by Sebastiano del Piombo. Niches on either side of the altar house sculptures by Bernini and Lorenzetto. Mosaics in the dome show God as creator of the seven heavenly bodies.

Kneeling Skeleton
This floor mosaic of the figure of death was added to the Chigi Chapel in the 17th century.

Entrance

KEY

① **Cybo Chapel**

② **The Tomb** of Giovanni della Rovere (1483) is by pupils of Andrea Bregno.

③ **The altarpiece** of *The Assumption* is by Annibale Carracci (1540–1609).

④ **The altar** houses the 13th-century painting known as the *Madonna del Popolo*.

⑤ **The Tomb** of Ascanio Sforza, who died in 1505, is by Andrea Sansovino.

Della Rovere Chapel
Pinturicchio painted the frescoes in the lunettes and the Nativity above the altar in 1490.

★ Caravaggio Paintings in Cerasi Chapel

One of two Caravaggios in the Cerasi Chapel, *The Crucifixion of St. Peter* uses dramatic foreshortening to highlight the sheer effort involved in turning the saint's crucifix upside down.

Stained Glass

In 1509 French artist Guillaume de Marcillat was invited to provide Rome's first two stained-glass windows.

★ Delphic Sibyl

This is one of a series of frescoes by Pinturicchio, some Classical and others Biblical, painted in 1508–10 to decorate the ceiling of the apse.

Nero's Ghost

Nero lived on in the imagination of the people long after the fall of the Roman Empire. In the Middle Ages a legend arose that a walnut tree growing here on the spot where his ashes were buried was haunted by the emperor. Ravens roosting in the tree were thought to be demons tormenting him for his hideous crimes. When the first church was built here in 1099 by Pope Paschal II, the tree was cut down, supposedly putting an end to the supernatural events that had terrified local people.

1213–27 Church enlarged under Gregory IX

Pinturicchio (c. 1454–1513)

1485–9 Della Rovere Chapel painted by Pinturicchio

1513–16 Raphael designs, and executes Chigi Chapel

1050   1200   1350   1500

1099 Paschal II builds chapel over tombs of the Domitia family (which included Nero) in honor of the Madonna

Pope Paschal II (reigned 1099–1118)

1472–8 Sixtus IV builds church (one of the first Renaissance churches in Rome)

1473 Main altar built

1530–34 Chigi Chapel altarpiece built by Sebastiano del Piombo

⑲ Ara Pacis

Lungotevere in Augusta. **Map** 4 F2.
Tel 06-0608. 🚌 70, 81, 117, 119, 186,
628. **Open** 9am–7pm Tue–Sun (last
adm: 6pm). **Closed** Jan 1, Dec 25. 📷
 🚻 📷 🅦 arapacis.it

Reconstructed at considerable
expense over many years, the
Ara Pacis (Altar of Peace) is
one of the most significant
monuments of ancient Rome. It
celebrates the peace created
throughout the Mediterranean
area by Emperor Augustus after
his victorious campaigns in Gaul
and Spain. The monument was
commissioned by the Senate in
13 BC and completed four years
later. It was positioned so that
the shadow of the huge obelisk
sundial on Campus Martius
(see p117) would fall upon it on
Augustus's birthday. It is a

Frieze on south wall showing procession with the family of Augustus

square enclosure on a low
platform with the altar in the
center. All surfaces are
decorated with magnificent
friezes, and reliefs carved in
Carrara marble. The reliefs
on the north and south walls
depict a procession that took
place on July 4, 13 BC, in which
the members of the emperor's
family can be identified, ranked
by their position in the
succession. At the time the heir
apparent was Marcus Agrippa,
husband of Augustus's
daughter Julia. All the portraits
in the relief are carved with
extraordinary realism, even

the innocent toddler clinging
to his mother's skirts.

The tale of the rediscovery of
the Ara Pacis dates back to the
16th century, when the first
panels were unearthed. One
section ended up in Paris,
another in Florence. Further
discoveries were made in
the late 19th century, when
archaeologists finally realized
just what they had found. What
we see today has all been
pieced together since 1938, in
part original, in part facsimile. In
1999 the architect Richard Meier
designed a building to house
the monument.

Marcus Agrippa (right)

The altar was used once
a year for a sacrifice on
the anniversary of the
monument's
inauguration.

East wall

South wall

West wall

North wall

Augustus's young
grandson, Lucius

An acanthus frieze
runs around the
lower half of the
outside wall.

⑳ Mausoleum of Augustus

Piazza Augusto Imperatore. **Map** 4 F2.
Tel 06-0608. 🚌 81, 117, 492, 628, 926.
Closed for restoration.

Now just a weedy mound ringed with cypresses, and sadly strewn with litter, this was once the most prestigious burial place in Rome. Augustus had the mausoleum built in 28 BC, the year he became sole ruler, as a tomb for himself and his descendants. The circular building was 285 ft (87 m) in diameter with two obelisks (now in Piazza del Quirinale and Piazza dell'Esquilino) at the entrance.

Inside were four concentric passageways linked by corridors where the urns containing the ashes of the Imperial family were placed. The first to be buried here was Augustus's favorite nephew, Marcellus, who had married Julia, the emperor's daughter. He died in 23 BC, possibly poisoned by Augustus's second wife Livia, who felt that her son, Tiberius, would make a more reliable emperor. When Augustus died in AD 14, his ashes were placed in the mausoleum, Tiberius duly became emperor, and dynastic poisonings continued to fill the family vault with urns.

This sinister monument was later used as a medieval fortress, a vineyard, a private garden, and even, in the 18th century, as an auditorium and theater.

Augustus, the first Roman emperor

Madonna, San Rocco, and Sant'Antonio with Victims of the Plague by Il Baciccia (1639–1709)

㉑ San Rocco

Largo San Rocco 1. **Map** 4 F2. **Tel**
06-689 6416. 🚌 81, 117, 492, 628,
926. **Open** 7:30–9:15am, 4:30–8pm
Mon–Sat; 8:30am–1pm, 4:30–8pm
Sun. **Closed** Aug 17–31. 🚻

This church, with a restrained Neo-Classical facade by Giuseppe Valadier, the designer of Piazza del Popolo, began life as the chapel of a 16th-century hospital with beds for 50 men – San Rocco was a healer of the plague-stricken. A maternity wing was added for the wives of Tiber bargees to save them from having to give birth in the unsanitary conditions of a boat. The hospital came to be used by unmarried mothers, and one section was set aside for women who wished to conceal their identities. They were even permitted to wear a veil for the duration of their stay. Unwanted children were sent to an orphanage, and if any mothers or children died, they were buried in anonymous graves. The hospital was abandoned in the early 20th century, and demolished in the 1930s during the excavation of the Mausoleum of Augustus.

The church sacristy is an interesting Baroque altarpiece (c. 1660) by Il Baciccia, the artist who decorated the ceiling of the Gesù *(see pp110–11).*

㉒ Santi Ambrogio e Carlo al Corso

Via del Corso 437. **Map** 4 F2. **Tel**
06-682 8101. 🚌 81, 117, 492, 628,
926. **Open** 7am–7pm daily. ✉

This church belonged to the Lombard community in Rome, and is dedicated to two canonized bishops of Milan, Lombardy's capital. In 1471, Pope Sixtus IV gave the Lombards a church, which they dedicated to Sant'Ambrogio, who died in 397. Then, in 1610, when Carlo Borromeo was canonized, the church was rebuilt in his honor. Most of the new church was the work of father and son Onorio and Martino Longhi, but the fine dome is by Pietro da Cortona. The altarpiece by Carlo Maratta (1625–1713) is the *Gloria dei Santi Ambrogio e Carlo.* An ambulatory leads behind the altar to a chapel housing the heart of San Carlo in a richly decorated reliquary.

Statue of San Carlo by Attilio Selva (1888–1970) behind the apse of Santi Ambrogio e Carlo

CAMPO DE' FIORI

Between Corso Vittorio Emanuele II, and the Tiber, the city displays many distinct personalities. The open-air market of Campo de' Fiori preserves the lively, bohemian atmosphere of the medieval inns that once flourished here, while the area also contains Renaissance palazzi, such as Palazzo Farnese, and Palazzo Spada, where powerful Roman families built their fortress-like houses near the route of papal processions. Close by, overlooking the picturesque Tiber Island, lies the former Jewish Ghetto, where many traces of daily life from past centuries can still be seen. The Portico of Octavia and the Theater of Marcellus are spectacular examples of the city's many-layered history, built up over the half-ruined remains of ancient Rome.

Sights at a Glance

Churches and Temples
5 Santissima Trinità dei Pellegrini
7 Santa Maria dell'Orazione e Morte
9 San Girolamo della Carità
10 Sant'Eligio degli Orefici
11 Santa Maria in Monserrato
18 San Carlo ai Catinari
20 Santa Maria in Campitelli
21 San Nicola in Carcere
29 San Giovanni dei Fiorentini

Museums and Galleries
6 Palazzo Spada
14 Piccola Farnesina
15 Burcardo Theatre Museum

Historic Buildings
2 Palazzo Pio Righetti
3 Palazzo del Monte di Pietà
8 Palazzo Farnese
12 Palazzo Ricci
13 Palazzo della Cancelleria
25 Casa di Lorenzo Manilio
26 Palazzo Cenci

Fountains
19 Fontana delle Tartarughe

Historic Streets and Piazzas
1 Campo de' Fiori
24 Ghetto and Synagogue
27 Tiber Island
28 Via Giulia

Famous Theaters
16 Teatro Argentina

Ancient Sites
4 Sotterranei di San Paolo alla Regola
17 Area Sacra dell'Argentina
22 Theater of Marcellus
23 Portico of Octavia

Restaurants
see pp311–15
1 Acchiappafantasmi
2 Angolo Divino
3 Al Bric
4 'Ba Ghetto Milky
5 Camponesci
6 Da Pancrazio
7 Enoteca il Goccetto
8 Giggetto
9 Il Sanlorenzo
10 Nonna Betta
11 Open Baladin
12 Pagliaccio
13 Percento
14 Pierluigi
15 Piperno
16 Polese
17 Roscioli
18 Settimio al Pellegrino
19 Sora Lella
20 Sora Margherita
21 Vinando
22 Vino e Camino

See also Street Finder maps 4, 8, 11, 12

◀ Theater of Marcellus

For map symbols *see back flap*

Street by Street: Campo de' Fiori

This fascinating part of Renaissance Rome is also an exciting area for shopping and nightlife, centered on the market square of Campo de' Fiori. Its stands supply many nearby restaurants, and young people shop for clothes in Via dei Giubbonari. Popular restaurants keep the area alive late into the night, when overcrowding and drunks can become problems. By day there are great buildings to admire, though few are open to the public. Two exceptions are the Piccola Farnesina, with its collection of Classical statues, and Palazzo Spada, home to many important paintings.

🔟 **Sant'Eligio degli Orefici**
A small Renaissance church designed by Raphael is concealed behind a later facade.

⓬ **Palazzo Ricci**
Painted Classical scenes were a favorite form of decoration for the facades of Renaissance houses.

9️⃣ **San Girolamo della Carità**
The chief attraction of this church is Borromini's fabulous Spada Chapel.

⓫ **Santa Maria in Monserrato**
This church, which has strong connections with Spain, houses a Bernini bust of Cardinal Pedro Foix de Montoya.

8️⃣ **Palazzo Farnese**
Michelangelo and other great artists helped create this monumental Renaissance palazzo.

Key

— Suggested route

0 meters	75
0 yards	75

7️⃣ **Santa Maria dell'Orazione e Morte**
A pair of dramatic winged skulls flank the doorway to this church dedicated to the burial of the dead.

❶ ★ Campo de' Fiori
This colourful market makes Piazza Campo de' Fiori one of Rome's most entertaining squares.

Locator Map
See Central Rome Map pp16–17

⓭ Palazzo della Cancelleria
The papal administration ran the affairs of the Church from this vast building.

⓮ Piccola Farnesina
This plaque honors Giovanni Barracco. His sculpture collection is housed in the palazzo.

❷ Palazzo Pio Righetti
Heraldic eagles stare down from the pediments of the palazzo's windows.

❺ Santissima Trinità dei Pellegrini
The principal role of this church was one of charity, caring for poor pilgrims arriving in Rome.

❹ Sotterranei di San Paolo alla Regola
Remains of a Roman house have survived in the basement of an old palace.

❸ Palazzo del Monte di Pietà
This was a papal institution, where the poor pawned their possessions in order to borrow small sums of money.

❻ ★ Palazzo Spada
The picture gallery houses a collection started by two wonderfully eccentric 17th-century cardinals.

❶ Campo de' Fiori

Piazza Campo de' Fiori. **Map** 4 E4 & 11 C4. 🚌 116 and routes to Largo di Torre Argentina or Corso Vittorio Emanuele II. *See Markets p344.*

The Campo de' Fiori (field of flowers), once a meadow, occupies the site of the open space facing the Theater of Pompey. Cardinals and noblemen used to rub shoulders with fishmongers and foreigners in the piazza's market, making it one of the liveliest areas of medieval and Renaissance Rome. Today's market retains much of the traditional lively atmosphere.

In the center of the square is a statue of the philosopher Giordano Bruno, burned at the stake for heresy here in 1600. The hooded figure is a grim reminder of the executions that were held here.

The piazza was surrounded by inns for pilgrims and other travelers. Many of these were once owned by the successful 15th-century courtesan Vannozza Catanei, mistress of Pope Alexander VI Borgia. On the corner between the piazza and Via del Pellegrino you can see Catanei's shield, which she had decorated with her own coat of arms and those of her husband, and her lover, the Borgia pope.

❷ Palazzo Pio Righetti

Piazza del Biscione 89. **Map** 4 E5 & 11 C4. 🚌 116 and routes to Largo Torre Argentina or Corso Vittorio Emanuele II. **Closed** to the public.

The vast 17th-century Palazzo Pio Righetti was built over the ruined Theater of Pompey. The windows of the palazzo are decorated with lions and pine cones from the coat of arms of the Pio da Carpi family, who lived here.

The curve of the Theater of Pompey, completed in 55 BC, is followed by Via di Grotta Pinta. Rome's first permanent theater was built of stone and concrete, and in the basement of the Pancrazio restaurant you can see early examples of *opus*

Window pediment with heraldic lion and pine cones, Palazzo Pio Righetti

reticulatum – small square blocks of tufa (porous rock) set diagonally as a facing for a concrete wall.

❸ Palazzo del Monte di Pietà

Piazza del Monte di Pietà 33. **Map** 4 E5 & 11 C4. **Tel** 06-54451. 🚌 116 and routes to Largo di Torre Argentina or Corso Vittorio Emanuele II. 🚋 8. Chapel: **Open** by appt. Ring in advance.

The Monte, as it is known, is a public institution, founded in 1539 by Pope Paul III Farnese as a pawn shop to staunch the usury then rampant in the city. The building still has offices and auction rooms for the sale of unclaimed goods. The stars with diagonal bands on the huge central plaque decorating the facade are the coat of arms of Pope Clement VIII Aldobrandini, added when Carlo Maderno enlarged the palace in the 17th century. The clock on the left was added later.

Within, the chapel is a jewel of Baroque architecture, adorned with gilded stucco, marble paneling, and reliefs. The decoration makes a perfect setting for the sculptures by Domenico Guidi – a bust of San Carlo Borromeo and a relief of the *Pietà*. There are also splendid reliefs by Giovanni Battista Théudon and Pierre Legros of biblical scenes illustrating the charitable nature of the institution.

❹ Sotterranei di San Paolo alla Regola

Via di San Paolo alla Regola. **Map** 11 C5. **Tel** 06-0608. 🚌 23, 116, 280 and routes to Largo di Torre Argentina. 🚋 8. **Open** by appt only.

An old palace hides the perfectly conserved remains of an ancient Roman house, dating from the 2nd–3rd centuries. Restoration works are being

Relief by Théudon of *Joseph Distributing Grain to the Egyptians* in Palazzo del Monte di Pietà

carried out in order to open this site to the public, but at present it is only possible to visit by special arrangement.

A ramp leads down well below today's street level, to reveal the locations of shops of the time. One level above is the Stanza della Colonna, at one time an open courtyard, with traces of frescoes and mosaics on its walls.

Guido Reni's *Holy Trinity*, in Santissima Trinità dei Pellegrini

❺ Santissima Trinità dei Pellegrini

Piazza della Trinità dei Pellegrini. **Map** 4 E5 & 11 C5. **Tel** 06-6830 0486. 23, 116, 280 and routes to Largo di Torre Argentina. 8. **Open** 7:30am–noon, 4:30–7:30pm Mon–Sat; 8am–12:30pm, 4:30–7:30pm Sun.

The church was donated in the 16th century to a charitable organization founded by San Filippo Neri to care for the poor and sick, in particular the thousands of paupers who flocked in pilgrimage to Rome during the special holy years known as Jubilees. The 18th-century facade has niches with statues of the Evangelists by Bernardino Ludovisi. The interior, with Corinthian columns, ends in a horseshoe vault and apse, dominated by Guido Reni's striking altarpiece of the Holy Trinity (1625). The frescoes in the lantern are also by Reni. Other interesting paintings include *St. Gregory the Great Freeing Souls from Purgatory*, by Baldassarre Croce (third chapel to the left);

Cavalier d'Arpino's *Virgin and Saints* (second chapel to the left); and a painting by Borgognone (1677) of the Virgin and recently canonized saints, including San Filippo Neri. In the sacristy are depictions of the nobility washing the feet of pilgrims, a custom that was started by San Filippo.

❻ Palazzo Spada

Piazza Capo di Ferro 13. **Map** 2 F5. **Tel** 06-686 1158 (Palazzo) or 06-683 2409 (Galleria). 23, 116, 280 and routes to Largo di Torre Argentina. 8. Galleria Spada: **Open** 8:30am–7:30pm Tue–Sun (last adm: 7pm). **Closed** Jan 1, Dec 25.

This majestic palazzo, built around 1550 for Cardinal Capo di Ferro, has an elegant stuccoed courtyard and facade decorated with reliefs evoking Rome's glorious past.

Cardinal Bernardino Spada, who lived here in the 17th century with his brother Virginio (also a cardinal), hired architects Bernini and Borromini to work on the building. The brothers' whimsical delight in false perspectives resulted in a colonnaded gallery by Borromini that appears four times longer than it really is.

The cardinals also amassed a superb private collection of paintings, which is now on display in the Galleria Spada. The collection features a wide range of artists, including Rubens, Dürer, and Guido Reni. The most important works on display include *The Visitation* by Andrea del Sarto (1486–1530), *Cain and Abel* by Giovanni Lanfranco (1582–1647), and *The Death of Dido* by Guercino (1591–1666).

❼ Santa Maria dell'Orazione e Morte

Via Giulia 262. **Map** 4 E5 & 11 B4. **Tel** 339-3484 378. 23, 116, 280. **Open** 10am–noon, 4–7pm daily (except Wed & Sat am).

A pious confraternity was formed here in the 16th century to collect the bodies of the

Offertory box in Santa Maria dell'Orazione e Morte

unknown dead and give them a Christian burial. The theme of death is stressed in this church, dedicated to St. Mary of Prayer and Death. The doors and windows of Ferdinando Fuga's dramatic Baroque facade are decorated with winged skulls. Above the central entrance there is a *clepsydra* (an ancient hourglass) – symbolic of death.

❽ Palazzo Farnese

Piazza Farnese. **Map** 4 E5 & 11 B4. 23, 116, 280 and routes to Corso Vittorio Emanuele II. **Open** for temporary exhibitions.

The prototype for numerous princely palaces, the imposing Palazzo Farnese was originally built for Cardinal Alessandro Farnese (who became Pope Paul III in 1534). He commissioned the greatest artists to work on it, starting with Antonio da Sangallo the Younger as architect in 1517. Michelangelo, who took over after him, contributed the great cornice and central window of the main facade, and the third level of the courtyard.

Michelangelo had a plan for the Farnese gardens to be connected by a bridge to the Farnese home in Trastevere, Villa Farnesina *(see pp220–21)*. The elegant arch spanning Via Giulia belongs to this unrealized scheme. The palazzo was completed in 1589, on a less ambitious scale, by Giacomo della Porta. It is now the home of the French Embassy, which moved in as early as 1635.

Spada Chapel in San Girolamo

❾ San Girolamo della Carità

Via di Monserrato 62A. **Map** 4 E5 & 11 B4. **Tel** 06-687 9786. 🚌 23, 40, 46, 62, 64, 116, 280. **Open** 10:30–noon Sun. 🚹

The church was built on a site incorporating the home of San Filippo Neri, the 16th-century saint from Tuscany who renewed Rome's spiritual and cultural life by his friendly, open approach to religion. He would have loved the frolicking putti shown surrounding his statue, in his chapel, reminding him of the Roman urchins he had cared for during his lifetime.

The breathtaking Spada Chapel was designed by Borromini, and is unique both as a work of art and as an illustration of the spirit of the Baroque age. All architectural elements are concealed so that the space of the chapel's interior is defined solely by decorative marblework and statues. Veined jasper and precious multicolored marbles are sculpted to imitate flowery damask and velvet hangings. Even the altar rail is a long swag of jasper drapery held up by a pair of kneeling angels with wooden wings.

Although there are memorials to former members of the Spada family, oddly, there is no indication as to which of the Spadas was responsible for endowing the chapel. It was probably art-lover Virgilio Spada, a follower of San Filippo Neri.

❿ Sant'Eligio degli Orefici

Via di Sant'Eligio 8A. **Map** 4 D4 & 11 B4. **Tel** 06-686 8260. 🚌 23, 40, 46, 62, 64, 116, 280. **Open** 9:30am–1:30pm Mon–Fri (stop first at Via di Sant'Eligio 7). **Closed** Aug. 🚹

The name of the church still records the fact that it was commissioned by a rich corporation of goldsmiths (orefici) in the early 16th century. The original design was by Raphael, who, like his master Bramante, had acquired a sense of the grandiose from the remains of Roman antiquity. The influence of some of Bramante's works, such as the choir of Santa Maria del Popolo (see pp140–41), is evident in the simple way the arches and pilasters define the structure of the walls.

The cupola of Sant'Eligio is attributed to Baldassarre Peruzzi, while the facade was added in the early 17th century by Flaminio Ponzio. Among the various 16th-century painters who decorated the interior was Taddeo Zuccari, who worked on Palazzo Farnese (see p149).

An early bust by Bernini of Cardinal Pedro Foix de Montoya

⓫ Santa Maria in Monserrato

Via di Monserrato. **Map** 4 E4 & 11 B3. **Tel** 06-686 5865. 🚌 23, 40, 46, 62, 64, 116, 280. **Open** 10am–1:30pm Sun; enquire at Via Giulia 151 for additional opening times. 🚹

The origins of the Spanish national church in Rome go back to 1506, when a hospice for Spanish pilgrims was begun by a brotherhood of the Virgin of Montserrat in Catalonia. Inside is Annibale Carracci's painting San Diego de Alcalà and, in the third chapel on the left, a copy of a Sansovino statue of St. James. Some beautiful 15th-century tombs by Andrea Bregno and Luigi Capponi are in the courtyard and side chapels. Don't miss Bernini's bust of Pedro Foix de Montoya, the church's benefactor, in the annex.

Statue of San Filippo Neri by Pierre Legros

San Diego by Annibale Carracci

⑫ Palazzo Ricci

Piazza de' Ricci. **Map** 4 D4 & 11 B4.
🚌 23, 40, 46, 62, 64, 116, 280, 870.
Closed to the public.

Palazzo Ricci was famous for its frescoed facade – now rather faded – originally painted in the 16th century by Polidoro da Caravaggio, a follower of Raphael.

In Renaissance Rome it was common to commission artists to decorate the outsides of houses with heroes of Classical antiquity. A fresco by a leading artist such as Polidoro, reputedly the inventor of this style of painting, was a conspicuous status symbol, in the nobility's attempts to outshine each other with their palazzi.

⑬ Palazzo della Cancelleria

Piazza della Cancelleria. **Map** 4 E4 & 11 C3. **Tel** 06-6989 3405. 🚌 40, 46, 62, 64, 70, 81, 87, 116, 492. **Open** by appointment only, Tue pm & Sat am (email: economato@apsa.va).

The palazzo, a supreme example of the confident architecture of the Early Renaissance, was begun in 1485. It was financed partly with the gambling winnings of Cardinal Raffaele Riario. Roses, the emblem of the Riario family, adorn the vaults and capitals of the beautiful Doric courtyard. The palazzo's interior was decorated after the Sack of Rome in 1527. Giorgio Vasari boasted that he had completed work on one enormous room in just 100 days; Michelangelo allegedly retorted, "It looks like it." Other Mannerist artists, Perin del Vaga and Francesco Salviati, frescoed the rooms of the cardinal in charge of the Papal Chancellery, the office that gave the palazzo its name when it was installed here by Pope Leo X. On the right of the main entrance is the unobtrusive and rather quaint church of San Lorenzo in Damaso, founded by Pope Damasus (reigned 366–84). It was reconstructed in 1495, and although Bernini made

Courtyard of Palazzo della Cancelleria

alterations to the transept and apse in 1638, it was later restored to its 15th-century lines. Its porticoes housed libraries for the first Papal Archives.

⑭ Piccola Farnesina

Corso Vittorio Emanuele II 168.
Map 4 E4 & 11 C3. **Tel** 06-0608. 🚌 40, 46, 62, 64, 70, 81, 87, 116, 492. **Open** Jun–Sep: 1–7pm Tue–Sun; Oct–May: 10am–4pm Tue–Sun.
🌐 **museobarracco.it**

This delightful miniature palazzo acquired its name from the lilies decorating its cornices. These were mistakenly identified as part of the Farnese family crest. In fact they were part of the coat of arms of a French clergyman, Thomas Le Roy, for whom the palazzo was built in 1523.

The entrance is in a facade built to overlook Corso Vittorio Emanuele II when the road was

Inner courtyard, Piccola Farnesina

constructed at the start of the 20th century. The original facade on the left of today's entrance is attributed to Antonio da Sangallo the Younger. Note the asymmetrical arrangement of its windows and ledges. The elegant central courtyard also retains its original appearance. The Piccola Farnesina now houses the Museo Barracco, a collection of ancient sculpture assembled during the last century by the politician Baron Giovanni Barracco. A bust of the baron can be seen in the courtyard. The collection includes an ancient Egyptian relief of the scribe Nofer, some Assyrian artifacts, and, among the Etruscan exhibits, a delicate ceramic female head. On the first floor is the Greek collection with a head of Apollo.

⑮ Burcardo Theater Museum

Via del Sudario 44. **Map** 4 F4 & 12 D4. **Tel** 06-5990 3805. 🚌 40, 46, 62, 64, 70, 81, 186, 492. 🚊 8. Museum: **Open** 9:15am–4:30pm Tue & Thu. **Closed** Aug. 🎫 🌐 **burcardo.org**

This late 15th-century house once belonged to Johannes Burckhardt, chamberlain to Pope Alexander VI Borgia, and author of a diary of Rome under the Borgias. His house now holds Rome's most complete collection of theater literature, plus Chinese puppets and comic masks from the various regions of Italy.

Detail of facade, Teatro Argentina

⑯ Teatro Argentina

Largo di Torre Argentina 52. **Map** 4 F4 & 12 D4. **Tel** 06-684 000 311. 🚌 40, 46, 62, 64, 70, 81, 87, 186, 492, 810. 🚋 8. Plays performed Oct–Jun. *See Entertainment pp352–3.* 🌐 teatrodiroma.net

One of the city's most important theaters was founded by the powerful Sforza Cesarini family in 1732, though the facade dates from a century later. Many famous operas, including those of Verdi, were first performed here. In 1816, the theater saw the ill-fated debut of Rossini's *Barber of Seville*, during which the composer insulted the unappreciative audience, who then pursued him, enraged, through the streets of Rome.

⑰ Area Sacra dell'Argentina

Largo di Torre Argentina. **Map** 4 F4 & 12 D4. 🚌 40, 46, 62, 64, 70, 81, 87, 186, 492, 810. 🚋 8. **Open** by appt only (call 06-0608).

The remains of four temples were discovered here in the 1920s. Dating from the Republican era, they are among the oldest in Rome. They are known as A, B, C, and D. The oldest (temple C) dates from the early 3rd century BC. It was placed on a high platform preceded by an altar and is typical of Italic plans. Temple A is from later in the 3rd century BC. In medieval times the church of San Nicola de' Cesarini was built over its podium: remains of its two apses are still visible. The north column stumps belonged to a great portico, the Hecatostylum

(portico of 100 columns). In Imperial times two marble lavatories were built here – the remains of one is visible behind temple A. Behind temples B and C are remains of a great platform of tufa blocks identified as part of the Curia of Pompey – a rectangular building with a statue of Pompey. It was here that the Senate met and Julius Caesar was murdered on March 15, 44 BC. At the southwest corner of the site is a cat sanctuary, home to Rome's abandoned felines (open afternoons).

⑱ San Carlo ai Catinari

Piazza B Cairoli. **Map** 4 F5 & 12 D4. **Tel** 06-6880 3554. 🚌 *see Area Sacra.* 🚋 8. **Open** 4–7pm daily, also 10am–noon Mon–Sat & 9:30am–12:30pm Sun. ✝ No visits during services.

In 1620, Rome's Milanese congregation decided to honor Cardinal Carlo Borromeo with this great church. It was called "ai Catinari" on account of the

San Carlo at Prayer by Guido Reni

bowl-makers' *(catinari)* shops in the area. The solemn travertine facade was completed in 1638 by the Roman architect Soria. The 16th-century basilican plan is flanked by chapels. The St. Cecilia chapel was designed and decorated by Antonio Gherardi, who added a family portrait. The church's paintings and frescoes by Pietro da Cortona and Guido Reni are mature works of the Counter-Reformation, depicting the life and acts of the recently canonized San Carlo.

The ornate crucifix on the sacristy altar, inlaid with marble and mother-of-pearl, is by the 16th-century sculptor Algardi.

Sacristy altar, San Carlo ai Catinari

⑲ Fontana delle Tartarughe

Piazza Mattei. **Map** 4 F5 & 12 D4. 🚌 46, 62, 63, 64, 70, 87, 186, 492, 810. 🚋 8.

The delightful Fontana delle Tartarughe (*tartarughe* are tortoises) was commissioned by the Mattei family to decorate "their" piazza between 1581 and 1588. The design was by Giacomo della Porta, but the fountain owes much of its charm to the four bronze youths each resting one foot on the head of a dolphin, sculpted by Taddeo Landini. Nearly a

Della Porta's graceful Fontana delle Tartarughe

century after the fountain was built, an unknown sculptor added the struggling tortoises to complete the composition.

⓴ Santa Maria in Campitelli

Piazza di Campitelli 9. **Map** 4 F5 & 12 E5. **Tel** 06-6880 3978. 🚌 40, 46, 62, 63, 64, 70, 87, 186, 780, 810. **Open** 7:30am–7pm daily. 🕇 🚻

In 17th-century Rome the plague could still strike fiercely, and there were no reliable, effective remedies. Many Romans simply prayed for a cure to a sacred medieval icon of the Virgin, the Madonna del Portico. When a particularly lethal outbreak of plague abated in 1656, popular gratitude was so strong that a new church was built to house the icon.

Lavish altar tabernacle in Santa Maria in Campitelli

The church, designed by a pupil of Bernini, Carlo Rainaldi, was completed in 1667. The main elements of the lively Baroque facade are the graceful columns, symbolizing the supporters of the true faith.

Inside the church stands a fabulously ornate, gilded altar tabernacle with spiral columns, which was designed by Giovanni Antonio de Rossi to contain the image of the Virgin. The side chapels are decorated by some of Rome's finest Baroque painters: Sebastiano Conca, Giovanni Battista Gaulli (known as Il Baciccia), and Luca Giordano.

Facade and medieval bell tower of San Nicola in Carcere

㉑ San Nicola in Carcere

Via del Teatro di Marcello 46. **Map** 5 A5 & 12 E5. **Tel** 06-6830 7198. 🚌 44, 63, 81, 160, 170, 628, 780, 781. **Open** 7am–7pm daily (from 10am Sun). 🎦 of excavations. 🎦 for tours. 🕇

The medieval church of San Nicola in Carcere stands on the site of three Roman temples of the Republican era that were converted into a prison (carcere) in the Middle Ages. The temples of Juno, Spes, and Janus faced a city gate leading from the Forum Holitorium, the city's vegetable and oil market, to the road down to the port on the Tiber. The columns embedded in the walls of the church belonged to two flanking temples whose platforms are

now marked by grass lawns. The church was rebuilt in 1599 and restored in the 19th century, but the bell tower and Roman columns are part of the original design.

The Theater of Marcellus by Thomas Hartley Cromek (1809–73)

㉒ Theater of Marcellus

Via del Teatro di Marcello. **Map** 4 A5 & 12 E5. **Tel** 06-0608. 🚌 44, 63, 81, 160, 170, 628, 780, 781. **Open** 9am–6pm (to 7pm in summer) daily.

The curved outer wall of this vast amphitheater has supported generations of Roman buildings. It was built by the Emperor Augustus (27 BC–AD 14), who dedicated it to Marcellus, his nephew and son-in-law, who had died at age 19 in 23 BC.

The Middle Ages were a turbulent time of invasions and local conflicts (see p32), and by the 13th century the theater had been converted into the fortress of the Savelli family. In the 16th century Baldassarre Peruzzi built a great palace on the theater ruins for the Orsini family. This included a garden that faced the Tiber. The lower arches were later occupied by humble dwellings and workshops.

Close to the theater stand three beautiful Corinthian columns and a section of frieze. These are from the Temple of Apollo, which housed many great works of art that the Romans plundered from Greece in the 2nd century BC.

❷❸ Portico of Octavia

Via del Portico d'Ottavia. **Map** 4 F5 & 12 E5. 46, 62, 63, 64, 70, 87, 186, 780, 810.

Built in honor of Octavia (the sister of Augustus and the abandoned wife of Mark Antony), this is the only surviving portico of what used to be the monumental piazza of Circus Flaminius. The rectangular portico enclosed temples dedicated to Jupiter and Juno, decorated with bronze statues. The part we see today is the great central atrium originally covered by marble facings.

In the Middle Ages a great fish market and a church, Sant'Angelo in Pescheria, were built in the ruins of the portico. As the church was associated with the fishing activities of the nearby river port, aquatic flora and fauna feature in many of its inlays. Links with the Tiber are also apparent in the stucco facade on the adjacent Fishmonger's Oratory, built in 1689. The church has a fresco of the Madonna and angels by the school of Benozzo Gozzoli.

❷❹ Ghetto and Synagogue

Synagogue, Lungotevere dei Cenci. **Map** 4 F5 & 12 E5. Tel 06-6840 0661. 23, 63, 280, 780 and routes to Largo di Torre Argentina. 8. Museum: **Open** mid-Jun–mid-Sep: 10am–7pm Sun–Thu, 10am–4pm Fri; mid-Sep–mid-Jun: 10am–5pm Sun–Thu, 9am–2pm Fri. **Closed** on Jewish public hols. **w museoebraico.roma.it** Ghetto: main street is Via del Portico d'Ottavia.

The first Jews came to Rome as traders in the 2nd century BC, and there has been a Jewish community in Rome ever since. Jews were much appreciated for their financial and medical skills during the time of the Roman Empire.

Systematic persecution began in the 16th century. From July 25, 1556, all of Rome's Jews were forced to live inside a high-walled enclosure erected on the orders of Pope Paul IV. The Ghetto was in an unhealthy part of Rome.

Inhabitants were only allowed out during the day, and on Sundays they were driven into the Church of Sant'Angelo in Pescheria to listen to Christian sermons – a practice abolished only in 1848.

Persecution started again in 1943 with the German occupation. Although many Jews were helped to escape or hidden by Roman citizens, thousands were deported to German concentration camps.

Today many Jews still live in the former Ghetto, and the medieval streets retain much of their old character. The Synagogue on Lungotevere was completed in 1904 and houses a Jewish museum that describes the history of the community through plans, Torahs, and other artifacts.

❷❺ Casa di Lorenzo Manilio

Via del Portico d'Ottavia 1D. **Map** 4 F5 & 12 D5. 46, 62, 63, 64, 70, 87, 186, 780, 810. **Closed** to the public.

Before the Renaissance, most Romans had only vague ideas of their city's past, but the 15th-century revival of interest in the philosophy, and arts of antiquity inspired some to build houses recalling the splendor of ancient Rome. In 1468 a certain Lorenzo Manilio built a great house for his family, decorating it with an elegant Classical plaque. The Latin inscription dates the building according to the ancient Roman method – 2,221 years after the foundation of the city – and gives the owner's name. Original reliefs

are embedded in the facades, as well as a fragment of an ancient sarcophagus. The Piazza Costaguti facade's windows are inscribed *Ave Roma* (Hail Rome).

Balcony of Palazzo Cenci

❷❻ Palazzo Cenci

Vicolo dei Cenci. **Map** 4 F5 & 12 D5. See Ghetto and Synagogue. **Closed** to the public.

Palazzo Cenci belonged to the family of Beatrice Cenci, who was accused, together with her brothers and stepmother, of witchcraft, and the murder of her tyrannical father. She was condemned to death, and beheaded at Ponte Sant'Angelo in 1599.

Most of the original medieval palazzo has been demolished, and the building you see today

Row of Roman busts decorating the Casa di Lorenzo Manilio

Tiber Island, with Ponte Cestio linking it to Trastevere

dates back to the 1570s, though its rather forbidding appearance seems medieval. Heraldic half-moons decorate the main facade on Via del Progresso, while pretty balconies open on the opposite side where a medieval arch joins the palace to Palazzetto Cenci, designed by Martino Longhi the Elder. Inside is a traditional courtyard with an Ionic-style loggia; many of the rooms retain the original 16th-century decoration that the unfortunate Beatrice would have known as a child.

㉗ Tiber Island

Isola Tiberina. **Map** 8 D1 & 12 D5. 23, 63, 280, 780. 8.

In ancient times, the island, which lay opposite the city's port, had large structures of white travertine at either end built to resemble the stern and prow of a ship.

Since 293 BC, when a temple was dedicated here to Aesculapius, the god of healing and protector against the plague, the island has been associated with the sick, and there is still a hospital here.

San Bartolomeo all'Isola, the church in the island's central piazza, was built on the ruins of the Temple of Aesculapius in the 10th century. Its Romanesque bell tower is clearly visible from across the river.

From the Ghetto area you can reach the island by a footbridge, the Ponte Fabricio. The oldest original bridge over the Tiber still in use, it was built in 62 BC. In medieval times, the Pierleoni, and then the Caetani, two powerful families, controlled this strategic point by means of

a tower, still in place. The other bridge to the island, the Ponte Cestio, is inscribed with the names of the Byzantine emperors associated with its restoration in AD 370.

Mask fountain in Via Giulia

㉘ Via Giulia

Map 4 D4 & 11 A3. 23, 116, 280, 870.

This picturesque street was laid out by Bramante for Pope Julius II della Rovere. Lined with 16th–18th century aristocratic palazzi, as well as fine churches and antique shops, Via Giulia makes a fascinating walk (see pp278–9).

㉙ San Giovanni dei Fiorentini

Via Acciaioli 2. **Map** 4 D4 & 11 A2. **Tel** 06-6889 2059. 23, 40, 46, 62, 64, 116, 280, 870. **Open** 7am–noon, 5–7pm daily.

The church of St. John of the Florentines was built for the large Florentine community living in this area. Pope Leo X wanted it to be an expression of the cultural superiority of Florence over Rome. Started in the early 16th century, the church took over a century to build. The principal architect was Antonio da Sangallo the Younger, but many others contributed before Carlo Maderno's elongated cupola was finally completed in 1620. The present facade was added in the 18th century.

The church was decorated mainly by Tuscan artists. One interesting exception is the 15th-century statue of San Giovannino by the Sicilian Mino del Reame in a niche above the sacristy. The spectacular high altar houses a marble group by Antonio Raggi, the Baptism of Christ. The altar itself is by Borromini, who is buried in the church along with Carlo Maderno.

This and San Lorenzo in Lucina (see p116) are the only churches in Rome that admit animals: the faithful can bring their pets, and an Easter lamb-blessing takes place.

Antonio Raggi's Baptism of Christ in San Giovanni dei Fiorentini

QUIRINAL

One of the original seven hills of Rome, the Quirinal was a largely residential area in Imperial times. To the east of the hill were the vast Baths of Diocletian, still standing in front of what is now the main train station. Abandoned in the Middle Ages, the district returned to favor in the late 16th century. The prime site was taken by the popes for Palazzo del Quirinale. Great families such as the Colonna and the Aldobrandini had their palazzi lower down the hill. With the end of papal rule in 1870, the surrounding area, especially Via Nazionale, was redeveloped as the Quirinal became the residence of the kings of Italy, then of the Italian president.

Sights at a Glance

Churches
- ④ Santi Apostoli
- ⑤ San Marcello al Corso
- ⑦ Santa Maria in Trivio
- ⑨ Santi Vincenzo e Anastasio
- ⑪ Sant'Andrea al Quirinale
- ⑫ San Carlo alle Quattro Fontane
- ⑮ Santa Maria degli Angeli
- ⑳ Santa Maria dei Monti
- ㉑ Sant'Agata dei Goti
- ㉓ Santi Domenico e Sisto

Museums and Galleries
- ⑧ Accademia Nazionale di San Luca
- ⑩ Acuderie del Quirinale
- ⑯ Museo Nazionale Romano (Palazzo Massimo)
- ⑲ Palazzo delle Esposizioni

Historic Piazzas
- ⑱ Piazza della Repubblica

Historic Buildings
- ② Palazzo del Quirinale
- ③ Palazzo Colonna
- ⑰ Baths of Diocletian

Fountains and Statues
- ① Castor and Pollux
- ⑥ Trevi Fountain
- ⑬ Le Quattro Fontane
- ⑭ Moses Fountain

Parks and Gardens
- ㉒ Villa Aldobrandini

☐ Restaurants
see pp315–17

1 Abruzzi ai SS Apostoli
2 Ai Tre Scalini
3 Antica Birreria Peroni
4 Asmara
5 Cavour 313
6 Colline Emiliane
7 Doozo
8 Il Baccano
9 Il Chianti
10 La Carbonara
11 L'Asino d'Oro
12 Open Colonna
13 Pipero al Rex
14 Taverna dei Fori Imperiali
15 Trimani il Wine Bar
16 Urbana 47
17 Vivendo

See also Street Finder maps 5, 6, 12

◀ Piazza della Repubblica's triumphal arch

For map symbols *see back flap*

Street by Street: The Quirinal Hill

Even though Palazzo del Quirinale is usually closed to the public, it is well worth walking up the hill to the palace to see the giant Roman statues of Castor and Pollux in the piazza and enjoy fine views of the city. Come down the hill by way of the narrow streets and stairways that lead to one of Rome's unforgettable sights, the Trevi Fountain. Many small churches lie hidden away in the back streets. Toward Piazza Venezia there are grand palazzi, including that of the Colonna, one of Rome's most ancient and powerful families.

Santa Maria in Via is famous for its medieval well and miraculous 13th-century icon of the Madonna.

7 Santa Maria in Trivio
The attractive facade of this tiny church conceals a rich Baroque interior.

8 Accademia Nazionale di San Luca
The art academy has works by famous former members, such as Canova and Angelica Kauffmann.

6 ★ Trevi Fountain
Rome's grandest and best-known fountain almost fills the tiny Piazza di Trevi.

9 Santi Vincenzo e Anastasio
The grand facade of this small Baroque church is on a corner facing the Trevi Fountain.

5 San Marcello al Corso
This stark *Crucifixion* by Van Dyck hangs in the sacristy of the church.

Palazzo Odescalchi has a Bernini facade from 1664, with a balustrade and richly decorated cornice. The building faces Santi Apostoli.

To Piazza Venezia

VIA POLI
VIA DELLE MURATTE
PIAZZA DI TREVI
VIA DI SAN V
VIA D
VIA DELLE VERGINI
VIA DELL'UMILTA
PIAZZA DE
VIA DEL CORSO

I Giardini del Quirinale
The magnificent gardens of the presidential palace are open to visitors just once a year, on June 2.

Locator Map
See Central Rome Map pp16–17

2 Palazzo del Quirinale
The old papal palace is now the home of the president of Italy. Palace guards in colorful dress uniform can often be seen outside.

1 Castor and Pollux
The statues are grouped with an obelisk and a fountain.

Piazza della Pilotta is dominated by the imposing facade of the Gregorian University.

PIAZZA DEL QUIRINALE

IA DELLA DATARIA

PIAZZA DELLA PILOTTA

3 Palazzo Colonna
One of the art gallery's finest Old Masters is Annibale Carracci's *The Bean Eater*.

Museo delle Cere, a wax museum opened in 1953, places its emphasis on horror.

4 Santi Apostoli
The figures of Christ and the Apostles on the balustrade were added by Carlo Rainaldi in 168.

Key

— Suggested route

| 0 meters | 75 |
| 0 yards | 75 |

Quirinal fountain and obelisk with Roman statues of Castor and Pollux

❶ Castor and Pollux

Piazza del Quirinale. **Map** 5 B4. 🚌 H, 40, 64, 70, 170 and many routes along Via del Tritone.

Castor and Pollux – the patrons of horsemanship – and their prancing horses stand in splendor in the Piazza del Quirinale. Over 18 ft (5.5 m) high, these statues are huge Roman copies of 5th-century BC Greek originals. They once stood at the entrance to the nearby Baths of Constantine. Pope Sixtus V had them restored and placed here in 1588. Formerly known as the "horse tamers," they gave the square its familiar name of Monte Cavallo (horse hill).

The obelisk that stands between them was brought here in 1786 from the Mausoleum of Augustus. In 1818 the composition was completed by the addition of a massive granite basin, once a cattle trough in the Forum.

❷ Palazzo del Quirinale

Piazza del Quirinale. **Map** 5 B3. **Tel** 06-469 91. 🚌 H, 40, 64, 70, 170 and many routes along Via del Tritone. **Open** 8:30am–noon Sun. **Closed** pub hols & late Jun–mid-Sep. 🖼 🌐 quirinale.it

By the 1500s, the Vatican had a reputation as an unhealthy location because of the high incidence of malaria, so Pope Gregory XIII chose this site on the highest of Rome's seven hills

as a papal summer residence. Work began in 1573. Piazza del Quirinale has buildings on three sides, while the fourth is open, with a splendid view of the city. Many great architects worked on the palace before it assumed its present form in the 1730s. Domenico Fontana designed the main facade, Carlo Maderno the huge chapel, and Bernini the narrow wing on Via del Quirinale.

Following the unification of Italy in 1870, it became the official residence of the king, then, in 1947, the president of the republic. The immaculately manicured palace gardens are open to the public only once a year, on Republic Day (June 2).

❸ Palazzo Colonna

Via della Pilotta 17. **Map** 5 A4 & 12 F3. **Tel** 06-678 4350. 🚌 H, 40, 64, 70, 170 and many routes to Piazza Venezia. **Open** 9am–1:15pm Sat only or by appt. **Closed** Aug & public hols. 🖼 🖼 🖼 🌐 galleriacolonna.it

Pope Martin V Colonna (reigned 1417–31) began building the palazzo, but most of the structure dates from the 18th century. The art gallery, built by Antonio del Grande between 1654 and 1665, is the only part open to the public. The pictures are numbered but unlabeled, so pick up a guide on the way in. Go up the stairs and through the antechamber leading to a series of three gleaming marble rooms with prominent yellow

Palazzo del Quirinale, official residence of the president of Italy

Canova's monument to Pope Clement XIV in Santi Apostoli, with figures of Humility and Modesty

columns, the Colonna family emblem (*colonna* means column).

The ceiling frescoes celebrate Marcantonio Colonna's victory over the Turks at the Battle of Lepanto (1571). On the walls are 16th- to 18th-century paintings, including Annibale Carracci's *The Bean Eater (see p159)*. The room of landscape paintings, many by Poussin's brother-in-law Gaspare Dughet, reflects the 18th-century taste of Cardinal Girolamo Colonna. Beyond is a room with a ceiling fresco of *The Apotheosis of Martin V*. The throne room has a chair reserved for visiting popes and a copy of Pisanello's portrait of Martin V. The gallery also offers a fine view of the private palace garden, site of the ruined Temple of Serapis.

❹ Santi Apostoli

Piazza dei Santi Apostoli. **Map** 5 A4 & 12 F3. **Tel** 06-699 571. 🚌 H, 40, 64, 70, 170 and many other routes to Piazza Venezia. **Open** 7:30am–noon, 4–7pm daily. 🚹

The original 6th-century church on this site was rebuilt in the 15th century by Popes Martin V Colonna and Sixtus IV della Rovere, whose oak-tree crest decorates the capitals of the late 15th-century portico. Inside the portico on the left is Canova's 1807 memorial to the engraver Giovanni Volpato. The church itself contains a much larger monument by Canova, his Tomb of Clement XIV (1789).

The Baroque interior by Francesco and Carlo Fontana was completed in 1714. Note the 3-D effect of Giovanni Odazzi's painted *Rebel Angels*, who really look as though they are falling from the sky. A huge 18th-century altarpiece by Domenico Muratori shows the martyrdom of the Apostles James and Philip, whose tombs are in the crypt.

Detail of Triton and "sea horse" at Rome's grandest fountain, the Trevi

❺ San Marcello al Corso

Piazza San Marcello 5. **Map** 5 A4 & 12 F3. **Tel** 06-69 93 01. 🚌 62, 63, 81, 85, 117, 119, 160, 175, 492, 628. **Open** 7am–noon (from 10am Sat, from 9am Sun), 4–7pm daily. 🕇

This church was originally one of the first places of Christian worship in Rome, which was known as *tituli*. A later Romanesque building burned down in 1519, and was rebuilt by Jacopo Sansovino with a single nave and many richly decorated private chapels on either side. The imposing travertine facade was designed by Fontana in late Baroque style.

The third chapel on the right has fine frescoes of the Virgin Mary by Francesco Salviati. The decoration of the next chapel was interrupted by the Sack of Rome in 1527. Raphael's follower Perin del Vaga fled, leaving the ceiling frescoes to be completed by Daniele da Volterra and Pellegrino Tibaldi when peace returned to the city. In the nave stands a splendid Venetian-style double tomb by Sansovino, a memorial to Cardinal Giovanni Michiel (victim of a Borgia poisoning in 1503) and his nephew, Bishop Antonio Orso.

❻ Trevi Fountain

Fontana di Trevi. **Map** 5 A3 & 12 F2. 🚌 52, 53, 61, 62, 63, 71, 80, 116, 119 and many other routes along Via del Corso and Via del Tritone.

Most visitors gathering around the coin-filled fountain assume that it has always been here, but by the standards of the Eternal City, the Trevi is a fairly recent creation. Nicola Salvi's theatrical design for Rome's largest and most famous fountain *(see p56)* was completed only in 1762. The central figures are Neptune flanked by two Tritons. One struggles to master a very unruly "sea horse," the other leads a far more docile animal. These symbolize the two contrasting moods of the sea.

The site originally marked the terminal of the Aqua Virgo aqueduct built in 19 BC. One of the first-story reliefs shows a young girl (the legendary virgin after whom the aqueduct was named) pointing to the spring from which the water flows.

Chapel in San Marcello al Corso, decorated by Francesco Salviati

Facade of Santa Maria in Trivio

❼ Santa Maria in Trivio

Piazza dei Crociferi 49. **Map** 5 A3 & 12 F2. **Tel** 06-678 9645. 🚌 52, 53, 61, 62, 63, 71, 80, 116, 119. **Open** 8am–noon, 4–7:30pm daily. 🛉

It has been said that Italian architecture is one of facades, and nowhere is this clearer than in the 1570s facade of Santa Maria in Trivio, delightfully stuck on to the building behind it. Note the false windows. There is illusion inside too, particularly in the ceiling frescoes, which show scenes from the New Testament by Antonio Gherardi (1644–1702).

The name of the tiny church probably means "St. Mary-at-the-meeting-of-three-roads."

❽ Accademia Nazionale di San Luca

Piazza dell'Accademia di San Luca 77. **Map** 5 A3 & 12 F2. **Tel** 06-679 8850. 🚌 52, 53, 61, 62, 63, 71, 80, 116, 119 and many routes along Via del Corso and Via del Tritone. **Open** 10am–2pm Mon–Sat. 🇼 accademiasanluca.it

St. Luke is supposed to have been a painter, hence the name of Rome's academy of fine arts. Appropriately, the gallery contains a painting of *St. Luke Painting a Portrait of the Virgin* by Raphael and his followers. The academy's heyday was in the 17th and 18th centuries, when many members gave their work to the collection. Canova

donated a model for his famous marble group, *The Three Graces*.

Of particular interest are three fascinating self-portraits painted by women: the 17th-century Italian Lavinia Fontana; the 18th-century Swiss Angelica Kauffmann, whose painting is copied from a portrait of her by Joshua Reynolds; and Elisabeth Vigée-Lebrun, the French painter of the years before the 1789 Revolution.

❾ Santi Vincenzo e Anastasio

Vicolo dei Modelli 73. **Map** 5 A3 & 12 F2. **Tel** 331-284 5596. 🚌 52, 53, 61, 62, 63, 71, 80, 116, 119. **Open** 9am–8pm daily. 🛉 (Bulgarian Orthodox services).

Overlooking the Trevi Fountain *(see p161)* is one of the most over-the-top Baroque facades in Rome. Its thickets of columns are crowned by the huge coat of arms of Cardinal Raimondo Mazzarino, who commissioned Martino Longhi the Younger to build the church in 1650. The female bust above the door is of one of the cardinal's

famous nieces, either Louis XIV's first love, Maria Mancini (1639–1715), or her younger sister, Ortensia. In the apse, memorial plaques record the popes whose *praecordia* (a part of the heart) are enshrined behind the wall. This gruesome tradition was started at the end of the 16th century by Pope Sixtus V and continued until Pius X stopped it in the early 20th century.

❿ Scuderie del Quirinale

Via 24 Maggio 16. **Map** 5 B4. **Tel** 06-3996 7500. 🚌 H, 40, 60, 64, 70, 170. **Open** for exhibitions 10am–8pm Sun–Thu, 10am–10:30pm Fri & Sat. ♿ 🚻 📷 🇼 scuderiequirinale.it

The Scuderie started life as stables for the nearby Palazzo del Quirinale. Built in the early 1700s by Ferdinando Fuga over the remains of the ancient Temple of Serapis, the stables were remodeled by Gae Aulenti at the end of the 20th century and now house some of the best temporary art exhibitions in the country.

Self-portrait by Lavinia Fontana in the Accademia Nazionale di San Luca

Interior of Bernini's oval Sant'Andrea al Quirinale

⓫ Sant'Andrea al Quirinale

Via del Quirinale 29. **Map** 5 B3. **Tel** 06-474 4872. 116, 117 and routes to Via del Tritone. **Open** 8:30am–noon, 2:30–6pm daily.

Known as the "Pearl of the Baroque" because of its beautiful roseate marble interior, Sant'Andrea was designed by Bernini and executed by his assistants between 1658 and 1670. It was built for the Jesuits, hence the many IHS emblems (*Iesus Hominum Salvator* – Jesus Savior of Mankind).

The site for the church was wide but shallow, so Bernini pointed the long axis of his oval plan not toward the altar, but toward the sides; he then leads the eye around to the altar end. Here Bernini ordered works of art in various media that function not in isolation, but together. The crucified St. Andrew (Sant'Andrea) of the altarpiece looks up at a stucco version of himself, who

in turn ascends toward the lantern and the Holy Spirit.

The many rooms of St. Stanislas Kostka in the adjacent convent should not be missed. The quarters of the Jesuit novice, who died in 1568 at age 19, reflect not only his own spartan taste, but also the richer style of the 17th-century Jesuits. The Polish saint has been brilliantly immortalized in an exquisite marble piece created by Pierre Legros (1666–1719).

⓬ San Carlo alle Quattro Fontane

Via del Quirinale 23. **Map** 5 B3. **Tel** 06-488 3261. 116, 117 & routes to Piazza Barberini. Ⓜ Barberini. **Open** 10am–1pm, 3–6pm Mon–Fri; 10am–1pm Sat & Sun.

In 1634, the Trinitarians, a Spanish order whose role was to pay the ransom of Christian hostages to the Arabs, commissioned Borromini to design a church and convent at the Quattro Fontane crossroads. The church, so small it would fit inside one of the piers of St. Peter's, is also known as "San Carlino."

Although dedicated to Carlo Borromeo, the 16th-century Milanese cardinal canonized in 1620, San Carlo is as much a monument to Borromini. Both facade and interior employ bold curves that give light and life to a small, cramped site. The oval dome and tiny lantern are particularly ingenious. The undulating lines of the facade are decorated with angels and a statue of San Carlo. Finished in 1667, the facade is one of Borromini's very last works.

There are further delights in the playful inverted shapes in the cloister and the stucco work in the refectory (now the sacristy), which houses a painting of San Carlo by Orazio Borgianni (1611).

In a small room off the sacristy hangs a portrait of Borromini himself wearing the Trinitarian cross. Borromini committed suicide in 1667, and in the crypt (which is now open to the public) a small curved chapel reserved for him remains empty.

Dome of San Carlo alle Quattro Fontane, lit by concealed windows

Fountain of Strength (or Juno)

⑬ Le Quattro Fontane

Intersection of Via delle Quattro Fontane and Via del Quirinale. **Map** 5 B3. 🚌 Routes to Piazza Barberini or Via Nazionale. Ⓜ Barberini.

These four small fountains are attached to the corners of the buildings at the intersection of two narrow, busy streets. They date from the great redevelopment of Rome in the reign of Sixtus V (1585–90). Each fountain has a statue of a reclining deity. The river god accompanied by the she-wolf is clearly the Tiber; the other male figure may be the Arno. The female figures represent Strength and Fidelity or the goddesses Juno and Diana.

The crossroads is at the highest point of the Quirinal hill and commands splendid views of three distant landmark obelisks: those placed by Sixtus V in front of Santa Maria Maggiore and Trinità dei Monti, and the one that stands in Piazza del Quirinale.

⑭ Moses Fountain

Fontana dell'Acqua Felice, Piazza San Bernardo. **Map** 5 C2. 🚌 36, 60, 61, 62, 84, 175, 492. Ⓜ Repubblica.

Officially known as the Fontana dell'Acqua Felice, this fountain owes its popular name to the grotesque statue of Moses in the central niche. The massive structure with its three elegant arches was designed by Domenico Fontana to mark the terminal of the Acqua Felice aqueduct, so called because it was one of the many great improvements commissioned by Felice Peretti, Pope Sixtus V. Completed in 1587, it brought clean piped water to this quarter of Rome for the first time.

The notorious statue of Moses striking water from the rock is larger than life and the proportions of the body are obviously wrong. Sculpted either by Prospero Bresciano or Leonardo Sormani, it is a clumsy attempt at recreating the awesome appearance of Michelangelo's Moses in the church of San Pietro in Vincoli *(see p172)*. As soon as it was unveiled, it was said to be frowning at having been brought into the world by such an inept sculptor. The side reliefs also illustrate water

Fontana's Moses Fountain

stories from the Old Testament: Aaron leading the Israelites to water and Joshua pointing the army toward the Red Sea. The fountain's four lions are copies of Egyptian originals (now in the Vatican Museums), which Sixtus V had put there for the public's "convenience" and "delight."

Gold coin with head of the Emperor Diocletian (AD 285–305)

⑮ Santa Maria degli Angeli

Piazza della Repubblica. **Map** 5 C3. **Tel** 06-488 0812. 🚌 36, 60, 61, 62, 64, 84, 90, 116, 170, 492, 910. Ⓜ Repubblica, Termini. **Open** 7am– 6:30pm daily. 🚻 ♿ 📷

Parts of the ruined Baths of Diocletian *(right)* provided building material and setting for this church, constructed by Michelangelo in 1563. The church was so altered in the 18th century that it has lost most of its original character.

An exhibition in the sacristy gives a detailed account of Michelangelo's original design.

Fidelity (or Diana) with her attendant dog, one of the Quattro Fontane

Part of the Museo Nazionale Romano in the Baths of Diocletian

⓰ Museo Nazionale Romano (Palazzo Massimo)

Palazzo Massimo, Largo di Villa Peretti 1. **Map** 6 D3. **Tel** 06-480 201. 🚌 36, 38, 40, 64, 86, 170, 175, H and other routes to Piazza dei Cinquecento. Ⓜ Repubblica, Termini. **Open** 9am–7:45pm Tue–Sun (last adm: 6:45pm). **Closed** Jan 1, Dec 25. 🎫 (the biglietto cumulativo gives entry to the museum's five branches). ♿ 📷 🎧 🛍

Founded in 1889, the Museo Nazionale Romano holds most of the antiquities found in Rome since 1870 as well as pre-existing collections, and is one of the world's leading museums of Classical art. It now has five branches: its original site, occupying part of the Baths of Diocletian; the Palazzo Massimo; the Palazzo Altemps (see p129); the Aula Ottagona (near the Baths of Diocletian); and Crypta Balbi at Via delle Botteghe Oscure 31, excavated from the foyer of the theater of Balbus (1st century BC) and housing findings from medieval Rome. The Palazzo Massimo, built in

1883–7 on the site of a villa that belonged to Sixtus V, used to be a Jesuit college. In 1981–97 it was restored to house a significant proportion of the museum's collections. The exhibits, contained on four floors, are originals dating from the 2nd century BC to the end of the 4th century AD.

The basement contains an excellent display of ancient coins, precious artifacts, and the only mummified child to be found in the ancient city. The ground floor is devoted to Roman statuary, with funeral monuments in Room 2 and Emperor Augustus in Pontifex Maximus guise in Room 5. Upstairs there are statues from Nero's summer villa in Anzio and Roman copies of famous Greek originals, such as the *Discobolos Ex-Lancellotti*. The real joy of the museum, however, is on the second floor, where entire rooms of wall paintings have been brought from various villas excavated in and around Rome. The most incredible frescoes are from Livia's Villa at Prima Porta. Her triclinium (dining room) was decorated with an abundance of trees, plants, and fruit, painted in a totally naturalistic style to fool guests that they were eating alfresco, rather than indoors.

Oaks, pine trees, cypresses, oleanders, roses, poppies, and irises are all clearly distinguishable. Other marvels include rooms brought from the first Villa Farnesina: the children's room has a predominantly white design, while the adults' bedroom is red, complete with erotic paintings. Equally impressive is the museum's display of mosaics on the same floor.

⓱ Baths of Diocletian

Terme di Diocleziano, Viale E de Nicola 79. **Map** 6 D3. **Tel** 06-3996 7700. 🚌 36, 60, 61, 62, 84, 90. Ⓜ Repubblica, Termini. **Open** 9am–7:45pm Tue–Sun (last adm: 6:45pm). **Closed** Jan 1, Dec 25.

Built in AD 298–306 under the infamous Emperor Diocletian, who murdered thousands of Christians, the baths (see pp26–7) were the most extensive in Rome and could accommodate up to 3,000 bathers at a time.

Part of the Museo Nazionale Romano, the complex houses a vast collection of Roman statues and inscriptions and incorporates the former Carthusian monastery of Santa Maria degli Angeli, which has a beautiful cloister designed by Michelangelo.

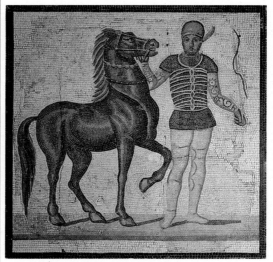

One of the Quattro Aurighe mosaics, Museo Nazionale Romano

⑱ Piazza della Repubblica

Map 5 C3. 🚌 36, 60, 61, 62, 64, 84, 90, 170, 175, 492, 646, 910.
Ⓜ Repubblica.

Romans often refer to the piazza by its old name, Piazza Esedra, so called because it follows the shape of an *exedra* (a semicircular recess) that was part of the Baths of Diocletian. The piazza was part of the great redevelopment undertaken when Rome became capital of a unified Italy. Under its sweeping 19th-century colonnades there were once elegant shops, but they have been ousted by banks, travel agencies, and cafés.

In the middle of the piazza stands the Fontana delle Naiadi. Mario Rutelli's four naked bronze nymphs caused something of a scandal when they were unveiled in 1901. Each reclines on an aquatic creature symbolizing water in its various forms: a sea horse for the oceans, a water snake for rivers, a swan for lakes, and a curious frilled lizard for subterranean streams. The

Piazza della Repubblica and the Fontana delle Naiadi

figure in the middle, added in 1911, is of the sea god Glaucus, who represents man victorious over the hostile forces of nature.

⑲ Palazzo delle Esposizioni

Via Nazionale 194. **Map** 5 B4. **Tel** 06-3996 7500. 🚌 40, 60, 64, 70, 116T, 170. **Open** 10am–8pm Tue–Thu & Sun, 10am–10:30pm Fri & Sat. 🚹 ♿ ⬚ from Via Piacenza or Via Milano 13 entrance. ♿ 🖥 📷
🔲 palaexpo.it

Facade of the Palazzo delle Esposizioni

This grandiose building, with wide steps, Corinthian columns, and statues, was designed as an exhibition center by the architect Pio Piacentini and built by the city of Rome in 1882 during the reign of Umberto I. The main entrance looks like a triumphal arch.

The restored palazzo is still used to house high-profile exhibitions of contemporary art. The exhibitions are changed every three months and include a variety of sculpture and paintings. Live performances, films, and lectures also take place here *(see p352)*. Foreign films are usually shown in the original language.

⑳ Santa Maria dei Monti

Via Madonna dei Monti 41. **Map** 5 B4. **Tel** 06-48 55 31. 🚌 75, 84, 117. Ⓜ Cavour. **Open** 7am–10pm daily. 🚻 ♿

Designed by Giacomo della Porta, this church, dating from 1580, has a particularly splendid dome. Over the high altar is a stunning medieval painting of the Madonna, patroness of this quarter of Rome. The altar in the left transept houses the tomb and effigy of the unworldly French saint Benoît-Joseph Labre, who died here in 1783, having spent his life as a solitary pilgrim. He slept rough in the ruins of the Colosseum, gave away any charitable gifts he received, and came regularly to Santa Maria dei Monti to worship. His faith could not sustain his body: still in his mid-thirties, he collapsed and died outside the church. The foul rags he wore are preserved.

One of the bronze nymphs of the fountain in Piazza della Repubblica

㉑ Sant'Agata dei Goti

Via Mazzarino 16 and Via Panisperna 29. **Map** 5 B4. **Tel** 06-4879 3531. 📧 40, 60, 64, 70, 71, 117, 170. **Open** 7–8:30am, 4–7pm Mon–Sat; 9am–noon Sun. 🚹 ♿

The Goths who gave their name to this church (*Goti* are Goths) occupied Rome in the 6th century AD. They were Aryan heretics who denied the divinity of Christ. The church was founded between AD 462 and 470, shortly before the main Gothic invasions, and the beautiful granite columns date from this period. The main altar has a well-preserved 12th-century Cosmatesque tabernacle, but the most delightful part of the church is the charming 18th-century courtyard built around an ivy-draped well.

18th-century courtyard of Sant'Agata dei Goti

㉒ Villa Aldobrandini

Via Panisperna. Entrance to gardens: Via Mazzarino 1. **Map** 5 B4. 📧 40, 60, 64, 70, 71, 117, 170. Gardens: **Open** dawn–dusk daily. Villa: **Closed** to the public.

Built in the 16th century for the Dukes of Urbino and acquired for his family by Pope Clement VIII Aldobrandini (reigned 1592–1605), the villa is now government property and houses an international law library.

The villa itself, decorated with the family's six-starred coat of arms, is closed to the public, but the gardens and terraces, hidden behind a high wall that runs along Via Nazionale, can be reached through an iron gate in

The imposing facade of Villa Aldobrandini

Via Mazzarino. Steps lead up past 2nd-century AD ruins into the gardens, highly recommended as an oasis of tranquillity in the center of the city. Gravel paths lead between formal lawns and clearly marked specimen trees, and benches are provided for the weary. Since the garden is raised some 30 ft (10 m) above street level, the views are excellent.

㉓ Santi Domenico e Sisto

Largo Angelicum 1. **Map** 5 B4. **Tel** 06-670 21. 📧 40, 60, 64, 70, 71 117, 170. **Open** 9am–noon Sat.

The church has a tall, slender Baroque facade rising above a steep flight of steps. This divides into two curving flights that sweep up to the terrace in front of the entrance. The pediment of the facade is crowned by eight flaming candlesticks.

The interior has a vaulted ceiling with a large fresco of *The Apotheosis of St. Dominic* by Domenico Canuti (1620–84). The first chapel on the right was decorated by Bernini, who may also have designed the sculpture of Mary Magdalene meeting the risen Christ in the Garden of Gethsemane. This fine marble group was executed by Antonio Raggi (1649). Above the altar is a 15th-century terra-cotta plaque of the Virgin and Child. On the left over a side altar is a large painting of the Madonna from the same period, attributed to Benozzo Gozzoli (1420–97), a pupil of Fra Angelico.

Chapel in Santi Domenico e Sisto

ESQUILINE

The Esquiline is the largest and highest of Rome's seven hills. In Imperial Rome, the western slopes overlooking the Forum housed the crowded slums of the Suburra. On the eastern side there were a few villas belonging to wealthy citizens like Maecenas, patron of the arts and adviser to Augustus. The essential character of the place has persisted through two millennia; it is still one of the poorer quarters of the city. The area is now heavily built up, except for a rather seedy park on the Colle Oppio, a smaller hill to the south of the Esquiline, where you can see the remains of the Baths of Titus, the Baths of Trajan, and Nero's Domus Aurea. The area's main interest, however, lies in its churches. Many of these were founded on the sites of private houses where Christians met to worship secretly in the days when their religion was banned.

Sights at a Glance

Churches

1. San Martino ai Monti
2. San Pietro in Vincoli
3. Santa Pudenziana
4. *Santa Maria Maggiore pp174–5*
5. Santa Prassede
7. Santa Bibiana

Museums

9. Museo Nazionale d'Arte Orientale

Historic Piazzas

8. Piazza Vittorio Emanuele II

Ancient Sites

10. Auditorium of Maecenas
11. Sette Sale
12. Domus Aurea

Arches

6. Arch of Gallienus

See also Street Finder maps 5, 6

Restaurants
see pp310–11

1. Agata e Romeo
2. Cuoco e Camicia
3. Da Danilo
4. Hang Zhou
5. La Gallina Bianca
6. Tempio di Iside
7. Trattoria Monti

◄ Detail from the apse mosaic at Santa Maria Maggiore

For map symbols *see back flap*

Street-by-Street: The Esquiline Hill

The sight that draws most people to this rather scruffy part of Rome is the great basilica of Santa Maria Maggiore. But it is also well worth searching out some of the smaller churches on the Esquiline: Santa Pudenziana, and Santa Prassede with their celebrated mosaics, and San Pietro in Vincoli, home to one of Michelangelo's most famous sculptures. To the south, in the Colle Oppio park, are the scattered remains of the Baths of Trajan.

3 Santa Pudenziana
The apse of this ancient church has a magnificent 4th-century mosaic of Christ surrounded by the Apostles.

Piazza dell'Esquilino was furnished with an obelisk in 1587 by Pope Sixtus V. This helped to guide pilgrims coming from the north to the important church of Santa Maria Maggiore.

2 ★ San Pietro in Vincoli
The church's treasures include Michelangelo's *Moses* and the chains that bound St. Peter.

To the Colosseum

The Baths of Trajan (AD 109) were the first to be built on the massive scale later used in the Baths of Diocletian and Caracalla.

The Torre dei Capocci, a restored medieval tower, is one of the area's most distinctive landmarks.

❹ ★ Santa Maria Maggiore
This imposing rear facade was added by Baroque architect Carlo Rainaldi in 1673. Santa Maria's interior is one of the most richly decorated in Rome.

Locator Map
See Central Rome Map pp16–17

The Tomb of Pius V (died 1572) by Domenico Fontana stands in this less-well-known Sistine Chapel, under the northeast dome of Santa Maria Maggiore.

To Vittorio Emanuele Metro

❻ Arch of Gallienus
This was built in the 3rd century AD to replace an entrance in the old Servian Wall.

❺ ★ Santa Prassede
The 9th-century mosaics in the Chapel of San Zeno are among the finest in Rome.

❶ San Martino ai Monti
The frescoes include 17th-century Roman landscapes and scenes from the life of Elijah by Gaspare Dughet.

Key

— Suggested route

| 0 meters | 75 |
| 0 yards | 75 |

Fresco of old San Giovanni in Laterano in San Martino ai Monti

① San Martino ai Monti

Viale del Monte Oppio 28. **Map** 6 D5.
Tel 06-478 4701. 🚌 16, 714.
Ⓜ Cavour, Vittorio Emanuele.
Open 8–11:30am, 4:30–7pm
Mon–Sat; 8am–noon, 4–8pm Sun.
🔔 ♿

Christians have been worshipping on the site of this church since the 3rd century, when they used to meet in the house of a man named Equitius. In the 4th century, after Constantine had legalized Christianity, Pope Sylvester I built a church, one of very few things he did during his pontificate. In fact, he was so insignificant that in the 5th century a more exciting life was fabricated for him – which included tales of him converting Constantine, curing him of leprosy, and forcing him to close all pagan temples. Pope Sylvester's fictional life was further enhanced in the 8th century, with the forgery of a document in which Constantine offered him the Imperial crown.

Pope Sylvester's church was replaced in about AD 500 by St. Symmachus, rebuilt in the 9th century, and then transformed completely in the 1630s. The only obvious signs of its age are the ancient Corinthian columns dividing the nave and aisles. The most interesting interior features are a series of frescoed landscapes of the countryside around

Rome *(campagna romana)* by the 17th-century French artist Gaspare Dughet, Poussin's brother-in-law, in the right aisle. The frescoes by Filippo Gagliardi, at either end of the left aisle, show old St. Peter's and the interior of San Giovanni in Laterano before Borromini's redesign. If you can find the sacristan, you can go beneath the church to see the remains of Equitius's house.

② San Pietro in Vincoli

Piazza di San Pietro in Vincoli 4A. **Map** 5 C5. **Tel** 06-9784 4950. 🚌 75, 84, 117. Ⓜ Cavour, Colosseo. **Open** 8am–12:30pm, 3–7pm (Oct–Mar: 6pm) daily. 🔔 ♿ 📷

According to tradition, the two chains *(vincoli)* used to shackle St. Peter while he was

Reliquary with St. Peter's chains

being held in the depths of the Mamertine Prison *(see p93)* were subsequently taken to Constantinople. In the 5th century, Empress Eudoxia deposited one in a church in Constantinople and sent the other to her daughter Eudoxia in Rome. She in turn gave hers to Pope Leo I, who had this church built to house it. Some years later the second chain was brought to Rome, where it linked miraculously with its partner.

The chains are still here, displayed below the high altar, but the church is now best known for Michelangelo's *Tomb of Pope Julius II*. When it was commissioned in 1505, Michelangelo spent eight months searching for perfect blocks of marble at Carrara in Tuscany, but Pope Julius became more interested in the building of a new St. Peter's and the project was laid aside. After the pope's death in 1513, Michelangelo resumed work on the tomb, but had only finished the statues of *Moses* and *The Dying Slaves* when Pope Paul III persuaded him to start work on the Sistine Chapel's *Last Judgment*. Michelangelo had planned a vast monument with over 40 statues, but the tomb that was built – mainly by his pupils – is simply a facade with six niches for statues. *The Dying Slaves* are in Paris and Florence, but the tremendous bearded *Moses* is here. The horns on Moses' head should really be beams of light – they are the result of the original Hebrew from the Old Testament being wrongly translated.

Michelangelo's *Moses* in San Pietro

❸ Santa Pudenziana

Via Urbana 160. **Map** 5 C4. **Tel** 06-481 4622. 🚌 16, 75, 84, 105, 714. Ⓜ Cavour. **Open** 8:30am–noon (from 9am Sun), 3–6pm daily. 🕆

Churches tend to be dedicated to existing saints, but in this case, the church, through a linguistic accident, created a brand new saint. In the 1st century AD a Roman senator called Pudens lived here, and, according to legend, allowed St. Peter to lodge with him. In the 2nd century a bath house was built on this site and in the 4th century a church was established inside the baths, known as the *Ecclesia Pudentiana* (the church of Pudens). In time it was assumed that "Pudentiana" was a woman's name, and a life was created for her – she became the sister of Prassede and was credited with caring for Christian victims of persecution. In 1969, both saints were declared invalid, though their churches both kept their names.

The 19th-century facade of the church retains an 11th-century frieze depicting both Prassede and Pudenziana dressed as crowned Byzantine empresses. The apse has a remarkable 4th-century mosaic, clearly influenced by Classical pagan art in its use of subtle colors. The Apostles are represented as Roman

Apse mosaics in Santa Prassede, showing the saint with St. Paul

senators in togas, but a clumsy attempt at restoration in the 16th century destroyed two of the Apostles and left other figures without legs.

❹ Santa Maria Maggiore

See pp174–5.

❺ Santa Prassede

Via Santa Prassede 9A. **Map** 6 D4. **Tel** 06-488 2456. 🚌 16, 70, 71, 75, 714. Ⓜ Vittorio Emanuele. **Open** 7:30am–noon, 4–6:30pm daily (afternoons only, Aug). 🕆 🚻

The church was founded by Pope Paschal II in the 9th century, on the site of a 2nd-century oratory. Although the interior has been altered and rebuilt, the structure of the original design of the 9th-century church is clearly visible. Its three aisles are separated by rows of granite columns. In the central nave, there is a round stone slab covering the well where, according to legend, St. Prassede buried the remains of 2,000 martyrs.

Artists from Byzantium decorated the church with glittering, jewel-colored mosaics. Those in the apse and choir depict stylized white-robed elders, the haloed elect looking down from the gold and blue walls of heaven, spindly legged lambs, feather-mop palm trees, and bright red poppies.

In the apse, Santa Prassede and Santa Pudenziana stand on either side of Christ, with the fatherly arms of St. Paul and St. Peter on their shoulders. Beautiful mosaics of saints, the Virgin, and Christ and the Apostles also cover the walls and vault of the Chapel of St. Zeno, built as a mausoleum for Pope Paschal's mother, Theodora. Part of a column brought back from Jerusalem, allegedly the one to which Christ was bound and flogged, also stands here.

Facade of the 19th-century church, Santa Pudenziana

❹ Santa Maria Maggiore

Of all the great Roman basilicas, Santa Maria has the most successful blend of different architectural styles. Its colonnaded nave is part of the original 5th-century building. The Cosmatesque marble floor and delightful Romanesque bell tower, with its blue ceramic roundels, are medieval. The Renaissance saw a new coffered ceiling, and the Baroque gave the church twin domes and its imposing front and rear facades. The mosaics are Santa Maria's most famous feature. From the 5th century come the biblical scenes in the aisle and the spectacular mosaics on the triumphal arch. Medieval highlights include a 13th-century enthroned Christ in the loggia.

Obelisk in Piazza dell'Esquilino
The Egyptian obelisk was erected by Pope Sixtus V in 1587 as a landmark for pilgrims.

★ Cappella Paolina
Flaminio Ponzio designed this richly decorated chapel (1611) for Pope Paul V Borghese.

Coffered Ceiling
The gilded ceiling, possibly by Giuliano da Sangallo, was a gift of Alexander VI Borgia at the end of the 15th century. The gold is said to be the first brought from America by Columbus.

356 Virgin appears to Pope Liberius

Pope Gregory VII

1347 Cola di Rienzo crowned Tribune of Rome in Santa Maria

1673 Carlo Rainaldi rebuilds apse

300 AD	600	900	1200	1500	18

432–40 Sixtus III completes church

420 Probable founding date

1075 Pope Gregory VII kidnapped by opponents while saying Christmas mass in Santa Maria

Coat of arms of Gregory VII

1288–92 Nicholas IV adds apse and transepts

1743 Ferdinando Fuga adds main facade on orders of Benedict XIV

★ **Coronation of the Virgin Mosaic**
This is the central image of a series of wonderful apse mosaics of the Virgin by Jacopo Torriti (1295).

Baldacchino (1740s)
Its columns of red porphyry and bronze were the work of Ferdinando Fuga.

★ **Tomb of Cardinal Rodriguez**
The Gothic tomb (1299) contains magnificent Cosmatesque marblework.

★ **Cappella Sistina**
This Sistine Chapel was built for Pope Sixtus V (1584–87) by Domenico Fontana and houses his tomb.

Column in Piazza Santa Maria Maggiore
A bronze of the Virgin and Child was added to this ancient marble column in 1615. The column came from the Basilica of Constantine in the Forum.

Legend of the Snow

In 356, Pope Liberius had a dream in which the Virgin told him to build a church on the spot where he found snow. When it fell on the Esquiline, on the morning of August 5, in the middle of a baking Roman summer, he naturally obeyed. The miracle of the snow is commemorated each year by a service during which thousands of white petals float down from the ceiling of Santa Maria. Originally roses were used, but nowadays the petals are more usually taken from dahlias.

❻ Arch of Gallienus

Via Carlo Alberto. **Map** 6 D4. 🚌 16, 71, 714. Ⓜ Vittorio Emanuele.

Squashed between two buildings just off Via Carlo Alberto is the central arch of an originally three-arched gate erected in memory of Emperor Gallienus, who was assassinated by his Illyrian officers in AD 262. It was built on the site of the old Esquiline Gate in the Servian Wall, parts of which are visible nearby.

National monument of Vittorio Emanuele II, built in honor of unified Italy's first king

Arch erected in memory of Emperor Gallienus

❼ Santa Bibiana

Via Giovanni Giolitti 154. **Map** 6 F4. **Tel** 06-446 5235. 🚌 71. 🚋 5, 14. Ⓜ Vittorio Emanuele. **Open** 7:30–9:45am, 5–7:30pm daily. 🔼 ♿

The deceptively simple facade of Santa Bibiana was Bernini's first foray into architecture. It is a clean, economic design with superimposed pilasters and deeply shadowed archways. The church itself was built on the site of the palace belonging to Bibiana's family. This is where the saint was buried after being flogged to death with leaded cords during the brief persecution of the Christians in the reign of Julian the Apostate (361–3). Just inside the church is a small column against which Bibiana is said to have been whipped. Her remains, along with those of her mother Dafrosa and her sister Demetria, who also suffered martyrdom, are preserved in an alabaster urn below the altar. In a niche above the altar stands a statue of Santa Bibiana by Bernini – the first fully clothed figure he ever sculpted. He depicts her standing beside a column, holding the cords with which she was whipped, apparently on the verge of a deadly swoon.

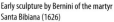

Early sculpture by Bernini of the martyr Santa Bibiana (1626)

❽ Piazza Vittorio Emanuele II

Map 6 E5. 🚌 4, 9, 71. 🚋 5, 14. Ⓜ Vittorio Emanuele. *See Markets p344.*

Piazza Vittorio, as it is called for short, was once one of the city's main open-air food markets, though now it has moved around the corner to new, covered premises. The arcaded square was built in the urban development undertaken after the unification of Italy in 1870. It was named after Italy's first king, but there is nothing regal about its appearance today.

However, the garden area in the center of the square has been restored. It contains a number of mysterious ruins, including a large mound, part of a Roman fountain from the 3rd century AD, and the Porta Magica, a curious 17th-century doorway inscribed with alchemical signs and formulae.

❾ Museo Nazionale d'Arte Orientale

Via Merulana 248. **Map** 6 D5. **Tel** 06-4697 4832. 🚌 16, 70, 71, 714. Ⓜ Vittorio Emanuele. **Open** 9am–2pm Tue, Wed & Fri; 9am–7:30pm Thu, Sat & Sun. 📷 ♿ 🌐 **museorientale. beniculturali.it**

The museum occupies part of the late 19th-century Palazzo Brancaccio, home of the Italian Institute of the Middle and Far East since 1957. The collection ranges from prehistoric Iranian ceramics to sculpture from Afghanistan, Nepal, Kashmir, and India to 18th-century Tibetan paintings on vellum.

From East Asia there are collections of Japanese screen paintings and Chinese jade.

The most unusual exhibits are the finds from the Italian excavation of the ancient civilization of Swat in northeast Pakistan. This fascinating Gandhara culture lasted from the 3rd century BC to about the 10th century AD. Its wonderfully exotic, sensual reliefs show an unusual combination of Hellenistic, Buddhist, and Hindu influences.

Nepalese Bodhisattva in the Museo Nazionale d'Arte Orientale

❿ Auditorium of Maecenas

Largo Leopardi 2. **Map** 6 D5. **Tel** 06-0608. 🚌16, 714. Ⓜ Vittorio Emanuele. **Open** by appt; phone in advance. ⊠ ♿

Maecenas, a dandy, gourmet, and patron of the arts, was also an astute adviser and colleague of the Emperor Augustus. Fabulously rich, he created a fantastic villa and gardens on the Esquiline hill, most of which has long disappeared beneath the modern city. The partially reconstructed auditorium, isolated on a traffic island, is all that remains.

Inside, a semicircle of tiered seats suggests that it may have been a place for readings and performances. If it was, then Maecenas would have been entertained here by his protégés, the lyric poet Horace and Virgil, author of the *Aeneid*, reading their latest works. However,

water ducts have also been discovered and it may well have been a *nympheum* – a kind of summerhouse – with fountains. Traces of frescoes remain on the walls: you can make out garden scenes and a procession of miniature figures – including one of a characteristically drunken Dionysus (the Greek god of wine) being propped upright by a satyr.

⓫ Sette Sale

Via delle Terme di Traiano. **Map** 5 C5. **Tel** 06-0608. 🚌 85, 87, 117, 186, 810, 850. 🚋 3. Ⓜ Colosseo. **Open** by appt; phone in advance.

Not far from Nero's Domus Aurea is the cistern of the Sette Sale. It was built here to supply the enormous quantities of water needed for the Baths of Trajan. These were built for Emperor Trajan in AD 104 on parts of the Domus Aurea that had been damaged by a fire.

A set of stairs leads down into the cistern, well below street level. There is not much to see here now, but a walk through the huge, echoing cistern where light rays illuminate the watery surfaces is still an evocative experience. The nine sections, 98 ft (30 m) long and 16 ft (5 m) wide, had a capacity of 2 million gallons (8 million liters).

⓬ Domus Aurea

Viale della Domus Aurea. **Map** 5 C5. **Tel** 06-0608. 🚌 85, 87, 117, 186, 810, 850. 🚋 3. Ⓜ Colosseo. **Closed** to the public (call for further information). ⊠ ♿ 🏛 🔍

After allegedly setting fire to Rome in AD 64, Nero decided to build himself an outrageous new palace. The Domus Aurea (sometimes called Nero's Golden House) occupied part of the Palatine and most of the Celian and Esquiline hills – an area approximately 25 times the size of the Colosseum. The vestibule on the Palatine side of the complex contained a colossal gilded statue of Nero. There was an artificial lake, with gardens and woods where

imported wild beasts were allowed to roam free. According to Suetonius in his life of Nero, the palace walls were adorned with gold and mother-of-pearl, rooms were designed with ceilings that showered guests with flowers or perfumes, the dining hall rotated, and the baths were fed with both sulfurous water and seawater.

Tacitus described Nero's debauched garden parties, with banquets served on barges and lakeside brothels serviced by aristocratic women, though since Nero killed himself in AD 68, he did not have long to enjoy his new home.

Nero's successors, anxious to distance themselves from the monster-emperor, did their utmost to erase all traces of the palace. Vespasian drained the lake and built the Colosseum *(see pp94–7)* in its place, Titus and Trajan each erected a complex of baths over the palace, and Hadrian placed the Temple of Venus and Rome *(see p89)* over the vestibule.

Rooms from one wing of the palace have survived, buried beneath the ruins of the Baths of Trajan on the Oppian hill. Excavations have revealed large frescoes and mosaics that are thought to be a panorama of Rome from a bird's-eye perspective. It is currently closed for safety reasons, but hopefully more areas will open to the public when considered safe from landslides.

Frescoed room in the ruins of the Domus Aurea

LATERAN

In the Middle Ages, the Lateran Palace was the residence of the popes, and the Basilica of San Giovanni beside it rivaled St. Peter's in splendor. After the return of the popes from Avignon at the end of the 14th century, the area declined in importance. Pilgrims still continued to visit San Giovanni and Santa Croce in Gerusalemme, but the area remained sparsely inhabited. Ancient convents were situated amid gardens and vineyards until Rome became capital of Italy in 1870 and a network of residential streets was laid out here to house the influx of newcomers. Archaeological interest lies chiefly in the Aurelian Wall and the ruins of the Aqueduct of Nero.

Sights at a Glance

Churches
1 San Giovanni in Laterano pp182–3
5 Santa Croce in Gerusalemme
11 Santi Quattro Coronati
12 San Clemente pp188–9
13 Santo Stefano Rotondo

Shrines
2 Scala Santa and Sancta Sanctorum

Arches and Gates
3 Porta Asinaria
7 Porta Maggiore

Ancient Sites
4 Amphiteatrum Castrense
8 Baker's Tomb
9 Aqueduct of Nero and the Freedmen's Tombs

Museums
6 Museum of Musical Instruments
10 Museo Storico della Liberazione di Roma

See also Street Finder maps 6, 9, 10

Restaurants
see pp310–11

1 Aroma
2 Bibenda
3 Charly's Saucière
4 I Clementini
5 Il Pentagrappolo
6 La Tavena dei 40
7 Maud

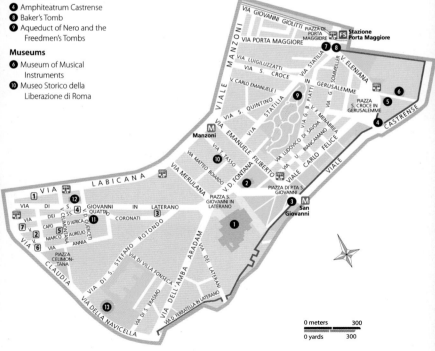

0 meters 300
0 yards 300

◀ The impressive interior of the Basilica of San Clemente

For map symbols see back flap

Street by Street: Piazza di San Giovanni

Both the Basilica of San Giovanni and the Lateran Palace look out over a huge open area, the Piazza di San Giovanni, laid out at the end of the 16th century with an Egyptian obelisk, the oldest in Rome, in the center. Unfortunately, the traffic streaming in and out of the city through Porta San Giovanni tends to detract from its grandeur. Across the square is the building housing the Scala Santa (the Holy Staircase), one of the most revered relics in Rome and the goal for many pilgrims. The area is also a venue for political rallies, and the feast of St. John on June 23 is celebrated with a fair at which Romans consume roast *porchetta (see p61)*.

The Chapel of Santa Rufina, originally the portico of the baptistry, has a 5th-century mosaic of spiraling foliage in the apse.

VIA DI SANTO STEFANO ROTONDO

VIA DELL'AMBA ARADAM

VIA DEI LATERANI

The Cloister of San Giovanni fortunately survived the two fires that destroyed the early basilica. A 13th-century masterpiece of mosaic work, the cloister now houses fragments from the medieval basilica.

Key

— Suggested route

0 meters 75

0 yards 75

The Chapel of San Venanzio is decorated with a series of 7th-century mosaics on a gold background. This detail from the apse shows one of the angels flanking the central figure of Christ. San Venanzio was an accomplished 6th-century Latin poet.

Piazza di San Giovanni in Laterano boasts an ancient obelisk, and parts of Nero's Aqueduct. This 18th-century painting by Canaletto shows how the piazza once looked.

Locator Map
See Central Rome Map pp16–17

The Lateran Palace, residence of the popes until 1309, was rebuilt by Domenico Fontana in 1586.

❶ ★ San Giovanni in Laterano
Borromini's interior dates from the 17th century, but the grand facade by Alessandro Galilei, with its giant statues of Christ, and the Apostles, was added in 1735.

PIAZZA DI SAN GIOVANNI IN LATERANO

VIA D. FONTANA

PIAZZA DI PORTA SAN GIOVANNI

❷ Scala Santa
This door at the top of the Holy Staircase leads to the Sancta Sanctorum.

The Triclinio Leoniano is a piece of wall, and a mosaic from the dining hall of 8th-century Pope Leo III.

❸ Porta Asinaria
This minor gateway, no longer in use, is as old as the Aurelian Wall, dating back to the 3rd century AD.

❶ San Giovanni in Laterano

Early in the 4th century, the Laterani family were disgraced, and their land taken by Emperor Constantine to build Rome's first Christian basilica. Today's church retains the original shape, but has been destroyed by fire twice and rebuilt several times. Borromini undertook the last major rebuild of the interior in 1646, and the main facade is an 18th-century addition. Before the pope's move to Avignon in 1309, the adjoining Lateran Palace was the official papal residence, and until 1870 all popes were crowned in the church. This is the city's main cathedral, and the seat of the Bishop of Rome, the Pope, who celebrates Maundy Thursday Mass here and attends the annual blessing of the people.

★ Baptistry
Though much restored, the domed baptistry dates back to Constantine's time. It assumed its present octagonal shape in AD 432 and the design has served as the model for baptistries throughout the Christian world.

Entrance to museum

KEY

① **Apse**

② **The Cappella di San Venanzio** chapel is attached to the baptistry, and is decorated with 7th-century mosaics.

③ **The original Lateran Palace** was almost destroyed by the fire of 1308, which devastated San Giovanni. Pope Sixtus V commissioned Fontana to replace it in 1586.

④ **Statues of Christ and the Apostles**

⑤ **A side door** is opened every Holy Year.

⑥ **The main entrance's** bronze doors originally came from the Curia (see p84).

Papal Altar
Only the Pope can celebrate mass at this altar. The Gothic *baldacchino*, decorated with frescoes, dates from the 14th century.

★ Cloisters
Built by the Vassalletto family in about 1220, the cloisters are remarkable for their twisted twin columns and inlaid marble mosaics.

North Facade
This was added by Domenico Fontana in 1586. The pope gives his blessing from the upper loggia.

Boniface VIII Fresco
This fragment showing the pope proclaiming the Holy Year of 1300 is attributed to Giotto.

VISITORS' CHECKLIST

Practical Information
Piazza di San Giovanni in Laterano 4.
Map 9 C2.
Tel 06-6988 6433.
Cathedral: **Open** 7am–6:30pm daily. Cloister: **Open** 9am–6pm daily. Museum: **Open** 9am–1pm Mon–Sat. Baptistry: **Open** 8am–noon, 4–7pm daily.
🎫 for museum, and cloister.
🚻 📷

Transportation
🚌 16, 81, 85, 87, 186, 650, 850 and other routes to Piazza San Giovanni. Ⓜ San Giovanni.
🚋 3.

Corsini Chapel
This chapel was built in the 1730s for Pope Clement XII. The altarpiece is a mosaic copy of Guido Reni's painting of Sant'Andrea Corsini.

Trial of a Corpse

Fear of rival factions led the early popes to extraordinary lengths. An absurd case took place at the Lateran Palace in 897 when Pope Stephen VI tried the corpse of his predecessor, Formosus, for disloyalty to the Church. The corpse was found guilty, its right hand was mutilated, and it was thrown into the Tiber.

Pope Formosus

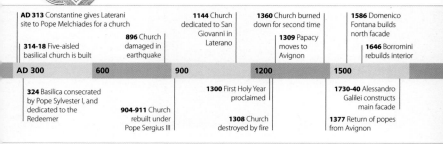

AD 313 Constantine gives Laterani site to Pope Melchiades for a church

314–18 Five-aisled basilical church is built

896 Church damaged in earthquake

1144 Church dedicated to San Giovanni in Laterano

1360 Church burned down for second time

1309 Papacy moves to Avignon

1586 Domenico Fontana builds north facade

1646 Borromini rebuilds interior

AD 300   **600**   **900**   **1200**   **1500**

324 Basilica consecrated by Pope Sylvester I, and dedicated to the Redeemer

904–911 Church rebuilt under Pope Sergius III

1300 First Holy Year proclaimed

1308 Church destroyed by fire

1730–40 Alessandro Galilei constructs main facade

1377 Return of popes from Avignon

Devout Christians climbing the Scala Santa on their knees

❷ Scala Santa and Sancta Sanctorum

Piazza di San Giovanni in Laterano 14. **Map** 9 C1. **Tel** 06-772 6641. 🚌 16, 81, 85, 87, 186 and other routes to Piazza di San Giovanni in Laterano. 🚊 3. Ⓜ San Giovanni. **Open** 6:30am–noon, 3–5pm daily (3:30–6pm in summer). ✝

On the east side of Piazza di San Giovanni in Laterano, a building designed by Domenico Fontana (1589) houses two surviving parts of the old Lateran Palace. One is the Sancta Sanctorum, the other the holy staircase, the Scala Santa. The 28 steps, said to be those that Christ ascended in Pontius Pilate's house during his trial, are supposed to have been brought from Jerusalem by St Helena, mother of the Emperor Constantine. This belief, however, cannot be traced back any earlier than the 7th century.

The steps were moved to their present site by Pope Sixtus V (reigned 1585–90) when the old Lateran Palace was destroyed. No foot may touch the holy steps, so they are covered by wooden boards. They may only be climbed by the faithful on their knees, a penance that is performed especially on Good Friday. In the vestibule there are various 19th-century sculptures including an *Ecce Homo* by Giosuè Meli (1874).

The Scala Santa and two side stairways lead to the Chapel of St Lawrence or Sancta

Sanctorum (Holy of Holies), built by Pope Nicholas III in 1278. Decorated with fine Cosmatesque marble-work, the chapel contains many important relics, the most precious being an image of Jesus – the *Acheiropoeton* or "picture painted without hands", said to be the work of St Luke, with the help of an angel. It was taken on procession in medieval times to ward off plagues.

On the walls and in the vault, restoration work has revealed 13th-century frescoes which for 500 years had been covered by later paintings. The frescoes, representing the legends of St Nicholas, St Lawrence, St Agnes and St Paul, show signs of the style that would characterize the frescoes of Giotto in Assisi, made a few years later.

❸ Porta Asinaria

Between Piazza di Porta San Giovanni and Piazzale Appio. **Map** 10 D2. 🚌 16, 81, 85, 87. 🚊 3. Ⓜ San Giovanni. *See Markets p345.*

The Porta Asinaria (Gate of the Donkeys) is one of the minor gateways in the Aurelian Wall *(see p198)*. Twin circular towers were added and a small enclosure built around the entrance; the remains are still visible. From outside the walls you can see the gate's white travertine facade and two rows of small windows, giving light to two corridors built into the wall above the gateway. In AD 546, treacherous barbarian soldiers serving in the Roman army opened this gate to the hordes of the Goth Totila, who mercilessly looted the city. In 1084 the Holy Roman Emperor Henry IV entered Rome via Porta Asinaria with the antipope Guibert to oust Pope Gregory VII. The gate was badly damaged in the conflicts that followed.

The area close to the gate, especially in the Via Sannio, is the home of a popular flea market *(see p345)*.

Shopping for bargain clothes at the Via Sannio flea market

❹ Amphiteatrum Castrense

Between Piazza di Santa Croce in Gerusalemme and Viale Castrense. **Map** 10 E1. 🚌 649. 🚊 3. **Open** by appt; call 06-0608.

This small 3rd-century amphitheater was used for games and baiting animals. It owes its preservation to the fact that it was incorporated in the Aurelian Wall *(see p198)*, which included several existing high buildings in its fortifications. The graceful arches framed by brick semicolumns were blocked up. The amphitheater is best seen from outside the walls, from where there is also a good view of the bell tower of Santa Croce in Gerusalemme.

Porta Asinaria from inside the wall

Discovery and Triumph of the Cross, attributed to Antoniazzo Romano, in Santa Croce in Gerusalemme

❺ Santa Croce in Gerusalemme

Piazza di Santa Croce in Gerusalemme 12. **Map** 10 E1. **Tel** 06-7061 3053. 🚌 16, 81, 649, 810. 🚋 3. **Open** 7am–12:45pm, 3:30–7:30pm daily. 🚹 📷

Emperor Constantine's mother St. Helena founded this church in AD 320 in the grounds of her private palace. Although the church stood at the edge of the city, the relics of the Crucifixion that St. Helena had brought back from Jerusalem made it a center of pilgrimage. Most important were the pieces of Christ's Cross (*croce* means cross) and part of Pontius Pilate's

18th-century statue of St. Helena on the facade of Santa Croce

inscription in Latin, Hebrew and Greek: "Jesus of Nazareth King of the Jews."

In the crypt is a Roman statue of Juno, found at Ostia (*see pp272–3*), transformed into a statue of St. Helena by replacing the head and arms and adding a cross. The 15th-century apse fresco shows the medieval legends that arose around the Cross. Helena is shown holding it over a dead youth and restoring him to life. Another episode shows its recovery from the Persians by the Byzantine Emperor Heraclitus after a bloody battle. In the center of the apse is a magnificent tomb by Jacopo Sansovino made for Cardinal Quiñones, Emperor Charles V's confessor (died 1540).

❻ Museum of Musical Instruments

Museo degli Strumenti Musicali, Piazza di Santa Croce in Gerusalemme 9a. **Map** 10 E1. **Tel** 06-701 4796. 🚌 16, 81, 649, 810. 🚋 3. **Open** 8:30am –7:30pm Tue–Sun. **Closed** Jan 1, Dec 25. 🚫 ♿ 🌐 **museostrumentimusicali.it**

One of Rome's lesser-known museums, the building stands on the site of the Sessorianum, the great Imperial villa belonging to Empress St. Helena, later included in the Aurelian Wall. Opened in 1974,

the museum has a collection of more than 3,000 instruments from all over the world, including instruments typical of the various regions of Italy, and wind, string, and percussion instruments of all ages (including Egyptian, Greek, and Roman). There are also sections dedicated to church and military music. The greater part of the collection is composed of Baroque instruments: don't miss the gorgeous Barberini harp, remarkably well-preserved, on the first floor in Room 13. There are spinets, harpsichords, and clavichords, and one of the first pianos ever made, dating from 1722. However, it is advisable to call before visiting since restoration is in progress.

Art Nouveau entrance to the Museum of Musical Instruments

❼ Porta Maggiore

Piazza di Porta Maggiore. **Map** 6 F5.
🚌 105. 🚊 3, 5, 14, 19.

Originally the two arches of
Porta Maggiore were not part
of the city wall, but part of an
aqueduct built by the Emperor
Claudius in AD 52. They carried
the water of the Aqua Claudia
over the Via Labicana and Via
Prenestina, two of ancient
Rome's main southbound roads.
You can still see the original
roadway beneath the gate. In
the large slabs of basalt – a hard
volcanic rock used in all old
Roman roads – note the great
ruts created by generations of
cart wheels. On top of the arches,
separate conduits carried the
water of two aqueducts: the
Aqua Claudia, and its offshoot,
the Aqueduct of Nero. They
bear inscriptions from the time
of the Emperor Claudius and
also from the reigns of Vespasian
and Titus, who restored them in
AD 71 and AD 81, respectively.
In all, six aqueducts from
different water sources entered
the city at Porta Maggiore.

The Aqua Claudia was
43 miles (68 km) long, with over
9 miles (15 km) above ground.
Its majestic arches are a
notable feature of the Roman
countryside, and a popular
mineral water bears its name.
One stretch of the Aqua Claudia
had its arches bricked up
when it was incorporated
into the 3rd-century Aurelian
Wall (see p198).

Porta Maggiore, a city gate formed by the
arches of an aqueduct

Relief showing breadmaking on the tomb of the baker Eurysaces

❽ Baker's Tomb

Piazzale Labicano. **Map** 6 F5. 🚌 105.
🚊 3, 5, 14, 19.

In the middle of the streetcar
intersection near Porta Maggiore
stands the tomb of the rich baker
Eurysaces and his wife Atistia,
built in 30 BC. Roman
custom forbade
burials within city walls,
and the roads leading
out of cities became
lined with tombs, and
monuments for the
middle and upper
classes. This tomb is
shaped like a baking
oven: a low-relief
frieze at the top
shows Eurysaces
presiding over his
slaves in the various phases of
breadmaking. The inscription
proudly asserts his origins, and
reveals him as a freed slave,
probably of Greek origin. Many
men like him saved money from
their meager slave salaries to
earn their freedom and set up
businesses, becoming the
backbone of Rome's economy.

Relief on the Tomb of
the Statilii freedmen

❾ Aqueduct of Nero and the Freedmen's Tombs

Intersection of Via Statilia and Via di
Santa Croce in Gerusalemme. **Map** 10
D1. 🚌 105, 649. 🚊 3, 5, 14, 19. **Open**
by appt only: call 06-0608.

The aqueduct was built by Nero
in the 1st century AD as an
extension of the Aqua Claudia
to supply Nero's Golden House
(see p177). It was later extended
to the Imperial residences on
the Palatine. Partly incorporated
into later buildings, the imposing arches make their way via
the Lateran to the Celian hill.
Along the first section of the
aqueduct, in Via Statilia, is a
small tomb in the
shape of a house,
dating from the
1st century BC,
bearing the names
and likenesses of a
group of freed slaves.
Their name, Statilii,
indicates that they
had been freed by the
Statilii, the family of
Claudius's notorious
wife Messalina.
Servants of families
often pooled funds in this way
to pay for a dignified burial in a
common resting place.

Well-preserved section of Nero's Aqueduct
near San Giovanni

⑩ Museo Storico della Liberazione di Roma

Via Tasso 145. **Map** 9 C1. **Tel** 06-700 3866. Ⓜ Manzoni, San Giovanni. 🚌 3. **Open** 3:30–7:30pm Tue, Thu & Fri; 9:30am–12:30pm Tue–Sun.

This museum, dedicated to the resistance to the Nazi occupation of Rome, is housed in the ex-prison of the Gestapo. The makeshift cells with bloodstained walls make a strong impact (see p268).

⑪ Santi Quattro Coronati

Via Santi Quattro Coronati 20. **Map** 9 B1. **Tel** 06-7047 5427. 🚌 85, 117. 🚋 3. **Open** 6:30am–12:30pm, 3:30–7:45pm daily. Cloister, St. Sylvester **Open** 10–11:45am (until 10:30am Sun) 4–5:45pm. 🔲 ♿

The name of this fortified convent (Four Crowned Saints) refers to four Christian soldiers martyred after refusing to worship a pagan god. For centuries it was the bastion of the pope's residence, the Lateran Palace. Its high apse looms over the houses below, while a Carolingian tower dominates the entrance. Erected in the 4th century AD, it was rebuilt after the invading Normans set fire to the neighborhood in 1084. Hidden within is the garden of the delightful inner cloister (admission on request), one of the earliest of its kind, built c. 1220.

The remains of medieval frescoes can be seen in the Chapel of Santa Barbara, but the convent's main feature is the Chapel of St. Sylvester – its remarkable frescoes (1246) recount the legend of the conversion to Christianity of the Emperor Constantine by Pope Sylvester I (reigned 314–35), then living as a hermit on Monte Soratte, north of Rome.

Stricken by the plague, Constantine is prescribed a bath in children's blood, to the horror of the matrons of Rome. Unable to bring himself to obey, Constantine is visited in a dream

Distinctive circular outline of Santo Stefano Rotondo

by St. Peter and St. Paul. They advise him to find Sylvester, who cures him and baptizes him. The final scene shows the emperor kneeling before the pope. The implied idea of the pope as heir to the Roman Empire would affect the whole course of medieval European history.

⑫ San Clemente

See pp188–9.

⑬ Santo Stefano Rotondo

Via di Santo Stefano Rotondo 7. **Map** 9 B2. **Tel** 06-42 11 99. 🚌 81, 117, 673. **Open** 9:30am–12:30pm, 3–6pm (2–5pm winter) Tue–Sun. 📷

One of Rome's earliest Christian churches, Santo Stefano Rotondo was constructed between 468 and 483. It has an unusual circular plan with four chapels

in the shape of a cross. The round inner area was surrounded by concentric corridors with 22 Ionic supporting columns. The high drum in the center is 72 ft (22 m) high and just as wide. It is lit by 22 high windows, a few of them restored or blocked by restorations carried out under Pope Nicholas V (reigned 1447–55), who consulted the Florentine architect Leon Battista Alberti. The archway in the center may have been added during this period.

In the 16th century the church walls were frescoed by Niccolò Pomarancio, with particularly gruesome illustrations of the martyrdom of innumerable saints. Some of the medieval decor remains: in the first chapel to the left of the entrance is a 7th-century mosaic of Christ with San Primo, and San Feliciano.

Fresco of St. Sylvester and Constantine in Santi Quattro Coronati

⑫ San Clemente

San Clemente provides an opportunity to travel back through three layers of history. At street level, there is a 12th-century church; underneath this lies a 4th-century church; and below that are ancient Roman buildings, including a Temple of Mithras. Mithraism, an all-male cult imported from Persia in the 1st century BC, was a rival to Christianity in Imperial Rome.

The upper levels are dedicated to St. Clement, the fourth pope, who was exiled to the Crimea, and martyred by being tied to an anchor, and drowned. His life is illustrated in some of the frescoes in the 4th-century church. The site was taken over in the 17th century by Irish Dominicans, who still continue the excavating work begun by Father Mullooly in 1857.

★ Cappella di Santa Caterina
The restored frescoes by the 15th-century Florentine artist Masolino da Panicale show scenes from the life of the martyred St. Catherine of Alexandria.

18th-century Facade
Twelfth-century columns were used in the arcade.

Piscina
This deep pit was discovered in 1967. It could have been used as a font or fountain.

★ 11th-century Frescoes
Commissioned by the de Rapiza family, one shows the story of a boy found alive in St. Clement's tomb beneath the Black Sea.

KEY

① **1st–3rd-century temple and buildings**

② **4th-century church**

③ **12th-century church**

④ **Entrance** to the church is through a door in Via di San Giovanni in Laterano.

⑤ **Temple of Mithras**

Catacomb
Discovered in 1938 and dating from the 5th or 6th century, it contains 16 wall tombs known as *loculi*.

★ Apse Mosaic
The 12th-century *Triumph of the Cross* includes beautifully detailed animals, and acanthus leaves.

VISITORS' CHECKLIST

Practical Information
Via di San Giovanni in Laterano.
Map 9 B1.
Tel 06-774 0021.
Open 9am–12:30pm, 3–6pm
Mon–Sat; noon–6pm Sun. Last
adm: 20 min before closing.
⚑ to excavations. 🚻 ✉ 📷
🔲 basilicasanclemente.com

Transportation
🚌 85, 87, 117, 186, 810, 850.
🚋 3. Ⓜ Colosseo.

Schola Cantorum
The 6th-century enclosure for the choir was retained for the new church, built in 1108.

Paschal Candlestick
This 12th-century spiral candlestick, striped with glittering mosaic, is a magnificent example of Cosmati work.

**★ Triclinium and
Altar of Mithras**
The altar, with a relief of Mithras slaying the bull, stands in the *triclinium*, a room used for ritual banquets.

2nd century Site possibly used for secret Christian worship

Late 2nd century Temple of Mithras built

867 Reputed transfer of remains of San Clemente to Rome

1108 New church built over 4th-century church

1857 Original 4th-century church rediscovered by Father Mullooly

| 10 | 500 | 1000 | 1500 | 2000 |

88-97 Papacy St. Clement

64 Nero's fire troys area

4th century First church built over courtyard of earlier Roman building

1084 Church destroyed during Norman invasion led by Robert Guiscard

1667 Church and convent given to Irish Dominicans

1861 Church is excavated. Roman ruins discovered

CARACALLA

The Celian Hill overlooks the Colosseum, and takes its name from Caelius Vibenna, the legendary hero of Rome's struggle against the Tarquins (see pp20–21). In Imperial Rome, this was a fashionable place to live, and some of its vanished splendor is still apparent in the vast ruins of the Baths of Caracalla. Today, thanks to the Archaeological Zone

established at the beginning of the 20th century, it is a peaceful area, a green wedge from the Aurelian Wall to the heart of the city. Through it runs the cobbled Via di Porta San Sebastiano, part of the old Via Appia. This road leads to Porta San Sebastiano, one of the best-preserved gates in the ancient city wall.

Sights at a Glance

Churches
1 Santi Giovanni e Paolo
2 San Gregorio Magno
4 Santa Maria in Domnica
6 San Sisto Vecchio
7 Santi Nereo e Achilleo
8 San Cesareo
9 San Giovanni a Porta Latina
10 San Giovanni in Oleo
16 Santa Balbina

Arches and Gates
3 Arch of Dolabella
13 Arch of Drusus
14 Aurelian Wall and Porta San Sebastiano
15 Sangallo Bastion

Historic Buildings
17 Baths of Caracalla

Tombs
11 Columbarium of Pomponius Hylas
12 Tomb of the Scipios

Parks and Gardens
5 Villa Celimontana

See also Street Finder maps 8, 9

0 meters 300
0 yards 300

◀ The Baths of Caracalla

For map symbols *see back flap*

Street-by-Street: The Celian Hill

In the course of a morning's exploration of the green slopes of the Celian hill, you will see a fascinating assortment of archaeological remains and beautiful churches. A good starting point is the church of San Gregorio Magno, from where the Clivo di Scauro leads up to the top of the hill. The steep, narrow street passes the ancient porticoed church of Santi Giovanni e Paolo with its beautiful Romanesque bell tower soaring above the surrounding medieval monastery buildings. Of the parks on the hill, the best kept and most peaceful is the Villa Celimontana with its formal walks and avenues. It is a good place for a picnic, since there are few bars or restaurants in the area.

Clivo di Scauro, the Roman *Clivus Scauri*, leads up to Santi Giovanni e Paolo, passing under the flying buttresses that support the church.

VIA DI SAN GREGORIO

CLIVO DI SCAURO

La Vignola is a delightful Renaissance pavilion, reconstructed here in 1911 after it was demolished during the creation of the Archaeological Zone around the Baths of Caracalla.

To Circo Massimo Metro

❷ **San Gregorio Magno**
A monastery and chapel were founded here by Pope Gregory the Great at the end of the 6th century.

❶ ★ **Santi Giovanni e Paolo**
The nave of the church, lit by a blaze of chandeliers, has been restored many times, assuming its present appearance in the 18th century.

❺ ★ **Villa Celimontana**
The beautiful 16th-century villa built for the Mattei family is now the center of a public park.

Streetcars passing over the Celian hill from the Colosseum rumble up a narrow, picturesque track through the Parco del Celio.

Locator Map
See Central Rome Map pp16–17

Ruins of the Temple of Claudius are visible over a large area of the Celian hill. These travertine blocks have been incorporated in the base of the bell tower of Santi Giovanni e Paolo.

3 Arch of Dolabella
Built in the 1st century AD, probably as an entrance to the city, this archway was later incorporated in Nero's aqueduct to the Palatine.

The gateway of San Tommaso in Formis is decorated with a wonderful 13th-century mosaic showing Christ with two freed slaves, one white, one black.

4 ★ Santa Maria in Domnica
This church is famed for its 9th-century mosaics. These Apostles appear on the triumphal arch above the apse, flanking a medallion containing the figure of Christ.

Key

— Suggested route

0 meters	75
0 yards	75

❶ Santi Giovanni e Paolo

Piazza Santi Giovanni e Paolo 13. **Map**
9 A1. **Tel** 06-772 711. 🚌 75, 81, 117,
175, 673. 🚋 3. Ⓜ Colosseo or Circo
Massimo. Church: **Open** 8:30am–
noon, 3:30–6pm daily. Roman houses:
Tel 06-7045 4544. **Open** 10am–1pm,
3–6pm Thu–Mon. 🚻 ♿ church only.
🆆 caseromane.it

Santi Giovanni e Paolo is
dedicated to two martyred
Roman officers whose house
originally stood on this site.
Giovanni (John) and Paolo (Paul)
had served the first Christian
emperor, Constantine. When
they were later called to arms
by the pagan emperor Julian
the Apostate, they refused and
were beheaded and buried in
secret in their own house
in AD 362.

Built toward the end of the
4th century, the church retains
many elements of its original
structure. The Ionic portico
dates from the 12th century,
and the apse and bell tower
were added by Nicholas
Breakspeare, the only English
pope, who reigned as Adrian IV
(1154–9). The base of the
superb 13th-century
Romanesque bell tower was
part of the Temple of Claudius
that stood on this site. The
interior, which was remodeled
in 1718, has granite piers and
columns. A tomb slab in the
nave marks the burial place of
the martyrs, whose relics are
preserved in an urn under
the high altar. In a tiny room

near the altar, a magnificent
13th-century fresco depicts the
figure of Christ flanked by his
Apostles (ask the sacristan, who
will be able to unlock the door).

Excavations beneath the
church have revealed two 2nd-
and 3rd-century Roman houses
used as a Christian burial place.
These are well worth a visit. The
two-story construction, with
20 rooms and a labyrinth of
corridors, has well-preserved
pagan and Christian paintings.
The arches to the left of the
church were part of a
3rd-century street of shops.

Facade of San Gregorio Magno

❷ San Gregorio Magno

Piazza di San Gregorio. **Map** 8 F2. **Tel**
06-700 8227. 🚌 75, 81, 117, 175, 673.
🚋 3. Ⓜ Circo Massimo. **Open**
9am–12:30pm daily. 🚻

To the English, this is one of the
most important churches in
Rome, for it was from here that
St. Augustine was sent on his
mission to convert England to

**Marble throne of Gregory the Great from
the 1st century BC**

Christianity. The church was
founded in AD 575 by San
Gregorio Magno (St. Gregory
the Great), who turned his
family home on this site into a
monastery. It was rebuilt in
medieval times and restored in
1629–33 by Giovanni Battista
Soria. The church is reached via
a flight of steps from the street.

The forecourt contains some
interesting tombs. To the left is
that of Sir Edward Carne, who
came to Rome several times
between 1529 and 1533 as
King Henry VIII's envoy to gain
the pope's consent to the
annulment of Henry's marriage
to Catherine of Aragon.

The interior, remodeled by
Francesco Ferrari in the mid-
18th century, is Baroque, apart
from the fine mosaic floor and
some ancient columns. At the
end of the right aisle is the
chapel of St. Gregory. Leading
off it, another small chapel,
believed to have been the
saint's own cell, houses his
episcopal throne – a Roman
chair of sculpted marble. The
Salviati Chapel on the left
contains a picture of the
Virgin said to have spoken
to St. Gregory.

Outside, amid the cypresses
to the left of the church, stand
three small chapels, dedicated
to St. Andrew, St. Barbara and
St. Sylvia (Gregory the Great's
mother). The chapels contain
frescoes by Domenichino and
Guido Reni.

Fresco of Christ and the Apostles in Santi Giovanni e Paolo

❸ Arch of Dolabella

Via di San Paolo della Croce. **Map** 9 A2. 🚌 81, 117, 673. 🚋 3. Ⓜ Colosseo.

The arch was built in AD 10 by consuls Caius Junius Silanus and Cornelius Dolabella, possibly on the site of one of the old Servian Wall's gateways. It was made of travertine blocks and later used to support Nero's extension of the Claudian aqueduct, built to supply the Imperial Palace on the Palatine Hill.

The restored Arch of Dolabella

❹ Santa Maria in Domnica

Piazza della Navicella 12. **Map** 9 A2. **Tel** 06-7720 2685. 🚌 81,117, 673. 🚋 3. Ⓜ Colosseo. **Open** 9am–noon, 3:30–7pm (to 6pm in winter) daily. 🚻 ♿

The church overlooks the Piazza della Navicella (little boat) and takes its name from the 16th-century fountain. Dating from the 7th century, the church was probably built on

the site of an ancient Roman firemen's barracks, which later became a meeting place for Christians. In the 16th century Pope Leo X added the portico and the coffered ceiling.

In the apse behind the modern altar is a superb 9th-century mosaic commissioned by Pope Paschal I. Wearing the square halo of the living, the pope appears at the feet of the Virgin and Child. The Virgin, surrounded by a throng of angels, holds a handkerchief like a fashionable lady at a Byzantine court.

❺ Villa Celimontana

Piazza della Navicella. **Map** 9 A2. 🚌 81, 117, 673. Park: **Open** 7am–dusk daily.

The Dukes of Mattei bought this land in 1553 and transformed the vineyards that covered the hillside into a formal garden. As well as palms and other exotic trees, the garden has its own Egyptian obelisk. Villa Mattei, built in the 1580s and now known as Villa Celimontana, houses the Italian Geographical Society.

The Mattei family used to open the park to the public on the day of the Visit of the Seven Churches, an annual event instituted by San Filippo Neri in 1552. Starting from the Chiesa Nuova (see p126), Romans went on foot to the city's seven major churches and, on reaching Villa Mattei, were given bread, wine,

salami, cheese, an egg, and two apples. The garden, now owned by the city of Rome, still makes an ideal place for a picnic. In summer it hosts an excellent jazz festival (see p350).

Park of Villa Celimontana

❻ San Sisto Vecchio

Piazzale Numa Pompilio 8. **Map** 9 A3. **Tel** 06-7720 5174. 🚌 160, 628, 671, 714. **Open** 9–11am, 3–5:30pm daily. 🚫

This small church is of great historical interest as it was granted to St. Dominic in 1219 by Pope Honorius III. The founder of the Dominican order soon moved his own headquarters to Santa Sabina (see p206), San Sisto becoming the first home of the order of Dominican nuns. The church, with its 13th-century bell tower and frescoes, is also a popular place for weddings.

Apse mosaic of the Virgin and Child in Santa Maria in Domnica

Fresco by Niccolò Pomarancio of the *Martyrdom of St. Simon* in Santi Nereo e Achilleo

❼ Santi Nereo e Achilleo

Via D. Terme di Caracalla 28. **Map** 9 A3. **Fax** 06 687 3124. 🚌 160, 628, 671, 714. **Open** 10am–noon, 4–6pm Thu–Mon (timings may vary). ♿

According to legend, St. Peter, after escaping from prison, was fleeing the city when he lost a bandage from his wounds. The original church was founded here in the 4th century on the spot where the bandage fell, but it was later rededicated to the 1st-century AD martyrs St. Nereus and St. Achilleus.

Restored at the end of the 16th century, the church has retained many medieval features, including some fine 9th-century mosaics on the triumphal arch. A magnificent pulpit rests on an enormous porphyry pedestal that was found nearby in the Baths of Caracalla. The walls of the side aisles are decorated with grisly 16th-century frescoes by Niccolò Pomarancio, showing in clinical detail how each of the Apostles was martyred.

❽ San Cesareo

Via di Porta San Sebastiano. **Map** 9 A3. **Tel** 06-5823 0140. 🚌 218, 628. **Open** 10am–noon Sun & by appt.

This splendid old church was built over Roman ruins of the 2nd century AD. You can still admire Giacomo della Porta's fine Renaissance facade, but by calling ahead to schedule a visit, you can also see Cosmatesque mosaic work, and carving to rival that of any church in Rome. The episcopal throne, altar, and pulpit are decorated with delightful birds and beasts. The church was restored in the 16th century by Pope Clement VIII, whose coat of arms decorates the ceiling.

❾ San Giovanni a Porta Latina

Via di San Giovanni a Porta Latina. **Map** 9 B3. **Tel** 06-7740 0032. 🚌 218, 360, 628. **Open** 7:30am–7pm daily. 🚻 ♿

Detail of mosaic, Santi Nereo e Achilleo

The church of "St. John at the Latin Gate" was founded in the 5th century, rebuilt in 720, and restored in 1191. This is one of the most picturesque of the old Roman churches. Classical columns support the medieval portico, and the 12th-century bell tower is superb. A tall cedar tree shades an ancient well standing in the forecourt. The interior has been restored, but it preserves the rare simplicity of its early origins with ancient columns of varying styles lining the aisles. Traces of early medieval frescoes can still be seen within the church. There are 12th-century frescoes showing 46 different biblical scenes, from both the Old and New testaments, which are among the finest of their kind in Rome.

❿ San Giovanni in Oleo

Via di Porta Latina. **Map** 9 C4. 🚌 628. 🔑 ask at S. Giovanni a Porta Latina.

The name of this charming octagonal Renaissance chapel means "St. John in Oil." The tiny building marks the spot where, according to legend, St. John was boiled in oil – and came out unscathed, or even refreshed. An earlier chapel is said to have existed on the site; the present one was built in the early 16th century. The design has been attributed to Baldassare Peruzzi or Antonio da Sangallo the Younger. It was restored by Borromini, who altered the roof, crowning it with a cross supported by a sphere decorated with roses. He also added a terra-cotta frieze of roses, and palm leaves. The wall paintings inside the chapel include one of St. John in a cauldron of boiling oil.

Fresco, San Giovanni a Porta Latina

Niches for funerary urns in the Columbarium of Pomponius Hylas

⑪ Columbarium of Pomponius Hylas

Via di Porta Latina 10. **Map** 9 B4. **Tel** 06-0608. 🚌 218, 360, 628. **Open** Guided tours only; phone ahead.

Known as a columbarium because it resembles a dovecote (*columba* is the Latin word for dove), this kind of vaulted tomb was usually built by rich Romans to house the cremated remains of their freedmen. Many similar tombs have been uncovered in this part of Rome, which up until the 3rd century AD lay outside the city wall. This one, excavated in 1831, dates from the 1st century AD. An inscription informs us that it is the tomb of Pomponius Hylas and his wife,

Mosaic inscription in the Columbarium of Pomponius Hylas

Pomponia Vitalinis. Above her name is a "V" that indicates that she was still living when the inscription was made. The tomb was probably a commercial venture. Niches in the interior walls of the columbarium were sold to people who could not afford to build vaults of their own.

⑫ Tomb of the Scipios

Via di Porta San Sebastiano 9. **Map** 9 B4. **Tel** 06-0608. 🚌 218, 360, 628. **Open** Guided tours only; call ahead.

The Scipios were a family of conquering generals. Southern Italy, Corsica, Algeria, Spain, and Asia Minor all fell to their victorious Roman armies. The most famous of these generals was Publius Cornelius Scipio Africanus, who defeated the great Carthaginian general Hannibal at the Battle of Zama in 202 BC (*see p25*). Scipio Africanus himself was not buried here in the family tomb, but at Liternum near Naples, where he owned a favorite villa.

The Tomb of the Scipios was discovered in 1780. It contained various sarcophagi, statues, and niches with terra-cotta burial urns. Many of the originals have now been moved to the Vatican Museums and copies stand in their place.

The earliest sarcophagus was that of Cornelius Scipio Barbatus, consul in 298 BC, for whom the tomb was built. Members of his illustrious family continued to be buried here up to the middle of the 2nd century BC. Excavations in the area have revealed a columbarium similar to that of Pomponius Hylas, a Christian catacomb, and a three-story house dating from the 3rd century AD, which was built over the Tomb of the Scipios.

⑬ Arch of Drusus

Via di Porta San Sebastiano. **Map** 9 B4. 🚌 218, 360.

Once mistakenly identified as a triumphal arch, the so-called Arch of Drusus merely supported the branch aqueduct that supplied the Baths of Caracalla. It was built in the 3rd century AD, so it had no connection with Drusus, a stepson of the Emperor Augustus. Its monumental appearance was due to the fact that it carried the aqueduct across an important route, Via Appia. The arch still spans the old cobbled road, just 160 ft (50 m) short of the gateway Porta San Sebastiano.

Arch of Drusus, part of the Aqua Antoniniana aqueduct

⓮ Aurelian Wall and Porta San Sebastiano

Museo delle Mura, Via di Porta San Sebastiano 18. **Map** 9 B4. 218, 360. **Tel** 06-7047 5284. **Open** 9am–2pm Tue–Sun. Last adm: 30 min before closing. **Closed** Jan 1, May 1, Dec 25. **museodellemuraroma.it**

Most of the Aurelian Wall, begun by the emperor Aurelian (AD 270–75) and completed by his successor Probus (AD 276–82), has survived. Aurelian ordered its construction as a defense against Germanic tribes, whose raids were penetrating deeper and deeper into Italy. Some 11 miles (18 km) around, with 18 gates and 381 towers, the wall took in all the seven hills of Rome. It was raised to almost twice its original height by Maxentius (AD 306–12).

The wall was Rome's main defense until 1870, when it was breached by Italian artillery near Porta Pia, close to today's British Embassy. Many of the gates are still in use, and although the city has spread, most of its noteworthy historical and cultural sights still lie within the walls.

Porta San Sebastiano, the gate leading to the Via Appia Antica (see p286), is the largest and best-preserved gateway in the Aurelian Wall. It was rebuilt by Emperor Honorius in the 5th century AD. Originally the Porta Appia, in Christian times it gradually became known as the Porta San Sebastiano, because the Via Appia led to the

Basilica and Catacombs of San Sebastiano, which were popular places of pilgrimage.

It was at this gate that the last triumphal procession to enter the city by the Appian Way was received in state – that of Marcantonio Colonna after the victory of Lepanto over the Turkish fleet in 1571. Today the gate's towers house a museum with prints, and models showing the walls' history. From here you can take a short walk along the restored walls. The views are spectacular.

Pope Paul III Farnese

⓯ Sangallo Bastion

Viale di Porta Ardeatina. **Map** 9 A4. 160. **Closed** for restoration.

Haunted by the memory of the Sack of Rome in 1527 and fearing attack by the Turks, Pope Paul III asked Antonio da Sangallo the Younger to reinforce the Aurelian Wall. Work on the huge projecting bastion began in 1537. For the moment its massive bulk can only be admired from outside.

The high altar of Santa Balbina

⓰ Santa Balbina

Piazza di Santa Balbina 8. **Map** 8 F3. **Tel** 06-578 0207. 160. 3. Circo Massimo. **Open** 12:30–1pm Mon–Fri, 10:30–11:30am Sun.

Overlooking the Baths of Caracalla, this isolated church is dedicated to Santa Balbina, a 2nd-century virgin martyr. It is one of the oldest in Rome, dating back to the fifth century, and was built on the remains of a Roman villa. Consecrated by Pope Gregory the Great, in the Middle Ages Santa Balbina was a fortified monastery, and over time it has changed in appearance several times, regaining its Romanesque aspect in the 1920s.

From the piazza in front of the church, a staircase leads up to a three-arched portico. Inside, light streams in from a series of high windows along the length of the nave. The remains of St. Balbina and her father, St. Quirinus, are in an urn at the high altar, though the church's real treasure is situated in the far right-hand corner: the magnificent sculpted and inlaid tomb of Cardinal Stefanis de Surdis by Giovanni di Cosma (1303).

Other features worth noting are a 13th-century episcopal throne and various fragments of frescoes. These include a lovely *Madonna and Child*, an example of the school of Pietro Cavallini, in the second chapel on the left. Fragments of first-century Roman mosaics were discovered in the 1930s. Depicting birds and signs of the zodiac, these are now set in the church floor.

Fortified gateway of Porta San Sebastiano

⓱ Baths of Caracalla

Viale delle Terme di Caracalla 52. **Map** 9 A3. **Tel** 06-3996 7700. 🚌 160, 628. 🚋 3. Ⓜ Circo Massimo. **Open** 9am–2pm Mon, 9am–approx 1hr before sunset Tue–Sun. **Closed** Jan 1, Dec 25. 🏛 🔲 📷 ♿

Completed by Emperor Caracalla in AD 217, the baths functioned for about 300 years, until the plumbing was destroyed by invading Goths. Over 1,600 bathers at a time could enjoy the facilities. A Roman bath was a serious business, beginning with a sort of Turkish bath, followed by a spell in the *caldarium*, a large hot room with pools of water to provide humidity. Then came the lukewarm *tepidarium*, a visit to the large central meeting place known as the *frigidarium*, and finally a plunge into

Fragment of mosaic pavement

the *natatio*, an open-air swimming pool. For the rich, this was followed by a rub-down with scented woolen cloth. As well as the baths, there were spaces for exercise, libraries, art galleries, and gardens – a true leisure center. Most of the rich marble decorations were removed by the Farnese family in the 16th

century to adorn the interior of Palazzo Farnese *(see p149)*. Open-air operas, mostly Verdi or Puccini, are performed in these settings in the summer months and are very well attended.

Key

- ▢ Caldarium (very hot)
- ▢ Tepidarium (lukewarm)
- ▢ Frigidarium (cold)
- ▢ Natatio (pool)
- ▢ Garden

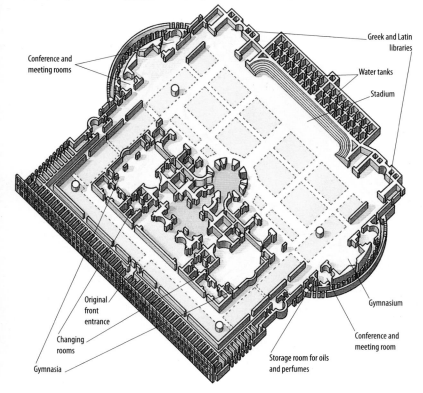

Part of one of the gymnasia in the Baths of Caracalla

Conference and meeting rooms

Greek and Latin libraries

Water tanks

Stadium

Original front entrance

Changing rooms

Gymnasia

Storage room for oils and perfumes

Gymnasium

Conference and meeting room

AVENTINE

This is one of the most peaceful areas within the walls of the city. Although it is largely residential, there are some unique historic sights. From the top of the Aventine Hill, crowned by the magnificent basilica of Santa Sabina, there are fine views across the river to Trastevere and St. Peter's. At the foot of the hill, ancient Rome is preserved in the two tiny Temples of the Forum Boarium and the Circus Maximus. The liveliest streets are in Testaccio, which has shops, restaurants, and clubs, while to the south, beside Rome's solitary pyramid, the Protestant Cemetery is another oasis of calm.

Sights at a Glance

Churches and Temples
1 Santa Maria in Cosmedin
3 San Giorgio in Velabro
4 San Teodoro
5 Santa Maria della Consolazione
6 San Giovanni Decollato
8 Temples of the Forum Boarium
9 Santa Sabina
10 Santi Bonifacio e Alessio
15 San Saba

Historic Buildings
7 Casa dei Crescenzi

Arches
2 Arch of Janus

Historic Streets and Piazzas
11 Piazza dei Cavalieri di Malta

Ancient Sites
12 Ponte Testaccio
16 Circus Maximus

Monuments and Tombs
13 Protestant Cemetery
14 Pyramid of Caius Cestius

Restaurants
see pp310–11

1 0, 75
2 Angelina a Testaccio
3 Checchino dal 1887
4 Da Oio a Casa Mia
5 Da Remo
6 Felice a Testaccio
7 Flavio al Velavevodetto
8 Oaso della Birra
9 Perilli

0 meters 300
0 yards 300

See also Street Finder
maps 7, 8, 12

◀ Mask fountain in the courtyard of Santa Sabina

For map symbols see back flap

Street-by-Street: Piazza della Bocca della Verità

The area attracts visitors eager to place their hands inside the Bocca della Verità (the Mouth of Truth) in the portico of Santa Maria in Cosmedin. There are many other sights to see in this quiet corner of the city beside the Tiber, which was the site of ancient Rome's first port and its busy cattle market. Substantial Classical remains include two small temples from the Republican age and the Arch of Janus from the later Empire. In the 6th century, the area became home to a Greek community from Byzantium, who founded the churches of San Giorgio in Velabro and Santa Maria in Cosmedin.

7 Casa dei Crescenzi
This 11th-century building used columns and capitals from ancient Roman temples.

Sant'Omobono, a late 16th-century church, now stands in isolation in the middle of an important archaeological site. The remains of sacrificial altars and two temples from the 6th century BC have been discovered.

Key

— Suggested route

0 meters — 75
0 yards — 75

Ponte Rotto, as this forlorn ruined arch in the Tiber is called, means simply "broken bridge." Built in the 2nd century BC, its original name was Pons Aemilius.

Tevere

LUNGOTEVERE DEI PIERLEONI

PONTE PALATINO

8 ★ Temples of the Forum Boarium
The tiny round Temple of Hercules and its neighbor, the Temple of Portunus, are the best preserved of Rome's Republican temples.

The Fontana dei Tritoni by Carlo Bizzaccheri was built here in 1715. The style shows the powerful influence of Bernini.

5 Santa Maria della Consolazione
This 16th-century church used to serve a hospital nearby.

4 San Teodoro
The 15th-century portal of this ancient round church is decorated with the insignia of Pope Nicholas V.

Locator Map
See Street Finder maps 7, 8 & 12

6 San Giovanni Decollato
The plain Renaissance facade was completed in about 1504.

VIA DEI FIENILI

VIA DI SAN TEODORO

DECOLLATO

3 San Giorgio in Velabro
The simple 12th-century portico of Ionic columns was destroyed by a bomb in 1993 but has been restored.

The Arco degli Argentari, dedicated to the Emperor Septimius Severus in AD 204, is decorated with scenes of religion and war.

2 Arch of Janus
This square structure with arches on each side dates from the 4th century AD.

PIAZZA DELLA BOCCA DELLA VERITA

VIA DEI CERCHI

1 ★ Santa Maria in Cosmedin
This medieval church has a fine marble mosaic floor and a Gothic baldacchino.

DELLA GRECA

❶ Santa Maria in Cosmedin

Piazza della Bocca della Verità 18.
Map 8 E1. **Tel** 06-678 7759. 🚍 23, 44, 81, 160, 170, 280, 628, 715, 716.
Open summer: 9:30am–6pm daily (to 5pm winter). 🚻 🚻 📷

This beautiful unadorned church was built in the 6th century on the site of the ancient city's food market. The elegant Romanesque bell tower and portico were added during the 12th century. In the 19th century, a Baroque facade was removed, and the church restored to its original simplicity. It contains many fine examples of Cosmati work, in particular the mosaic pavement, the raised choir, the bishop's throne, and the canopy over the main altar.

Set into the wall of the portico is the Bocca della Verità (Mouth of Truth). This may have been a drain cover, dating back to before the 4th century BC. Medieval tradition had it that the formidable jaws would snap shut over the hand of those who told lies – a useful trick for testing the faithfulness of spouses.

Bocca della Verità at Santa Maria in Cosmedin

❷ Arch of Janus

Via del Velabro. **Map** 8 E1. 🚍 23, 44, 63, 81, 160, 170, 280, 628, 715, 716, 780.

Probably dating from the reign of Constantine, this imposing four-faced marble arch stood at the crossroads on the edge of the Forum Boarium, near the ancient docks. Merchants did business in its shade. On the keystones above the four arches you can see small figures of the goddesses Roma, Juno, Ceres, and Minerva. In medieval times the arch formed the base of a tower fortress. It was restored to its original shape in 1827.

San Giorgio in Velabro after its restoration in 1999

❸ San Giorgio in Velabro

Via del Velabro 19. **Map** 8 E1.
Tel 06-6979 7536. 🚍 23, 44, 63, 81, 95, 160, 170, 280, 628, 715, 716, 780.
Open 9am–7pm daily.

In the hollow of the street named after the Velabrum, the swamp where Romulus, and Remus are said to have been found by the she-wolf, is a small church dedicated to St. George, whose bones lie under the altar.

The 7th-century basilica has suffered over time from periodic floods, and in 1993 a bomb damaged the front of the church. Careful restoration has, however, returned it to its original appearance.

A double row of granite, and marble columns (taken from ancient Roman temples) divides the triple nave. The austerity of the gray interior is relieved by golden frescoes in the apse (attributed to Pietro Cavallini, 1295). The bell tower dates from the 12th century.

❹ San Teodoro

Via di San Teodoro 7. **Map** 8 E1.
Tel 06-678 6624. 🚍 23, 44, 81, 95, 160, 170, 280, 628, 715, 716.
Open 9:30am–12:30pm Sun–Fri.

If you are in the area on a Sunday morning, you will find this small round 6th-century church at the foot of the Palatine a delight to visit for the Greek Orthodox services. Inside, the 6th-century mosaics in the apse are breathtaking, as is the Florentine cupola dating from 1454. The fetching outer courtyard was designed by Carlo Fontana in 1705.

❺ Santa Maria della Consolazione

Piazza della Consolazione 84.
Map 5 A5. **Tel** 06-678 4654. 🚍 23, 44, 63, 81, 160, 170, 280, 628, 715, 716, 780. **Open** 7am–7pm Mon–Sat; 8am–6pm Sun. 🚻 🚻

The church stands near then foot of the Tarpeian Rock, the site of public execution of traitors since the time of the Sabine War (see p76).

The Arch of Janus, where cattle dealers sheltered from the midday sun

Facade of Santa Maria della Consolazione

In 1385, Giordanello degli Alberini, a condemned nobleman, paid two gold florins for an image of the Virgin Mary to be placed here, to provide consolation to prisoners in their final moments before execution – hence the name of the church that was built here in 1470. It was reconstructed between 1583 and 1600 by Martino Longhi, who provided the early Baroque facade at the same time.

The church's 11 side-chapels are owned by noble families and local crafts guild members. Taddeo Zuccari is responsible for the 1556 frescoes depicting scenes from the Passion (first chapel on the right), while the Mannerist artist Niccolò Circignani painted the scenes from the life of Mary and Jesus in the fifth chapel. In the presbytery is the image of Mary, attributed to Antoniazzo Romano.

❻ San Giovanni Decollato

Via di San Giovanni Decollato 22. **Map** 8 E1. **Tel** 06-679 1890. 🚌 23, 44, 63, 81, 160, 170, 280, 628, 715, 716, 780. **Open** near the feast of St. John (Jun 24).

The main altar is dominated by Giorgio Vasari's *The Beheading of St. John* (1553) from which the church takes its name, San Giovanni Decollato. In 1490 Pope Innocent VIII gave this site to build a church for a very specialized Florentine confraternity. Clad in black

robes and hoods, their task was to encourage condemned prisoners to repent, and to give them a decent burial after they had been hanged. In the cloisters there are seven manholes (one for women), which received the bodies.

The oratory holds a cycle of frescoes depicting events in the life of St. John the Baptist by leading Florentine Mannerists Jacopino del Conte and Francesco Salviati. In style, the figures resemble some of those in the Sistine Chapel. The confraternity exists to this day, with church funds assisting prisoners' families.

❼ Casa dei Crescenzi

Via Luigi Petroselli. **Map** 8 E1. 🚌 23, 44, 63, 81, 160, 170, 280, 628, 715, 716, 780.

Studded with archaeological fragments, the house is what remains of an 11th-century tower fortress. The powerful Crescenzi family built it to keep an eye on the docks (now the site of the Anagrafe or Public Records Office) and on the bridge where they collected a toll.

❽ Temples of the Forum Boarium

Piazza della Bocca della Verità. **Map** 8 E1. 🚌 23, 44, 81, 160, 170, 280, 628, 715, 716.

These miraculously well-preserved Republican temples are particularly appealing by moonlight, in their grassy enclave under the umbrella pines beside the Tiber. They date from the 2nd century BC and were saved for posterity when they were reconsecrated as Christian churches in the Middle Ages. They offer rare examples of combined elements from Greek, and Roman architecture.

The rectangular temple (formerly known as the Temple of Fortuna Virilis) was in fact dedicated to Portunus, the god of rivers and ports – a reference to the nearby port of ancient Rome. Set on a podium, it has four Ionic travertine columns fluted at the front and 12 half-columns, embedded in the tufa wall of the *cella* – the room that housed the image of the god. Nearby is the small circular Temple of Hercules, with its slender Corinthian columns surrounding the central *cella*. Built around 120 BC, the temple is thought to be the earliest marble edifice in ancient Rome that has survived to the present day. It is often referred to as the Temple of Vesta because of its similarity to the one in the Forum.

Ancient Roman fragments in the Casa dei Crescenzi

Luminous interior of Santa Sabina

❾ Santa Sabina

Piazza Pietro d'Illiria 1. **Map** 8 E2.
Tel 06-5794 0600. 🚌 23, 280, 716.
Ⓜ Circo Massimo. **Open** 6:30am–
12:45pm, 3–7pm daily (to 6pm
winter). ♿

High on the Aventine stands an
early Christian basilica, founded
by Peter of Illyria in AD 425, and
restored to its original simplicity
in the early 20th century. Light
filters through 9th-century
windows upon a wide nave
framed by white Corinthian
columns supporting an arcade
decorated with a marble frieze.
Over the main door is a 5th-
century blue and gold mosaic
dedicatory inscription. The
pulpit, carved choir, and bishop's
throne date from the 9th century.
The church was given to the
Dominicans in the 13th century
and in the nave is the
magnificent mosaic tombstone
of one of the first leaders of the
order, Muñoz de Zamora
(died 1300).
The side portico has
5th-century paneled doors
carved from cypress wood,
representing scenes from the
Bible, including one of the
earliest Crucifixions in existence.

❿ Santi Bonifacio e Alessio

Piazza di Sant'Alessio 23. **Map** 8 D2.
Tel 06-574 3446. 🚌 23, 280, 716.
Ⓜ Circo Massimo. **Open** 8:30am–
12:15pm, 3–6:30pm daily. ♿

The church is dedicated to two
early Christian martyrs, whose
remains lie under the main altar.

Legend has it that Alessio, son
of a rich senator living on the
site, fled to the East to avoid
an impending marriage, and
became a pilgrim. Returning
home after many years, he died
as a servant, unrecognized, under
the stairs of the family entrance
hall, clutching the manuscript of
his story for posterity.
The original 5th-century
church has undergone many
changes over time. Noteworthy
are the 18th-century facade
with its five arches, the restored
Cosmati doorway, and pavement, and the magnificent
Romanesque five-story bell
tower (1217).
An 18th-century Baroque
chapel by Andrea Bergondi
houses part of the famous
staircase. Other relics include
the well from Alessio's family
home and the glowing
Byzantine Madonna of the
Intercession brought from
Damascus to Rome at the end
of the 10th century.

⓫ Piazza dei Cavalieri di Malta

Map 8 D2. 🚌 23, 280, 716.
Ⓜ Circo Massimo.

Surrounded by cypress trees,
this ornate walled piazza
decorated with obelisks, and
military trophies was designed
by Piranesi in 1765. It
is named after the
Order of the Knights
of Malta (Cavalieri di
Malta), whose priory
(at No. 3) is famous
for the bronze
keyhole through
which there is a
miniature view of St.
Peter's, framed by a
tree-lined avenue.
The priory church,
Santa Maria del
Priorato, was restored
in Neo-Classical style
by Piranesi in the
18th century. To visit
the church, ask
permission in person
at the Order's
building at 48 Via
Condotti. At the

southwest corner of the square
is Sant'Anselmo, the international
Benedictine church, where
Gregorian chant may be heard
on Sundays (see p348).

Doorway of the Priory of the
Knights of Malta

⓬ Monte Testaccio

Via Galvani. **Map** 8 D4. Ⓜ Piramide.
🚌 23, 63, 719. 🚋 3. **Open** by appt
only; call 06-0608.

From about 140 BC to AD 250
this hill was created by
dumping millions of *testae*
(hence Testaccio) – pieces of the
amphorae used to carry goods
to nearby warehouses. The full
archaeological significance of
this 118-ft- (36-m-) high artificial
hill was not realized until the
late 18th century.

Facade of Santi Bonifacio e Alessio

⑬ Protestant Cemetery

Cimitero Acattolico, Via Caio Cestio 6. **Map** 8 D4. **Tel** 06-574 1900. ▦ 23, 280, 716. ▦ 3. Ⓜ Piramide. **Open** 9am–5pm Mon–Sat; 9am–1pm Sun (last adm: 30 min before closing). Donation expected. ▦

The peace of this well-tended cemetery beneath the Aurelian Wall is profoundly moving. Non-Catholics, mainly English, and German, have been buried here since 1738. In the oldest part are the graves of John Keats (died 1821), whose epitaph reads: "Here lies One Whose Name was writ in Water," and his friend Joseph Severn (died 1879); not far away are the ashes

Tombstone of John Keats

of Percy Bysshe Shelley (died 1822). Goethe's son Julius is also buried here.

Memorial pyramid of Caius Cestius

⑭ Pyramid of Caius Cestius

Piazzale Ostiense. **Map** 8 E4. ▦ 23, 280, 716. ▦ 3. Ⓜ Piramide.

Caius Cestius, a wealthy *praetor* (senior Roman magistrate), died in 12 BC. His one claim to fame is his tomb, an imposing pyramid faced in white marble set in the Aurelian Wall near Porta San Paolo. It stands 118 ft (36 m) high and, according to an inscription, took 330 days to build. Unmistakable as a landmark, it must have looked almost as incongruous when it was built as it does today.

Detail of carving on sarcophagus in the portico of San Saba

⑮ San Saba

Via di San Saba. **Map** 8 F3. **Tel** 06-6458 0140. ▦ 75, 175, 673. ▦ 3. **Open** 8am–noon, 4–7pm Mon–Sat; 9:30am–1pm, 4–7:30pm Sun. ✝

Tucked away in a residential street on the Little Aventine hill, San Saba began life as an oratory for Palestinian monks fleeing from Arab invasions in the 7th century. The existing church dates from the 10th century, and has undergone much restoration. The portico houses a fascinating collection of archaeological remains.

The church has three naves in the Greek style and a short fourth 11th-century nave to the left with vestiges of 13th-century frescoes of the life of St. Nicholas of Bari. Particularly intriguing is a scene of three naked young ladies lying in bed, who are saved from penury by the gift

of a bag of gold from St. Nicholas, the future Santa Claus. The beautiful marble inlay in the main door, the floor, and the remains of the choir are all 13th-century Cosmati work.

⑯ Circus Maximus

Via del Circo Massimo. **Map** 8 F2. ▦ 81, 160, 628, 715. ▦ 3. Ⓜ Circo Massimo.

What was once ancient Rome's largest stadium is today little more than a long grassy esplanade. Set in the valley between the Palatine, and Aventine hills, the Circus Maximus was continually embellished and expanded from the 4th century BC until AD 549, when the last races were held. The grandstands held some 300,000 spectators, cheering wildly at the horse, and chariot races, athletic contests, and wild animal fights, betting furiously throughout.

The Circus had a central dividing barrier *(spina)* with seven large egg-shaped objects on it used for counting the laps of a race. These were joined in 33 BC by seven bronze dolphins that served a similar purpose. In 10 BC, Augustus built the Imperial box under the Palatine and decorated the *spina* with the obelisk that now stands in the center of Piazza del Popolo *(see p139)*. A second obelisk, which was added in the 4th century by Constantine II, is now in Piazza di San Giovanni in Laterano *(see pp180–81)*.

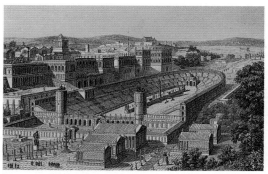

Reconstruction of the Circus Maximus in its heyday

TRASTEVERE

The proud and aggressively independent inhabitants of Trastevere, the area "across the Tiber," consider themselves the most authentic of Romans. In one of the most picturesque old quarters of the city, it is still possible to glimpse scenes of everyday life that seem to belong to bygone centuries. There are, however, signs that much of the earthy, proletarian character of the place may soon be destroyed by the proliferation of fashionable clubs, restaurants, and

boutiques. Some of Rome's most fascinating medieval churches lie hidden away in the patchwork of narrow, cobbled backstreets, the only clue to their location an occasional glimpse of a Romanesque bell tower. Of these, Santa Cecilia was built on the site of the martyrdom of the patron saint of music; San Francesco a Ripa commemorates St. Francis of Assisi's visit to Rome; and Santa Maria in Trastevere is the traditional center of the spiritual and social life of the area.

Sights at a Glance

Churches
3 Santa Maria della Scala
5 *Santa Maria in Trastevere pp214–15*
6 San Crisogono
8 Santa Cecilia in Trastevere
10 San Francesco a Ripa

Museums and Galleries
4 Sant'Egidio and Museo di Roma in Trastevere

Historic Buildings
1 Casa della Fornarina
7 Caserma dei Vigili della VII Coorte
9 San Michele a Ripa Grande

Bridges
2 Ponte Sisto

Parks and Gardens
11 Villa Sciarra

See also Street Finder maps 4, 7, 8, 11

Restaurants
see pp317–19
1 Akropolis
2 Bir & Fud
3 Da Gildo
4 Da Lucia
5 Dar Poeta
6 Da Teo
7 Glass
8 Il Capriccio
9 In Vino Veritas
10 Ivo a Trastevere
11 La Gensola
12 Meridionale
13 Pizzeria ai Panattoni
14 Rajdhani
15 Roma Sparita
16 Spirito Divino
17 Taverna Trilussa

 Cobbled street in Trastevere district

For map symbols see back flap

Street by Street: Trastevere

Trastevere is a major attraction both for its restaurants, clubs, and movie theaters, and for its picturesque maze of narrow cobbled alleyways. On summer evenings the streets are packed with jostling groups of pleasure-seekers, especially during the noisy local festival, the Festa de' Noantri *(see p61)*. Everywhere café and restaurant tables spill out over sidewalks, especially around Piazza di Santa Maria in Trastevere and outside the pizzerias along Viale di Trastevere. There are also kiosks selling slices of watermelon and *grattachecca*, a mixture of syrup and grated ice. It is usually easier to appreciate the antique charm of Trastevere's narrow streets in the more tranquil atmosphere of the early morning.

① Casa della Fornarina
Raphael's beautiful mistress is said to have lived here. There is now a flourishing restaurant in the back garden.

The church of Santa Maria dei Sette Dolori (1643) is a minor work by Borromini.

③ Santa Maria della Scala
The church's unassuming facade conceals a rich Baroque interior.

④ Sant'Egidio and Museo di Roma in Trastevere
This 17th-century fresco of Sant' Egidio by Pomarancio decorates the left-hand chapel in the church. The convent next door is a museum of Roman life and customs.

Vicolo del Piede is one of the picturesque narrow streets lined with restaurant tables leading off Piazza di Santa Maria in Trastevere.

⑤ ★ Santa Maria in Trastevere
The church is famous for its mosaics by Pietro Cavallini, but it also has earlier works such as this mosaic of the prophet Isaiah to the left of the apse.

The fountain of Piazza di Santa Maria in Trastevere by Carlo Fontana (1692) is a popular meeting place. At night it is floodlit and dozens of young people sit on the steps around its octagonal base.

Key

— Suggested route

0 meters   75
0 yards   75

Locator Map
See Central Rome Map pp16–17

② Ponte Sisto
This bridge was built on the orders
of Sixtus IV in 1474 to link
Trastevere to central Rome.

**The Torre degli
Anguillara** (13th century)
is the only survivor of the
many medieval towers
that once dominated the
Trastevere skyline.

Piazza Belli is named after Giuseppe Gioacchino
Belli (1791–1863), who wrote satirical sonnets in
Roman dialect rather than academic Italian.
At the center of the piazza stands a statue of
the poet (1913).

**⑦ Caserma dei
Vigili della VII
Coorte**
The courtyard of this
antique Roman fire
station still stands.

⑥ San Crisogono
The Romanesque bell tower
dates from the early 12th century.
The plain portico is a later addition
(1626), but is in keeping with the spirit
of this ancient church.

❶ Casa della Fornarina

Via di Santa Dorotea 20. **Map** 4 D5 & 11 B5. 🚌 23, 280.

Not much is known about Raphael's model and lover, La Fornarina, yet over the centuries she has acquired a name, Margherita, and even a biography. Her father was a Sienese baker (*la fornarina* means the baker's girl), and his shop was here in Trastevere near Raphael's frescoes in the Villa Farnesina (*see pp220–21*).

Margherita earned a reputation as a "fallen woman," and Raphael, wishing to be absolved before dying, turned her away from his deathbed. After his death she took refuge in the convent of Santa Apollonia in Trastevere.

She is assumed to have been the model for Raphael's famous portrait *La Donna Velata* in the Palazzo Pitti in Florence.

❷ Ponte Sisto

Map 4 E5 & 11 B5. 🚌 23, 280.

Named after Pope Sixtus IV della Rovere (reigned 1471–84), who commissioned it, this bridge was built by Baccio Pontelli to replace an ancient Roman bridge. The enterprising pope also built the Sistine Chapel (*see pp242–5*), the Hospital of Santo Spirito (*see p246*), and restored many churches, and monuments. This caused him great financial difficulties and he had to sell personal collections in order to finance his projects.

Another method of financing projects was to levy a tax on the city's prostitutes. Several popes are known to have resorted to this unpopular form of taxation.

Pope Sixtus IV

Gilded Baroque altar of Santa Maria della Scala

❸ Santa Maria della Scala

Piazza della Scala 23. **Map** 4 D5 & 11 B5. **Tel** 06-580 6233. 🚌 23, 280. **Open** 10am–12:30pm, 4–7pm daily. 🕇

This church belongs to a time of major building activity that lasted about 30 years from the end of the 16th to the early 17th century. Its simple facade contrasts with a rich interior decorated with multicolored marbles, and a number of spirited Baroque altars, and reliefs. In 1849, the church was used as a hospital to treat Garibaldi's soldiers (*see pp40–41*).

❹ Sant'Egidio and Museo di Roma in Trastevere

Piazza Sant'Egidio 1. **Map** 7 C1. 🚌 H, 23, 280. 🚋 8. Church: **Tel** 06-58 56 61. **Open** 10am–12:30pm Sat. Museo di Roma in Trastevere: **Tel** 06-581 6563. **Open** 10am–8pm Tue–Sun (last adm: 7pm). ♿
Ⓦ **museodiromaintrastevere.it**

Built in 1630, Sant'Egidio was the church of the adjoining Carmelite convent, one of many founded in the area to shelter the poor and destitute. The convent is now a museum, containing a wealth of material relating to the festivals, pastimes, superstitions, and customs of the Romans when they lived under papal rule.

There are old paintings and prints of the city and tableaux showing scenes of everyday life in 18th- and 19th-century Rome, including reconstructions of shops and a tavern.

The museum also has manuscripts by the much-loved poets Belli and Trilussa, who wrote in local dialect.

Watercolor of public scribe (1880) in the Museo di Roma in Trastevere

❺ Santa Maria in Trastevere

See pp214–15.

❻ San Crisogono

Piazza Sonnino 44. **Map** 7 C1. **Tel** 06-5810 0076. 🚌 H, 23, 280, 780. 🚋 8. **Open** 7:30am–noon, 4:15–7:30pm Mon–Sat; 8:30am–1pm, 4:15–7:30pm Sun. 📷 for excavations. 🕇 ♿

This church was built on the site of one of the city's oldest *tituli* (private houses used for Christian worship). An 8th-century church with 11th-century frescoes can still be seen beneath the present church. This dates from the early 12th century, a period of intense building activity in Rome. San Crisogono was decorated by Pietro Cavallini – the apse mosaic remains. Most of the church's columns

Apse mosaic in San Crisogono

were taken from previous buildings, including the great porphyry ones of a triumphal arch. The mosaic floor is the result of recycling precious marble from various Roman ruins.

❼ Caserma dei Vigili della VII Coorte

Via della VII Coorte 9. **Map** 7 C1. **Tel** 06-0608. H, 23, 280, 780. 8. **Closed** for restoration work; call for details.

Not all Roman ruins are Imperial villas or grand temples; one that illustrates the daily life of a busy city is the barracks of the guards of the VII Coorte (7th Cohort), the Roman fire department. It was built in Augustus's reign, in the 1st century AD, and the excavated courtyard is where the men would rest while waiting for a callout.

❽ Santa Cecilia in Trastevere

Piazza di Santa Cecilia. **Map** 8 D1. **Tel** 06-589 9289. H, 23, 44, 280. 8. **Open** 9:30am–12:30pm, 4–6:30pm daily. for excavations. Cavallini fresco can be seen 10am–12:30pm Mon–Sat.

St. Cecilia, aristocrat, and patron saint of music, was martyred here in AD 230. After an attempt at scalding her to death, she was beheaded. A church was founded – perhaps in the 4th century – on the site of her house. (The house, beneath the church with the remains of a Roman tannery, is well worth a visit.) Her body turned up in the Catacombs of San Callisto (see p267), and was buried here in the 9th century by Pope Paschal I, who rebuilt the church. A fine apse mosaic survives from this period.

The altar canopy by Arnolfo di Cambio and the fresco of The Last Judgment by Pietro Cavallini, reached through the adjoining convent, date from the 13th century, one of the few periods when Rome had a distinctive artistic style of its own. In front of the altar is a

Detail of 13th-century fresco by Pietro Cavallini in Santa Cecilia

statue of St. Cecilia by Stefano Maderno, who used her miraculously preserved remains as a model when she was briefly disinterred in 1599.

❾ San Michele a Ripa Grande

Via di San Michele 25. **Map** 8 D2. **Tel** 06-584 31. 23, 44, 75, 280. **Open** for special exhibitions only.

This huge, imposing complex, now housing the Ministry of Culture, stretches 985 ft (300 m) along the Tiber River. It was built on the initiative of Pope Innocent XII and contained a home for the elderly, a boys' reform school, a

woolen mill, and various chapels. Today, contemporary exhibitions are occasionally held here.

❿ San Francesco a Ripa

Piazza San Francesco d'Assisi 88. **Map** 7 C2. **Tel** 06-581 9020. H, 23, 44, 75, 280. 8. **Open** 7:30am–1pm, 2–7pm daily.

St. Francis of Assisi lived here in a hospice when he visited Rome in 1219, and his stone pillow and crucifix are preserved in his cell. The church was rebuilt by his follower, the nobleman Rodolfo Anguillara, who is portrayed on his tombstone wearing the Franciscan habit.

Entirely rebuilt in the 1680s by Cardinal Pallavicini, the church is rich in sculptures. Particularly flamboyant are the 18th-century Rospigliosi and Pallavicini monuments in the transept chapel.

The Paluzzi-Albertoni chapel (fourth on the left, along the nave) contains Bernini's breathtaking Ecstasy of Beata Ludovica Albertoni.

⓫ Villa Sciarra

Via Calandrelli 35. **Map** 7 B2. 44, 75. Park: **Open** 9am–sunset daily.

In Roman times the site of this small, attractive public park was a nymph's sanctuary. It is especially picturesque in spring when its wisterias are in full bloom. The paths through the park are decorated with Romantic follies, fountains, and statues, and there are splendid views over the bastions of the Janiculum.

Bernini's Ecstasy of Beata Ludovica Albertoni (1674) in San Francesco a Ripa

❺ Santa Maria in Trastevere

Probably the first official Christian place of worship to be built in Rome, this basilica became the focus of devotion to the Virgin Mary. According to legend, the church was founded by Pope Callixtus I in the 3rd century, when Christianity was still a minority cult. Today's church is largely a 12th-century building, remarkable for its mosaics, in particular those by Pietro Cavallini. The 22 granite columns in the nave were taken from the ruins of ancient Roman buildings. Despite some 18th-century Baroque additions, Santa Maria has retained its medieval character. This friendly church has strong links with the local community.

Piazza Santa Maria in Trastevere
The piazza in front of the church is the traditional heart of Trastevere. Today it is surrounded by lively bars and restaurants. Carlo Fontana built the octagonal fountain in the late 17th century.

★ Facade Mosaics
The 12th-century mosaic shows Mary feeding the baby Jesus and ten women holding lamps. Eight of the lamps are lit, symbolizing virginity; the veiled women whose lamps have gone out are probably widows.

Modest Donors

Many of Rome's mosaics include a portrait of the pope or cardinal responsible for the building of the church. Often the portrait is dwarfed by the rest of the picture, which glorifies the saint to whom the church is dedicated. On the facade of Santa Maria, two tiny unidentified figures kneel at the Virgin's feet. Were they to stand up, the men would barely reach her knees.

Facade mosaic, detail

KEY

① **The portico** was remodeled in 1702 by Carlo Fontana. Statues of four popes decorate the balustrade above.

② **The bell tower** was built in the 12th century. At the top is a small mosaic of the Virgin.

③ **The floor**, relaid in the 1870s, is a recreation of the Cosmatesque mosaic floor of the 13th century.

④ **15th-century wall tabernacle** by Mino del Reame.

Front entrance

Apse Mosaic
The 12th-century mosaic in the basin of the apse shows the Coronation of the Virgin. She sits on Christ's right hand, surrounded by saints.

VISITORS' CHECKLIST

Practical Information
Via della Paglia 14c, Piazza Santa Maria in Trastevere.
Map 7 C1.
Tel 06-581 4802.
Open 7:30am–8:30pm daily. 🕇
9am & 5:30pm daily. ♿ 📷

Transportation
🚌 H & 780 to Piazza S. Sonnino, 23 & 280 along Lungotevere Sanzio. 🚊 8 from Largo Argentina.

Madonna della Clemenza
The life-size icon probably dates from the 7th century. A replica is displayed above the altar of the Cappella Altemps.

★ Cavallini Mosaics
The details in the six mosaics of the Life of the Virgin (1291) display a touching realism.

Tomb of Cardinal Pietro Stefaneschi
The last of his line, Pietro Stefaneschi died in 1417. His tomb is by an otherwise unknown sculptor called Paolo.

AD 217–22 Church founded by Pope Callixtus I

Pope Innocent II

1291 Pietro Cavallini adds mosaics of scenes from the life of the Virgin for his patron, Bertoldo Stefaneschi

1866–77 Church restored by Virginio Vespignani

50 BC	0	600	1200	1800

38 BC Jet of mineral oil spouts from the ground on this site. Later interpreted as a portent of the coming of Christ

c. 1138 Pope Innocent II starts rebuilding the church

1580 Martino Longhi the Elder restores church and builds family chapel for Cardinal Marco Sittico Altemps

1702 Pope Clement XI has portico rebuilt

1617 Domenichino designs coffered ceiling with octagonal panel of the Assumption of the Virgin

JANICULUM

Overlooking the Tiber on the Trastevere side of the river, the Janiculum Hill has often played its part in the defense of the city. The last occasion was in 1849, when Garibaldi held off the attacking French troops. The park at the top of the hill is filled with monuments to Garibaldi and his men. A popular place for walks, the park provides a welcome escape from the densely packed streets of Trastevere. You will often come across puppet shows and other children's amusements. In medieval times, most of the hill was occupied by monasteries and convents. Bramante built his miniature masterpiece, the Tempietto, in the convent of San Pietro in Montorio. The Renaissance also saw the development of the riverside area along Via della Lungara, where the rich and powerful built beautiful houses such as the Villa Farnesina.

Sights at a Glance

Churches and Temples
- ⑥ Sant'Onofrio
- ⑦ San Pietro in Montorio
- ⑧ Tempietto

Museums and Galleries
- ② Palazzo Corsini and Galleria Nazionale d'Arte Antica

Historic Buildings
- ① *Villa Farnesina pp220–21*

Fountains
- ⑨ Fontana dell'Acqua Paola

Monuments
- ⑤ Garibaldi Monument

Arches and Gates
- ③ Porta Settimiana

Parks and Gardens
- ④ Botanical Gardens

See also Street Finder maps 3, 4, 7, 11

☐ **Restaurants**
see pp317–19
1 Antica Arco
2 Antico Arco
3 Isole di Sicilia
4 Lo Scarpone

| 0 meters | 300 |
| 0 yards | 300 |

◀ View of Garibaldi Monument, Janiculum Hill

For map symbols *see back flap*

A Tour of the Janiculum

The long hike to the top of the Janiculum is rewarded by wonderful views over the city. The park's monuments include a lighthouse and statues of Garibaldi and his wife Anita. There is also a cannon that is fired at noon each day. In Via della Lungara, between the Janiculum and the Tiber, stand Palazzo Corsini with its national art collection and the Villa Farnesina, decorated by Raphael for his friend and patron, the fabulously wealthy banker Agostino Chigi.

Tasso's Oak is a memorial to the poet Torquato Tasso, who liked to sit here in the days before he died in 1595. The tree was struck by lightning in 1843.

The Manfredi Lighthouse, built in 1911, was a gift to the city of Rome from Italians in Argentina.

The Monument to Anita Garibaldi by Mario Rutelli was erected in 1932. The great patriot's Brazilian wife lies buried beneath the statue.

The view from Villa Lante, a beautiful Renaissance summer residence, gives a magnificent panorama of the whole city.

❺ **Garibaldi Monument**
The inscription on the base of the equestrian statue says "Rome or Death."

❹ Botanical Gardens
These were established in 1883 when part of the grounds of Palazzo Corsini was given to the University of Rome.

❶ ★ Villa Farnesina
The suburban villa of the banker Agostino Chigi is celebrated for its frescoes by Raphael, Baldassarre Peruzzi, and other Renaissance masters.

Locator Map
See Central Rome Map pp16–17

❷ ★ Palazzo Corsini
This 15th-century triptych by Fra Angelico hangs in the Galleria Nazionale d'Arte Antica.

VICOLO DELLA PENITENZA

VIA DELLA PENITENZA

VIA DEI RIARI

VIA DELLA LUNGARA

VIA CORSINI

VIA G. GARIBALDI

Key

— Suggested route

0 meters	75
0 yards	75

❸ Porta Settimiana
Looking through this Renaissance gateway from Via della Lungara, you catch a glimpse of Trastevere's warren of narrow streets.

❶ Villa Farnesina

The wealthy Sienese banker Agostino Chigi, who had established the headquarters of his far-flung financial empire in Rome, commissioned the villa in 1508 from his compatriot Baldassare Peruzzi. The simple, harmonious design, with a central block and projecting wings, made this one of the earliest true Renaissance villas. The decoration was carried out between 1510 and 1519, and this has been restored. Peruzzi frescoed some of the interiors himself. Later, Sebastiano del Piombo, Raphael, and his pupils added more elaborate works. The frescoes illustrate Classical myths, and the vault of the main hall, the Sala di Galatea, is adorned with astrological scenes showing the position of the stars at the time of Chigi's birth. Artists, poets, cardinals, princes, and the pope himself were entertained here in magnificent style by their wealthy and influential host. In 1577 the villa was bought by Cardinal Alessandro Farnese. Since then, it has been known as the Villa Farnesina.

North Facade
The Loggia of Cupid and Psyche looks out on formal gardens that were used for parties and putting on plays.

Entrance

The Wedding of Alexander and Roxanne by Sodoma
Cherubs are shown helping the bride Roxanne to prepare for her marriage.

★ Triumph of Galatea by Raphael
The beautiful sea nymph Galatea was one of the 50 daughters of the god Nereus.

The Architect

Baldassare Peruzzi, painter and architect, arrived in Rome from Siena in 1503 at age 20 and became Bramante's chief assistant. Although his architectural designs were typical of Classicism, his painting owes more to Gothic influences, as his figurework is very highly stylized. On Raphael's death, he became Head of Works at St. Peter's, but was captured in the Sack of Rome (see p35), exiled to Siena until 1535, and died in 1536.

Baldassare Peruzzi

Frescoes in the Room of Galatea
Perseus beheads Medusa in a scene from one of Peruzzi's series of mythological frescoes.

★ **Salone delle Prospettive**
Peruzzi's frescoes create the illusion of looking out at views of 16th-century Rome through a marble colonnade.

VISITORS' CHECKLIST

Practical Information
Via della Lungara 230.
Map 4 D5 & 11 A5.
Tel 06-6802 7268.
Open 9am–2pm Mon–Sat and second Sun of every month.
Closed Aug. 🏛 📷 🎧 📅 ♿

Transportation
🚌 23, 280 to Lungotevere Farnesina.

Fresco from the Salone delle Prospettive
This scene shows the Torre delle Milizie *(see p92)* as it looked in the 1500s.

★ **Loggia of Cupid and Psyche**
The model for the figure on the left in Raphael's painting of *The Three Graces* was Agostino Chigi's mistress, the courtesan Imperia.

Lunette in the Room of Galatea
This giant monochrome head by Peruzzi was once attributed to Michelangelo.

Queen Christina's bedroom in the Palazzo Corsini

❷ Palazzo Corsini and Galleria Nazionale d'Arte Antica

Via della Lungara 10. **Map** 4 D5 & 11 A5. **Tel** 06-6880 2323. 🚌 23, 280. **Open** 8:30am–7:30pm Tue–Sun. **Closed** Jan 1, Dec 25. 🚫 🚻 📷 ♿ 📷 🌐 galleriaborghese.it

The history of Palazzo Corsini is intimately entwined with that of Rome. Built for Cardinal Domenico Riario in 1510–12, it has boasted among its many distinguished guests Bramante, the young Michelangelo, Erasmus, and Queen Christina of Sweden, who died here in 1689. The old palazzo was completely rebuilt for Cardinal Neri Corsini by Ferdinando Fuga in 1736. Via della Lungara is too narrow for a good frontal view, so Fuga designed the facade so it could be seen from an angle.

Palazzo Corsini houses the Galleria Nazionale d'Arte Antica, also known as Galleria Corsini. This outstanding collection includes paintings by Rubens, Van Dyck, Murillo, Caravaggio, and Guido Reni, together with 17th- and 18th-century Italian regional art. The palazzo is also home to the Accademia dei Lincei, a learned society founded in 1603, which once included Galileo among its members.

In 1797 Palazzo Corsini was the backdrop to momentous events: French General Duphot (the fiancé of Napoleon's sister Pauline) was killed here in a skirmish between papal troops and Republicans. The consequent French occupation of the city, and the deportation of Pope Pius VI led to the proclamation of a short-lived Roman Republic (1798–99).

❸ Porta Settimiana

Between Via della Scala and Via della Lungara. **Map** 4 D5 & 11 B5. 🚌 23, 280.

This gate was built in 1498 by Pope Alexander VI Borgia to replace a minor passageway in the Aurelian Wall. The Porta Settimiana marks the start of Via della Lungara, a long, straight road built in the early 16th century.

❹ Botanical Gardens

Largo Cristina di Svezia 24, off Via Corsini. **Map** 4 D5. **Tel** 06-4991 7107. 🚌 23, 280. **Open** Apr–Sep: 9am–6:30pm Mon–Sat (Oct–Mar: to 5:30pm). **Closed** public hols. 🚫 📷 (call to book).

Sequoias, palm trees, and collections of orchids and bromeliads are housed in Rome's Botanical Gardens *(Orto Botanico)*. These tranquil gardens contain more than 7,000 plant species from all over the world. Indigenous and exotic species are grouped to illustrate their botanical families and their adaptation to different climates and ecosystems.

There are also plants such as the ginkgo that have survived virtually unchanged from earlier eras. The gardens were originally part of the Palazzo Corsini, but since 1983 have belonged to the University of Rome.

Base of the Garibaldi Monument

❺ Garibaldi Monument

Piazzale Giuseppe Garibaldi. **Map** 3 C5. 🚌 870.

This huge equestrian statue is part of a commemorative park, recalling the heroic events witnessed on the Janiculum when the French army attacked the city in 1849. Garibaldi's Republicans fended off the greatly superior French forces for weeks, until the Italians were overwhelmed. Garibaldi and his men escaped. The monument, erected in 1895, was the work of Emilio Gallori. Around the pedestal are four smaller sculptures in bronze showing battle scenes and allegorical figures.

Steps and tiered fountains at the Botanical Gardens

Courtyard of Sant'Onofrio

❻ Sant'Onofrio

Piazza di Sant'Onofrio 2. **Map** 3 C4.
Tel 06-686 4498. 🚌 870. **Open**
9am–1pm Mon–Sat. **Closed** Aug. 🛆
Museum **Open** by appt only. **Tel**
06-686 9040.

Beato Nicola da Forca Palena, whose tombstone guards the entrance, founded this church in 1419 in honor of the hermit Sant'Onofrio. It retains the flavor of the 15th century in the simple shapes of the portico and the cloister. In the early 17th century the portico was decorated with frescoes by Domenichino.

The monastery next to the church houses a small museum dedicated to the 16th-century Italian poet Torquato Tasso, who died there.

❼ San Pietro in Montorio

Piazza San Pietro in Montorio 2.
Map 7 B1. **Tel** 06-581 39 40. 🚌 44, 75.
Open 8am–noon daily, 3–4pm
(4–6pm summer) Mon–Fri. If closed,
ring bell at door to right of church. 🛆

San Pietro in Montorio – the church of St. Peter on the Golden Hill – was founded in the Middle Ages near the spot where St. Peter was presumed to have been crucified. It was rebuilt by order of Ferdinand and Isabella of Spain at the end of the 15th century, and decorated by outstanding artists of the Renaissance.

The facade is typical of a time when clean, geometric shapes derived from Classical architecture were in vogue. The single nave ends in a deep apse that once contained Raphael's

Transfiguration, now in the Vatican. Two wide chapels, one on either side of the nave, were decorated by some of Michelangelo's most famous pupils. The left-hand chapel was designed by one of the few artists Michelangelo openly admired, Daniele da Volterra, also responsible for the altar painting, *The Baptism of Christ*. The chapel on the right was the work of Giorgio Vasari, who included a self-portrait (in black, on the left) in his altar painting, *The Conversion of St. Paul.*

The first chapel to the right of the entrance contains a powerful *Flagellation*, by the Venetian artist Sebastiano del Piombo (1518); Michelangelo is said to have provided the original drawings. Work by Bernini and his followers can be seen in the second chapel on the left and in the flanking De Raymondi tombs.

❽ Tempietto

Piazza San Pietro in Montorio (in
courtyard). **Map** 7 B1. **Tel** 06-581 2806.
🚌 44, 75. **Open** 9:30am–12:30pm,
2–4:30pm Tue–Sat. *See The History of
Rome pp34–5.*

Around 1502, Bramante completed what many consider to be the first true Renaissance building in Rome: the Tempietto. The name means simply "little temple." Its circular shape echoes early Christian *martyria*, chapels built on the site of a saint's martyrdom. This was believed to be the place where St. Peter was crucified.

Bramante chose the Doric order for the 16 columns surrounding the domed chapel. Above the columns is a Classical frieze and a delicate balustrade. Though the scale of the Tempietto is tiny, Bramante's masterly use of Classical proportions creates a satisfyingly harmonious whole. The Tempietto illustrates the great Renaissance

dream that the city of Rome would once again relive its ancient glory.

Fontana dell'Acqua Paola

❾ Fontana dell'Acqua Paola

Via Garibaldi. **Map** 7 B1. 🚌 44, 75.

This monumental fountain commemorates the reopening in 1612 of an aqueduct originally built by Emperor Trajan in AD 109. The aqueduct was renamed the "Acqua Paola" after Paul V, the Borghese pope who ordered its restoration. When it was first built, the fountain had five small basins, but in 1690 Carlo Fontana altered the design, adding the huge basin you can see today. Despite many laws intended to deter them, generations of Romans used this convenient pool of fresh water for bathing and washing their vegetables.

Bramante's round chapel, the Tempietto

VATICAN

As the site where St. Peter was martyred and buried, the Vatican became the residence of the popes who succeeded him. Decisions made here have shaped the destiny of Europe, and the great Basilica of St. Peter's draws pilgrims from all over the Christian world. The papal palaces beside St. Peter's house the Vatican Museums. With the added attractions of Michelangelo's Sistine Chapel and the Raphael Rooms, their wonderful collections of Classical sculpture make them the finest museums in Rome. The Vatican's position as a state within a state was guaranteed by the Lateran Treaty of 1929, marked by the building of a new road, the Via della Conciliazione. This leads from St. Peter's to Castel Sant'Angelo, a monument to a far grimmer past. Built originally as the Emperor Hadrian's mausoleum, this papal fortress and prison has witnessed many fierce battles for control of the city.

Sights at a Glance

Churches and Temples
- ① St. Peter's pp228–9
- ④ Santo Spirito in Sassia
- ⑨ Santa Maria in Traspontina

Museums and Galleries
- ② Vatican Museums pp232–9

Historic Buildings
- ⑤ Hospital of Santo Spirito
- ⑥ Palazzo del Commendatore
- ⑦ Palazzo dei Convertendi
- ⑧ Palazzo dei Penitenzieri
- ⑫ Palazzo Torlonia
- ⑬ Castel Sant'Angelo pp250–51
- ⑭ Palazzo di Giustizia

Gates
- ③ Porta Santo Spirito

Historic Streets and Piazzas
- ⑩ The Borgo
- ⑪ Vatican Corridor

☐ Restaurants
see pp317–19
1. Arlù
2. Da Benito e Gilberto
3. Da Cesare
4. Taverna Angelica
5. Velando
6. Veranda

0 meters 300
0 yards 300

See also Street Finder maps 3, 4

◀ The statue of St. Peter, St. Peter's Square

For map symbols *see back flap*

A Tour of the Vatican

The Vatican, a center of power for Catholics all over the world and a sovereign state since February 1929, is ruled by the pope. About 1,000 people live here, staffing the Vatican's facilities. These include a post office and shops; Vatican radio, broadcasting to the world in over 20 languages; a daily newspaper (*L'Osservatore Romano*); Vatican offices; and a publishing house.

The Madonna of Guadalupe shows the miraculous image of the Madonna that appeared on the cloak of a Mexican Indian in 1531.

Papal heliport

The Grotto of Lourdes is a replica of the grotto in the southwest of France, where in 1858 the Virgin appeared to St. Bernadette.

The Vatican Train Station, opened in 1930, connects with the line from Rome to Viterbo, but is now used only for freight.

Radio Vatican is broadcast from this tower, part of the Leonine Wall built in 847.

The Papal Audience Chamber, by Pier Luigi Nervi, was opened in 1971. It seats up to 12,000.

The information office gives details of tours of the Vatican Gardens.

PIAZZA DEL SANT UFFIZIO

❶ ★ St. Peter's
The Chapel of St. Peter is in the Grottoes under the basilica. The rich marble decoration was added by Clement VIII at the end of the 16th century.

Piazza San Pietro was laid out by Bernini between 1656 and 1667. The narrow space in front of the church opens out into an enormous ellipse flanked by colonnades.

Key

— Suggested route

0 meters 75

0 yards 75

The Eagle Fountain was built to celebrate the arrival of water from the Acqua Paola aqueduct at the Vatican. The eagle is the Borghese crest.

Locator Map
See Central Rome Map pp16–17

The Casina of Pius IV is a delightful summer house in the Vatican Gardens built by Pirro Ligorio in the mid-16th century.

Entrance to Vatican Museums

❷ ★ Vatican Museums
Raphael's *Madonna of Foligno* (1513) is just one of the Vatican's many Renaissance masterpieces.

The Galleon Fountain is a perfect scale model of a 17th-century ship in lead, brass, and copper. It was made by a Flemish artist for Pope Paul V.

VIA DI PORTA ANGELICA

PIAZZA SAN PIETRO

PIAZZA PIO XII

The obelisk was erected here in 1586 with the help of 150 horses and 47 winches.

To Via della Conciliazione

The Cortile della Pigna is mostly the work of Bramante. The niche for the pine cone, once a Roman fountain, was added by Pirro Ligorio in 1562.

❶ St. Peter's

The center of the Roman Catholic faith, St. Peter's draws pilgrims from all over the world. Few are disappointed when they enter the sumptuously decorated basilica beneath Michelangelo's vast dome.

A shrine was erected on the site of St. Peter's tomb in the 2nd century, and the first great basilica, ordered by the Emperor Constantine, was completed around AD 349. By the 15th century it was falling down, so in 1506 Pope Julius II laid the first stone of a new church. It took more than a century to build, and all the great architects of the Roman Renaissance and Baroque had a hand in its design.

★ Dome of St. Peter's
Designed by Michelangelo, though not finished in his lifetime, the spectacular cupola, 448 ft (136.5 m) high, gives unity to the majestic interior of the basilica.

Papal Altar
The present altar dates from the reign of Clement VIII (1592–1605). The plain slab of marble found in the Forum of Nerva stands under Bernini's baldacchino, overlooking the well of the *confessio,* the crypt where St. Peter's body is reputedly buried.

Baldacchino
This magnificent canopy of gilded bronze, supported on spiral columns 66 ft (20 m) high, was designed by Bernini in the 17th century.

KEY

① **The nave's** total length is 715 ft (218 m).

② **The two minor cupolas** at the corners of the transept are by Vignola.

③ **Facade by Carlo Maderno** (1614).

④ **Stairs to the dome**.

Pope Urban VIII's Keys
At the base of the columns of the baldacchino, the coat of arms of Pope Urban VIII features the keys to the Kingdom of Heaven.

★ **View from the Dome**
The superb symmetry of Bernini's colonnade can be appreciated from the dome.

Piazza San Pietro
On Sundays and religious occasions, the Pope blesses the crowds from his balcony above the square.

Entrance

Filarete Door
Finished in 1445, Antonio Averulino's bronze door came from the original basilica.

AD 61 Burial of St. Peter				1506 Julius II lays first stone	1547 Michelangelo named as chief architect of St. Peter's		1593 Dome completed	1626 New basilica of St. Peter's consecrated
	324 Constantine builds basilica	1452 Nicholas V plans restoration						

AD 60		800		1500		1550		1600	
	200 Altar built marking grave of St. Peter		1503 Pope Julius II chooses Bramante as architect for new basilica		1538 Antonio da Sangallo the Younger made director of works		1606 Carlo Maderno extends basilica		1614 Maderno finishes the facade
	800 Charlemagne crowned Emperor of Romans in St. Peter's			1514 Raphael director of works		1564 Death of Michelangelo			

A Guided Tour of St. Peter's

The vast basilica's 615-ft- (187-m-) long, marble-encrusted interior contains 11 chapels and 45 altars and a wealth of precious works of art. Some were salvaged from the original basilica and others commissioned from late Renaissance and Baroque artists, but much of the elaborate decoration is owed to Bernini's mid-17th-century work. The two side aisles are 250 ft (76 m) long and converge under Michelangelo's enormous dome. The building's central focus is the Papal Altar beneath Bernini's great baldacchino, filling the space between the four piers that support the dome. From the basilica you can visit the Grottoes, where the late Pope John Paul II is buried, the Treasury and St. Peter's Sacristy, or the terrace for panoramic views.

⑤ Baldacchino by Bernini

Commissioned by Pope Urban VIII in 1624, the extravagant Baroque canopy dominates the nave and crowns the Papal Altar, at which only the pope may celebrate mass.

Bernini's Monument to Urban VIII

④ Throne of St. Peter in Glory

In the domed apse, look up to the window above Bernini's Baroque sculpture of 1656–65. It lights the image of the Holy Spirit, shown as a dove amid clouds, rays of sunlight, and flights of angels.

Entrance to Treasury and Sacristy

Entrance to Necropolis

Historical Plan of the Basilica of St. Peter's

St. Peter was buried c. AD 64 in a necropolis near his crucifixion site at the Circus of Nero. Constantine built a basilica on the burial site in AD 324. In the 15th century the old church was found to be unsafe and had to be demolished. It was rebuilt in the 16th and 17th centuries. By 1614 the facade was ready, and in 1626 the new church was consecrated.

Key
- ■ Circus of Nero
- □ Constantinian
- ■ Renaissance
- □ Baroque

③ Monument to Pope Alexander VII

Bernini's last work was finished in 1678 and is in an alcove on the left of the transept. The pope sits among the figures of Truth, Justice, Charity, and Prudence.

② Monument to Leo XI

On the left beneath the aisle arch is Alessandro Algardi's white marble 1650 monument to Leo XI, whose reign as pope lasted only 27 days.

Key
- — Tour route

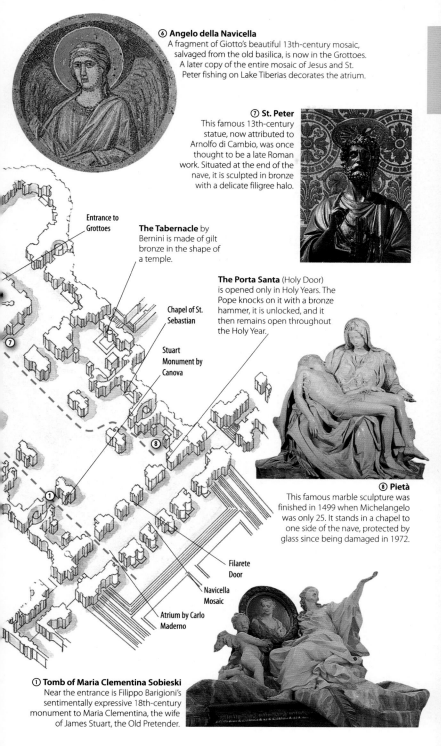

⑥ Angelo della Navicella
A fragment of Giotto's beautiful 13th-century mosaic, salvaged from the old basilica, is now in the Grottoes. A later copy of the entire mosaic of Jesus and St. Peter fishing on Lake Tiberias decorates the atrium.

⑦ St. Peter
This famous 13th-century statue, now attributed to Arnolfo di Cambio, was once thought to be a late Roman work. Situated at the end of the nave, it is sculpted in bronze with a delicate filigree halo.

Entrance to Grottoes

The Tabernacle by Bernini is made of gilt bronze in the shape of a temple.

Chapel of St. Sebastian

Stuart Monument by Canova

The Porta Santa (Holy Door) is opened only in Holy Years. The Pope knocks on it with a bronze hammer, it is unlocked, and it then remains open throughout the Holy Year.

⑧ Pietà
This famous marble sculpture was finished in 1499 when Michelangelo was only 25. It stands in a chapel to one side of the nave, protected by glass since being damaged in 1972.

Filarete Door

Navicella Mosaic

Atrium by Carlo Maderno

① Tomb of Maria Clementina Sobieski
Near the entrance is Filippo Barigioni's sentimentally expressive 18th-century monument to Maria Clementina, the wife of James Stuart, the Old Pretender.

❷ Vatican Museums

The buildings that house one of the world's finest art collections were once papal palaces built for Renaissance popes such as Sixtus IV, Innocent VIII, and Julius II. The long courtyards and galleries, linking Innocent VIII's Belvedere Palace to the other buildings, are by Donato Bramante and were commissioned for Julius II in 1503. Most of the later additions to the buildings were made in the 18th century, when priceless works of art were first put on display. This complex of museums also houses the Sistine Chapel and the Raphael Rooms, and should not be missed. Note that no bare knees or shoulders are allowed.

★ Atrium of the Four Gates
Built by Camporese in 1792–3, this vast domed edifice was the original entrance to the Vatican Museums.

★ Cortile della Pigna
This huge bronze pine cone, part of an ancient Roman fountain, once stood in the courtyard of old St. Peter's. Its niche was designed by Pirro Ligorio.

KEY

① **Cortile di San Damaso**

② **Raphael Loggia**

③ **Borgia Apartment**

④ **Borgia Tower**

⑤ **Sistine Chapel**

⑥ **Apartment of Pius V**

⑦ **Cortile del Belvedere**

⑧ **Cortile della Biblioteca**

⑨ **Braccio Nuovo**

⑩ **The Belvedere Palace** was commissioned in the late 15th century by Pope Innocent VIII.

Spiral Ramp
The spectacular stairway leading down from the museums to the street was designed by Giuseppe Momo in 1932.

Entrance

VISITORS' CHECKLIST

Practical Information
Città del Vaticano. Entrance in Viale Vaticano. **Map** 3 B2. **Tel** 06-6988 4676. **Open** 9am–6pm (last adm: 4pm) Mon–Sat, 9am–2pm (last adm: 12:30pm) last Sun of each month. Also occasionally 7–11pm Fri (book in adv). **Closed** public & relig hols. Special permit needed for Raphael Loggia, Vatican Library, Lapidary Gallery & Vatican Archives. **W** mv.vatican.va (free last Sun of month). ♿ special routes. Temp exhibitions, lectures. Gardens & tours: 06-6988 3145.

Transportation
49 to entrance, 23, 81, 492, 990 to Piazza del Risorgimento or 62 to St. Peter's. **M** Cipro Musei Vaticani, Ottaviano S. Pietro.

Simonetti Stairway
Built in the 1780s with a vaulted ceiling, the stairs were part of the conversion of the Belvedere Palace into the Pio-Clementine Museum.

★ Bramante Stairway
Pope Julius II built the spiral staircase within a square tower as an entrance to the palace. The staircase could be ridden up on horseback in case of emergency.

Cortile Ottagonale
The inner court of the Belvedere Palace was given its octagonal shape in 1773.

1198 Innocent III creates papal palace

1503 Bramante lays out Belvedere Courtyard

1509 Raphael begins work on Rooms

1756 Foundation of Christian Museum

1655 Bernini designs Scala Regia

1800–23 Chiaramonti Museum founded

1837 Etruscan Museum founded

1000	1500	1600	1700	1800	1900

1473 Pope Sixtus IV builds Sistine Chapel

1503–13 Pope Julius II starts Classical sculpture collection

1758 Museum of Pagan Antiquities founded

1776–84 Pius VI enlarges museum

Bramante (1444–1514)

1822 Braccio Nuovo is opened

1970 Pope Paul VI opens Gregorian Museum of Pagan Antiquities

Exploring the Vatican Museums

Four centuries of papal patronage and connoisseurship have resulted in one of the world's great collections of Classical and Renaissance art. The Vatican houses many of the great archaeological finds of central Italy, including the *Laocoön* group, discovered in 1506 on the Esquiline, the *Apollo del Belvedere*, and the Etruscan bronze known as the *Mars of Todi*. During the Renaissance, parts of the museums were decorated with wonderful frescoes commissioned for the Sistine Chapel, the Raphael Rooms, and the Borgia Apartment.

Gallery of the Candelabra
Once an open loggia, this gallery of Greek and Roman sculpture has a fine view of the Vatican Gardens.

Room of the Biga

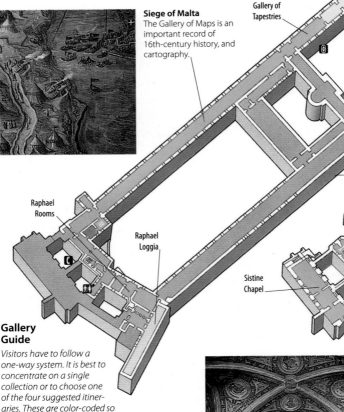

Siege of Malta
The Gallery of Maps is an important record of 16th-century history, and cartography.

Gallery of Tapestries

Upper floor

Raphael Rooms

Raphael Loggia

Sistine Chapel

Gallery Guide

Visitors have to follow a one-way system. It is best to concentrate on a single collection or to choose one of the four suggested itineraries. These are color-coded so that you can follow them through the museums. They vary in length from 90 minutes to 5 hours. If you are planning a long visit, make sure you allow plenty of time for resting. Conserve your stamina for the Sistine Chapel and Raphael Rooms; they are 20–30 minutes' walk from the entrance, without allowing for any viewing time along the way.

Sala dei Misteri
This is one of the rooms of the Borgia Apartment, richly decorated with Pinturicchio frescoes.

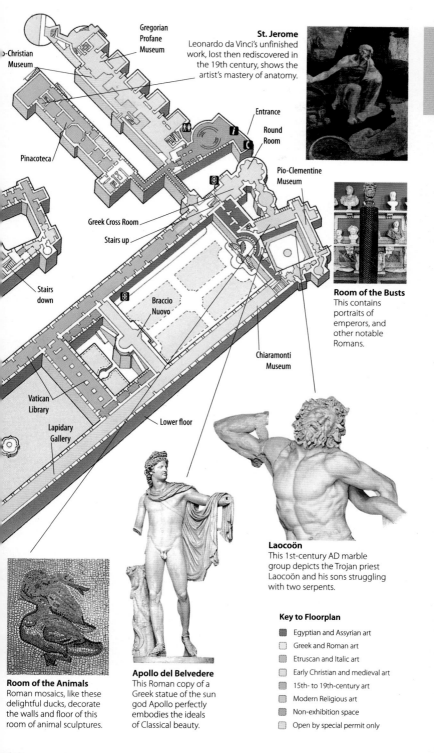

Gregorian Profane Museum

o-Christian Museum

St. Jerome
Leonardo da Vinci's unfinished work, lost then rediscovered in the 19th century, shows the artist's mastery of anatomy.

Entrance

Round Room

Pinacoteca

Pio-Clementine Museum

Greek Cross Room

Stairs up

Room of the Busts
This contains portraits of emperors, and other notable Romans.

Stairs down

Braccio Nuovo

Chiaramonti Museum

Vatican Library

Lower floor

Lapidary Gallery

Laocoön
This 1st-century AD marble group depicts the Trojan priest Laocoön and his sons struggling with two serpents.

Apollo del Belvedere
This Roman copy of a Greek statue of the sun god Apollo perfectly embodies the ideals of Classical beauty.

Room of the Animals
Roman mosaics, like these delightful ducks, decorate the walls and floor of this room of animal sculptures.

Key to Floorplan
- Egyptian and Assyrian art
- Greek and Roman art
- Etruscan and Italic art
- Early Christian and medieval art
- 15th- to 19th-century art
- Modern Religious art
- Non-exhibition space
- Open by special permit only

Exploring the Vatican's Collections

The Vatican's greatest treasures are its Greek and Roman antiquities. These have been on display since the 18th century. The 19th century saw the addition of exciting discoveries from Etruscan tombs and excavations in Egypt. In the Pinacoteca (art gallery) there is a small, choice collection of paintings, including works by Raphael, Titian and Leonardo. Works by great painters and sculptors are also on view throughout the older parts of the museums in the form of sumptuous decorations commissioned by the Renaissance popes.

Coloured bas-relief from an Egyptian tomb (c.2400 BC)

Egyptian and Assyrian Art

The Egyptian collection contains finds from 19th and 20th-century excavations in Egypt and statues which were brought to Rome in Imperial times. There are also Roman imitations of Egyptian art from Hadrian's Villa (see p271) and from the Campus Martius district of ancient Rome. Egyptian-style statuary from Hadrian's Villa was used to decorate the Greek Cross Room, the entrance to the new wing built in 1780 by Michelangelo Simonetti.

The genuine Egyptian works, exhibited on the lower floor of the Belvedere Palace, include statues, mummies, mummy cases and funerary artifacts. There is also a large collection of documents written on papyrus, the paper the ancient Egyptians made from reeds. Among the main treasures is a colossal granite statue of Queen Tuia, the mother of Rameses II, found on the site of the Horti Sallustiani gardens (see p253) in 1714. The statue, which dates from the 13th century BC, may have been brought to Rome by the Emperor Caligula (reigned AD 37–41), who had an unhealthy interest in pharaohs and in his own mother, Agrippina.

Also noteworthy are the head of a statue of Montuhotep IV (21st century BC), the beautiful mummy case of Queen Hetepheres, and the tomb of Iri, the guardian of the Pyramid of Cheops (26th century BC).

The Assyrian Stairway is decorated with fragments of reliefs from the palaces of the kings of Nineveh (8th century BC). These depict the military exploits of King Sennacherib and his son Sargon II, and show scenes from Assyrian and Chaldean mythology.

Etruscan and Other Pre-Roman Art

This collection comprises artifacts from pre-Roman civilizations in Etruria and Latium, from Neolithic times to the 1st century BC, when these ancient populations were assimilated into the Roman state. Pride of place in the Gregorian Etruscan Museum goes to the objects found in the Regolini-Galassi tomb, excavated in 1836 at the necropolis of Cerveteri (see p273). The tomb was found intact and yielded numerous everyday household objects, plus a throne, a bed and a funeral cart, all cast in bronze, dating from the 7th century BC. Beautiful black vases, delightful terracotta figurines and bronze statues such as the famous Mars of Todi, displayed in the Room of the Bronzes, show the Etruscans to have been a highly civilized, sophisticated people.

A number of Greek vases that were found in Etruscan tombs are on display in the Vase Collection. The Room of the Italiot Vases contains only vases produced locally in the Greek cities of Southern Italy and in Etruria itself. These date from the 3rd to the 1st century BC.

Etruscan gold clasp (fibula) from the 7th century BC

Head of an athlete in mosaic from the Baths of Caracalla

Greek and Roman Art

The greater part of the Vatican Museums is dedicated to Greek and Roman art. Exhibits line connecting corridors and vestibules; walls and floors display fine mosaics; and famous sculptures decorate the main courtyards.

The first serious organization of the collection took place in the reign of Julius II (1503–13) around Bramante's Belvedere Courtyard. The prize pieces form the nucleus of the 18th-century Pio-Clementine Museum. In the pavilions of the Octagonal Courtyard and in the surrounding rooms are sculptures considered among the greatest achievements of Western art. The *Apoxyomenos* (an athlete wiping his body after a race) and the *Apollo del Belvedere* are high-quality Roman copies of Greek originals of about 320 BC. The magnificent *Laocoön*, sculpted by three artists from Rhodes, had long been known to exist from a description by Pliny the Elder. It was rediscovered near the ruins of the Domus Aurea *(see p177)* in 1506. Classical works such as these had a profound influence on Michelangelo and other Renaissance artists.

The much smaller Chiaramonti Museum, named after Pope Pius VII Chiaramonti, was laid out by Canova in the early 19th century. It includes a striking colossal head of the goddess Athene. The Braccio Nuovo, an extension of the Chiaramonti, decorated with Roman floor mosaics, contains a statue of Augustus from the villa of his wife Livia at Prima Porta. Its pose is based on the famous *Doryphoros* by the Greek sculptor Polyclitus, of which there is a Roman copy on display opposite.

Exhibits in the Vase Rooms range from the Greek geometric style (8th century BC) to black-figure vases from Corinth, such as the famous vase by Exekias, with Achilles and Ajax playing a game similar to draughts (530 BC), and the later red-figure type, such as the *kylix* (a wide shallow cup) with Oedipus and the Sphinx from the 5th century BC. A stairway links this section to the Gallery of the Candelabra and the Room of the Biga (a two-horse chariot). The horses and harness were added in the 18th century.

The Gregorian Profane Museum charts the evolution of Roman art from

dependence upon Greek models to a recognizably Roman style. Original Greek works include large marble fragments from the Parthenon in Athens. There is also a Roman copy of *Athene and Marsyas* by Myron, which was part of the decoration of the Parthenon. Totally Roman in character are two reliefs known as the *Rilievi della Cancelleria*, because they were discovered beneath the Palazzo della Cancelleria *(see p151)* in the 1930s. They show military parades of the Emperor Vespasian and his son Domitian. This section also has fine Roman floor mosaics. There are two from the Baths of Caracalla *(see p199)*, depicting athletes and referees. They date from the 3rd century AD. Most striking of all is a mosaic that creates the impression of an unswept floor, covered with debris after a meal.

Away from the main Classical collections, in one of the rooms of the Vatican Library, is the *Aldobrandini Wedding*, a beautiful Roman fresco of a bride being prepared for her marriage, dating from the 1st century AD.

The *Doryphoros* or spear-carrier, a Roman copy in marble of an original Greek bronze

Floor mosaic from the Baths of Otricoli in Umbria, in the Chiaramonti Museum

Detail from Giotto's *Stefaneschi Triptych*

Early Christian and Medieval Art

The main collection of early Christian antiquities is in the Pio-Christian Museum, founded in the last century by Pope Pius IX and formerly housed in the Lateran Palace. It contains inscriptions and sculpture from catacombs and early Christian basilicas. The sculpture consists chiefly of reliefs decorating sarcophagi, though the most striking work is a freestanding 4th-century statue of the *Good Shepherd*. The sculpture's chief interest lies in the way it blends Biblical episodes with pagan mythology. Christianity adopted Classical images so that its doctrines could be understood in clear visual terms. The idealized pastoral figure of the shepherd, for example, became Christ himself, while bearded philosophers turned into the Apostles. At the same time, Christianity laid its claim as the spiritual and cultural heir of the Roman Empire.

The first two rooms of the Pinacoteca are dedicated to late medieval art, mostly tempera-painted wooden panels that served as altarpieces. The outstanding work is Giotto's altarpiece dating from about 1300, known as the *Stefaneschi Triptych*. It expresses much the same theme as the early Christian works: the continuity between the Classical world of the Roman Empire and the new order of Christian Europe. The crucifixion of St. Peter takes place between two landmarks of ancient Rome, the Pyramid of Caius Cestius *(see p207)*, and the pyramid known in the Middle Ages as the Tomb of Romulus, which stood near the Vatican. The triptych, which decorated the main altar of old St. Peter's, includes portraits of Pope St. Celestine V (reigned 1294), and of the donor, Cardinal Jacopo Stefaneschi, shown offering the triptych to St. Peter.

The Vatican Library has a number of medieval treasures exhibited rather haphazardly in showcases; these include woven and embroidered cloths, reliquaries, enamels, and icons. One of the aims of the 18th-century reorganization of the Vatican collections was to glorify Christian works by contrasting them with earlier pagan creations. In the long Lapidary Gallery over 3,000 stone tablets with Christian and pagan inscriptions are displayed on opposite walls. The world's greatest collection of its kind, it may be visited only with special permission.

15th- to 19th-Century Art

The Renaissance popes, many of whom were cultured connoisseurs of the arts, considered it their duty to sponsor the leading painters, sculptors, and goldsmiths of the

Pietà by the Venetian artist Giovanni Bellini (1430–1516)

Raphael's Last Painting

When Raphael died in 1520, the *Transfiguration* was found in his studio, almost complete. The wonderful luminous work was placed at the head of the bier where the great artist's body lay. It depicts the episode in the Gospels in which Christ took three of the Apostles to the top of a mountain, where he appeared to them in divine glory. In the detail shown here, Christ floats above the ground in a halo of ethereal light.

age. The galleries around the Cortile del Belvedere were all decorated by great artists between the 16th and the 19th centuries. The Gallery of Tapestries is hung with tapestries woven in Brussels to designs by students of Raphael; the Apartment of Pope Pius V has beautiful 15th-century Flemish tapestries; and the Gallery of Maps is frescoed with 16th-century maps of ancient and contemporary Italy. When you go to visit the Raphael Rooms *(see pp240–41)*, you should not overlook the nearby Room of the Chiaroscuri and Pope Nicholas V's tiny private chapel, frescoed by Fra Angelico between 1447, and 1451. Similarly, before reaching the Sistine Chapel *(see pp242–5)*, visit the Borgia Apartment, frescoed in a decorative, flowery style by Pinturicchio and his students in the 1490s. The contrast with Michelangelo's Sistine Chapel ceiling, begun in 1508, could hardly be greater. Another set of fascinating frescoes decorates the Loggia of Raphael, but this requires special permission to visit.

Many important works by Renaissance masters are on display in the Pinacoteca (art gallery). Highlights among the works by 15th-century painters are a fine *Pietà* by the Venetian Giovanni Bellini, and Leonardo da Vinci's unfinished *St. Jerome*. Of the great 16th-century works, do not miss the fine altarpiece by Titian, the *Crucifixion of St. Peter* by Guido Reni, the *Deposition* by Caravaggio, and the *Communion of St. Jerome* by Domenichino. Raphael has a whole room dedicated to his work. It contains the beautiful *Madonna of Foligno* and the *Transfiguration* as well as eight tapestries made to his designs.

Lunette of the *Adoration of the Magi* by Pinturicchio in the Room of the Mysteries in the Borgia Apartment

Modern Religious Art

Modern artists exhibited in the Vatican Museums face daunting competition from the great works of the past. Few modern works are displayed conspicuously, the exceptions being Momo's spiral staircase of 1932, which greets visitors as they enter the museums, and Giò Pomodoro's abstract sculpture in the center of the Cortile della Pigna.

In 1973 a contemporary art collection was inaugurated by Pope Paul VI. Housed in the Borgia Apartment, it includes over 800 exhibits by modern artists from all over the world, donated by collectors or the artists themselves. Works in a great variety of media show many contrasting approaches to religious subjects. There are paintings, drawings, engravings and sculpture by 19th- and 20th-century artists, as well as mosaics, stained glass, ceramics, and tapestries. Well-known modern painters such as Georges Braque, Paul Klee, Edvard Munch, and Graham Sutherland are all represented. There are also drawings by Henry Moore, ceramics by Picasso, and stained glass by Fernand Léger. Projects for modern church ornaments include Matisse's decorations for the church of St. Paul de Vence, Luigi Fontana's models for the bronze doors of Milan cathedral, and Emilio Greco's panels for the doors of Orvieto cathedral.

Town with Gothic Cathedral by Paul Klee (1879–1940)

Raphael Rooms

Pope Julius II's private apartments were built above those of his hated predecessor, Alexander VI, one of the Borgias, who died in 1503. Julius was impressed with Raphael's work, and chose him to redecorate the four rooms (stanze). Raphael and his pupils began the task in 1508, replacing existing

Detail from *The Expulsion of Heliodorus from the Temple*, showing Pope Julius II watching the scene from his litter

works by several better-known artists, including Raphael's own teacher, Perugino. The work took over 16 years and Raphael himself died before its completion. The frescoes express the religious and philosophical ideals of the Renaissance. They quickly established Raphael's reputation as an artist in Rome, putting him on a par with Michelangelo, then working on the ceiling of the Sistine Chapel.

Cortile del Belvedere

Key to Floorplan
① Hall of Constantine
② Room of Heliodorus
③ Room of the Segnatura
④ Room of *The Fire in the Borgo*

① Hall of Constantine

The frescoes in this room were started in 1517, three years before Raphael's death, but Raphael himself probably had little hand in their execution. As a result they are not held in the same high regard as those in the other rooms. The work was completed in 1525 in the reign of Pope Clement VII by Giulio Romano, and two other former pupils of Raphael, Giovanni Francesco Penni, and Raffaellino del Colle.

The theme of the decoration is the triumph of Christianity over paganism. The four major frescoes show scenes from the life of Constantine, and include his *Vision of the Cross*, and his victory over his rival Maxentius at *The Battle of the Milvian Bridge*, for which Raphael had provided a preparatory sketch. In both *The Baptism of Constantine* and *The Donation of Constantine*, the figure of Pope Sylvester (see p172) was given the features of Clement VII.

② Room of Heliodorus

This private antechamber was decorated by Raphael between 1512 and 1514. The main frescoes show the miraculous protection granted to all the Church's ministers, doctrines, and property. The room's name refers to the fresco on the right, *The Expulsion of Heliodorus from the Temple*. This shows a story from Jewish history, in which a thief called Heliodorus is felled by a horseman as he tries

Swiss guards waiting with papal chair in *The Mass at Bolsena*

to make off with the treasure from the Temple of Jerusalem. The scene is witnessed by the pope, borne on a litter by courtiers. The incident is also a thinly veiled reference to Julius II's success in driving foreign armies out of Italy. In *The Meeting of Leo I and Attila* Raphael pays a similar compliment to the pope's political skill. Pope Leo was originally given the face of Julius II, but after his death, Raphael substituted the features of Julius's successor, Leo X.

The Mass at Bolsena depicts a miracle that occurred in 1263. A priest who doubted that the

The Battle of the Milvian Bridge, completed by one of Raphael's assistants

The Liberation of St Peter, a three-part composition, shows the saint asleep in his cell in the middle section, led out of prison by an angel on the right, while, on the left, the prison guards cower in terror.

The most famous, *The Fire in the Borgo*, was painted from Raphael's designs, and reflects his maturity as an artist. It celebrates the miracle that took place in 847, when Pope Leo IV extinguished a fire raging in the Borgo *(see p248)* by making the sign of the cross. The incident is likened to the flight of Aeneas from Troy described by Virgil. The figure of Aeneas appears in the foreground carrying his father on his back. This borrowing of an event from Classical legend shows a new willingness to experiment on the part of Raphael. Sadly, his pupils did not always follow his designs faithfully and this, combined with some poor restoration, has spoilt the work.

bread, and wine really were the body and blood of Christ suddenly saw the host bleed while he was celebrating mass. Julius II appears in this fresco, accompanied by a colorful group of Swiss guards.

Julius appears yet again as St Peter in *The Liberation of St Peter*. This fresco is remarkable for its dramatic lighting effects, achieved despite the painting's awkward shape and its position above a window.

truth between Greek philosophers Plato and Aristotle. It also features portraits of many of Raphael's contemporaries, including Leonardo da Vinci, Bramante and Michelangelo. The other works include a portrait of the bearded Pope Julius II, who in 1511 vowed not to shave until he managed to rid Italy of all usurpers.

③ Room of the Segnatura

The name is derived from a special council which met in this room to sign official documents. The frescoes here were completed between 1508 and 1511. The scheme Raphael followed was dictated by Pope Julius II. It reflects the Humanist belief that there could be perfect harmony between Classical culture and Christianity in their mutual search for truth.

The Dispute over the Holy Sacrament, the first fresco completed by Raphael for Pope Julius, represents the triumph of religion, and spiritual truth. The consecrated host is shown at the center of the painting. This links the group of learned scholars, who discuss its significance, to the Holy Trinity, and the saints floating on clouds up above.

On the opposite wall, *The School of Athens (see p34)* is a bustling scene centered around the debate on the search for

④ Room of *The Fire in the Borgo*

This was originally the dining room, but when the decoration was completed under Pope Leo X, it became a music room. All the frescoes exalt the reigning pope by depicting events in the lives of his namesakes, the 9th-century popes Leo III and IV. The main frescoes were finished by two of Raphael's assistants between 1514, and 1517, following their master's own plans.

Detail from *The Fire in the Borgo*, showing Aeneas, the Trojan hero, with his father on his back, fleeing from the fire

The Dispute over the Holy Sacrament, the first fresco completed in the Raphael Rooms

Sistine Chapel: The Walls

The massive walls of the Sistine Chapel, the main chapel in the Vatican Palace, were frescoed by some of the finest artists of the 15th and 16th centuries. The 12 paintings on the side walls, by artists including Perugino, Ghirlandaio, Botticelli, and Signorelli, show parallel episodes from the lives of Moses and Christ. The decoration of the chapel walls was completed between 1534 and 1541 by Michelangelo, who added the great altar wall fresco, *The Last Judgment*.

Key to the Frescoes: Artists and Subjects

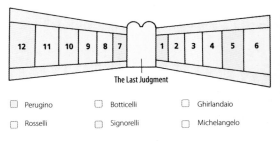

The Last Judgment

☐ Perugino   ☐ Botticelli   ☐ Ghirlandaio

☐ Rosselli   ☐ Signorelli   ☐ Michelangelo

1 Baptism of Christ in the Jordan
2 Temptations of Christ
3 Calling of St. Peter and St. Andrew
4 Sermon on the Mount
5 Handing Over the Keys to St. Peter
6 Last Supper

7 Moses's Journey into Egypt
8 Moses Receiving the Call
9 Crossing of the Red Sea
10 Adoration of the Golden Calf
11 Punishment of the Rebels
12 Last Days of Moses

The Last Judgment by Michelangelo

Revealed in 1993 after a year's restoration, *The Last Judgment* is considered to be the masterpiece of Michelangelo's mature years. It was commissioned by Pope Paul III Farnese, and required the removal of earlier frescoes and two windows over the altar. A new wall was erected that slanted inward to stop dust from settling on it. Michelangelo worked alone on the fresco for seven years, until its completion in 1541.

The painting depicts the souls of the dead rising up to face the wrath of God, a subject that is rarely used for an altar decoration. The pope chose it as a warning to Catholics to adhere to their faith in the turmoil of the Reformation. In fact, the work conveys the artist's own tormented attitude to his faith. It offers neither the certainties of Christian orthodoxy nor the ordered view of Classicism.

In a dynamic, emotional composition, the figures are caught in a vortex of motion. The dead are torn from their graves and hauled up to face Christ the Judge, whose athletic, muscular figure is the focus of all the painting's movement. Christ shows little sympathy for the agitated saints around him, clutching the instruments of their martyrdom. Neither is any pity shown for the damned, hurled down to the demons in hell. Here, Charon, pushing people off his boat into the depths of Hades, and the infernal judge Minos, are taken from Dante's *Inferno*. Minos has ass's ears, and is a portrait of courtier Biagio da Cesena, who had objected to the nude figures in the fresco. Michelangelo's self-portrait is on the skin held by the martyr St. Bartholomew.

Souls meeting the wrath of Christ in Michelangelo's *Last Judgment*

Wall Frescoes

Detail from Botticelli's fresco *Temptations of Christ*

When the Sistine Chapel was built, the papacy was a strong political power with vast accumulated wealth. In 1475 Pope Sixtus IV was able to summon some of the greatest painters of his day to decorate the chapel. Among the artists employed were Perugino, who was Raphael's master and is often credited with overseeing the project; Sandro Botticelli; Domenico Ghirlandaio; Cosimo Rosselli; and Luca Signorelli. Their work on the chapel's frescoes took from 1481 to 1483.

Although frequently overlooked by visitors who concentrate on Michelangelo's work, the frescoes along the side walls of the chapel include some of the finest works of 15th-century Italian art. The two cycles of frescoes represent scenes from the lives of Moses and Christ. Above them in the spaces between the windows are portraits of the earliest popes, painted by various artists, including Botticelli.

The fresco cycles start at the altar end of the chapel, with the story of Christ on the right-hand wall and that of Moses on the left. Originally there were two paintings, *The Birth of Christ* and *The Finding of Moses*, on the wall behind the altar, but these were both destroyed to make way for Michelangelo's *Last Judgment*. The final paintings of the two

cycles are also lost. They were on the entrance wall, which collapsed during the 16th century. When the wall was restored, they were replaced with poor substitutes.

As was customary at the time, each fresco contains a series of scenes, linked thematically to the central episode. Hidden meanings and symbols connect each painting with its counterpart on the opposite wall, and there are also many allusions to contemporary events.

The elaborate architectural details in the frescoes include familiar Roman monuments. The Arch of Constantine *(see p93)* provides the backdrop for the *Punishment of the Rebels* by Botticelli, the fifth panel in the cycle of Moses, in which the artist himself appears as the second-last figure on the right. Two similar arches appear in the painting opposite, Perugino's *Handing Over the Keys to St. Peter.*

Moses was both spiritual and temporal leader of his people. He called down the wrath of God on those who challenged his decisions, thus setting a precedent for the power

The crowd of onlookers in the *Calling of St. Peter and St. Andrew* by Ghirlandaio

exercised by the pope. In *Handing Over the Keys to St. Peter*, Christ confers spiritual and

temporal authority on St. Peter by giving him the keys to the kingdoms of Heaven and Earth. The golden-domed building in the center of the vast piazza represents both the Temple of Jerusalem and the Church, as founded by Peter, the first pope. The fifth figure on the right is thought to be a self-portrait by Perugino.

The central episode in Botticelli's *Punishment of the Rebels*

Botticelli's *Temptations of Christ* includes a view of the Hospital of Santo Spirito, rebuilt in 1475 by Sixtus IV *(see p246)*. Here the devil is disguised in the habit of a Franciscan monk. Portraits of both Botticelli and Filippino Lippi are visible in the left hand corner. A portrait of the pope's nephew, Girolamo Riario, appears in the painting of the *Crossing of the Red Sea* by Rosselli, in which the sea is literally red. This painting also commemorates the papal victory at Campomorto in 1482.

Perugino's *Handing Over the Keys to St. Peter*

Sistine Chapel: The Ceiling

Michelangelo frescoed the ceiling for Pope Julius II between 1508 and 1512, working on specially designed scaffolding. The main panels, which chart the Creation of the World and Fall of Man, are surrounded by subjects from the Old and New Testaments – except for the Classical Sibyls, who are said to have foreseen the birth of Christ. In the 1980s the ceiling was restored, revealing colors of an unsuspected vibrancy.

Libyan Sibyl
The pagan prophetess reaches for the Book of Knowledge. Like most female figures Michelangelo painted, the beautiful Libyan Sibyl was probably modeled on a man.

Creation of the Sun and Moon
Michelangelo depicts God as a dynamic but terrifying figure commanding the sun to shed light on the earth.

KEY

① **Illusionistic architecture**

② **The lunettes** are devoted to frescoes of the ancestors of Christ, like Hezekiah.

③ **The Ignudi** are athletic male nudes whose significance is uncertain.

Key to Ceiling Panels

Genesis: 1 God Dividing Light from Darkness; **2** Creation of the Sun and Moon; **3** Separating Waters from Land; **4** Creation of Adam; **5** Creation of Eve; **6** Original Sin; **7** Sacrifice of Noah; **8** The Deluge; **9** Drunkenness of Noah.

Ancestors of Christ: 10 Solomon with Mother; **11** Parents of Jesse; **12** Rehoboam with Mother; **13** Asa with Parents; **14** Uzziah with Parents; **15** Hezekiah with Parents; **16** Zerubbabel with Parents; **17** Josiah with Parents.

Prophets: 18 Jonah; **19** Jeremiah; **20** Daniel; **21** Ezekiel; **22** Isaiah; **23** Joel; **24** Zechariah.

Sibyls: 25 Libyan Sibyl; **26** Persian Sibyl; **27** Cumaean Sibyl; **28** Erythrean Sibyl; **29** Delphic Sibyl.

**Old Testament Scenes of Salvation
30** Punishment of Haman; **31** Moses and the Brazen Serpent; **32** David and Goliath; **33** Judith and Holofernes.

Original Sin
This shows Adam and Eve tasting the forbidden fruit from the Tree of Knowledge, and their expulsion from Paradise. Michelangelo represents Satan as a snake with the body of a woman.

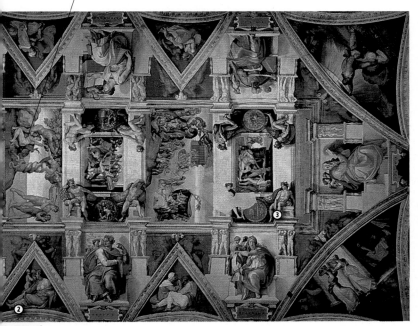

Restoration of the Sistine Ceiling

Restorers used computers, photography, and spectral analysis to inspect the fresco before cleaning began. They were therefore able to detect and remove the changes previous restorers had made to Michelangelo's original work. Analysis showed that the ceiling had been cleaned with materials ranging from bread to retsina wine. The restoration then revealed the familiarly dusky, eggshell-cracked figures to have creamy skins and lustrous hair and to be dressed in brightly colored, luscious robes: "a Benetton Michelangelo," mocked one critic, claiming that a layer of varnish that the artist had added to darken the colors had been removed. However, after examining the work, most experts agreed that the new colors probably matched those painted by Michelangelo.

A restorer cleaning the Libyan Sibyl

❸ Porta Santo Spirito

Via dei Penitenzieri. **Map** 3 C3. 🚌 23, 34, 46, 62, 64, 98, 870, 881, 982.

This gate is situated at what was the southern limit of the "Leonine City," the area enclosed within walls by Pope Leo IV as a defense against the Saracens, who had sacked Rome in AD 845. The walls measure 2 miles (3 km) in circumference.

Work on the walls started in AD 846. Pope Leo personally supervised the army of laborers, and thanks to his encouragement, the job was completed in 4 years. He then consecrated his massive feat of construction.

Since the time of Pope Leo, the walls have needed much reinforcement and repair. The gateway visible today at Porta Santo Spirito was built by the architect Antonio da Sangallo the Younger in 1543–4. It is framed by two huge bastions that were added in 1564 by Pope Pius IV Medici. Sangallo's design for a monumental entrance to the Vatican was never completed; the principal columns come to an end abruptly in a modern covering of cement.

Nave of Santo Spirito in Sassia

❹ Santo Spirito in Sassia

Via dei Penitenzieri 12. **Map** 3 C3. **Tel** 06-687 9310. 🚌 23, 34, 46, 62, 64, 98, 870, 881, 982. **Open** 7:30am–noon (9:30am–1pm Sun), 3–7:30pm daily. 🔔 ♿

Sixtus V's arms over door of Santo Spirito

Built on the site of a church erected by King Ine of Wessex, who died in Rome in the 8th century, the church is the work of Antonio da Sangallo the Younger. It was rebuilt (1538–44) after the Sack of Rome left it in ruins in 1527.

The facade was added under Pope Sixtus V (1585–90). The nave and side chapels are decorated with a series of light, lively frescoes. The pretty bell tower is earlier, dating from the reign of Sixtus IV (1471–84). It was probably the work of the pope's architect, Baccio Pontelli, who also built the Hospital of Santo Spirito, and the Ponte Sisto *(see p212)* farther down the Tiber River.

❺ Hospital of Santo Spirito

Borgo Santo Spirito 2. **Map** 3 C3. 🚌 23, 34, 46, 62, 64. Complex & chapel: **Open** for tours; call 06-6821 0854. 📷

The oldest hospital in Rome, this is said to have been founded as a result of a nightmare experienced by Pope Innocent III (1198–1216). In the dream, an angel showed him the bodies of Rome's unwanted babies dredged up from the Tiber River in fishing nets. As a result, the pope hastened to build a hospice for sick paupers. In 1475 the hospital was reorganized by

Fresco of an angel in the octagonal chapel of the Hospital of Santo Spirito

Pope Sixtus IV to care for the poor pilgrims expected for the Holy Year. Sixtus's hospital was a radical building. Cloisters divided the different types of patients; one area is still reserved for orphans, and their nurses.

Unwanted infants were passed through a revolving barrel-like contraption called the *rota*, still visible to the left of the central entrance in Borgo Santo Spirito, to guarantee anonymity. Martin Luther, who visited in 1511, was shocked by the number of abandoned children he saw, believing them to be "the sons of the pope himself."

In the center, under the hospital's conspicuous drum, is an octagonal chapel, where mass was said for patients. This room can be visited while the rest of the building still functions as a hospital.

Rusticated doorway of the Palazzo dei Convertendi

The *rota* of Santo Spirito, where mothers left unwanted babies

❻ Palazzo del Commendatore

Borgo Santo Spirito 3. **Map** 3 C3.
🚌 23, 34, 46, 62, 64. **Closed** for restoration; call 06-6821 0854 for information.

As director of the Hospital of Santo Spirito, the Commendatore not only oversaw the running of the hospital, he was also responsible for its estates and revenues. This important post was originally given to members of the pope's family.

The palazzo, built next door to the hospital, has a spacious 16th-century frescoed loggia appropriate to the dignity and sobriety of its owners. The frescoes represent the story of the founding of the Hospital of Santo Spirito. To the left of the entrance is the Spezieria, or Pharmacy. This still has the wheel used for grinding the bark of the cinchona tree to produce the drug quinine, first introduced here in 1632 by Jesuits from Peru as a cure for malaria.

Above the courtyard is a splendid clock (1827). The dial is divided into six; it was not until 1846 that the familiar division of the day into two periods of 12 hours was introduced in Rome by Pope Pius IX.

Della Rovere arms

❼ Palazzo dei Convertendi

Via della Conciliazione 43. **Map** 3 C3.
🚌 23, 34, 62, 64. **Closed** to the public.

With the building of Via della Conciliazione in the 1930s, Palazzo dei Convertendi was taken down and later moved to this new site nearby. The house, partly attributed to the architect Bramante, is where the artist Raphael died in 1520.

❾ Palazzo dei Penitenzieri

Via della Conciliazione 33. **Map** 3 C3.
Tel 06-682 8121. 🚌 23, 34, 62, 64.
Open by appt (call first, then fax 06-6880 2298 or email: gmag@oessh.va). 🖼 (donation) for groups.

The palazzo owes its name to the fact that the place was once home to the confessors (*penitenzieri*) of St. Peter's. Now partly housing the Hotel Columbus, it was originally built by Cardinal Domenico della Rovere in 1480. The palazzo still bears the family's coat of arms, the oak tree (*rovere* means oak), on its graceful courtyard wellhead. On the cardinal's death, the palazzo was acquired by Cardinal Francesco Alidosi, Pope Julius II della Rovere's favorite. Suspected of treason, the cardinal was murdered in 1511 by the pope's nephew, the Duke of Urbino, who took over the palazzo. A few of the rooms of the palazzo still contain beautiful frescoes.

View of the Tiber and the Borgo between Castel Sant'Angelo and St. Peter's by Gaspare Vanvitelli (1653–1736)

❾ Santa Maria in Traspontina

Via della Conciliazione 14. **Map** 3 C3.
Tel 06-6880 6451. 🚌 23, 34, 62, 64.
Open 7:30am–noon, 4:30–7pm daily.
🚻 ♿

The church occupies the site of an ancient Roman pyramid, believed in the Middle Ages to have been the Tomb of Romulus. The pyramid was destroyed by Pope Alexander VI Borgia, but representations of it survive in the bronze doors at the entrance to St. Peter's and in a Giotto triptych housed in the Vatican Pinacoteca (see p238).

The present church was begun in 1566 to replace an earlier one that had been in the line of fire of the cannons defending Castel Sant'Angelo during the Sack of Rome in 1527. The papal artillery officers insisted that the dome of the new church should be as low as possible, so it was built without a supporting drum. The first chapel to the right is dedicated to the gunners' patron saint, Santa Barbara, and is decorated with warlike motifs. In the third chapel on the left are two columns, popularly thought to be the ones that saints Peter and Paul were bound to before going to their martyrdom nearby.

The facade of the Carmelite church of Santa Maria in Traspontina

❿ The Borgo

Map 3 C3. 🚌 23, 34, 40, 62.

The Borgo's name derives from the German *burg*, meaning town. Rome's Borgo is where the first pilgrims to St. Peter's were housed in hostels, and hospices, often for quite lengthy periods. The first of these foreign colonies, called "schools," was founded in AD 725 by a Saxon, King Ine of Wessex, who wished to live a life of penance and to be buried near the Tomb of St. Peter. These days, hotels, and hostels have made the Borgo a colony of international pilgrims once again. Much of the area's character was lost after redevelopment in the 1930s, but it is still enjoyable to stroll the old narrow streets on either side of Via della Conciliazione.

Clement VII, who used the Vatican Corridor to evade capture in 1527

⓫ Vatican Corridor

Castel Sant'Angelo to the Vatican.
Map 3 C3. 🚌 23, 34, 40, 62. **Closed** to the public.

Locally known as the Passetto (small corridor), this long passageway was built into the fortifications during medieval times. Intended as a link between the Vatican, and the fortress of Castel Sant'Angelo, it constituted a fortified escape route that could also be used to control the strategic Borgo area. Arrows and other missiles could be fired from its bastions onto the streets, and houses below. The corridor was used in 1494 by Pope Alexander VI Borgia when Rome was invaded by King Charles VIII of France. In 1527 it enabled Pope Clement VII to take refuge in Castel Sant'Angelo, as the troops commanded by the Constable of Bourbon began the Sack of Rome.

⑫ Palazzo Torlonia

Via della Conciliazione 30. **Map** 3 C3.
🚌 23, 34, 40, 62, 64. **Closed** to the public.

The palazzo was built in the late 15th century by the wealthy Cardinal Adriano Castellesi, in a style closely resembling Palazzo della Cancelleria (see p151). The cardinal was a much-traveled rogue who collected vast revenues from the bishopric of Bath, and Wells, which he was given by his friend King Henry VII of

Palazzo Torlonia (1496), unaffected by changes to the surrounding area

Pope Leo X

England. In return, he gave Henry his palazzo for use as the seat of the English ambassador to the Holy See. Castellesi was finally stripped of his cardinalate by Pope Leo X Medici, and disappeared from history.

Since then, the palazzo has had many owners and tenants. In the 17th century it was rented for a time by Queen Christina of Sweden. The Torlonia family, who acquired the building in 1820, owed its fortune to the financial genius of shopkeeper-turned-banker Giovanni Torlonia. He lent money to the impoverished Roman nobility and bought up their property during the Napoleonic Wars.

⑬ Castel Sant'Angelo

See pp250–51.

⑭ Palazzo di Giustizia

Piazza Cavour. **Map** 4 E3. 🚌 34, 49, 70, 87, 186, 280, 492, 913, 926, 990. **Closed** to the public.

The monumental Palazzo di Giustizia (Palace of Justice) was built between 1889 and 1910 to house the national law courts.

Its riverside facade is crowned with a bronze chariot and fronted by giant statues of the great men of Italian law.

The building was supposed to embody the new order replacing the injustices of papal rule, but it has never endeared itself to the Romans. It was soon dubbed the Palazzaccio (roughly, "the ugly old palazzo") both for its appearance and for the nature of its business. By the 1970s the building was collapsing under its own weight, but it has now been restored.

The ornate travertine facade of the Palazzo di Giustizia

⓭ Castel Sant'Angelo

The massive fortress of Castel Sant'Angelo takes its name from the vision that Pope Gregory the Great had of the Archangel Michael on this site. It began life in AD 139 as Emperor Hadrian's mausoleum. Since then, it has had many roles: as part of Emperor Aurelian's city wall, as a medieval citadel and prison, and as the residence of the popes in times of political unrest. From the dank cells in the lower levels to the fine apartments of the Renaissance popes above, a 58-room museum covers all aspects of the castle's history.

Mausoleum of Hadrian
This artist's impression shows the tomb before Aurelian fortified its walls in AD 270–75.

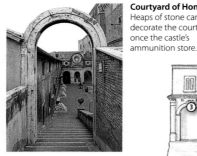

Courtyard of Honor
Heaps of stone cannonballs decorate the courtyard, once the castle's ammunition store.

KEY

① **The spiral ramp** was the entrance to the mausoleum.

② **The Rooms of Clement VIII** are inscribed with the family crest of the Aldobrandini pope (1592–1605).

③ **Loggia of Paul III**

④ **Hall of the Library**

⑤ **Hall of the Columns**

⑥ **The Treasury** was probably the original site of Hadrian's burial chamber.

⑦ **The Round Hall** houses the original model from which Verschaffelt's angel was cast.

⑧ **The Hall of Justice** is decorated with a fresco of *The Angel of Justice* by Domenico Zaga (1545).

⑨ **Hall of Apollo** The room is frescoed with scenes from mythology attributed to the pupils of Perin del Vaga (1548).

⑩ **Ventilation shaft**

⑪ **Bridge**

⑫ **The Chamber of the Urns** housed the ashes of members of Hadrian's family

★ **View from Terrace**
The castle's terrace, scene of the last act of Puccini's *Tosca*, offers splendid views in every direction.

Protecting the Pope

The Vatican Corridor leads from the Vatican Palace to Castel Sant'Angelo. It was built in 1277 to provide an escape route when the pope was in danger. The pentagonal ramparts built around the castle during the 17th century improved its defenses in times of siege.

▨ Walls and fortifications
☐ Vatican Corridor

Bronze Angel
The gigantic statue of the Archangel Michael is by the 18th-century Flemish sculptor Pieter Verschaffelt.

★ Sala Paolina
The illusionistic frescoes by Perin del Vaga and Pellegrino Tibaldi (1546–8) include one of a courtier entering the room through a painted door.

★ Staircase of Alexander VI
This staircase cuts right through the heart of the building.

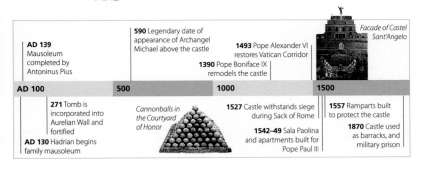

AD 139 Mausoleum completed by Antoninus Pius

590 Legendary date of appearance of Archangel Michael above the castle

1493 Pope Alexander VI restores Vatican Corridor

1390 Pope Boniface IX remodels the castle

Facade of Castel Sant'Angelo

AD 100 | **500** | **1000** | **1500**

271 Tomb is incorporated into Aurelian Wall and fortified
AD 130 Hadrian begins family mausoleum

Cannonballs in the Courtyard of Honor

1527 Castle withstands siege during Sack of Rome
1542–49 Sala Paolina and apartments built for Pope Paul III

1557 Ramparts built to protect the castle
1870 Castle used as barracks, and military prison

VIA VENETO

In Imperial Rome, this was a suburb where rich families owned luxurious villas and gardens. Ruins from this era can be seen in the excavations in Piazza Sallustio, named after the most extensive gardens in the area, the Horti Sallustiani. After the Sack of Rome in the 5th century, the area reverted to open countryside. Not until the 17th century did it recover its lost splendor, with the building of Palazzo Barberini and the now-vanished Villa Ludovisi. When Rome became capital of Italy in 1870, the Ludovisi sold their land for development. They kept a lot for a new house, but tax on the profits from the sale was so high, they had to sell that too. By 1900, Via Veneto had become a street of stylish modern hotels and cafés. It featured prominently in Fellini's 1960 film *La Dolce Vita*, a scathing satire on the lives of movie stars and the idle rich, but since then has lost its position as the meeting place of the famous.

Sights at a Glance

Churches and Temples
❸ Santa Maria della Concezione
❼ Santa Susanna
❽ Santa Maria della Vittoria

Historic Buildings
❷ Casino dell'Aurora
❻ Palazzo Barberini

Famous Streets
❶ Via Veneto

Fountains
❹ Fontana delle Api
❺ Fontana del Tritone

See also Street Finder map 5

Restaurants
see pp315–17

1 Edoardo
2 Filippo La Mantia
3 Harry's Bar
4 La Terrazza
5 L'Olimpo
6 Mirabelle
7 Papà Baccus
8 San Marco

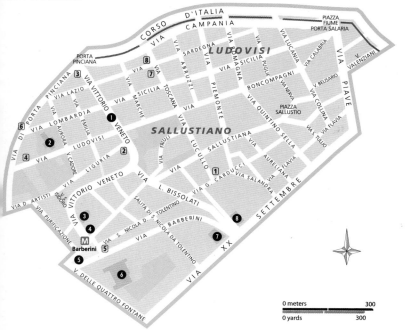

0 meters 300
0 yards 300

◀ The magnificent interior of Santa Maria della Vittoria

For map symbols *see back flap*

Street by Street: Via Veneto

The streets around Via Veneto, though within the walls of ancient Rome, contain little dating from before the unification of Italy in 1870. With its hotels, restaurants, bars, and travel agencies, the area is the center of 21st-century tourism in the way that Piazza di Spagna was the hub of the tourist trade in the Rome of the 18th-century Grand Tour. However, glimpses of the old city can be seen among the modern streets. These include Santa Maria della Concezione, the church of the Capuchin friars, whose convent once stood in its own gardens. In the 17th century, Palazzo Barberini was built here for the powerful papal family. Bernini's Fontana del Tritone and Fontana delle Api have stood in Piazza Barberini since it was the meeting place of cart tracks entering the city from surrounding vineyards.

❸ Santa Maria della Concezione
This church is best known for the macabre collection of bones in its crypt.

❹ Fontana delle Api
Bernini's drinking fountain is decorated with bees, emblem of his Barberini patrons.

Barberini station

PIAZZA BARBERINI

VIA VENETO

VIA DI SAN BA

VIA DI SAN NICOLA DA TOLENTINO

VIA BARBERINI

❺ Fontana del Tritone
Bernini's muscular sea god has been spouting water skyward for 350 years.

❻ ★ Palazzo Barberini
Pietro da Cortona worked on his spectacular ceiling fresco *The Triumph of Divine Providence* between 1633 and 1639.

VIA XX SETTEMBRE

The Porta Pinciana was built in AD 403. Only the central arch of white travertine is original.

Locator Map
See Central Rome Map pp16–17

② Casino dell'Aurora
A pavilion is all that remains of the great Ludovisi estate that once occupied most of this quarter of Rome.

① Via Veneto
Built during the redevelopment of Rome at the end of the 19th century, this street of chichotels and spacious sidewalk cafés enjoyed its heyday during the 1950s and 1960s.

Key

Suggested route

0 meters 75
0 yards 75

⑦ Santa Susanna
This church is dedicated to a martyr executed during Diocletian's persecution of Christians in the 3rd century AD.

⑧ ★ Santa Maria della Vittoria
The highlight of this Baroque church is the Cornaro Chapel, designed to resemble a theater. The center of the stage is occupied by Bernini's thrilling sculpture of *The Ecstasy of St. Teresa.*

Sidewalk café in Via Veneto

❶ Via Veneto

Map 5 B1. 🚌 52, 53, 63, 80, 116, 119, 160 and many routes to Piazza Barberini. Ⓜ Barberini.

Via Veneto descends in a lazy curve from the Porta Pinciana to Piazza Barberini, lined in its upper reaches with exuberant late 19th-century hotels and canopied sidewalk cafés. It was laid out in 1879 over a large estate sold by the Ludovisi family in the great building boom of Rome's first years as capital of Italy. Palazzo Margherita, intended to be the new Ludovisi family palazzo, was completed in 1890. It now houses the American embassy.

In the 1960s this was the most glamorous street in Rome, its cafés patronized by movie stars and plagued by the paparazzi. Most of the people drinking in the cafés today are tourists, since celebrities now seem to prefer the livelier bohemian atmosphere of Trastevere.

❷ Casino dell'Aurora

Via Lombardia 46. **Map** 5 B2. **Tel** 06-8346 7000. 🚌 52, 53, 63, 80, 116, 119. Ⓜ Barberini. **Open** First day of every month (except Jan) 10am–noon, 3–5pm or by appt. Call above number, then email: aurorapallavicini@saita.it.

The Casino (a stately country residence) was a summer-house on the grounds of the Ludovisi Palace. It was built by Cardinal Ludovisi in the 17th century, and frescoed by Guido Reni. The ceiling fresco makes it seem as if the Casino has no roof, but lies open to a cloudy sky, across which horses pull the carriage of Aurora, the goddess of dawn, from darkness toward light.

❸ Santa Maria della Concezione

Via Veneto 27. **Map** 5 B2. **Tel** 06-487 1185. 🚌 52, 53, 61, 62, 63, 80, 116, 119, 175. Ⓜ Barberini. **Open** 7am–noon, 3–7pm daily. Crypt: **Open** 9am–7pm daily. **Closed** some religious holidays. 🚫 🎟

Pope Urban VIII's brother, Antonio Barberini was a cardinal and a Capuchin friar. In 1626 he founded this plain, unassuming church at what is now the foot of the Via Veneto. When he died he was buried not in a grand marble sarcophagus, like most cardinals, but below a simple flagstone near the altar, with the bleak epitaph in Latin: "Here lies dust, ashes, nothing."

The grim reality of death is illustrated even more graphically in the crypt beneath the church, where generations of Capuchin friars decorated the walls of the five vaulted chapels with the bones and skulls of their departed brethren. In all, some 4,000 skeletons were used over about 100 years to create this macabre *memento mori* started in the late 17th century. Some of the bones are wired together to form Christian symbols such as crowns of thorns, sacred hearts, and crucifixes. There are also some complete skeletons, including one of a Barberini princess who died as a child. At the exit, an inscription in Latin reads: "What you are, we used to be. What we are, you will be."

❹ Fontana delle Api

Piazza Barberini. **Map** 5 B2. 🚌 52, 53, 61, 62, 63, 80, 116, 119, 175. Ⓜ Barberini.

The fountain of the bees – *api* are bees, symbol of the Barberini family – is one of Bernini's more modest works. Tucked away in a corner of Piazza Barberini, it is quite easy to miss. Dating from 1644, it pays homage to Pope Urban VIII Barberini, and features rather crablike bees that appear to be sipping the water as it dribbles down into the basin. A Latin inscription informs us that the water is for the use of the public and their animals.

Bernini's Fontana delle Api

❺ Fontana del Tritone

Piazza Barberini. **Map** 5 B3. 🚌 52, 53, 61, 62, 63, 80, 116, 119, 175. Ⓜ Barberini.

In the center of busy Piazza Barberini is one of Bernini's liveliest creations, the Triton Fountain. It was created for Pope Urban VIII Barberini in 1642, shortly after the completion of his palace on the ridge above. Acrobatic dolphins stand on their heads, twisting their tails

Pope Urban VIII

The Triton and his conch shell in Bernini's Fontana del Tritone

together to support a huge scallop shell on which the sea god Triton kneels, blowing a spindly column of water up into the air through a conch shell. Entwined artistically among the dolphins' tails are the papal tiara, the keys of St. Peter, and the Barberini coat of arms.

❻ Palazzo Barberini

Via delle Quattro Fontane 13. **Map** 5 B3. **Tel** 06-482 4184. 🚌 52, 53, 61, 62, 63, 80, 116, 175, 492, 590. Ⓜ Barberini. **Open** 8:30am–7pm Tue–Sun (last adm: 6pm). **Closed** Jan 1, Dec 25. 🚫 📷 📹 🎧 🔊 ♿ ✉ 🅆 **galleriaborghese.it**

When Maffei Barberini became Pope Urban VIII in 1623, he decided to build a grand palace for his family on the fringes of the city, overlooking a ruined temple. The architect, Carlo Maderno, designed it as a typical rural villa, with wings extending into the surrounding gardens. Maderno died in 1629 and Bernini took over, assisted by Borromini. The peculiar pediments on some of the top floor windows, and the oval staircase inside, are almost certainly by Borromini.

Of the many sumptuously decorated rooms, the most striking is the Gran Salone, with a dazzling illusionistic ceiling fresco by Pietro da Cortona. The palazzo also houses paintings from the 13th to the 16th centuries, part of the Galleria Nazionale d'Arte Antica, with important works by Filippo Lippi, El Greco, and Caravaggio. There is also a Holbein portrait of King Henry VIII of England dressed for his wedding to Anne of Cleves. Of greater local significance are Guido Reni's *Beatrice Cenci*, the young woman executed for planning her father's murder *(see p154)*, and *La Fornarina*, traditionally identified as a portrait of Raphael's mistress *(see p212)*, although not necessarily painted by him.

Facade of Santa Susanna

❼ Santa Susanna

Via XX Settembre 14. **Map** 5 C2. **Tel** 06-4201 4554. 🚌 60, 61, 62, 84, 175, 492, 910. Ⓜ Repubblica. **Open** 9am–noon, 4–7pm daily (to 5:30pm Sun). ✝

Santa Susanna's most striking feature is its vigorous Baroque facade by Carlo Maderno, finished in 1603. Christians have worshiped on the site since at least the 4th century. In the nave, there are four huge frescoes by Baldassarre Croce (1558–1628), painted to resemble tapestries. These depict scenes from the life of Susanna, an obscure Roman saint who was martyred here, and the rather better-known life of the Old Testament Susanna, who was spotted bathing in her husband's garden by two lecherous judges.

Santa Susanna is the Catholic church for Americans in Rome and holds services in English every day.

❽ Santa Maria della Vittoria

Via XX Settembre 17. **Map** 5 C2. **Tel** 06-4274 0571. 🚌 60, 61, 62, 84, 492, 910. Ⓜ Repubblica. **Open** 9am–noon, 3:30–6:30pm daily. ✝ ✉

Santa Maria della Vittoria is an intimate Baroque church with a lavishly decorated candlelit interior. It contains one of Bernini's most ambitious sculptural works, *The Ecstasy of St. Teresa* (1646), centerpiece of the Cornaro Chapel, built to resemble a miniature theater. It even has an audience: sculptures of the chapel's benefactor, Cardinal Federico Cornaro, and his ancestors sit in boxes, as if watching and discussing the scene occurring in front of them.

Visitors may be shocked or thrilled by the apparently physical nature of St. Teresa's ecstasy. She lies on a cloud, her mouth half open, and her eyelids closed, with rippling drapery covering her body. Looking over her with a smile, which from different angles can appear either tender or cruel, is a curly-haired angel holding an arrow with which he is about to pierce the saint's body for a second time. The marble figures are framed and illuminated by rays of divine light materialized in bronze.

Bernini's astonishing *Ecstasy of St. Teresa*

FARTHER AFIELD

The more inquisitive visitor to Rome may wish to try a few excursions to the large parks and some of the more isolated churches on the outskirts of the city. With a day to spare, you can explore the villas of Tivoli and the ruins of the ancient Roman port of Ostia. Traditional haunts of the Grand Tour *(see p132)*, such as the catacombs, and the ruined aqueducts of Parco Appio Claudio, still offer glimpses of the rapidly vanishing Campagna, the countryside around Rome. More modern sights include the suburb of EUR, built in the Fascist era, and the memorial at the Fosse Ardeatine.

Sights at a Glance

Towns and Areas
- ⑮ EUR
- ⑲ Tivoli

Historic Roads
- ⑨ Via Appia Antica

Churches
- ⑥ Santa Costanza
- ⑦ Sant'Agnese fuori le Mura
- ⑧ San Lorenzo fuori le Mura
- ⑯ San Paolo fuori le Mura

Museums and Galleries
- ② Museo e Galleria Borghese pp262–3

- ③ Villa Giulia pp264–5
- ④ MAXXI
- ⑤ Museo di Arte Contemporanea di Roma
- ⑰ Centrale Montemartini

Ancient Sites
- ㉒ Hadrian's Villa
- ㉓ Ostia Antica

Parks and Gardens
- ① Villa Borghese
- ⑱ Villa Doria Pamphilj

- ⑳ Villa d'Este
- ㉑ Villa Gregoriana

Tombs and Catacombs
- ⑩ Catacombs of San Callisto
- ⑪ Catacombs of San Sebastiano
- ⑫ Catacombs of Domitilla
- ⑬ Fosse Ardeatine
- ⑭ Tomb of Cecilia Metella

Key

- Main sightseeing areas
- Freeway
- Main road
- Train line

0 kilometers 2
0 miles 1

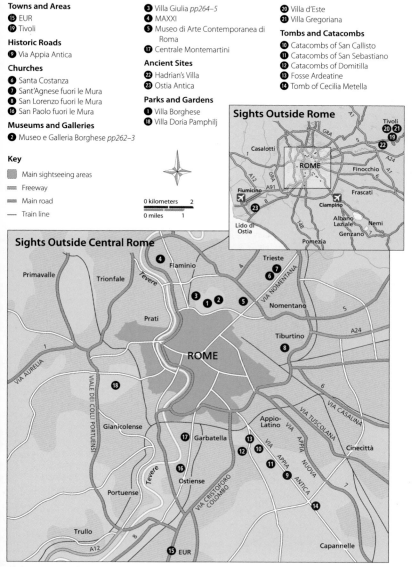

Sights Outside Rome

Sights Outside Central Rome

ROME

◄ A picturesque waterfall in the grounds of Villa d'Este

For map symbols *see back flap*

❶ Villa Borghese

Map 2 E5. ▦ 52, 53, 88, 95, 116, 490, 495. ▦ 3, 19. Park: **Open** dawn to sunset. Bioparco: Viale del Giardino Zoologico 20. **Map** 2 E4. **Tel** 06-360 8211. ▦ 52. ▦ 3, 19. **Open** daily. **Closed** Dec 25. ♿ 🚻 🅿 📷 🅦 **bio parco.it**. Galleria Nazionale d'Arte Moderna: Viale delle Belle Arti 131. **Map** 2 D4. **Tel** 06-3229 8221. ▦ 3, 19. **Open** 8:30am–7:30pm Tue–Sun (last adm: 6:45pm). **Closed** Jan 1, May 1, Dec 25. ♿ 🚻 🚻 🅿 📷 Museo Carlo Bilotti: Viale F. La Guardia. **Map** 2 D5. **Open** Oct–May: 10am–4pm; Jun–Sep: 1–7pm Mon–Fri, 10am–7pm Sat–Sun. **Closed** Jan 1, May 1, Dec 25. 📷 📷

British School at Rome, designed by Edwin Lutyens in 1911

The villa and its park were designed in 1605 for Cardinal Scipione Borghese, nephew of Pope Paul V. The park was the first of its kind in Rome. It contained 400 newly-planted pine trees, garden sculpture by Bernini's father, Pietro, and dramatic waterworks built by Giovanni Fontana. The layout of the formal gardens was imitated by other prominent Roman families at Villa Ludovisi and Villa Doria Pamphilj.

In the early 19th century, Prince Camillo Borghese assembled the family's magnificent art collection in the Casino Borghese, now the home of the Galleria and Museo Borghese.

In 1901 the park became the property of the Italian state. Within its 4-mile (6-km) circumference there are now museums and galleries, foreign academies and schools of archaeology, a zoo, a riding school, a grassy amphitheater, an artificial lake, an aviary, and an array of summer houses, fountains, Neo-Classical statuary, and exotic follies.

There are several ways into the park, including a monumental entrance on Piazzale Flaminio, built for Prince Camillo Borghese in 1825 by Luigi Canina. Other conveniently sited entrances are at Porta Pinciana at the end of Via Veneto and from the Pincio Gardens (see p138). Piazza di Siena, a pleasantly open, grass-covered amphitheater surrounded by tall umbrella pines, was the inspiration for Ottorino Respighi's famous symphonic poem The Pines of Rome, written in 1924. Near Piazza di Siena are the so-called Casina di Raffaello, said to have been owned by Raphael, and the 18th-century Palazzetto dell' Orologio. These were summerhouses from which people enjoyed the beautiful vistas across the park.

Statue of the English poet Byron by Thorvaldsen

Many buildings in the park were originally surrounded by formal gardens: the Casino Borghese and the nearby 17th-century Casino della Meridiana and its aviary (uccelliera) have both kept their geometric flowerbeds. Throughout the park, the intersections of paths, and avenues are marked by fountains, and statues. West of Piazza di Siena is the Fontana dei Cavalli Marini (the Fountain of the Seahorses), added during the villa's 18th-century remodeling. Walking through the park you will encounter statues of Byron, Goethe, and Victor Hugo, and a gloomy equestrian King Umberto I.

Dotted around the park are picturesque temples made to look like ruins, including a circular Temple of Diana between Piazza di Siena, and Porta Pinciana, and a Temple of Faustina, wife of Emperor Antoninus Pius, on the hill north of Piazza di Siena. The nearby medieval-looking Fortezzuola by Canina contains the works of the sculptor Pietro Canonica, who lived in the building, and died there in 1959. In the garden stands Canonica's Monument to the Alpino and his Mule, which honors the humblest protagonists in Italy's alpine battles against Austria in World War I.

Neo-Classical Temple of Diana

Ionic temple dedicated to Aesculapius, built on the lake island

In the center of the park is the Giardino del Lago, its main entrance marked by an 18th-century copy of the Arch of Septimius Severus. The garden has an artificial lake complete with an Ionic temple to Aesculapius, the god of healing, by the 18th-century architect Antonio Asprucci. Rowboats, and ducks make the lake a favorite with children, banana trees, and bamboo grow around the shore, and clearings are studded with sculptures.

Surrounded by flowerbeds south of the lake is the Art Nouveau Fontana dei Fauni, one of the garden's prettiest sculptures. In a clearing close to the entrance on Viale Pietro Canonica are the original Tritons of the Fontana del Moro in Piazza Navona (see p122) – they were moved here and replaced by copies in the 19th century.

From the northwest, the park is entered by the Viale delle Belle Arti, where the Galleria Nazionale d'Arte Moderna houses a good collection of 19th- and 20th-century paintings. The Art Nouveau character of the area dates from the International Exhibition held here in 1911, for which pavilions were built by many nations, the most impressive being Edwin Lutyens' British School at Rome, with a facade adapted from the upper west portico of St. Paul's Cathedral in London. It is now a research institute for Classical studies, history, and the visual arts. Nearby statues include one of Simón Bolívar, and other liberators of Latin America.

In the northeastern corner of the park lie the Museo Zoologico and a small zoo, the Bioparco, where the emphasis is on conservation. Nearby, the pretty 16th-century Villa Giulia houses a world-famous collection of Etruscan and other pre-Roman remains. Another Renaissance building of importance is the Palazzina of Pius IV, designed by the architect Vignola in 1552. It now houses the Italian embassy to the Holy See.

Named after its principal benefactor, the Museo Carlo Bilotti is situated in the center of the Villa Borghese. This former orangery has been transformed into a modern art gallery boasting works by Giorgio de Chirico, Andy Warhol, and Gino Severini.

❷ Museo e Galleria Borghese

See pp262–3.

❸ Villa Giulia

See pp264–5.

❹ MAXXI (National Museum of 21st Century Arts)

Via Guido Reni 4A. **Map** 1 A2. **Tel** 06-3996 7350. 🚊 53, 217, 225, 910. 🚋 2. **Open** 11am–7pm Tue–Sun (to 10pm Sat). **Closed** May 1, Dec 25. ♿ 🚻 🖥 📷 🖼 (free up to age 14). 📷 🌐 **fondazionemaxxi.it**

Along with the nearby Parco della Musica (see p350), MAXXI, the National Museum of 21st Century Arts, has put Rome on the contemporary arts map. Located in a stunning building designed by architect Zaha Hadid, it showcases emerging Italian, and international artists. An impressive amount of space is also dedicated to architecture.

MAXXI, the National Museum of 21st Century Arts, designed by Zaha Hadid

❷ Museo e Galleria Borghese

The villa and park were laid out by Cardinal Scipione Borghese, favorite nephew of Paul V, who had the house designed for pleasure, and entertainment. The hedonistic cardinal was also an extravagant patron of the arts, and he commissioned sculptures from the young Bernini that now rank among his most famous works. Scipione also opened his pleasure park to the public. Today the villa houses the superb private Borghese collection of sculptures, and paintings in the Museo and Galleria Borghese.

Facade of the Villa Borghese
This painting (1613) by the villa's Flemish architect Jan van Santen shows the highly ornate facade of the original design.

Rear entrance

Sleeping Hermaphrodite
This is a marble Roman copy of the Greek original by Polycles, dated around 150 BC. The head and mattress were added by Andrea Bergondi in the 17th century.

★ **Rape of Proserpine**
One of Bernini's finest works shows Pluto (Hades) abducting his bride. The sculptor's amazing skill with marble can be seen clearly in the twisting figures.

The Egyptian Room
Frescoes show episodes in Egyptian history and Egyptian motifs.

Gladiator Mosaic
The floor is decorated with the fragments of a 4th-century AD mosaic from a villa in Torrenova.

1613 15-year-old Bernini sculpts *Aeneas and Anchises*	**Early 1800s** Statues, and reliefs are considered too ornate and stripped from the villa's facade	**1902** Villa, grounds, and collection bought by the state
1622–25 Bernini sculpts *The Rape of Proserpine*		**1809** Much of the collection is sold by Prince Camillo Borghese to France and goes to Louvre
1610	**1710**	**1810**
1622–25 Bernini sculpts *Apollo and Daphne*	**1805** Canova sculpts the seminude, reclining Pauline Borghese	
1613–15 The Flemish architect Jan van Santen designs, and builds Villa Borghese	*Daphne's fingers turning into leaves*	**Early 1900s** Balustrade around the forecourt is bought by Lord Astor for the Cliveden estate in England

★ Apollo and Daphne

Bernini's most famous masterpiece depicts the nymph Daphne fleeing the sun god Apollo at the moment of Daphne's dramatic transformation into a tree.

★ Galleria Borghese

The gallery has Old Master paintings, such as Titian's *Sacred and Profane Love* (detail) dating from 1514.

★ Pauline Borghese

Napoleon's sister Pauline posed as Venus for this sculpture. Once the statue was finished, her husband locked it away, even from its sculptor Canova.

Front entrance

Key to Floor plan

☐ Exhibition space
▨ Non-exhibition space

Museum Guide

The museum is divided into two sections: the sculpture collection (Museo Borghese) occupies the entire ground floor and the picture gallery (Galleria Borghese) is on the upper floor. The museum also hosts wonderful temporary exhibitions.

David

This sculpture, by Bernini (1624), captures the moment just before David attacks Goliath with a rock. Bernini modeled David's face on his own.

❸ Villa Giulia

This villa was built as a country retreat for Pope Julius III, and was designed for entertaining rather than as a permanent home. It once housed an impressive collection of statues – 160 boatloads were sent to the Vatican after the pope died in 1555. The villa, gardens, pavilions, and fountains were designed by exceptional architects: Vignola (designer of the Gesù), Vasari, and the sculptor Ammannati. Michelangelo also contributed. The villa's main features are its facade, the courtyard, and garden, and the *nymphaeum*. Since 1889 Villa Giulia has housed the Museo Nazionale Etrusco, with its outstanding collection of pre-Roman antiquities from central Italy.

★ Ficoroni Cist
Engraved and beautifully illustrated, this fine bronze marriage coffer dates from the 4th century BC.

★ Sarcophagus of the Spouses
This 6th-century BC masterpiece, from Cerveteri, shows a dead couple at the eternal banquet.

Votive Offering
The religious Etruscans made artifacts, such as this model of a boy feeding a bird, in their gods' honor.

Museum Guide

This is the most important Etruscan museum in Italy, housing artifacts from most of the major excavations in Tuscany and Lazio. Rooms 1–13b and 31–37 are arranged by site and include Vulci, Todi, Veio, and Cerveteri, while private collections are in rooms 14–24.

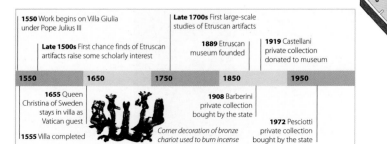

1550	1650	1750	1850	1950

1550 Work begins on Villa Giulia under Pope Julius III

Late 1500s First chance finds of Etruscan artifacts raise some scholarly interest

Late 1700s First large-scale studies of Etruscan artifacts

1889 Etruscan museum founded

1919 Castellani private collection donated to museum

1655 Queen Christina of Sweden stays in villa as Vatican guest

1555 Villa completed

Corner decoration of bronze chariot used to burn incense

1908 Barberini private collection bought by the state

1972 Pesciotti private collection bought by the state

Facade
The villa's facade dates from 1551. The entrance is designed in the form of a triumphal arch.

VISITORS' CHECKLIST

Practical Information
Piazzale di Villa Giulia 9.
Map 1 C4.
Tel 06-322 6571.
Open 8:30am–7:30pm Tue–Sun (last adm: 6:30pm).
Closed Jan 1, Dec 25. 🅿️ 🎟️ with seven days' notice. 🏛️ 🛍️ 📷 ♿ 📧 It is also possible to visit the museum's additional collections at the nearby Villa Poniatowski, 9am–1:45pm Tue–Sat.

Transportation
🚌 52, 926 to Viale Bruno Buozzi, 88, 95, 490, 495 to Viale Washington. 🚊 3, 19 to Piazza Thorwaldsen.

Chigi Vase
Battle and hunting scenes adorn this Corinthian vase from the 6th century BC.

Faliscan Crater of the Dawn
This ornate vase, painted in the free style of the 4th century BC, shows Dawn rising in a chariot.

★ Reconstruction of an Etruscan Temple
Count Adolfo Cozza built the Temple of Alatri here in 1891. He based his design on the accounts of Vitruvius and 19th-century excavations.

Main entrance

Key to Floor plan
- ▢ Lower ground floor
- ▢ Ground floor
- ▣ First floor
- ▢ Non-exhibition space

Nymphaeum
Literally, the "area dedicated to the nymphs," this is a sunken courtyard decorated with Classical mosaics, statues, and fountains.

❺ Museo di Arte Contemporanea di Roma

Via Cagliari (corner Via Nizza). **Map** 6 E1. **Tel** 06-671 070 400. ▣ 36, 60, 84, 90. **Open** 11am–7pm Tue–Sun (until 10pm Sat) Also at: Piazza Giustiniani 4 (Testaccio). **Map** 7 C4. ▣ 23, 95, 280, 719. **Open** for exhibitions 4–10pm Tue–Sun. ▣ ▣ ▣ ▣ **macro. roma.museum**

The historic Peroni beer factory is now home to the MACRO gallery of contemporary art. Apart from a permanent collection of late 20th-century art, featuring artists such as Carla Accardi and Mario Schifano, there are interesting exhibitions – both here and at the Testaccio outpost – showcasing the latest on the local, and national scene.

Interior of Santa Costanza

❻ Santa Costanza

Via Nomentana 349. **Tel** 06-861 0840. ▣ 36, 60, 84, 90. Ⓜ Annibaliano. **Open** 9am–noon, 4–6pm Mon–Sat; 4–6pm Sun. ▣ ▣ ▣

The round church of Santa Costanza was first built as a mausoleum for Emperor Constantine's daughters Constantia and Helena, in the early 4th century. The dome and its drum are supported by a circular arcade resting on 12 magnificent pairs of granite columns. The ambulatory that runs around the outside of the

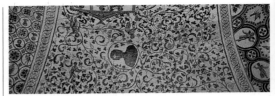

Part of the 4th-century mosaic in the ambulatory of Santa Costanza

central arcade has a barrel-vaulted ceiling decorated with wonderful 4th-century mosaics of flora and fauna and charming scenes of a Roman grape harvest. In a niche on the far side of the church from the entrance is a replica of Constantia's ornately carved porphyry sarcophagus. The original was moved to the Vatican Museums in 1790.

Constantia's sanctity is debatable – she was described by the historian Marcellinus as fury incarnate, constantly goading her equally unpleasant husband Hannibalianus to violence. Her canonization was probably the result of some confusion with a saintly nun of the same name.

❼ Sant'Agnese fuori le Mura

Via Nomentana 349. **Tel** 06-861 0840. ▣ 36, 60, 84, 90. Ⓜ Annibaliano. **Open** 7:30am–noon, 4–7:45pm daily. ▣ to catacombs. ▣ ▣

The church of Sant'Agnese stands among a group of early Christian buildings that includes the ruins of a covered cemetery, some

extensive catacombs, and the crypt where the 13-year-old martyr St. Agnes was buried in AD 304. Agnes was exposed naked by order of Emperor Diocletian, furious that she should have rejected the advances of a young man at his court, but her hair miraculously grew to protect her modesty (see p123).

The church is said to have been built at the request of the Emperor Constantine's daughter, Constantia, after she had prayed at the Tomb of St. Agnes for delivery from leprosy.

Though much altered over the centuries, the form, and much of the structure of the 4th-century basilica remain intact. In the 7th-century apse mosaic St. Agnes appears as a bejeweled Byzantine empress in a stole of gold, and a violet robe. According to tradition, she appeared like this eight days after her death holding a white lamb. Every year on January 21, two lambs are blessed on the church altar, and a vestment called the *pallium* is woven from their wool. Every newly appointed archbishop is sent a *pallium* by the pope.

Apse mosaic in Sant'Agnese, showing the saint flanked by two popes

Cloister, San Lorenzo fuori le Mura

❽ San Lorenzo fuori le Mura

Piazzale del Verano 3. **Tel** 06-49 15 11.
71, 492. 3, 19. **Open** 7:30am–
noon, 4–7pm daily.

Just outside the eastern wall of the city stands the church of San Lorenzo. Roasted slowly to death in AD 258, San Lorenzo was one of the most revered of Rome's early Christian martyrs. The first basilica erected over his burial place by Constantine was largely rebuilt in 576 by Pope Pelagius II. Close by stood a 5th-century church dedicated to the Virgin Mary. The intriguing two-level church we see today is the result of these two churches being merged into one. This process, started in the 8th century, was completed in the 13th century by Pope Honorius III, when the nave, the portico, and much of the decoration were added. The remains of San Lorenzo are in the choir of the 6th-century church (beneath the 13th-century high altar).

Romanesque bell tower of San Lorenzo

❾ Via Appia Antica

118, 218. **W** parcoappiaantica.it
See Walks pp286–7.

The first part of the Via Appia was built in 312 BC by the Censor Appius Claudius Caecus. When it was extended to the ports of Benevento, Taranto, and Brindisi in 190 BC, the road became Rome's link with its expanding empire in the East. It was the route taken by the funeral processions of the dictator Sulla (78 BC) and Emperor Augustus (AD 14) and it was along this road that St. Paul was led a prisoner to Rome in AD 56. Gradually abandoned during the Middle Ages, the road was restored by Pope Pius IV in the mid-16th century. It is lined with ruined family tombs and collective burial places known as columbaria. Beneath the fields on either side lies a vast maze of catacombs. Today the road starts at Porta San Sebastiano (see p198). Major Christian sights include the church of Domine Quo Vadis, built where St. Peter is said to have met Christ while fleeing from Rome, and the Catacombs of San Callisto and San Sebastiano. The tombs lining the road include those of Cecilia Metella (see p268) and Romulus (son of Emperor Maxentius) who died in 309. The ancient Villa dei Quintilli is nearby, at Via Appia Nuova 1092 (phone 06-3996 7700).

❿ Catacombs of San Callisto

Via Appia Antica 126. **Tel** 06-5130 151.
118, 218. **Open** 9am–noon,
2–5pm Thu–Tue. **Closed** Jan 1, late
Jan–late Feb, Easter Sun & Dec 25.
W catacombe.roma.it

In burying their dead in underground cemeteries outside the city walls, the early Christians were obeying the laws of the time: it was not because of persecution. So many saints were buried that the catacombs became shrines and places of pilgrimage.

The vast Catacombs of San Callisto are on four different levels and only partly explored. The rooms and connecting passageways are hewn out of volcanic tufa. The dead were placed in niches, known as *loculi*, which held two or three bodies. The most important rooms were decorated with stucco and frescoes. The area that can be visited includes the Crypt of the Popes, where many of the early popes were buried, and the Crypt of Santa Cecilia, where the saint's body was discovered in 820 before being moved to her church in Trastevere (see p213).

⓫ Catacombs of San Sebastiano

Via Appia Antica 136. **Tel** 06-785 0350.
118, 218. **Open** 10am–4:30pm
Mon–Sat. **Closed** Jan 1, late Nov–late
Dec, Dec 25.
W catacombe.org

The 17th-century church of San Sebastiano, above the catacombs, occupies the site of a basilica. Preserved at the entrance to the catacombs is the *triclia*, a building that once stood above ground, and was used by mourners for taking funeral refreshments. Its walls are covered with graffiti invoking St. Peter and St. Paul, whose remains may have been moved here during one of the periods of persecution.

Cypresses lining part of the Roman Via Appia Antica

⓬ Catacombs of Domitilla

Via delle Sette Chiese 282. **Tel** 06-511 0342. 🚌 218, 716. **Open** 9am–noon, 2–5pm Wed–Mon. **Closed** mid-Dec– mid-Jan, Easter Sun. 🎫 ♿ 📷
ⓦ domitilla.info

This network of catacombs is the largest in Rome. Many of the tombs from the 1st and 2nd centuries AD have no Christian connection. In the burial chambers there are frescoes of both Classical and Christian scenes, including one of the earliest depictions of Christ as the *Good Shepherd*. Above the catacombs stands the basilica of Santi Nereo e Achilleo. After rebuilding and restoration, little remains of the original 4th-century church.

Bronze entrance gates to the Fosse Ardeatine by Mirko Basaldella

⓭ Fosse Ardeatine

Via Ardeatina 174. **Tel** 06-513 6742. 🚌 218, 716. **Open** 8:15am–3:15pm Mon– Fri, 8:15am–4:30pm Sat & Sun. **Closed** public hols.

On the evening of March 24, 1944, Nazi forces took 335 prisoners to this abandoned quarry south of Rome, and shot them at point-blank range. The execution was in reprisal for a bomb attack that had killed 32 German soldiers. The victims included various political prisoners, 73 Jews, and 10 other civilians, among them a priest and a 14-year-old boy. The Germans blew up the tunnels where the massacre had taken place, but a local peasant had witnessed the scene, and later

helped find the corpses. The site is now a memorial to the values of the Resistance against the Nazi occupation, which gave birth to the modern Italian Republic (*see p187*). A forbidding bunker-like monument houses the rows of identical tombs containing the victims.

Beside it is a museum of the Resistance. Interesting works of modern sculpture include *The Martyrs*, by Francesco Coccia, and the gates shaped like a wall of thorns by Mirko Basaldella.

⓮ Tomb of Cecilia Metella

Via Appia Antica, km 3. **Tel** 06-3996 7700. 🚌 118, 660. **Open** 9am–approx 1 hr before sunset Tue–Sun.

One of the most famous landmarks on the Via Appia Antica is the huge tomb built for the noblewoman Cecilia Metella. Her father, and husband were rich patricians, and successful generals of late Republican Rome, but hardly anything is known about the woman herself. Byron muses over her unknown destiny in his poem *Childe Harold*.

In 1302 Pope Boniface VIII donated the tomb to his family, the Caetani. They incorporated it in a fortified castle that blocked the Via Appia, allowing them to control the traffic on the road and exact high tolls. The marble facing of the tomb was pillaged by another pope, Sixtus V, at the end of the 16th century.

On the opposite side of the road stands what remains of the early 14th-century church of San Nicola.

Fragments of marble relief on the Tomb of Cecilia Metella

EUR's Palazzo della Civiltà del Lavoro, the "Square Colosseum"

⓯ EUR

🚌 170, 671, 714 and other routes. Ⓜ EUR Fermi, EUR Palasport. Museo della Civiltà Romana: Piazza G. Agnelli 10. **Tel** 06-5422 0919. **Open** 9am–2pm Tue–Sun; last adm: 1 hr before closing. **Closed** Jan 1, May 1, Dec 25. 🎫

The Esposizione Universale di Roma (EUR), a suburb south of the city, was built for an international exhibition, a kind of "Work Olympics," that was planned for 1942, but never took place because of the war. The architecture was intended to glorify Fascism, and the style of the public buildings is very overblown, and rhetorical. The eerie shape of the Palazzo della Civiltà del Lavoro (The Palace of the Civilization of Work) is an unmistakable landmark for people arriving from Fiumicino airport.

The plan was completed in the 1950s. In terms of town planning, EUR has been quite successful, and people are still eager to live here. The great marble halls house several government offices, and museums.

The Museo della Civiltà Romana displays a vast scale model of Rome at the time of Constantine and casts of the reliefs on Trajan's Column. These, and the interesting planetarium, make the museum worth a visit.

To the south is a lake, and park, and the huge domed Palazzo dello Sport built for the 1960 Olympics.

⓰ San Paolo fuori le Mura

Via Ostiense 186. **Tel** 06-541 0341.
🚌 23, 128, 170, 670, 707, 761, 769.
Ⓜ San Paolo. **Open** 7am–6:30pm daily. Cloister: **Open** 9am–6pm daily.

19th-century mosaic on facade of San Paolo fuori le Mura

Today's church is a faithful reconstruction of the great 4th-century basilica destroyed by fire on July 15, 1823. Few fragments of the original church survived. The triumphal arch over the nave is decorated on one side with restored 5th-century mosaics. On the other side are mosaics by Pietro Cavallini, originally on the facade. The splendid Venetian apse mosaics (1220) depict the figures of Christ with St. Peter, St. Andrew, St. Paul, and St. Luke.

The fine marble canopy over the high altar is signed by the sculptor Arnolfo di Cambio (1285) "together with his partner Pietro," who may have been Pietro Cavallini. Below the altar is the *confessio*, the tomb of St. Paul. To the right is an impressive Paschal candlestick by Nicolò di Angelo and Pietro Vassalletto.

The cloister of San Paolo, with its pairs of colorful inlaid columns supporting the arcade, was spared completely by the fire. Completed around 1214, it is considered one of the most beautiful in Rome.

⓱ Centrale Montemartini

Via Ostiense 106. **Tel** 06-574 8042.
🚌 23, 769. **Open** 9am–7pm Tue–Sun (last adm: 6:30pm). **Closed** Jan 1, May 1, Dec 25.

An enormous old industrial site has been restored to house the ACEA art center. Originally, the building was used as Rome's first power station, and its two huge generators still occupy the central machine room, creating quite an intriguing contrast to the exhibitions. On display are Roman statues and artifacts belonging to the Capitoline Museums *(see pp70–73)*. Many of the statues were discovered during excavations in the late 19th and early 20th centuries, including some from the Area Sacra di Largo Argentina *(see p152)*.

Casino del Bel Respiro, summer residence in Villa Doria Pamphilj

⓲ Villa Doria Pamphilj

Via di San Pancrazio. 🚌 31, 44, 75, 710, 870. Park: **Open** dawn–dusk daily.

One of Rome's largest public parks, the Villa Doria Pamphilj was laid out in the mid-17th century for Prince Camillo Pamphilj. His uncle, Pope Innocent X, paid for the magnificent summer residence, the Casino del Bel Respiro, and the fountains and summer-houses, some of which still survive.

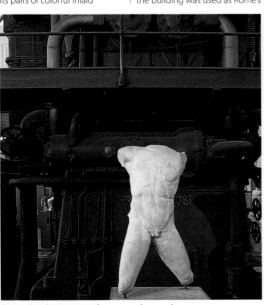

Statue in Centrale Montemartini, former power plant turned art center

Day Trips around Rome

Tivoli, a favorite place to escape the heat of the Roman summer

⑲ Tivoli

Town is 20 miles (31 km) northeast of Rome. FS from Tiburtina. COTRAL from Ponte Mammolo (on Metro line B).

Tivoli has been a popular summer resort since the days of the Roman Republic. Among the famous men who owned villas here were the poets Catullus and Horace, Caesar's assassins Brutus and Cassius, and the Emperors Trajan and Hadrian. Tivoli's main attractions were its clean air and beautiful situation on the slopes of the Tiburtini hills, its healthy sulfur springs, and the waterfalls of the Aniene – the Emperor Augustus said these had cured him of insomnia. The Romans' luxurious lifestyle was revived in Renaissance times by the owners of the Villa d'Este, the town's most famous sight.

In the Middle Ages, Tivoli suffered frequent invasions; its position made it an ideal base for an advance on Rome. In 1461 Pope Pius II built a fortress here, the Rocca Pia, declaring: "It is easier to regain Rome while possessing Tivoli, than to regain Tivoli while possessing Rome." After suffering heavy bomb damage in 1944, Tivoli's main buildings and churches were speedily restored.

The town's cobbled streets are still lined with medieval houses. The Duomo (cathedral) houses a beautiful 13th-century life-size wooden group representing the *Deposition from the Cross*.

⑳ Villa d'Este

Piazza Trento 5, Tivoli. **Tel** 0774-31 2070. COTRAL from Ponte Mammolo (on Metro line B). **Open** 8:30am–approx 1 hr before sunset Tue–Sun. **Closed** Jan 1, Dec 25. 🖼 🖥 W villadestetivoli.info

The villa occupies the site of an old Benedictine convent. In the 16th century the estate was developed by Cardinal Ippolito d'Este, son of Lucrezia Borgia. A palace was designed by Pirro Ligorio to make the most of its hilltop situation, but the villa's fame rests more on the terraced gardens and fountains laid out by Ligorio and Giacomo della Porta.

The gardens have suffered neglect in the past, but the grottoes and fountains still give a vivid impression of the great luxury that the princes of the church enjoyed. From the great loggia of the palace you descend through the privet-lined paths to the Grotto of Diana and Bernini's Fontana del Bicchierone. Below to the right is the Rometta (little Rome), a model of Tiber Island with allegorical

Detail of Fontana dell'Organo at Villa d'Este

figures and the legendary she-wolf. The Rometta is at one end of the Viale delle Cento Fontane, 100 fountains in the shapes of grotesques, obelisks, ships, and the eagles of the d'Este coat of arms. Other fountains are now being restored to their former glory. The Fontana dell'Organo is a water-organ, in which the force of the water pumps air through the pipes. The garden's lowest level has flower beds and fountains as well as some splendid views out over the plain below.

Terrace of 100 Fountains in the gardens of Villa d'Este

㉑ Villa Gregoriana

Largo Sant'Angelo, Tivoli. FS Tivoli, then short walk. **Tel** 06-3996 7701. **Open** 10am–6:30pm Tue–Sun (to 2:30pm Mar, Oct 16–Nov 30). Last adm: 1 hour before close. **Closed** Dec–Feb. 🖼 🏛

The main attractions of this steeply sloping park are the waterfalls and grottoes created by the Aniene River. The park is named after Pope Gregory XVI, who in the 1830s ordered the building of a tunnel to protect against flooding. This tunnel created a new waterfall, called the Grande Cascata, which plunges 525 ft (160 m) into the valley behind the town.

The Canopus, extensively restored, with replicas of its original caryatids lining the canal

㉒ Hadrian's Villa

Villa Adriana, Via Tiburtina. Site is 4 miles (6 km) southwest of Tivoli. **Tel** 0774-38 27 33. **FS** Tivoli, then local bus No. 4. ⬛ COTRAL from Ponte Mammolo (on Metro line B). **Open** 9am–approx 1 hr before sunset daily (last adm: 1 hour before). **Closed** Jan 1 , May 1, Dec 25. ⬛ ⬛ ⬛ ⬛

Built as a private summer retreat between AD 118 and 134, Hadrian's Villa was a vast open-air museum of the finest architecture of the Roman world. The grounds of the Imperial Palace covered an area of 300 acres (120 hectares) and were filled with full-scale reproductions of the emperor's favorite buildings from Greece and Egypt. Although excavations on this site began in the 16th century, many of the ruins lying scattered in the surrounding fields have yet to be identified with any certainty. The grounds of the villa make a very picturesque site for a picnic, with scattered fragments of columns lying among olive trees and cypresses.

For an idea of how the whole complex would have looked in its heyday, study the scale model in the building by the parking lot. The most important buildings are signposted, and several have been partially restored or reconstructed. One of the most impressive is the so-called Maritime Theater. This is a round pool with an island in the middle, surrounded by columns. The island, reached by means of a swing bridge, was

Pair of Ionic columns in the vaulted baths of Hadrian's Villa

probably Hadrian's private studio, where he withdrew from the cares of the Empire to indulge in his two favorite pastimes, painting, and architecture. There were also theaters, Greek, and Latin libraries, two bathhouses, extensive housing for guests, and the palace staff, and formal gardens with fountains, statues, and pools.

Hadrian also loved Greek philosophy. One part of the gardens is thought to have been Hadrian's reproduction of the Grove of Academe, where Plato lectured to his students. He also had a replica made of the Stoà Poikile, a beautiful painted colonnade in Athens, from which the Stoic philosophers took their name. This copy enclosed a great piazza with a central pool. The so-called Hall of the Philosophers close to the Poikile was probably a library.

The most ambitious of Hadrian's replicas was the Canopus, a sanctuary of the god Serapis near Alexandria. For this, a canal 130 yd (119 m) long was dug and Egyptian statues were imported to decorate the temple and its grounds. This impressive piece of engineering has been restored, and the banks of the canal are lined with caryatids.

Another picturesque spot in the grounds is the Vale of Tempe, the legendary haunt of the goddess Diana, with a stream representing the Peneios River. Below ground the emperor even built a fanciful recreation of the underworld, Hades, reached through underground tunnels, of which there were many linking the various parts of the villa.

Plundered by barbarians who camped here in the 6th and 8th centuries, the villa fell into disrepair. Its marble was burned to make lime for cement, and Renaissance antiquarians contributed even further to its destruction. Statues unearthed in the grounds are on display in museums around Europe. The Vatican's Egyptian Collection (see p236) has many fine works that were found here.

㉓ Ostia Antica

Viale dei Romagnoli 717. Site is 16 miles (25 km) southwest of Rome. **Tel** 06-5635 8099. Ⓜ Piramide, then train from Porta San Paolo station. Excavations and museum: **Open** 8.30am–6pm Tue–Sun (to 4pm Nov–Feb, to 5pm Mar). Last adm: 1 hour before close. **Closed** Jan 1, May 1, Dec 25. 🔛 🏛 💻 ♿
Ⓦ ostiantica.info

Ruins of shops, offices, and houses near Ostia's theater

In Republican times, Ostia was Rome's main commercial port and a military base defending the coastline and the mouth of the Tiber. The port continued to flourish under the Empire, despite the development of Portus, a new port slightly to the northwest, in the 2nd century AD. Ostia's decline began in the 4th century, when a reduction in trade was combined with the gradual silting up of the harbor. Then malaria became endemic in the area, and the city, whose population may have been nearly 100,000 at its peak, was totally abandoned.

Buried for centuries by sand, the city is remarkably well preserved. The site is less spectacular than Pompeii or Herculaneum because Ostia died a gradual death, but it gives a more complete picture of life under the Roman Empire. People of all social classes and from all over the Mediterranean lived and worked here.

Visitors can understand the layout of Ostia's streets almost at a glance. The main road through the town, the Decumanus Maximus, would have been filled with hurrying slaves and citizens, avoiding the jostling carriages and carts, while tradesmen pursued their business under the porticoes lining the street. The floorplans of the public buildings along the road are very clear. Many were bathhouses, such as the Baths of the Cisiarii (carters) and the grander Baths of Neptune, named after their fine black-and-white floor mosaics. Beside the theater, three large masks, originally part of the decoration of the stage, have been mounted on large blocks of tufa. Beneath the great brick arches that supported the semicircular tiers of seats were taverns and shops. Classical plays are put on here in the summer.

The Tiber's course has changed considerably since Ostia was the port of Rome. It once flowed past just to the north of Piazzale delle Corporazioni, the square behind the theater. The corporations were the guilds of the various trades involved in equipping and supplying ships: tanners and rope-makers, ship-builders and timber merchants, ships' chandlers, and grain weighers. There were some 60 or 70 offices around the square. Mosaics showing scenes of everyday life in the port and the names, and symbols of the corporations can still be seen. There were also offices used by ship owners and their agents from places as far apart as Tunisia, and southern France, Sardinia, and Egypt. In one office, belonging to a merchant from the town of Sabratha in North Africa, there is a delightful mosaic of an elephant.

The main cargo coming into Rome was grain from Africa. Much of this was distributed free to prevent social unrest. Although only men received this *annona*, or grain dole, at times over 300,000 were eligible. In the center of the square was a temple, probably dedicated to Ceres, goddess of the harvest. Among the

Mask decorating the theater

Mural from Ostia of merchant ship being loaded with grain

buildings excavated are many large warehouses in which grain was stored before it was shipped on to Rome.

The Decumanus leads to the Forum and the city's principal temple, erected by Hadrian in the 2nd century AD, and dedicated to Jove, Juno, and Minerva. In this rather romantic, lonely spot, it is hard to imagine the Forum as a bustling center, where justice was dispensed and officials met to discuss the city's affairs. In the 18th century

Floor mosaic of Nereid and sea monster in the House of the Dioscuri

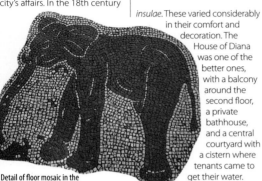

Detail of floor mosaic in the Piazzale delle Corporazioni

it was used as a sheepfold. Away from the main street are the buildings where Ostia's inhabitants lived. The great majority were housed in rented apartments in blocks three or four stories high known as

insulae. These varied considerably in their comfort and decoration. The House of Diana was one of the better ones, with a balcony around the second floor, a private bathhouse, and a central courtyard with a cistern where tenants came to get their water. Around the ground floor of the block were shops, taverns, and bars selling snacks and drinks. In the bar at the House of Diana you can see the marble counter used by customers buying their sausages and hot wine sweetened with honey.

For the wealthy there were detached houses (*domus*) such as the House of the Dioscuri, which has fine mosaics, and the House of Cupid and Psyche, named after a statue there. This is now in the site's Museo Ostiense, near the Forum, along with other sculptures and reliefs found in Ostia.

Among the houses and shops there are other fascinating buildings, including a laundry and the firemen's barracks. The religions practiced in Ostia reflect the cosmopolitan nature of the port. There are also no fewer than 18 temples dedicated to the Persian god Mithras, as well as a Jewish synagogue dating from the 1st century AD, and a Christian basilica. A plaque records the death of St. Augustine's mother in a hotel here in AD 387.

Also Worth Seeing

Anagni FS from Termini (60 min), then local bus (infrequent) or long walk.
Picturesque hill-town with papal palace, and famous cathedral.

Bracciano FS from Ostiense (about 70 min). ▭ from Saxa Rubra, reached by train from Roma Nord (bus 90 min).
Volcanic lake with villages and wooded hills. Nice for walks or a visit to Orsini Castle. Swimming in summer.

Cerveteri FS from Termini, Tiburtina or Ostiense to Cerveteri-Ladispoli, then local bus (70 min). ▭ from Cornelia, on Metro line A (bus 80 min).
One of the greatest Etruscan cities. Necropolis with complete streets, and houses.

Nemi ▭ from Anagnina, on Metro line A (bus 75 min); may need to change at Genzano.
Charming village at volcanic lake in the Castelli Romani. Famous for its wine, and strawberries.

Palestrina ▭ from Anagnina, on Metro line A (bus 70 min).
Impressive Roman sanctuary to goddess Fortuna. Museum, and the Mosaic of the Nile.

Pompeii FS from Termini to Naples, then local train (130 min). ▭ Special tours from tourist agents.
Excavations of the wealthy and bustling Roman city where busy daily life was put to a sudden end by the eruption of Vesuvius in AD 79.

Subiaco ▭ from Ponte Mammolo, on Metro line B (bus about 100 min).

Birthplace of St. Benedict. Two monasteries to visit.

Tarquinia FS from Termini or Ostiense plus local bus (100 min). ▭ from Lepanto, on Metro line A. Change at Civitavecchia (150 min).
Outstanding collection of Etruscan objects and frescoes from Tarquinia's necropolis.

Viterbo FS from Ostiense (115 min) or train from Roma Nord, Piazzale Flaminio, on Metro line A (120 min). ▭ from Saxa Rubra reached by the train above (bus 90 min).
Medieval quarter, papal palace, and archaeological museum within 13th-century walls.

NINE GUIDED WALKS

Rome is an excellent city for walking. The distances between major sights in the historic downtown are easily covered on foot, and many streets are pedestrianized. When you get tired, stop at one of the sidewalk cafés in lovely settings, such as Piazza Navona and Campo de' Fiori. If you are interested in archaeology, then a walk across the Forum *(see pp78–89)*, and over the Palatine *(see pp98–103)* takes you away from the roaring traffic of modern Rome to a different world of scattered ruins and shady pine trees.

The first of the nine suggested walks takes in picturesque quarters on either side of the Tiber. The second walk, along the perfectly straight Via Giulia, gives a vivid impression of the Renaissance city. The next three walks

each follow a particular theme. You can savor the glory of ancient Rome through the triumphal arches of the emperors, tour early Christian churches with well-preserved mosaics, and explore the great contribution of Bernini to the appearance of the city.

The sixth walk is outside the downtown along the best-known of all Roman roads, the Via Appia Antica, parts of which are still intact after more than 2,000 years of use. The seventh walk explores some macabre points of interest, including a park said to be haunted by the Emperor Nero. The next couples Trastevere's atmospheric backstreets with the romantic viewpoints of the Janiculum. Lastly, there is a tour of churches and ancient ruins on, and around the tranquil, leafy Aventine.

Choosing a Walk

The Nine Walks
The routes of eight of the walks are marked on the larger map, which also shows the main sightseeing areas of Rome. The smaller inset map shows the location of the Via Appia walk in relation to the central area.

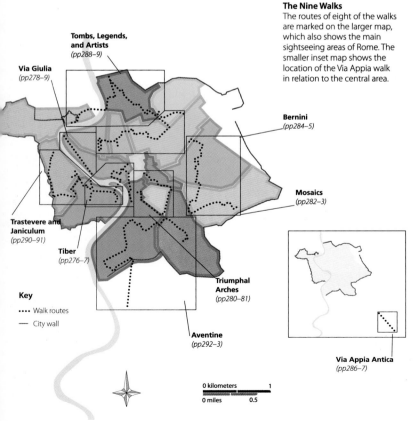

Tombs, Legends, and Artists
(pp288–9)

Via Giulia
(pp278–9)

Bernini
(pp284–5)

Trastevere and Janiculum
(pp290–91)

Tiber
(pp276–7)

Mosaics
(pp282–3)

Triumphal Arches
(pp280–81)

Aventine
(pp292–3)

Via Appia Antica
(pp286–7)

Key

•••• Walk routes

—— City wall

0 kilometers 1
0 miles 0.5

◄ Cobbled street leading to the Pantheon

A Two-Hour Walk by the Tiber River

Rome owes its very existence to the Tiber; the city grew up around an easy fording point where a marketplace developed. The river could also be a hazard; shallow and torrent-like, it flooded the city every winter up to 1870, when work began on the massive Lungotevere embankments that run along both sides of the river. These provide many fine views from points along their avenues of plane trees. The walk also explores the neighborhoods along the riverside, in particular the Jewish Ghetto and Trastevere, which have preserved much of their character from earlier periods in the colorful history of Rome.

From the old port of Rome to Via dei Funari

Starting from the church of Santa Maria in Cosmedin ① *(see p204)*, cross the piazza to the Temples of the Forum Boarium ② *(see p201)*. This was the cattle market that stood near the city's river port. The river here has preserved two less obvious structures from ancient Rome: the mouth of the Cloaca Maxima ③, the city's great sewer, and one arch of a ruined bridge, known as the Ponte Rotto ④. In Via Petroselli stands the rather extraordinary medieval Casa dei Crescenzi ⑤ *(see p201)*, decorated with fragments of Roman temples. Passing the modern Anagrafe (public records office) ⑥, built on the site of the old Roman port, you come to San Nicola in Carcere ⑦ *(see p153)*.

You are now in the Foro Olitorio, Rome's ancient vegetable market. To the east stand the ruins of a Roman portico and the medieval house of the Pierleoni family. Head for the massive Theater of Marcellus

Santa Maria in Cosmedin ①

⑧ *(see p153)*; go and look at the three Corinthian columns of the Temple of Apollo beside it. Turn into Piazza Campitelli and walk up to Santa Maria in Campitelli ⑨ *(see p153)*. The church honors a miraculous image of the Virgin credited with halting the plague in 1656. The 16th-century piazza was the home of Flaminio Ponzio, its architect, who lived at No. 6. Take Via dei Delfini to Piazza Margana, where you should look up at the 14th-century tower of the Margani family ⑩. Retrace your steps, then go up Via dei Funari (Street of the Ropemakers) to the 16th-century facade of Santa Caterina dei Funari ⑪.

The Ghetto

From Piazza Lovatelli take Via Sant'Angelo in Pescheria, which leads to the ruined Portico of Octavia ⑫ *(see p154)* in the Jewish Ghetto *(see p154)*. The Roman portico, once Rome's fish market, houses the church of Sant'Angelo in Pescheria. Find the marble plaque on the facade: fish longer than this slab were given to the city's *conservatori* (governors). Turn into the Ghetto: two column stumps belonging to the Portico stand in front of a patched-up doorway made of fragments of Roman sculpture. The cramped buildings, and streets around Via del Portico

Arch of the Ponte Rotto ④

Main altar of Santa Maria in Campitelli ⑨

d'Ottavia are typical of old Rome: see the Casa di Lorenzo Manilio ⑬ *(see p154)*, and turn down Via del Progresso, past Palazzo Cenci ⑭ *(see p154)*, towards the river. On Lungotevere walk past the Synagogue ⑮ *(see p154)* to the small church of San Gregorio ⑯. Here stood the Ghetto's gates, which were locked at sundown.

Across the river to Trastevere

Crossing to Tiber Island *(see p155)* by Ponte Fabricio, with its two ancient stone heads on the parapet, you can enjoy a

Classical relief of Medusa above the doorway of Palazzo Cenci ⑭

Piscinula, and the surrounding streets retain much of the spirit of old Trastevere. Walk up to the start of Viale di Trastevere at

As you go down Via della Lungaretta to Piazza Santa Maria in Trastevere, don't miss the old-fashioned pharmacy at No. 7. The piazza itself, in front of the magnificent church of Santa Maria in Trastevere ㉒ *(see pp214–15)*, has a cheerful atmosphere, and the fountain steps are a favorite meeting place. Go back a little way to Via del Moro. This leads to Piazza Trilussa, dominated by the fountain of the Acqua Paola ㉓, where you emerge onto the bank of the river again. Note the lifelike statue, near the fountain, of Roman poet Trilussa, who wrote in the local dialect. From Ponte Sisto ㉔ *(see p212)*, look back to Tiber Island and, beyond it, to the medieval bell tower of Santa Maria in Cosmedin, set against the pine trees on the summit of the Palatine.

Fountain of the Acqua Paola ㉓

Tips for Walkers

Starting point: Piazza della Bocca della Verità.
Length: 2 miles (3.5 km).
Getting there: The 23, 44, 81, 160, 280, 628, 715, and 716 buses stop near Santa Maria in Cosmedin.
Best time for walk: This walk can be very romantic in the evening but is enjoyable at any time.
Stopping points: Piazza Campitelli and Piazza Margana have elegant restaurants, and Via del Portico d'Ottavia has many restaurants and a bakery. Tiber Island has a bar and the famous Sora Lella restaurant (see p314). In Viale Trastevere there are bars and pizzerias. Piazza Santa Maria in Trastevere has lively bars, and restaurants with outdoor tables.

Key

• • • Walk route

0 meters — 250
0 yards — 250

good view of the river in both directions. On the island itself, you should not miss the Pierleoni Tower ⑰ or the church of San Bartolomeo all'Isola ⑱.

Trastevere

As you cross into Trastevere, you can see the medieval house of the powerful Mattei family ⑲, with its fragments of ancient sculpture. Beyond it, Piazza in

Piazza Belli. After crossing the road look back at the medieval tower of the Anguillara ⑳ and the statue honoring the poet Gioacchino Belli ㉑ *(see p207)*.

Piazza in Piscinula, old Trastevere

A One-Hour Walk along Via Giulia

Laid out by Bramante for Pope Julius II in the early 16th century, Via Giulia was one of the first Renaissance streets to slice through Rome's jumble of medieval alleys. The original plan included new law courts in a central piazza, but this project was abandoned for lack of cash. The street is now dominated by antique shops and furniture restorers. On summer evenings, hundreds of oil lamps light the street, while cloisters and courtyards provide romantic settings for a special season of concerts.

Baroque capital on the facade of Sant'Eligio degli Orefici ⑦

From Lungotevere to Largo della Moretta

Starting from Lungotevere dei Tebaldi ① at the eastern end of Via Giulia, you will see ahead of you an archway ② spanning the road. This was the start of Michelangelo's unrealized project linking Palazzo Farnese and its gardens (see p149) with the Villa Farnesina (see pp220–21) on the other side of the river.

Just before you reach the archway, you will see to your left the curious Fontana del Mascherone ③, in which an ancient grotesque mask and granite basin were combined to create a Baroque fountain.

Beyond the Farnese archway on the left is the lively Baroque facade of the church of Santa Maria dell'Orazione e Morte ④ (see p149). A bit farther along on the same side of the road stands Palazzo Falconieri ⑤, enlarged by Borromini in 1650. Note its two stone falcons glowering at each other across the width of the facade. On the other side of the road you pass the yellowish facade of Santa Caterina da Siena ⑥, church of the Sienese colony in Rome, which has pretty 18th-century reliefs. The figures of Romulus and Remus

Relief of Romulus and Remus on Santa Caterina da Siena ⑥

symbolize Rome and Siena – there is a legend that the city of Siena was founded by the less fortunate of the twins. After passing the short street that leads down to Sant'Eligio degli Orefici ⑦ (see p150) and the facade of Palazzo Ricci ⑧ (see p151), you come to an area of half-demolished buildings around the ruined church of San Filippo Neri ⑨, called Vicolo della Moretta. If you look to the left down to the river, you can see Ponte

Fontana del Mascherone ③

Mazzini and the huge prison of Regina Coeli on the other side of the Tiber. At this point you may like to make a small detour to the right to the beginning of Via del Pellegrino, where there is an inscription ⑩, defining the *pomerium*, or boundary, of the city in the time of the Emperor Claudius.

From Largo della Moretta to the Sofas of Via Giulia

Farther on, facing the narrow Vicolo del Malpasso, are the imposing prisons, the Carceri

Nuove ⑪, built by Pope Innocent X Pamphilj in 1655. When first opened, they were a model of humane treatment of prisoners, but they were replaced by the Regina Coeli prison across the river at the end of the 19th century. The buildings now house offices of the Ministry of Justice, and a small Museum of Crime.

At the corner of Via del Gonfalone, a small side street running down to the river, you

Key

••• Walk route

| 0 meters | 250 |
| 0 yards | 250 |

Farnese archway across Via Giulia, built to a design by Michelangelo ②

originates from the traditional distribution of bread to the poor that took place on the saint's feast day.

On the corner there are more travertine blocks belonging to the foundations of Julius II's projected law courts, known because of their curious shape as the "Sofas of Via Giulia."

The Florentine Quarter

Your next stop should be the imposing Palazzo Sacchetti at No. 66 ⑮. Originally this was the house of Antonio da Sangallo the Younger, the architect of Palazzo Farnese, but it was greatly enlarged by later owners. The porticoed courtyard houses a 15th-century Madonna and a striking Roman relief of the 3rd century AD. Just opposite Palazzo Sacchetti, note the beautiful late Renaissance portal of Palazzo Donarelli ⑯. The 16th-century house at No. 93 is richly decorated with stuccoes and coats of arms ⑰. No. 85 is another typical Renaissance palazzo with a heavily rusticated ground floor ⑱. There is a tradition that, like

Plaque honoring Antonio da Sangallo on Palazzo Sacchetti ⑮

many houses of the period, it once belonged to Raphael. Palazzo Clarelli ⑲ was built by Antonio da Sangallo the Younger as his own house. The inscription above the doorway bears the name of Duke Cosimo II de' Medici, whose family later bought the palazzo.

This whole area used to be inhabited by a flourishing Florentine colony, which had its own water mills built on pontoons along the Tiber. Their national church is San Giovanni dei Fiorentini ⑳ (see p155), the final great landmark at the end of Via Giulia. Many Florentine artists, and architects had a hand in its design, including Sangallo, and Jacopo Sansovino.

Coat of arms of Pope Paul III Farnese on the facade of Via Giulia No. 93 ⑰

Tips for Walkers

Starting point: Lungotevere dei Tebaldi, by Ponte Sisto.

Length: 1,100 yd (1 km).

Getting there: The 116 goes to and along Via Giulia, or you can take 46, 62, or 64 to Corso Vittorio Emanuele II, then walk down Via dei Pettinari, or take a 23 or 280 along Lungotevere. Best time for walk: On summer evenings, oil lamps often light the street. At Christmas, there are nativity scenes in many shop windows.

Stopping points: There are bars in Via Giulia, at Nos. 18 and 84. Campo de' Fiori has better bars, with outdoor tables, and a wide choice of places to eat. These include a fried fish restaurant in Piazza Santa Barbara dei Librari (closed Sun).

can see part of the foundations of Julius II's planned law courts. Just down the street stands the small Oratorio di Santa Lucia del Gonfalone ⑫, which is often used for concerts.

The next interesting facade is Carlo Rainaldi's 17th-century Santa Maria del Suffragio ⑬ on the left. On the same side is San Biagio degli Armeni ⑭, the Armenian church in Rome. It is often referred to by local people as San Biagio della Pagnotta (of the loaf of bread). The nickname

Detail on the side of the door of Santa Maria del Suffragio ⑬

A 90-Minute Tour of Rome's Triumphal Arches

Rome's greatest gift to architecture was the arch, and the Roman people's highest tribute to its victorious generals was the triumphal arch. In Imperial times, arches were erected to honor an emperor's campaign victories almost as a matter of course, promoting his personal cult and ensuring his subsequent deification. Spectacular processions passed through these arches. Conquering generals, cheered by rapturous crowds, rode in their chariots to the Capitol, accompanied by their legions bearing spoils from their campaigns.

Part of the Via Sacra, once spanned by the Arch of Augustus ③

Relief of barbarian captives on the Arch of Septimius Severus ①

Arches of the Forum

This walk through the Forum and around the base of the Palatine takes in Rome's three great surviving triumphal arches and two arches of more humble design that were used simply as places of business. It starts from the Arch of Emperor Septimius Severus ① and his sons Geta and Caracalla (see p85) in the Forum. Erected in AD 203, it celebrates a successful campaign in the Middle East. Eight years later, when Caracalla had his brother killed, all mention of Geta was removed from the inscription.

Look up at the reliefs showing phases of the campaigns. Set in tiers, they are probably the sculptural counterparts of the paintings illustrating the general's feats that were borne aloft in the triumphal procession. On the right, the inhabitants of a fortified city surrender to the Romans' siege machines. Below are smaller friezes showing the triumphal procession itself.

Heading east, make your way through the Forum to the ruins

of the Temple of Julius Caesar ②. The temple was built by Augustus in 29 BC, on the site where Caesar's body was cremated after Mark Antony's famous funerary oration. A nearby sign marks the ruins of one of the arches dedicated to Augustus ③, spanning the Via Sacra between the Temple of Castor and Pollux ④ (see p86), and the Temple of Caesar. This arch, erected after Augustus had defeated Mark Antony, and Cleopatra, was finally demolished in 1545, and its materials were used in the new St. Peter's. From here, proceed uphill toward the elegant Arch of Titus ⑤ (see p89). Compared with Septimius Severus's arch, it shows an earlier, simpler style. Look up at the beautiful lettering of the inscription before you examine the inner bas-reliefs. These show Roman legionaries carrying the spoils looted from the conquest of Jerusalem, heralds holding plaques with the names of vanquished peoples and cities, and Titus riding in triumph in his chariot.

The medieval Frangipane family turned the Colosseum into a vast impregnable stronghold and incorporated the Arch of Titus into their fortifications. Notice the

Capital from Temple of Castor and Pollux ④

[Map of the area showing walk route with numbered locations including PIAZZA DEL COMPIDOGLIO, VIA DEL TEATRO DI MARCELLO, LUNGOT. PIERLEONI, ISOLA TIBERNA, Ponte Palatino, VIA D. CONSOLAZIONE, V. DEI FIENILI, PIAZZA D. BOCCA DELLA VERITÀ, MON PALAT, PARCO DEL CIRCO MASSIMO, VIA DEI CE]

Key

• • • Walk route

0 meters 250
0 yards 250

wheel marks scratched on the inside walls of the arch by generations of carts; they indicate the steady rise in the level of the Forum floor before it was eventually excavated in the 18th and 19th centuries. Many of the carts that passed through the arch would have been

Arch of Titus in a 19th-century watercolor by the English artist Thomas Hartley Cromek ⑤

hectic battle scenes just above the smaller arches, sculpted in AD 315. In the curious dwarflike soldiers, you can see the transition from Classicism to a cruder medieval style of sculpture.

Now take Via di San Gregorio, which runs the length of the valley between the Palatine and Celian hills. This was the ancient route taken by most triumphal processions. Passing the entrance to the Palatine ⑧ and the well-preserved arches of the Claudian Aqueduct ⑨ on the right, you come to Piazza di Porta Capena ⑩, named after the gate that stood here to

Four-sided Arch of Janus in the Forum Boarium ⑬

take shelter from the sun or rain when discussing business. Like the Arch of Titus, it became part of a fortress built by the Frangipane family during the Middle Ages.

Tucked away beside the nearby church of San Giorgio in Velabro ⑭ (see p204) is what looks like a large rectangular doorway. This is the Arco degli Argentari, or Moneychangers' Arch ⑮. Look up at the inscription, which says that it was erected by local silversmiths in honor of Septimius Severus and his family in AD 204. As in the emperor's triumphal arch, the name of Geta has been obliterated by his brother and murderer, Caracalla. Geta's figure has also been removed from among the portraits on the panels inside the arch. Triumph in Imperial Rome could be very short-lived.

Arches of Domitian's extension to the Claudian Aqueduct ⑨

carrying building materials quarried from the Forum's many ruined monuments.

Arch of Constantine

Leave the Forum by heading down the hill toward the Colosseum ⑥ (see pp94–7) and the nearby Arch of Constantine ⑦ (see p93). This arch, hastily built to commemorate the emperor's victory over his rival Maxentius in AD 312, is a patchwork of reliefs from different periods. Stand on the Via di San Gregorio side and compare the earlier panels at the top (AD 180–193) with the

mark the beginning of the Via Appia (see p286). After rounding the back of the Palatine, follow Via dei Cerchi, which runs alongside the grassy area that preserves, in an oval outline, all that remains of the Circus Maximus ⑪ (see p207).

Arches of the Forum Boarium

When you reach the church of Sant'Anastasia ⑫, turn right up Via di San Teodoro, then first left down Via del Velabro. Straddling the street is the four-sided Arch of Janus ⑬ (see p204), erected in the 3rd century AD. This is not a triumphal arch but a covered area where merchants could

Tips for Walkers

Starting point: The Roman Forum, entrance Largo Romolo e Remo, on Via dei Fori Imperiali.
Length: 1.5 miles (2.5 km).
Getting there: The closest Metro station is Colosseo on line B. Buses 75, 85, 87, 117, 175, 186, and 810 stop in Via dei Fori Imperiali, near Forum entrance.
Best time: Any time during Forum opening hours (see p84).
Stopping points: Several bars and restaurants overlook the Colosseum. There is a small bar on the corner of Via dei Cerchi and Via di San Teodoro, and a gelateria at the start of Via di San Teodoro. For a meal, try Alvaro al Circo Massimo (closed Mon) in Via di San Teodoro.

A Three-Hour Tour of Rome's Best Mosaics

In imitation of the audience chambers of Imperial palaces, Rome's early Christian churches were decorated with colorful mosaics. These were pieced together from cubes of marble, colored stone, and fragments of glass. To create a golden background, gold leaf was placed between pieces of glass. These were then heated so that they fused. The glorious colors and subjects portrayed gave the faithful a glimpse of the heavenly court of the King of Kings. This walk concentrates on a few of the churches decorated in this wonderful medium.

Apse mosaic in the Chapel of Santa Rufina ③

Obelisk and side facade of San Giovanni in Laterano ②

San Giovanni

Start from Piazza di Porta San Giovanni, where you can visit the heavily restored mosaic of the Triclinio Leoniano (see p181). Originally in the banqueting hall of Pope Leo III (795–816) ①, it shows Christ among the Apostles. On the left are Pope Sylvester and the Emperor Constantine, on the right, Pope Leo and Charlemagne just before he was crowned Emperor of the Romans in AD 800. Inside the basilica of San Giovanni in Laterano ② (see pp182–3), the 13th-century apse mosaic shows Christ as he appeared miraculously during the consecration of the church. In the panels by the windows, look for the small figures of two Franciscan friars; these are the artists Jacopo Torriti (left) and

Jacopo de Camerino (right). Leave by the exit on the right near the splendid 16th-century organ and head for the octagonal Baptistry of San Giovanni ③, where the Chapel of Santa Rufina has a beautiful apse mosaic, dating from the 5th century. In the neighboring Chapel of San Venanzio, there are golden 7th-century mosaics, showing the strong influence of the Eastern Church at this time.

Santo Stefano Rotondo to San Clemente

Leave the piazza by the narrow road that leads to the round church of Santo Stefano Rotondo ④ (see p187). One of its chapels contains a 7th-century Byzantine mosaic honoring two martyrs buried here. Farther on, in Piazza della Navicella, is the church of Santa Maria in Domnica ⑤ (see p195). It houses the superb mosaics commissioned by Pope Paschal I, who gave new impetus to Rome's mosaic production in the 9th century. He is represented kneeling beside the Virgin. On leaving the church, notice the facade of San Tommaso in Formis ⑥, which has a charming mosaic of Christ flanked by two freed slaves, one black and one

Ceiling mosaic, Baptistry of San Giovanni ③

Interior of Baptistry of San Giovanni ③

white, dating from the 13th century. From here, head up the steep hill, past the forbidding apse of Santi Quattro Coronati ⑦ *(see p187)*, to the fascinating church of San Clemente ⑧ *(see pp188–9)*. Its 12th-century apse mosaic shows the cross set in a swirling pattern of acanthus leaves. San Clemente also has a fine 12th-century Cosmatesque mosaic floor.

The Colle Oppio
Passing the old entrance to the church, cross Via Labicana, and walk up the hill to the small Colle Oppio park ⑨. This has fine views of the Colosseum and contains the ruins of the Domus Aurea ⑩ *(see p177)* and the Baths of Trajan ⑪. Across the park lie San Martino ai Monti ⑫ *(see p172)*, which has a 6th-century mosaic portrait of Pope St. Sylvester near the crypt, and Santa Prassede ⑬ *(see p173)*. Here the Chapel of St. Zeno contains the most important Byzantine mosaics in Rome, reminiscent of the fabulous mosaics of Ravenna. Pope Paschal I erected the chapel as a mausoleum for his

Inside, the 5th-century mosaics in the nave depict Old Testament stories, while the triumphal arch has scenes relating to the birth of Christ, including one of the Magi wearing striped stockings. In the apse there is a *Coronation of the Virgin* by Jacopo Torriti (1295).

On leaving Santa Maria, pass the obelisk ⑮ in the piazza behind the church and go downhill to Via Urbana and Santa Pudenziana ⑯ *(see p173)*. The figures in the apse mosaic, one of the oldest in Rome (AD 390), are remarkable for their naturalism. The two women with crowns are traditionally identified as Santa Prassede and Santa Pudenziana. When you leave the church, you can either retrace your steps to Santa Maria Maggiore or walk down Via Urbana to Via Cavour Metro station.

Mosaic saint in Santa Prassede ⑬

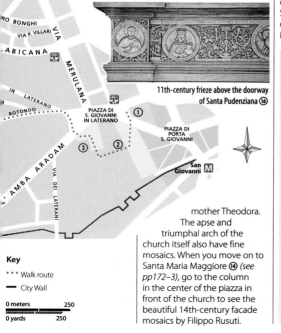

11th-century frieze above the doorway of Santa Pudenziana ⑯

mother Theodora. The apse and triumphal arch of the church itself also have fine mosaics. When you move on to Santa Maria Maggiore ⑭ *(see pp172–3)*, go to the column in the center of the piazza in front of the church to see the beautiful 14th-century facade mosaics by Filippo Rusuti.

Key

• • • Walk route

— City Wall

| 0 meters | 250 |
| 0 yards | 250 |

Tips for Walkers

Starting point: Piazza di Porta San Giovanni.
Length: 2 miles (3.5 km).
Getting there: The nearest Metro station is San Giovanni, on line A, in Piazzale Appio, just outside Porta San Giovanni. The 16, 81, 85, 87, 218, and 650 buses and the 3 tram stop in front of San Giovanni in Laterano, while 117 stops around the corner on Piazza San Giovanni in Laterano.
Best time for walk: Go in the morning, in order to appreciate the mosaics in the best light.
Stopping points: The bars, and restaurants in Piazza del Colosseo are popular with tourists. In the Parco del Colle Oppio there is a café kiosk with tables. There are several bars around Santa Maria Maggiore, some with outdoor tables.

For map symbols *see back flap*

A Two-Hour Walk around Bernini's Rome

Gian Lorenzo Bernini (1598–1680) is the artist who probably left the strongest personal mark on the appearance of the city of Rome. Favorite architect, sculptor, and town planner of three successive popes, he turned Rome into a uniquely Baroque city. This walk traces his enormous influence on the development and appearance of the center of Rome. It starts from the busy Largo di Santa Susanna just north of Termini station, at the church of Santa Maria della Vittoria.

Facade of Santa Maria in Via ⑬

(see p159), built by Bernini's rival Borromini, take Via del Quirinale. The long wing of the Palazzo del Quirinale ⑦ (see p160), nicknamed the *Manica Lunga* (long sleeve), is by Bernini. On the other side of the road is the facade of Sant'Andrea al Quirinale ⑧ (see p163), one of Bernini's greatest churches. When you reach the Piazza del Quirinale ⑨, note the doorway of the palazzo, attributed

Bernini's Fontana del Tritone ②

Leave the piazza along Via delle Muratte, where the composer Donizetti lived at No. 77, and turn into Via di Santa Maria in

Through Piazza Barberini

Santa Maria della Vittoria ① (see p257) houses the Cornaro Chapel, the setting for one of Bernini's most revolutionary and controversial sculptures, *The Ecstasy of St. Teresa* (1646). From here, take Via Barberini to Piazza Barberini. In its center is Bernini's dramatic Fontana del Tritone ② (see p256), and at one side stands the more modest Fontana delle Api ③ (see p256). As you go up Via delle Quattro Fontane, you catch a glimpse of Palazzo Barberini ④ (see p257), built by Bernini and several other artists for Pope Urban VIII. The gateway and cornices are decorated with the bees that made up part of the Barberini family crest. Next, make your way to the crossroads, decorated by Le Quattro Fontane ⑤ (see p164), to enjoy the splendid views in all four directions.

Passing the diminutive San Carlo alle Quattro Fontane ⑥

to Bernini. From the piazza, go down the stairs to Via della Dataria, and into Vicolo Scanderbeg, which leads to a small piazza with the same name ⑩. Scanderbeg was the nickname of the Albanian prince Giorgio Castriota (1403–68), the "Terror of the Turks." His portrait is preserved on his house.

The Trevi Fountain

Go along the narrow Vicolo dei Modelli ⑪, where male models waited to be chosen by artists, then turn toward the Trevi Fountain ⑫ (see p161). Its energy is clearly inspired by Bernini's work, a tribute to his lasting influence on Roman taste.

Neptune Fountain at the north end of Piazza Navona ⑱

Via, where the church ⑬ has a fine Baroque facade by Bernini's follower Carlo Rainaldi. At the top of this street, turn left down to Via del Corso. On the other side of the road, you will see the towering Column of Marcus Aurelius ⑭ (see p117) in Piazza Colonna. Beyond this is Palazzo Montecitorio ⑮, begun in 1650 by Bernini, and now the home of the Italian parliament (see p116).

Key

• • • Walk route

Statue of the Nile River from the Fontana dei Quattro Fiumi

0 meters 250

0 yards 250

central fountain, the Fontana dei Quattro Fiumi (see p122), was by Bernini, though the figures symbolic of the four rivers were sculpted by other artists. The central figure in the Fontana del Moro, however, is by Bernini himself. Bernini's contemporaries were fascinated by the innovative use of shells, rocks, and other natural forms in his fountains, and his expert handling of water to create constant movement.

An Extended Walk

More energetic walkers may like to head toward the river to see the Ponte Sant'Angelo and its Bernini angels, and then on to St. Peter's (see pp228–31), where they can admire Bernini's great colonnaded piazza in front of the church, the papal tombs, his altar decorations, and the bronze baldacchino.

Angel on Ponte Sant'Angelo

Pantheon to Piazza Navona

Via in Aquiro leads you to the Pantheon ⑯ (see pp114–15). Refusing Pope Urban VIII's request for him to redecorate the dome, Bernini said that although St. Peter's had a hundred defects, the Pantheon did not have any. From the Pantheon, make a small detour to Piazza della Minerva where you can see the obelisk, supported by Bernini's small, bizarre elephant, by the church of Santa Maria sopra Minerva ⑪ (see p112). Then retrace your steps, and take Salita dei

Crescenzi to reach the fabulous Piazza Navona ⑱ (see p122) which was remodeled by Bernini for Pope Innocent X Pamphilj. The design for the

Tips for Walkers

Starting point: Largo di Santa Susanna.

Length: 2 miles (3.5 km).

Getting there: Take Metro line A to Repubblica or any bus to Termini, then walk. Buses 61, 62, 175, and 492 stop in Via Barberini.

Best time for walk: Go either between 9am and noon for good lighting conditions in the churches, or between 4 and 7pm.

Stopping points: The Piazza Barberini and Fontana di Trevi areas have lots of bars and pizzerias. The many elegant cafés en route include the famous Caffè Giolitti (see p113), and outdoor cafés and restaurants are plentiful around Piazza della Rotonda, and Piazza Navona.

For map symbols see back flap

⓿ A 90-Minute Walk Along the Via Appia Antica

Lined with cypresses and pines as it was when the ancient Romans came here by torchlight to bury their dead, the Via Appia is wonderfully atmospheric. The fields are strewn with ruined tombs set against the picturesque background of the Alban hills to the south. Although the marble or travertine stone facings of most tombs have been plundered, a few statues and reliefs survive or have been replaced by copies.

Tomb of Sixtus Pompeus the Righteous ⑨

Capo di Bove

Start from the Tomb of Cecilia Metella ① (see p268). In the Middle Ages, this area acquired the name Capo di Bove (ox head) from the frieze of festoons and ox heads still visible on the tomb. On the other side of the road you can see the ruined

Gothic windows in the church of San Nicola ②

Gothic church of San Nicola ②, which, like the Tomb of Cecilia Metella, was part of the medieval fortress of the Caetani family.

Proceed to the crossroads ③, where there are still many original Roman paving slabs, huge blocks of extremely durable volcanic basalt. Just past the next

tombs, some still capped with the remains of the medieval towers that were built over them. On the right, after passing what remains of a thermal complex, you come to a military zone around the Forte Appio ⑤, one of a series of forts built around the city in the 19th century. On the left, a little farther along, stand the ruins of the Tomb of Marcus Servilius ⑥, showing fragments of reliefs excavated in 1808 by the Neo-Classical sculptor Antonio Canova. He was one of the first to work on the principle that

The ruined church of San Nicola ②

turn (Via Capo di Bove), you will see on your left the nucleus of a great mausoleum overgrown with ivy, known as the Torre di Capo di Bove ④. Beyond it, on both sides of the Appia, are other

excavated tombs and their inscriptions and reliefs should be allowed to remain in situ. On the other side of the road stands a tomb with a relief of a man, naked except for a short cape,

known as the "Heroic Relief" ⑦. On the left of the road are the ruins of the so-called Tomb of Seneca ⑧. The great moralist Seneca owned a villa near here, where he committed suicide in

Key

••• Walk route

0 meters   250
0 yards   250

Artist's impression of how the mausoleums and tombs lining the Via Appia looked in the 2nd century AD

Section of the Via Appia Antica, showing original Roman paving stones

AD 65 on the orders of Nero. The next major tomb is that of the family of Sixtus Pompeus the Righteous, a freed slave of the 1st century AD ⑨. The verse inscription records the father's sadness at having to bury his own children, who died young.

From Via dei Lugari to Via di Tor Carbone

Just past Via dei Lugari on the right, screened by trees, is the Tomb of Pope St. Urban (reigned 222–230) ⑩. Set back from the road on the left stands a large ruined podium, probably part of a Temple of Jupiter ⑪. The next stretch was excavated by the architect Luigi Canina early in the 19th century. On the right is the Tomb of Caius Licinius ⑫, followed by a smaller Doric tomb ⑬ and the imposing Tomb of Hilarius Fuscus ⑭, with five portrait busts in relief of members of his family. Next comes the Tomb of Tiberius Claudius Secondinus ⑮, where a group of freedmen of the Imperial household were buried in the 2nd century AD.

Passing a large ruined columbarium, you reach the Tomb of Quintus Apuleius ⑯

and the reconstructed Tomb of the Rabirii freed slaves (1st century BC) ⑰. This has a frieze of three half-length figures above an inscription.

The figure on the right is a priestess of Isis. Behind her you can see the outline of a *sistrum*, the metal rattle used at ceremonies of the cult.

The majority of the tombs are little more than shapeless stacks of eroded brickwork. Two exceptions in the last stretch of this walk are the Tomb of the Festoons ⑱, with its reconstructed frieze of festive putti, and the Tomb of the Frontispiece ⑲, which has a copy of a relief with four portraits. The two central figures are holding hands.

When you reach Via di Tor Carbone, the Via Appia still stretches out ahead of you in a straight line and, if you wish to extend your walk, there are many more tombs and ruined villas to visit along the way.

Figure on the Tomb of the Heroic Relief ⑦

Tips for Walkers

Starting point: Tomb of Cecilia Metella.

Length: 2 miles (3 km).

Getting there: Reach the tomb by taxi, or take the Archeobus (see p390), the 118 from Piazzale Ostiense, or the 660 from Colli Albani on Metro Line A.

Best time: On Sunday, when the road is closed to traffic. Go fairly early, before it gets too hot.

Stopping points: There is a bar on the corner of Via Metella and a pleasant picnic area in the grounds of a thermal complex just beyond Vicolo di Tor Carbone. There are also several restaurants on the first stretch of the Appia, including the Cecilia Metella, Via Appia Antica 129, tel 06-512 6769 (closed Mon).

A Two-Hour Tour of Roman Tombs, Legends, and Artists

The northern half of central Rome with its air of mystery is a great place for families to explore. Following this trail of creepy places and famous deaths interspersed with glimpses of the city's historic artists' center, visitors can see Imperial mausoleums, a death mask, and a crypt decorated with monks' bones. This is also a Rome where art isn't just in the museums – it's everywhere – so you'll see working art studios, pass Rome's Gallery of Fine Arts, and wander down the famous "artists' row."

Castel Sant'Angelo, site of the Emperor Hadrian's tomb ①

Imperial Tombs

Begin at Emperor Hadrian's tomb, deep in the heart of the papal Castel Sant'Angelo ① *(see pp250–51)*. From the castle's riverside entrance, turn left then left again along the star-shaped walls, before turning right into Piazza Cavour, surrounded on the south by the huge, ostentatious Palazzo di Giustizia ② *(see p249)*, slowly sinking under its own weight since 1910. Turn right down Via Colonna to cross the Tiber on Ponte Cavour. Once across the busy Lungotevere, turn left to go into the church of San Rocco ③ *(see p143)*. Just beyond it lies the Mausoleum of Augustus ④ *(see p143)*, sprouting a miniature grove of cypresses. To its left sits the ancient altar, Ara Pacis ⑤ *(see p142)*.

Frieze from Ara Pacis

Camporese. On the right, at the corner of Via Canova, is the church of Santa Maria Portae Paradisi ⑦, designed in 1523 by Antonio Sangallo the Younger with a 1509 *Madonna and Child* by sculptor Sansovino. The octagonal interior dates to 1645. Turn right down Via

Canova (named after the sculptor Antonio Canova) to see the exterior of his studio ⑧ at No. 16, a corner building studded with ancient statues and carvings. Turn left onto Via del Corso ⑨, Rome's "Main Street. "This is just under a mile (1.5 km) of *palazzi*, and shops that has hosted parades, carnivals, races, and processions for centuries, and still functions as the main drag for Rome's evening stroll, the *passeggiata*. As you pass San Giacomo on your left (once the church of a hospital founded in 1339 as a

The Tridente

Continue heading north up Via di Ripetta. On your left is the graffiti-covered courtyard of the Accademia di Belle Arti ⑥, Rome's fine art academy, designed in 1845 by Pietro

0 meters 200
0 yards 200

Key

• • • Walk route

Baroque magnificence inside the Chiesa di Gesù e Maria ⑩

The Piazza di Spagna, and the famous Spanish Steps, usually busy with visitors but quiet on rare occasions ⑱

Tips for Walkers

Starting point: Castel Sant'Angelo.
Length: 2.2 miles (3.6 km).
Getting there: Take bus 30, 34, 40, 49, 62, 70, 87, 130, 186, 224, 280, 492, 913, 926, or 990.
Best time for walk: Go in the afternoon, when the area starts to come alive.
Stopping points: Piazza del Popolo is flanked by two great Roman cafés with clear political affiliations – leftist Rosati (see p321) on the west side, right-wing Canova on the east. The Spanish Steps area has some great eateries as well as the usual fast food chains (see pp315–17).

hospice for pilgrims), you'll see on the right Chiesa di Gesù e Maria ⑩, Carlo Rinaldi's 1675 Baroque masterpiece. Farther along, at No. 18, is the Casa di Goethe ⑪ (see p138). The Corso ends in the dramatic Piazza del Popolo ⑫ (see p139).

from Old Master Madonnas to Modernist abstracts. Take the third left, then right onto quiet Via Margutta ⑯, home of artists' studios and galleries for centuries. Turn right again down Via Orto di Napoli to return to Via del Babuino, then left. On your right, reclining on a fountain, and surrounded by various graffiti, and placards, is one of the ugliest – and most respected – statues in Rome. The Babuino ⑰ (like the famous Pasquino, see p126)

Zuccari turned the door, and window frames of his Palazzetto Zuccari ㉒ into monsters. At the bottom of Via Gregoriana, turn left up to Via F. Crispi, then right down Via Sistina into Piazza Barberini ㉓, noting Bernini's fountain (see p254). Turn left up the square, cross Via V. Veneto, and left again. A few dozen paces up on the right is the staircase to the church of Santa Maria della Concezione. To finish off, stop at the first landing to enter the creepy Capuchin Crypt ㉔ (see p256), where there are four chapels decorated with mosaics, and skeletal displays. When you leave the crypt, head for Piazza Barberini, and the Metro station.

The square is named after the church on its north end, Santa Maria del Popolo ⑬ (see pp140–41). The church, which is full of art treasures, is called "St. Mary of the People" because it was built to help exorcise the ghost of Nero from a walnut grove on this site, once Nero's family estate where the disgraced emperor was secretly buried. The estate once continued up the slopes of what are now the Pincio Gardens ⑭ (see p138), above the piazza to the east, and locals declare that the ravens' screams are those of the dead emperor. Leave Piazza del Popolo from the southeast corner to stroll down Via del Babuino ⑮, lined with art galleries hawking everything

has served as a soapbox for political, and social dissent for centuries. Via del Babuino ends in Piazza di Spagna ⑱ (see p135), usually thronged with tourists. The pink house to the right of the Spanish Steps is the Keats-Shelley Memorial House ⑲ (see p136). Take a look inside to see Keats' death mask.

The Spanish Steps to the Capuchin Crypt
Go up the famed Spanish Steps ⑳ (see p136–7) to Trinità dei Monti ㉑ (see p137). Turn right down Via Gregoriana to No. 28, where painter Federico

Bones, and skulls from monks in the Capuchin Crypt ㉔

For map symbols see back flap

A Two-Hour Walk Around Trastevere and Janiculum Hill

This walk begins in the warren of cobbled, medieval streets of Trastevere, which is becoming ever more popular, and shows you the neighborhood's hidden gems rather than its major sights. In the morning, enjoy the mosaics and frescoes in the local churches before pausing for lunch in central Trastevere. Then go for a gentle climb up the Gianicolo, or Janiculum Hill. This long crest parallels the Tiber, and is blessed with the best panoramic views in Rome. At sunset, couples find it a romantic place to go for a stroll.

The high altar of San Benedetto ③

Southern Trastevere

Start at Santa Cecilia in Trastevere ① *(see p213)*, a church that hides its best – the basement excavations of St. Cecilia's house and Pietro Cavallini's sole surviving Roman fresco inside the cloistered convent – behind a bland 18th-century interior. Turn left out of the church, left again onto Via dei Salumi, then right on Via in Piscinula into Piazza in Piscinula ②, named for the remains of a bathing pool underneath. On the piazza's south side, below an 11th-century belltower, sits the tiny church of San Benedetto in Piscinula ③ (ring the doorbell for entry). It contains parts of a beautiful Cosmati mosaic pavement, 13th-century frescoes, and the saint's cell. Head west along Via della Lungaretta, and cross the Viale di Trastevere to visit the excavations of a 5th-century basilica and fragments of its later frescoes below San Crisogono ④ *(see p212)*.

Central Trastevere

Turn left out of the church, and left again to continue along Via della Lungaretta to Piazza Santa Maria in Trastevere ⑤,

a communal outdoor parlor, busy with cafés, guitar-strumming backpackers on the fountain steps, and visitors to the gorgeous Santa Maria in Trastevere ⑥ *(see p214–15)*. Exit the square on the south side into tiny Piazza San Callisto, and take the right fork down Via di San Cosimato into the large triangular Piazza di San Cosimato ⑦, bustling (until 2pm) with an open-air food market. Backtrack to Piazza Santa Maria in Trastevere. Along the square's north side you'll see a tiny street called Fonte d'Olio, the entrance into the twisting maze of alleys, and ivy-covered buildings at the heart of Trastevere. The street bends sharply left, then turn right onto Vicolo del Piede to arrive at the diminutive Piazza de' Renzi, lined with medieval houses. Turn left to follow Via della Pelliccia, then left again at the pedestrian intersection. This will bring you into the elongated triangle of Piazza di Sant'Egidio ⑧, alive with cafés and bars. A short

staircase at No. 9 leads to the Museo di Roma in Trastevere ⑨ *(see p212)*, devoted to the history of everyday Roman life. Exit the piazza at the northwest corner, and cross Vicolo del Cedro to continue straight on Via della Scala, past shops, and

Piazza Santa Maria in Trastevere and its enchanting church ⑤

Raphael's *Galatea* in the Villa Farnesina ⑬

of frescoing the Villa Farnesina ⑬ *(see pp220–21)*, just up Via della Lungara, he spent so much time with his lover that, unlike the famed *Galatea* in the dining room, the "Raphael" work in the Loggia of Cupid and Psyche was executed largely by his assistants. Across from the Farnesina squats the Palazzo Corsini and the Galleria Nazionale d'Arte Antica ⑭ *(see p222)*. Tucked behind the gallery – accessible by backtracking down Via della Lungara and turning right on Via Corsini – are the Botanical Gardens ⑮ *(see p222)*.

The Gianicolo
Continue back south on Via della Lungara through the Porta Settimiana, and turn right up Via G. Garibaldi to climb Janiculum Hill. After the road makes a sharp left turn, veer right up a set of steps to San Pietro in Montorio, home to

Tips for Walkers
Starting point: Santa Cecilia in Trastevere.
Length: 2.9 miles (4.7 km).
Getting there: Take bus 23, 44, or 280.
Best time for walk: Weekdays (to see the Cavallini fresco in Santa Cecilia), starting mid-morning while the churches of southern Trastevere are still open.
Stopping points: Trastevere is the most restaurant-intensive district in Rome, so it has plenty of eateries, and bars (see pp324–5).

Bramante's Tempietto ⑯ *(see p223)*. Go on up Via G. Garibaldi to the broad basin of the Fontana dell'Acqua Paola ⑰ *(see p223)*. Continue along Via G. Garibaldi to the 1644 Porta San Pancrazio ⑱, which had to be rebuilt in 1849 due to cannon damage *(see pp38–9)*. Turn right onto Passeggiata del Gianicolo to enter the park, where the first wide space with a panoramic

Key
• • • Walk route

bars into Piazza della Scala, where the Carmelite convent of Santa Maria della Scala ⑩ *(see p212)* has an ornate interior.

Northern Trastevere
The far northern part of Trastevere, between the Gianicolo and the river, is where the artist Raphael dallied with a baker's daughter at the Casa della Fornarina ⑪ *(see p212)*, on the right just before the Porta Settimiana ⑫ *(see p222)*. Instead

Steps at the tranquil Botanical Gardens ⑮

vista over Rome is Piazzale Garibaldi with its equestrian monument to the general ⑲ *(see p222)*. Here, paths are lined with marble busts of other Risorgimento heroes. When you reach the Lighthouse of Manfredi ⑳ *(see p218)*, the dome of St. Peter's appears to the north. Continue down the steps at the Passeggiata's first bend to the 400-year-old remains of Tasso's Oak ㉑ *(see p218)*. At the foot of the steps, rejoin the Passeggiata. Beyond it, a few steps up, finish at the church of Sant'Onofrio ㉒ *(see p223)*. From Viale Aldo Fabrizi catch bus No. 870 back.

For map symbols *see back flap*

A Two-Hour Walk Around the Aventine

Rising just across the Circus Maximus from the Palatine, the residential Aventine Hill has served as a leafy haven of villas and mansions since Imperial times. This southernmost of Rome's legendary seven hills is still an oasis where traffic noise all but disappears. Yet few visitors walk here – despite the lure of fine old churches, lovely city panoramas, and rarely visited ancient ruins. You'll also explore Testaccio, a fine area for authentic restaurants, and see a Roman pyramid.

The gymnasium at the northwest side of the Baths of Caracalla ①

The Aventine

Begin at one of Rome's most magnificent ancient sites, the massive Baths of Caracalla ① *(see p199)*, where plebeian, and patrician alike once bathed (and, much later, where the poet Shelley found inspiration for *Prometheus Unbound*). Just outside the Baths' entrance sits the church of SS Nero e Achilleo ② *(see p196)*, with 9th-century mosaics. Across Viale delle Terme di Caracalla lies tiny San Sisto Vecchio ③, first home of the Dominican nuns *(see p195)*. Turning northwest up Viale delle Terme di Caracalla, take the first right onto Via di Valle delle Camene, a tree-lined avenue parallel to the main road. Angle right up Salita di San Gregorio, and ascend the imposing staircase of San Gregorio Magno ④ *(see p194)* for great views of the Palatine. Look for the third-century marble table (in the St. Barbara chapel, on the left side of the church) at which St. Gregory the Great shared meals with the poor and, once,

an angel in disguise. Turn left down Via di San Gregorio, and cross wide Piazza di Porta Capena, keeping the long, dusty oval of the Circus Maximus ⑤ *(see p207)* on your right. At the start of Viale Aventino you'll see the modernist bulk of FAO ⑥, originally intended to be the Ministry of Italian Africa when Mussolini was launching his ill-fated conquest of the Horn of Africa. Since its 1952 completion, it has housed the UN's Food and Agriculture Organization.

Across the Aventine

Turn right on Via del Circo Massimo, and immediately left onto Via della Fonte di Fauno to start climbing the Aventine Hill. This leads you to a small piazza before the church of Santa Prisca ⑦, built in the third century atop the house where the martyred saint's parents hosted

The apse of Santa Prisca ⑦

St. Peter. The current church dates largely to a Renaissance-era remodeling, and includes a Passignano altarpiece. Continue north up Via di Santa Prisca, angle left through Largo Arrigo VII, turn left on Via Eufemiano, and immediately right onto Via Sant'Alberto Magno. This leads right into Parco Savello ⑨, a garden of orange trees with a panoramic river view over Trastevere. Leaving the park, turn right onto Via di Santa Sabina to the

gorgeous basilica of Santa Sabina ⑨ *(see p206)*, where its rare, 5th-century wooden doors incorporate one of the earliest Crucifixion representations. Continue along Via di Santa Sabina to see the fine Cosmati work in SS Bonifacio e Alessio ⑩ *(see p206)*. The street ends in the Piazza dei Cavaliere di Malta ⑪ *(see p206)*, where you get a tiny view of St. Peter's dome through the keyhole at number 3. Turn left down Via di Porta Lavernate,

Keats' gravestone at the Protestant Cemetery on Via Caio Cestio ⑮

that have long burrowed into its flanks to take advantage of the terra cotta's constant, cool temperature for storing wine. Turn left through Piazza Orazio Giustiniani to continue skirting the hill along Via di Monte Testaccio. Across the street, you'll see the blind arcades of the Ex-Mattatoio ⑭, a defunct abattoir whose workers were paid, in part, with the day's offal. They would carry this *quinto quarto* (fifth quarter) of the animal across the street to one of Testaccio's early eateries,

where it would be turned into such (now) classic Roman delicacies as oxtail stew, and *pajata* (calf intestines). Continue along Via di Monte Testaccio, which becomes Via Caio Cestio, to the Protestant Cemetery ⑮ *(see p207)* where such luminaries as Keats and Shelley lie in peace. At Via Marmorata, turn right to pass the Porta San Paolo ⑯, a city gate dating to AD 402. As you walk through the remains of the Aurelian Wall into Piazzale Ostiense, you can't miss on your right the Pyramid of Caius Cestius ⑰ *(see p207)*. The final leg is a long stroll down Via Ostiense or, alternatively, hop on the bus (Nos. 23, 271, or 769) to see the wonderfully weird Centrale Montemartini ⑱, an early Industrial Age power plant now stuffed with ancient sculptures *(see p269)*. Bus numbers 23 and 769 will take you back to within walking distance of Piramide Metro.

Tips for Walkers

Starting point: The Baths of Caracalla entrance on Viale delle Terme di Caracalla 52.
Length: 3 miles (5 km).
Getting there: You can walk from the Circo Massimo Metro stop, or take bus 118 or 628.
Best time for walk: Start in the morning, timing your walk so that you can eat lunch in Testaccio.
Stopping points: There are many options, since fantastic, and authentic local eateries abound in, and around Piazza Testaccio, from cheap pizza places to traditional Roman restaurants.

Key

• • • Walk route

passing the facade of Sant'Anselmo ⑫. Built in 1900, the church houses a 3rd-century mosaic scene of Orpheus found during excavations. From Piazza dei Servili, turn right on Via Asinio Pollione to go down off the Aventine.

Testaccio and South

Cross Via Marmorata and continue down Via Galvani. As you cross Via Nicola Zabaglia, you see Testaccio market ahead on your right, while the ground on your left rises to form Monte Testaccio ⑬ *(see p206)*, an ancient garbage dump made up entirely of potsherds. It is lined with various restaurants

Ancient sculptures on display in the Centrale Montemartini ⑱

For map symbols *see back flap*

TRAVELERS' NEEDS

WHERE TO STAY

Rome has been a major tourist centre since the Middle Ages, when pilgrims from all over Europe came to visit the home of Catholicism and its relic-packed churches. The nostalgic can still sleep in a 15th-century hotel, or stay around the Campo de' Fiori market, where visiting ecclesiastics were entertained by courtesans in the Renaissance era. Those who prefer their history a little less raffish could opt for an ex-monastery or convent, or stay in a still-functioning religious house. Romantics can sleep in the house once occupied by Keats, while stargazers can stay in former palaces graced by celebrities of the

past and present. Rome can offer the full range of accommodations, mostly in historical buildings, very little purpose-built. *Pensione* (guesthouse) no longer refers to a specific type of establishment, but in practice many retain the name and more personal character that has made them so popular with travelers. Other possibilities include hostels, residential hotels and self-catering accommodation.

Hotel listings *(pp300–303)* are organized according to their theme and area, with DK Choice entries highlighted – see Recommended Hotels on p298–9 for more information.

Hotel Prices

Prices are set by the state, and hotels should display the official rate on the door of each room. VAT (IVA in Italian) is usually included, and has been taken into account in the price categories on page 300.

Hotels in Rome generally have low and high season rates. April to June, September and October are high season. Double-check tariffs when booking hotels at other times of year as you may initially be quoted the higher rate. Excepting Christmas and New Year, there are some real bargains to be had between November and February, and also in July and August. Many hotels also offer special Internet booking deals, especially if made

far in advance, or at the last minute. Discounts for long-stay visitors, and groups are often negotiable. Rooms without a bathroom can cost about 30 per cent less. Single travelers are badly catered for, and though it is possible to find a single room for 60 per cent of the price of a double, on average you'll pay as much as 70 per cent, and occasionally even more.

Hidden Extras

Even if the price of your room includes service, you are frequently expected to tip bellboys and for room service.

Rates are often not inclusive of breakfast, especially at some luxury hotels, where it may cost

up to €50. Hotels usually add hefty surcharges to international phone calls, and may charge for parking and air conditioning. The cost of drinks in minibars can also be high.

All hotels, B&Bs and campsites in Rome must add a city tax *(contributo di soggiorno)* to the final bill. At present this tax is for the first ten days of any stay and is fixed at €1 per day per person for campsites, €2 for establishments up to and including three-star hotels, and €3 for four- and five-star hotels. Children under ten are exempt, as are visitors staying in youth hostels.

Facilities

Internet access, air conditioning and bathrooms with hair dryers are common in most mid-range hotels, and phones in middle- to lower-price rooms, although budget travellers staying in cheaper hotels shouldn't expect much more than a clean room.

Because most hotels occupy historic buildings, room sizes can vary dramatically even within the same establishment (and this is often reflected in the pricing), so do ask to see your room before you check in. Swimming pools are rare, but roof terraces or gardens are common across the range of hotels.

Top-class hotels will usually have some soundproofing; otherwise noise levels can be dreadful, in which case ask for a room facing away from the road.

The Verdi Room in Via Veneto's Majestic Hotel *(see p302)*

◀ One of the many charming restaurants in Rome

Grand Hotel de la Minerve *(see p302)*

Parking in central Rome is a problem, though a few hotels have a limited number of parking spaces of their own.

Business visitors to the capital are well catered for, with practical hotel facilities such as conference rooms.

Making Reservations

It is best to book through the hotel website, by phone or email. You should do this at least two months in advance if you want a particular hotel during peak season. If you require any particular features, such as a view, insist on confirmation in writing to ensure that you get what you have been promised.

If a deposit is required you can usually pay by debit or credit card. Under Italian law a booking is valid as soon as the

The Portoghesi Hotel *(see p300)*

deposit is paid, so you could lose money if you pull out. Double-check bookings prior to departure. Many hotels have a fierce cancellation policy and there is every chance that you will be charged for at least one night, even if you don't stay. Another reason for checking bookings is that some hotels deliberately overbook and then offer unsatisfactory alternative accommodation.

If you arrive by train, touts may descend on you at the station with offers of hotels. They can be of some use if you are looking for a budget hotel, but exercise the usual caution. A better bet if you have not booked in advance is to head for one of the tourist board offices *(see p299)*, where staff will reserve you a room within the price range you specify.

Checking In and Out

Italian hoteliers are legally obliged to register you with the police, which is the reason they always ask for your passport. Everyone in Italy is supposed
to carry with them some sort of identification.

In some of Rome's cheaper *pensioni*, do not be surprised if you are asked to pay on arrival. Mention in advance if you intend to pay by credit card. A common tax dodge by many hotels is to ask for payment in cash; you are entitled to refuse.

Disabled Travelers

Provision for disabled travelers is poor. Hotels that occupy parts of buildings often start their rooms up several flights of stairs, while others can only accommodate disabled guests on the ground floor. Ramps, wide doorways and bathroom handrails are rare.

Contact the hotel entries in the listings directly, before booking, to check whether they are wheelchair accessible and can provide any other specific requirements (for more information *see p368*).

There is a useful website

Villa San Pio garden *(see p300)*

(Roma Pertutti) dedicated to mobility within Rome, while the Lazio region provides advice on accessibility further afield (800 27 1027). Public transportation authority **Bus Abile** offers a pick-up service and bus tourism for travelers with disabilities and must be reserved in advance.

Travelling with Children

Italians love children and they are usually welcome across the range of hotels. Most hotels can provide cribs or small beds, but high chairs, children's meals and babysitting services are rare.

Many hotels do not have special rates for children and charge a standard rate if you require an extra bed in a room, whether for a baby or an adult, which can add anything from a few euros to 40 percent on to the price. For a family with older children, two-room suites are sometimes available.

Contact the hotel in advance of booking for more information on family rates and children's facilities.

Bed & Breakfast

A popular option for visitors to Rome is bed & breakfast accommodations. This can be anything from a spare room in an apartment to something more like a small hotel. The type of breakfast can also vary depending on the owner. Contact the **Bed & Breakfast Association** of Rome for details, **Rome Bed & Breakfast** in the US, or visit Rome's

Residential Hotels

If you want the comfort and privacy of your own apartment coupled with the services of a hotel, you could opt to stay in a *residenza*. Prices range from around €300 to over €3,000 for a week in a room with two beds, though some *residenze* are only available for two-week or one-month rentals.

A full list of residential hotels is available from tourist board offices; some of the most central are listed in the directory on page 299.

Religious Institutions

If you do not mind an early curfew, quite a few religious institutions take in paying guests. All religions are welcome, and you do not have to be a practicing Catholic. Reserve well in advance, since all of the following places cater to groups of students and pilgrims. **Casa Il Rosario** convent is located near the Colosseum, while **Nostra Signora di Lourdes**, and the **Casa di Santa Brigida** are in the center of Rome. Prices are in the same range as for the cheaper hotels.

Budget Accommodations

Even if you are traveling on a shoestring, it is possible to find a decent room in Rome. More, and more mid-range options are now available, and dormitory accommodations can be found at rock-bottom prices in simple establishments, such as the Ottaviano. Youth hostels are also a good option. At the **Alessandro Palace**, bed, breakfast, and shower can all be had at a reasonable cost. **Fawlty Towers** has good facilities for the price, including a roof terrace; like **Stargate**, it is located near Termini station.

Women can get rooms at the **Foresteria Orsa Maggiore** in Trastevere or at the **Young Women's Christian Association (YWCA)** near Termini (those arriving in Termini at night should be careful). There are also several downtown budget hotels

The reception area of the Regina Hotel Baglioni *(see p302)*

offering clean rooms, and often a free breakfast. See websites like www.venere.com and www.eurocheapo.com for more options.

Self-Service Apartments

Independent apartments are a good alternative and allow you more freedom. Apartments range from luxury locations with a daily cleaning service to smaller basic facilities. Most come equipped with cooking utensils, towels, and bed linens. **RetRome Bed & Breakfast** provides apartments at various locations around town.

Camping

Camping has come a long way since the simple tent and trailer. Campsites around Rome offer everything from fully equipped cabins (with private bath) to Jacuzzis and on-site discos. Most campsites are located quite far out of town but offer a shuttle

Bedroom at the Residenza Cellini *(see p303)*

service, as well as airport transportation; **Flaminio Village** is one exception, at only 4 miles (6 km) north of the downtown. Like many sites, it has a pool, coffee bar, restaurant, and Internet access.

Tourist Boards

Provincial and city tourist boards can provide advice on accommodations. Hotel Reservation is a booking service with offices at Termini station, as well as both of the city's airports.

Recommended Hotels

We've divided our recommended hotels into five categories: Boutique, Budget, Historic, Luxury, and Pensions and B&B. Boutique hotels are smaller and designed with an artistic eye, whether it be modern or ancient in style. Budget accommodations, while the least expensive option, are not limited to hostels and B&Bs. Surprisingly, Rome has some great options for frugal travelers who know where to look. The city is also full of historic accommodations, since many Renaissance palaces and villas have been turned into hotels. Antique furniture and exposed architectural elements make them the most romantic choices. Luxury hotels provide 5-star service and facilities, most with stunningly beautiful rooms, panoramic rooftop terraces, and award-winning restaurants.

Pensions and B&Bs may provide more basic facilities, but

are often full of character at an affordable price.

Our hotels are divided into five geographical areas. In Central Rome, from Piazza Navona to the Jewish Ghetto and southward as far as the Tiber, you will find a plethora of hotels for all budgets. Many exclusive boutique hotels can be found here, as well as a number of mid-range options. Ancient Rome, from the Colosseum to the Esquiline Hill, including the Lateran and the Aventine, offers varied accommodations, including a number of budget options, particularly near Termini station. Most of the luxury hotels can be found in the Spanish Steps and Via Veneto neighborhoods, categorized under Spagna, Veneto, and Around, which also includes the Quirinal Hill. Trastevere and Around,

The pool in the Aldrovandi Palace garden *(see p303)*

including the Vatican and Janiculum areas, offer some great historical choices and many B&Bs. The Farther Afield section covers hotels outside the downtown and in nearby Tivoli.

Throughout our listings, we've marked recommended hotels

as DK Choice. These hotels are chosen because they offer a special experience – either for superlative service, beautiful interiors and rooms, top-notch amenties and gadgets, an excellent on-site restaurant, or a combination of these.

DIRECTORY

Disabled Travelers

Bus Abile
Tel 800-469 540 (call between 9am and 1pm Mon–Fri). **w** atac.roma.it

Roma per Tutti
w romapertutti.it

Bed & Breakfast

Bed & Breakfast Association of Rome
Via A. Pacinotti 73.
Tel 06-5530 2248.
w b-b.rm.it

Rome Bed & Breakfast
Tel 1-800 872 2632.
w romebandb.com

Residential Hotels

Di Ripetta
Via di Ripetta 231, 00186.
Tel 06-323 1144.
w ripetta.it

In Trastevere
Vicolo Moroni 35–36,
00153. **Tel** 06-808 3375.
w romerenting.com

Residence Babuino
Via del Babuino 172,
00187. **Tel** 06-361 1663.

Vittoria
Via Vittoria 60-64, 00187.
Tel 06-679 7533.
w residencevittoria.com

Religious Institutions

Casa di Santa Brigida
Piazza Farnese 96, 00186.
Tel 06-6889 2596.

Casa Il Rosario
Via Sant'Agata dei Goti 10,
00184. **Tel** 06-679 2346.

Nostra Signora di Lourdes
Via Sistina 113, 00187.
Tel 06-474 5324.

Budget Accommodations

Alessandro Palace
Via Vicenza 42, 00185.
Tel 06-446 1958.
w hostelsalessandro.com

Associazione Italiana Alberghi per la Gioventù
(Youth Hostels Association)

Via Cavour 44, 00184.
Tel 06-487 1152.
w aighostels.com

Fawlty Towers
Via Magenta 39, 00185.
Tel 06-445 0374.
w fawltytowers.org

Foresteria Orsa Maggiore
Via di San Francesco di Sales 1A, 00165.
Tel 06-689 3753.
w casainternazionale delledonne.org

Ottaviano
Via Ottaviano 6, 00192.
Tel 06-3973 8138.
w pensioneottaviano.com

Stargate
Via Palestro 88, 00185.
Tel 06-445 7164.
w stargatehotels.com

YWCA
Via C. Balbo 4, 00184.
Tel 06-488 3917.
w ywca-ucdg.it

Self-Service

RetRome Bed & Breakfast
Tel 06-9555 7334.
w retrome.net

Camping

Flaminio Village
Via Flaminia Nuova 821,
00189. **Tel** 06-333 2604.
w campingflaminio.com

Tourist Board

Hotel Reservation
Termini Station, 00185,
and Terminal 3 (arrivals),
Leonardo da Vinci Airport,
Fiumicino.
Tel 06-699 1000.
Open 7am–10pm daily.
w hotelreservation.it

Rome City Tourist Board
Termini Station 00185.
Tel 06-0608.
Open 8am–7.30pm daily.
w 060608.it

Terminal 3 (arrivals),
Leonardo da Vinci Airport,
Fiumicino.
Open 8am–7.30pm daily.

Where to Stay

Boutique

Ancient Rome

Canada   €
Via Vicenza 58, 00185
Tel *06-445 7770*   **Map** 6 E2
w hotelcanadaroma.com
Rooms vary at this above-average
three-star; some have canopy
beds. Access to Wi-Fi for a fee.

Domus Aventina   €
Via di Santa Prisca 11b, 00153
Tel *06-574 6135*   **Map** 8 E3
w hoteldomusaventina.com
Simple but elegantly decorated
rooms open directly onto a lush,
quiet courtyard.

Hotel Celio   €
*Via dei Santissimi Quattro 35/c,
00184*
Tel *06-7049 5333*   **Map** 9 A1
w hotelcelio.com
Elegant three-star with a touch of
whimsy. Reproduction artwork
is found in every room.

San Anselmo   €€
Piazza Sant'Anselmo 2, 00153
Tel *06-570 057*   **Map** 8 D3
w aventinohotels.com
A romantic choice, San Anselmo
offers four-poster beds, and claw-
foot tubs for a memorable stay.

Villa San Pio   €€
Via Santa Melania 19, 00153
Tel *06-570 057*   **Map** 8 E3
w aventinohotels.com
This quiet and secluded hotel is a
stone's throw from downtown.
Free parking and breakfast.

Fortyseven   €€€
Via Luigi Petroselli 47, 00186
Tel *06-678 7816*   **Map** 8 E1
w fortysevenhotel.com
Stellar views of the ancient city
from this retro-style hotel that
prides itself on its hospitality.

Central Rome

Campo de'Fiori Hotel   €€
Via del Biscione 6, 00186
Tel *06-6880 6865*   **Map** 11 C4
w hotelcampodefiori.com
Romantically decorated rooms
with charming details, and views
of rooftops and domes.

Hotel Santa Chiara   €€
Via di Santa Chiara 21, 00186
Tel *06-687 2979*   **Map** 12 D3
w albergosantachiara.com
Well-located hotel with an
impressive, spacious lobby, and
simply furnished rooms.

Contemporary interior of the
Babuino181 hotel

Locanda Cairoli   €€
Piazza Benedetto Cairoli 2, 00186
Tel *06-6880 9278*   **Map** 12 D5
w locandacairoli.it
Centrally located, and
comfortable hotel with a cozy
family-style breakfast room.
Quirky, and eclectic furnishings.

Portoghesi   €€
Via dei Portoghesi 1, 00186
Tel *06-686 4231*   **Map** 11 C2
w hotelportoghesiroma.it
A good-value hotel nestled in
a quiet cobbled alley. It has a
lovely breakfast terrace.

Teatropace33   €€
Via del Teatro Pace 33, 00186
Tel *06-687 9075*   **Map** 11 C3
w hotelteatropace.com
Charming hotel decorated in
ornate Baroque style with an
excellent price/quality ratio.

Sole al Pantheon   €€€
Piazza della Rotonda 63, 00186
Tel *06-678 0441*   **Map** 12 D3
w solealpantheonrome.com
Nice rooms with unparalleled
views of the Pantheon. Can
be noisy.

Spagna, Veneto, and Around

Art   €€
Via Margutta 56, 00187
Tel *06-328 711*   **Map** 4 F1
w hotelart.it
While the art-inspired public
spaces may be overdone,
the rooms are sleek.

Deko Rome   €€
Via Toscana 1, 00187
Tel *06-4202 0032*   **Map** 5 C1
w dekorome.com

Small but comfortable rooms in
minimalist style. Spacious, and
luxurious bathrooms.

Parlamento   €€
Via delle Convertite 5, 00187
Tel *06-6992 1000*   **Map** 12 E1
w hotelparlamento.it
Simple but romantic rooms
with whimsical touches. Rooftop terrace with a lovely view
for breakfast.

Babuino181   €€€
Via del Babuino 181, 00187
Tel *06-3229 5295*   **Map** 4 F1
w romeluxurysuites.com
A Renaissance palace remodeled
with a sleek, modern look, and
luxurious details.

Piranesi   €€€
Via del Babuino 196, 00187
Tel *06-328 041*   **Map** 4 F1
w hotelpiranesi.com
This tiny hotel exudes quiet
elegance and is in an ideal location. Facilities include a small gym.

Portrait Suites   €€€
Via Bocca di Leone 23
Tel *06-6938 0742*   **Map** 5 A2
w lungarnocollection.com
Stylish hotel owned by Salvatore
Ferragamo. Individually
decorated rooms.

Trastevere and Around

Domus Tiberina   €
Via in Piscinula 37, 00153
Tel *06-581 3648*   **Map** 8 D1
w hoteldomustiberina.it
A quaint hotel on a picturesque,
vine-covered alleyway. Steps
away from the Tiber.

Hotel Ponte Sisto   €€
Via dei Pettinari 64, 00186
Tel *06-686 3100*   **Map** 11 C5
w hotelpontesisto.it
Comfortable rooms with
panoramic views, and a
delightful roof terrace.

Palazzo Cardinal Cesi   €€
Via della Conciliazione 51, 00193
Tel *06-684 0390*   **Map** 3 C3
w palazzocesi.it
Former cardinal's palace with
original moldings, coffered
ceilings, and a romantic garden.

San Francesco €€
Via Jacopa de' Settesoli 7, 00153
Tel *06-5830 0051*   **Map** 7 C2
Ⓦ hotelsanfrancesco.net
An unassuming entrance hides a gem of a hotel. San Francesco has tasteful rooms and a chic rooftop bar.

Sant'Anna €€
Borgo Pio 134, 00193
Tel *06-6880 1602*   **Map** 3 C3
Ⓦ santannahotel.net
Modern convenience with an old-fashioned feel. Exquisite courtyard provides respite from the busy street.

Budget
Ancient Rome
Blue Hostel €
Via Carlo Alberto 13, 00185
Tel *340-925 8503*   **Map** 6 D4
Ⓦ bluehostel.it
The accommodations are an excellent buy at this impressive, spotless hostel.

Hostel des Artistes €
Via Villafranca 20, 00185
Tel *06-445 4365*   **Map** 6 E2
Ⓦ hostelrome.com
Friendly, and clean hostel with dorm accommodation. Simple private rooms are also available.

DK Choice
The Beehive €
Via Marghera 8, 00185
Tel *06-4470 4553*   **Map** 6 E3
Ⓦ the-beehive.com
This gem of a hotel is owned by an American couple, and offers both private rooms and small dormitories. Accommodations are basic, but clean and comfortable. There are many extras available, such as yoga lessons, massage sessions, and a café serving freshly baked bread and organic coffee. An excellent choice for frugal travelers, but reserve early.

Central Rome
Mimosa €
Via di Santa Chiara, 61, 00186
Tel *06-6880 1753*   **Map** 12 D3
Ⓦ hotelmimosa.net
Affordable accommodations with basic rooms that are comfortable, clean, and air conditioned.

Palazzo Olivia €
Via dei Leutari 15, 00186
Tel *06-6821 6986*   **Map** 11 C3
Ⓦ palazzo-olivia.it

Set in a 17th-century palace. Self-service apartments, each named after an opera character.

Spagna, Veneto and Around

Hotel Grifo €
Via del Boschetto 144, 00184
Tel *06-487 1395*   **Map** 5 B4
Ⓦ hotelgrifo.com
The compact, functional rooms are kept immaculately clean. Breakfast is served on a cozy terrace with a charming view.

Trastevere and Around

Casa Internazionale della Donna €
Via di San Francesco di Sales 1A, 00165
Tel *06-6889 2465*   **Map** 4 D5
Ⓦ casainternazionaledelle donne.org
Basic and inexpensive accommodations in a quiet but central area. For women only.

Centro Diffusione Spiritualità €
Via dei Riari 44, 00153
Tel *06-6880 6122*   **Map** 11 A5
Ⓦ villariari.it
Rock-bottom prices at this religious center located on a quiet street. It has a lovely garden.

Hotel Ottaviano €
Via Ottaviano 6, 00192
Tel *06-3973 8138*   **Map** 3 C2
Ⓦ pensioneottaviano.com
This simple but central hostel is a backpacker's paradise. Just steps away from the Vatican museums.

Hotel Trastevere €
Via Luciano Manara 24a, 00153
Tel *06-581 4713*   **Map** 7 C1
Ⓦ hoteltrastevere.net
A good buy for the area, with basic service and large and bright, though unimaginative, rooms.

Historic
Ancient Rome
Hotel Forum €€
Via Tor de' Conti 25, 00184
Tel *06-679 2446*   **Map** 5 B5
Ⓦ hotelforum.com
Dark wooden floors and rich fabrics evoke an old-world feel. Stunning views of ancient Rome.

Palazzo Manfredi €€€
Via Labicana 125, 00184
Tel *06-7759 1380*   **Map** 9 B1
Ⓦ palazzomanfredi.com
Converted Renaissance palace with elegantly decorated rooms. The Colosseum is just steps away.

Central Rome
Sole al Biscione €
Via del Biscione 76, 00186
Tel *06-6880 6873*   **Map** 11 C4
Ⓦ solealbiscione.it
This functional but charming hotel claims to be the oldest in Rome. Fantastic rooftop terrace.

Casa di Santa Brigida €€
Via Monserrato 54, 00186
Tel *06-6889 2596*   **Map** 11 C4
Ⓦ brigidine.org
Not the cheapest convent in town, but the location, and rooftop terrace are worth it.

Due Torri €€
Vicolo del Leonetto 23, 00186
Tel *06-6880 6956*   **Map** 11 C1
Ⓦ hotelduetorriroma.com
Converted Renaissance palace with small but well-appointed rooms and friendly service.

Teatro di Pompeo €€
Largo del Pallaro 8, 00186
Tel *06-6830 0170*   **Map** 11 C4
Ⓦ hotelteatrodipompeo.it
This simple but evocative hotel was built on the ruins of Pompey's ancient theater. Attentive staff.

Warm and inviting room at the Due Torri hotel

For more information on types of hotels see p296–7

Spagna, Veneto, and Around

Locarno €€€
Via della Penna 22, 00186
Tel *06-361 0841* **Map** 4 F1
w hotellocarno.com
Many classic movies have been shot on the exquisite rooftop terrace of this Art Deco masterpiece.

Trastevere and Around

Relais Casa della Fornarina €
Via di Porta Settimiana 7, 00153
Tel *06-6456 2268* **Map** 11 B5
w casadellafornarina.com
Set in the house where Raphael's muse, the famous baker's daughter, lived. Busy area at night.

Bramante €€
Vicolo delle Palline 24, 00193
Tel *06-6880 6426* **Map** 3 C3
w hotelbramante.com
On a quaint and cobbled backstreet in the shadow of St. Peter's Basilica. Quiet, and tasteful rooms.

DK Choice

Donna Camilla Savelli €€
Via Garibaldi 27, 00153
Tel *06-588 861* **Map** 7 B1
w hoteldonnacamilla
savelli.com
This restored monastery still belongs to the nuns of the original order, but is now a four-star hotel. It was recently voted among the top 100 hotels in the world. All rooms are decorated with antique furniture, and some have Jacuzzi tubs. The cloister is an oasis in the heart of the city.

Luxury

Ancient Rome

Hotel Mediterraneo €€€
Via Cavour 15, 00184
Tel *06-488 4051* **Map** 6 D3
w romehotelmediterraneo.it
This four-star boasts Art Deco design, comfortable rooms, and a terrace with sweeping views.

Kolbe Hotel €€€
Via di San Teodoro 48, 00186
Tel *06-679 8866* **Map** 8 E1
w kolbehotelrome.com
Modern furnishings mix with ancient architectual elements. Some rooms look directly over the Forum.

Radisson Blu ES €€€
Via Filippo Turati 171, 00185
Tel *06-444 841* **Map** 6 E4
w radissonblu.com

A magnificent rooftop pool, cutting-edge design, and breath-taking views make for an unforgettable stay.

Central Rome

Grand Hotel de la Minerve €€€
Piazza della Minerva 69, 00186
Tel *06-695 201* **Map** 12 D3
w grandhoteldela
minerve.com
Postcard views from nearly every room and an unbeatable rooftop terrace. Luxurious service and decor.

Hotel St George €€€
Via Giulia 62, 00186
Tel *06-686 611* **Map** 11 B4
w stgeorgehotel.it
Discreet, romantic hotel with a rooftop terrace offering chic *aperitivo* (apértifs) and river views.

Nazionale €€€
Piazza di Monte Citorio 131, 00186
Tel *06-695 001* **Map** 12 E2
w hotelnazionale.it
Antique furniture, and rich fabrics at this elegant four-star. Ask for the Jacuzzi with a view.

Raphael €€€
Largo Febo 2, 00186
Tel *06-682 831* **Map** 11 C2
w raphaelhotel.com
World-class service, a panoramic terrace, and gorgeous decor make for a romantic stay.

Spagna, Veneto, and Around

Boscolo Aleph €€€
Via di San Basilio 15, 00185
Tel *06-422 901* **Map** 5 B2
w aleph-roma.boscolo
hotels.com
Modern opulence reigns at this five-star. Elegant conference rooms, and a luxurious spa.

Boscolo Exedra €€€
Piazza della Repubblica 47, 00185
Tel *06-4893 8012* **Map** 5 C3
w exedra-roma.boscolo
hotels.com

Lavish, modern five-star hotel with an award-winning spa and a rooftop infinity pool.

De Russie €€€
Via del Babuino 9, 00187
Tel *06-328 881* **Map** 4 F1
w hotelderussie.it
Spectacular gardens surround this Renaissance villa-turned hotel. It has a fully-equipped spa.

Eden €€€
Via Ludovisi 49, 00187
Tel *06-478 121* **Map** 5 B2
w edenroma.com
Outstanding service, and an award-winning rooftop terrace restaurant at this elegant hotel.

DK Choice

Hassler €€€
Piazza Trinità Dei Monti 6, 00187
Tel *06-699 340* **Map** 5 A2
w hotelhasslerroma.com
Impeccable service, plush furnishings, and incomparable views have made this legendary hotel the favorite Roman *pied-à-terre* for many celebrities. Each room is individually styled, and every possible comfort is available for a price. It is enviably located atop the Spanish Steps.

Hotel d'Inghilterra €€€
Via Bocca di Leone 14, 00187
Tel *06-699 811* **Map** 5 A2
w hoteldinghilterrarome.com
Sumptuous accommodations in an enviable location. There is a candlelit rooftop terrace.

Regina Hotel Baglioni €€€
Via Veneto 72, 00187
Tel *06-421 111* **Map** 5 B2
w baglionihotels.com
A gem of Liberty-style decor, and architecture, with opulent furnishings and every comfort.

Majestic €€€
Via Veneto 50, 00187
Tel *06-4214 4705* **Map** 5 B2
w hotelmajestic.com

Impressive lobby of the Grand Hotel de la Minerve

Charming touches at the inviting Pantheon View

Luxurious fabrics, antique elements, and a colorful, eclectic style at this high-end hotel.

St Regis Hotel €€€
Via Vittorio Emanuele Orlando 3, 00185
Tel *06-470 91*   **Map** 5 C3
W starwoodhotels.com
Extravagant decor at this over-the-top palace hotel. There is an on-site spa and fitness center.

Villa Spalletti Trivelli €€€
Via Piacenza 4, 00184
Tel *06-4890 7934*   **Map** 5 B3
W villaspalletti.it
Understated elegance, and impeccable taste at this villa nestled in a lush garden setting.

Westin Excelsior €€€
Via Veneto 125, 00187
Tel *06-470 81*   **Map** 5 B2
W westinrome.com
A favorite with honeymooners; the perfect spot to indulge in *la dolce vita*.

Farther Afield

Grand Hotel Duca d'Este €€
Via Tiburtina Valeria 330, 00019, Tivoli
Tel *07-743 883*
W ducadeste.com
Comfortable business hotel with a well-equipped wellness center. Near the famous thermal baths.

Aldrovandi Palace €€€
Via Ulisse Aldrovandi 15, 00197, Villa Borghese
Tel *06-322 3993*   **Map** 2 D4
W aldrovandi.com
Spectacular five-star with airy rooms, a poolside restaurant, and views of the Borghese gardens.

Pension and B&B
Ancient Rome
La Casa di Amy €
Via Principe Amedeo 85A, 00185
Tel *06-446 0708*   **Map** 6 D4
W lacasadiamy.com

Funky decoration, and a friendly atmosphere at this family-run B&B. Bright, spotlessly clean rooms.

Paba €
Via Cavour 266, 00184
Tel *06-4782 4902*   **Map** 5 B5
W hotelpaba.com
Proximity to the Forum makes Paba a convenient budget option. Rooms are simply furnished.

Piccolo Principe €
Via Giovanni Giolitti 255, 00185
Tel *32-0699 3110*   **Map** 6 E4
W bebromatermini.it
Brightly painted rooms with basic furnishings, and clean bathrooms. Located near the Termini station.

Central Rome
Casa Banzo €
Piazza del Monte di Pietà 30, 00186
Tel *06-683 3909*   **Map** 11 C4
W casabanzo.it
Impressive details, and period-style furniture make this low-priced option quite enjoyable.

DK Choice
Pantheon View €
Via del Seminario 87, 00186
Tel *06-699 0294*   **Map** 12 D3
W pantheonview.it
This pension offers the comforts of a hotel, in addition to details such as wood-beamed ceilings, antique furniture, exposed brickwork, chandeliers, and original copper faucets. Most rooms have Pantheon views.

Spagna, Veneto, and Around

DK Choice
Casa Howard €
Via di Capo le Case 18, 00187 and Via Sistina 149, 00187
Tel *06-6992 4555*   **Map** 12 F1

W casahoward.com
This B&B inspired by E. M. Forster's novel *Howard's End* has 10 unique rooms. What it lacks in round-the-clock service, it makes up for in style, and character. Some rooms do not have private baths, but kimonos are provided for convenience.

Panda €
Via della Croce 35, 00187
Tel *06-678 0179*   **Map** 5 A2
W hotelpanda.it
Simply furnished rooms are warmed by terra-cotta-tiled floors and wood-beamed ceilings.

Hotel Julia €€
Via Rasella 29, 00187
Tel *06-488 1637*   **Map** 5 B3
W hoteljulia.it
A well-priced three-star with simple, comfortable rooms. The staff is friendly.

Hotel Suisse €€
Via Gregoriana 54, 00187
Tel *06-678 3649*   **Map** 5 A2
W hotelsuisserome.com
Great value and warm service at this well-appointed, and superbly located pension.

Oceania €€
Via Firenze 38, 00187
Tel *06-482 4696*   **Map** 5 C3
W hoteloceania.it
Plenty of old-world charm, and eccentric details at this simple but tasteful hotel.

Residenza Cellini €€
Via Modena 5, 00184
Tel *06-4782 5204*   **Map** 5 C3
W residenzacellini.it
Spacious rooms with basic furnishings. Some bathrooms have Jacuzzi tubs.

Trastevere and Around
Arco del Lauro €
Via dell'Arco de' Tolomei 27, 00153
Tel *06-9784 0350*   **Map** 8 D1
W arcodellauro.it
A tiny hotel with simple but lovely rooms in a picturesque medieval location.

Farther Afield
Palazzo Maggiore €
Via Domenico Giuliani 89, 00019, Tivoli
Tel *39-3104 4937*
W palazzomaggiore.com
This sweet B&B with cozy, individually decorated rooms is the perfect base to explore Tivoli's incredible villas.

For more information on types of hotels *see p298–9*

WHERE TO EAT AND DRINK

In Rome, eating out can be both a joy and an entertainment. On warm summer evenings, tables spill out into every conceivable open space, and diners dedicate long hours to the popular social activity of people-watching (and of being noticed and admired themselves) in a confusion of passers-by, buskers, rose sellers, and traffic. Although Romans have always loved to linger at the table, the lavish feasts of ancient Rome have slimmed down, and today's cooking is based on simplicity, freshness, and good-quality local ingredients in what is

essentially a seasonal cuisine. Fast food is available, but it is fundamentally alien to the Roman temperament and way of life.

The restaurants reviewed in this chapter have been selected from the best that Rome can offer across all price ranges. Their descriptions, including the highlighted DK Choice entries, will help you narrow down your choice and enjoy a variety of cuisine types. The section on *Light Meals and Drinks* on pages 320–25 has details of recommended cafés, pizzerias, wine bars, and other places for more casual eating.

Types of Restaurants

In general, a *trattoria* is a family-run establishment with good home cooking, while a *ristorante* is more upmarket, more elegant, and thus more expensive.

Some eating places – where paper tablecloths give a clue to low prices – simply have no name. They offer excellent, basic home cooking. A number of them offer a great deal more than that, and your chances of finding authentic Roman cooking are higher in the best of these establishments than in expensive restaurants.

There will probably be times when you do not want a large meal, and Rome offers a huge variety of places for more casual eating (*see pp320–25*). One type of place offering snacks or more

substantial dishes is the *enoteca*, which doubles as a well-stocked wine shop for browsers and connoisseurs.

Other places for a sit-down, informal lunch or dinner are *birrerie*, which are not only for beer drinkers, but also offer pizzas and even four-course meals.

There is always interesting take-out food for sale – *pizza rustica* or *pizza al taglio* (pizza by the slice) is available all over the city. For the best full-size pizzas, choose places with wood stoves (*forno a legna*). Other take-outs such as a whole roast chicken, or *pomodori al riso* (tomatoes stuffed with rice), can be found at a *rosticcerie*. A self-service *tavola calda* will serve an impressive array of hot food and is ideal for lunchtime.

Fresh artichokes, a Roman specialty

Vegetarian Food

Purely vegetarian restaurants are few and far between in Rome, but everywhere you will find pasta and rice dishes (*risotto*). Most menus include an extensive list of vegetable-based side dishes (*contorni*), which could be anything from artichokes (stewed – *alla Romana* – or

fried – *alla giudia*) to grilled or au gratin vegetables to sautéed spinach, chard, or chicory. Vegetables stuffed with rice then baked in the oven are also menu staples. Most menus are adaptable, as dishes are prepared to order. Tell your waiter that you are *vegetariano* (female: *vegetariana*) and he will advise accordingly.

The Price of a Meal

What you pay will depend on your choice of establishment. In a *tavola calda* or Roman pizzeria, for example, you can still eat for as little as €15 a head. A local *trattoria* costs perhaps €25, while in a fancier restaurant, plan on around €30 and up. Bottled wine, as opposed to a jug or carafe of house wine (*vino della casa*), will cost more but should offer a more interesting range of tastes (*see p308*). House wine can be a hit-or-miss affair.

Reading the Menu

Not every restaurant provides a menu – the waiter will often tell you the day's specialties (*piatti del giorno*), usually not mentioned on the menu but almost always worth ordering. Or, ask for *la lista* (the menu) and then allow yourself to be guided.

A meal could begin with *antipasti* (appetizers) or *primi*

Interior of a hotel restaurant

piatti – the latter consisting of *pasta asciutta* (pasta with some kind of sauce), *pasta in brodo* (clear broth with pasta in it), *pasta al forno* (baked pasta), risotto, or a substantial soup. You then move on to the *secondi*, the main meat or fish course, for which you will usually need to order vegetables (*contorni*) separately. Afterward you have *formaggi* (cheeses), *frutta* (fruit), or *dolci* (desserts). Romans do not usually eat cheese as well as a sweet dish. Strong espresso coffee, and perhaps a liqueur (*amaro or digestivo*) rounds off the meal (*see p309*). You may want to skip the first course, or prefer to choose a salad or vegetable dish. Pasta alone is not seen traditionally as a full meal.

Opening Times

Restaurants are generally open from about noon to 3pm and from 8pm to 11pm or later. The busiest times tend to be 9pm–9:30pm for dinner and 1pm–1:30pm at lunchtime. Dinner is generally the preferred time for relaxed eating, particularly in summer. Bars are open all day, often from the early hours, serving all kinds of drinks (alcohol can be sold at any time of day) and snacks. The quietest month is August, when many restaurant owners take their annual vacation (shown by *chiuso per ferie* signs).

Making Reservations

Reservations (*prenotazione*) are generally advisable. Sunday is the main lunchtime of the week

One of many Trastevere cafés

Outdoor café life in the piazza outside Santa Maria in Trastevere

when you should definitely book; the same usually goes for Saturday evening. Check the weekly closing day if you do not book. Many places are closed on Mondays, and Sunday evening can also be difficult.

In summer, try to reserve a shady table outside, since air conditioning is not universal.

Wheelchair Access

Rome is becoming more solicitous toward those in wheelchairs, but a call to the restaurant in advance will help secure the right table.

Taking Children Along

Children are made very welcome, particularly in family-run places. You can usually order half-portions, or just ask for an extra plate. High chairs (*seggioloni*) may also be available.

Smoking

Smoking is banned in restaurants, bars, and cafés.

Recommended Restaurants

Every area of Rome has its own culinary delights (*see Flavors of Rome pp306–7*). Our restaurants are divided into five geographical areas: Ancient Rome, Central Rome, Spagna, Veneto and Around, Trastevere and Around, and Farther Afield. Ancient Rome begins near the Forum, stretching past the Colosseum to encompass Testaccio, the Aventine Hill, the Lateran and the Esquiline Hill (where Termini station is found). Central Rome is the very heart of town, from

Piazza Navona and the Pantheon down to the river, including Campo de' Fiori and the Jewish Ghetto. Spagna, Veneto, and Around covers the heavily-trafficked areas from Piazza del Popolo to Piazza Barberini, as well as the Quirinal Hill and the gastronomically rich neighborhood of Monti. Trastevere and Around includes the Vatican and the foothills of the Janiculum as well. Farther Afield covers anything from areas just outside the downtown, like Monteverde and Parioli, to nearby cities Tivoli, and Fiumicino.

Each restaurant listed is given a cuisine category. Traditional Roman cuisine is hearty and meat-based, although vegetarian dishes do exist. Modern Italian restaurants use traditional recipes as a springboard to create new and modern dishes using unexpected ingredients. Every Italian region has its own local cuisine, and they vary drastically. Opt for a regional Italian restaurant to sample these varieties. Pizzerias abound, but keep in mind that some serve a range of other dishes, while others offer nothing but the beloved dough. The *enotecas* and *birrerias* listed offer food to go with drinks, from cheese platters to full meals. For an extraordinary meal, try a fine dining option, but be prepared for a hefty bill. Rome's international restaurants are great when pasta and pizza begin to get old.

Throughout our listings, we've marked recommended restaurants as DK Choice. We've highlighted these because they offer a special experience – either for the superb cuisine, for enjoying a particularly Italian night out, for the excellent value, or a combination of these.

The Flavors of Rome

There are few more enduring pleasures than lingering over a leisurely alfresco meal in a piazza in the Eternal City. Roman food is tasty, nutritious, simple, and extremely varied. Menus tend to be seasonal, and there are even specialties eaten on specific days of the week. Traditionally, Thursday is *gnocchi* day, Friday is for salted cod *(baccalà)*, and Saturday for tripe. Food is redolent of aromatic herbs, olive oil, garlic, and onions, and there are many signature dishes, including pasta. But much authentic Roman cuisine is based on organ meats, and slow, inventive cooking transforms these tradtionally "poor" cuts into rich and flavorsome dishes.

Olives and olive oil

Pasta being made by hand in traditional style

Cucina Romana

Traditional Roman cuisine originated in the Testaccio area, near the old slaughterhouse, whose butchers *(vaccinari)* were paid partly in cash and partly in variety meats. The "fifth quarter" *(quinto quarto)* included head, trotters, tail, intestines, brain, and other unmentionable parts of the beast, which, when carefully cooked and richly flavored with herbs and spices, are transformed into culinary delight. These robust dishes, such as *coda alla vaccinara* (literally, "oxtail cooked in the style of the slaughterhouse butcher") still feature on the menus of many of Rome's top restaurants.

For more squeamish carnivores, lamb is popular, often served simply roasted. Veal is another specialty, as is piglet flavored with herbs. Authentic *cucina romana* also has roots in the Jewish cuisine of the Ghetto area. Local globe artichokes are fried whole in olive oil *(carciofi alla giudia)* or served *alla romana*, with oil, garlic, and Roman mint. Zucchini flowers are also deep-fried, as are Jewish-style salt cod fillets *(filetti di baccalà)*.

Seafood and fish restaurants are among the best in Rome,

Marinated artichokes · Roast peppers · Sun-dried tomatoes · Sweet baby peppers · Olives · Marinated mushrooms

Selection of delicious, typically Roman *antipasti* (appetizers)

Regional Dishes and Specialties

As an appetizer, *bruschetta* (Roman dialect for "lightly burned bread") may be topped with a selection of intense flavors. Other *antipasti* include crispy-fried or marinated vegetables. A favorite pasta dish is *bucatini all'amatriciana* – pasta tubes in a spicy tomato, and sausage or bacon sauce, sprinkled with grated tangy pecorino cheese. Veal is a great favorite and delicacies include *rigatoni alla pajata* (pasta with milk-fed veal intestines). Lamb is also very popular, in dishes such as *abbacchio al forno* (roasted milk-fed lamb) or *alla cacciatore* ("huntsman's style" with anchovy sauce). The generic word for organ meats is *animelle,* and Roman delicacies include *cervelle* (calves' brains), *pajata* (veal intestines), and *trippa* (tripe).

Bruschetta

Supplì These tasty fried rice croquettes are stuffed with mozzarella cheese that oozes out when they are cut.

Selecting fresh vegetables at a market in central Rome

although they can be very expensive. Everything is available, from sumptuous seafood platters to small fish caught off the Lazio coast, and served fried or used in soups, as well as superb sea bass cooked Roman-style with porcini mushrooms.

Pasta, Pasta

Pasta is the mainstay of the Roman meal, especially spaghetti. *Spaghetti alla carbonara*, made with *pancetta* (cured bacon) or *guanciale* (pig's cheek), egg yolks, and cheese, is a classic Roman dish, as is *spaghetti alle vongole*, with clams. Many menus also include *spaghetti cacio e pepe* (with pecorino cheese and pepper) and *bucatini all'amatriciana* (with a spicy tomato and bacon sauce). At a conservative estimate, there is

one type of pasta for every day of the year. Many have wonderfully descriptive or poetic names, such as *capelli d'angelo* (angel's hair), *strozzapreti* (priest chokers), or *ziti* (bridegrooms), whose shape is best left to the imagination.

Huge wheels of pecorino cheese ready to be cut and enjoyed

La Dolce Vita

For those with a taste for "the sweet life," nuts, fruits, and versatile ricotta cheese are often combined in mouthwatering delicious sweets. Ice cream is an art form in Rome, where some parlors offer over 100 flavors of homemade *gelati*. Types vary from the classic *crema*, and *frutta* to *grattachecca* (water ice), from *semifreddo* (a half-frozen sponge cake, similar to *tiramisù* in consistency) to *granità* (ice shavings flavored with fruit syrups). Glorious *gelato* is one of the great pleasures here, to be enjoyed at any time of the day – or night.

On the Menu

Abbacchio alla cacciatora Lamb simmered in Castelli Romani wine with anchovies, garlic, rosemary, and olive oil.

Bruschetta Toasted bread rubbed with garlic, drizzled with olive oil, may be served with a variety of toppings.

Gnocchi alla romana Little semolina dumplings served with a tomato or *ragù* sauce, or just with butter.

Pecorino romano The traditional Roman cheese, made from ewe's milk.

Spigola alla romana Sea bass with *porcini* mushrooms, shallots, garlic, Castelli Romani wine, and olive oil.

Spaghetti alla carbonara The creamy sauce thickens as the hot pasta mixes into the egg yolks and cheese.

Saltimbocca alla romana Veal slices are rolled with prosciutto and sage. Saltimbocca means "jump in the mouth."

Crostata di ricotta This rich, baked cheesecake is made using ricotta and flavored with Marsala and lemon.

What to Drink in Rome

Italy is one of Europe's most significant wine-producing countries, keeping up a tradition started in the hills around Rome over 2,000 years ago. Today, wine is usually drunk with meals as a matter of course, and knowing the difference between *rosso* (red) and *bianco* (white) may be all the vocabulary you need to get by. Beer is widely available, too, as well as good ranges of apéritifs and digestifs. Rome's drinking water, another debt to the ancient Romans, is particularly good, fresh, and sweet, and in abundant supply.

The vineyards of Frascati, southeast of Rome

White Wine

Orvieto   Frascati

Vines thrive in the warm climate of Lazio, the region around Rome, producing abundant supplies of inexpensive dry white wine for the city's cafés and restaurants. It is usually sold by the carafe. Of local bottled wines, Frascati is the best-known, but Castelli Romani, Marino, Colli Albani, and Velletri are very similar in style. All are made from one grape variety, the Trebbiano, though better-quality versions contain a dash of Malvasia for perfume and flavor. Other central Italian whites worth trying are Orvieto and Verdicchio. Quality white wines from all over Italy, including fine whites from Friuli in the northeast, are widely available in Rome.

Calcaia comes from Barberani, a reliable producer of Orvieto.

Bigi produces good-quality Orvieto, especially the single-vineyard Torricella.

Wine Type	Good Vintages	Good Producers
White Wine		
Friuli (Pinot Bianco, Chardonnay, Pinot Grigio, Sauvignon)	The most recent	Gravner, Jermann, Puiatti, Schiopetto, Volpe Pasini
Orvieto/ Orvieto Classico	The most recent	Antinori, Barberani, Bigi, Il Palazzone
Red Wine		
Chianti/ Chianti Classico/ Chianti Rufina	2007, 2006, 2001, 2000, 99, 97, 95, 90, 88, 85	Antinori, Castello di Ama, Castello di Cacchiano, Castello di Volpaia, Felsina Berardenga, Fontodi, Frescobaldi, Isole e Olena, Il Palazzino, Riecine, Rocca delle Macie, Ruffino, Vecchie Terre di Montefili, Villa Cafaggio
Brunello di Montalcino/ Vino Nobile di Montepulciano	2007, 2004, 2001, 99, 97, 95, 90, 88, 85	Altesino, Avignonesi, Biondi Santi, Caparzo, Case Basse, Lisini, Il Poggione, Poliziano, Villa Banfi
Barolo/Barbaresco	2006, 2004, 2000, 99, 98, 97, 95, 90, 89, 88	Aldo Conterno, Altare, Ceretto, Clerico, Gaja, Giacomo Conterno, Giacosa, Mascarello, Ratti, Voerzio

Casal Pilozzo is an easy-drinking white wine from Frascati producers Colli di Catone. Choose the youngest vintage.

Colle Gaio, with its rich, fruity flavor, stands out among the dry white Frascatis.

Red Wine

Though some local red wine is made, most of the bottled red wine in Rome comes from other parts of Italy. Regions like Tuscany, and Piedmont produce very good everyday drinking as well as top-class wines like Barolo. Price should reflect quality – try Dolcetto, Rosso di Montalcino, or Montepulciano for good-value reds.

Tuscan table wine   Barolo

Montepulciano d'Abruzzo, a rich and juicy red wine, is always a good buy. It is produced in the Abruzzi region east of Rome.

Chianti Classico Riserva is older and stronger than a normal Chianti Classico.

Torre Ercolana is produced in small quantities, and is generally regarded as one of Lazio's best red wines. It is made from Cesanese, and Cabernet grapes and requires at least five years' aging.

Reading the Label

Italy has a two-tier system for labeling quality wine. DOC (*denominazione di origine controllata*) means you can be sure the wine is from the region declared on the label and is made from designated grape varieties. A higher classification – DOCG (*denominazione di origine controllata e garantita*) – is given to top wines such as the reds Barolo, Barbaresco, Chianti Classico, and Brunello di Montalcino.

Chianti Classico

Apéritifs and Other Drinks

Bitter, herb-flavored drinks like Martini, Campari, or Aperol are the most popular apéritifs. (Ask for an *analcolico* if you prefer a non-alcoholic one.) Italians drink their apéritifs straight or with ice and soda. Strong after-dinner drinks, known as *digestivi* or *amari*, are worth trying, as is aniseed *sambuca*, served with coffee beans. Italian brandy, and grappa can be very fiery, and Italian beer is made in lager style.

Campari

Drinking Water

Unlike many Mediterranean cities, Rome benefits from a constant supply of fresh drinking water, piped down from the hills through a system of pipes, and aqueducts that has changed little from ancient Roman times. Only if there is a sign saying *acqua non potabile* is the water not safe to drink.

One of Rome's many fresh water drinking fountains

Soft Drinks

Italian fruit juices are good, and most bars squeeze fresh orange juice (*spremuta di arancia*) on the spot. Iced coffee, and fruit-flavored tea, such as peach, are popular.

Refrigerated storage for wine and beer

Coffee is almost more important to Roman life than wine. Choose espresso for strong black coffee at any time of day; milky cappuccino for breakfast or mid-afternoon; and caffè latte for extra milk.

Espresso

Cappuccino

Caffè latte

Where to Eat and Drink

Ancient Rome

0,75 €
Enoteca **Map** 8 E1
*Via dei Cerchi 65,
00186*
Tel 06-687 5706
Named for the size of a bottle
of wine, this friendly *enoteca*
offers a meal at almost any
time of day.

Angelina a Testaccio €
Traditional Roman **Map** 8 D4
*Via Galvani 24a,
00153*
Tel 06-5728 3840
The gem of Testaccio, this
shabby-chic bistro offers
a tempting Sunday brunch.

Asmara €
Ethiopian/Eritrean **Map** 6 D2
Via Cernaia 36, 00185
Tel 06-481 4409
A surprising combination
of flavors enliven the mostly
meat-based dishes; many
vegetarian options are
also available. Asmara has
a lively atmosphere.

Bibenda €
Enoteca **Map** 9 A1
*Via Capo d'Africa 21,
00184*
Tel 06-7720 6673
The official wine bar of Rome's
most important sommelier
academy, Bibenda also offers a
wide selection of tasty snacks to
pair with white or red.

Charly's Saucière €
French-Swiss **Map** 9 B1
*Via di San Giovanni in
Laterano 270, 00184*
Tel 06-7049 5666
Hearty soups, warming au gratin
dishes, and fondue are a few of
the specialties available at this
popular restaurant.

Da Oio a Casa Mia €
Traditional Roman **Map** 8 D3
*Via Galvani 43,
00153*
Tel 06-578 2680
Friendly though unrefined
service at this family-style
restaurant serving traditional
Roman recipes. Do not miss the
lip-smacking oxtail stew.

Da Remo €
Pizzeria **Map** 8 D3
*Piazza di Santa Maria
Liberatrice 44, 00153*
Tel 06-574 6270
Thin, crispy pizzas baked in
a wood-burning oven, plus
plenty of fried appetizers, are
offered here. Arrive early to
avoid the long lines.

Felice a Testaccio €
Traditional Roman **Map** 8 D3
*Via Mastro Giorgio 29,
00153*
Tel 06-574 6800
Black-and-white checkered
floors, and exposed brickwork
make a charming setting.
Roman cuisine, including plenty
of organ meat, is offered.

I Clementini €
Traditional Roman **Map** 9 B1
*Via di San Giovanni in
Laterano 106, 00184*
Tel 06-4542 6395
The chefs at this simple,
authentic, and traditional
restaurant take pride in using
their grandmothers' recipes.

Il Pentagrappolo €
Enoteca **Map** 9 A1
Via Celimontana 21b, 00184
Tel 06-709 6301
A modern wine bar,
Il Pentagrappolo serves both
creative snacks, and full
meals. Live jazz on most
weekend nights.

La Gallina Bianca €
Pizzeria **Map** 6 D4
*Via Antonio Rosmini 9,
00184*
Tel 06-474 3777
Excellent pizza and much
more at this casual restaurant
with country-style decor. Do
not miss the tempting home-
made desserts.

La Taverna dei 40 €
Traditional Roman **Map** 9 A1
*Via Claudia 24,
00184*
Tel 06-700 0550
Family-run establishment
serving classic Roman dishes.
Sit outside to see the
Colosseum in the distance.

Oasi della Birra €
Birreria **Map** 8 D3
*Piazza Testaccio 39,
00153*
Tel 06-574 6122
The name says it all – this beer
oasis starts serving drinks and
food in the early afternoon, and
no guest leaves thirsty.

The bar area at 0,75, a trendy *enoteca*

Trattoria Monti €
Traditional Roman **Map** 6 D4
Via di San Vito 13,
00185
Tel *06-446 6573*
The daily specials at this heavenly *trattoria* feature seasonal ingredients that are explained to guests in detail by the brothers who own the place.

Trimani il Wine Bar €
Enoteca **Map** 6 D2
Via Cernaia 37b,
00185
Tel *06-446 9630*
Modern wine bar with a vast selection of labels perfectly paired with cold, and hot dishes as well as a range of Italian cheeses.

Checchino dal 1887 €€
Traditional Roman **Map** 8 D4
Via di Monte Testaccio 30,
00153
Tel *06-574 3816*
Hearty Roman dishes, lovingly prepared, make Checchino dal 1887 a favorite spot for discerning diners.

Da Danilo €€
Traditional Roman **Map** 6 E5
Via Petrarca 13,
00185
Tel *06-7720 0111*
Typical Roman dishes are served at this homey *trattoria* run by mother and son. Also boasts an impressive list of artisanal beers.

Enoteca Provincia Romana €€
Enoteca **Map** 5 B5
Largo di Foro Traiano 82-84,
00187
Tel *06-6994 0273*
Both the wine list, and the menu ingredients are refreshingly local at this *enoteca*, sponsored by the province of Rome.

Flavio al Velavevodetto €€
Traditional Roman **Map** 8 D4
Via di Monte Testaccio 97,
00153
Tel *06-574 4194*
Simple and satisfying Roman pasta and meat dishes, plus a few seafood options, all at reasonable prices. Lots of outdoor seating space in good weather.

Hang Zhou €€
Chinese **Map** 6 E5
Via Principe Eugenio 82,
00184
Tel *06-487 2732*
This is unanimously touted as serving the best Chinese food

Seating at the well-reviewed Checchino dal 1887

in town. The all-you-can-eat buffet is a steal, but generally prices are higher than average.

Maud €€
Modern Italian **Map** 9 A1
Via Capo d'Africa 6,
00184
Tel *06-8956 2910*
Maud is a great choice for both a creatively prepared meal, and an after-dinner drink. Sleek, modern decor, and useful for people-watching.

Perilli €€
Traditional Roman **Map** 8 D3
Via Marmorata 39,
00153
Tel *06-575 5100*
Generous portions of Roman favorites are served here. Authentic food, although the prices are a bit high.

Tempio di Iside €€
Seafood **Map** 9 B1
Via Labicano 50, 00184

Vibrant interior at the stellar Agata e Romeo

Tel *06-700 4741*
Fish of all kinds, much of it raw, including several varieties of oysters. Romantic, candlelit interior with exposed brickwork.

Agata e Romeo €€€
Fine Dining **Map** 6 D4
Via Carlo Alberto 45,
00185
Tel *06-446 6115*
High-end dining with exceptional taster menus. Even traditional recipes have a sophisticated twist. Cavernous wine cellar.

Aroma €€€
Fine Dining **Map** 9 A1
Via Labicana 125,
00184
Tel *06-7759 1380*
A well-reviewed restaurant with sleek interiors, and unequaled views of the Colosseum. Seasonal menu with regional favorites.

Central Rome

Acchiappafantasmi €
Pizzeria **Map** 11 B3
Via dei Cappellari 66,
00186
Tel *06-687 3462*
This pizzeria, whose name means "Ghostbusters," serves tasty, and crunchy ghost-shaped pizzas.

Al Duello €
Traditional Roman **Map** 12 D2
Vicolo della Vaccarella 11,
00186
Tel *06-687 3348*
Hearty Roman fare is served in this *trattoria* named for the infamous duel in which the painter Caravaggio (1571–1610) killed his opponent.

Diners at the cozy Nonna Betta, known for its authentic Jewish cuisine

Baffetto €
Pizzeria **Map** 11 C3
*Via del Governo Vecchio
114, 00186*
Tel *06-686 1617*
The thin, crisp Roman-style pizza
served here is considered by
many to be the best in Rome. Be
prepared for a long wait.

Coso €
Enoteca **Map** 12 E1
Via in Lucina 16L, 00186
Tel *06-6821 0420*
Coso is a trendy wine
bar serving pan-Italian dishes
including meat, fish, and
vegetarian specialties. Choose
from fantastic desserts, and
a stellar wine list.

Da Pancrazio €
Traditional Roman **Map** 11 C4
*Piazza del Biscione 92,
00186*
Tel *06-686 1246*
Dine here for a slice of history:
Da Pancrazio is set above the
ruins of Pompey's 1st-century
BC theater. Lovingly prepared
traditional Roman recipes
are offered.

Enoteca il Goccetto €
Enoteca **Map** 11 B3
*Via dei Banchi Vecchi 14,
00186*
Tel *06-686 4268*
A casual wine bar that serves
top-quality bottles at fair prices;
delicious snacks are also
available. Popular with locals.

Enoteca il Piccolo €
Enoteca **Map** 11 C3
*Via del Governo Vecchio 74,
00186*
Tel *06-6880 1746*
This tiny wine bar spills out onto
a busy piazza and boasts an
ample selection of Italian labels
at great prices.

Il Corallo €
Traditional Roman **Map** 11 B3
Via del Corallo 10, 00186
Tel *06-6830 7703*
Located on a charming street,
simple yet imaginative dishes
are served by friendly staff. The
wine list is impressive.

Le Streghe €
Traditional Roman **Map** 11 B2
*Vicolo del Curato 13,
00186*
Tel *06-686 1381*
A no-frills *osteria*, Le Streghe
serves a small selection of time-
honored recipes. Authentic
home-style cooking.

DK Choice

Nonna Betta €
Traditional Roman **Map** 12 D5
*Via del Portico d'Ottavia 16,
00186*
Tel *06-6880 6263*
An authentic kosher restaurant
in the heart of the Jewish
quarter, the renowned
Nonna Betta specializes in
delectable Jewish-Roman
cuisine. The fried mozzarella
balls are highly recommended.
The ambience is warm
and cozy.

Old Bear €
Regional Italian **Map** 11 C2
*Via dei Gigli d'Oro 2–4,
00186*
Tel *06-6821 0009*
Dark wood beams and low
ceilings create a warm, inviting
ambience. The Tuscan soup with
truffle oil is recommended.

Open Baladin €
Birreria **Map** 11 C5
*Via degli Specchi 6,
00186*
Tel *06-683 8989*

Over 120 labels of craft beers,
as well as original all-natural
sodas, are available.

Osteria del Gallo €
Traditional Roman **Map** 11 C2
*Vicolo di Montevecchio 27,
00186*
Tel *06-687 3781*
Classic Roman dishes, and tasty
seafood options are served at
this informal spot with plenty
of outdoor seating on a
secluded piazza.

Osteria del Sostegno €
Modern Italian **Map** 12 D2
Via delle Colonnelle 5, 00186
Tel *06-679 3842*
Tucked away in a tiny alley,
this charming little restaurant
creates inventive versions of
classic Roman recipes.

Polese €
Traditional Roman **Map** 11 B3
*Piazza Sforza Cesarini 40,
00186*
Tel *06-686 1709*
Authentic traditional recipes
are served with a smile here.
Outdoor seating on a large
square ensures a table even
on a busy night.

Sora Margherita €
Traditional Roman **Map** 12 D5
*Piazza delle Cinque Scole 30,
00186*
Tel *06-687 4216*
A simple and authentic eatery,
Sora Margherita whips up classic
Italian fare. Do not expect
English translations on the
handwritten menu.

Angolo Divino €€
Enoteca **Map** 11 C4
*Via dei Balestrari 12,
00186*
Tel *06-686 4413*
An intimate and romantic

restaurant with an impressive wine list. Try the divine warm chocolate cake.

Armando al Pantheon €€
Traditional Roman   **Map** 12 D3
Salita i Crescenzi 31,
00186
Tel *06-6880 3034*
Two brothers own and run this typical Roman *trattoria*. Classic dishes, and some interesting vegetarian options available.

Ba Ghetto Milky €€
Traditional Roman   **Map** 12 D5
Via Portico D'Ottavia 57,
00186
Tel *06-6830 0077*
Heavenly Jewish-Roman cuisine served strictly kosher; only vegetarian fare is available. Outdoor seating on a bustling pedestrian street.

Capricci Siciliani €€
Regional Italian   **Map** 11 B2
Via di Panico 83, 00186
Tel *06-4543 3823*
Elegant Sicilian food in the heart of the historic city. Specialties include swordfish medallions, and anchovy rolls.

Casa Bleve €€
Enoteca   **Map** 12 D3
Via del Teatro Valle 48,
00186
Tel *06-686 5970*
Vaulted ceilings, and ceramic-tiled floors add a sense of occasion to any meal at this sophisticated wine bar. Ample buffet lunch.

Clemente alla Maddalena €€
Modern Italian   **Map** 12 D2
Piazza della Maddalena 4,
00186
Tel *06-683 3633*
The head chef creates imaginative takes on cuisines from all over Italy. Outdoor seating in a lovely square.

Cul de Sac €€
Enoteca   **Map** 11 C3
Piazza di Pasquino 73,
00186
Tel *06-6880 1094*
This narrow wine bar boasts hundreds of labels as well as a wide variety of tasty eats.

Da Giggetto €€
Traditional Roman   **Map** 12 E5
Via del Portico d'Ottavia
21/22, 00186
Tel *06-686 1105*
Dine in the shadow of ancient ruins at this famous Jewish-Roman eatery. The deep-fried artichokes are delectable.

Enoteca Capranica €€
Enoteca   **Map** 12 D2
Piazza Capranica 99, 00186
Tel *06-6994 0992*
Numerous bottles line the walls of this large yet cozy wine bar. Mouthwatering dishes pair with excellent wines.

Il Bacaro €€
Modern Italian   **Map** 12 D2
Via degli Spagnoli 27, 00186
Tel *06-687 2554*
This restaurant is romantic and centrally located. Specialties include the *trofie* with asparagus or beef *carpaccio* with chicory and truffles.

Il Convivio-Troiani €€
Fine Dining   **Map** 11 C2
Vicolo dei Soldati 31, 00186
Tel *06-686 9432*
This elegant restaurant takes pride in its handmade products, from bread to pasta. Exquisite wine list.

DK Choice

La Pallacorda €€
Seafood   **Map** 12 D1
Piazza Cardelli 5, 00186

Convivial atmosphere at the popular Jewish-Roman Da Giggetto

Tel *06-683 4026*
This sophisticated restaurant excels at seafood dishes with a touch of imagination. Oysters are the house specialty and several varieties are available here, while the generous antipasto buffet boasts delicacies such as salmon tartare. Many pasta options are also on the menu, in addition to excellent desserts. A miniature chocolate cake with a liquid center makes the perfect end to a memorable meal.

Maccheroni €€
Traditional Roman   **Map** 12 D2
Piazza delle Coppelle 44,
00186
Tel *06-6830 7895*
A Roman institution, this large restaurant relies on tried and true recipes, served in a rustic and warm atmosphere by a jovial staff.

Montevecchio €€
Traditional Roman   **Map** 11 C2
Piazza Montevecchio 22/a,
00186
Tel *06-686 1319*
This tiny, sophisticated restaurant is where well-heeled locals converse in hushed tones over delectable pasta and meat dishes.

Osteria del Pegno €€
Traditional Roman   **Map** 11 C2
Vicolo di Montevecchio 8,
00186
Tel *06-6880 7025*
Small and intimate restaurant with lovingly prepared staples of the Roman tradition. A few more inventive options also feature on the menu. There is an ample wine list.

Wine bottles adorning the walls of Enoteca Capranica

For more information on types of restaurants *see p304*

Charming outdoor seating and helpful staff at Piperno

Percento
Modern Italian   €€   **Map** 11 C4
*Via del Pellegrino 160,
00186*
Tel *06-689 554*
The chefs at this modern restaurant prepare pan-Italian dishes in a glass-enclosed kitchen. Large selection of international cheeses.

Pierluigi
Modern Italian   €€   **Map** 11 B4
*Piazza de' Ricci 144,
00186*
Tel *06-686 8717*
A sprawling outdoor seating area in a cobbled piazza enhances the heavenly, and imaginative inventions that come out of Pierluigi's kitchen.

Piperno
Traditional Roman   €€   **Map** 12 D5
*Via Monte de' Cenci 9,
00186*
Tel *06-6880 6629*
Set in a pretty piazza, this place serves traditonal Roman cuisine. Large selection of seafood plus excellent fried artichokes.

Roscioli
Enoteca   €€   **Map** 11 C4
*Via dei Giubbonari 21,
00186*
Tel *06-687 5287*
Part wine bar and part *salumeria* (delicatessen). Delicious meats and cheeses accompany a dizzying selection of wine labels.

Sangallo ai Coronari
Modern Italian   €€   **Map** 11 B2
*Via dei Coronari 180,
00186*
Tel *06-686 5549*
Time-honored recipes from Rome and the area immediately south of the city. Tempting tasting menu and helpful sommelier for wine suggestions.

Settimio al Pellegrino
Traditional Roman   €€   **Map** 11 B3
*Via del Pellegrino 117,
00186*
Tel *06-688 01976*
Knock if the door is closed at this old-fashioned favorite with locals. Simple food, and friendly service.

Sora Lella
Traditional Roman   €€   **Map** 8 D1
*Via di Ponte Quattro Capi 16,
00186*
Tel *06-686 1601*
The only restaurant on Tiber Island, this historic *trattoria* has been in the same family for generations. Serves lighter versions of Roman recipes.

Terra di Siena
Regional Italian   €€   **Map** 11 C3
*Piazza di Pasquino 77,
00186*
Tel *06-6830 7704*
Serves hearty Tuscan dishes such as Florentine steak and ribollita soup. Sit in a cheerful dining room or on the buzzing piazza.

The Library
Modern Italian   €€   **Map** 11 C3
*Vicolo della Cancelleria 7,
00186*
Tel *334 806 1200*
Located on a narrow back street, this miniscule, and romantic spot has just a few tables. Great wine and first courses.

Vinando
Enoteca   €€   **Map** 12 E4
*Piazza Margana 23,
00186*
Tel *06-6920 0741*
Great vegetarian options, as well as meat and fish dishes, are served at this chic wine bar. Open all day.

Vino e Camino
Regional Italian   €€   **Map** 11 A2
Piazza dell'Oro 6, 00186

Tel *06-6830 1332*
Wine bottles line the walls and there is a working fireplace at this cozy restaurant with lovingly prepared food and excellent wine.

Vitti
Traditional Roman   €€   **Map** 12 E1
Piazza di San Lorenzo in Lucina 33, 00186
Tel *06-687 6304*
Grab a table outside in one of the most stylish piazzas in town. The food is basic but the location makes up for it.

Al Bric
Fine Dining   €€€   **Map** 11 C4
*Via del Pellegrino 51,
00186*
Tel *06-687 9533*
An impeccable wine list is matched by the tempting creations from the kitchen. A warm, charming setting.

Camponeschi
Fine Dining   €€€   **Map** 11 C4
*Piazza Farnese 50/50a,
00186*
Tel *06-687 4927*
World-class dining in the heart of the city. Try the tagliolini with lobster, and black truffles. Wild game is the house specialty.

Hostaria dell'Orso
Fine Dining   €€€   **Map** 11 C2
*Via dei Soldati 25c,
00186*
Tel *06-6830 1192*
Inviting, traditional dining raised to an art form. This legendary restaurant and nightclub has been welcoming guests for 500 years.

Il Pagliaccio
Fine Dining   €€€   **Map** 11 A3
*Via dei Banchi Vecchi 129,
00186*
Tel *06-6880 9595*

Intimate interior of the elegant
Al Bric restaurant

Surprising blend of pan-Asian, and Mediterranean cuisines. For true gourmands, the tasting menus have up to 12 courses.

Il Sanlorenzo €€€
Seafood **Map** 11 C4
Via dei Chiavari 4,
00186
Tel *06-686 5097*
Pricy, but worth it for some of the best seafood in town. Try the tasting menu to make your money go farther.

La Rosetta €€€
Seafood **Map** 12 D2
Via della Rosetta 8/9,
00186
Tel *06-686 1002*
Top-quality seafood served right in front of the Pantheon. Be sure to reserve an outdoor table at this lovely restaurant.

Spagna, Veneto, and Around

Gusto €
Pizzeria **Map** 4 F2
Piazza Augusto Imperatore 9,
00186
Tel *06-322 6273*
Gusto has a unique factory-like setting with exposed brick, and iron. Serves thick-crusted, and chewy Neapolitan-style pizzas.

Abruzzi ai SS Apostoli €
Regional Italian **Map** 12 F3
Via del Vaccaro 1, 00187
Tel *06-679 3897*
The wide selection of cold appetizers makes an excellent start to specialties from the Abruzzo region.

Ai Tre Scalini €
Enoteca **Map** 5 B4
Via Panisperna 251,
00184
Tel *06-4890 7495*
One of the hippest wine bars in town. Impressive wines, beers, and savory delicacies.

Antica Birreria Peroni €
Birreria **Map** 12 F3
Via di San Marcello 19,
00187
Tel *06-679 5310*
A casual spot that has been serving beer since 1906. All-Italian beef, and pork dishes prepared on the grill.

Cavour 313 €
Enoteca **Map** 5 B5
Via Cavour 313, 00184
Tel *06-678 5496*

Features a wood-paneled wine bar. The staff can help guests select a memorable vintage.

Colline Emiliane €
Regional Italian **Map** 5 B3
Via degli Avignonesi 22, 00187
Tel *06-481 7538*
Elegant *trattoria* serving hearty Bolognese specialties such as handmade tortellini and filling meat dishes.

La Carbonara €
Traditional Roman **Map** 5 B4
Via Panisperna 214, 00184
Tel *06-482 5176*
This welcoming *osteria* serves hearty local fare including the pasta dish it was named for, a Roman favorite.

San Marco €
Pizzeria **Map** 5 C1
Via Sardegna 38D, 00187
Tel *06-4201 2620*
Also a wine bar and grill, but noted most for its excellent pizzas. Chalkboard-covered walls list the day's specials.

Tati' al 28 €
Enoteca **Map** 4 F2
Piazza Augusto Imperatore 28,
00030
Tel *06-6813 4221*
Chic wine bar that also serves cocktails, tea, and coffee. Tasty snacks and lots of desserts available as well.

Taverna dei Fori Imperiali €
Traditional Roman **Map** 5 B5
Via della Madonna dei
Monti 9, 00184
Tel *06-679 8643*
The whole family pitches in to make this inviting *trattoria* a favorite with locals and visitors alike. The burrata ravioli is divine.

Babette €€
Modern Italian **Map** 4 F1
Via Margutta 1d, 00187
Tel *06-321 1559*
Inspired by the movie *Babette's Feast*, this large and boisterous restaurant whips up unusual versions of popular dishes from around the country. Reservations are recommended at this popular spot.

Baccano €€
Modern Italian **Map** 12 F2
Via delle Muratte 23, 00184
Tel *06-6994 1166*
Retro decor dominates at this restaurant serving classic Italian dishes with alternative ingredients. Gourmet burgers, and sandwiches are also available.

Cuoco e Camicia €€
Modern Italian **Map** 5 C5
Via Monte Polacco 2/4,
00184
Tel *06-8892 2987*
A cheerful eatery that prides itself on using only the freshest local ingredients. Interesting tasting menu.

Exposed brickwork and subtle lighting at Gusto

For more information on types of restaurants *see p304*

Spectacular city views and romantic interiors at Imàgo

Edoardo €€
Regional Italian **Map** 5 C2
Via Lucullo 2, 00187
Tel *06-486 428*
Taste delicious traditional dishes from the Abruzzo region at this elegant restaurant. Service is refined. Live music on weekends.

Filippo La Mantia €€
Fine Dining **Map** 5 B2
Via Liguria 1, 00187
Tel *06-4214 4715*
Exalted versions of Sicilian cuisine mainstays at this luxurious place inside the Majestic Hotel.

Hamasei €€
Japanese **Map** 12 F1
Via della Mercede 35/36, 00187
Tel *06-679 2134*
Minimalist black, and white setting includes low tables for authentic Nipponese dining. Serves ultra-fresh sushi, and sashimi.

Il Chianti €€
Modern Italian **Map** 12 F2
Via del Lavatore 81, 00187
Tel *06-678 7550*
Elegantly arranged cheese, and salami platters are followed by creative pan-Italian appetizers, and entrées.

Il Palazzetto €€
Traditional Roman **Map** 5 A2
Vicolo del Bottino 8, 00187
Tel *06-69934 1000*
Sip excellent wine and dig into classic Roman dishes on the tiny roof terrace at the top of the Spanish Steps.

La Campana €€
Traditional Roman **Map** 12 D1
Vicolo della Campana 18, 00186
Tel *06-687 5273*

Packed with Romans on any night of the week, this quaint, historic eatery dates back nearly 500 years.

L'Asino d'Oro €€
Regional Italian **Map** 5 B4
Via del Boschetto 73, 00184
Tel *06-4891 3832*
A reincarnation of a famous *trattoria* in Orvieto. Serves Umbrian specialties as well as Roman classics. Dishes are creative and tasty.

Open Colonna €€
Modern Italian **Map** 5 B4
Via Milano 9/a, 00184
Tel *06-4782 2641*
Perched above the PalaExpo, this modern, glassed-in open space provides an airy setting to enjoy tempting, creative dishes.

Papà Baccus €€
Regional Italian **Map** 5 C1
Via Toscana 36, 00187
Tel *06-4274 2808*
Every product used in this Tuscan restaurant is selected from trusted non-industrial producers. Guaranteed fresh and organic dishes.

Pipero al Rex €€
Fine Dining **Map** 5 C3
Via Torino 149, 00184
Tel *06-482 4828*
Sumptuous and meticulously prepared dishes are served at this magnificent restaurant.

DK Choice

Rhome €€
Modern Italian **Map** 4 F2
Piazza Augusto Imperatore 46, 00186
Tel *06-6830 1430*

As its name implies, the objective of this restaurant is to make its guests feel at home. Plush couches and overstuffed armchairs pull right up to the table. The dining experience here gives a whole new meaning to the term "comfort food." Carefully prepared classic dishes mingle with more daring recipes.

Canova-Tadolini Museum Atelier €€€
Traditional Roman **Map** 4 F2
Via del Babuino 150/a, 00187
Tel *06-3211 0702*
Dine amid dozens of artworks at the studio of the legendary 18th-century sculptor Canova.

Doozo €€€
Japanese **Map** 5 C4
Via Palermo 51, 00184
Tel *06-481 5655*
Courses in origami, a Bonsai exhibit, and book presentations, plus mouthwatering sushi, feature at this restaurant, and Japanese cultural center.

Harry's Bar €€€
Fine Dining **Map** 5 B2
Via Veneto 150, 00187
Tel *06-474 2103*
Take a bite of *la dolce vita* at this iconic bar and café serving exquisite meals and the famous Bellini cocktail.

Imàgo €€€
Fine Dining **Map** 5 A1
Piazza Trinità dei Monti 6, 00187
Tel *06-6993 4726*
Stellar dining with an exceptional view from the top of the Spanish Steps. Chef Apreda serves creative Italian cuisine.

L'Olimpo €€€
Fine Dining   **Map** 5 B2
Piazza Barberini 23, 00187
Tel 06-48 8931
Dine high atop the Hotel Bernini Bristol, with its sweeping views of the entire city. Good deals at lunchtime.

La Terrazza dell'Eden €€€
Fine Dining   **Map** 5 B2
Via Ludovisi 49, 00187
Tel 06-4781 2752
Special culinary events, and sensational tasting menus make this award-winning rooftop restaurant a special venue.

Le Jardin de Russie €€€
Fine Dining   **Map** 4 F1
Via del Babuino 9, 00187
Tel 06-3288 8870
Delectable Mediterranean dishes served with flair, and artistry in a refined, and sumptuous setting.

Mirabelle €€€
Fine Dining   **Map** 5 B1
Via di Porta Pinciana 14, 00187
Tel 06-4216 8838
Impeccable service and a panoramic view at this rooftop restaurant. Imaginative yet subtle Mediterranean dishes.

Osteria Margutta €€€
Modern Italian   **Map** 5 A2
Via Margutta 82, 00187
Tel 06-323 1025
Historic restaurant on an idyllic vine-covered street. Serves classic Roman dishes with a modern twist.

Vivendo €€€
Modern Italian   **Map** 5 C3
Via Vittorio Emanuele Orlando 3, 00185
Tel 06-4709 2736
Luxurious decor provides an elegant backdrop to the fabulous Mediterranean cuisine. Wine tasting in the elegant cellar.

Trastevere and Around

Akropolis €
Greek   **Map** 7 C2
Via di San Francesco a Ripa 103, 00153
Tel 06-5833 2600
A wide selection of tempting appetizers include stuffed vine leaves and spanakopita (Greek savory pastry). Fantastic gyros.

Arian €
Persian   **Map** 4 D2
Via Tacito 54a, 00193
Tel 06-4544 1122
Authentic Iranian cuisine in a vibrant atmosphere. Live belly dancing Friday and Saturday night.

Arlù €
Traditional Roman   **Map** 3 C3
Borgo Pio 135, 00193
Tel 06-686 8936
The most authentic restaurant in the busy Vatican area. A husband-and-wife team serve up delectable Roman cuisine.

Bir & Fud €
Birreria   **Map** 11 B5
Via Benedetta 23, 00153
Tel 06-589 4016
Artisanal beers and microbrews from around Italy; perfect for washing down the crusty pizzas and gourmet potato chips.

Da Gildo €
Traditional Roman   **Map** 7 C1
Via della Scala 31, 00153
Tel 06-580 0733
Try the simple and divine gnocchi alla romana. Quirky decoration and outdoor seating.

In Vino Veritas €
Enoteca   **Map** 4 D5
Via Garibaldi 2a, 00153
Tel 06-5833 2012.0.
A cozy and informal wine bar, with chess and other games in the tiny seating area.

Ivo a Trastevere €
Pizzeria   **Map** 7 C1
Via di San Francesco a Ripa 158, 00153
Tel 06-581 7082
Delicious super-thin-crust Roman pizza has this simple eatery bustling with locals and the occasional celebrity.

Meridionale €
Regional Italian   **Map** 7 C1
Via dei Fienaroli 30a, 00153
Tel 06-589 7196
Friendly and bright, this delightful restaurant specializes in fresh cuisine from southern Italy. Seafood options are particularly tempting.

Pizzeria ai Panattoni €
Pizzeria   **Map** 7 C1
Viale di Trastevere 53, 00153
Tel 06-580 0919
This pizzeria is nicknamed "the morgue" for its long marble-topped tables. Try the supplì al telefono (fried rice balls).

Rajdhani €
Indian   **Map** 8 D1
Via di Santa Cecilia 8, 00153
Tel 06-581 8508
Tandoori chicken (cooked in a clay oven) and creamy tikka masala (spicy roasted chicken) are the specialties at this friendly spot. The set menu is a particularly good buy.

Sushi and other Japanese delicacies laid out on a table at Doozo

For more information on types of restaurants see p304

Wine cellar at Spirito Divino, located within a 10th-century synagogue

Roma Sparita €
Traditional Roman **Map** 8 D1
Piazza di Santa Cecilia 24,
00153
Tel *06-580 0757*
Set in an enviable position in
front of a gorgeous church, this
traditional spot serves the best
cacio e pepe (cheese and pepper
pasta) in town.

Da Benito e Gilberto €€
Seafood
Via del Falco 19, 00193
Tel *06-686 7769*
This small and friendly restaurant,
run by a father and son, prepares
classic pasta dishes and elaborate
seafood delicacies.

Da Cesare €€
Traditional Roman **Map** 4 D2
Via Crescenzio 13, 00193
Tel *06-686 1227*
The owners of this local
favorite are dedicated to
using only local, seasonal, and
non-industrial products.

Da Teo €€
Traditional Roman **Map** 8 D1
Piazza del Ponziani 7a,
00153
Tel *06-581 8355*
Situated in a charming and quiet
piazza, this casual yet elegant
spot offers classic local recipes
and flavorful marinated dishes.

Il Capricco €€
Regional Italian **Map** 7 C2
Via Roma Libera 19, 00153
Tel *06-581 6469*
Every meal can be served
gluten-free at this jovial spot
know for its traditional Sicilian
cuisine. There are traditional
music performances
on weekends.

DK Choice

Isole di Sicilia €€
Regional Italian **Map** 7 B1
Via Garibaldi 68, 00153
Tel *06-5833 4212*
This cheerful restaurant dishes
up some of the best Sicilian
food in town. Inspired by the
native cuisine of the tiny islands
surrounding Sicily, the elaborate
dishes use delectable
ingredients such as eggplant,
capers, peppers, almonds, basil,
and, of course, lots and lots of
super-fresh fish. A vast antipasto
spread kicks off a memorable
meal. Sidewalk seating on the
tree-lined street in good
weather.

La Gensola €€
Modern Italian **Map** 8 D1
Piazza della Gensola 15, 00153
Tel *06-581 6312*
This sweet little *osteria* whips up
excellent seafood and has a
surprisingly pleasant take on
traditional Roman cuisine.

Lo Scarpone €€
Traditional Roman **Map** 7 A2
Piazza di San Pancrazio 15, 00152
Tel *06-5814094*
Nestled in a lush garden with
plenty of outdoor seating. The
cozy interior has a working
fireplace. The menu features
lots of meat options.

Taverna Angelica €€
Modern Italian **Map** 3 C2
Piazza Amerigo Capponi 6, 00193
Tel *06-687 4514*
Creative seafood and meat
specialties are popular at this
cozy restaurant. The Sunday
lunches are superb.

Velando €€
Modern Italian **Map** 3 C3
Borgo Vittorio 26, 00193
Tel *06-6880 9955*
This fantastic little restaurant
presents modern takes on well-
loved classic dishes from Rome,
and beyond. It pays much
attention to detail.

Antica Pesa €€€
Fine Dining **Map** 7 B1
Via Garibaldi 18, 00153
Tel *06-580 9236*
The walls of this decadent
restaurant are covered with
murals by top international
artists. Meals are served in a leafy
courtyard in warm weather.

Antico Arco €€€
Fine Dining **Map** 7 A1
Piazzale Aurelio 7, 00152
Tel *06-581 5274*
Truffles, wild strawberries,
and other such delights fill the
menu. The vast wine list is
equally tantalizing.

Glass €€€
Modern Italian **Map** 4 E5
Vicolo del Cinque 58, 00153
Tel *06-5833 5903*
This Michelin-starred, sleekly
modern restaurant offers
glorified Mediterranean
cuisine with a dash of
international flavor.

DK Choice

Spirito Divino €€€
Modern Italian **Map** 8 D1
Via dei Genovesi 31, 00153
Tel *06-589 6689*
An elegant, family-run
establishment, housed in a
10th-century synagogue, but

thoroughly modernized inside. The owner delights in describing to guests each exquisite dish on the ever-changing menu, while his wife lovingly prepares them in the kitchen. Take a peek into the 2,100-year-old wine cellar.

Taverna Trilussa €€€
Traditional Roman **Map** 4 E5
Via del Politeama 23, 00153
Tel 06-581 8918
This bustling yet elegant spot serves classic Roman recipes. Some pasta dishes are served in the pan they were cooked in.

Veranda €€€
Fine Dining **Map** 3 C3
Via della Conciliazione 33, 00193
Tel 06-687 2973
Stunning setting in a frescoed palace with vaulted ceilings and low lighting. Selective menu offers finely tuned pasta, plus meat, and fish dishes.

Farther Afield

Vivi Bistrot €
International
Via Vitellia 102, 00152
Tel 06-582 7540
Nestled in the sprawling grounds of Villa Pamphilj. Serves American-style breakfast as well as picnic options, and *aperitivos* on the grass in summer.

Ambasciata d'Abruzzo €€
Regional Italian **Map** 2 D3
Via Pietro Tacchini 26, 00197
Tel 06-807 8256
Traditional Abruzzese dishes, such as maccheroni with lamb ragù, mingle with Roman favorites in a convivial setting.

Avec 55 €€
Modern Italian
Via Domenico Giuliani 55,

00019, Tivoli
Tel 07-7431 7243
A restaurant and culinary work-shop combined. Chef Raoul Reperi teaches amateur cooks how to recreate his gastronomic feats. The menu changes regularly.

Brasserie 4:20 €€
Birreria **Map** 7 C3
Via Portuense 82, 00153
Tel 06-5831 0737
Craft beers from around the world are meticulously paired with select dishes, particularly fish.

La Gatta Mangiona €€
Pizzeria
Via Federico Ozanam 30, 00152
Tel 06-534 6702
Creative toppings, and daily specials make this Monteverde pizzeria popular with locals, and savvy visitors.

La Sibilla €€
Regional Italian
Via della Sibilla 50, 00019, Tivoli
Tel 07-7433 5281
Sweeping views of Villa Gregoriana and Roman ruins provide an unforgettable setting for indulging in high-quality regional cuisine.

DK Choice

Mò Mò Republic €€
Pizzeria
Piazza Forlanini 10, 00151
Tel 06-537 3087
A 19th-century mansion nestled in a leafy garden is the setting for this modern, and trendy pizzeria. Oversized chandeliers and parquet floors add to the glamorous ambience, yet prices are surprisingly affordable. Large round tables on the massive terrace make it the perfect spot for a big group of friends. In summer, start with *aperitivos* on the lawn. Pasta, meat, and fish dishes are also available.

Osteria Flaminio €€
Modern Italian **Map** 1 B3
Via Flaminia 297, 00196
Tel 06-323 6900
This restaurant, just north of downtown, offers a range of innovative, and original Italian dishes.

Osteria Scaloni €€
Traditional Roman
Via Carlo Mirabello 8, 00195
Tel 06-372 1593
Dishes based on simple, local cuisine are taken a step further with unexpected ingredients, and creative touches. The wine list is excellent.

Bastianelli al Molo €€€
Fine Dining
Via Torre Clementina 312, 00054, Fiumicino
Tel 06-650 5358
A vast terrace overlooking the Tyrrhenian Sea is the setting for a memorable meal of the freshest seafood in Lazio.

DK Choice

La Pergola €€€
Fine Dining
Via Alberto Cadlolo 101, 00136
Tel 06-35 091
Universally recognized as Rome's finest restaurant, La Pergola is also the only one to earn the coveted three Michelin stars. Chef Heinz Beck dazzles diners with his exquisite Mediterranean creations. Perched atop Monte Mario hill, the restaurant offers stunning views of St. Peter's Basilica, and the entire city skyline. The award-winning wine cellar boasts over 3,000 labels and more than 53,000 bottles, the oldest dating to 1888. Reserve well in advance.

Oliver Glowig €€€
Fine Dining **Map** 2 D4
Via Ulisse Aldrovandi 15, 00197
Tel 06-321 6126
This impressive poolside restaurant serves rich Mediterranean delicacies such as scampi with artichoke hearts and burrata cheese.

Settembrini €€€
Modern Italian
Via Luigi Settembrini 25, 00195
Tel 06-323 2617
Talented chef Gigi Nastri serves creative Italian cuisine that is both well-presented, and tasty. The seafood options are particularly delectable.

Seating amid bright flowers at Vivi Bistrot

For more information on types of restaurants *see p304*

Light Meals and Drinks

Rome can delight the most demanding gourmet and satisfy the biggest appetite, whatever the hour. An enticing array of *gelaterie, pasticcerie, pizzerie, enoteche, rosticcerie,* and *gastronomie* means that good food and drink are, literally, around the corner.

Hotel breakfasts often aren't very good, and you would be better off starting the day with a genuine Italian breakfast at your local stand-up bar: a cappuccino or latte with a hot *cornetto* (croissant) or *fagottino* (similar to a *pain au chocolat*). If you are in Italy during late winter, when blood-red oranges from Sicily are in season, order a *spremuta,* a freshly squeezed orange juice.

A heavy morning's sightseeing may leave you ready for a coffee or an apéritif in one of Rome's elegant 19th-century bars, followed by lunch at a wine bar or Roman-style fast food joint. Later, enjoy tea in a tearoom or coffee and cakes at a *pasticceria.* Once the sun starts to set, there are many places to sip a drink, linger over ice cream, and ponder another wonderful day in the city.

Pizzerias

Roman *pizzerias* are an obvious choice if you feel like an informal meal: they are noisy, convivial, and great fun. Many, however, open only in the evening. Look for the *forno a legno* (wood-burning oven) sign – electric ovens simply don't produce the same results. In the best *pizzerias* you can sit in view of the vast marble slabs where the *pizzaioli* flatten the dough and whip the pizzas in and out of the oven on long-handled pallets. The turnaround is fast and lines are common, so you may not be encouraged to linger after you have eaten.

The progression is fairly straightforward: you might have a *bruschetta* (toasted tomato or garlic bread) to start with, some *supplì* (fried rice croquettes), or *fiori di zucca* (zucchini flowers in batter, filled with hot mozzarella, and a single anchovy). Alternatively, try the *filetti di baccalà* (battered cod fillets) or perhaps a plate of *cannellini* beans in oil. Follow this with a crisp *calzone* (folded-over pizza) or the classic Roman pizza – round, thin, and crunchy – with a variety of toppings: the basic *margherita* (tomato, mozzarella), *napoletana* (tomato, anchovies, mozzarella), *capricciosa* (ham, artichokes,

eggs, olives) or anything else the *pizzaiolo* fancies. Draft beer or *birra alla spina* is the classic drink, but wine is always available, even if limited in choice and quality. You should expect to pay around €14 a head for a meal.

The most representative Roman *pizzerias*, from all points of view, are **Da Baffetto**, which can be easily found by looking for the line outside, and its offspring, **La Montecarlo. Remo** in Testaccio and **Dar Poeta** and **Pizzeria Ivo** in Trastevere, where tables line the road in summer, are also typically Roman. Another place not to be missed is **Panattoni – I Marmi**, where a huge variety of customers patiently wait for a sidewalk seat on Viale Trastevere in summer, or clamor for one of the marble-topped tables (which gives it its nickname of "the mortuary") inside. For slick interiors and Neapolitan-style (high-rise) pizza, try **'Gusto**, but once again, be prepared to wait in line.

Enoteche

Enoteche or wine bars offer a very fine selection of wines, mainly from Italy, but often from around the world. Usually run by experts eager to share their

knowledge and advise on the best combinations of wine and food, many are simply shops for browsing, and buying wine. Others, such as **Achilli al Parlamento** (see p343) and **L'Angolo Divino** (see p354), offer the traditional *mescita* – wine, and champagne tasting by the glass, accompanied by snacks and canapés. Prices are fairly reasonable: about €3 for a glass on tap, €5 upward for a quality wine or for a *prosecco* or *spumante,* Italian champagne. **La Vineria** (see p342) in Campo de' Fiori is a typical spot for *mescita,* especially at night. Nearby, the beautiful **Il Goccetto**, with original painted ceilings, serves excellent wines and delicious food.

Some of the oldest wine bars are inside historic buildings, such as **Caffè Novecento**, which serves excellent food, mainly vegetarian. The prize for one of the most ancient must go to **La Curia di Bacco**, set in an atmospheric candlelit cave dating back to 70 BC.

For more substantial food for around €15–20 per head, try the bistro- or restaurant-style *enoteche,* open from lunch until late. Particularly recommended are the innovative **Cul de Sac, Trimani** (see p343), **Il Tajut** (serving specialties from Friuli), and **Cavour 313**. Food emporium **'Gusto** (see p343) has a wine bar with a gourmet cheese selection, while the specialty at **Al Bric** is *sarcofage bretone* – beef stroganoff with Barolo and a Jerusalem artichoke. The **Antico Forno Roscioli** is particularly creative, with great dishes such as pasta with *radicchio,* and orange peel and pear pastry with coconut.

Enoteche are often tucked away near famous sights or in unlikely places. **Vinando** is extremely convenient for the Capitol, while the Tuscan **Vineria Il Chianti** is near the Trevi Fountain. Over in Testaccio, **Divinare** offers fine labels alongside top quality preserves and chocolate. There are a growing number of wine bars across the river. Crowds at **Enoteca Trastevere** spill on to the sidewalk outside, while **Cantina Paradiso** is a quieter venue with a reasonable evening menu. When night falls, try the lively **In Vino Veritas Art Bar** at the foot of the Janiculum Hill.

Birrerie

Roman *birrerie* or beer houses had their heyday in the early 1900s, often with sumptuous interiors and abundant stained glass. Although many subsequently closed, thanks to their growing popularity with most Italian teenagers they are today undergoing something of a revival. Many British- and Irish-style pubs have also opened. At German-style beer houses you can still enjoy beer and substantial snacks in traditional wood-paneled rooms. The **Old Bear** pub is a jewel inside a 17th-century convent, with romantic candlelight and excellent food and beer. **Löwenhaus** is bedecked in old oil paintings depicting typical Bavarian scenes, again with low lighting for a mellow evening. The ever-crowded **Birreria Peroni**, serving classic beer-drinkers' fare, is also well worth a visit for its local beer and lovely decor. Attracting Italians and foreigners alike is the lively **Ma Che Siete Venuti a Fà** with its excellent range of well-selected ales. Across the river in Testaccio is the equally charming **L'Oasi della Birra**, which also serves good food. Other beer houses with a great atmosphere, food, and late closing times are **The Fiddler's Elbow**, often with live music, **La Pace del Cervello** (meaning "peace of mind" – or **Trinity College**, a favorite of expatriates and Romans.

Fast Food

The term "fast food" in Rome encompasses a cornucopia of choices. The most prolific establishments are *pizza a taglio* shops where slices of freshly baked pizza are available for €1 or €2 – these are sold by weight.

Many of these places also sell spit-roasted chickens (*pollo allo spiedo*), *supplì*, and other fried fare. **Forno La Renella** in Trastevere is one of the finest. Figs and ham or potatoes and rosemary are typical pizza toppings. At **La Pratolina**, near the Vatican, pizza with sausage, potatoes, and truffles is on the menu. **Chagat**, in the Ghetto, prepares tasty kosher food, while **Rosticceri**, with branches in Testaccio and near Piazza Navona, specializes in classic Roman carry-out with an inventive twist.

Rosticcerie and *gastronomie* also offer roast chicken and potatoes, as well as ready-made pasta dishes, cooked vegetables *sott'olio* (in oil), salads, and desserts – useful for picnics. Many also offer stools and narrow bars where you can devour your purchases on the spot. Near the Vatican are some of the finest, such as **Franchi** (*see p342*) and **Ercoli dal 1928**.

For a sit-down snack, bars with a *tavola calda* (hot table) have a similar selection, especially at lunchtime. One of the best is **Volpetti Più** in Testaccio. For a taste of traditional deep-fried fast food, try **Cose Fritte** near Piazza del Popolo. In the Galleria Alberto Sordi, opposite the Piazza Colonna, the excellent **Trevi e Tritone** offers hot and cold food until 10pm.

Most *alimentari* (food stores) or *salumerie* (delicatessens) will make you a *panino* (filled roll). Especially delicious are **Lo Zozzone's** hot plain pizza pockets stuffed with choices from the shop's counters, where you can also sip a glass of wine. Try a typical local specialty if you see the sign *porchetta* – whole aromatic roast pig with crackling, sliced into *rosette* (rolls) or thick country-bread sandwiches. A good place to try this is the **Antico Chiosco** in the small park in Viale Carlo Felice, near San Giovanni in Laterano. Alternatively, go to the hole-in-the-wall **Er Buchetto**, where you can sit down in (relative) comfort with a glass of wine. For a really typical Roman snack,

make a late-afternoon detour to **Filetti di Baccalà** serving, as the name suggests, fried cod fillets.

For cheese, go to **Obiká** near the Pantheon. This bar offers a vast choice of fresh buffalo and cow mozzarella; eat it as it should be – unadulterated – or prepared in a variety of creative ways.

Termini now has two good options for those waiting or rushing for trains – the self-service restaurant **Chef Express Gusto** or **Vyta** (*see p342*), which serves up gourmet sandwiches to go.

Bars, Cafés, and Tearooms

Roman bars are the city's lifeline: places to meet, eat, drink, buy milk or coffee, make phone calls, or find a restroom. Some are small, stand-up, basic one-counter bars for grabbing a quick *cornetto* and cappuccino; some may be more luxurious, doubling as a cake shop, ice-cream parlor, tearoom, or *tavola calda*; or a combination of all these. Most open early at about 7:30am and close late, particularly on weekends, at around midnight or 2am. If you sit down you will be served by a waiter and pay for the privilege. At busy times, or at popular bars, the crowds at the counter will be large and you will have to wait your turn. If you choose to stand, you pay for your drink at the register beforehand. A small tip (5 or 10 cents per drink) may increase your chances of speedy service. In summer, tables cover all available outdoor space, and the fight for a place in the shade is never-ending.

Traditionally elegant – and expensive – bars for people-watching are the admirably located **Rosati** and **Doney**, as well as **Caffè Greco**, the 19th-century haunt of artists, writers, and composers (*see p135*), or the carefully restored **La Caffettiera**, near the Pantheon. Other popular, and well-established bars are the **Antico Caffè della Pace** and **Café Romano**; both of these places are recommended for late-night drinks. **Zodiaco** on Monte Mario pulls in the crowds for its panoramic views, as does **Oppio Café** near the Domus Aurea. For sheer decadence, go to **Stravinsky** at the Hotel de Russie for wonderful martinis or a relaxed cup of coffee.

Tearooms are becoming increasingly popular. **Babington's Tea Rooms** (see p136) on Piazza di Spagna serves an outrageously expensive cup of tea and scones in genteel surroundings, while **Dolci e Doni** is more relaxed. Much better deals can be found at **Il Giardino del Te** and **Makasar**. For serious luxury, you can have a full afternoon tea at the **Grand Bar** in the St. Regis Grand (see p303).

Coffee fiends should try a **gran caffè speciale** at the counters of **Caffè Sant' Eustachio**, or one of Rome's best espressos at **La Tazza d'Oro** (see p106). Less familiar to tourists, however, are the excellent **Antico Caffè del Brasile** (see p343), **Bar del Cappuccino**, **Ciamei**, or **Spinelli**. **Ciampini al Café du Jardin**, with its garden setting and rooftop views, is unbeatable in summer, particularly at the apéritif hour, as is the **Caffè Parnaso** in Parioli. Gradually becoming common in Rome are bookshop cafés – **Caffè la Feltrinelli** and **Biblioteq** are two examples – and museum cafés. The **Caffetteria D'Art al Chiostro del Bramante** is in an art gallery on the upper loggia of a beautiful cloister. The bar at the Capitoline Museums has breathtaking views, if average food, while the café in the **Palazzo delle Esposizioni** (see p166) is open throughout the day with an attractive selection of snacks, and drinks.

Pasticcerie

On Sunday mornings you will often see Romans emerging from the local pastry shop or *pasticceria* with a beautifully wrapped package. This can contain dainty individual pastries, whole cakes or tarts, traditional Easter *colombe* (doves), or the Christmas *panettoni* – huge cakes with raisins and candied citrus peel – all for consumption by large gatherings of friends or family after lunch. The window displays of cake shops are often fantastic. These, and the aroma of brewing coffee, will tempt even those who claim not to have a sweet tooth. The selection is vast, from a hot *cornetto* or *brioche* in the early morning, a midday *pizzetta* or savory tart at lunch, or a choux pastry or fruit tart in the afternoon. **Cipriani** (see p339), open since 1906, has delicious biscuits, ricotta cake, and apple tart. Nearby **Regoli** has wonderful *mille feuilles* and *torta con crema e pinoli* (pine nuts). **Dagnino** prepares hundreds of Sicilian specialties every day, while **Boccione** specializes in traditional Roman-Jewish cakes. As well as cakes, numerous shops offer handmade chocolates. At some, such as **Rivendita di Cioccolata e Vino** (see p350), you can pause over a cup of coffee or glass of wine while deciding which you like best.

Gelaterie

Ice cream (*gelato*) is one of summer's main delights and at Rome's ice-cream parlors, you are certainly in for a lavish treat. Look for the word *artigianale*, if you want to savor the best. The choice is endless – water ices made with a phenomenal variety of fruit; lemon and coffee *granite* (crushed ice); as well as more exotic ice-cream specialties such as rice pudding, *zuppa inglese* (English trifle), *zabaglione*, and *tiramisù*. Choose as many varieties as the size of your cone or cup will hold, ask for an optional topping of cream (*panna*), and go for a sensation-filled stroll. Or take a seat and rest awhile – you will be served an obscenely sized creation at the table (at a price). *Gelaterie* are open all day, many until late at night, and are very much an integral part of Roman socializing. **Tre Scalini** in Piazza Navona is a famous spot for enjoying the pricy, yet so heavenly, chocolate *tartufo* (truffle), while a summer evening in EUR, especially with children, nearly always ends in a trip to **Giolitti**, a historic ice-cream name. The strategically placed, crowded original near the Pantheon deserves at least one visit too. Gourmet fans of *gelato* should not miss **San Crispino**, which offers homemade delicacies made with the best ingredients. Its *zabaglione* is made with 20-year-old barrel-aged Marsala. In summer, try the mouth-watering *susine* (yellow plum) flavor; in winter, the *arancia selvatica* (wild orange) should not be missed.

Adults may prefer to pick their nighttime treat at **Chalet del Lago**, again in EUR, while sitting beside the lake. If you come across a small kiosk with the sign *grattachecche* (most likely in Trastevere, and Testaccio), try one of Rome's oldest traditions: ice grated by a gloved hand on the spot, and enlivened with a variety of classic flavorings. Try **Sora Mirella**, near the Tiber Island.

Everyone has their own favourite flavors, and preferred *gelateria*, but the quest for perfection is an ongoing pleasure. For top *zabaglione*, try **Fiocco di Neve**, **Giolitti** of Via Vespucci, or **Petrini dal 1926**. **Palazzo del Freddo** makes an exceptionally wonderful rice pudding flavor, and its own *La Caterinetta* – one of the secret ingredients is honey. **Al Settimo Gelo**, a witty play on words (*settimo* is seventh, *cielo* is heaven and *gelo* is ice), creates exciting chestnut sorbet, chocolate with *peperoncino*, ginger and ice cream made from Greek yogurt. For those with dairy allergies, visit the Sicilian *gelateria* **Gelarmony**, which also uses soy milk and has 14 different flavors. At **Fior di Luna** in Trastevere, all ingredients are organic. Excellent ingredients also distinguish **Neve di Latte**, located near the MAXXI gallery (see p259), and the more central **GROM**.

DIRECTORY

Capitol

BARS, CAFÉS, AND TEAROOMS

Caffè Capitolino
Piazzale Caffarelli.
Map 12 F5.

Piazza della Rotonda

PIZZERIAS

Barroccio
Via dei Pastini 13.
Map 12 D2.

Er Faciolaro
Via dei Pastini 123.
Map 12 D2.

La Sagrestia
Via del Seminario 89.
Map 12 E3.

ENOTECHE

Achilli al Parlamento
Via dei Prefetti 15.
Map 12 D1.

Corsi
Via del Gesù 88.
Map 12 E3.

BIRRERIE

Trinity College
Via del Collegio Romano 6. **Map** 12 E3.

FAST FOOD

Obikà
Piazza Firenze 28.
Map 12 D1.

BARS, CAFÉS, AND TEAROOMS

Caffè Sant'Eustachio
Piazza Sant'Eustachio 82.
Map 12 D3.

La Caffettiera
Piazza di Pietra 65.
Map 12 E2.

Ciampini
Piazza S. Lorenzo in Lucina 29. **Map** 12 D1.

La Tazza d'Oro
Via degli Orfani 82/84.
Map 12 D2.

Teichner
Piazza San Lorenzo in Lucina 15–17. **Map** 12 D1.

Vitti
Piazza San Lorenzo in Lucina 33. **Map** 12 E1

GELATERIE

Fiocco di Neve
Via del Pantheon 51.
Map 12 D2.

Giolitti
Via degli Uffici del Vicario 40. **Map** 12 D2.

Grom
Via della Maddalena 30A.
Map 12 D2.

Piazza Navona

PIZZERIAS

Da Baffetto
Via del Governo Vecchio 114. **Map** 11 B3.

Da Francesco
Piazza del Fico 29.
Map 11 B2.

La Montecarlo
Vicolo Savelli 12/13.
Map 11 C3.

ENOTECHE

Bevitoria Navona
Piazza Navona 72.
Map 11 C2.

Caffè Novecento
Via del Governo Vecchio 12. **Map** 11 B3.

Cul de Sac
Piazza Pasquino 73.
Map 11 C3.

Giulio Passami l'Olio
Via di Monte Giordano 28.
Map 11B2.

Il Piccolo
Via del Governo Vecchio 74–75. **Map** 11 C3.

BIRRERIE

Old Bear
Via dei Gigli d'Oro 62–4.
Map 11 C2.

FAST FOOD

Lo Zozzone
Via del Teatro Pace 32.
Map 11 B3.

BARS, CAFÉS, AND TEAROOMS

Antico Caffè della Pace
Via della Pace 5.
Map 11 C3.

Caffeteria D'Art al Chiostro del Bramante
Via della Pace. **Map** 11 C2.

PASTICCERIE

La Deliziosa
Vicolo Savelli 50.
Map 11 B3.

GELATERIE

Bar Navona
Piazza Navona 67.
Map 11 C3.

Da Quinto
Via di Tor Millina 15.
Map 11 C3.

Tre Scalini
Piazza Navona 28.
Map 11 C3.

Piazza di Spagna

PIZZERIAS

'Gusto Piazza Augusto Imperatore 9. **Map** 4 F2.

PizzaRé
Via di Ripetta 14.
Map 4 F1.

ENOTECHE

Antica Enoteca di Via della Croce
Via della Croce 76B.
Map 5 A2.

Buccone
Via di Ripetta 19.
Map 4 F1.

'Gusto
See Pizzerias.

Il Brillo Parlante
Via della Fontanella 12.
Map 4 F1.

BIRRERIE

Löwenhaus
Via della Fontanella 16B.
Map 4 F1.

FAST FOOD

Cose Fritte
Via di Ripetta 3. **Map** 4 F1.

Difronte A
Via della Croce 38.
Map 4 F2.

Fratelli Fabbi
Via della Croce 27.
Map 4 F2.

BARS, CAFÉS, AND TEAROOMS

Babington's Tea Rooms
Piazza di Spagna 23.
Map 5 A2.

Café Romano
Via Borgognona 4.
Map 12 E1.

Caffè Greco
Via Condotti 86.
Map 5 A2.

Ciampini al Café du Jardin
Viale Trinità dei Monti.
Map 5 A2.

Dolci e Doni
Via delle Carrozze 85B.
Map 4 F2.

Rosati
Piazza del Popolo 5.
Map 4 F1.

Stravinsky Bar
Hotel de Russie, Via del Babuino 9. **Map** 5 A2.

GELATERIE

Venchi
Via della Croce 25.
Map 5 A2.

Campo de' Fiori

PIZZERIAS

Acchiappafantasmi
Via dei Cappellari 66.
Map 11 B3.

ENOTECHE

Al Bric
Via del Pellegrino 51.
Map 11 B3.

Antico Forno Roscioli
Via dei Giubbonari 21.
Map 11 C4.

La Curia di Bacco
Via del Biscione 79.
Map 11 C4.

Il Goccetto
Via dei Banchi Vecchi 14.
Map 11 B3.

L'Angolo Divino
Via dei Balestrari 12.
Map 11 C4.

Vinando
Piazza Margana 23.
Map 12 E4.

DIRECTORY

La Vineria
Piazza Campo de' Fiori 15.
Map 11 C4.

FAST FOOD

Chagat
Via Santa Maria del Pianto
66. **Map** 12 D5.

Da Benito
Via dei Falegnami 14.
Map 12 D4.

Filetti di Baccalà
Largo dei Librari 88.
Map 11 C4.

**Forno Campo de'
Fiori**
Piazza Campo de' Fiori 22.
Map 11 C4.

Pizza Florida
Via Florida 25. **Map** 12 D4.

**BARS, CAFÉS, AND
TEAROOMS**

Alberto Pica
Via della Seggiola 12.
Map 12 D5.

Bar del Cappuccino
Via Arenula 50.
Map 12 D4.

Bernasconi
Piazza Cairoli 16.
Map 12 D4.

Bibliotèq
Via dei Banchi Vecchi 124.
Map 11 B3.

Caffè la Feltrinelli
Largo Torre Argentina 5.
Map 12 D4.

PASTICCERIE

Boccione
Via del Portico d'Ottavia 1.
Map 12 E5.

La Dolceroma
Via del Portico d'Ottavia
20B. **Map** 12 E5.

GELATERIE

L'Angolo dell'Artista
Largo dei Librari 86. **Map**
11 C4.

Blue Ice
Via dei Baullari 130 and
141. **Map** 11 C4.

Quirinal

PIZZERIAS

Al Giubileo
Via Palermo 7. **Map** 5 B4.

Est! Est! Est!
Via Genova 32. **Map** 5 C4.

ENOTECHE

Cavour 313
Via Cavour 313. **Map** 5 B5.

Vineria Il Chianti
Via del Lavatore 81.
Map 12 F2.

BIRRERIE

The Albert
Via del Traforo 132.
Map 5 B3.

Birreria Peroni
Via San Marcello 19.
Map 12 F3.

Da Valentino
Via del Boschetto 37.
Map 5 B4.

FAST FOOD

Er Buchetto
Via Viminale 2. **Map** 5 C3.

Fior di Pizza
Via Milano 33. **Map** 5 B4.

Trevi e Tritone
Galleria Alberto Sordi.
Map 12 E2.

**BARS, CAFÉS, AND
TEAROOMS**

**Antico Caffè del
Brasile**
Via dei Serpenti 23.
Map 5 B4.

La Bottega del Caffè
Piazza della Madonna dei
Monti 5.
Map 5 B5.

Il Giardino del Tè
Via del Boschetto 107.
Map 5 B4.

**Palazzo delle
Esposizioni**
Via Milano 15–17.
Map 5 B4.

Spinelli
Piazza del Viminale 18.
Map 5 C3.

Theatre Café
Largo Magnanapoli 157A.
Map 5 B4.

PASTICCERIE

Dagnino
Galleria Esedra, Via Vittorio
Emanuele Orlando 75.
Map 5 C2.

GELATERIE

San Crispino
Via della Panetteria 42.
Map 12 F2.

Termini

PIZZERIAS

Formula Uno
Via degli Equi 13.
Map 6 F4.

San Marco
Via Sardegna 38D.
Map 5 B1.

ENOTECHE

Enoteca Chirra
Via Torino 132–133.
Map 5 C3.

Trimani
Via Cernaia 37B.
Map 6 D2.

FAST FOOD

Chef Express Gusto
Galleria Termini – Exit Via
Marsala. **Map** 6 D3.

Vyta
Galleria Termini – Exit Via
Marsala. **Map** 6 D3.

Wok
Stazione Termini (Lower
Level). **Map** 6 D3.

**BARS, CAFÉS, AND
TEAROOMS**

Grand Bar
St Regis Grand Via Vittorio
Emanuele Orlando 3.
Map 6 C3.

Esquiline

BIRRERIE

The Fiddler's Elbow
Via dell'Olmata 43.
Map 6 D4.

Old Marconi
Via di Sante Prassede 9C.
Map 6 D4.

FAST FOOD

Panella
Via Merulana 54.
Map 6 D5.

**BARS, CAFÉS, AND
TEAROOMS**

Ciamei
Via Emanuele Filiberto 57.
Map 6 E5.

Oppio Café
Via delle Terme di Tito 72.
Map 5 C5.

PASTICCERIE

Cipriani
Via C. Botta 21. **Map** 6 D5.

Regoli
Via dello Statuto 60.
Map 6 D5.

GELATERIE

Palazzo del Freddo
Via Principe Eugenio
65/67. **Map** 6 E5.

Lateran

BIRRERIE

La Pace del Cervello
Via dei SS Quattro 63.
Map 9 A1.

ENOTECHE

Il Tajut
Via di San Giovanni in
Laterano 244–246.
Map 9 B1.

FAST FOOD

Antico Chiosco
Viale Carlo Felice.
Map 10 D1.

PASTICCERIE

Paci
Via dei Marsi 33. Off
Map 6 F4.

GELATERIE

Gelateria Fantasia
Via La Spezia 100/102.
Map 10 E1.

San Crispino
Via Acaia 56. **Map** 9 C4.

Aventine

PIZZERIAS

Remo
Piazza Santa Maria
Liberatrice 44. **Map** 8 D3.

BIRRERIE

L'Oasi della Birra
Piazza Testaccio 41.
Map 8 D3.

ENOTECHE

Divinare
Via Manuzio 13.
Map 8 D3.

FAST FOOD

Farinando
Via Luca della Robbia 30.
Map 8 D3.

Rosticceri
Piazza Testaccio 24–5.
Map 8 D3.

Volpetti Più
Via Alessandro Volta 8.
Map 8 D3.

GELATERIE

Café du Parc
Piazza di Porta San Paolo.
Map 8 E4.

Giolitti
Via Vespucci 35.
Map 8 D3.

Trastevere

PIZZERIAS

Da Vittorio
Via di S. Cosimato 14A.
Map 7 C1.

Dar Poeta
Vicolo del Bologna 45.
Map 11 B5.

Panattoni – I Marmi
Viale Trastevere 53.
Map 7 C1.

Pizzeria Ivo
Via S. Francesco a Ripa
158. **Map** 7 C1.

ENOTECHE

Cantina Paradiso
Via San Francesco a Ripa
73. **Map** 7 C2.

Ferrara
Via del Moro 1A.
Map 7 C1.

Trastevere
Via della Lungaretta 86.
Map 7 C1.

BIRRERIE

**Ma Che Siete Venuti
a Fà**
Via Benedetta 25.
Map 11 B5.

FAST FOOD

Forno La Renella
Via del Moro 15.
Map 7 C1.

BARS, CAFÉS, AND
TEAROOMS

Caffè Settimiano
Via di Porta Settimiana 1.
Map 11 B5.

PASTICCERIE

Innocenti
Via della Luce 21A.
Map 7 C2.

Pasticceria Trastevere
Via Natale del Grande 49.
Map 7 C1.

**Rivendita di
Cioccolata e Vino**
Vicolo del Cinque 11A.
Map 11 B5.

GELATERIE

Fior di Luna
Via della Lungaretta 96.
Map 7 C1.

La Fonte della Salute
Via Cardinale Marmaggi
2–4. **Map** 7 C1.

Sora Mirella
Lungotevere degli
Anguillara (corner with
Ponte Cestio). **Map** 8 D1.

Janiculum

ENOTECHE

**In Vino Veritas
Art Bar**
Via Garibaldi 2A.
Map 11 B5.

Vatican

PIZZERIAS

L'Archetto
Via Germanico 105.
Map 3 C1.

Napul'è
Viale Giulio Cesare 91.
Map 3 C1.

ENOTECHE

Costantini
Piazza Cavour 16.
Map 4 E2.

Del Frate
Via degli Scipioni 118.
Map 3 C1.

Il Pane e Le Rose
Via Quirino Visconti 61A.
Map 4 E2.

Birrerie

Cantina Tirolese
Via Vitelleschi 23.
Map 3 C2.

The Proud Lion
Borgo Pio 36. **Map** 3 C3.

FAST FOOD

Ercoli dal 1928
Via Montello 26.
Off **Map** 1 A5.

Franchi
Via Cola di Rienzo 200.
Map 4 D2.

La Pratolina
Via degli Scipioni 248.
Map 3 C1.

BARS, CAFÉS, AND
TEAROOMS

Art Studio Café
Via dei Gracchi 187A.
Map 4 D2.

Faggiani
Via Ferrari 23. **Map** 1 A5.

Makasar
Via Plauto 33. **Map** 3 C3.

PASTICCERIE

Antonini
Via Sabotino 19–29. Just
off **Map** 1 A5.

Gran Caffè Esperia
Lungotevere Mellini 1.
Map 4 E1.

GELATERIE

Al Settimo Gelo
Via Vodice 21A. Just off
Map 1 A5.

Gelarmony
Via Marcantonio Colonna
34. **Map** 4 D1.

Via Veneto

PIZZERIAS

San Marco
Via Sardegna 38D.
Map 5 C1.

BARS, CAFÉS, AND
TEAROOMS

Café de Paris
Via Veneto 90.
Map 5 B2.

Cine Caffè
Largo M. Mastroianni 1.
Map 5 B1.

Doney
Via Veneto 141.
Map 5 B2.

EUR

ENOTECHE

La Cave des Amis
Piazzale Ardigò 27–29.

BARS, CAFÉS, AND
TEAROOMS

Palombini
Piazzale Adenauer 12.

GELATERIE

Chalet del Lago
Lake, EUR.

Giolitti
Casina dei Tre Laghi, Viale
Oceania 90.

Farther Afield

PIZZERIAS

Al Forno della Soffita
Via Piave 62. **Map** 6 D1.

La Pantera Rosa
Piazzale del Verano 84. Off
Map 6 F4.

BARS, CAFÉS, AND
TEAROOMS

Caffè Parnaso
Piazzale delle Muse 22.
Map 2 E2.

Zodiaco
Viale Parco Mellini 88–92.
Off **Map** 3 A1.

PASTICCERIE

Mondi
Via Flaminia 468. Off
Map 1 A1.

GELATERIE

Neve di Latte
Via L. Poletti 6. **Map** 1 A2.

Petrini dal 1926
Piazza dell'Alberone 16A.
Map 10 F4.

SHOPS AND MARKETS

Rome has been a thriving center for design and cosmopolitan shopping since ancient times. In the heyday of the Empire, the finest craftsmen were drawn to Rome, and artifacts and products of all kinds, including gold, furs, wine, and slaves, were imported from far-flung corners of the Empire to service the needs of the wealthy Roman population. Shopping in Rome today in many ways reflects this diverse tradition. Italian designers have an international reputation for their luxuriously chic style in fashion, knitwear, and leather goods (especially shoes and handbags) as well as in interior design, fabrics, ceramics, and glass. The artisan-craftsman tradition is strong and the love of good design filters through into the smallest items. Rome is not a city for bargains (although there are often better buys here than Florence or Milan), but the joys of window shopping here will offer plenty of compensation.

Best Buys

Leather goods of all kinds, including shoes, and bags, are a strong point. Ready-to-wear Italian designer clothes are not cheap, but they are certainly less expensive than in other countries. Armani jeans are a good example *(see p331)*. You are also likely to find designer lighting fixtures, for example, at lower prices here. Both modern, and traditional Italian ceramics, and handicrafts can be very beautifully made, and, if you have time to wander around the back streets, really unusual and individual gifts can often be found.

Sales

Bargain hunters may like to visit Rome during sale time *(saldi)*, from mid-July to mid-September and the period from just after Christmas to the first week in March. Top designers *(see p330)* can slash prices by half, but their clothes are still very expensive even then. Good bargains can be found in the young designer-wear shops *(see p331)* and good-quality small and large shoe sizes are sold off very cheaply. In general, though, sales in Rome tend to offer moderate rather than huge discounts.

Both the original, and the sale price should be marked on each reduced item. *Liquidazioni* (closing-down sales) are usually genuine and can sometimes be worth investigating. However, other signs in shop windows such as *vendite promozionali* (special introductory prices) and *sconti* (discounts) are often only lures to get you into the shop. The sign on the door saying *entrata libera* means "browsers welcome."

When to Shop

Shops are generally open from 9am to 1pm and from 3:30pm

Antiques at Acanto *(see p340)*

to 7:30pm (4pm to 8pm in the summer months). Some downtown shops stay open all day from 10am to 7:30pm.

Most shops are closed on Sunday (except immediately before Christmas). Shops are also closed on Monday morning, apart from most food stores, which close on Thursday afternoons in winter, and Saturday afternoons in high summer.

August brings the city to a virtual standstill as Roman families flee the heat to the sea or the mountains, but this is gradually changing, with Romans taking shorter summer holidays. Most shops close for at least 2 weeks around August 15, the national holiday.

Shopping Etiquette

Apart from a few department stores, most Roman shops are

Flower stalls in Piazza Campo de' Fiori *(see p344)*

small, specializing in just one field. Browsing at leisure may at first seem daunting if you are used to large shopping centers. Customers will almost always receive better attention if they dress stylishly – the emphasis on *fare una bella figura* (making a good impression) is taken seriously.

Sizes are not always uniform, so it is wise to try clothes on if possible before buying, since refunds and exchanges are not always given.

Stylish leather gloves on display

How to Pay

Most shops accept all the major credit cards, whose signs are displayed on the shop window. Some will also accept foreign currency, though the exchange rate may not be good. When you make a purchase, you are bound by Italian law to leave the shop with a *scontrino fiscale* (receipt). You can try asking for a discount if paying cash, and you may be lucky, though many shops have a *prezzi fissi* (fixed prices) sign.

VAT Exemption

Value Added Tax – VAT (IVA in Italy) – ranges from 12 percent on clothing to 35 percent on luxury items such as jewelry, and furs. Marked or advertised prices normally include the IVA. It is possible for non–European Union residents to obtain an IVA

One of many designer shops around Piazza di Spagna

refund for individual purchases that exceed €155, but be prepared for a long, and bureaucratic process. The simplest method is to shop at a place displaying the "Euro Free Tax" sign. Present your passport when you make your purchase and ask for a tax refund check. On leaving Italy, show your new purchases, and receipts at customs, and get the check stamped. You can then collect your refund at Fiumicino airport by presenting the check at the **Global Blue** desk, where you will be reimbursed.

If you wish to buy something from a shop that is not part of the "Euro Free Tax" program, you must get an Italian customs agent to stamp the vendor's receipt at your departure, showing them the purchased article; then mail the receipt back to the shop, which should send you a refund.

Mercato delle Stampe *(see p344)*

Department Stores and Shopping Centers

Department stores, known as *grandi magazzini*, are few, and far between in Rome, but they tend to have longer opening hours than smaller shops. **La Rinascente,** and **Coin** are good for ready-to-wear clothes for both men, and women, household linens, and sewing notions, and have well-stocked perfume counters. The **Oviesse** and **Upim** chain stores offer moderately priced medium-quality clothes, and a variety of household goods.

Another alternative for the zealous shopper is to head for one of Rome's shopping malls. **Cinecittà Due Centro Commerciale**, built in 1988, offers around 100 shops

Bargains in Via Sannio *(see p345)*

plus bars, banks, and restaurants within easy reach of downtown by Metro (line A to Cinecittà).

DIRECTORY

Shopping

Cinecittà Due Centro Commerciale
Viale Palmiro Togliatti 2.
Tel 06-722 0902.

Coin
Termini Station. **Map** 6 D3.
Tel 06-4782 5909.

Piazzale Appio 7. **Map** 10 D2.
Tel 06-708 0020.

Via Cola di Rienzo 173. **Map** 3 C2.
Tel 06-3600 4298.

Global Blue
Terminal 3, Gate H1 and Terminal 5, Fiumicino airport.
Tel 00800 32 111 111 (toll free).
🇼 global-blue.com

La Rinascente
Galleria Alberto Sordi. **Map** 12 E2.
Tel 06-678 4209.

Piazza Fiume. **Map** 6 D1.
Tel 06-884 1231.

Oviesse
Viale Trastevere 62. **Map** 7 C2.
Tel 06-5833 3633.

Via Appia Nuova 181–5. **Map** 10 D2. **Tel** 06-702 3214.

Upim
Circonvallazione Gianicolense 78.
Map 7 A5. **Tel** 06-536 692.

Via Goberti 64. **Map** 6 D4.
Tel 06-446 5579.

Rome's Best: Shopping Streets and Markets

The most interesting shops in Rome are in the oldest part of the city, so shopping is easy to combine with sightseeing. Shops are often housed in medieval or Renaissance buildings, and their window displays can be exquisite. Just like shopkeepers in past centuries, traders tend to specialize in one type of merchandise. Street names often refer to the old tradesmen: locksmiths in Via dei Chiavari, leather jerkin makers in Via dei Giubbonari, and chairs in Via dei Sediari. Today, antiques merchants have taken over from the rosary sellers on Via dei Coronari. The top names in fashion and modern design dominate the Via Condotti area, and the artisan-craftsman tradition is still strong around Campo de' Fiori and Piazza Navona.

Via Cola di Rienzo
Situated close to the Vatican Museums, this long, wide street has the finest food shops and is also good for clothes, books, and gifts.

Via dei Coronari
Art Nouveau and antique collectors will love browsing in the shops that line this charming street just northwest of Piazza Navona. But be prepared for high prices, since most of the items are imported.

Pia
Sp

Vatican

R

Piazza
Navona

Janiculum

Ca
de

Via del Pellegrino
Book and art shops abound here next to working artisans in the historic downtown. Do not miss the mirror-lined alley near Campo de' Fiori.

Traste

Via dei Cappellari
This narrow, medieval street is a great place for watching furniture restorers and other artisans plying their trade in the open air.

Porta Portese
You can buy anything from antiques to a tin whistle at Trastevere's Sunday morning flea market. *(See p345.)*

Via Margutta
Upscale antique shops mix with genteel restaurants on this peaceful, cobbled street.

Via del Babuino
This street is renowned for designer furniture, lighting, and glass, as well as interesting antique and fashion shops.

0 meters 500
0 yards 500

Via Veneto

Quirinal

apitol

Forum

Palatine

Esquiline

Lateran

entine

Caracalla

VIA DELLA CROCE · VIA · D&G · Missoni · Prada · PIAZZA DI SPAGNA · VIA DELLE CARROZZE · Giorgio Armani · BOCCA DI LEONE · VIA MARIO DE' FIORI · Gucci · PIAZZA MIGNANELLI · Trussardi · CONDOTTI · DI LEONE · Valentino · BORGOGNONA · VIA · VIA DI PROPAGANDA · VIA · BELSIANA · VIA FRATTINA · Max Mara · VIA DELLA VITE · VIA DEL CORSO · VIA DELLA MERCEDE

Designer Shopping

All the well-known stars of the Italian fashion scene, plus exclusive jewelers, gift shops, shoe designers, and tailors, are concentrated in this cluster of chic, and stylish shopping streets by the Spanish Steps *(see pp330–35)*. Romans love to stroll here in the early evening.

Testaccio Market
A visual feast of fruit and vegetables greets the eye in this lively market. *(See p344.)*

Via Borgognona
Crowds flock here to buy, or just gaze at, high-fashion clothes, shoes, leather bags, and other accessories.

Men's and Women's Fashion

Italy is one of the leading lights in high-class fashion, or *alta moda*. Many of the most famous designers are based in Milan, but Rome is home to a cluster of sophisticated and internationally distinguished fashion houses. There is also a wonderful selection of *alta moda* shops. Boutiques displaying an eclectic mix of designer goods rub shoulders with showrooms devoted to single collections. But even for those of us unable to splurge on genuine designer-wear, much fun can be gained from a stroll down the glittering streets that radiate out from the Piazza di Spagna, since some of the window displays are truly spectacular.

The "atelier" made-to-measure fashions are beyond most pockets, but the designers also offer ready-to-wear alternatives in their boutiques. These are not cheap, but cost far less than a tailor-made garment.

Women's High Fashion

Rome's most famous designer internationally is probably **Valentino**, who retired in 2008 but whose boutique on Piazza di Spagna is still a mecca for the younger fashionista. Just up the Spanish Steps, in chic Via Sistina, is the Rome branch of **Gattinoni**, which showcases the subtly extravagant haute couture, and ready-to-wear designs of Guillermo Mariotto.

The equally impressive **Fendi** occupies a 19th-century palazzo in Largo Goldoni. Fendi made its name with high-fashion furs, then branched out into leather goods, accessories, and ready-to-wear, collaborating with Karl Lagerfeld, who designed the coveted double-F logo that emblazons its very collectible products. Third-generation family members design the younger, less expensive Fendissime line.

For well over a decade, **Laura Biagiotti** has reigned as Rome's queen of discreet, conservative couture. From her headquarters in a castle just outside Rome, she designs a range of timelessly elegant knitwear and silk separates for women who don't want to sacrifice style for comfort. She is famous for her use of cashmere and white as well as her creative use of fabrics and quality of finish. Her flagship showroom in Via Mario de' Fiori stocks her complete collection, which now includes hosiery, perfumes, swimwear, and leather goods. Her scarves make wonderful presents, and are often reduced in price during sales; other items from previous collections are available in the shop all year at very good discounts. Meanwhile, in nearby Via Condotti, there is the temple to the creations of **Salvatore Ferragamo**.

Other internationally known Rome-based designers include **Renato Balestra**, who produces tailored suits and glamorous evening wear.

Milan's miraculous fashion house **Prada** has an alluring branch on Via Condotti, featuring clothes, shoes, and accessories in unmistakable style. The window display is always worth a look. Other luminaries of Italian fashion who have shops in Rome include **Gianni Versace**, **Trussardi**, and **Giada Curti**. Top designers **Giorgio Armani** and **Dolce & Gabbana** also have stores in the Via Condotti area.

An affirmed star in ready-to-wear is **Roberto Cavalli**, whose design team produces some coolly imaginative and stylish collections.

If you're looking for clothes from more unconventional designers, **Gente** is the place to go – its Roman showrooms have exclusive rights to the original couture collections of Dolce & Gabbana, Moschino, and Jean-Paul Gaultier.

MaxMara also has a number of branches here. Chic suits and separates are the mainstays of this popular label. The quality of fabric and finish is superb and, with suits available for around €500, its prices are much lower than other *alta moda* couture designers' ready-to-wear lines.

Men's Tailors and Designer Wear

Italian men are every bit as fashion-conscious as the women, and there is no shortage of choice in Rome for the well-dressed man. Suits tend to begin at around €620, jackets €415, and pants €155.

Most of the "star" designers of women's *alta moda* have a shop for men, like **Salvatore Ferragamo**, **Prada**, and **Gianni Versace**. The designs are generally less dramatic than the women's, with the accent on understated sophistication and casual sportiness. **Valentino**'s distinctive monogrammed accessories are relatively affordable. **Battistoni** is probably the

Valentino

One of the high priests of Italian fashion, **Valentino Garavani**, opened the doors of his Roman studio in 1959 to a distinguished clientele that included Sophia Loren, Audrey Hepburn, and Jackie Kennedy. Before retiring in 2008, Valentino created some of the most dramatic and flattering evening dresses of the last 50 years. In the 1970s he began designing ready-to-wear lines for both men and women alongside his *alta moda* collections, and you can now find his very distinctive "V" logo on a wide range of accessories. The Valentino brand is still based in a huge palazzo in Piazza Mignanelli, and there are separate ready-to-wear boutiques nearby *(see p334)*.

most prestigious designer concentrating on menswear. Giorgio Battistoni and family's fine custom-made shirts and suits have been in demand with movie stars and top society for over 50 years. **Etro** sells classically cut clothes, and accessories for men, and women in exotic Italian-designed printed fabrics.

Ermenegildo Zegna is housed in a Baroque palazzo setting. It offers elegant ready-to-wear, and the master tailor Gaetano will also make to measure. **Davide Cenci** has been a mecca for those in search of the English country gentleman look since 1926. **Brioni** offers traditional tailor-made and own-label ready-to-wear men's clothing, **Trussardi** sells beautifully tailored classics, and **Testa** has impeccably tailored suits that appeal to younger Romans. **Degli Effetti** stocks more avant-garde designers such as Romeo Gigli and Jean-Paul Gaultier.

Young Designer Wear

There is a huge choice for the young. Top designers Dolce & Gabbana and Armani offer their particular styles translated into more affordable lines at **D&G** and **Emporio Armani** (Armani jeans are a good buy at around €100). **Fendi** has its Fendissime line; **Ermanno Scervino** also has a boutique at Piazza di Spagna, not far from **Gianfranco Ferré**'s youth-inspired label. Aimed at the younger set, these are good places to pick up stylish, sporty clothes. **Timberland** is another casual label very popular with young Italians. Average prices are in the region of €52 for a shirt and €210 for raincoats.

Energie is a big hit, and has some of the best window displays in Rome. Teenagers flock here for jeans and T-shirts, both the shop's own, and other labels. Trussardi's casual line is found at **Tru Trussardi**, and **Aria**, **Diesel**, and **SBU** are also very popular. **Eventi** represents the more avant-garde styles – *dark*, as they call it here – fusing

Gothic, New Age, and punk influences, which can result in some outrageous window creations. For women, Via del Governo Vecchio is the place to head for. **Arsenico e Vecchi Merletti**, **Luna e L'altra**, and **Maga Morgana** offer some unconventional designer clothes in a pleasant, friendly atmosphere.

Retail Fashion

Rome is not a good place to look for everyday wear, since there is a distinct lack of mid-price shops bridging the huge gap between the dazzlingly priced *alta moda* designer exclusives, and the ultra-cheap goods sold in markets *(see pp344–5)*. Lower-budget stores do exist, but quality is often poor. If you have the stamina, you may find a bargain along Via del Corso, Via del Tritone, Via Nazionale, Via Cavour, Via Cola di Rienzo, Via Ottaviano, or the Via dei Giubbonari.

The most convenient places to shop are department stores like La Rinascente, Coin, and Upim *(see p327)*. They may not sound exciting, but you can browse at leisure and occasionally find nice things. It is also worth trying shops mentioned under Young Designer Wear – particularly the *alta moda* designers' cheaper lines such as **Emporio Armani**. At the different branches of **Discount dell'Alta Moda** you can find end-of-season designer labels at 50 percent less than the boutique prices. And while you don't need to come all the way to Rome to shop at **Benetton**, there are many branches here, which sell the authentic garments in their universal colors.

Knitwear

Knitwear is a particular strength in Italian design, and in Rome there are plenty of specialty shops. **Laura Biagiotti** is celebrated for her luxurious cashmere separates, and **Missoni** for spectacular kaleidoscopic patterns and colors.

Krizia no longer has a shop in Rome, but sophisticated knitwear can be purchased at **Liz**.

Other shops, such as the **Luisa Spagnoli** outlets, offer a wider selection, including lower-priced items, as does **Stefanel**, which has various branches in the city.

Lingerie

This is another Italian specialty excelling in both style and quality, with lines like La Perla exported worldwide. Lingerie is traditionally sold in top household linen shops *(see p337)* – **Cesari**, for example, has its own complete range. There are also boutiques specializing in lingerie and swimwear.

Marisa Padovan has a range of swimwear that's ideal for Italian beaches, as well as light, bright summer dresses. **Brighenti** is said to be where movie stars go for their lingerie. **Schostal** has more traditional underwear with a very good men's section.

Secondhand Clothes

Those who are willing to browse will find a wide variety of secondhand clothes, whether inspired by a collector's interest in vintage clothes or a low budget. Apart from Via Sannio and Porta Portese markets *(see p345)*, which have many second-hand clothing stands, the mecca is Via del Governo Vecchio. Among the best shops in this ancient street near Piazza Navona is **Mado**, which has mostly 1920s dresses and some hats, and jewelry.

Le Gallinelle offers a marvelous selection of second-hand, and vintage clothes, as well as their own line. At **Daniela e Daniela** in Via Mastro Giorgio, Testaccio, there is an excellent range of women's clothes, mostly with designer labels. Via del Pellegrino is also a good street for shops selling secondhand clothes, and for independent stores.

Shoes and Accessories

Italy's leather industry is renowned all over the world, and shoes, bags, and belts are a good buy in Rome. Accessories in general are not just an afterthought but an integral part of an outfit for the well-dressed Roman. The choice of stylish jewelry, scarves, ties, and other accessories is excellent.

Shoes

Rome is full of shoe shops, ranging from high-quality stores in the Via Condotti area (where prices tend to start at €170) to the more economical shops around the Trevi fountain, and every big market has bargain shoe stands on its fringes.

Probably the best-known shop is **Ferragamo** – one of the world's top shoe shops. It stocks classic yet fashion-conscious shoes, as well as women's clothing and leather goods. The silk signature scarves are famous.

Fratelli Rossetti is a close contender for the number one position. Founded by brothers Renzo and Renato some 50 years ago, this company produces classic men's shoes and beautiful, dressy low-heeled shoes for women that reflect the most up-to-the-minute trends. Along with shops like **Tod's** in Via Condotti, it represents the epitome of elegance. The prices, of course, are sky-high, but you can buy something small, and at least you'll have the bag!

Boccanera's retail outlets, over in Testaccio, offer the latest men's and women's shoe styles from top Italian and British designers, with prices to match.

Silvano Lattanzi is one of the longer-lived shoe shops in Rome, having been in business for almost two decades, but it can't compete with **Domus**, which opened in 1938. Silvano Lattanzi sells made-to-measure footwear for both men and women, particularly shoes for special occasions and to customers' personal specifications. Domus sells a selection of high-quality footwear, specializing in classic shoes for women. They also stock a limited range of

leather bags and accessories. **De Bach** has colorful shoe styles for women.

Via Frattina has several more great shoe shops, such as **Campanile**, which specializes in footwear for both men and women in trendy and imaginative styles. Native designer **Fausto Santini** stocks original, stylish, colorful designs for younger people. Beautiful, bright designs for both men and women can also be found at **Baldinini**.

Borini stocks simple and elegant, low-heeled designs. The **Mr Boots** chain of shops stocks a wide range of trendy boots and casual shoes for men and women, while **Nuyorica** sells quirky, chic footwear for women alongside its select clothes range. If comfort is your priority, head to the **Geox** flagship store on Via del Corso.

Leather Bags and Accessories

The most famous of Rome's leather shops is the super-trendy **Gucci**, a dandy's paradise selling shoes, suitcases, handbags, wallets, belts, and other accessories. It has a fashion boutique for men and women and is well-known for its silk ties and scarves. **Fendi** also has exquisite leather goods as well as some lower-priced lines in synthetic materials and a range of gift items. Although their famous "stripe" line of leather-finished synthetic handbags cost €130 (and their all-leather ones start at €155), they are at least cheaper to buy here than abroad. **Skin**, situated around the Via Sistina area, is also quite pricey. Located a short walk to the south of Skin, near the Trevi Fountain, is **La Sella**. It sells all things leather,

including a range of shoes, bags, purses, and belts.

Mandarina Duck's brightly colored fabric bags and range of luggage are very much in fashion and make an attractive (and vegetarian) alternative to the more traditional leather styles. For sleek, utterly fashionable handbags, check out the latest creations from **Furla** or go for one of **Alviero Martini**'s famous "map" bags.

For a more unusual men's present, try **La Cravatta** in Trastevere. In addition to their selection of classy handmade ties, they also manufacture ties to customers' specifications. You can choose the design, material, length, and shape of the tie to create the perfect gift.

Classic Jewelry

What Cartier is to Paris, Tiffany & Co. is to New York and Asprey's is to London, **Bulgari** is to Rome. This internationally revered jeweler has passers-by glued to the windows gazing at its large gemstones. These "windows" are rather curious small boxes inserted into a wall with one or two pieces of jewelry in each of them, which adds to the feeling of looking at precious items in a case at a museum. Bulgari's watches, especially the men's, are popular and very elegant, as are the famous mesh necklaces. It specializes in large, colorful stones in High Renaissance–style settings but also produces a selection of contemporary designs. This was one of Andy Warhol's favorite shops, and it is definitely the most palatial shop on Via Condotti. Inside, the shop's atmosphere is one of almost religious awe and contemplation.

Buccellati is an offshoot of the famous Florentine dynasty, which was begun by Mario Buccellati in the 1920s and patronized by the poet Gabriele D'Annunzio. Its delicately engraved designs are inspired by the Italian

Renaissance, and are real classics, displaying superb craftsmanship.

Ansuini designs are fashionable yet classic, with strong, imaginative themes being introduced for each new collection. **Massoni**, founded in 1790, is one of Rome's oldest jewelry houses. Its refined brooches and one-of-a-kind pieces are outstanding.

At **Moroni Gioielli** you will also find imaginative, unique pieces of the highest-quality workmanship.

Peroso is an old-fashioned shop that has been in existence since 1891 and specializes in antique jewelry and silverware. **Boncompagni Sturni** sells traditional designs with the emphasis on quality and craftsmanship. You have to ring the bell to be admitted to both of these shops, and they are extremely expensive.

Tiffany & Co. sells its classic designs in jewelry, watches, accessories, and gifts at an exquisite outlet on elegant Via del Babuino.

Costume Jewelry

For less conventional tastes, there are several shops selling innovative, avant-garde pieces, often using semiprecious metals and stones. **Granuzzo**, in Via dei Coronari, is worth trying.

Tempi Moderni has an interesting collection of Art Deco and Liberty (Art Nouveau) period jewelry, including Bakelite brooches. There is also a range of designer pieces from the fifties and sixties.

Danae makes interesting pieces using silver and precious stones, inspired by Coco Chanel, while **Paola Volpi** uses industrial materials and is one of the most interesting designers of modern jewelry in Italy.

Traditional Goldsmiths and Silversmiths

The mainstays of Rome's jewelry industry are still the traditional artisan goldsmiths and silversmiths, working

to order in tiny studio workshops. These are concentrated in the old Jewish Ghetto area by the Tiber River, Campo de' Fiori, Ponte Sisto near Via Giulia, and in Montepietà (which is also where the city's pawnbrokers are situated).

Artisan jewelry can also be found in Via dei Coronari, Via dell'Orso and Via del Pellegrino. The jewelers create individual pieces to their own designs and have often learned their profession from their parents, and grandparents. They will also do repair work, or take old gold jewelry, melt it down, and make it into something new to the customer's specifications.

Gioie d'Arte produces some traditional artisan jewelry and always works to customers' commissions.

Gloves, Hats, and Hosiery

If you're looking for top quality, you will find an expensive line in gloves at **Di Cori**, and **Sermoneta**, both of which stock every imaginable kind.

To find stylish leather gloves to match your new shoes, and handbags, whatever their color, pay a visit to **Settimio Mieli** which is sure to have something suitable, and at a reasonable price.

Catello d'Auria specializes in gloves and hosiery. **Borsalino** is a good place to go for all sorts of hats, including its namesake. **Calzedonia** has several branches in the city, and will provide you with almost any color or pattern of tights, and stockings that you could wish for.

Size Chart

For Australian sizes follow British and American convention.

Children's clothing

Italian	2-3	4-5	6-7	8-9	10-11	12	14	14+ (years)
British	2-3	4-5	6-7	8-9	10-11	12	14	14+ (years)
American	2-3	4-5	6-6x	7-8	10	12	14	16 (size)

Children's shoes

Italian	24	25½	27	28	29	30	32	33	34
British	7	8	9	10	11	12	13	1	2
American	7½	8½	9½	10½	11½	12½	13½	1½	2½

Women's dresses, coats, and skirts

Italian	38	40	42	44	46	48	50
British	8	10	12	14	16	18	20
American	6	8	10	12	14	16	18

Women's blouses and sweaters

Italian	81	84	87	90	93	96	99 (cms)
British	31	32	34	36	38	40	42 (inches)
American	6	8	10	12	14	16	18 (size)

Women's shoes

Italian	36	37	38	39	40	41
British	3	4	5	6	7	8
American	5	6	7	8	9	10

Men's suits

Italian	44	46	48	50	52	54	56	58 (size)
British	34	36	38	40	42	44	46	48 (inches)
American	34	36	38	40	42	44	46	48 (inches)

Men's shirts (collar size)

Italian	36	38	39	41	42	43	44	45 (cms)
British	14	15	15½	16	16½	17	17½	18 (inches)
American	14	15	15½	16	16½	17	17½	18 (inches)

Men's shoes

Italian	39	40	41	42	43	44	45	46
British	6	7	7½	8	9	10	11	12
American	7	7½	8	8½	9½	10½	11	11½

DIRECTORY

Women's High Fashion

Dolce & Gabbana
Via Condotti 51–52.
Map 5 A2.
Tel 06-6992 4999.

Fendi
Largo Goldoni 419.
Map 12 E1.
Tel 06-69 66 61.

Gattinoni
Via Sistina 44.
Map 5 A2.
Tel 06-678 3972.

Gente
Via del Babuino 81.
Map 4 F1.
Tel 06-320 7671.
Also: Via Frattina 69.
Map 5 A2.
Tel 06-678 9132.

Giada Curti
Rampa Mignanelli 12.
Map 5 A2.
Tel 06-6979 7794.

Gianni Versace
Via Bocca di Leone 26–27.
Map 5 A2.
Tel 06-678 0521.

Giorgio Armani
Via Condotti 77.
Map 5 A2.
Tel 06-699 1461.

Laura Biagiotti
Via Mario de' Fiori 26.
Map 12 F1.
Tel 06-679 1205.

Max & Co
Via Condotti 46.
Map 5 A2.
Tel 06-678 7946.

MaxMara
Via Frattina 28. **Map** 5 A2.
Tel 06-679 3638.

Prada
Via Condotti 92–95.
Map 5 A2.
Tel 06-679 0897.

Renato Balestra
Via Abruzzi 3. **Map** 5 C1.
Tel 06-482 1723.

Roberto Cavalli
Via Borgognona 25.
Map 5 A2.
Tel 06-6992 5469.

Salvatore Ferragamo
Via Condotti 73–74.
Map 5 A2.
Tel 06-679 1565.

Trussardi
Via Condotti 49–50.
Map 5 A2.
Tel 06-678 0280.

Valentino
Via Condotti 15.
Map 5 A2.
Tel 06-673 9420.

Men's Tailors, and Designer Wear

Battistoni
Via Condotti 61A.
Map 5 A2.
Tel 06-697 6111.

Brioni
Via Condotti 21A.
Map 5 A2.
Tel 06-678 3428.

Davide Cenci
Via Campo Marzio 1–7.
Map 4 F3 & 12 D2.
Tel 06-699 0681.

Degli Effetti
Piazza Capranica 79.
Map 4 F3 & 12 D2.
Tel 06-679 0202.

Ermenegildo Zegna
Via Condotti 58.
Map 5 A2.
Tel 06-6994 0678.

Etro
Via del Babuino 102.
Map 5 A2.
Tel 06-678 8257.

Gianni Versace
Via Bocca di Leone 26–27.
Map 5 A2.
Tel 06-678 0521.

Gucci
Via Condotti 8. **Map** 5 A2.
Tel 06-679 0405.

Salvatore Ferragamo
Via Condotti 65.
Map 5 A2.
Tel 06-678 1130.

Testa
Via Borgognona 13.
Map 12 E1.
Tel 06-679 0660.
Also: Piazza Euclide 27.
Map 2 D2.
Tel 06-807 0118.

Trussardi
See Women's High Fashion.

Young Designer Wear

Aria
Via Nazionale 239.
Map 5 C3.
Tel 06-48 44 21.

Armani Jeans
Via del Babuino 70A.
Map 4 F1.
Tel 06-3600 1848.

Arsenico e Vecchi Merletti
Via del Governo Vecchio 36.
Map 11 B3.
Tel 06-683 3936.

D&G
Via Belsiana 66.
Map 4 F2.
Tel 06-6938 0870.

Diesel
Via del Corso 186.
Map 4 F3 & 12 E1.
Tel 06-678 3933.

Emporio Armani
Via del Babuino 140.
Map 4 F1.
Tel 06-322 1581.

Energie
Via del Corso 486.
Map 4 F2.
Tel 06-322 7046.

Ermanno Scervino
Piazza di Spagna 82–83.
Map 5 A2.
Tel 06-679 2294.

Eventi
Via dei Serpenti 134.
Map 5 B4.
Tel 06-48 49 60.

Gianfranco Ferré
Piazza di Spagna 70.
Map 5 A2.
Tel 06-679 1451.

Luna e L'Altra
Piazza Pasquino 76.
Map 4 E4 & 11 C3.
Tel 06-6880 4995.

Maga Morgana
Via del Governo Vecchio 27 & 98.
Map 4 E4 & 11 C3.
Tel 06-687 9995.

Sbu
Via S. Pantaleo 68.
Map 11 C3.
Tel 06-6880 2547.

Timberland
Via del Corso 488.
Map 4 F2.
Tel 06-324 3363.

Tru Trussardi
Via Frattina 42.
Map 5 A2.
Tel 06-6938 0939.

High Street Fashion

Benetton
Via del Corso 288.
Map 12 E1.
Tel 06-6810 2520.

Discount dell'Alta Moda
Via di Gesù e Maria 14 & 16A. **Map** 4 F2.
Tel 06-361 3796.
Also: Via de Pretis 88.
Map 5 C3.
Tel 06-4782 5672.

Emporio Armani
See Young Designer Wear

Zara
Galleria Alberto Sordi.
Map 12 E2.
Tel 06-6992 5401.
Also:
Via del Corso 129–135.
Map 12 E2.
Tel 06-6992 3196.

Knitwear

Laura Biagiotti
See Women's High Fashion.

Liz
Via Appia Nuova 90.
Map 10 D2.
Tel 06-700 3609.

Luisa Spagnoli
Via del Tritone 30.
Map 5 A3–B3 & 12 F1.
Tel 06-6992 2769.
Also:
Via Vittorio Veneto 130.
Map 5 B1.
Tel 06-4201 1281.

Missoni
Piazza di Spagna 78.
Map 5 A2.
Tel 06-679 2555.

Stefanel
Via Frattina 31–33.
Map 5 A2.
Tel 06-679 2667.

Lingerie

Brighenti
Via Borgognona 27.
Map 5 A2.
Tel 06-678 3898.

Cesari
Via del Babuino 195.
Map 5 B3.
Tel 06-638 1241.

Marisa Padovan
Via delle Carrozze 81–82.
Map 5 A2.
Tel 06-679 3946.

Schostal
Via Fontanella Borghese
29. **Map** 12 D1.
Tel 06-679 1240.

Secondhand Clothes

Daniela e Daniela
Via Mastro Giorgio 79B.
Map 8 D3.
Tel 06-5728 5208.

Le Gallinelle
Via Panisperna 61.
Map 5 B4.
Tel 06-488 1017.

Mado
Via del Governo Vecchio
89A. **Map** 4 E4 & 11 B3.
Tel 06-687 5028.

Shoes

Baldinini
Via del Babuino 150.
Map 4 F2.
Tel 06-3601 0347.

Boccanera
Via Luca della Robbia
34–36. **Map** 8 D3.
Tel 06-575 6804.

Borini
Via dei Pettinari 86–87.
Map 4 E5 & 11 C5.
Tel 06-687 5670.

Campanile
Via Frattina 25.
Map 12 E1.
Tel 06-6994 0621.

De Bach
Via del Babuino 123.
Map 4 F1.
Tel 06-678 3384.

Domus
Via Belsiana 52. **Map** 4 F2.
Tel 06-67 8 9083.

Fausto Santini
Via Frattina 120.
Map 5 A2.
Tel 06-678 4114.

Ferragamo
Via Condotti 73–74.
Map 5 A2.
Tel 06-679 1565.
Also: Via Condotti 65.
Map 5 A2.
Tel 06-678 1130.

Fratelli Rossetti
Via Borgognona 5A.
Map 5 A2.
Tel 06-678 2676.

Geox
Via del Corso 443.
Map 4 F2.
Tel 06-6889 2720.

Mr Boots
Piazza Re di Roma 10.
Map 10 D3.
Tel 06-7720 8672.
Also: Via A Brunetti 2.
Map 4 F1.
Tel 06-321 5733.

Nuyorica
Piazza della Pollarola
36–7.
Map 11 C4.
Tel 06-6889 1243.

Silvano Lattanzi
Via Bocca di Leone 59.
Map 5 A2.
Tel 06-678 6119.

Tod's
Via Condotti 52–53A.
Map 5 A2.
Tel 06-699 1089.

Leather Bags and Accessories

Alviero Martini
Via Frattina 116.
Map 5 A2.
Tel 06-6992 3381.

La Cravatta
Via di Santa Cecilia 12.
Map 8 D1.
Tel 06-8901 6941.

Furla
Via Condotti 56.
Map 5 A2.
Tel 06-679 1973.
Also: Via Nazionale 54–55.
Map 5 C3.
Tel 06-487 0127.

Gucci
Via Borgognona 7D.
Map 5 A2. **Tel** 06-6919
0661.
Also: Via Condotti 8.
Map 5 A2.
Tel 06-679 0405.

Mandarina Duck
Via Due Macelli 59F/G.
Map 12 F1.
Tel 06-678 6414.

La Sella
Via del Lavatore 56.
Map 5 A3 & 12 F2.
Tel 06-679 6654.

Skin
Via Capo le Case 41.
Map 5 A3 & 12 F1.
Tel 06-678 5531.

Classic Jewelry

Ansuini
Corso Vittorio Emanuele
151.
Map 4 E4 & 11 C3.
Tel 06-6880 6909.

Boncompagni
Via Vittoria 4A.
Map 4 F2.
Tel 06-321 3950.

Buccellati
Via Condotti 31.
Map 5 A2. **Tel** 06-679
0329.

Bulgari
Via Condotti 10.
Map 5 A2. **Tel** 06-696 261.

Massoni
Via Margutta 74.
Map 4 F1.
Tel 06-321 6916.

Moroni Gioielli
Via Belsiana 32A. **Map**
4 F2. **Tel** 06-678 0466.

Peroso
Via Sistina 29A.
Map 5 B3.
Tel 06-474 7952.

Tiffany & Co.
Via del Babuino 118.
Map 5 A2.
Tel 06-679 0717.

Costume Jewelry

Danae
Via della Maddalena 40.
Map 12 D2.
Tel 06-679 1881.

Granuzzo
Via dei Coronari 193.
Map 4 E3 & 11 B2.
Tel 06-6880 1503.

Paola Volpi
Piazza dei Satiri 55.
Map 11 C4.
Tel 06-687 3366.

Tempi Moderni
Via del Governo
Vecchio 108.
Map 4 E4 & 11 B3.
Tel 06-687 7007.

Traditional Goldsmiths, and Silversmiths

Gioie d'Arte
Via de' Gigli d'Oro 10.
Map 4 E3 & 11 C2.
Tel 06-687 7524.

Gloves, Hats, and Hosiery

Borsalino
Piazza del Popolo 20.
Map 4 F1.
Tel 06-3265 0838.
Also: Via Sistina 58A.
Map 5 B2.
Tel 06-678 8821.

Calzedonia
Via del Corso 106.
Map 4 F2.
Tel 06-6992 5436.

Catello d'Auria
Via dei Due Macelli 55.
Map 5 A2 & 12 F1.
Tel 06-679 3364.

Di Cori
Piazza di Spagna 53.
Map 5 A2.
Tel 06-678 4439.

Fendi
See Women's High
Fashion.

Sermoneta
Piazza di Spagna 61.
Map 5 A2.
Tel 06-679 1960.

Settimio Mieli
Via San Claudio 70.
Map 5 A3 & 12 E2.
Tel 06-678 5979.

Interior Design

Italian design belongs to a long-established tradition based on the skills of the master craftsman, and some firms have a history going back hundreds of years. Rome's stylish interior design shops are worth seeking out, even if only to look around and enjoy the ambience. You might well pick up some design ideas for your home, or find some interesting or unusual things to buy. They are an excellent place to buy souvenirs, and presents to take home.

Furniture

Italy is well-known for its stylish, well-made furniture. Although there is no distinct area of Rome that is renowned for its furniture shops, many of the top stores are located to the north of the downtown.

In the heart of historic Rome, on Via della Scrofa, is **Arcon**. This airy outlet is packed with various slick furniture designs, particularly chairs, desks, and lighting, though there are some smaller, and more affordable household items.

Tucked in a side street off Via Giulia, **Sfera** displays a provocative blend of classic, and modern well-upholstered chairs, and divans matched with more minimalist designs.

Spazio Sette, near Largo Argentina, is worth visiting for the building itself. The store has a spectacular showroom on three levels in the Palazzo Lazzaroni, a former cardinal's palace. Spazio Sette is one of Rome's premier home furnishing stores and, as well as furniture, the shop stocks plenty of items that would make interesting gifts. The furniture, including modern, laminated stack-up chairs, and the vases, glass, bowls, and kitchen equipment are jumbled together in a fascinating display.

Nearby, on Piazza Cairoli, stands **Confalone**, a furniture shop that specializes in well-upholstered sofas and armchairs, though dining tables and chairs also crowd the display area. The shop's wide range of classical designs suits any interior.

Benedetti, which occupies a line of shops on the Via Marmorata, offers a range of fine modern wood furniture, while **Fattorini**, on Via Arenula, gives a modern Italian take on 1970s retro styling.

Light Fixtures

Light fixtures are one of the most popular and more easily transportable items, and there are several superb showrooms in Rome that are worth a visit.

Flos is a merger of two design houses whose Roman showroom displays its lights as if they were museum exhibits. The design style is chic, and minimalist, with plenty of black and white, chrome and steel.

Nearby **Artemide** is, like Flos, a design house in its own right, and is similarly well known abroad, above all for its classic anglepoise lamps in a variety of colors. Its showroom in Rome is elegant, with expensive, high-tech lighting design. Just across the road from the Palazzo delle Esposizioni, the **Targetti** store showcases their famous range: sleek, occasionally space-age designs that respond to any internal or external lighting requirement. **Borghini** sells less famous names, and is therefore more economical.

To see examples of light fixtures from all of Italy's leading producers, head to **Obor**, where high-tech items are displayed alongside more traditional designs.

Italian electrical equipment is designed for 220–240 volts. If you are going to use it in countries with lower voltage, always ask the shop whether the product needs a transformer, as this can depend on the model.

Light fixtures generally take standard screw-in light bulbs, but double-check before you buy.

Kitchens and Bathrooms

Although you won't be able to take one home with you, you may want to take a look at the ultra-modern high-tech kitchen designs in Rome.

For an overview of the latest chic stainless steel designs, visit **Arclinea**, near Ponte Garibaldi, for its select display of state-of-the-art kitchens. Equally inspiring are the kitchens on display at **Emporio Cucina**, just off Piazza Navona.

Italian bathroom shops concentrate almost exclusively on modern designs, some of which are luxuriously decadent. **Ravasini** has very decorative floral fixtures with some matching accessories. **Materia** is another bathroom shop that sells all the latest styles.

Tiles

The Italian ceramic tile tradition is an ancient one. A great variety of tiles are displayed in kitchen and bathroom showrooms, but there are also one or two specialty shops.

Ceramiche Musa specializes in modern tiles incorporating decorative floral and ancient Roman motifs, which are popular, especially with foreign visitors.

Glass

Decorative glass objects are a popular buy in Rome. **Murano Più**, just behind Piazza Navona, sells Murano and other glass items at reasonable prices. This shop is one of the few that open on Sundays – which can be useful for visitors on short trips to Rome.

Archimede Seguso also specializes in Murano glass but includes smaller pieces, and also offers a range of gift-sized items. **Arteque** is a very beautiful shop that has a more traditional flavor.

For less expensive gifts, try **Stilvetro**. It is the ideal place for pasta bowls, glass, and ceramics.

An added advantage is that shipment abroad can usually be arranged at any of these glass establishments, so you can make your purchase without worrying about transporting it home.

Fabrics

Beautiful fabrics and wallpapers to order are offered by **Il Sigillo**, which has a rich assortment of samples.

At **Celsa** you can find all manner of fabrics, some at bargain discount prices.

If you are looking for further bargains, take a walk around the old Jewish quarter, Il Ghetto, which runs from Largo Argentina down to the Tiber; the area contains numerous fabric shops such as **Paganini**. During sale times (*see p326*), remnants of fabrics (*scampoli*) are always sold off cheaply, and if you are lucky you could find just the right fabric for just the right price.

Household Linen and Kitchenware

Shops selling household goods abound in Rome. For a selection of lovely sheets, and other bed linens, head to **Frette**.

If you enjoy designer kitchenware, don't miss **c.u.c.i.n.a.** which is tucked away in No. 65 Via Mario de' Fiori. The shop stocks kitchen utensils from all over the world, as well as pots, and pans in both rustic and sleek styles, and countless space-saving kitchen accessories.

Right next to Piazza Venezia, **House & Kitchen** specializes in articles for the table, and kitchen, selling every accessory, and gadget imaginable.

The Roman pizzeria **'Gusto** (*see p323*) also offers an interesting range of kitchen utensils and essentials in its ground-floor shop.

Finally, there is **Limentani**, whose basement shop in the old ghetto area is well stocked with interesting gift ideas. Here, you will find an extraordinary array of household and kitchenware, including silver, china, and crystal items.

DIRECTORY

Furniture

Arcon
Via della Scrofa 104.
Map 12 D1.
Tel 06-686 8354.

Benedetti
Via Marmorata 141.
Map 8 D3.
Tel 06-574 6610.

Confalone
Piazza Cairoli 110.
Map 12 D4.
Tel 06-6880 3684.

Fattorini
Via Arenula 55.
Map 12 D5.
Tel 06-6813 6615.

Sfera
Via delle Carceri 6.
Map 11 B3.
Tel 06-6889 2630.

Spazio Sette
Via dei Barbieri 7.
Map 4 F5 & 12 D4.
Tel 06-6880 4261.

Light Fixtures

Artemide
Via Margutta 107.
Map 4 F1.
Tel 06-3600 1802.

Borghini
Via Belsiana 87–89.
Map 4 F2.
Tel 06-679 0636.

Flos
Via del Babuino 84.
Map 5 A2.
Tel 06-320 7631.

Obor
Piazza San Lorenzo in Lucina 28.
Map 12 E1.
Tel 06-687 1496.

Targetti
Via Nazionale 193.
Map 5 B4.
Tel 06-474 4694.

Kitchens and Bathrooms

Arclinea
Lungotevere dei Cenci 4B.
Map 4 F5 & 12 D5.
Tel 06-686 5104.

Emporio Cucina
Piazza delle Cinque Lune 74. **Map** 11 C2.
Tel 06-6880 3685.

Materia
Corso Vittorio Emanuele II 189.
Map 11 C3.
Tel 06-686 1896.

Ravasini
Via di Ripetta 69–71.
Map 4 F2.
Tel 06-322 7096.

Tiles

Ceramiche Musa
Via Campo Marzio 39.
Map 4 F3 & 12 D1.
Tel 06-687 1204.

Glass

Archimede Seguso
Via dei Due Macelli 56.
Map 5 A2.
Tel 06-679 1781.

Arteque
Via Giulia 13. **Map** 4 D4 & 11 A3. **Tel** 06-687 7388.

Murano Più
Corso Rinascimento 43–45.
Map 4 E3.
Tel 06-6880 8038.

Stilvetro
Via Frattina 56. **Map** 5 A2.
Tel 06-679 0258.

Fabrics

Celsa
Via delle Botteghe Oscure 44. **Map** 12 E4.
Tel 06-6994 0872.

Paganini
Via Aracoeli 23.
Map 4 F5 & 12 E4.
Tel 06-678 6831.

Il Sigillo
Via Laurina 15.
Map 4 F1.
Tel 06-361 3247.

Household and Kitchenware

c.u.c.i.n.a.
Via Mario de' Fiori 65.
Map 5 A2.
Tel 06-679 1275.

Frette
Piazza di Spagna 10.
Map 5 A2.
Tel 06-679 0673.

'Gusto
Piazza Augusto Imperatore 7.
Map 4 F2.
Tel 06-323 6363.

House & Kitchen
Via del Plebiscito 103.
Map 12 E3.
Tel 06-679 4208.

Limentani
Via del Portico D'Ottavia 48. **Map** 12 E5.
Tel 06-6880 6949.

Books and Gifts

Rome offers huge scope for gift buying, both in the well-established tourist stores in the *centro storico* (historic center) and in smaller shops in less frequented parts of the city. Seeking out the smaller shops can be an adventure in itself; many are in attractive parts of the city that you might not otherwise visit.

Unusual artisan ceramics, wonderful books on Italian art, and architecture, paper products, vintage Italian movie posters, beautiful prints of historic views of Rome, and specialty candies and cakes make ideal souvenirs to take home. While masterpieces by Michelangelo, Raphael, and Caravaggio are popular icons for T-shirts, statuettes, and postcards, religious artifacts are also readily available in the city that hosts the papal seat.

Bookshops

Rome is rich in bookshops, from the encyclopaedic to the very specialized. Italian books, both hardback and softback, are generally very attractive but also tend to be expensive.

As Italy's largest and most renowned bookshop chain, **Feltrinelli** dedicates its endless shelf space to both modern and classic Italian literature, and also houses a wide selection of non-fiction titles. **Feltrinelli International** in Via Emanuele Orlando has an excellent range of foreign-language fiction and specialty nonfiction, covering various subjects including art, cooking, travel, and history. It also stocks some superb photographic, art, and movie posters. Magazines, and stationery are available as well, and the notice-board is a lifeline for information on rooms for rent and Italian language courses.

Specialty English bookstores include the **Anglo-American Book Co.**, which is located near Piazza di Spagna. In Trastevere, the **Almost Corner Bookshop**, though small, has probably the most extensive selection of English language fiction in the capital, as well as nonfiction titles – from ancient Rome to modern Italian culture, and politics.

The **Libreria del Viaggiatore** is jam-packed with maps and travel guides (some in English). The charming **Libreria Godel** is good for browsing, as is the more modern **Mel Bookstore**, while **Bibli** is a cultural focal point across the Tiber, in Trastevere. For prospective chefs, fantastic recipe books on Italian, and international cuisine can be found at **Emporio Libreria 'Gusto** *(see p343)* in Piazza Augusto Imperatore.

As an alternative to traditional bookstores, there are lots of discount deals at the second-hand book stands in Via delle Terme di Diocleziano and in Largo della Fontanella di Borghese.

Multimedia and Music

The split-level **Feltrinelli** in Galleria Alberto Sordi on Via del Corso, and its sister store in Largo Argentina, represent the closest Rome gets to a multimedia megastore. At both these stores, in addition to their stock of fiction, and nonfiction titles, there is a reasonable selection of CDs and DVDs that cover mainstream tastes.

For harder-to-find albums, visit **Ricordi**, which is considered Rome's biggest specialty music store. Besides the fine collection of records, cassettes, and CDs, it sells instruments and musical scores in its four central outlets.

Stationery and Paper Crafts

Near the Pantheon, the Florentine **Il Papiro** sells a great range of illustrious paper-based products that include notebooks, diaries, envelopes, and beautiful seal-and-wax sets that make for an ideal gift.

In a similar vein, a wide selection of pretty marbled notebooks, writing papers, and files and boxes in various sizes are also offered at **Laboratorio Scatole**. **Pineider**, stationery suppliers to the Roman gentry, will print sets of exquisite visiting cards for you. The more modern **Vertecchi** is filled with original paper gifts, including boxes of every shape and size, while **Fabriano** has its own fabulous line of stationery and notebooks.

Posters and Prints

Near Piazza Navona, **L'Image** has an extensive range of artistic, photographic, and movie posters for sale, as well as a decent range of stationery, souvenirs, and calendars. Geared more toward antiques, **Galleria Trincia** sells good-quality and reasonably priced prints of 17th-century panoramic paintings of Rome, as well as watercolors. It also undertakes restoration work.

For superb posters on past exhibitions as well as stylish souvenirs and postcards, visit Rome's museum shops – for example, **Il Chiostro del Bramante** near Piazza Navona, or **Complesso del Vittoriano** next to the Forum.

Artisan Handicrafts and Design

The central Via del Pellegrino is a street crammed with small specialty outlets such as **Le Tre Ghinee**, which sells ceramics and glass objects. **La Chiave** is a good choice for gifts, selling all things ethnic, with the emphasis on bright furnishings and original jewelry.

If you are more interested in contemporary design, visit the **Palazzo delle Esposizioni** *(see p166)*, where a wide range of objects by famous designers is available. For a really original gift, try **Bottega del Marmoraro**, a workshop that reproduces ancient Roman and Pompeian inscriptions on marble. The owner will recreate any design you choose to order.

Souvenirs and Religious Artifacts

Most of the tobacconists in central Rome sell postcards, stamps, and a variety of souvenirs. Cheap, and sometimes appealingly kitsch souvenirs are also found at the mobile stands around the major tourist attractions.

Bookshops near the main basilicas, such as **Libreria Belardetti**, sell souvenirs, and religious mementos. Other shops specialize in religious articles for both the clergy and the layperson. Facing the Vatican gates in Via di Porta Angelica there are several shops, such as **Al Pellegrino Cattolico**, selling artifacts to visiting pilgrims.

Candy and Cookies

In addition to the several bars and cafés that sell cakes and cookies to take our *(da portare via)*, there are a number of specialty stores in Rome well worth taking the time to visit.

Downtown near Piazza Navona, **La Deliziosa** *(see p323)*, though small, offers a great range of classic Italian desserts and cakes; the ricotta-based variety deserves a special mention. In the Galleria Esedra, near Piazza della Repubblica, **Dagnino** is renowned throughout the city as one of the best places for sugary Sicilian delicacies such as *cannoli* and *cassate*.

For a wonderful range of fresh and appetizing Italian cookies to suit all occasions and every whim, head for **Cipriani** *(see p322)* in Esquilino near Termini station, or **Innocenti** *(see p323)*, a historic *pasticceria* famed for its elaborate cookies made with varied ingredients including almonds, pine nuts, and honey. Innocenti is situated across the Tiber from the *centro storico* in Trastevere.

DIRECTORY

Bookshops

Almost Corner Bookshop
Via del Moro 45.
Map 7 C1.
Tel 06-583 6942.

Anglo-American Book Co.
Via della Vite 102.
Map 12 E1.
Tel 06-679 5222.

Bibli
Via dei Fienaroli 28.
Map 7 C1.
Tel 06-581 4534.

Emporio Libreria 'Gusto
Piazza Augusto Imperatore 7. **Map** 4 F2.
Tel 06-323 6363.

Feltrinelli
Largo Argentina 5A.
Map 4 F4. **Tel** 06-6880 3248. Also: Galleria Alberto Sordi 31–35.
Map 12 E2.
Tel 06-6975 5001.

Feltrinelli International
Via E. Orlando 84–86.
Map 5 C3.
Tel 06-482 7878.

Libreria del Viaggiatore
Via del Pellegrino 78.
Map 11 B3.
Tel 06-6880 1048.

Libreria Godel
Via Poli 46. **Map** 12 F2.
Tel 06-679 8716.

Mel Bookstore
Via Nazionale 254–255.
Map 5 C3.
Tel 06-488 5405.

Multimedia and Music

Feltrinelli
See bookshops

Ricordi
Via del Corso 506. **Map** 12 E1. **Tel** 06-361 2370.

Stationery and Paper Crafts

Fabriano
Via del Babuino 173.
Map 4 F2.
Tel 06-3260 0361.

Laboratorio Scatole
Via della Stelletta 27. **Map** 12 D2. **Tel** 06-6880 2053.

Il Papiro
Via del Pantheon 50 (leading to Via Degli Orfani). **Map** 12 D2.
Tel 06-679 5597.

Pineider
Via dei Due Macelli 68.
Map 12 F1.
Tel 06-679 5884.

Vertecchi
Via della Croce 70. **Map** 4 F2. **Tel** 06-332 2821.

Posters and Prints

Il Chiostro del Bramante
Via della Pace 5. **Map** 11 C2. **Tel** 06-880 9098.

Complesso del Vittoriano
Via San Pietro In Carcere.
Map 5 A5.
Tel 06-678 0664.

Galleria Trincia
Via Laurina 12. **Map** 4 F1.
Tel 06-361 2322.

L'Image
Via della Scrofa 67. **Map** 12 D2. **Tel** 06-686 4050.

Artisan Handicrafts and Design

Bottega del Marmoraro
Via Margutta 53B. **Map** 5 A2. **Tel** 06-320 7660.

La Chiave
Largo delle Stimmate 28.
Map 12 D4.
Tel 06-6830 8848.

Palazzo delle Esposizioni
Via Milano 15–17. **Map** 5 B4. **Tel** 06-4891 3361.

Le Tre Ghinee
Via del Pellegrino 90.
Map 11 B3.
Tel 06-687 2739.

Souvenirs and Religious Artifacts

Al Pellegrino Cattolico
Via di Porta Angelica 83.
Map 3 C2.
Tel 06-6880 2351.

Libreria Belardetti
Via della Conciliazione 4A.
Map 3 C3.
Tel 06-686 5502.

Candy and Cookies

Cipriani
Via C. Botta 21. **Map** 6 D5.
Tel 06-7045 3930.

Dagnino
Galleria Esedra, Via Vittorio Emanuele Orlando 75.
Map 5 C2.
Tel 06-481 8660.

La Deliziosa
Vicolo Savelli 50.
Map 11 B3.
Tel 06-6880 3155.

Innocenti
Via della Luce 21A.
Map 7 C2.
Tel 06-580 3926.

Art and Antiques

Rome's art and antique shops range from exclusive establishments to contemporary art galleries. In response to a fashion for collecting early-20th-century artifacts, new dealers and galleries are springing up throughout Rome – Venini's Murano glass is popular, as are lighting and furniture. Many more sell general bric-a-brac and jewelry. Copies of antique prints can be picked up for a fraction of the original's price. Rome is not good for antique bargains, but it is worth looking in shops along Via dei Cappellari and Via del Pellegrino or going to the Porta Portese Sunday market *(see p345)*.

Antiques and Old Master Paintings

There are antique shops dotted all over the center of Rome, though the cream of the crop tend to be concentrated in distinct areas. Discreet haggling in the shops is accepted practice, but even if you get a reduction in price, make sure the dealer provides you with the relevant export documents.

The famous Via del Babuino, and to a lesser extent Via Margutta, which is better known for its art galleries, are home to around 30 of Rome's grandest showrooms for antique furniture, Old Master paintings, and *objets d'art*. **Cesare Lampronti** is owned by the top dealer of that name. Aided and complemented by his partner Carlo Peruzzi, he sells 16th- to 18th-century European paintings, with an emphasis on Roman and Italian works in general.

Alberto di Castro, situated in Piazza di Spagna, is a fourth-generation dealer specializing in statues, paintings, and other precious objects from the medieval to the Neo-Classical periods. Nearby, **M Simotti-Rocchi** stocks Greek and Roman statuary, as well as more luggage-friendly coins and figurines.

Via Giulia *(see p155)* has over 20 high-quality antique shops to choose from. Definitely worth a visit is **Antichità Cipriani**, which is a temple to owner Paola Cipriani's love of simply elegant Neo-Classical furniture and paintings. She also sells the occasional modern piece. Another shop not to miss on Via Giulia is **Antiquariato Valligiano**. This is the only place in Rome where you can find 19th-century Italian country furniture, a rustic antidote for those overpowered by the grandiose Baroque.

Via Monserrato, running parallel, is worth scouring for slightly lower-quality pieces at more realistic prices. The area just to the north of Via Giulia is also a good hunting ground. **Mario Prilli**, on Via Banchi Nuovi, is tiny, but don't let that deter you. With every inch of space occupied by a wide variety of antiques, this fascinating shop is worth a look even if you are only browsing.

Via dei Coronari is largely devoted to antiques, with over 30 shops lining both sides of the street. Quality is very high – as are the prices. It is a good place for Baroque and Empire elaborate inlaid vases, secretaries, and consoles. **Ad Antiqua Domus** is a treasure trove of antique Italian furniture. Pieces dating from ancient Rome through to the 19th century are for sale.

Liberty specializes in high-quality Art Nouveau (usually called *Liberty* here), while the **Art Deco Gallery** sells furniture and sculpture from that period. **Galleria dei Coronari** has a superb collection of tapestries, clocks, paintings, and statuary. **Antichità Arredamenti** also specializes in Italian light fixtures and candlesticks.

Slightly farther away is Via della Stelletta, which is home to a handful of unusual, and fascinating shops. **Acanto** is an inexpensively priced Aladdin's cave with an eclectic mix of *objets d'art*. It is the perfect place to search for religious memorabilia, Italian curiosities, and prints.

Bilenchi is yet another specialist, this time in exquisite, early 20th-century lamps.

Another relatively undiscovered area is the one around Via del Boschetto and Via Panisperna. Shops around here tend to specialize in early 20th-century artifacts, with some English Victorian pieces thrown in. **Goffi Carboni** is more Asian in outlook, with Chinese, and Japanese ceramics, and prints alongside its 17th–19th-century European art collection.

Of course there are many perennial favorites apart from these streets. The best way to discover them is through word of mouth or just by chance as you stroll along. **Antichità Carnovale** is a shop full of interesting 19th- and 20th-century canvases, while **Agostini** is one of the oldest antique shops in Rome, and definitely one of the largest. It offers an impressive collection of European antiques.

Modern Art

Rome is rich in avant-garde galleries exhibiting paintings by recognized Modern Masters through to the up-and-coming generation of young, mainly Italian, artists.

Rome's art galleries are usually open 10am–1pm and 5–8pm Tue–Sat. Some open only in the afternoon; others also stay open on Monday afternoon. The best times to visit are afternoons, and early evenings.

As with Rome's antique shops, the art galleries tend to be concentrated in a couple of distinct areas. The largest of these covers the triangular area between Via del Babuino, and Via di Ripetta and adjoining streets, known locally as the Trident. Via Margutta is also home to several prestigious private galleries.

The **Galleria Valentina Moncada** exhibits contemporary Italian and international art, and also showcases 20th- century photography, while **Monogramma Arte Contemporanea** deals with promising young artists from Italy and abroad. One of this area's highlights is the Via Margutta art fair *(see p345)*, which usually takes place around Christmas, and in springtime.

The enterprising **Fontanella Borghese** gallery shows works by foreign artists such as Sam Francis and Andy Warhol. Also on view at the gallery are Italian artists like Boetti, Festa, and Turcato.

Via Giulia and its surroundings is the next area to investigate: **Galleria Giulia** is a gallery/bookshop with works by artists such as Argeles, Boille, Cano, Cascella, Echaurren, Erba, and Lionni, as well as Bauhaus artists and German Expressionists. Fabio Sargentini at **L'Attico**

follows the latest trends in Italian art from Del Giudice to Corsini and Fabiani.

Another innovative downtown venture is **Galleria Bonomo** (owned by Alessandra Bonomo), which spotlights Italian and foreign painters such as Schifano, Boetti, Twombly, Nunzio, Tremlett, LeWitt, and Dokoupil.

On the other side of the Tiber, the **Galleria Lorcan O'Neill** showcases contemporary Italian and international art. Past exhibitions have included works by Tracey Emin, and Rachel Whiteread.

Antique Prints and Photographs

The justifiably celebrated **Nardecchia**, named after its erudite owner Plinio, is the cream of Rome's print dealers. Look out for originals by the 18th-century engraver Piranesi, as well as views of the city, and depictions of ancient Roman life.

Another Roman institution, **Casali**, has been trading for over 100 years. The family now runs two shops specializing in 16th- to 19th-century drawings and engravings of Roman scenes ranging from museum-standard Piranesi down to relatively inexpensive unknown and delightfully decorative floral scenes.

The Florence-based **Alinari** family is renowned for its old sepia photographs of Italy from 1890 onward, including shots of Rome a century ago. At its Roman outlet, prices of photographs from the original plates start at around €30 and mounted prints at €280. Larger sizes can be mounted on wood or posterboard.

Another place definitely worth heading for in search of that perfect print of old Rome, and some enjoyable, relaxing, and maybe persuasive browsing is the **Mercato delle Stampe** *(see p344).*

DIRECTORY

Antiques and Old Master Paintings

Acanto
Via della Stelletta 10.
Map 4 F3 & 12 D2.
Tel 06-686 5481.

Ad Antiqua Domus
Via dei Coronari 39–43.
Map 4 E3 & 11 B2.
Tel 06-686 1186.

Agostini
Piazza Borghese 1. **Map** 12 D1. **Tel** 06-687 3632.

Alberto di Castro
Piazza di Spagna 5. **Map** 5 A2. **Tel** 06-679 2269.

Antichità Arredamenti
Via dei Coronari 218. **Map** 4 E3. **Tel** 06-6880 1254.

Antichità Carnovale
Via del Governo Vecchio 71. **Map** 11 C3.
Tel 06-686 4850.

Antichità Cipriani
Via Giulia 122.
Map 4 D4 & 11 A3.
Tel 06-6830 8344.

Antiquariato Valligiano
Via Giulia 193. **Map** 4 E5 & 11 B5. **Tel** 06-686 9505.

Art Deco Gallery
Via dei Coronari 14.
Map 4 E3 & 11 C2.
Tel 06-686 5330.

Bilenchi
Via della Stelletta 17.
Map 4 F3 & 12 D2.
Tel 06-687 5222.

Cesare Lampronti
Via del Babuino 174–75
(also Via del Babuino 182).
Map 4 F1.
Tel 06-322 7194.

Galleria dei Coronari
Via dei Coronari 59.
Map 4 E3 & 11 B2.
Tel 06-687 4049.

Goffi Carboni
Via Margutta 9. **Map** 5 A2.
Tel 06-322 7184.

Liberty
Via dei Coronari 8. **Map** 11 C2. **Tel** 06-687 5634.

Mario Prilli
Via dei Banchi Nuovi 42.
Map 4 D3 & 11 A2.
Tel 06-686 8816.

M Simotti-Rocchi
Largo Fontanella
Borghese 76. **Map** 12 D1.
Tel 06-687 6656.

Modern Art

L'Attico
Via del Paradiso 41.
Map 4 E4 & 11 C4.
Tel 06-686 9846.

Fontanella Borghese
Via Fontanella Borghese 31. **Map** 12 D1.
Tel 06-687 3741.

Galleria Bonomo
Via del Gesù 62. **Map** 12 E3. **Tel** 06-6992 5858.

Galleria Giulia
Via della Barchetta 13.
Map 4 D4 & 11 B4.
Tel 06-686 1443.

Galleria Lorcan O'Neill
Via Orti D'Alibert 1E. **Map** 4 D4. **Tel** 06-6889 2980.

Galleria Valentina Moncada
Via Margutta 54. **Map** 5 A2. **Tel** 06-320 7956.

Monogramma Arte Contemporanea
Via Margutta 57. **Map** 5 A2. **Tel** 06-3265 0297.

Antique Prints and Photographs

Alinari
Via Alibert 16A. **Map** 5 A2. **Tel** 06-679 2923.

Casali
Piazza della Rotonda 81A/82. **Map** 4 F4 & 12 D3. **Tel** 06-678 3515. Also: Via dei Coronari 115.
Map 11 B2. **Tel** 06-687 3705.

Nardecchia
Piazza Navona 25.
Map 4 E4 & 11 C3.
Tel 06-686 9318.

Food and Drink

Having sampled the local cuisine during your stay in Rome, you may be tempted to take home some irresistible delicacies that are typical of Italy. The traditional Italian food stores, *alimentari*, offer an extensive range of goods, and are a great place to start. However, specialty shops are also well worth a visit. Shop around, and choose from many typically Italian products such as pecorino romano cheese, Parma ham, extra-virgin olive oil, dried porcini mushrooms, sun-dried tomatoes, olives, and grappa, as well as superb wines from Lazio, and elsewhere. If coffee or chocolate feature on your list, then there's plenty of opportunity to satisfy those cravings too.

Do bear in mind, however, that customs restrictions can apply to certain foodstuffs. Also, when on your shopping sprees, a decent pocket-sized dictionary can be very useful in helping you decipher the labels.

Alimentari

The well-stocked **Fratelli Fabbi**, near Piazza di Spagna, has an exceptional selection of delicious cold meats, and cheeses from every corner of Italy, as well as carefully chosen quality wines, and sparkling wines to accompany them. A few doors down Via della Croce, **Focacci** is a stiff competitor with its wonderful array of Italian delicacies, while nearby **Cambi** caters to its loyal clientele with similarly first-rate fare.

Elsewhere downtown, near Campo de' Fiori, **Roscioli** (see p320), with a reputation for quality and friendly service, is a favorite among locals. In the Campo itself is the **Antica Norcineria Viola**, which is the place to go for an excellent range of sausages and salami.

Farther afield, **Franchi** (see p321) in Prati is recognized as one of the best delicatessens in the capital for its tempting window display of seafood platters, pâtés, regional cheeses, and cold meats that continue to pull in the crowds. The historic but expensive **Volpetti** in Testaccio is synonymous with great service, and uncompromising quality. Aside from specializing in unusual cheeses, olive oils, vinegars, and a fabulous selection of food hampers, it also stocks a variety of Italian lard and caviar – you can even try before you buy.

Nearby is the well-stocked **La Fromagerie**, though those who favor organic produce may prefer to head for **Canestro**.

In the vicinity of Via Veneto is **Carlo Gargani**, with its elaborate variety of food items.

A savior for commuters, and tourists is **Vyta** (see p321) located inside Termini station; you can choose from a selection of appetizing sandwiches or wines by the glass (*alla mescita*) and enjoy them at the bar. An excellent weekend farmers' market, **Campagna Amica**, is tucked away behind the church of Santa Maria in Cosmedin, and is well worth visiting for its stands of organic, locally produced food and wine.

Cheese Specialists

For the ultimate cheese lover, a wider choice of regional, and national cheeses, including the best buffalo mozzarella in town, can be found in a select number of specialty shops. In the Pinciano district, the **Casa dei Latticini Micocci** sells a comprehensive range of cheeses from even the most remote regions of Italy. While in Trastevere, the family-run store **Antica Caciara Trasteverina** also has a vast assortment of local and regional products, which include sheep's ricotta and the Piemontese *toma del fen*. Branches of **Cisternino** sell well-priced local cheeses.

Chocolate Specialists

The capital boasts a number of specialty shops designed to fulfill the needs of the ever-expanding luxury food market. In the *centro storico*, **Chocolat** sells brand-name, and home-made chocolate and also organizes occasional tastings and dinners for connoisseurs. In Santa Croce, **La Bottega del Cioccolato** is known for its creativity – try their chocolate Colosseums. Elsewhere, close to the Pantheon, the landmark **Moriondo e Gariglio** has been in operation since 1850, serving up strictly Piedmontese treats. Across the Tiber in Trastevere, **Dolce Idea** produces bizarre but interesting concoctions such as white chocolate with lemon liqueur filling and dark chocolate laced with ginger. **Rivendita di Cioccolata e Vino** (see p322) can also be recommended for its selection.

Enoteche

Although most *alimentari* and supermarkets stock a decent selection of reasonably priced Italian wines, Rome's many *enoteche* (see p320) represent a more characteristic, and gratifying alternative. As well as being wine bars and sometimes even restaurants, they also sell carefully selected wines, after-dinner liqueurs, spirits, and beers to take out.

Downtown, the cramped but friendly **Mr Wine** displays a superb range of mainly Italian and a few French wines, as well as a host of sparkling wines, whiskeys, grappa, rum, liqueurs, and some classic Italian food. **La Vineria** (see p320) in Campo de' Fiori, while maintaining its status as an institution for many bohemian drinkers, also successfully doubles as a well-stocked and competitively priced wine shop.

Better known for its Neapolitan pizza parlor, chic restaurant, and lively wine bar, **'Gusto** (see p320) in Piazza Augusto Imperatore offers an outstanding assortment of wines for sale too. Don't pass by the shop either – it is full of designer kitchen accessories, and specialty cookbooks with recipes for both Italian, and international cuisine.

The central **Achilli Enoteca al Parlamento** *(see p320)* and **L'Angolo Divino** both warrant a visit for a refined alternative, especially if you want to relax with an apéritif while you select wines to carry home. **Ferrazza** *(see p354)* in San Lorenzo and **Il Vinaietto** near Campo de' Fiori also deserve special mentions for their extensive wine lists, and memorable ambience.

In Trastevere, the well-stocked liquor store **Bernabei** has good deals, as does the family-run **Trimani** *(see p320)* near Termini, which has an astounding variety of wines and liquor.

Others that should not be overlooked include the **Costantini** in Piazza Cavour, the beer-oriented **Palombi** in Testaccio, and **Marchetti** in Pinciano, which is the wine experts' not-so-closely-guarded secret.

Coffee Specialists

Italian brand coffee has been internationally available for many years, but if you are looking for something rarer or more exotic, then make your way to **Antico Caffè del Brasile** *(see p322)* in Monti for four mouth-watering blends, from Brazilian gem (the 90 percent pure variety) to economy, and family mixes. In the shadow of the Pantheon, the historic **Tazza d'Oro** *(see p106)* also offers a fantastic selection of blends, including the Queen of Coffees and Jamaican Blue Mountain.

DIRECTORY

Alimentari

Antica Norcineria Viola
Campo de' Fiori 43.
Map 11 C4.
Tel 06-6880 6114.

Cambi
Via del Leoncino 30.
Map 12 D1.
Tel 06-687 8081.

Campagna Amica
Via di San Teodoro 74.
Map 8 E1. **Tel** 06-489 931.

Canestro
Via Luca della Robbia 12.
Map 8 D2.
Tel 06-574 6287.

Carlo Gargani
Via Lombardia 15. **Map** 5 B2. **Tel** 06-474 0865.

Focacci
Via della Croce 43.
Map 4 F2.
Tel 06-679 1228.

Franchi
Via Cola di Rienzo 200.
Map 3 C2.
Tel 06-687 4651.

Fratelli Fabbi
Via della Croce 28.
Map 4 F2.
Tel 06-679 0612.

La Fromagerie
Piazza Testaccio 35.
Map 8 D2.
Tel 06-5725 0185.

Roscioli
Via dei Giubbonari 21.
Map 11 C4.
Tel 06-687 5287.

Volpetti
Via Marmorata 47.
Map 8 D2.
Tel 06-574 2352.

Vyta
Galleria Termini (Termini Station). **Map** 6 D3.
Tel 06-4201 4301.

Cheese Specialists

Antica Caciara Trasteverina
Via San Francesco a Ripa 140a/b. **Map** 7 C1.
Tel 06-581 2815.

Casa dei Latticini Micocci
Via Collina 14–16.
Map 6 D2.
Tel 06-474 1784.

Cisternino
Vicolo del Gallo 18–19.
Map 11 C4.
Tel 06-687 2875.

Chocolate Specialists

La Bottega del Cioccolato
Via Leonina 82.
Map 5 C5.
Tel 06-482 1473.

Chocolat
Via del Teatro Valle 54.
Map 12 D3.
Tel 06-6813 5545.

Dolce Idea
Via San Francesco a Ripa 27. **Map** 7 C1.
Tel 06-5833 4043.

Moriondo e Gariglio
Via del Piè di Marmo 21.
Map 12 E3.
Tel 06-699 0856.

Rivendita di Cioccolata e Vino
Vicolo del Cinque 11A.
Map 11 B5.
Tel 06-5830 1868.

Enoteche

Achilli Enoteca al Parlamento
Via dei Prefetti 15. **Map** 12 D1. **Tel** 06-687 3446.

L'Angolo Divino
Via dei Balestrari 12–14.
Map 11 C4.
Tel 06-686 4413.

Bernabei
Via San Francesco a Ripa 48. **Map** 7 C1.
Tel 06-581-2818.

Costantini
Piazza Cavour 16. **Map** 11 B1. **Tel** 06-321 3210.

Ferrazza
Via dei Volsci 59. **Map** 6 F4. **Tel** 06-490 506.

'Gusto
Piazza Augusto Imperatore 9. **Map** 4 F2.
Tel 06-322 6273.

Marchetti
Via Flavia 28. **Map** 5 C2.
Tel 06-474 1745.

Mr Wine
Piazza del Parlamento 7.
Map 12 E1.
Tel 06-6813 4141.

Palombi
Piazza Testaccio 38.
Map 8 D3.
Tel 06-574 6122.

Trimani
Via Goito 20. **Map** 6 D2.
Tel 06-446 9661.

Il Vinaietto
Via Monte della Farina 37–38. **Map** 12 D4.
Tel 06-6880 6989.

La Vineria
Campo de' Fiori 15.
Map 11 C4.
Tel 06-6880 3268.

Coffee Specialists

Antico Caffè del Brasile
Via dei Serpenti 23.
Map 5 B4.
Tel 06-488 2319.

Tazza d'Oro
Via degli Orfani 84.
Map 12 D4.
Tel 06-678 9792.

Street Markets

Rome's open-air markets are essential to visit if you are interested in soaking up the bustling atmosphere of Italian market-life. The markets can be incredibly colorful and vivid as Italian stallholders have raised the display of even the humblest vegetable to an art form.

The city is dotted with popular, small local food markets, and there are several fascinating well-established markets near the center of the city, along with the famous flea market over in Trastevere.

It is important to keep your wits about you in markets because pickpockets work with lightning speed in the bustling crowds. But that said, Roman markets provide a vibrant source of entertainment and it would be a shame to let such caveats deter you from joining in.

The street fairs that take place throughout the year are fun to go to, if they coincide with your visit, since they normally sell a good variety of local produce, handicrafts, and clothes. Seasonal fairs also occur, especially around Christmas, when you can stock up on Italian specialties.

Campo de' Fiori

Piazza Campo de' Fiori. **Map** 4 E4 & 11 C4. 40, 46, 62, 64, 70, 81, 116, 492, 628. 8. **Open** 7am–1:30pm Mon–Sat. See p148.

Right in the heart of the old city, Rome's most picturesque market is also its most historic. Its name, Campo de' Fiori, which translates as field of flowers, sometimes misleads people into expecting a flower market. In fact, the name is said to derive from Campus Florae (Flora's square) – Flora being the lover of the great Roman general Pompey. A market has actually been held in this beautiful piazza for many centuries. Every morning except Sunday, the piazza is transformed by an array of stands selling fruit and vegetables, meat, poultry, and fish. One or two stands specialize in beans, rice, dried fruit, and nuts, and there are also flower stands situated near the fountain. But the huge open baskets of broccoli and spinach, chopped vegetables, and freshly prepared green salad mixes are the main attraction for visitors. They provide a striking visual display as well as an edible feast.

The excellent delicatessens on the square, and bread shops nearby, complement the market. They make it a great place to stock up for an impromptu picnic if the weather is pleasant and you are tempted to do some alfresco dining in one of Rome's many parks. The market gets extremely busy on Saturdays, so be prepared to fight your way through the crowds.

Mercato delle Stampe

Largo della Fontanella di Borghese. **Map** 4 F3 & 12 D1. 81, 116, 117, 492, 628. **Open** 7am–1pm Mon–Sat.

This market is a veritable haven for lovers of old prints, books (both genuine antiquarian and less-exalted secondhand), magazines, and other printed ephemera. The quality varies, but it is a good deal more specialized than the *banche* or stands near Termini station, which are a more obvious tourist trap. Italian-speaking collectors can enjoy a field day leafing through back issues of specialty magazines. Other visitors might prefer the wonderful selection of illustrated art books and old prints of Rome. It is a good place to pick up that Piranesi print of your favorite Roman vista, ruin, or church – but be prepared to bargain hard.

Mercato dei Fiori

Via Trionfale. **Map** 3 B1. Ottaviano S. Pietro. 23, 51, 70, 490. **Open** 10:30am–1pm Tue.

Essentially a trade market, the Flower Market, just north of Via Andrea Doria, is open to the public only on Tuesdays. Housed in a covered hall, it has two floors overflowing with cut flowers upstairs, and all kinds of potted plants on the lower floor.

Anyone who has an interest in flowers will enjoy this wonderful array of Mediterranean blooms, which are sold at giveaway prices.

Mercato Andrea Doria

Via Andrea Doria. **Map** 3 B1. Ottaviano S. Pietro. 23, 70, 490. **Open** 7am–1:30pm Mon–Sat.

The market used to stretch the whole length of this wide avenue. It has now been transferred to a modern, covered state-of-the- art building. Apart from the magnificent displays of fruit and vegetables, it has numerous stands selling meat, poultry, fish, and groceries, as well as an interesting clothing, and shoe section. Situated northwest of the Vatican Museums, it is a little off the normal beaten track, and has remained very much a Roman market that caters to the needs of the large local population.

Nuovo Mercato Esquilino

Via Principe Amedeo. **Map** 6 E5. Vittorio Emanuele. 105. **Open** 7am–2pm Mon–Sat. See p176.

In the past, bustling Piazza Vittorio was perhaps the most Roman of the city's larger markets.

Rechristened, and housed in covered premises, it is still the place where bargain-hunting *popolari*, Rome's bustling shoppers, buy their food. Vendors offer bargain prices if you buy by the kilo (2.2 lb), but watch out for bad fruit.

This is also one of the city's more international markets, and features African and Asian food stands that cater to the area's many ethnic groups. Definitely a place to go to capture the atmosphere of a traditional but changing city.

Mercato di Testaccio

Between Via A. Volta and Via Galvani. **Map** 8 D3. Piramide. 23, 75, 280. 3. **Open** 7:30am–1:30pm Mon–Sat.

Filled with stands selling fresh produce of every kind, the local market for this most Roman of areas is a stage set of seductive colors and textures. Uniquely, it also houses the Roman remains found on the site during the construction of the present building; appropriately enough, archaeologists think that the ruins testify to a market that stood here in ancient times. Popular with local residents, who insist on high-quality produce at reasonable prices, the market also appeals to visitors for its relaxed and friendly atmosphere.

Porta Portese

Via Portuense & Via Ippolito Nievo. **Map** 7 C3. ▥ H, 23, 44, 75. ▥ 3, 8. **Open** 6:30am–2pm Sun.

The *mercato delle pulci* or flea market is a relatively new market in Roman terms. Established shortly after the end of World War II, it is said to have grown out of the thriving black market that operated at Tor di Nona opposite Castel Sant'Angelo during those lean years. Vendors come from as far away as Naples and set up shop in the early hours of the morning – if you are strolling in that direction after a late night in Trastevere, it is well worth pausing just to watch them.

Anything and everything seems to be for sale, piled high on stands in carefully arranged disorder – clothes, shoes, bags, luggage, camping equipment, linen, towels, pots, pans, kitchen utensils, plants, pets, spare parts, cassettes, and CDs, old LPs and 78s.

Furniture stands tend to be concentrated around Piazza Ippolito Nievo along with what they call "antiques," though you may have to sort through an awful lot of junk before finding a real one. And then you will have to bargain for it. The technique is to offer them half the asked price, and then walk away. A lot of people go just for the fun of it and end up buying something.

There are also secondhand clothes – leather or sheepskin coats and jackets go for €10 – with many of the Via Sannio vendors relocating here for the Sunday market. In recent years, Porta Portese has become much frequented by customers belonging to the various immigrant groups in the capital. If you have a Sunday morning to spare, a visit to the market is now one of the most cosmopolitan experiences that the city offers.

Mercato di Via Sannio

Via Sannio. **Map** 9 C2. Ⓜ San Giovanni. ▥ 16, 81, 87. **Open** 8am–1pm Mon–Fri, 8am–6pm Sat.

In the 1960s and 1970s this used to be Italy's answer to London's Carnaby Street. Today, at first glance, it seems not to have anything special to offer – random stands selling inexpensive casual clothes, shoes, bags, belts, jewelry, toys, kitchen utensils, and music cassettes. But toward the end of the street there is a large covered section that extends back to the Aurelian Wall *(see p198)* with many stands piled high with second-hand clothes at very low prices for those who like to rummage. There is also a section that sells military-style goods plus some camping, and fishing equipment.

Some of these stands move their wares to Porta Portese on Sunday morning.

Local Markets

Generally Open *7am–1pm Mon–Sat.*

Piazza delle Coppelle (**Map** 4 F3 & 12 D2), near the Pantheon, is probably the most picturesque of the food markets sprinkled around the city. A tiny market devoted to food, fruit, and flowers, it offers a charming splash of color in the heart of the city.

Piazza San Cosimato (**Map** 7 C1) in Trastevere hosts another lively local market with some tempting cheeses and salami.

There is a fairly big market on **Via Alessandrina** (**Map** 6 D1) in Nomentana, and other smaller ones in **Via della Pace** (**Map** 4 E4 & 11 C3) near Piazza Navona, and in **Via Balbo** (**Map** 5 C4) and **Via Milazzo** (**Map** 6 E3) near Termini station.

All markets usually have at least one stand selling household goods, and basic Italian kitchen gadgets.

Street Fairs

A special and interesting feature of shopping in Rome is the street fair.

Neglected and under-exploited for most of the year, the lower banks of the Tiber come into their own in summer during the mid-June–early September **Lungo il Tevere** festival. This takes place daily from 6pm until after midnight on the stretch of river between Ponte Palatino and Ponte Sisto. Stands sell a variety of goods, from regional produce and ethnic bric-a-brac to books and confectionery. You can also take a break at one of the many bars and eateries lining the route.

There are various open-air antique markets held in the city throughout the year. One of the most central and best known is **La Soffitta sotto i Portici** (The Attic beneath the Porticoes), which is held 8am–7pm every other Sunday (except August) along the eastern edge of Piazza Augusto Imperatore. Professional and weekend sellers run stands offering antique (or simply retro) furniture, lamps, jewelry and *objets d'art*.

The **Via Margutta Art Fair** usually takes place around Christmas and in springtime. Set in one of the most charming and exclusive streets of the city, this is an event not to be missed, although it is more for browsing, since prices are very high.

The utterly glamorous **Spanish Steps Alta Moda Fashion Show** is a must for fashionistas but does not have a set date. The limited seating space is filled by invitation only. However, the public can squeeze in behind to enjoy this display of all-Italian designer fashion. So far it has been held mid-to late July.

The traditional **Christmas Fair** held in Piazza Navona from mid-December until January 6 is now rather down-at-heel, but still fascinating for those who have not seen it before, or for children. Stands selling clay statues for nativity scenes and candies that look like pieces of coal are the main attraction.

Natale Oggi is a well-established event taking place near Christmas at the Fiera di Roma in the Portuense district, and worth visiting to take a look at the Italian Christmas treats.

Via Giulia hosts art fairs now and then, and open evenings when the antique and art galleries stay open late, offering food and wine to all visitors.

Every year Trastevere hosts its very own carnival, the **Festa de Noantri**, in late July, when Viale Trastevere is overrun with the typical *porchetta* stands *(see p347)*, party lights, gift stands, and people.

The details given here may change, so consult the local listings, the tourist office, or the tourist call center *(see p369)*.

ENTERTAINMENT IN ROME

There's a particular excitement attached to Roman entertainment. Soccer and opera, for example, are both worth experiencing for sheer atmosphere alone, whether or not you are a fan. The jazz scene is especially good, with international stars appearing alongside local talent. And concerts and movies take on an added dimension when performances take place beneath the stars in the many open-air arenas spread across the city.

Unexpectedly, given the general shutdown among shops and restaurants, the summer remains Rome's liveliest time for live music, and other cultural events. Rome's graceful Renaissance squares, vast parks, villa gardens, Classical ruins, and other open spaces host various major arts festivals. For those who prefer sports, or want to try out some Roman nightclubs, there's plenty available too.

Saxophonist at Alpheus *(see p350)*

Practical Information

A good source of information about what's going on is *Trova-Roma*, the weekly Thursday supplement to *La Repubblica* newspaper. It has a day-by-day rundown of what's on, and where, and covers music, exhibitions, theater, movies, guided tours, restaurants, and children's entertainment. The weekly listings magazine *Roma c'è* has an English section. Daily newspapers like *Il Messaggero*, *Il Manifesto* and *La Repubblica* usually list that evening's entertainment.

The magazine *Wanted in Rome*, found at Via Veneto newsstands or English-language bookshops, provides less detailed listings in English. Also worth getting hold of is *L'Evento*, a free booklet that is available from tourist information offices around the city *(see p369)*. Published every two months, it gives details in English of classical music, festivals, theater, exhibitions, and more in the city and surroundings. Up-to-date information can also be found on various websites.

Punctuality is not what Italians are renowned for, so

don't be surprised if events start later than advertised.

Buying Tickets

Booking in advance is not part of the Italian lifestyle, though this is slowly changing. Two ticket agencies that will reserve tickets for some performances for you (for a small fee) are **Orbis**, and the Internet-based **Ticketeria**. Many theaters themselves do not accept phone bookings – you have to visit the box office in person. They will charge you a *prevendita* supplement (about 10 percent of the normal price) for any tickets sold in advance. The price of a theater ticket can be anything between €8 and €52.

Tickets for classical concerts are usually sold on the spot, and are sometimes for that night only, an arrangement that favors the last-minute decision to go. Opera is the exception. Tickets are sold months in advance, with just a few held back until two days before

the performance. It is usually easier (and also a bit cheaper) to get tickets for the open-air summer performances.

Stage at Caffè Latino *(see pp350–51)*

The **Teatro dell'Opera** box office *(see p349)* handles sales for both summer and winter seasons, and they have a high-tech booking system, with a computer that color-codes unsold seats.

Tickets for most big rock and jazz events can be bought at **Orbis** and at larger record shops such as **Ricordi**.

Remember that if you are trying to get hold of a ticket for a particular performance that has already sold out, you are extremely unlikely to be able to obtain one from unofficial sources – there are very few ticket scalpers in Rome, except at major soccer games such as important finals.

Member of contemporary dance group Momix *(see p349)*

Discount Tickets

Theaters and concert venues tend not to offer discounts directly, although there is a centralized service (**Last Minute Teatro**) offering up to

50 percent off seats on the day of the performance.

Movie theaters occasionally offer people over 60, and disabled people a 30 percent reduction on weekdays. Many theaters also have cheaper ticket prices for weekday afternoon screenings, and for all shows on Wednesdays.

Some clubs offer reductions: look for *due per uno* coupons in local bars that allow two people entrance for the price of one.

Facilities for the Disabled

Few Roman venues provide easy access for people with restricted mobility, and any disabled visitors and their companions are likely to find the lack of provisions for them very frustrating.

The situation does improve a little in summer, however, when a great many performances in the city are held at open-air venues. The classical concerts held in the beautiful gardens of Villa Giulia *(see pp354–5)* have wheelchair access.

For more general information on facilities for disabled people visiting Rome, see pages 368–9.

Open-Air Entertainment

Open-air opera, movies, and concerts fill the calendar from late June until the end of

The Teatro dell'Opera *(see p348)*

Summer night outdoor performance among Roman ruins

September. These outdoor performances can be wonderful, with spectacular settings and enthusiastic audiences. Some of them are grand affairs, but smaller events may be just as evocative – a recital in the grounds of the Theater of Marcellus *(see p153)*, for example, or jazz in the gardens of Villa Celimontana *(see p195)*.

Some movie theaters roll back their ceilings in summer for open-air screenings, or else move to outdoor arenas, and there are also annual open-air movie festivals. The Cineporto along the Tiber, and the Festival di Massenzio offer films, food, and small exhibitions in July and August. Theater, too, moves outside in summer. Greek and Roman plays are staged at Ostia Antica *(see p272)*, and other shows take place at the Anfiteatro del Tasso *(see p353)*.

The Basilica of Constantine and Maxentius in the Forum *(see p88)* hosts the Festa della Letteratura (mid-May–mid-Jun), with major international writers reading from their works. Hadrian's Villa *(see p271)* is the equally stunning setting for the Villa Adriana Festival of music and modern dance (Jun–Jul). Consult listings in newspapers, magazines, or websites *(see p346)*, or watch for posters around the city for the most up-to-date information.

Singers performing the *Barber of Seville*

More traditional is Trastevere's community festival, Festa de Noantri *(see p61)*, with music, fireworks, and processions. This religious festival begins on the Saturday after July 16, but celebrations continue into August. The Festa dell'Unità, run by the DS (the former Communist Party), but not limited to politics, is generally held in summer. The program includes games, stands, food, and drinks.

Finally, if you like your entertainment less structured, do as the Romans do and take part in the *passeggiata* (early evening stroll) – the city's favorite spots are Piazza Navona *(see p122)* and along Via del Corso.

DIRECTORY

Ticket Agencies

Box Office (inside Feltrinelli)
Largo Argentina 11. **Map** 4 F4. **Tel** 06-6830 8596. Classical music, rock, pop, and jazz concerts, and some sporting events.

Last Minute Teatro
Via Bari 18 (just off Piazza Salerno). **Map** 6 F1. **Tel** 06-4411 7799. **Open** 2–8pm Tue–Sat, 2–4pm Sun.

Orbis
Piazza dell'Esquilino 37. **Map** 6 D4. **Tel** 06-474 4776.

Useful Websites

🆆 helloticket.it
🆆 listicket.it
🆆 romaturismo.it
🆆 ticketeria.it

Classical Music and Dance

Classical concerts take place in a surprising number of venues; tickets for opera premieres may be hard to get, but soloists, groups, or orchestras playing in gardens, churches, villas, or ancient ruins are more accessible. World-renowned soloists and orchestras make appearances throughout the year; past visitors have included Luciano Pavarotti and Placido Domingo, the Berlin Philharmonic, and prima ballerina Sylvie Guillem.

Programs are generally international in scope but sometimes you will find a festival dedicated to one of Italy's own, like Palestrina, the great 16th-century master of polyphonic church music, or Arcangelo Corelli, inventor of the Baroque *concerto grosso*.

Music in Churches

One of Rome's main attractions for classical music is the rich repertoire in the city's churches. Always sacred in theme (by decree of Pope John Paul II), music is mainly performed as concerts rather than during services.

Programs are posted around the city and outside the churches. You will often find very good musicians playing in the main churches, while the smaller, out-of-the-way churches frequently have young musicians, and amateur choirs as well.

St. Peter's (see p228) hosts one major RAI (national broadcasting company) concert on December 5, attended by the Pope and free to the general public. It has two established choirs. The Coro della Cappella Giulia sings at the 10:30am and 5pm vespers on Sunday. The Coro della Cappella Sistina sings whenever the Pope celebrates mass here, as on June 29 (St. Peter and St. Paul's Day).

Important choral masses also take place on January 25 in **San Paolo fuori le Mura** (see p269), when the Pope attends, on June 24 in **San Giovanni in Laterano** (p182), and on December 31 at the **Gesù** (pp110–11) where the *Te Deum* is sung. The church of **Sant'Ignazio di Loyola** (p108) is another favorite venue for choral concerts.

Plainsong and Gregorian chant can be heard in **Sant' Anselmo** (p206) every Sunday (Oct–Jul) at the 8:30am mass and 7:15pm vespers. Easter and the Christmas festivities are a great time for cheap (and chilly) concerts.

Orchestral, Chamber, and Choral Music

Up until the opening of the Renzo Piano–designed **Parco della Musica** on the Via Flaminia, with its three auditoriums and open-air arena, the **Auditorium Conciliazione**, and the **Teatro dell'Opera** had been Rome's two main auditoriums. All venues have their own resident orchestras and choirs, and offer varied seasons that include visiting groups, and soloists from all over the world. Rome's own Orchestra e Coro dell'Accademia di Santa Cecilia performs at the Parco della Musica throughout the year.

The season at the **Teatro Olimpico** usually offers good chamber music, some orchestral concerts, and ballet, with at least one concert a week.

Although a variety of classical concerts take place at the **Accademia Filarmonica Romana**, the emphasis is on chamber and choral music, with an internationally renowned series of concerts running from mid-October to mid-May. Performances take place in the Sala Casella, which seats around 180.

Ticket prices for classical concerts depend a lot on performers and venue. The **Auditorium del Foro Italico** sells tickets for most concerts for under €15; a ticket for the **Teatro Olimpico** costs between €15–€25, but seats for an important concert at **Teatro dell'Opera** may cost more than €80.

The Associazione Musicale Romana, dedicated to Renaissance and Baroque music, organizes three annual festivals in the **Palazzo della Cancelleria** (see p151): the Festival Internazionale di Cembalo (harpsichord festival) in March; Musica al Palazzo in May; and the Festival Internazionale di Organo in September. Classical music fans should also watch for performances by the Orchestra di Roma e del Lazio at **Teatro Argentina** or **Teatro Valle** (see p353).

It is always worth checking which musicians are due to be playing at the **Teatro Ghione**, the **Oratorio del Gonfalone,** and especially the **Aula Magna dell'Università La Sapienza**, which has one of the most innovative programs of classical, and contemporary music.

Open-Air Summer Concerts

In the summer, music lovers can enjoy concerts in cloisters, palazzo courtyards, and ancient ruins. Concerts can be one-time events or part of a festival program, regular fixtures or impromptu. Do as the Romans do: wait until the last moment and keep an eye on the posters and listings pages (see p346).

Open-air opera, and dance have their summer home in the Baths of Caracalla, which provide a splendid backdrop to performances. Classical concerts are often part of festivals like Roma-Europa (see p347) but there are also open-air festivals, and concert series dedicated to classical music. Among the more interesting are those that take place in some of the city's historic churches. It is well worth checking out the summer programs for Sant'Ivo alla Sapienza (see p124) and San Clemente (see p189).

The Associazione Musicale Romana organizes Serenate in

Chiostro – a lively and varied program of concerts during July in the cloisters of **Santa Maria della Pace** *(see p123)* with tickets at reasonable prices. The Concerti del Tempietto are a real summer treat with concerts held almost every evening from July to September in the **Area Archeologica del Teatro di Marcello** *(see p153)* or in the park of the Villa Torlonia.

Festival Villa Pamphilj in Musica, in July, is a series of concerts in the gardens of **Villa Doria Pamphilj** *(see p269)*. Programs range from comic opera to jazz and 20th-century classical music.

Brass bands can be heard in the **Pincio Gardens** *(see p138)* on Sunday mornings from the end of April until mid-July – they usually strike up at around 10:30am.

Contemporary Music

The Parco della Musica and the Accademia Filarmonica Romana (usually at the **Teatro Olimpico**) often include contemporary pieces in their programs, but these are less popular than the classical pieces and there is no set venue with a regular contemporary program.

International names appear on festival programs, and at special concerts at the **Aula**

Magna dell'Università La Sapienza. The most interesting contemporary music festival is organized by the Nuova Consonanza in the fall, while electronic, and digital music is showcased at the Dissonanze festival, which is generally held in May. Also worth keeping an eye out for are performances by scholars of the French Academy at **Villa Medici** *(see p137)*.

Opera

Italy and opera are to many people synonymous. Critics will tell you (justifiably) that Rome's opera is not up to the standard of Milan's La Scala or Naples's San Carlo. But that doesn't mean it is not worth visiting – world-class singers do appear here *(see p42)*, mainly in premières or solo recitals. However you judge the quality of the performances, the surroundings in which they take place are often incomparable. In summer the visual spectacle of *Aida*, say, performed in the open air, is quite magnificent.

The season starts late at **Teatro dell'Opera**, between November and January. In recent years programs have concentrated on the great popular operas, rather than staging experimental

productions. Tickets range from €17 to €130.

The Teatro dell'Opera moves outdoors in July and August to stage opera and ballet in the ancient Baths of Caracalla *(see p199)*. Popular works by Verdi and Puccini are performed, and although the acoustics are not perfect, the unique setting makes up for it.

Ballet and Dance

Opportunities to watch ballet or contemporary dance can be limited in Rome. The opera house's resident company Corpo di Ballo del Teatro dell'Opera di Roma performs the great classics as well as Roland Petit–style modern choreographies. Performances are staged at **Teatro dell'Opera**.

Contemporary dance is best seen during the Equilibrio Festival in February or at summer festivals, but foreign companies also perform at **Teatro Olimpico**. American modern dance groups of the Moses Pendleton school – Pilobolus, Momix, ISO, and Daniel Ezralow – are popular visitors. **Teatro del Vascello** is another venue noted for its experimental dance performances.

In fall, top visiting companies from all over the world perform during the **RomaEuropa Festival**.

DIRECTORY

For information about festivals and open-air concerts, see Trovaroma or similar listings *(see pp346 & 367)*.

Orchestral, Chamber, and Choral Music

Accademia Filarmonica Romana
Via Flaminia 118. **Map** 1 A1. **Tel** 06-320 1752.
W filarmonicaromana.org

Auditorium Conciliazione
Via della Conciliazione 4. **Map** 3 C3. **Tel** 800-904 560. W auditorium conciliazione.it

Aula Magna dell'Università La Sapienza
Piazzale Aldo Moro 5. **Tel** 06-361 0051.
W concertiiuc.it

Oratorio del Gonfalone
Via del Gonfalone 32A. **Map** 4 D4 & 11 A3. **Tel** 06-687 5952.

Parco della Musica
Viale de Coubertin 30. **Map** 1 C2. **Tel** 06-8024 1281 (for information); **Tel** 892 982 (for credit card sales). W auditorium. com

Sant'Anselmo
Piazza Cavalieri di Malta 5. **Map** 8 D2. **Tel** 06-579 11.

Teatro Ghione
Via delle Fornaci 37. **Map** 3 B4. **Tel** 06-637 2294.
W teatroghione.it

Teatro Olimpico
Piazza Gentile da Fabriano 17. **Tel** 06-326 5991.
W teatroolimpico.it

Opera

Teatro dell'Opera
Piazza Beniamino Gigli 1. **Map** 5 C3. **Tel** 06-4816 0255. W operaroma.it

Ballet & Dance

RomaEuropa Festival
Via dei Magazzini Generali 20A. **Tel** 06-4555 3050.
W romaeuropa.net

Teatro Olimpico
Piazza Gentile da Fabriano 17. **Tel** 06-326 5991.

Teatro dell'Opera
Piazza Beniamino Gigli 1. **Map** 5 C3.
Tel 06-4816 0255.

Teatro Vascello
Via G Carini 78. **Map** 7 A2. **Tel** 06-588 1021.
W teatrovascello.it

Rock, Jazz, Folk, and World Music

Rome's non-classical music scene is unpredictable and subject to vast seasonal changes, but there is a huge variety of music at the many clubs and stadiums, with visiting foreign and homegrown stars. Summer months bring excellent open-air rock, jazz, and world music festivals.

The music sections of *Trova-Roma* and *Roma c'è (see p346)* give a good idea of what's on, and ticket agencies at Orbis and Feltrinelli will have details of the latest tours. For smaller venues, you might need to buy a *tessera* (monthly or annual membership card) costing anything from €2 to €11, which often includes the entrance fee for smaller bands.

Rock Music

Big-name rock concerts are held in sports venues at the **Palalottomatica** and the legendary **Stadio Olimpico**, though it is also a good idea to keep an eye on who's performing at the **Atlantico**. The **Palladium** and Testaccio's **Villaggio Globale** at the Ex-Mattatoio (a converted abattoir) are other large-scale venues for concerts and other events, while the **Parco della Musica** also hosts top acts. Entrance can cost above €25, but there are plenty of opportunities for smaller budgets. If you're in Rome on May 1, join the crowds at the massive open-air concert that is usually held at Piazza San Giovanni. Bands also play for free during the European Festival of Music celebrations, on and around June 21. For all mega-concerts, it is always a good idea to show up an hour or so before the act gets under way to be sure of a good place.

Not far from the Vatican, **Fonclea** and **The Place** are also worth checking out.

One of the city's most interesting venues is **Forte Prenestino**, a former prison taken over by squatters, and turned into a social center with a characteristically alternative feel. It now hosts rock concerts, debates, and art exhibitions. Meanwhile, **Locanda Atlantide**, with its low entrance fee and central location, is a place where many up-and-coming

Roman bands, and soloists cut their teeth. **Init** is also worth checking out.

Discos often double as live music venues, too, so check to see if there are any midweek surprises at **Piper** or weekend concerts at the **Circolo degli Artisti** and the slightly more alternative **Brancaleone**.

Jazz

Rome's taste for jazz has developed over the years as a result of visits from American and other foreign musicians. Miles Davis played one of his last concerts here, and other jazz gurus such as Pat Metheny, Michael Brecker, Sonny Rollins, and Joe Zawinul's Syndicate are all frequent visitors. On no account should *aficionados* miss a visit to the excellent **Casa del Jazz**. Top musicians also play at **Alexanderplatz** and Trastevere's **Big Mama** club, one of the city's legendary addresses for important names, offering everything from trad R&B to progressive jazz and rock. It is also worth checking out what's on at **Gregory's**, **Boogie Club**, and **Be Bop** jazz and blues club. **Alpheus** is unique in offering separate concert halls, and interesting festivals featuring high-quality ensembles. Otherwise, check local listings to see what's on at **Caffè Latino** or **Caruso – Café de Oriente**. Some of Rome's smaller venues, like **Charity Cafè**, also

showcase formidable new talent.

If you want to mix music with your meal, then try **'Gusto**, a slick downtown pizzeria/restaurant with live jazz performances on most nights. If Creole cuisine is more to your taste, then reserve a table in advance at Alexanderplatz.

Local names to look for include pianist Antonello Salis, who mingles jazz, and Caribbean rhythms, and respected soul-singer Fulvio Tomaino. Other leading lights on the blues scene are Roberto Gatto and Maurizio Gianmarco, frequent visitors at Big Mama.

The Roman summer abounds in jazz. The principal event is the Alexanderplatz Jazz Image festival in June and July, with nightly alfresco performances at the Villa Celimontana park, just behind the Colosseum. Tickets cost around €10, and are available at the park itself. Another important fixture is the yearly fall Roma Jazz Festival with big names from the Italian, and international jazz scene visiting the Parco della Musica.

Folk Music

Since the sad demise of Rome's historic Folkstudio, there is no single venue for folk aficionados in the city, though those prepared to scour the listings may uncover a country evening at **Four Green Fields**, an interesting acoustic set at **Caffè Latino**, or a soulful soloist at **Lettere Caffè**.

Traditional Roman folk music has been more or less reduced to tourist-diluted serenades at outdoor restaurants; besides, young locals tend to favor the folk music of other regions and countries. Many bands from various parts of Italy, such as Mau Mau and Agricantus, have found success by drawing on regional rhythms and singing in dialect. Italians' love of all things Irish also means that strains of the fiddle and drum can be heard in many of the Irish pubs dotted throughout the city. If you have to choose one, then make it the Guinness-enriched **Fiddler's Elbow** near Santa Maria Maggiore.

World Music

As capital of a Latin country that has strong links with other Mediterranean cultures, Rome is a place where world music flourishes. Whether you are looking for South American salsa, African rhythms, or Arab cadences, you are unlikely to be disappointed.

Latin American music is no passing fad, as the well-established festivals, dance schools, and sellout tours by the likes of Brazilian mega-star Caetano Veloso testify. Many venues offer opportunities to enjoy Latin American music throughout the year. **Arriba Arriba** serves up a choice menu of strictly spicy Latin rhythms. Also check what's on at **Caruso – Café de Oriente** in Testaccio, where you can enjoy a cocktail or two along with the predominantly Cuban music.

But it is summer when Latin American music really comes into its own. The two-month Fiesta festival at the **Ippodromo delle Capannelle** has become by far the most popular feature of the long list of Roman summer events, racking up in excess of a million ticket sales.

If your tastes are more eclectic, there's also the excellent "Roma Incontra Il Mondo." This summer festival of world music takes place at **Villa Ada**, a large park north of downtown, from mid-June to early August. Fans gather each evening to appreciate the talents of names like Angelique Kidjo and South African pianist Abdullah Ibrahim.

World music is also well served at the aptly named **Villaggio Globale**, which hosts regular concerts. For a somewhat more eclectic experience, try **Lettere Caffè**, Rome's first literary café, which offers occasional evenings of world music, with performances of anything from Australian aborigine to Greek syrtaki sounds.

DIRECTORY

Alexanderplatz
Via Ostia 9. **Map** 3 B1.
Tel 06-3974 2171.

Alpheus
Via del Commercio 36–38.
Map 8 D5.
Tel 06-574 7826.

Arriba Arriba
Via delle Capannelle 104.
Tel 06-721 3772.

Atlantico
Viale dell'Oceano
Atlantico 271D, EUR.
Tel 06-591 5727.

Be Bop
Via Giulietti 14. **Map** 8 E4.
Tel 340 556 0112.

Big Mama
Vicolo San Francesco a
Ripa 18. **Map** 7 C2.
Tel 06-581 2551.

Boogie Club
Via Gaetano Astolfi 63–65
(southeast of Stazione
Trastevere).
Tel 06-6066 4283.

Brancaleone
Via Levanna 13 (in Monte
Sacro). **Tel** 06-8200 4382.

Caffè Latino
Via di Monte Testaccio 96.
Map 8 D4.
Tel 06-578 2411.

**Caruso – Café de
Oriente**
Via di Monte Testaccio 36.
Map 8 D4.
Tel 06-574 5019.

Casa del Jazz
Viale di Porta Ardeatina
55. **Map** 9 A4.
Tel 06-704 731.

Charity Cafè
Via Panisperna 68. **Map** 5
C4. **Tel** 06-4782 5881.

Circolo degli Artisti
Via Casilina Vecchia 42.
Map 10 F1.
Tel 06-7030 5684.

Feltrinelli
Galleria Alberto Sordi
31–35. **Map** 12 E2.
Tel 06-679 4957.

Fiddler's Elbow
Via dell'Olmata 43.
Map 6 D4.
Tel 06-487 2110.

Fonclea
Via Crescenzio 82A.
Map 3 C2.
Tel 06-689 6302.

Forte Prenestino
Via F. Delpino (east of city,
along Via Prenestina).
Tel 06-2180 7855.

Four Green Fields
Via Morin 40. **Map** 3 B1.
Tel 06-372 5091.

Gregory's
Via Gregoriana 54D.
Map 5 A2.
Tel 06-679 6386.

'Gusto
Via della Frezza 23.
Map 4 F2.
Tel 06-322 6273.

Init
Via della Stazione
Tuscolana 133. **Map** 10
F3. **Tel** 06-9727 7724.

**Ippodromo delle
Capannelle**
Via Appia Nuova 1245
(km 12). **Tel** 06-718 2139.

Lettere Caffè
Via San Francesco a Ripa
100. **Map** 7 C1.
Tel 06-9727 0991.

Locanda Atlantide
Via dei Lucani 22B (San
Lorenzo district).
Tel 06-4470 4540.

Orbis
Piazza Esquilino 37. **Map**
6 D4. **Tel** 06-474 4776.

Palalottomatica
Piazzale dello Sport, EUR.
Tel 199 128 800.

Palladium
Piazza B. Romano 8 (to
the south of Stazione
Ostiense).
Tel 06-5706 7761.

Parco della Musica
Viale de Coubertin 15.
Map 1 C2.
Tel 06-8024 1281.
W auditorium.com

Stadio Olimpico
Viale dei Gladiatori (northwest of downtown, across
the Tiber by Monte
Mario).

The Place
Via Alberico II 27.
Map 3 C2.
Tel 06-6830 7137.

Villa Ada
Via Salaria 197 (north of
downtown).
Tel 06-4173 4712.

Villaggio Globale
Ex-Mattatoio,
Lungotevere Testaccio 2.
Map 8 D4.
Tel 347 413 1205.

Movies and Theater

Going to the movies is a popular Roman pastime, with around 40 different films on show in any week. The excellent Casa del Cinema and high-profile International Festival of Cinema reflect the city's enduring love of the big screen.

The great majority of Roman movie theaters are *prima visione* (first run) and show the latest international movies in dubbed versions. The smaller arthouse theaters are more likely to show subtitled versions of foreign films.

Theater productions are performed in Italian whether the plays are national classics or by foreign playwrights. The main theaters offer a selection by great Italian playwrights. There are also performances of traditional cabaret, avant-garde theater, and dance theater. Theater tickets cost between €8 and €50 and can be bought in advance by visiting the theater box office, or through the last-minute booking service *(see p347)*.

Prima Visione

There are over 80 *prima visione* movie theaters in the city. The best ones for decor, and comfort are the **Fiamma** (two screens) and **Barberini** (three screens).

Foreign movies are usually dubbed. Films in the original language are shown at the **Nuovo Olimpia** (daily), on Mondays at the **Alcazar**, and occasionally at the **Greenwich**.

Tickets for new movies cost around €7, but a few theaters listed as *prima visione* charge less, namely **Farnese** and **Reale**. People over 60, and disabled people are normally entitled to a 30 percent discount on weekdays. Tickets are reduced in many theaters on weekday afternoons, and on Wednesdays. Check the newspaper or listings such as *TrovaRoma* or *Roma c'è* for details *(see p346)*.

Arthouse Movie Theaters

True film buffs flock to Rome in October for the International Festival of Cinema (www.romacinemafest.it) with events centering on the **Parco della Musica**.

There are two main types of arthouse movie theaters in Rome: *cine-clubs* and *cinema d'essai*. Both are good if you're interested in catching older classics and new foreign films as well as movies by contemporary Italian directors.

The *d'essai* theaters now and then show films in the original language (indicated by *v.o.* for *versione originale* in the listings). Try the **Azzurro Scipioni** (one of the few to be open throughout summer), **Filmstudio**, or Nanni Moretti's **Nuovo Sacher**. Some of the smaller theaters are called *cine-clubs* and require membership.

The **Palazzo delle Esposizioni** shows interesting series of international films, though you should head for the **Casa del Cinema** for the real arthouse experience.

Cartoons and children's favorites are shown at **Dei Piccoli**, in the leafy surrounds of the Villa Borghese.

English-Language Films

As well as occasional undubbed showings of American, British, and Australasian films in arthouse theaters and the **Nuovo Olimpia** and **Space Cinema Moderno**, the excellent **Casa del Cinema** has a policy of screening all movies in their original language.

Summer Movies

Some Roman cinemas have roll-back ceilings that are in use during the summer, while the others close down. The **Nuovo Sacher** has an outdoor arena. Rome also has various summer film festivals: Cineporto and Massenzio, to name but two.

These show several films each night from 9pm until the small hours, with food and drinks for sale and often live music during intermissions. Cineporto takes place in the Parco della Farnesina nightly between July and September, but Massenzio moves around *(see listings)*.

Sci-fi enthusiasts should keep an eye out for the Fantafestival (early June), a science fiction, fantasy, and horror film festival. The Venezia a Roma event in September gives movie buffs a chance to see movies presented at the summer Venice Film Festival.

The listings pages *(see p346)* have details on retrospectives and avant-garde film seasons at the **Azzurro Scipioni** and the open-air arts festivals like RomaEuropa *(see p347)* and Festa dell'Unità *(see p347)*.

Mainstream Theater

The backbone of Rome's theatrical repertoire are Luigi Pirandello's dramas, and comedies by 18th-century Venetian Carlo Goldoni, 20th-century Neapolitan Eduardo de Filippo, and Nobel Prize winner Dario Fo. Major foreign playwrights are also performed from time to time.

The best classic productions are staged at the **Teatro Argentina**, **Teatro Quirino**, **Teatro Eliseo**, and **Teatro Piccolo Eliseo**. **Teatro Argentina** is state-owned and home of Rome's permanent theater company. Its sister theater, **Teatro India**, stages more innovative works. The historic **Teatro Ambra Jovinelli**, near Termini station, is the best place to go for comedy acts. Plays at the **Quirino** often feature famous Italian actors. The **Eliseo** and **Piccolo Eliseo** are among the city's best private theaters.

At **Teatro Sistina** and **Teatro Brancaccio** you can see hit musicals by visiting foreign companies and shows by popular Italian actors, while **Teatro Vittoria** goes in for plays by Noël Coward or Neil Simon.

Contemporary Theater

The home of contemporary theater is the ever-dynamic **Vascello**, the **Orologio**, and, beyond these well-known names, in a host of small theaters, ingeniously rigged up in cellars, garages, small apartments, or even tents.

The **Colosseo** hosts some alternative fringe-type productions (known here as *teatro off*), while the **Palladium** and the **Vascello** tend to stage works by contemporary authors and occasional avant-garde productions. Some of them, like **Teatro India** and Orologio, also put on foreign-language productions.

Folk, Cabaret, and Puppet Theater

Roman and Neapolitan folk songs and cabaret can be enjoyed in Trastevere's tourist-trade restaurants, like **Meo Patacca**, while **Tina Pika Village** offers more alternative cabaret.

Puppet theater is another Roman tradition. Shows take place early in the evening on weekends, and sometimes during the week, at **Teatro Verde** and **Teatro Mongiovino**. In the Villa Borghese, the **Teatro San Carlino** also presents plays with the younger audience in mind. Among the most popular are the adventures of *Pulcinella* (the Italian Punch).

Open-Air Theater

The open-air summer theater season usually features Greek and Roman plays at **Ostia Antica** (*see pp272–3*).

The **Anfiteatro Quercia del Tasso** in the Janiculum Park takes its name from the oak tree under which 16th-century poet Tasso used to sit. Comedy shows are staged here in July to September, when the weather permits. In winter the company performs at the **Teatro Anfitrione**.

Nearby is a Neapolitan street puppet theater booth featuring *Pulcinella*. Shows are usually on in the afternoons, with morning shows on Sundays.

DIRECTORY

Prima Visione

Alcazar
Via Card. Merry del Val 14.
Map 7 C1. **Tel** 06-588 0099.

Barberini
Piazza Barberini 24.
Map 5 B3. **Tel** 06-482 1082.

Farnese
Piazza Campo de' Fiori 56.
Map 4 E5.
Tel 06-686 4395.

Fiamma
Via Bissolati 47. **Map** 5 C2.
Tel 06-485 526.

Greenwich
Via Bodoni 59. **Map** 7 C3.
Tel 06-574 5825.

Nuovo Olimpia
Via in Lucina 16. **Map** 12
E1. **Tel** 06-686 1068.

Reale
Piazza Sonnino 7.
Map 7 C1. **Tel** 06-5810 234.

Space Cinema Moderno
Piazza della Repubblica
45. **Map** 5 C3.
Tel 06-892 111.

Arthouse Movie Theaters

Azzurro Scipioni
Via degli Scipioni 82. **Map** 3
C2. **Tel** 06-3973 7161.

Casa del Cinema
Largo M. Mastroianni 1.
Map 5 B1. **Tel** 06-423 601.
w casadelcinema.it

Dei Piccoli
Viale della Pineta 15.
Map 5 B1.
Tel 06-855 3485.

Filmstudio
Via degli Orti d'Alibert 1C.
Map 4 D4.
Tel 334 178 0632.

Nuovo Sacher
Largo Ascianghi 1.
Map 7 C2.
Tel 06-581 8116.

Palazzo delle Esposizioni
Via Nazionale 194.
Map 5 B4.
Tel 06-3996 7500.
w palazzoesposizioni.it

Parco della Musica
Viale de Coubertin 30.
Map 1 C2.
Tel 06-8024 1281.
w romacinemafest.org

Mainstream Theater

Teatro Ambra Jovinelli
Piazza G. Pepe 43. **Map** 6
E4. **Tel** 06-8308 2620.

Teatro Argentina
Largo Argentina 56.
Map 4 F4. **Tel** 06-684 001.
w teatrodiroma.net

Teatro Brancaccio
Via Merulana 244.
Map 6 D5.
Tel 06-9826 4500.

Teatro Eliseo
Via Nazionale 183. **Map** 5
B4. **Tel** 06-488 2114.
w teatroeliseo.it

Teatro India
Via L. Pierantoni 6.
Map 7 C5.
Tel 06-684 0001.

Teatro Piccolo Eliseo
Via Nazionale 183.
Map 5 B4.
Tel 06-488 2114.

Teatro Quirino
Via delle Vergini 7.
Map 5 A4 & 12 F2.
Tel 06-679 4585.
w teatroquirino.it

Teatro Sistina
Via Sistina 129. **Map** 5 B2.
Tel 06-420 0711.

Teatro Vittoria
Piazza S. Maria Liberatrice
8. **Map** 8 D3.
Tel 06-574 0598.

Contemporary Theater

Palladium
Piazza B. Romano 8 (south
of Stazione Ostiense).
Tel 06-5706 7761.

Teatro Anfitrione
Via di San Saba 24.
Map 8 E3.
Tel 06-575 0827.

Teatro Colosseo
Via Capo d'Africa 29A.
Map 9 A1.
Tel 06-700 4932.

Teatro dell'Orologio
Via dei Filippini 17A. **Map**
11 B3. **Tel** 06-687 5550.

Teatro Olimpico
Piazza Gentile da Fabriano
17 (off Via Guido Reni).
Map 1 A2.
Tel 06-326 5991.

Teatro Vascello
Via G. Carini 72. **Map** 7 A2.
Tel 06-588 1021.

Folk, Cabaret, Puppet Theater

Meo Patacca
P. dei Mercanti 30. **Map** 8
D1. **Tel** 06-581 6198.

Teatro Mongiovino
Via Genocchi 15.
Tel 06-513 9405.

Teatro San Carlino
Viale dei Bambini (Pincio).
Map 4 F1. **Tel** 06-6992
2117. w sancarlino.it

Teatro Verde
Circonvall. Gianicolense
10. **Map** 7 B4.
Tel 06-588 2034.

Tina Pika Village
Via Fonteiana 57
(Monteverde district).
Tel 06-588 5754.

Open-Air Theater

Anfiteatro Quercia del Tasso
Passeggiata del Gianicolo.
Map 3 C5. **Tel** 06-575 0827.

Nightlife

Rome's nightlife has never been as diverse or vibrant as it is today. The city has witnessed a sharp rise in the number of bar and club openings that cater to an ever more demanding clientele. Where once the choice was limited to the Irish theme bars near Termini, the few well-established but crowded bars in the downtown, and the hugely popular clubs in Testaccio, the capital now offers a wide range of options to satisfy all tastes and budgets. Depending on your mood, head first for a stylish pre-clubbing bar and then on to one of the exclusive clubs, or simply relax with friends and a bottle of good wine in an earthy wine bar in one of the historic downtown's breathtaking squares. For a memorable first stop, enjoy spectacular views with an apéritif from a rooftop terrace bar.

On the downside, despite the greater number of bars and clubs, prices have soared in Rome since the euro was introduced – today you can be charged up to €10 for a cocktail. For cheaper alternative nights out, away from the tourist traps, visit a bar in San Lorenzo.

What's On

As in any major city, Rome's nightlife is constantly evolving. Roman club-goers are an extremely varied group, and most clubs arrange different nights to appeal to the diverse range of tastes – so it is essential to keep up to date on what's happening by checking listings magazines *(see p346)* that hit the newsstands every Thursday.

Flyers for many nightclubs are handed out in some of the busier squares in and around the downtown, such as Campo de' Fiori and Piazza del Fico. They are also distributed inside the many pre-clubbing bars dotted around Testaccio, such as **Il Seme e La Foglia**.

Practicalities

Preferred clubbing nights are Friday and Saturday, when the cars, and scooters of revelers clog the streets of the downtown. Lines at the most popular venues can be very long at peak entrance time (around midnight), so it is advisable to get there an hour or so earlier. However, if you are unable do so, and don't feel like waiting, try calling in advance and charming your way onto the guest list. Instead of an entrance fee, some smaller clubs require a *tessera*, a monthly or yearly membership card, which you can buy, and fill out on the spot. If you're paying just to get through the door that night, hold on to your entrance ticket as it usually entitles you to a free first drink *(la consumazione)*; your second could be expensive, and cost as much as €15.

As a general rule, remember that all-male groups are rarely welcome, and in some exclusive clubs neither are unaccompanied men. Also, to enter any of the more select venues, you'll need both an introduction from one of the regulars, and clothes that aim to impress.

Bars

Despite increased competition, especially from the revitalized rustic wine bar **Il Nolano**, **La Vineria** *(see p320)* in Campo de' Fiori has maintained its cult status among Romans of all ages, and backgrounds for unpretentious, lively drinking at reasonable prices. Just around the corner, **L'Angolo Divino** *(see p320)* is less well-known, and consequently not as bustling. It nonetheless remains a perfect spot for socializing over great wines and heartwarming food. Another landmark in the *centro storico* (historic center), though for a more well-to-do and fashion-conscious crowd, is the in-vogue **Antico Caffè della Pace**, a popular choice near Piazza Navona for those who want to see and be seen. **Fluid**, on Via del Governo Vecchio, is much livelier, and has made its mark in the capital as the perfect venue to get you in the mood for late-night clubbing. A few doors down but really a world away, the comfortable and candlelit **Mimì e Cocò** is a great place to relax (alfresco or inside) and linger over subtle wines, served with a smile. Just off the top end of the same street, moving away from Corso Vittorio Emanuele II, is **Giulio Passami l'Olio**, a warm, welcoming, and animated *enoteca*, tucked away from the usual *passaggiate* (promenade) routes. Closer to Piazza di Spagna, the striking interior and extensive choice of wines by the glass make the **Antica Enoteca di Via della Croce** a favorite spot for wine connoisseurs. Although it's definitely not cheap, the impressive bar buffet is well worth sampling.

In Trastevere, too, the romantic streets are full of tiny bars aimed at diverse crowds. Find a table if you can outside **Ombre Rosse** in the wonderful Piazza Sant'Egidio and watch the world go by. If Ombre Rosse is too crowded, **Caffè della Scala**, just a few minutes' walk away, is a good alternative. Other bars in the area include the lively **Nylon** and **Friends Art Café**, which is a perfect spot to enjoy a refreshing, though expensive, apéritif with complimentary but elaborate snacks – a growing trend in the Eternal City. The simple, but vintage, **Bar San Callisto**, located just off Piazza Santa Maria, draws strictly nonconventional patrons.

Elsewhere in the city, the sophisticated **Ferrazza** (see p343), in San Lorenzo, serves up exceptional wines for more sophisticated customers, while the monumental student bar **Rive Gauche** does great business as the biggest pub in the area. The slick surf-bar **Duke's** in Parioli is slightly away from the center, but is worth it for star-spotting. Duke's has tried to curb its soaring popularity by closing on Saturday nights, but to no avail. It remains the number one place to be seen in north Rome.

Finally, and not just for hopeless romantics, breathtaking views of Rome can be enjoyed at the lavish rooftop terrace bars at hotel **Eden** (see p302), near Via Veneto, and the **Radisson Blu ES** hotel (see p302) near Termini. At dusk, particularly after a sunny day, these stunning venues offer a great place to start an unforgettable evening out.

Clubs

To brush shoulders with TV starlets and parliamentary undersecretaries, head for **Gilda**. Its glitzy dance-floor and restaurant have made it a favorite with the Roman jet set and hangers-on. The famous Sixties nightclub, **Jackie O**, revamped in lavish style, with a lush interior, a piano bar, and an expensive eatery, draws an international, thirty-something crowd.

Bòeme is a safe option for commercial music among Roman twenty-somethings, though **Heaven** is slightly funkier with its marked preference for house. More challenging is the eclectic **Micca Club** with the chance to hear live sets, while the more traditional disco is at its best at **Piper**, which changes its look each season and organizes imaginative floor shows and other events. There are a few disco-pubs downtown that offer a compromise between a straightforward bar and

an all-out club. **The Nag's Head** is one that is especially worth noting.

In and around Testaccio, the undisputed clubbing heart of Rome, you'll find it difficult to decide which club to visit. Many think that **Muzak** is one of the best dance clubs around; the stylish **Caruso – Café de Oriente** concentrates on Latin, R&B, and salsa sounds, while the multifunctional **Distillerie Clandestine** is the place for eating, drinking, relaxing, and dancing. **Caffè Latino** changes gear on weekends, with clubbers dancing to covers bands, while nearby are the trendy **La Saponeria** and **Neo**, a stronghold of underground music. Saturday night at **Big Bang** signifies all things dark and new wave, while at the equally alternative **Alpheus**, you can drift between three rooms offering three completely different DJ sets. Last but by no means least, the legendary **Goa** remains the champion of Roman clubs, attracting the best of Italian as well as international DJs.

The wine bar at **'Gusto** offers live music, and the chance to explore the venue's various restaurant areas while enjoying a glass of wine from the vast selection available. On the other side of Corso Vittorio Emanuele, the select **La Maison** attracts a slightly older crowd with its less commercial music, and elegant ambience. However, if you're in the mood for a mainstream alternative that is free of charge, and easier to gain entry to, then head to the upbeat **Habana Café** for a continuous program of live music, and DJ sets every evening.

For something a little different, the **Radio Café** is a multifunctional venue with a lounge, café, disco, and meeting spaces frequented by a trendy media set.

Gay Scene

Rome is no longer the provincial backwater it once

was. This is clearly reflected in both the rise in the number of gay bars, and clubs, and their increasing popularity. While some are exclusively gay, others attract a mixed clientele.

Across the river from the *centro storico* in Trastevere is the exclusive **Il Giardino dei Ciliegi**, a living-room-style bar that specializes in cocktails. It also stocks a wide variety of teas and serves exciting salads, and an excellent Sunday brunch – even on public holidays. For livelier social drinking, head for **Anfiteatro My Bar** and **Coming Out**, between San Giovanni, and the Colosseum, to mingle with a mixed crowd that usually spills out onto the street. Nearby, the men-only bar **Hangar** continues to pack them in.

When it comes to clubbing, the ever-growing number of gay one-nighters in both alternative and mainstream clubs in many ways present the best venues for drinking and dancing until the early hours. **Goa**, just off Via Ostiense, occasionally hosts gay nights such as the women-only Venus Rising once a month; Mucca Assassina (quite literally "homicidal cow") pulls in the crowds every Friday at the monumental **Qube** in Tiburtino; the rival Omogenic crew takes over the **Circolo degli Artisti** on the same evening, while the **Alpheus** hosts the Gorgeous I Am one-nighters every Saturday. These clubs are in addition to the justly famous gay-friendly disco **Alibi** in Testaccio with its explosive mix of house music, and retro classics.

Pride Week, a yearly event held at the end of June/early July, is a time when gay Romans hit the streets for seven days of nonstop partying. The program, and date change from year to year, so it is wise to consult listing magazines for full details.

In summer, as with most clubs, Rome's gay venues move outdoors in an attempt to beat the stifling heat.

In recent years, many of these have been hosted at **Gay Village**, a summer-long outdoor party. This is yet another important indication that gay culture is finally beginning to be accepted on the mainstream entertainment scene.

Centri Sociali

Centri sociali, or illegally occupied buildings that have been converted into centers for the arts and entertainment, give an alternative edge to Rome's vivacious nightlife and cultural scene. While some centers are run on a professional basis and are able to successfully compete with many of the capital's swankier

and established venues, others have continued to maintain their staunch anti-establishment stance.

Top billing must go to **Brancaleone** in north Rome, which regularly features progressive Italian and international DJs for the very best in electronic and house tunes. This well-run establishment is also home to an organic café and shop, superb art exhibitions, and a cinema club.

Near the Baths of Caracalla, the **Angelo Mai Center** regularly organizes a multitude of cultural events, including exhibitions and showings of art house films – sometimes even in their original non-dubbed

version. On weekends, the venue dedicates its space primarily to club nights, covering a spectrum of tastes from underground and ethnic live bands to wild DJ sets. They also boast their own eatery.

Farther away from downtown, the abandoned fort, **Forte Prenestino**, is a magical maze of spooky rooms and endless corridors and represents the most bizarre of Rome's social center venues. Famous for its anti-establishment Labor Day concert – the official and free rock concert is held in Piazza San Giovanni in Laterano – it also holds theater productions, film festivals, and club nights throughout the year for a young but alternative crowd. Closer to

DIRECTORY

Bars

Angelo Mai
Viale delle Terme di Caracalla 55A.
Map 9 A2.
Tel 329 448 1358.

L'Angolo Divino
Via dei Balestrari 12–14.
Map 11 C4.
Tel 06-686 4413.

Antica Enoteca di Via della Croce
Via della Croce 76B.
Map 4 F2.
Tel 06-679 0896.

Antico Caffè della Pace
Via della Pace 3–7.
Map 11 C3.
Tel 06-686 1216.

Bar San Callisto
Piazza San Callisto 3–4.
Map 7 C1.
Tel 06-583 5869.

Caffè della Scala
Via della Scala 4.
Map 7 C1.
Tel 06-580 3610.

Duke's
Viale Parioli 200.
Map 2 D1.
Tel 06-8066 2455.

Eden
Via Ludovisi 49.
Map 5 B2.
Tel 06-478 121.

Ferrazza
Via dei Volsci 59.
Map 6 F4.
Tel 06-490 506.

Fluid
Via del Governo Vecchio 46/47. **Map** 11 C3.
Tel 06-683 2361.

Friends Art Café
Piazza Trilussa 34.
Map 4 E5.
Tel 06-581 6111.

Giulio Passami l'Olio
Via di Monte Giordano 28.
Map 11 B2.
Tel 06-6880 3288.

Mimì e Cocò
Via del Governo Vecchio 72. **Map** 11 C3.
Tel 06-6821 0845.

Il Nolano
Campo de' Fiori 11/12.
Map 11 C4.
Tel 06-687 9344.

Nylon
Via del Politeama 12.
Map 11 C5.
Tel 06-5834 0692.

Ombre Rosse
Piazza Sant'Egidio 12.
Map 7 C1.
Tel 06-588 4155.

Radisson Blu ES
Via Filippo Turati 171.
Map 6 D4.
Tel 06-444 841.

Rive Gauche
Via dei Sabelli 43.
Map 6 F4.
Tel 06-445 6722.

Il Seme e la Foglia
Via Galvani 18.
Map 8 D4.
Tel 06-574 3008.

La Vineria
Campo de' Fiori 15.
Map 11 C4.
Tel 06-6880 3268.

Clubs

Alpheus
Via del Commercio 36/8.
Map 8 D5.
Tel 06-574 7826.

Big Bang
Via Monte Testaccio 22.
Map 8 D4.
Tel 392 901 1993.

Bòeme
Via Velletri 13.
Map 6 D1.
Tel 06-841 2212.

Caffè Latino
Via di Monte Testaccio 96.
Map 8 D4.
Tel 06-578 2411.

Caruso – Café de Orient
Via di Monte Testaccio 36.
Map 8 D4.
Tel 06-574 5019.

Distillerie Clandestine
Via Libetta 13.
Tel 06-5730 5102.

Gilda
Via Mario de' Fiori 97.
Map 12 F1.
Tel 06-678 4838.

Goa
Via Libetta 13.
Tel 06-574 8277.

'Gusto
Via delle Frezza 23.
Map 4 F2.
Tel 06-322 6273.

Habana Café
Via dei Pastini 120.
Map 12 D2.
Tel 06-678 1983.

Heaven
Viale di Porta Ardeatina 119. **Map** 9 B5.
Tel 06-574 3772.

Jackie O
Via Boncompagni 11.
Map 5 B2.
Tel 06-4288 5457.

La Maison
Vicolo dei Granari 4.
Map 11 C3.
Tel 06-683 3312.

the center, **Villaggio Globale**, situated on a vast area of open space at the edge of Testaccio, has a very similar philosophy and range of services. In summer, it regularly hosts open-air concerts, occasionally beating out the competition to feature big-name Italian bands such as Tiromancino.

Jazz, Salsa, and African Sounds

Rome offers countless venues for jazz, from trad and swing to modern fusion (see p350). Several jazz and Latin American clubs combine live music with dancing, eating, and drinking. For South American style music, **Fonclea** and **Arriba Arriba** (see p351) or **Alpheus** all pay homage to Latin American and world music, although **Caffè Latino** in Testaccio is far and away the best place to check out on weekends.

Clubbing in Summer

At the height of the sweltering summer, when virtually everything closes down in the capital, **Art Cafè** in Villa Borghese stands out as the supreme club venue for the fun-loving, young, and hip. A number of smaller venues open up on the Tiber too, while some of the bigger clubs hit the coast from July through to December – most notably in Ostia and in Fregene, where the revamped **Janga Beach** is a permanent fixture. Also worth checking out is the sophisticated **Singita** beach club, where they hold a special sunset ceremony accompanied by a DJ set.

After Hours

Most Roman clubs stay open until 2am or 3am. However, night owls may find one or two dance havens that see in the dawn, especially during the beach-party season. Before heading off to bed, you could join the other diehard clubbers for a final drink at one of the city's 24-hour watering holes, or else make for one of the early-morning bakers, and feast on sweet breakfast cornetti straight from the oven.

DIRECTORY

Micca Club
Via P. Micca 7A.
Map 6 F5.
Tel 06-8744 0079.

Muzak
Via di Monte Testaccio 38.
Map 8 D4.
Tel 06-574 4712.
The Nag's Head Via IV
Novembre 138B.
Map 5 A4.
Tel 06-679 4620.

Neo
Via degli Argonauti 18 (to the south of Stazione Ostiense).
Tel 06-9652 1094.

Piper
Via Tagliamento 9 (north of downtown).
Tel 06-855 5398.

Radio Café
Via Principe Umberto 67.
Map 6 E5.
Tel 06-4436 1110.

La Saponeria
Via degli Argonauti 20 (to the south of Stazione Ostiense, off Via Ostiense).
Tel 06-574 6999.

Gay Scene

Alibi
Via di Monte Testaccio
39–44. **Map** 8 D4.
Tel 06-574 3448.

Alpheus
See clubs.

Anfiteatro My Bar
Via San Giovanni in
Laterano 12. **Map** 9 A1.
Tel 06-700 4425.

Circolo degli Artisti
Via Casilina Vecchia 42.
Map 10 F1.
Tel 06-7030 5684.

Coming Out
Via San Giovanni In
Laterano 8. **Map** 9 A1.
Tel 06-700 9871.

Gay Village
Phone or check website
for venue. **Tel** 340-753
8396. **w** gayvillage.it

Il Giardino dei Ciliegi
Via dei Fienaroli 4.
Tel 06-580 3423.

Goa
See clubs.

Hangar
Via in Selci 69. **Map** 5 C5.
Tel 06-488 1397.

Qube
Via di Portonaccio 212
(north of downtown).
Tel 06-438 5445.

Centri Sociali

Brancaleone
Via Levanna 11 (in
Montesacro).
Tel 06-8200 4382.

Forte Prenestino
Via F. Delpino (in
Prenestino).
Tel 06-2180 7855.

Villaggio Globale
Lungotevere Testaccio 2/
Via di Monte Testaccio 22.
Map 7 4C.
Tel 347 413 1205.

Jazz, Salsa, and African Sounds

Alpheus
See clubs.

Arriba Arriba
Via delle Capannelle 104.
Tel 06-721 3772.

Caffè Latino
Via di Monte Testaccio 96.
Map 8 D4.
Tel 06-5728 8556.

Fonclea
Via Crescenzio 82A.
Map 3 C2. **Tel** 06-689
6302. **w** fonclea.it

Clubbing in Summer

Art Cafè
Viale del Galoppatoio, 33
(Villa Borghese).
Map 5 A1.
Tel 06-3600 6578.

Janga Beach
Lungomare di Ponente
11, Fregene.
Tel 06-6656 0649.

Singita
Villaggio dei Pescatori
Fregene.
Tel 06-6196 4921.

Sports

Do not be surprised if the peace of a Sunday afternoon in Rome is interrupted by the honking of cars and people shouting. It simply means that one of the home soccer teams has won at the stadium and the whole city appears to be celebrating the result.

Soccer is Italy's national sport, but other sports also attract a large following, and Roman sports fans have a varied choice of events and activites to watch or participate in.

You will find times and venues for most spectator sports listed in *Trova-Roma or Roma c'è (see p346)*, as well as the local sections of *La Gazzetta dello Sport* or *Corriere dello Sport*.

Soccer

An Italian soccer match is an experience not to be missed for the quality of the play and the fun atmosphere, though hooliganism has begun to raise its ugly head.

Rome has two teams, Roma and Lazio, and they take turns playing at the **Stadio Olimpico** on a Sunday afternoon at 3pm, in the Campionato Italiano (Italian championship league).

Seats can be scarce, so get tickets in advance from the stadium (€15 to €80) from noon onward on the day itself, or through club websites (www.sslazio.it and www.asroma.it). The cheapest seats are in the Le Curve stand; the mid-price and most expensive are in Le Gradinate, and La Tribuna respectively.

On Wednesday evenings there may be international competitions – the UEFA Cup or the Coppa dei Campioni (European Championship Cup). In between these, teams battle it out for the national Coppa Italia.

Tennis

A major event, the International Championships go on at **Foro Italico** for two weeks in May. The world's top tennis stars thrash it out on clay courts at 1pm, and 8:30pm from Tuesday to Friday, and at 1pm only on weekends. Buy tickets in advance either directly from the Foro Italico or from a ticket agency.

If you wish to play yourself, there are now more than 350 tennis clubs in Rome. It is often essential to reserve at least a week in advance and there is usually a moderate court fee.

Clubs where membership is not required include **Tennis Club Nomentano** and the **Circolo Tennis della Stampa** in northern Rome and the **Oasi di Pace**, just off the Via Appia Antica. Large hotels offer tennis for a reasonable price. The **Crowne Plaza** requires a small annual membership fee on top of the court price, which includes the gym and the pool (in the summer).

Horse-Racing, Trotting, and Leisure Riding

Important races include the Derby in May and the Premio Roma in November. There are trotting races at the **Ippodromo di Tor di Valle** and both flat races and steeplechases at the **Ippodromo delle Capannelle**.

The International Horse Show, organized by the Federazione Italiana Sport Equestri (**FISE**), is held in May in Piazza di Siena, Villa Borghese *(see p350)*. It is one of the most important social, and sporting events in the calendar, and has a great setting.

Through the FISE, it may be possible to find a riding club that will take you on a trail ride in the countryside around Rome, but most do not accept short-term members.

Golf

Even the most elite golf clubs will accept a touring golfer with a home membership, and handicap. Many clubs close on Mondays and on weekends, when they host competitions and guests cannot play. Prices range from €55 to €100.

The **Olgiata Golf Club** is open to everybody, though it is best to call first if you want to play on the weekend, when demand and fees are much higher. **Country Club Castel Gandolfo** is the newest club and **Circolo del Golf di Roma Acquasanta** the oldest and most prestigious. Within the city's ring road is the course at the **Sheraton Golf Hotel** (closed Tuesdays).

One of the many important competitions on the various golf courses around Rome is the Circolo Golf Roma Coppa d'Oro (Gold Cup) in April.

Car and Motorcycle Racing

Formula 1 and Formula 3 races take place on Sundays at **Vallelunga**; be prepared for some expensive entrance fees. Frequently on Saturdays official trials are open to spectators, and on some non-racing Sundays Italy's car designers show new models.

Rugby

Rugby is becoming increasingly popular, thanks to Italy's participation in the Six Nations tournament. This means that in winter (usually Feb–Mar) there are a couple of international matches in Rome. The home team is drawn against two other member "nations" each year: France, England, Scotland, Ireland, or Wales.

Rowing

In mid-June, an Oxford/Cambridge crew challenges the historic Aniene crew to a race taking place alternately on the Tiber, and on the Thames in England. The best place to watch is between the Margherita and Sant'Angelo bridges. The race usually starts at around 6pm. Another event is the battle between the Roma, and Lazio crews, from Ponte Duca d'Aosta to Ponte Risorgimento, on the same variable date as the Roma-Lazio soccer derby.

Swimming

Swimming pools are scarce, and definitely not geared to the short-term visitor. It is often necessary to pay an expensive membership plus a monthly fee. Most pools also require you to produce a medical certificate assuring your good health, and have lane-only swimming. The state-owned pools can be slightly cheaper, but you still have to pay an initial membership fee.

The **Shangri-La Hotel** opens its pool to non-residents in the summer, as does the **Cavalieri Rome Hotel**, for an entry fee. The best deal is on a Sunday, when the sports club and swimming pool **La Margherita** opens to non-members 10am–1pm, for a reasonable entry fee. **Piscina delle Rose** is an Olympic-sized pool open from June to September 9am–5:30pm daily (to 7pm at weekends). Overlooking the Colosseum, the **All'Ombra del Colosseo** festival also has a popular open-air pool in summer.

Health Clubs

Like the swimming pools, Roman health clubs usually require both a membership fee and monthly payments. For a short stay in Rome, it is more sensible to try the facilities in your hotel, or, if you are willing to pay, head for one of the private clubs. Use of club facilities may be negotiable.

The **Roman Sport Center** welcomes daily members for a reasonable price (€30) and you can use the pools, the gym, and the sauna. The facilities are open 7am–10:30pm on weekdays (until 8:30pm Saturday, 9am–3pm Sunday). Any shorts worn must be made of Lycra.

Jogging and Cycling

Rome's perfect climate, and stunning scenery attract thousands of well-dressed joggers and cyclists into the city's many parks. Early on weekday mornings or at any time on a Sunday you'll find the more popular locations looking like high-speed fashion shows. Each March, however, serious runners take part in the Rome Marathon.

Villa Doria Pamphilj (see p269) is an extensive park situated above the Janiculum, where you can choose from various tracks, plenty of open spaces, and a network of paths. **Villa Borghese** (see p260) is another vast, popular place with a running track.

Alternatively, jog under the acacia trees and palms at Villa Torlonia, on the spotlit track at Villa Glori, or combine sports with culture by running the **Via Appia Antica** (see p267) branching off into Parco Caffarella. Other favorite places are Viale delle Terme di Caracalla, Circo Massimo, Parco degli Aquedotti, and Parco di Colle Oppio.

All of the above are also ideal for cyclists, and you can rent bikes from many places, including **Collalti** and **Treno e Scooter Rent**.

DIRECTORY

Soccer

Stadio Olimpico
Via Foro Italico.
Tel 06-368 51.

Tennis

Circolo Tennis della Stampa
Piazza Mancini 19.
Map 1 A2.
Tel 06-323 2454.

Crowne Plaza
Via Aurelia Antica 415.
Tel 06-66420.

Foro Italico
Viale dei Gladiatori 31.
Tel 06-3272 3301.
W ctforoitalico.coni.it

Oasi di Pace
Via degli Eugenii 2.
Tel 06-718 4550.
W ct-oasidipace.it

Tennis Club Nomentano
Viale Rousseau 124.
Tel 06-8680 1888.
W clubnomentano.it

Horse Racing and Riding

FISE
Tel 06-836 6841.
W fise.it

Ippodromo delle Capannelle
Via Appia Nuova 1255.
Tel 06-71 67 71.

Ippodromo di Tor di Valle
Via dell'Ippica 20.
Tel 06- 524 761.
W tordivalle.ippocity.com

Golf

Circolo del Golf di Roma Acquasanta
Via Appia Nuova 716A.
Tel 06-780 3407.
W golfroma.it

Country Club Castel Gandolfo
Via di Santo Spirito 13,
Castelgandolfo.
Tel 06-931 2301.

Olgiata Golf Club
Largo dell'Olgiata 15.
Tel 06-3088 9141.

Sheraton Golf Hotel
Viale Salvatore Rebecchini 39. **Tel** 06-655 3477.

Car and Motor-cycle Racing

Vallelunga
Autodromo di Roma, Via Cassia km 34.5. **Tel** 06-901 5501. **W** vallelunga.it

Rugby

Federazione Italiana Rugby
Tel 06-4521 3117.
W federugby.it

Swimming

All'Ombra del Colosseo
Via di San Gregorio. **Map** 8 F1. **Tel** 333-509 4637.

ARCA Swimming Club
Via Monti Tiburtini 511.
Tel 06-451 0552.

Cavalieri Rome Hotel
Via Cadlolo 101.
Tel 06-350 91.
W romecavalieri.com

Piscina delle Rose
Viale America 20.
Tel 06-5422 0333.
W piscinadellerose.com

Shangri-La Hotel
Viale Algeria 141.
Tel 06-591 6441.

Health Clubs

Roman Sport Center
Via del Galoppatoio 33.
Map 5 A1.
Tel 06-320 1667.

Jogging and Cycling

Collalti
Via del Pellegrino 82.
Map 4 E4.
Tel 06-6880 1084.

Maratona di Roma
Tel 06-406 5064.
W maratonadiroma.it

Treno e Scooter Rent
Termini Station.
Map 6 D3.
Tel 06-4890 5823.

CHILDREN'S ROME

Italians love having children around, and you can be sure yours will be made welcome wherever they go. But there are few special facilities for children, and the heat, crowds, and lack of clean restrooms mean that Rome is not an ideal city for a vacation with babies or children under seven. It does, however, have plenty to offer slightly older children, especially those who are interested in history or art. The temptation may be to wear yourself and your children out by packing too many sights into one day. Plan in advance, and leave plenty of time to wander around the city, looking at the quirkier fountains, and monuments, watching knife-grinders at work in the markets, and spending time pondering the choice of ice cream flavors and special pizza toppings.

Practical Advice

If you are planning to bring your children to Rome, try to come in early spring or late fall, when the weather is good, but not too hot. Easter is best avoided, as the city is more crowded than usual, and you're constantly jostled on packed buses and streets. Where you stay is crucial. A hotel near the Villa Borghese park will give your children plenty of chances to relax and let off steam, though you may end up spending a lot of time and money to get to and from the downtown. A hotel in the historic center is ideal, since you can easily come back during the day for a rest, and a clean bathroom. Hygienic toilets and changing facilities are rare within the city, so it is really not advisable to bring a baby to Rome unless you are visiting friends or family. As with many historic cities, Rome may not instantly appeal to all children, but there is plenty to inspire their imaginations. Use this book to make the buildings and history come alive. Children might also enjoy learning a few Italian words and phrases so they can order food and buy things by themselves. If lingering over drinks on café terraces is what you enjoy best, bring your offspring something to keep them busy once they have finished their treats: crayons and paper, a computer game or an MP3 player. Alternatively, most other adults are very tolerant of children running around, and making noise while they relax and, if yours are reason-ably outgoing, they could join in with the local children playing ball games in early evenings on piazzas like Campo de' Fiori.

If you feel the need for a total break from the kids, most hotels will be able to provide a babysitter or help you contact a licensed babysitting agency.

In case of accident or illness, see pages 370–71 for information on what to do and a list of emergency numbers.

Getting Around

Bumpy cobblestones, narrow streets without sidewalks, and overcrowded buses make tiring work of pushing children around in strollers.

Fairground in the Villa Borghese park

Mothers with young children are, however, usually allowed to cut in line. Outside rush hours, the Metro is often less busy. Kids under 3 ft 3 in (1 m) tall travel free on public transportation.

Although the city is not good for cyclists, families with older children could rent bikes to ride along the Tiber on the cycle tracks to the north of the city, or to take on a regional train into the country. The bikes, tandems, and rickshaws for rent in Villa Borghese are good fun, and the bike rental hut in the Pincio gardens has free baby seats.

Anyone over the age of 14 is permitted to ride a scooter under 50cc, although Rome is not the best place for novices (see p386).

Eating Out

Children are normally warmly welcomed in neighborhood pizzerias and trattorias, and high

Children playing in the park at Villa Borghese

Pony trains in the Villa Borghese park

markets, there are lots of scrumptious take-out foods. Many of them are appealingly messy, so it is wise to take paper tissues. Try deep-fried fruit, and vegetables from Cose Fritte on Via di Ripetta *(see p323)* and *supplì al telefono*, rice croquettes with a gooey string of mozzarella inside, from *pizza al taglio* or *pizza rustica* outlets. A *tramezzino* comes quite close to a basic sandwich and if your kids are miserable without peanut butter, you can find it (and other foreign foods) at Castroni on Via Cola di Rienzo.

chairs are often available for toddlers and babies. If there is no high chair, be prepared for the waiters to improvise for you with armloads of cushions or telephone directories. Most places are perfectly happy to serve half portions, or to let children share meals.

In trattorias it can sometimes be difficult to be exactly sure what a certain dish contains (especially when there is no menu and the dishes of the day are reeled off, usually at top speed, by the waiter), so picky eaters are likely to be happier in pizzerias *(see pp320–21)*. Here they can choose their own toppings (remember that *prosciutto,* which is usually translated in menus as ham, is cured). The most entertaining pizzerias for kids are the old-fashioned ones where they can watch the chefs pound, stretch,

and flip the pizza dough. Restaurants open in the evening at or soon after 7pm, and the best places get busy from around 8:30pm, so it is wise to go early to avoid having to wait for a table.

Picnics

Picnics in the parks are ideal, and shopping for the food is often half the fun. There is no problem finding cartons of fruit juice and branded canned drinks, but these are expensive unless you go to a super-market – various outlets are dotted around the downtown.

Water from the drinking fountains is potable, so it is worth carrying plastic cups around with you.

As well as picnic food from bakeries and

Ice Cream

Rome, of course, is famous for ice cream; you and your

Fontana della Barcaccia, Piazza di Spagna

children are likely to be tempted at every turn. Real ice cream fans may even want to plan their day's sightseeing round one of the best *gelaterie (see pp322–5)*.

It is far cheaper to buy either a cone or tub of ice cream to eat in the street, but in some of the more traditional places it is worth paying to sit down, as the interiors can be fun and attractive to children.

At Fassi, they have an old-fashioned ice cream making machine on display and at Giolitti, you can enjoy gargantuan sundaes in the elegant parlor *(see p113)*.

Investigating some of the hundreds of Italian ice cream flavors

Sightseeing with Children

Entrance to the Villa Borghese Zoo

General Tips

Rome does not have many museums with the kind of exciting hands-on exhibits that many other cities provide for children. However, Bernini's marble elephant *(see p112)*, and the fat *facchino*, or porter *(p109)*, tend to appeal to kids. The Capuchin cemetery at Santa Maria della Concezione *(p256)*, the catacombs *(pp266–8)*, and the Mamertine Prison *(p93)* will capture more ghoulish imaginations, and children will also enjoy putting their hands into the Bocca della Verità *(p204)*.

Keep your children's interest alive by looking for details like the dirty toenails on figures in Caravaggio's paintings; the Etruscan votives, which were offered to the gods, at the Villa Giulia *(pp264–5)*; and the illusory collapsing ceiling in the Chiesa Nuova, as well as the fake dome of Sant'Ignazio di Loyola *(see p108)*.

Museums your children will enjoy include **Museo Explora**, full of interesting hands-on exhibits for children, and the Museo delle Mura, which explores a short length of the Aurelian Wall *(p198)*. Among the churches, St. Peter's *(see p228)* and San Clemente *(see pp188–9)* are the most fun.

At the Vatican, children will like the animal statues and mosaics in the Animal Gallery and also the Sistine Ceiling *(p244)*, especially once they know that Michelangelo had to paint it hunched up on a scaffolding platform. Remember that Vatican dress etiquette *(see p229)* applies to kids too.

Ancient Ruins

The ancient ruins best appreciated by children are the Colosseum *(see pp94–7)*, and Trajan's Markets *(see pp90–91)*. You can still make out

what both these buildings looked like from their remains. The scant ruins of the Forum and Palatine, on the other hand, may not appeal so strongly. Ostia Antica, where the remains include a theater, shop, and 20-seater public toilet, is much more likely to interest them *(see pp272–3)*.

Mosaics

There are scores of vivid, sometimes quirky, mosaics in buildings all over Rome.

Mosaic from the Vatican

Many of these are particularly appealing to children. Details in the mosaics range from brilliantly colored flowers, leaves, animals, and buildings (in the churches of San Clemente, Santa Prassede, and Santa Maria in Trastevere, *see* p188, p173 and pp214–15) to the debris of a banquet (in the Vatican's Museo Gregorio Profano, *see* pp232–3).

Entertainment

To find out what's going on for children in Rome, scour the movie pages of newspapers and the listings in *Trova-Roma* and *Wanted in Rome*, and entertainment websites *(see pp346–7)*. Most theaters, and movie theaters have reduced entry fees for children, but shows are often only in Italian. There are cartoons shown at Villa Borghese's Cinema dei Piccoli and traditional puppet shows every afternoon, except Wednesday, on Janiculum Hill. Located in EUR, **Sea Life** is a state-of-the-art aquarium that is worth a

Miniature train in Villa Borghese

Stand at the Christmas toy fair on Piazza Navona

DIRECTORY

General Tips

Museo Explora
Via Flamino 82.
Map 1 C5.
Tel 06-361 3776 (book ahead).
W mdbr.it

Entertainment

Sea Life
Viale America 93.
Tel 06-9970 6701.
W visitsealife.com/roma

Toys

Al Sogno
Piazza Navona 53.
Map 4 E4 & 11 C3.
Tel 06-686 4198.

Città del Sole
Via della Scrofa 65.
Map 4 F3 & 12 D2.
Tel 06-6880 3805.

Children's Clothes

Benetton
Via del Corso 288.
Map 4 F2.
Tel 06-6810 2520.

Lavori Artigianali Femminili
Via Capo le Case 6.
Map 5 A3 & 12 F1.
Tel 06-679 2992.

Rachele
Vicolo del Bollo 6–7 (off Via del Pellegrino).
Map 11 C4.
Tel 06-686 4975.

visit at any time of year. An appealing time for kids to be in Rome is over Christmas, when Piazza Navona hosts a Christmas toy fair, with stands selling toys and sweets.

Parks

Villa Borghese *(see p260)* has rowboats for rent; pony-cart rides; bikes to rent; a mini movie theater; a small fair; and a zoo. Villa Celimontana *(see p195)* has bike trails, " and open-air theater performances in the summer. Technotown, a multimedia playhouse, in the grounds of Villa Torlonia is fun. In EUR *(see p268)* is the Piscina delle Rose, a swimming pool open in the summer *(see p359)*. The Bomarzo Monster Park, 60 miles (95 km) north of Rome, was built in the 16th century for a mad duke. Children can clamber over its giant stone monsters.

Toys

A visit to a Roman toy shop can be a lot of fun. **Città del Sole** sells educational toys and games, while the window display at **Al Sogno** is a delight for kids who love stuffed animals.

Children's Clothes

Italians adore dressing their children up, especially on Sunday afternoons. Many shops sell beautifully hand-crafted children's shoes, and clothes. The downside is that they can often be expensive and impractical: dry-clean-only clothes are common and shoes are not made for mud. **Lavori Artigianali Femminili** sells handmade silk, and wool clothes for children up to the age of eight. **Rachele** offers top-quality handmade clothes for children, while **Benetton** has more wallet-friendly casuals.

Children enjoying pony-cart rides at Villa Borghese

SURVIVAL GUIDE

ONT·M

PRACTICAL INFORMATION

Romans often seem unconcerned by the priceless art treasures and ancient ruins that lie casually among the streets and buildings of their hectic 21st-century city. However, it's not always easy for visitors to make the most of these wonders; relaxed local attitudes make for dozens of variations in opening hours, and many places – including shops, banks, and offices – close for 2 or 3 hours over lunch, reopening in the late afternoon. On a more positive note, most of the main sights are within easy walking distance of one another. Start your day early and wear comfortable shoes. Rome can be a delightfully informal city to visit, but remember to observe dress rules and cover up in churches, since this is one area where regulations are strictly enforced.

Steps heading to Michelangelo's Piazza del Campidoglio

When to Go

Rome enjoys a Mediterranean climate, with hot, dry summers and mild-to-cold, rainy winters. From late March to June, and from September to October, the pleasant, sunny weather allows for plenty of time outdoors. Visitors can expect to pay more to stay during the high season, between March, and November. In hot August, most Romans are on vacation, and the smaller shops, and restaurants are closed, but all tourist sights stay open, the city is quieter, and you can find good hotel deals.

Visas and Passports

Italy is part of the Schengen agreement, which means travelers moving from one Schengen country to another are not subject to border controls, although there are occasional spot checks.

All visitors to Italy must register with the police within eight working days of arrival. If you are staying in a hotel, this will be done for you. Otherwise, contact the local *questura* (police station). European Union nationals, and citizens of the US, Canada, Australia, and New Zealand do not need visas for stays of up to three months.

Anyone wishing to stay for more than three months (eight working days for citizens from countries other than those mentioned above) will have to obtain a *permesso di soggiorno* (permit to stay). European Union citizens can apply for a permit at any main police station. Non-EU citizens must apply in advance in their home country for a permit to stay; it is very difficult for non-EU citizens to obtain a work permit. If you lose your passport, contact your embassy (see p369).

Customs Information

Duty-free allowances are as follows: non-EU citizens can bring into Italy 200 cigarettes or 50 cigars or 100 cigarillos or 250 grams of tobacco, 1 liter of spirits or 2 liters of wine, and 50 grams of perfume. EU residents do not need to declare goods, but random checks are often made to look for drug traffickers. To find out what you can take back from Italy to a non-EU country, contact that country's customs department. The refund system for Value Added Tax (IVA in Italy) for non-EU residents is very complex (see p327).

Tourist Information

Information kiosks run by the Comune di Roma are dotted around the downtown and have English-speaking staff who provide free maps, leaflets, and advice. Alternatively, call their **Rome City Tourist Office** for information in English. Rome Council's two useful websites have information on all the sights as well as on current exhibitions, events, and hotels in the city. The **American Express** office can also be helpful to visitors. A privately run company called **Enjoy Rome** has an informative website and offices close to the Termini train station. Note that admission prices, and opening times change often, and sights can be closed for long periods for restoration (*chiuso per restauro*) or because of a strike (*sciopero*).

Tourist information sign

Opening Hours and Admission Prices

Museums are generally open all day, although most close on Mondays and on some public holidays. Open-air sights such as the Forum are open daily year-round, closing 1 hour before sunset.

The three-day **Roma Pass** (€30) provides free travel within Rome, free entrance to two museums or archaeological sites, and discounts for various exhibitions, events, and services. National and city museums offer entrance free of charge to EU passport holders who are under 18 or over 65, and discounted entry for those between 18 and 25 with a valid student ID card.

Entrance to churches is free, and many contain extraordinary works of art: keep in mind that you may be charged a small fee to see a certain area, such as a chapel, cloister, or underground ruins.

Some of Rome's sights, such as Nero's Aqueduct, and the Vatican Gardens, are accessible only on personal application or by written appointment (see below). The Area by Area section of this guide gives opening times for each sight, and tells you whether there is an admission charge.

During the Beni Culturali (Ministry for Culture, and Heritage) week in April, admission to all state-run sites is free.

The weekly supplement TrovaRoma (see p375) has a small English section with details of current exhibitions.

Sightseeing Permits

To visit certain sights in Rome, you need to obtain a written permit, and arrange your visit in advance, particularly for archaeological sites, which may sometimes be closed during excavations. Call the **Rome City Tourist Office** number on page 377, giving your name, the number of people in your party (individual visits are generally not possible), and when you would like to visit. You may then be asked to send written confirmation by email or fax.

Social Customs and Etiquette

Romans are generally courteous and friendly to foreign visitors. Italians are delighted at any effort to speak their language, so it is worth learning a few phrases (see p439). Italians tend to drink only with meals and are unlikely to be seen drunk – obvious drunkenness is frowned upon. Smoking is banned on public transportation, and in restaurants, bars, and cafés.

Visiting Churches

Many of Italy's churches are very dark, but they usually have electric, coin-operated light meters to illuminate chapels and works of art. Recorded information in several languages is also often available. Dress codes (see below) are firmly upheld in churches and should be respected. St. Peter's (see pp228–31) is especially strict – you cannot wear shorts.

Catholic Services

For many Catholics, a visit to Rome means an audience with the pope. General audiences are usually held every Wednesday at 10:30am either in St. Peter's Square, indoors at the Sala Paolo

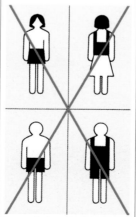
Unacceptable dress in church: both sexes should cover torsos, upper arms, and legs

The altar in church of Santa Maria Maggiore

VI, or at Castel Gandolfo. To attend an audience, call the **Prefettura della Casa Pontificia** (see p229) or go in person to the office through the bronze doors on the right of the colonnade in St. Peter's Square (9am–1pm). Travel agencies can also arrange an audience as part of a coach tour.

Mass is held daily in the main churches of Rome (High Mass is on Sunday). Confession is heard in St. Peter's (see pp228–31), San Giovanni in Laterano (pp182–3), San Paolo fuori le Mura (p269), Santa Maria Maggiore (pp174–5), the Gesù (pp110–11), Santa Sabina (p206), and Sant'Ignazio (p108). English-speaking Catholic churches include San Clemente (see p189) and Santa Susanna (see p257).

For details of non-Catholic services see p369.

Tipping

Service is sometimes included in the bill at restaurants, bars and cafés. Italians usually tip a few euros if the service was good. It is not necessary to tip taxi drivers, though you should round up to the next euro. Keep small change handy for sacristans, cleaners, doormen, and porters.

Accessibility to Public Restrooms

Public restrooms are few and far between. There are clean ones by the Colosseum (with facilities for the disabled) and at St. Peter's. Most cafés will let you use theirs if you ask.

Disabled access sign at the Vatican

Travelers with Special Needs

Rome is not particularly well-equipped for disabled visitors. The **Disabled Customer Assistance** center at Termini station offers help, and advice on train travel. Disabled travelers needing assistance getting on and off the train should reserve a special lift service 12 hours in advance, stating the names of all the stations at which they require help. A limited number of buses and streetcars have wheelchair access, and only a few metro stations have elevators. Ramps, elevators, and modified restrooms are available in an increasing number of places, including Termini station, although you may find an elevator out of order or a ramp blocked by an illegally parked car. Some restaurants have wheelchair access to the dining area, but not to the restroom.

If you are traveling without an escort, consider a specially designed package tour, or contact an organization for disabled travelers before you go.

The Vatican Museums, Sistine Chapel, and St. Peter's are all accessible by wheelchair.

Senior Travelers

EU citizens over 65 have free entry to many museums, and discounts for *anziani* (elderly citizens) are available at most other sights and on some Trenitalia *(see p379)* tickets.

Student Information

If you are an EU passport holder, it is worth having an International Student Identity Card (ISIC) or a Youth International Educational Exchange Card (YIEE) because you will receive reduced admission prices to national museums. Non-EU members with an ISIC or a YIEE card can also benefit from discounts at some private museums.

Contact the **Centro Turistico Studentesco** for general student information. The **Associazione Italiana Alberghi per la Gioventù** (the Italian YHA) operates four hostels across the city.

International Student Identity Card

Gay and Lesbian Travelers

The main venue for Rome's gay community is the gay-friendly bar **Coming Out** *(see p355)*, near the Colosseum. The Gay Pride parade takes place in June. The two-month-long **Gay Village** event (one of Europe's largest gay festivals) begins in July. In Rome, displays of public affection between same-sex individuals are not common, and some violence against homosexuals has been reported in the past.

Rome Time

Rome is 1 hour ahead of Greenwich Mean Time (GMT). Examples of the time difference with Rome for other major cities are as follows: London: –1 hour; New York: –6 hours; Dallas: –7 hours; Los Angeles: –9 hours; Perth: +7 hours; Sydney: +9 hours; Auckland: +11 hours; Tokyo: +8 hours. These figures can vary slightly for brief periods during local changes in summer. For all official purposes, Italians use the 24-hour clock.

Electrical Adapters

Electric current in Italy is 220V AC, with two- or three-pin round-pronged plugs. Adapters can be bought in most countries. Most hotels of three or more stars have hair dryers and shaver outlets in all bedrooms.

Conversion Table

US to Metric
1 inch = 2.54 centimeters
1 foot = 30 centimeters
1 mile = 1.6 kilometers
1 ounce = 28 grams
1 pound = 454 grams
1 pint = 0.47 liters
1 gallon = 3.8 liters

Metric to US
1 centimeter = 0.4 inches
1 meter = 3 feet 3 inches
1 kilometer = 0.6 miles
1 gram = 0.04 ounces
1 kilogram = 2.2 pounds
1 liter = 2.1 pints

A Gay Pride march passing the Colosseum

Responsible Tourism

Rome is aware of the need to become more "green," and environmental initiatives are taking place across the city. Italian cooking has always placed an emphasis on local seasonal food, but Italians are also starting to understand the importance of reducing carbon emissions. Eating local is a good way to support the area's economy, as well as helping the environment.

Organic shops and restaurants are springing up across Rome. Buy regional food at **Spazio Bio**, inside the Città dell'Altra Economia, a large expo space dedicated to the promotion of an organic and sustainable lifestyle, fair trade, ethical tourism, and recycling (which is

Shady terrace at Rome's Bed & Breakfast Bio

gradually being introduced in Rome). Shops can also no longer use non-biodegradable plastic bags. Those dreaming of greener nights can book a room in one of the mini-boutique hotels and B&Bs offering an eco-friendly stay.

Two such establishments are **EcoHotel** and **Bed & Breakfast Bio**, both of which guarantee energy- and water-saving rooms, serve organic breakfasts, and offer free bicycles for rides in the surrounding parks and nature preserves.

DIRECTORY

Tourist Information

American Express
Piazza di Spagna 38.
Map 5 A2.
Tel 06-6764 2250.

Enjoy Rome
Via Marghera 8A.
Map 6 E3. **Tel** 06-445 1843.
W enjoyrome.com

Rome City Tourist Office
Termini Station (Platform 24). **Map** 6 D3. **Tel** 06-0608.
W turismoroma.it and
W 060608.it

Opening Hours and Admission Prices

Roma Pass
Tel 06-0608.
W romapass.it

Embassies

Australia
Via A. Bosio 5.
Tel 06-85 27 21.
W italy.embassy.gov.au

Canada
Via Zara 30. **Tel** 06-85 444 2911. **W** canada.it

New Zealand
Via Clitunno 44.
Tel 06- 853 7501.
W nzembassy.com/italy

United Kingdom
Via XX Settembre 80A.
Map 6 D2.
Tel 06-4220 0001.
W ukinitaly.fco.gov.uk

United States
Via Veneto 119A/121.
Map 5 B2. **Tel** 06-467 41.
W italy.usembassy.gov

Religious Services

American Episcopal
St. Paul's, Via Napoli 58.
Map 5 C3.
Tel 06-488 3339.

Anglican
All Saints, Via del Babuino 153. **Map** 4 F2.
Tel 06-3600 1881.

Jewish
Sinagoga (Tempio Maggiore), Lungotevere Cenci. **Map** 4 F5 & 12 D5.
Tel 06-684 0061.

Methodist
Via del Banco di Santo Spirito 3.
Map 4 E3 & 11 A2.
Tel 06-686 8314.

Muslim
The Mosque (Grande Moschea). Viale della Moschea 85 (Parioli district). **Map** 2 F1.
Tel 06-808 2258.

Prefettura della Casa Pontificia
Città del Vaticano.
Map 3 B3.
Tel 06-6988 3114.

Presbyterian
St. Andrew's, Via XX Settembre 7.
Map 5 C3.
Tel 06-482 7627.

Travelers with Special Needs

Disabled Customer Assistance
Termini Station (Platform 1). **Map** 6 D3.
Tel 199-30 30 60.

Student Information

Associazione Italiana Alberghi per la Gioventù
Via Cavour 44. **Map** 3 D3.
Tel 06-487 1152.
Fax 06-488 0492.
W aighostels.com

Centro Turistico Studentesco
Via Solferino 6A.
Map 6 D3.
Tel 06-462 0431.

Piazza Sforza Cesarini 26.
Map 11 B3.
Tel 06-6880 3290.
W cts.it

Gay and Lesbian Travelers

Coming Out
Via San Giovanni, Laterano 8.
Map 9 A1.
Tel 06-700 9871.
W comingout.it

Gay Village
Parco del Turismo (EUR).
W gayvillage.it

Responsible Tourism

Bed & Breakfast Bio
Via Cavalese 28.
Tel 335-7151 749.
W bedandbreakfastbio.com

EcoHotel
Via di Bravetta 91.
Tel 06-6615 6920.
W ecohotelroma.com

Spazio Bio
Città dell'Altra Economia
Largo Dino Frisullo.
Map 8 D4.
Tel 06-5730 0419.
W cittadellaltra economia.org

Personal Security and Health

On the whole, Rome is a safe, unthreatening place for visitors, but petty street crime is a problem. Do not carry more money than needed for the day, and leave other valuables or documents in a hotel safe. Cameras are less likely to be snatched if they are in a carrier bag rather than an obvious case. Take particular care in crowded places, such as train stations, or on full buses, and steer clear of bands of innocent-looking children – they may be skillful professional pickpockets.

Carabinieri in dress uniform

Police

There are several different police forces in Rome. The *polizia* (state police) wear blue uniforms with white belts and berets. They deal with all kinds of crimes and are the ones who issue *permessi di soggiorno* (residence permits) to foreigners and passports to Italian citizens (see p366).

The *vigili urbani* (municipal police) wear blue uniforms in winter and white in summer, and can issue heavy fines for traffic and parking violations. They can usually be seen patrolling the streets, enforcing laws or regulating traffic.

The *carabinieri* (military police) wear red striped trousers. They deal with everything from fine-art thefts to speeding tickets.

The *guardia di finanza* are the tax police and wear gray uniforms. They deal with tax evasion and with customs; you will see them at the airport, behind the "goods to declare" counter.

To report stolen or lost items, go to the nearest police station (*questura*) or *carabinieri* office. If you believe your car may have been towed away, you should

find a member of the *vigili urbani* on the streets or have the Comune put you through to them by calling 06-0606.

What to Be Aware of

Be wary of bag-snatchers on mopeds who operate in quiet streets. Carry your bag at your side away from the road, or carry a discreet money belt or a securely fastened, long-strapped shoulder bag across your body. Equipment like video cameras should be disguised. Pickpockets (sometimes children) adopt highly sophisticated distraction techniques with pieces of paper or newspaper while they part you from your possessions in seconds. Take extra care of your valuables in market places or on public transportation. Bus routes 40 and 64, which run between Termini station and the Vatican, are notorious for pickpockets.

Thefts from cars are also rife. Jackets or bags should never be left visible inside a car parked on Rome's streets. Do not carry luggage on a roof rack. The streets to the east and south of Termini station are well-known for prostitution and drug-peddling, and are seedy at night.

Women traveling alone (or even in small groups) may need to take extra care. Women without male escorts attract more attention than they do in much of the rest of Europe and North America.

Beware of unauthorized minicab drivers who are probably not insured and frequently overcharge. They operate in particular at the airport and Termini station, waiting to profit from new arrivals. Hotel touts and unofficial tour guides are also best avoided; instead, stick to the official tourist agencies (see p297 and p369).

In an Emergency

For emergency phone numbers, see the Directory. For other medical attention, contact the First Aid (*Pronto Soccorso*) department of a major hospital such as **Policlinico Umberto I**, or **Ospedale di Santo Spirito**, or check the Yellow Pages (*Pagine Gialle*) for a doctor (*medico*) or dentist (*dentista*). For children, the **Ospedale Pediatrico Bambino Gesù** is renowned. Emergency care in public hospitals is free, even for foreigners.

Municipal police officer directing traffic

Poliziotto – a member of the state police

Carabiniere – a member of the military police

Police car

Ambulance

Fire truck

Lost Property

For items lost on a bus or on the Metro, contact the numbers in the Directory. Otherwise, ask at a police station. To make an insurance claim, report your loss to a police station and get a signed form. For lost passports, contact your embassy or consulate (see p369); for lost credit cards or traveler's checks, contact the issuing company's office (see p372).

Hospitals and Pharmacies

English-speaking doctors can be found at **Rome American Hospital** or by looking in the English Yellow Pages, which is available at some hotel receptions and international bookshops. For access to paediatricians, visit the **Ospedale Pediatrico Bambino Gesù**. The **Ospedale Odontoiatrico G Eastman** can help with serious dental problems.

Pharmacists display late-opening rosters (several stay open all night), and can usually supply the local equivalent of foreign medicines. The **Vatican Pharmacy** stocks some American and British pharmaceutical products. For minor problems, pharmacists can give advice and recommend over-the-counter medications.

Minor Hazards

No inoculations are needed for Rome, but take mosquito repellent and sunscreen in the summer. Be sure to wash your hands frequently if you use public transportation, especially in winter when colds and flu are rampant. The Tiber is polluted, but water from faucets, and potable street fountains is piped straight from the hills, and is fresh and palatable.

Travel and Health Insurance

All visitors should carry insurance for property and medical care. When buying airline tickets, ask if there are any waivers included in your particular ticket for medical problems, death in the family, or other emergencies.

Take out adequate property insurance before you travel (it is difficult to buy once you are in Italy), and look after your belongings while you are in Rome. Be particularly careful when using public transportation and when visiting crowded tourist sights, where pick-pocketing is common. If possible, leave valuables at your hotel instead of carrying them around with you. Some hotels provide personal safes in the bedrooms. You can set these with your own memorable number. (Do not use your date of birth; it is on your passport and registration slip.) To be prepared for all eventualities, it is advisable to keep a separate photocopy of vital documents, such as your passport and plane tickets, to minimize the problem of replacing them if they are lost or stolen. It is also useful to take along a spare passport-sized photograph or two.

Non-EU residents should purchase a primary medical travel insurance policy before leaving their home country. EU residents are officially entitled to reciprocal medical care, but the bureaucracy involved can be daunting. Before you travel, make sure you obtain the European Health Insurance Card (EHIC) from your department of health or a post office.

DIRECTORY

In an Emergency

Ambulance
Tel 118 (free from any telephone).

Fire
Tel 115 (free from any telephone).

General SOS
Tel 113 (free from any telephone).

Police
Tel 112 (Carabinieri); 113 (Police) (free from any telephone).

Samaritans
Tel 800-860 022.
Open 1–10pm daily.

Traffic Police
Tel 06-676 91.

Lost Property

Buses and Streetcars
Tel 06-6769 3214.

Metro
Line A Tel 06-4695 7068.
Open 9:30am–12:30pm Mon, Wed, Fri. Line B Tel 06-4695 8165.
Open 8am–1pm Mon–Sat.
After 10–15 days:
Tel 06-6769 3214.

Hospitals and Pharmacies

Ospedale Odontoiatrico G Eastman
Viale Regina Elena 287B.
Map 6 F2. Tel 06-8448 3258.

Ospedale Pediatrico Bambino Gesù
Piazza S. Onofrio 4.
Map 3 C4. Tel 06-68 591.

Ospedale di Santo Spirito
Lungotevere in Sassia 1.
Map 3 C3. Tel 06-683 51.

Policlinico Umberto I
Viale del Policlinico 155. Map 6 F2. Tel 06-499 71.

Rome American Hospital
Via E Longoni 69. Tel 06-225 51.

Vatican Pharmacy
Porta Sant'Anna, Via di Porta Angelica. Map 3 C2.
Tel 06-6988 9806.

Banking and Local Currency

ATMs are easily found across Rome. Many businesses will accept credit cards, but some smaller family-run establishments still only accept cash. Exchanging money and traveler's checks can involve a lot of paperwork. Banks and post office exchange rates are generally more favorable than those offered by travel agents. Carry some small change, since coins are needed for tips and illuminating works of art and chapels in churches *(see p367)*.

The Banca d'Italia, Italy's central bank

Banks and Bureaux de Change

It is best to have a few euros when you arrive, so you won't have to change money immediately. However, ATMs are found everywhere, including the airports.

For the best exchange rates, change money at a bank (look for the sign *Cambio*). Exchange offices and hotels tend to give poor rates, even if they charge modest commissions. At the Vatican Museums *(see p233)*, you won't be charged any commission. The American Express office *(see p369)* offers good rates and is open on Saturday mornings.

Lines at banks can be long and the form-filling involved in changing money can take up a lot of time. Take some form of identification with you, such as a passport. You may be asked to leave handbags, shopping bags, and metal objects in the small lockers outside the bank.

Post offices also give good exchange rates, but lines can be long here as well. Currency can

only be changed at the main post offices, such as the one near Piramide Metro station.

Banks are usually open 8:30am–1:20pm and 3–4:30pm Mon–Fri, but opening times vary. They are always closed on public holidays.

Bureaux de change have more generous opening times, similar to shop hours. The two exchange offices at Termini station *(see p378)* are also open on Sundays.

ATMs

ATM machines (*Bancomat*) can be found throughout the city and accept a wide range of credit and debit cards. The daily limit for withdrawals is usually €250. A fee is charged for each withdrawal. ATM crime (mainly related to card cloning rather than to theft) has been reported in the past. Always use caution at an ATM machine: cover the hand that is typing the code with the other hand, and avoid withdrawing cash from any machine you are unsure about.

Credit Cards and Traveler's Checks

Credit cards, are now much more widely accepted in hotels, restaurants, and shops. All major credit and charge cards (American Express, MasterCard, Visa, Diners Club) are well known. Banks and ATMs are more likely to accept Visa cards for cash advances, but MasterCard is accepted by many retail outlets in Italy. Take both if you have them. Paying for anything in foreign currency will almost always be expensive.

Some restaurants and shops set a minimum expenditure level, below which they will not accept credit card payment. Ask first or check you have some cash just in case.

Traveler's checks are not as popular as they used to be, and tourists are finding it increasingly hard to cash or spend them. If you decide to use them, choose a well-known name such as American Express. Record the traveler's check numbers and refund addresses separately from the checks themselves in case they are stolen.

DIRECTORY

Banks and Bureaux de Change

Banca Intesa San Paolo
Piazza di Spagna 18. **Map** 5 A2.
Tel 06-697 7471. **Open**
8:30am–1:30pm, 2:45–4:15pm
Mon–Fri; 8:30am–12:45pm Sat.

Banca Nazionale del Lavoro BNL
Piazza Venezia 6. **Map** 12 F4.
Tel 06-678 2979. **Open**
8:35am–1:35pm, 2:45–4:15pm
Mon–Fri.

Lost and Stolen Credit Cards

American Express
Tel 06-7290 0347 or 06-72282.

Diners Club
Tel 800-864 064 (toll free).

Visa and MasterCard
Tel 800-819 014 (toll free).

The Euro

The euro (€) is the common currency of the European Union. It went into general circulation on January 1, 2002, initially for 12 participating countries. Italy was one of those 12 countries.

The area comprising the EU member states using the euro as sole official currency is known as the eurozone. Several EU members have opted out of joining this common currency.

Euro notes are identical throughout the eurozone, each one including designs of fictional architectural structures. The coins, however, have one side identical (the value side), and one side with an image unique to each country. Notes and coins are exchangeable in all participating euro countries.

Euro Bills

Euro bills come in seven denominations. The €5 bill (gray in color) is the smallest, followed by the €10 bill (pink), €20 bill (blue), €50 bill (orange), €100 bill (green), €200 note (yellow), and €500 bill (purple). All bills show the stars of the European Union.

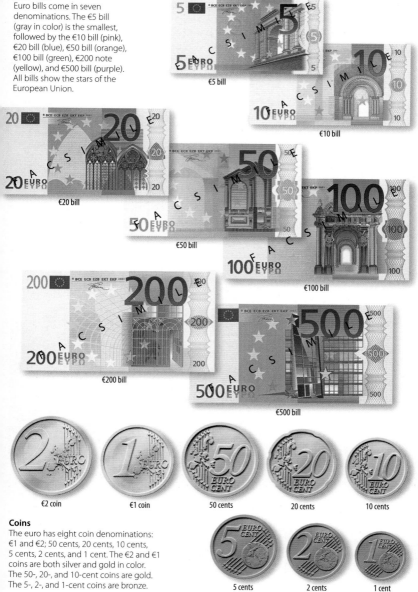

€5 bill

€10 bill

€20 bill

€50 bill

€100 bill

€200 bill

€500 bill

€2 coin

€1 coin

50 cents

20 cents

10 cents

Coins

The euro has eight coin denominations: €1 and €2; 50 cents, 20 cents, 10 cents, 5 cents, 2 cents, and 1 cent. The €2 and €1 coins are both silver and gold in color. The 50-, 20-, and 10-cent coins are gold. The 5-, 2-, and 1-cent coins are bronze.

5 cents

2 cents

1 cent

Communications and Media

With the most recent advances in technology, it is easier, and cheaper than ever to stay in touch with family, and friends while abroad. Even if you don't have a phone with Internet capabilities, you'll find that Wi-Fi and Internet cafés are everywhere in Rome, and phone cards offering very reasonable call rates abound. You can stay abreast of the news at home through BBC World (most likely available in your hotel) or the English-language publications available at many newsagents in the center of Rome.

Telephone company logo

International and Local Telephone Calls

Privately owned "call centers" offer a convenient way of making private long-distance calls. They are equipped with several metered telephones in sound-proof booths. An assistant will assign you a booth and meter your call. You pay at the desk when you are finished, so coins are not needed. Call centers tend to be open from early morning until late night and many also offer fax, Internet, and photocopying facilities.

Reaching the Right Number

- The code for Rome is 06 (required also within the city).
- Multilingual directory assistance is at 1254 (press 2).
- Operator assistance is at 170. Collect calls, and credit card calls are also accepted.
- Italian directory assistance is at 1254 (press 1).
- To reach the operator in your own country to place a collect or credit card call, dial 800 172 then: 444 for AT&T, US; 401 for Verizon, US; 405 for US Sprint; 441 for the UK; 610 for Telstra, Australia; and 611 for Optus, Australia.

In the wake of the cell phone revolution, demand for public telephones has decreased considerably. However, there are some payphones around the city, mostly located at train stations, metro stations, and other main hubs. From these you can direct-dial long-distance and most international calls. The newest phones take coins; the older ones only take telephone cards (ask for a *scheda telefonica*), available in several denominations. Telephone cards are sold in shops, and tobacconists *(tabacchi)*. Break off the marked corner, insert the card arrow-first, and the value of the unexpired units will show in a display window. After your call, the card can be retrieved and reused until it expires.

Public telephone sign

International phone cards, such as the Europa card, are by far the cheapest option if calling overseas from Italy. They come in either €5 or €10 cards, which give 120 (or more) minutes of calling time. To use them, dial the main number on the card, key in the PIN, and then dial the number required.

Any Italian landline telephone number dialed needs to have the full relevant local code (including the zero) dialed in front of it, even if you are calling within the same city. Cell phone number prefixes begin with a 3, and do not require a 0.

Keep in mind that telephone calls from hotel rooms are usually very expensive, sometimes marked up by as much as several hundred percent.

Cell Phones

If you are staying in Rome for a considerable period of time, it is probably worth buying an Italian SIM card, with its own telephone number, to use with your own phone, provided you have a GSM-compatible phone with a removable SIM card. You must show an official ID (such as a passport) when buying a SIM card. There are four main cell carriers: Vodafone, TIM, Tre, and Wind. The SIM cards cost around €15 and usually come with €5 of free credit. They can be purchased, and recharged, from various cell phone retailers throughout the city.

Once you have the SIM, you can also recharge your credit with a scratch-off card *(ricarica)* bought at tobacconist's shops or some newsstands. Some tobacconist's shops have a computerized system where they key in your cell phone number, and put the credit on your phone for you, which is easier, and faster than following the instructions on the scratch-off card.

Internet café sign

Internet Access

Many hotels now offer Internet connection or Wi-Fi access so you can access the Internet and email with your own laptop (sometimes for an extra fee). There are also a number of Internet cafés (Italians call them *Internet point*) throughout Rome where you can go online, and use email; some even offer headphones and webcams so customers can use Skype or other chat programs.

There are plenty of Internet cafés, found all around the downtown. Many Internet points have Wi-Fi so you can access the Internet through your laptop with a password provided by the assistant. An anti-terrorism law requires Internet café staff to take your information from an official ID (such as a passport), so staff may want to take a photocopy before allowing customers to use the Internet on their computers. This does not apply to customers using their own laptops.

Post office sign

Postal Services

Post offices are multi-functional in Italy, used not only for postal services, but also for paying bills, managing certain bank accounts, and more. Lines can be long, and disorganized, so if you are just sending a regular letter or postcard, save yourself the exasperation, and buy a stamp at a tobacconist's shop. Then drop your letter in one of the mailboxes on walls around the city; most are red, with a slot for mail within Rome (*Roma e provincia di Roma*) and one for mail outside Rome (*per tutte le altre destinazioni*). There are also some blue mailboxes exclusively for foreign destinations (marked *estero*).

The postal service is quite reliable and efficient, though it tends to be slower around Christmas time. For urgent items,

Vatican post office sign

Vatican postage stamps

use the post office's express or registered service.

The Italian post office offers a *poste restante* service, where letters and packages addressed to you can be picked up directly at the post office. Post should be sent care of (*c/o*) *Fermo Posta* and the name of the relevant post office. Print your last name clearly in block capitals and underline it to make sure it is filed correctly. To collect your mail, you have to show your passport and pay a small charge.

Regular post office hours are generally from around 8:30am to 2pm (8:30am to noon on Saturdays and on holiday eves), but main offices stay open until well into the evening for some services (such as registered letters).

Newspapers, TV, Radio

Rome's main newspapers are *La Repubblica* and *Il Messaggero*. British and American newspapers are readily available, with the *International Herald Tribune* and the *Guardian* on sale on the day of issue. The *TrovaRoma* supplement in the Thursday edition of *La Repubblica* is generally considered the main guide to what's happening in the capital. The magazines *Wanted in Rome* (www.wantedinrome.com) and *Where Rome* (www.whererome. it) also have English listings. Some of these publications also have websites full of information.

The state TV channels are RAI Uno, Due, and Tre, matched by four private channels. Analog TV has been replaced by digital across the region, so all TVs must now have a digital decoder to

Vatican Post

The Vatican postal service costs the same as the state postal service, but is faster. Buy cards and stamps at the post office near the Vatican Museums entrance, or in Piazza San Pietro. Letters bearing Vatican stamps can only be mailed within Vatican City.

Foreign papers at a newsstand

pick up any channels; with the decoder, you can access these basic Italian networks, plus some other channels including BBC World in English.

Vatican Radio transmits on 93.3MHz and 105MHz (FM) and also broadcasts news in English.

DIRECTORY

Internet Cafés

Bibli
Via dei Fienaroli 28. **Map** 7 C1.
Tel 06-581 4534.
Open 5:30pm–midnight Mon, 11am–11pm Tue–Sun.

Internet Café
Via Cavour 213. **Map** 5 C5.
Tel 06-4782 3051.
Open 11am–1am daily.

Interpoint Yex
Piazza Sant'Andrea della Valle 3.
Map 12 D4. **Tel** 06-9727 3136.
Open 10am–10pm daily (to 8:30pm in winter).

Also: Corso Vittorio Emanuele 106. **Map** 12 D4.
Tel 06-4542 9818.
Open 11am–7pm Mon–Sat.

Also: Via dei Pastini 21.
Map 12 E2. **Tel** 06-9760 3301.
Open 11am–7pm daily.

Post Offices

Termini Station, Via Giolitti 14.
Map 6 E4. **Tel** 06-488 8741.
Open 8am–7pm Mon–Fri, 8am–1:15pm Sat.

Piazza San Silvestro 19.
Map 5 A3.
Tel 06-6973 7205.
Open 8am–7pm Mon–Fri, 8am–1:15pm Sat.

GETTING TO ROME

Many national airlines, including Italy's Alitalia, fly direct to Rome from most European cities and several in North America. Fiumicino airport now has a high-security terminal, Terminal 5, for flights to the US, and Israel. Ciampino airport is smaller and mainly caters to low-cost airlines flying in from other European cities. Rome also has train and long-distance bus links with the rest of Europe. These take a lot longer than flights (about 24 hours from London, for example, compared with about 2½ hours by air), but tend to cost about the same, so are they only really worthwhile if you want to travel overland. Trains are often crowded during the summer.

Arriving by Air

If you are flying from the United States, **Delta**, **American Airlines**, **US Airways**, and **Alitalia** operate regular direct scheduled flights to Rome, with services from New York. Flying time is about 8½ hours. **Air Canada** and **Qantas** operate from Canada and Australia, respectively. There are also direct flights from Boston, Atlanta, Miami, Philadelphia, and Toronto. However, it may be considerably cheaper for intercontinental travelers to take a budget flight to London, Paris, Athens, Frankfurt, or Amsterdam and continue the journey to Rome from there. **British Airways** and Alitalia both operate direct scheduled flights from London Heathrow to Rome (Fiumicino), and you can also fly from Gatwick. **Swiss** and **KLM** also fly to Rome from London, and other British cities. A plane change in Zurich or Amsterdam is usually involved.

Excursion fares generally offer the best value in scheduled flights, but you must purchase them well in advance. They are subject to penalty clauses if you

Part of the extension to Fiumicino airport

cancel, so it is advisable to take out insurance as soon as you buy your ticket.

In addition to BA and Alitalia, you can buy low-cost tickets direct from airlines **easyJet** and **Ryanair**, which have daily flights from London, and other locations to Rome. Hotels, and car rental can also be booked via these airlines' websites, and both offer their own privately chartered bus to transport incoming passengers from Ciampino airport to Termini.

Alitalia flight tickets

Regular charter flights from the UK to Ciampino airport run year-round. Most leave from Stansted, Gatwick, and Luton, but there are also flights that leave from Manchester, Glasgow, and Birmingham. The price of fares varies, peaking in summer and in Holy Week for the Pope's Easter blessing. In Rome, the American Express travel office (see p369) will also book flights.

Fiumicino Airport

Rome has two international airports. Leonardo da Vinci – known as Fiumicino – is the largest one and handles most scheduled flights, as well as several easyJet routes. It is located about 18 miles (30 km) southwest of the city and has four terminals: 1 for domestic flights, 2 for EU flights, 3 for international flights, and 5 for flights to the US or Israel. The vast shopping area inside the airport offers a variety of stores, selling the most important Italian brands.

From Fiumicino there are two types of trains to Rome: one (€8) runs every 15–30 minutes

Check-in area at Fiumicino, Rome's main international airport

(5:57am–11:27pm) to Fara Sabina station, stopping at Trastevere, Ostiense, Tuscolana, and Tiburtina, but not Termini. The other train, known as the "Leonardo Express," is faster and more expensive (€14), running nonstop to Termini every half-hour (6:37am–11:37pm). If the ticket office is not open, try the automatic ticket machine (you can choose to see the instructions in English). Remember to specify which train you want when buying your ticket.

Ostiense station is linked with Piramide Metro (Line B) where you can catch an underground train to the downtown from 5:30am until 11:30pm daily (to 1:30am Fri and Sat). It can be hard to find a taxi at Ostiense after 9pm, but there are buses (Nos. 63 and 30) to Piazza Venezia. At night there is a coach service from Fiumicino to Tiburtina station. Car rental is available from offices at the airport (see p387).

Check-in area at Rome's Ciampino airport

Train linking Fiumicino airport to Stazione Termini

Ciampino Airport

The other airport that serves Rome is Giovanni Battista Pastine Airport, known as Ciampino. It is located approximately 12 miles (20 km) southeast of the city and used by the majority of charter flights and low-cost airlines. Ciampino airport is always busy and sometimes chaotic,

so it is advisable to arrive there well in advance of your departure time.

Major car rental firms have branches at the airport (see p387), though you may find it less harrowing to travel into central Rome on public transportation or by taxi.

The fastest way to get to the center of Rome is by the private **Terravision**, **Atral/Schiaffini**, or **SITBusShuttle** bus services. Buses go direct to Termini station and tickets cost between €4 and €6 one way. You can buy them on board the bus. A cheaper option is by **COTRAL** bus to Anagnina Metro station, then by underground train to Termini. Tickets (€1.50, plus €1.50 for each large bag) can be bought on the bus. A local bus service also links the airport to Ciampino train station.

Airport Taxis

Always use the official white taxis with a "taxi" sign on the roof. They usually line up in the yellow TAXI lanes in front of the airports and stations. The Rome Comune has established a flat fee for taxi rides from, and to the airports: €45 to/from Fiumicino from/to anywhere downtown (inside the Aurelian walls) and €35 to/from Ciampino from/to downtown. The fare covers a maximum of four people with baggage included. If a taxi refuses to apply the flat fee, you should report the driver by calling 06-6710 70721 and stating the cab number, which is found on both the inside and the outside of the car.

DIRECTORY

Arriving by Air

Air Canada
Tel 06-8351 4955.
W aircanada.com

Alitalia
W alitalia.com

American Airlines
W aa.com

British Airways
Tel 02-6963 3602.
W britishairways.com

Delta
W delta.com

easyJet
W easyjet.com

KLM
W klm.com

Qantas
Tel 848 350 010.
W qantas.com

Ryanair
W ryanair.com

Swiss
W swiss.com

US Airways
Tel 8488 13177.
W usairways.com

Fiumicino and Ciampino Airports

Atral (Ciampino)
Tel 800 700 805 (toll free).
W atral-lazio.com

COTRAL (both airports)
Tel 800 174 471 (toll free).
W cotralspa.it

SITBusShuttle (both airports)
Tel 06-5916 826.
W sitbusshuttle.it

Terravision (Ciampino)
Tel 06-9761 0632.
W terravision.eu

Arriving in Rome by Train, Bus, or Car

Any overland journey to Rome is fastest by train, though there are bus connections to most major European cities. Within Italy, journeys between large cities are usually also best done by train, but when traveling from towns that are not on the main Intercity rail routes, buses can be quicker. For drivers, the Italian Automobile Club *(see p379)* provides free assistance, and excellent maps to members of affiliated automobile clubs from all over the world.

A Eurostar train

The concourse at Stazione Termini

Stazione Termini

Stazione Termini, Rome's main train station, is also the hub of the urban transportation system. Beneath it is the only interchange between the city's two Metro lines, and outside, on Piazza dei Cinquecento, is the central bus terminus. Though it is one of Rome's most stunning 20th-century buildings, it also has some unsavory aspects, so don't linger longer than necessary at night.

If you do arrive here late, there are usually taxis available (go to the official taxi stand) even in the small hours, and many of the city's night buses start at Termini.

In summer, the station gets crowded, and you can expect long lines. Termini has baggage lockers, a police station, a bureau de change, and tourist, and travel information offices. Other facilities include many tobacconists and newsstands (where you can buy bus and Metro tickets), as well as various bars and restaurants on the mezzanine floor, with more eateries and shops, including a bookstore, on the lower Termini Forum level. A post office is adjacent to platform 24, as are car rental desks. There is only one waiting room, located next to platform 1.

Of Rome's other stations, four are most likely to be of interest to tourists. They are Ostiense and Trastevere, for trains to Fiumicino airport and Viterbo *(see p273)*; Tiburtina, for some of the late-night and high-speed trains on the north–south line through Italy; and Roma Nord, for trains to Prima Porta.

Traveling by Train

Trenitalia, the Italian state rail company, has several levels of service, including the Regionale trains. These stop at almost every station, often have no air conditioning, and are much cheaper than the other trains. On Regionale and Inter-regionale trains, sometimes first-class seats are "declassed" so second-class ticket holders can sit there. The Eurostar, a cleaner, faster train, offers a first- and second-class service. It runs between Rome and Milan, Turin, Genoa, Bari, Naples, and Venice, with an extra fast *(alta velocità)* service operating on the Naples–Rome–Milan and Venice–Rome lines, although it now faces stiff competition from the high-speed **NTV** trains. You have to reserve a seat and you are charged hefty supplements for the privileges of speed and attendant services. Intercity trains, which are for fast long-distance journeys, also charge a supplement. First- and second-class tickets are available to the larger cities. From Rome you can also take international or Eurocity (EC) trains to destinations all over Europe.

Reservations are required on

Trenitalia logo

Termini, the heart of Italy's rail network and Rome's transport system

all trains except those on Regionale and Inter-regionale routes. Tickets for immediate travel can be bought at the station, but you should allow plenty of time to wait in line.

The Trenitalia website *(see below)* is useful for planning trips, checking scheduled train times, and buying tickets. If you book in advance or are a family with a child, you may be able to get a cheaper rate. However, it is easiest to go to a travel agency when booking a discounted ticket because Trenitalia's offers and fares change all the time.

An Intercity train

Traveling by Bus

Long-distance coaches (buses) terminate at Tiburtina, which is the city's main coach station. Information and tickets for travel to European cities are available from the **Eurolines**, **Baltour**, or **Italybus** websites. The **Appian Line** offers regular services within Italy. Its itineraries include Florence, Naples, Capri, Sorrento, and Pompeii, and, in summer, Venice, and Assisi. Local buses, serving villages and towns within the Lazio region, are run by **COTRAL**. All bus stations used by COTRAL in Rome are linked to Metro stations. Tickets are purchased on the spot and cannot be booked in advance. Some day trips from Rome by bus are described on pages 270–73.

Machines for Trenitalia Rail Tickets

These machines are easy to use, and most have instructions on screen in a choice of six languages. They accept coins, bills, and credit cards.

1 Touch screen: choose destination, train, and ticket type, make seat reservations, and choose payment method.

2 Insert coins here.

3 Payment with credit card: touchpad with slot for card below.

4 Receive train tickets, seat reservations, and change here.

5 Insert bills here.

Traveling by Car

To drive your own car in Italy, you need your driver's license, an international Green Card (for insurance purposes), and the vehicle registration document. A translation of your driver's license, available at Italian tourist offices abroad, is useful. Wearing seatbelts is mandatory in Italy. Headlights must be turned on even during the day on freeways and outside of built-up areas. Heavy fines are imposed for using a cell phone while driving. You must also carry a warning triangle and a reflective orange or yellow vest to wear if you leave your car in case of breakdown. Main routes to Rome connect with the Grande Raccordo Anulare (GRA), Rome's "ring road" (bypass). Tolls are charged on most Italian freeways. You take a ticket when you enter a toll road, and pay on

exit. Tolls can be paid with cash, credit cards, or a prepaid ViaCard. The latter is widely available (even at highway rest stops), and the toll is deducted from the card on leaving the freeway. Prices vary according to road type.

Official speed limits are 30–50 km/h (equivalent to 18–30 mph) in town, 80–110 km/h (50–70 mph), on two-lane roads outside town, and 130 km/h (90 mph) on freeways.

Directory

Traveling by Train

NTV
W ntvspa.it

Trenitalia
Tel 89 20 21.
W trenitalia.com

Traveling by Bus

Appian Line
W appianline.it

Baltour
W baltour.it

COTRAL
W cotralspa.it

EUROLINES
W eurolines.com

Italybus
W italybus.it

Eurolines bus connecting Rome with the rest of Europe

Arriving in Rome

This map shows the main bus, rail, and Metro links used by travelers arriving in Rome. The connections between Rome's two airports and the center of the city are shown, as well as links between Rome and the rest of Italy, and international rail routes from neighboring European countries. Travel information, including details of trip times and service frequency, is listed separately in each box.

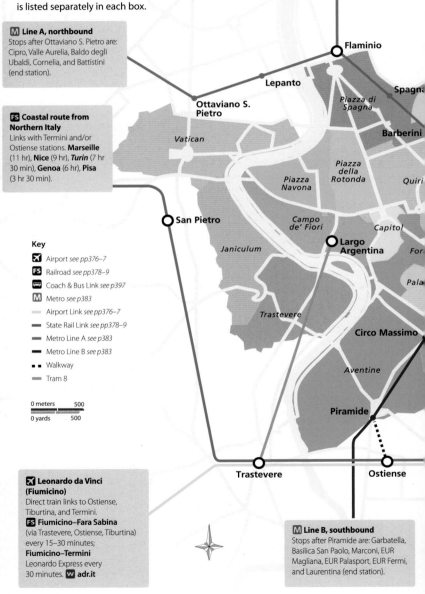

Local train connections
Links to Flaminio (Roma Nord station) from **Viterbo** (2 hr 30 min).

Ⓜ **Line A, northbound**
Stops after Ottaviano S. Pietro are: Cipro, Valle Aurelia, Baldo degli Ubaldi, Cornelia, and Battistini (end station).

Ⓕ **Coastal route from Northern Italy**
Links with Termini and/or Ostiense stations. **Marseille** (11 hr), **Nice** (9 hr), **Turin** (7 hr 30 min), **Genoa** (6 hr), **Pisa** (3 hr 30 min).

Flaminio

Lepanto

Spagna

Piazza di Spagna

Ottaviano S. Pietro

Barberini

Vatican

Piazza della Rotonda

Quiri

Piazza Navona

San Pietro

Campo de' Fiori

Capitol

For

Janiculum

Largo Argentina

Pala

Trastevere

Circo Massimo

Aventine

Piramide

Trastevere

Ostiense

Key

🛪 Airport *see pp376–7*
Ⓕ Railroad *see pp378–9*
🚍 Coach & Bus Link *see p397*
Ⓜ Metro *see p383*
⋯ Airport Link *see pp376–7*
— State Rail Link *see pp378–9*
— Metro Line A *see p383*
— Metro Line B *see p383*
▪▪ Walkway
— Tram 8

0 meters   500
0 yards   500

🛪 **Leonardo da Vinci (Fiumicino)**
Direct train links to Ostiense, Tiburtina, and Termini.
Ⓕ **Fiumicino–Fara Sabina**
(via Trastevere, Ostiense, Tiburtina) every 15–30 minutes;
Fiumicino–Termini
Leonardo Express every 30 minutes. 🆆 **adr.it**

Ⓜ **Line B, southbound**
Stops after Piramide are: Garbatella, Basilica San Paolo, Marconi, EUR Magliana, EUR Palasport, EUR Fermi, and Laurentina (end station).

For additional map symbols *see back flap*

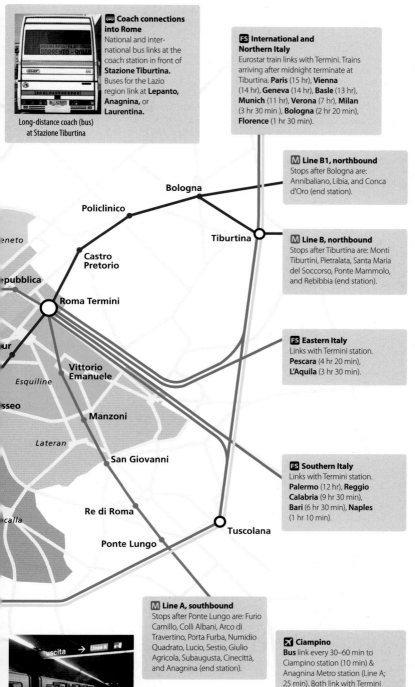

Coach connections into Rome
National and international bus links at the coach station in front of **Stazione Tiburtina.** Buses for the Lazio region link at **Lepanto, Anagnina,** or **Laurentina.**

Long-distance coach (bus) at Stazione Tiburtina

FS International and Northern Italy
Eurostar train links with Termini. Trains arriving after midnight terminate at Tiburtina. **Paris** (15 hr), **Vienna** (14 hr), **Geneva** (14 hr), **Basle** (13 hr), **Munich** (11 hr), **Verona** (7 hr), **Milan** (3 hr 30 min), **Bologna** (2 hr 20 min), **Florence** (1 hr 30 min).

M Line B1, northbound
Stops after Bologna are: Annibaliano, Libia, and Conca d'Oro (end station).

M Line B, northbound
Stops after Tiburtina are: Monti Tiburtini, Pietralata, Santa Maria del Soccorso, Ponte Mammolo, and Rebibbia (end station).

FS Eastern Italy
Links with Termini station. **Pescara** (4 hr 20 min), **L'Aquila** (3 hr 30 min).

FS Southern Italy
Links with Termini station. **Palermo** (12 hr), **Reggio Calabria** (9 hr 30 min), **Bari** (6 hr 30 min), **Naples** (1 hr 10 min).

Bologna

Policlinico

Tiburtina

eneto

Castro Pretorio

epubblica

Roma Termini

ur

Vittorio Emanuele

Esquiline

sseo

Manzoni

Lateran

San Giovanni

calla

Re di Roma

Tuscolana

Ponte Lungo

M Line A, southbound
Stops after Ponte Lungo are: Furio Camillo, Colli Albani, Arco di Travertino, Porta Furba, Numidio Quadrato, Lucio, Sestio, Giulio Agricola, Subaugusta, Cinecittà, and Anagnina (end station).

Ciampino
Bus link every 30–60 min to Ciampino station (10 min) & Anagnina Metro station (Line A; 25 min). Both link with Termini station. Private coach services to Termini station are also available.
W adr.it

Termini Metro station

GETTING AROUND ROME

Rome's downtown is compact and, even though walking absolutely everywhere would be overambitious, it is a city in which you can spend much of your time on foot. Since the main streets in the central city are usually clogged with traffic, driving, and cycling are not recommended, but brave motorbike or scooter riders can have great fun buzzing around on a rented Vespa. Traveling by bus and streetcar can be very slow, so use overground transportation only when you have a long way to go. The Metro, designed to connect the suburbs with the downtown, has no stops in the historic city center near the Pantheon or Piazza Navona, though it is certainly the fastest way of crossing the city.

Green Travel

As the largest, and most advanced city of the ancient world, Rome was the first to face (and combat) air pollution from burning wood. The fight against smog continues today, as many Romans rely exclusively on their cars. Car-sharing programs, city-owned bicycles, and some (but not enough) bike lanes, **electric-car charging stations**, and car-free Sundays (in the springtime) are among the initiatives. Video cameras prevent unauthorized cars from entering the *centro storico*, where many bus lines (three of which are electric) cover almost everything there is to see. Though often busy and chaotic, public transportation is always a better option than driving, and some used bus tickets will buy you discounted entry to selected exhibitions (see instructions on the ticket itself). Walking around the downtown is pleasant, so if you want to enjoy the warm sunshine and avoid public transportation, make sure you wear sturdy, comfortable shoes.

Bus stop listing details of routes served

Buses and Streetcars

Rome's mass transit company is called **ATAC** (Azienda Tramvie e Autobus del Comune di Roma). Scores of buses and a few streetcars cover most parts of the city. Most run from early morning until midnight, meaning the last bus leaves from the end of the line at midnight. There are also a few night buses.

Apart from some small electric minibuses (like the 116 and 119), no buses can run through the narrow streets of the city's historic center. But there are plenty of bus routes to take you within a short walk of the main sights *(see inside back cover)*.

Bus stops list the details of routes taken by all buses using that stop. Night buses are indicated by an "N" before the number.

There are several streetcars in the city, but the only line of tourist interest is the 8, which runs from Torre Argentina to Casaletto, going through Trastevere and Monteverde.

Special Bus Services

There are two tourist bus services: the 110 and the Archeobus service. The 110, a red, open-topped double-decker, is a hop-on/hop-off service that passes many of the city's tourist attractions. It leaves from Piazza dei Cinquecento every 15 minutes between 8:30am and 8:30pm (to 7pm in winter). Linking the downtown with the catacombs and the monuments on the Via Appia Antica, the Archeobus leaves Piazza Venezia every half-hour between 9am and 4:30pm.

Using Buses and Streetcars

The main terminus is on Piazza dei Cinquecento outside Termini station, but there are other major route hubs throughout the city, most usefully those at Piazza del Risorgimento and Piazza Venezia. Information on mass transit can be obtained from ATAC kiosks, the customer service office, or the ATAC website. Board the bus at the front or the back; the central door is reserved for people getting off. You must stamp your

A modern streetcar taking passengers through the city

One of Rome's red and gray ATAC buses

ticket in the yellow machine once you get on the bus. Timed tickets, *biglietto integrato a tempo* (BIT), can be used on all means of transportation.

Tickets

Tickets for buses, streetcars, and the Metro should be bought in advance, and stamped in the appropriate machine as soon as you start your trip. You can buy tickets at bars, some newsstands, and tobacconists, and Metro stations and bus terminals. There are automatic ticket machines at main bus stops, and Metro stations that take coins. Some

buses have a machine on board for buying tickets, but there is no way of knowing which buses have one, so purchase a ticket before you board.

BIT tickets are valid for 100 minutes, during which time you can take one Metro ride and as many buses, and streetcars as you like. If you are going to make four or more trips in one day, buy a daily (BIG) ticket. There are also three-day, seven-day, and monthly passes. To travel farther afield in Lazio, consider buying a regional BIRG ticket. Fare-dodging incurs a hefty on-the-spot fine.

Metro logo

Metropolitana

Rome's underground system, the Metropolitana, has two lines (A and B) that cross the city in a rough X-shape, converging at Termini station (*see inside back cover*). Line A (red) leads from Battistini in the west to Anagnina in the southeast of the city, from where buses go to Ciampino airport. Line B (blue) runs from Rebibbia in the northeast, branches off at Bologna station, then goes down to EUR in the southwest, where buses leave for the coast.

Stations are clearly marked by the Metro logo, a white M on a red background. Among the most useful stations are Colosseo, Spagna, San Giovanni, Ottaviano S. Pietro, and Piramide (for trains to Fiumicino). Both lines run from 5:30am until 11:30pm every day (to 1:30am Friday and Saturday). For more details, visit www.atac. roma.it. A third Metro line, C, is scheduled to open in 2015. A fourth line is also planned.

Useful Bus Routes

This map shows some of the buses that go through interesting parts of Rome with good views of major sights. The 40 Express is always full of tourists, since it goes from Termini to St. Peter's and the Vatican. The other routes are likely to be less crowded.

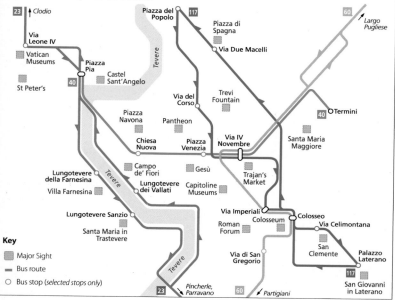

Key

◼ Major Sight

▬ Bus route

○ Bus stop (*selected stops only*)

Walking

Wandering through Rome's old center is one of the most enjoyable aspects of the city. You can take in the architectural details, absorb the streetlife, take detours at will, and peek into any church, shop, or bar that catches your interest. You can easily visit several of the main tourist sights in a few hours.

Explore the city area by area, using public transportation when distances are too far. Although some parts of historic Rome are now pedestrianized, a street that is closed to cars may still be used by cyclists and, illegally, by scooter riders. There have been many plans to create more traffic-free zones, but imposing such measures on a population as insubordinate as Rome's is not easily done.

During the height of summer, you'll have a more enjoyable time if you follow the example of the Italians. Walk slowly on the shady side of the street; have a long lunch followed by a siesta during the hottest part of the day. Continue exploring in the late afternoon, when churches and shops reopen, and the streets are at their liveliest. Wandering at night is delightful, as the streets are cool, and many facades floodlit.

Crossing the Street

First impressions suggest that there can be only two kinds of pedestrians in Rome: the quick and the dead. Even if you cross

Passengers sightseeing on an open-top tour bus

roads at traffic lights, and pedestrian crossings strictly in your favor, there is sure to be some van or Vespa hurtling toward you with apparently homicidal intent. Fortunately, Roman drivers have quick reactions and accidents are relatively rare. The best tactic is to be as alert and confident as Romans. The roads are very busy. When crossing, you should try to leave as large a gap as possible between yourself, and oncoming traffic. Step purposefully into the road, making eye contact with approaching drivers, and don't hesitate or change your course. Once a driver sees that you are determined to cross, he will stop, or at least swerve. Pedestrians must take particular care at night, when the traffic lights are switched to a constantly flashing yellow, turning the crossings into free-for-alls.

Street Signs

Theoretically, although it may not always seem to be the case, pedestrians have right of way at crossings when the green *avanti* sign is lit up. The red sign *alt* means you must wait. Underground crossings are indicated by a sign reading *sottopassaggio*.

It is easy to get lost in the maze of streets and piazzas of the historic downtown. Until you know your way around, you can follow yellow signs marking routes between the sights and piazzas of particular

interest to tourists. Routes leading to other landmarks are indicated by signs on a brown or gray background.

Guided Tours

Several companies offer guided tours in English; these include the excellent **Walks of Italy**, **Green Line Tours**, **Context**, and **Carrani Tours**. Full-day city tours including lunch cost around €100; half-day tours around €40. Alternatively, the **No. 110 Bus** passes many of the main sights on a 2-hour circuit. Tickets cost around €18, and the bus leaves from Termini every 15 minutes between 8:30am, and 8:30pm (to 7pm in winter); the website has further details as well as information on the Archeobus tours of the ancient

Directions for walkers

Watch out for children

Pedestrian crossing

Nuns walking in downtown Rome

Avanti: go! Pedestrians have right of way

Alt: stop! Traffic has right of way

monuments. Tour guides can often be hired at major sights, such as the Roman Forum *(see pp80–89)*. Employ only official guides and establish the fee in advance; they usually charge at least €50 for a half-day tour.

Driving

Driving in Rome can be an extremely intimidating experience for visitors. The flamboyant aggression of Italian drivers is notorious, pedestrians step out into the roads without warning, and the one-way system operating in much of the downtown makes maintaining a sense of direction impossible. You'll also find drivers passing on the wrong side, while scooters, and Vespas zoom among the lanes of traffic and go the wrong way down one-way streets. One rule to remember is to yield to the right. Additionally, non-resident drivers cannot enter the central city's ZTL (Limited Traffic Zone) during the day and on some weekend nights. There are cameras at the entrance of the ZTL, and cars without a permit will incur a fine each time they pass in front of the camera. The cameras are very visible, and there is always an electronic sign saying whether access is open to everyone *(varco aperto)* or restricted *(varco chiuso)*. You can call 06-57003 or check www.atacmobile.it for ZTL times.

No stopping

No parking

One-way street

No through road

Unless you are accustomed to driving in Italian cities and fully aware of the ZTL regulations and zones, leave your car at home – or, failing that, in a guarded parking lot.

Thefts from cars are rife in Rome, so never leave anything of value in your vehicle, even out of sight: areas such as Campo de' Fiori are patrolled by gangs on the lookout for anyone leaving cameras and other costly items in the car. You should also remove the car radio and GPS

if you can – you won't be the only person carrying these items around with you.

Take extra care if driving late at night. Not only do traffic lights switch to flashing yellow, but some drivers are astonishingly cavalier about driving under the influence of alcohol or drugs. In case of a breakdown, call the **ACI** *(see pp386–7)*.

Parking

The most convenient parking lot is below the Villa Borghese. Much of the downtown is reserved for residents with permits, but there are around 2,000 metered parking spaces marked with a blue line (from 8am–8pm or 8am–11pm, depending on the area). If you do find a legal place to park, however, you may return to find you have been hemmed in by double-parked cars. Locations of some of the most useful parking lots are listed on page 387.

Beware of illegal parking attendants, found especially at night in busy areas where parking is free, who direct you to a space (sometimes even an unauthorized one) in exchange for some change. This practice is against the law, but Italians often pay, for fear the attendant will damage their car if they don't.

Gasoline

Gasoline is very expensive. It can be bought from roadside gas pumps (many of which are self-service, which is cheaper; these pumps take bills or debit/credit cards), as well as from regular garages. Check whether your car uses unleaded gas *(benzina senza piombo* or *benzina verde)* or not. Late-night gas stations are listed on page 387. At night, most self-service stations are attended by illegal gas station attendants, who will put the gas in for you in exchange for a tip.

The state oil company logo

Illegal Parking

Rome's traffic police are vigilant. If you park illegally, your car may be clamped or (if it's causing an obstruction) towed away, so call 06-67 691 or 06-0606 before reporting it stolen. No-parking zones should be clearly marked, but check in case the sign is hidden by a tree.

zona rimozione fermata consentita per salita e discesa con conducente a bordo

Signpost for a tow-away area *(zona rimozione)*

A tow truck at work

Car Rentals

Major international firms (**Avis**, **Hertz**, **Europcar**) and **Sixt** have rental offices at the airports, Termini station, and in the city. However, you may get a better deal by reserving a car before you arrive through a travel agent or online, or by using a local firm (such as **Maggiore**). Make sure breakdown service and collision damage waiver are included. Prospective renters usually need to be at least 25 years old and have held a driver's license for at least a year. You will also need to leave a deposit – a credit card number is usually enough. Some firms also ask for an international license (available from your national automobile association).

Accident rates on Italian roads are high, so make sure you are fully insured against all eventualities. It is a good idea to join an internationally affiliated automobile association (such as the AAA in the US or the AA in Britain) so that if you do break down, the **ACI** (Italian Automobile Club) will tow your car without charging.

Details of road and traffic conditions (in Italian) are available from a special **Road Conditions** number. For more information on driving and parking in the city, as well as understanding road signs, and buying fuel, *see page 385.*

Moped and Bicycle Rental

Rome's narrow streets, and heavy traffic, combined with the seven steep hills on which it was built, make it a challenging place for even the most serious of cyclists. However, there are a few areas, such as the Villa Borghese, the banks of the Tiber, and some pockets in the historic downtown (around the Pantheon and Piazza Navona), where bike lanes make for a relaxing way to see the city.

Mopeds *(motorini)*, and scooters – like the classic Piaggio Vespa, meaning "wasp" – are good for getting through the traffic. You may want to stick to quiet streets to begin with, though.

Bikes and scooters can be rented from **Collalti**, **Bici & Baci**, and **Barberini Scooters for Rent**. There are also **Bike Rental** spots dotted around the city. Motorcyclists, scooter drivers, and their passengers must wear helmets by law; these can be rented from most rental shops. You may be asked to leave a credit card number or cash as a deposit when you pick up the vehicle *(see p359).*

The **Roma Bikesharing** program is good for short rides in the central city. You must enrol and pay a €10 deposit for a "smartcard," which can be recharged. You then have access to bikes at stands across the city, though these may be few and far between.

Taxi on a busy street in downtown Rome

Taxis

Official taxis in Rome are white, say "Comune di Roma" on the side, and bear a "taxi" sign on the roof. Do not use the taxis offered by touts at stations, and tourist spots; official taxi drivers do not solicit customers. Official taxis can be hailed at specially marked taxi stands or on the street (drivers are not supposed to stop in the street but many of them do). You can nearly always find them at the main tourist sights, airports, and stations (including Termini and Ostiense). Roman taxi drivers are not renowned for their friendliness and may even refuse to take you if you're going too far from the lucrative downtown or, conversely, if the ride is too short.

Taxis are not particularly cheap, so, unless you have heavy luggage or screaming toddlers, public transportation is usually a better option. Taxi drivers charge supplements for more than one bag, night rides (10pm–7am), and ravel on Sundays or public holidays.

Customers should make sure the meter is turned on and visible. The meter continues running while you are at a standstill, so traffic jams can become expensive. Drivers may take suspiciously circuitous routes. Italians don't tip taxi drivers; they simply round up to the nearest euro. You can call for a taxi (but you will pay from the time the driver gets the call from the switchboard) from: **Mondo Taxi**, **Radiotaxi 3570** or **La Capitale Radio Taxi**. Taxi rides to and from the city's

Motorbikes and scooters, a popular means of transportation in Rome

airports incur a flat fee for up to four passengers and their luggage (see p377).

River Tour

The summer service offered by **Battelli di Roma** runs from embarkation points near the Ponte Sant'Angelo, and Tiber Island. Boats depart every hour, starting at 10am, and all-day tickets cost €16 (see website for details). There are also dinner cruises on weekends.

Horse-Drawn Carriages

You can rent horse-drawn caleches (carrozzelle) for a gentle tour of the historic downtown. Carriages carry up to five people

Horse-drawn carriage offering tours from St. Peter's Square

and can be rented from many points: Piazza di Spagna, the Colosseum, Trevi Fountain, St. Peter's, Via Veneto, Villa Borghese, Piazza Venezia, and Piazza Navona. Trips last half an hour, an hour, half a day or a day. They tend to be expensive, but prices for longer rides are negotiable; establish the price before you set off, and make sure you understand whether the rate is per person, or for the whole carriage.

DIRECTORY

Electric-Car Charging Stations

Via Cola di Rienzo.
Map 4 D2.

Piazza Mastai. **Map** 7 C1.
🆆 colonnineelettriche.it.

Buses and Trams

Atac
Piazza dei Cinquecento.
Map 6 D3. **Tel** 06-46951.
🆆 atac.roma.it

Traffic Info
Piazzale degli Archivi 40.
Tel 06-57003.
🆆 agenziamobilita. roma.it

Guided Tours

Carrani Tours
Via V. E. Orlando 95. **Map** 5 C3. **Tel** 06-474 2501.
🆆 carrani.com

Context
Tel 06-9672 7371.
🆆 contexttravel.com/ city/rome

Green Line Tours
Via Amendola 32. **Map** 6 D3. **Tel** 06-482 7480.
🆆 greenlinetours.com

No. 110 Bus and Archeobus
Piazza dei Cinquecento.
Map 6 D3.
Tel 800-281 281.
🆆 trambusopen.com

Walks of Italy
Tel 1-202 684 6916
🆆 walksofitaly.com

Main Car Parks

Acqua Acetosa station.
Map 2 E1. Also: Lepanto Metro station. **Map** 4 D1.
Also: Villa Borghese.
Map 5 A1. Also: Piazzale dei Partigiani. **Map** 8 E4.

Useful 24-Hour Petrol Stations

Portuense
Piazzale della Radio.
Map 7 B5.

Trastevere
Lungotevere Ripa.
Map 8 D1.

Car Breakdown Services

ACI Breakdown
Tel 803 116.

Road Conditions
Tel 1518.

Car Rental

Avis
Tel 199-100 133
(centralized booking).
Also: Ciampino airport.
Tel 06-7934 0195.
Also: Fiumicino airport.
Tel 06-6501 1531.

Also: Via Sardegna 38A.
Map 5 C1.
Tel 06-4282 4728.
🆆 avisautonoleggio.it

Europcar
Tel 199 307 030
(centralized free booking).
Also: Fiumicino airport.
Tel 06-6576 1211.
Also: Stazione Termini.
Map 6 D3.
Tel 06-488 2854.
🆆 europcar.it

Hertz
Via Gregorio VII 207.
Tel 06-3937 8807.
Also: Stazione Termini.
Map 6 D3.
Tel 06-474 0389.
Also: Fiumicino airport.
Tel 06-6501 1553.
🆆 hertz.it

Maggiore
Stazione Termini. **Map** 6 D3. **Tel** 06-488 0049.
Also: Via Po 8A. **Map** 5 C1.
Tel 06-854 8698.
🆆 maggiore.it

Sixt
Stazione Termini. **Map** 6 D3. **Tel** 06-4782 6000.
Also: Ciampino airport.
Tel 06-7934 0802.
Also: Fiumicino airport.
Tel 06-6595 3547.
🆆 sixt.it

Moped and Bicycle Rental

Barberini Scooters for Rent
Via della Purificazione 84.
Tel 06-488 5485.

Bici & Baci
Via del Viminale 5.
Map 5 C3.
🆆 bicibaci.com

Bike Rental
Piazza del Popolo.
Map 4 F1.
Also: Piazza di Spagna.
Map 5 A2.

Collalti
Via del Pellegrino 82.
Map 4 E4 & 11 C4.
Tel 06-6880 1084 (bikes).

Roma Bikesharing
Tel 06-57003.
🆆 bikesharing.roma.it

Taxis

La Capitale Radio Taxi
Tel 06-49 94.

Mondo Taxi
Tel 06-88 22.

Radiotaxi 3570
Tel 06-35 70.

River Tour

Battelli di Roma
Tel 06-9774 5498.
🆆 battellidiroma.it

STREET FINDER

Map references given with sights, hotels, restaurants, shops, and entertainment venues refer to the maps in this section (see How the Map References Work, opposite). A complete index of the street names and places of interest marked on the maps follows on pages 390–99. The key map below shows the area of Rome covered by the Street Finder only. This includes the sightseeing areas (which are color-coded) as well as the whole of central Rome with all the districts important for restaurants, hotels, and entertainment venues. Because the historic downtown is so packed with sights, there is a large-scale map of this area on maps 11 and 12.

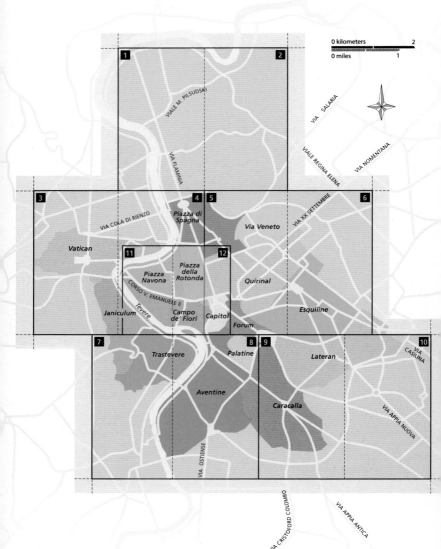

How the Map References Work

The first number tells you which *Street Finder* map to turn to.

❼ Trevi Fountain

Fontana di Trevi. **Map 5** A3 & 12 F2. 🚌 52, 53, 61, 62, 63, 71, 80, 116, 119.

The letter and number give the grid reference. Letters go across the map's top and bottom; numbers on its sides.

The second reference refers to the large-scale maps of central Rome (11 & 12). It is read in exactly the same way as the first.

The map continues on map 8 of the *Street Finder*.

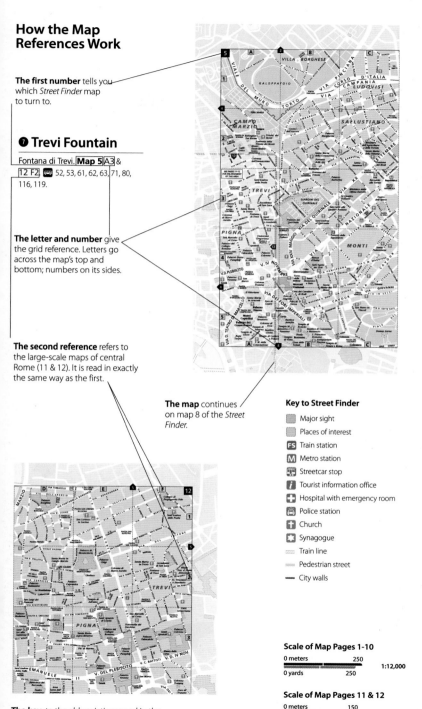

Key to Street Finder

- Major sight
- Places of interest
- **FS** Train station
- **M** Metro station
- Streetcar stop
- *i* Tourist information office
- Hospital with emergency room
- Police station
- Church
- Synagogue
- Train line
- Pedestrian street
- City walls

The key to the abbreviations used in the Street Finder is on page 390.

Scale of Map Pages 1-10

0 meters	250	
0 yards	250	1:12,000

Scale of Map Pages 11 & 12

0 meters	150	
0 yards	150	1:7,600

Street Finder Index

Key to Abbreviations used in the Street Finder

B.go	Borgo	P.	Piazza	S.	San, Sant', Santa
d.	di, del, dell', dello, della, dei, delle, degli	P.etta	Piazzetta	S. M.	Santa Maria
		P.le	Piazzale	SS.	Santi, Santissima
Gall.	Galleria	Princ.	Principe	V.	Via
L.go	Largo	P.ta	Porta	Vic.	Vicolo
Lungot.	Lungotevere	P.te	Ponte	V.le	Viale
M.te	Monte	Reg.	Regina		

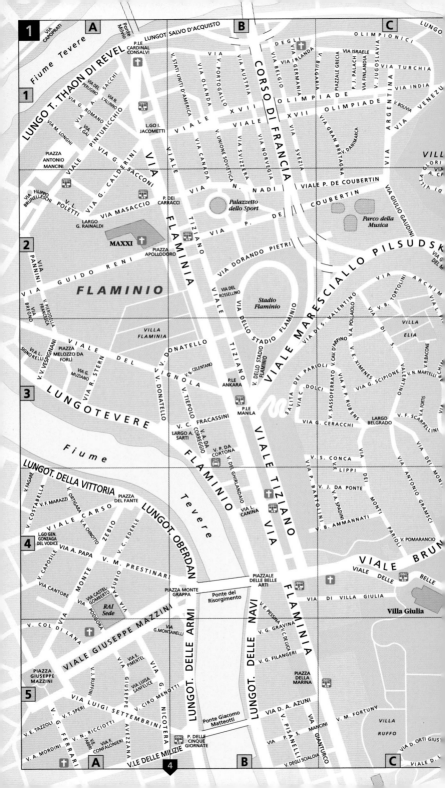

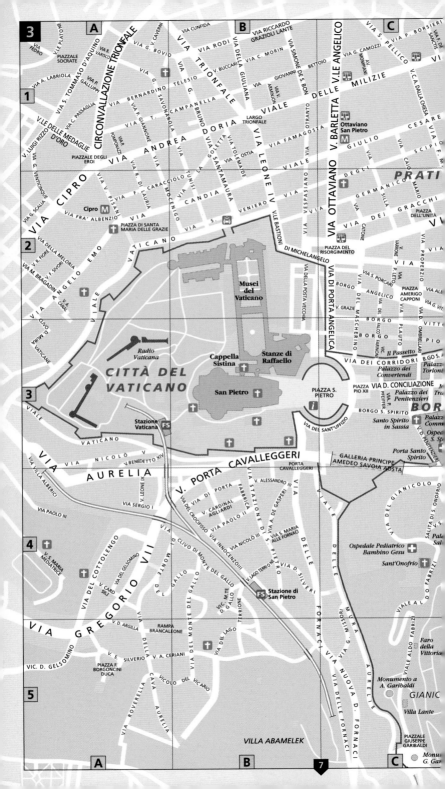

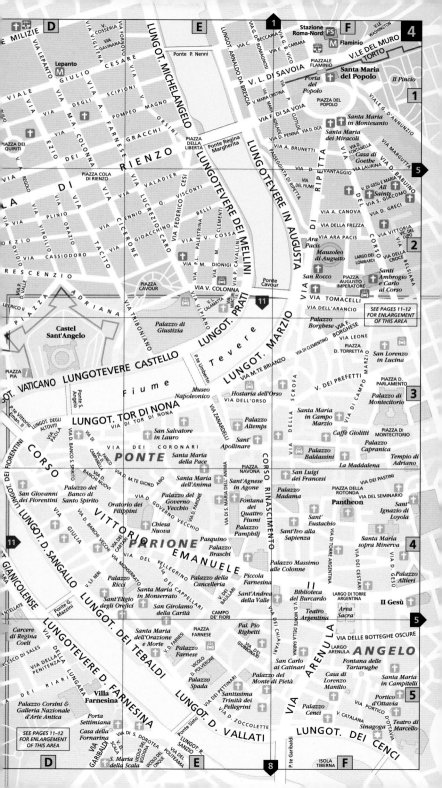

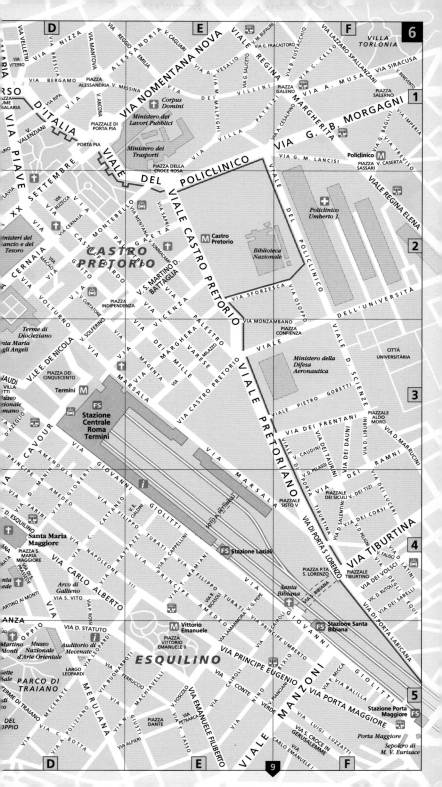

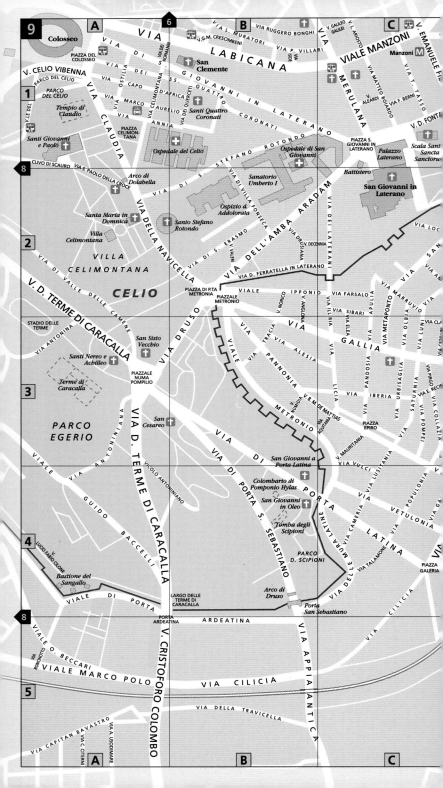

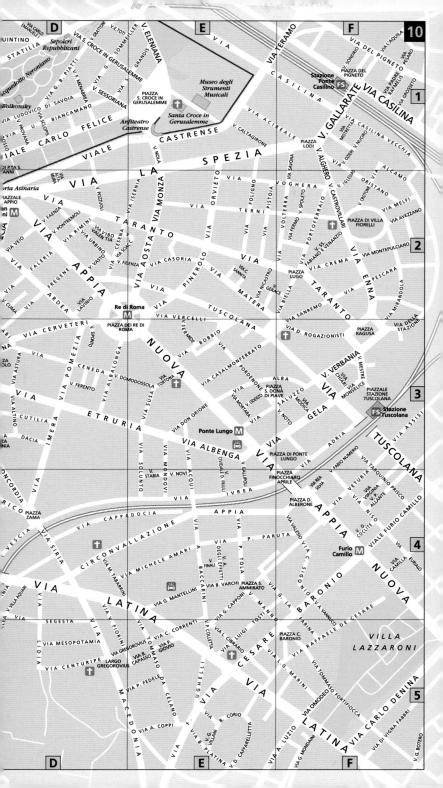

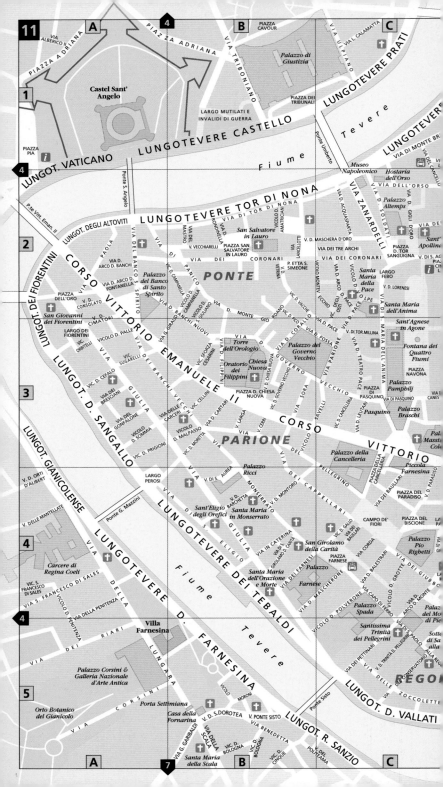

General Index

Acknowledgments

Dorling Kindersley would like to thank the many people whose help and assistance contributed to the preparation of this book.

Main Contributors

Olivia Ercoli is an art historian and tour guide, who has lived all her life in Rome. Bilingual in English and Italian, she lectures on art history and writes on a range of subjects for English and Italian publications.
Travel writer Ros Belford conceived the idea of the Virago Woman's Guides, of which she is now series editor, and wrote the *Virago Woman's Guide to Rome*. She has travelled widely in Europe and as well as writing guide books contributes to a variety of publications including *The Guardian*.
Roberta Mitchell heads the editorial section of the UN's Publishing Division in Rome, where she has lived for many years. An experienced writer and editor with extensive knowledge of the city, she has contributed to a number of guides to Rome including the *American Express Guide to Rome*.

Contributors

Reid Bramblett, Sam Cole, Mary Jane Cryan Pancani, Daphne Wilson Ercoli, Laura Ercoli, Lindsay Hunt, Adrian James, Leonie Loudon, Christopher McDowall, Davina Palmer, Rodney Palmer, Pardeep Sandhu, Debra Shipley. Dorling Kindersley wishes to thank the following editors and researchers at Websters International Publishers: Sandy Carr, Matthew Barrell, Siobhan Bremner, Serena Cross, Valeria Fabbri, Annie Galpin, Gemma Hancock, Celia Woolfrey.

Additional Photography

Max Alexander, Marta Bescos, Giuseppe Carfagna, Demetrio Carrasco, Andy Crawford, Peter Douglas, Mike Dunning, Philip Enticknap, Steve Gorton, John Heseltine, Britta Jaschinski, Neil Mersh, Ian O'Leary, Poppy, Rough Guides/James McConnachie, Alessandra Santarelli, David Sutherland, Martin Woodward.

Additional Illustrations

Anne Bowes, Robin Carter, Pramod Negi, Gillie Newman, Chris D Orr.

Additional Picture Research

Sharon Buckley.

Cartography

Advanced Illustration (Cheshire), Contour Publishing (Derby), Euromap Limited (Berkshire), Alok Pathak, Kunal Singh. Street Finder maps: ERA Maptec Ltd (Dublin) adapted with permission from original survey and mapping from Shobunsha (Japan).

Cartographic Research

James Anderson, Donna Rispoli, Joan Russell.

Research Assistance

Janet Abbott, Flaminia Allvin, Fabrizio Ardito, Licia Bronzin, Lupus Sabene.

Revisions and Relaunch Team

Namrata Adhwaryu, Beverley Ager, Emma Anacootee, Jasneet Arora, Rupanki Arora Kaushik, Shruti Bahl, Meghna Baruah, Sreemoyee Basu, Marta Bescos Sanchez, Tessa Bindloss, Peter Bently, Vandana Bhagra, Subhashree Bharati, Hilary Bird, Divya Chowfin, Lucinda Cooke, Michelle Crane, Vanessa Courtier, Kristin Dolina-Adamczyk, Peter Douglas, Vidushi Duggal, Claire Edwards, Jon Eldan, Simon Farbrother, Emer FitzGerald, Karen Fitzpatrick, Anna Freiberger, Vanessa Hamilton, Marcus Hardy, Kaberi Hazarika, Sasha Heseltine, Sally Ann Hibbard, Paul Hines, Stephanie Jackson, Claire Jones, Steve Knowlden, Priya Kukadia, Rakesh Kumar Pal, Mary Lambert, Maite Lantaron, Jude Ledger, Janette Leung, Carly Madden, Shahid Mahmood, Nicola Malone, Alison McGill, Jane Middleton, Ian Midson, Fiona Morgan, Jane Oliver-Jedrzejak, Helen Partington, Catherine Palmi, Naomi Peck, Marianne Petrou, Carolyn Pyrah, Pete Quinlan, Salim Qurashi, Rada Radojicic, Pamposh Raina, Marisa Renzullo, Ellen Root, Collette Sadler, Sands Publishing Solutions, Mathew Baishakhee Sengupta, Jane Shaw, Azeem Siddiqui, Susana Smith, Clare Sullivan, Avantika Sukhia, Rachel Symons, Andrew Szudek, Alka Thakur, Daphne Trotter, Ajay Verma, Karen Villabona, Diana Vowles, Lynda Warrington, Stewart J. Wild.

Special Assistance

Dottore Riccardo Baldini, Mario di Bartolomeo of the Soprintendenza dei Beni Artistici e Storici di Roma, Belloni, Dorling Kindersley picture department, David Gleave MW, Debbie Harris, Emma Hutton and Cooling Brown Partnership, Marina Tavolato, Dottoressa Todaro and Signora Camimiti at the Ministero dell'Interno, Trestini.

Photography Permissions

Dorling Kindersley would like to thank the following for their kind permission to photograph at their establishments: Bathsheba Abse at the Keats-Shelley Memorial House, Accademia dei Lincei, Accanto, Aeroporti di Roma, Aldrovandi Palace, Alpheus, Banco di Santo Spirito at Palazzo del Monte di Pietà, Rory Bruck at Babington's, Caffè Giolitti, Caffè Latino, Comune di Roma (Ripartizione X), Comunità Ebraica di Roma, Guido Cornini at Monumenti Musei e Gallerie Pontificie, Direzione Sanitaria Ospedale di Santo Spirito, Dottoressa Laura Falsini at the Soprintendenza Archeologica di Etruria Meridionale, Hotel Gregoriana, Hotel Majestic, Hotel Regina Baglioni, Marco Marchetti at Ente EUR, Dottoressa Mercalli at the Museo Nazionale di Castel Sant'Angelo, Ministero dell' Interno, Plaza Minerva, Ristorante Alberto Ciarla, Ristorante Filetti di Baccalà, Ristorante Romolo, Signor Rulli and Signor Angeli at the Soprintendenza Archeologica di Roma, Soprintendenza Archeologica per il Lazio, Soprintendenza per i Beni Ambientali e Architettonici,

Soprintendenza per i Beni Artistici e Storici di Roma, Daniela Tabo at the Musei Capitolini, Villa d'Este, Villa San Pio, Mrs Marjorie Weeke at St Peter's.

Picture Credits

a - above; b - below/bottom; c - centre; f - far; l - left; r - right; t - top..

Works of art have been reproduced with the permission of the following copyright holders: *Town with Gothic Cathedral*, Paul Klee © DACS, London 2011 239br.

The publishers are grateful to the following individuals, companies and picture libraries for permission to reproduce their photographs:

Accademia Nazionale di San Luca, Rome: 162br; **AFE:** 59bc, 63cra; Sandro Battaglia 61c, 63bl, 63br, 328br; **Aeroporti di Roma:** 376bl, 377tr; **Agenzia Sintesi:** 370bl, 370br, 370cla; Marco Marcotulli 370bc; **AKG-Images:** Andrea Jemolo 10br; **Alamy Images:** Caro 151tr; Cubolmages srl/Gimmi 387tr; Kathy DeWitt 307tl; Michele Flazone 44; Lautaro 194c; Prisma Archivo 241tl; Travel Division Images 310b; Travel Ink/Jim Gibson 374crb; Jozef Sedmak 200; Sklifas Steven 216; Superstock 64-5; John G. Wilbanks 274; Robin Wilkinson 371tl; Wilmar Topshots 252; AGF foto: 42–3c; **Aldrovandi Palace Hotel:** 299tr; **Alitalia:** 376cr; **Ancient Art and Architecture:** 20bl, 25tl,29bc, 38crb, 39tc, 48clb; **Artothek,** Städelsches Kunstinstitut Frankfurt, Goethe in the Roman Campagna by JHW Tischbein 138tr.

Babuino 181, Rome: 300tc; Baglioni hotels SPA: 298tr; Banca d'Italia: 372cla; Bed and Breakfast Bio: 369tr; **Biblioteca Reale,** Torino: 32–3c; Al Bric, Rome: 314br; **Bridgeman Art Library, London/New York:** 22br, 41tr, 164crb; Agnew & Sons, London 55tr; Antikenmuseum Staatliches Museum, Berlin 23bc; Bibliothèque da la Sorbonne 32c, British Museum, London 31cra; Christie's, London 97tr; The Fine Art Society, London 153tr, 281tl; Galleria degli Uffizi, Florence 35bl; Giraudon/Château de Versailles, France 37tr; Greek Museum, University of Newcastle-upon-Tyne 20br; Index/Biblioteca Publica Episcopal, Barcelona 110bl, /Piacenza Town Hall, Italy/31br; King Street Galleries, London 37bc; Lauros-Giraudon/Louvre 30br, 58br; Roy Miles Gallery, 29 Bruton St, London 248t; Musée des Beaux-Arts, Nantes 57cr; Museo e Gallerie Nazionali di Capodimonte, Naples, Detail from the predella of San Ludovico by Simone Martini 30tr; Musée Condé, Chantilly f.71v Très Riches Heures, 30tc; Museum of Fine Arts, Budapest 114br; Museo Archeologico di Villa Giulia 52cl; Palazzo Doria Pamphilj, Rome 109br; Private Collection 23br, 26bc, 28bc, 31tr, 181tl; Pushkin Museum, Moscow 115tc; Sotheby's, London 22bl; Vatican Museums & Galleries 45c, 235tr.

Capitoline Museums, Rome: 73cr; Enoteca Capranica, Rome: 313bl; **Cephas Picture Library:** Mick Rock 308tr; **Corbis:** Art on File 12bl; Alessandra Benedetti 367tr; Bettmann 8-9; epa/Ettore Ferrari 100cla; Owen Franken

306cla; Robert Harding World Imagery/Bruno Morandi 258; Ken Kaminesky 156; Bob Krist 307c; Araldo de Luca 70tr; Reuters/Max Rossi 42cb; Checchino dal 1887, Rome: 311tr; Corpo Nazionale dei Vigili del Fuoco: 371cl; Croce Bianca Italiana: 371cla.

Il Dagherrotipo: 147tc, 327bl, 378cla; Stefano Chieppa 291bc, 292bc; Andrea Getuli 289tl; Stephano Occhibelli 290cla, 290br; Paolo Priori 206tr; Giovanni Rinaldi 198tr, 288cla, 288br, 289br, 292cla, 293br, 293tc, 383tl; **CM Dixon:** 21bl, 28c, 272bl, 273tr, 273cl; Dorling Kindersley: Courtesy of Basilica San Clemente 178; Courtesy of the Ministero della Pubblica Instruzione 263bc; Dreamstime: Avorym 13br; Bramble100 66; Danileon 12tr, 190; Dennis_dolkens 107br; Krylon80 98; Luis007 294-5; Maui01 144; Monick79 167bl.

Ecole Nationale Superieure des Beaux-Arts: 25cb, 26–7, 250tr; **ET Archive:** 18, 21tc, 21clb, 23tl, 23tc, 27t, 31clb, 35crb, 36br, 41bc; Eurolines: 379bl; **Mary Evans Picture Library:** 22cla, 27cb, 28cl, 33cb, 34cb, 34bc, 35tl, 38cr, 38bl, 69br, 76tr, 83b, 93tc, 95br, 97tl, 137tr, 215bc.

Coraldo Falsini: 43tl, 346b, 347t, 347c; **Ferrovie dello stato:** 379cl, 379tr; **Werner Forman Archive:** 21cr, 24bc, 27crb, 27bl, 27br, 51ca, 177br; **Folklore Museum, Rome:** 212cra.

Garden Picture Library: Bob Challinor 175br; **Getty Images:** AFP 61br; AFP/Andreas Olaro 368br; Sylvain Grandadam 171tc, 364-5; Andre Thijssen 368tl; Stone/Richard Passmore 1c; Visions of our land 78; **Giraudon:** 19b, 32br, 40bc; Grandi Stazioni S.p.A: 378b; Grand Hotel de la Minerve, Rome: 302br; **Ronald Grant:** 56br.

Sonia Halliday: 23ca, 26br, 29cb; Laura Lushington 28bl; **Robert Harding Picture Library:** 27cra, 36bl, 81cr, 272c; Mario Carrieri 39tr; 347bl; Sheila Terry 43clb; G White 61bl; Hotel Due Torri, Rome: 301br.**Hulton Deutsch:** 59cr, 365c.

Imago, Hassler Roma: 316t.

Le Jardin de Russie, Rome: 317b.

Magnum: Erich Lessing 21tl, 91crb; **Mansell:** 23tr, 29bl, 30cb, 35ca, 58cl, 59cl, 77cla, 77c, 80cra, 94cb, 116c, 127tr, 134br, 135cr, 138bl, 141bl, 141bc, 174bl, 174bc, 176cl, 183crb, 198c, 212bl, 220bl, 247cb; Alinari 143bl, 256bc; Anderson 141crb, 165tl, 248crb; **Marka:** V Arcomano 37cr; D. Donadoni 11br; Lorenzo Sechi 10cla, 226bc; **MAXXI:** Roberto Galasso 261br; **Moro Roma:** 40cla, 41cl, 42bc, 43tr, 42br. Museo Nazionale Romano: Fabio Ratti 129tr, 129br, 165br.

National Portrait Gallery, London: 58tr, 59tr; **Grazia Neri:** Vision/Giorgio Casulich 116br, 158bc, Vision/Roberta Krasnig 126tr, 285tr; © **Nippon Television Network Corporation,** Tokyo 1999: 242bl and all pictures on 244-5; Nonna Betta, Rome: 312t.

Pantheon View, Rome: Gantcho Beltchev Photography 303tl.

Residenza Cellini: 298bc; **Rex Features:** Steve Wood 43crb.

Scala Group S.p.A: 51tr, 96tr, 127tl, 231tl, 280cl; Chiesa del Gesù 111tl, Galleria Borghese 36cla, 262tr, Galleria Colonna 159crb, Galleria Doria Pamphilj 50br, 107cr, Galleria Spada 50cl, Galleria degli Uffizi 20–21, 31bl, Museo d'Arte Orientale 177cl, Musei Capitolini 51br, Museo della Civiltà Romana 52tr, 52b, Museo delle Terme 25tr, Museo Napoleonico 53cr, Museo Nazionale, Napoli 25cl, Museo Nazionale, Ravenna 26cl, Museo del Risorgimento, Milano 40cb, 40–1c, Museo del Risorgimento, Roma 41tl, Palazzo Barberini 254bl, Palazzo Ducale 23cla, 25tr, Palazzo della Farnesina 220clb, Palazzo Madama 24cr, Palazzo Venezia 51cr, 68bl, San Carlo alle Quattro Fontane 37c, San Clemente 39clb, Santa Costanza 28–9c, Santa Maria dell'Anima 123tr, Santa Maria Maggiore 47tr, Santa Maria del Popolo 141tc, 141cra, Santa Prassede 30bl, 32clb, Santa Sabina 29ca, 33cb, Vatican Museums 23crb, 29tl, 29cr, 29cra, 31crb, 33tl, 33cr, 34cla, 35cr, 35br, 36c, 36clb, 45cra, 50cla, 52cr, 53bl, 226clb, 227cra, 233tl, 236 all, 238-9 all, 240 -1 all except 241tl, 243 all, 291tl; **Lourens Smak**: 11tl; Spirito Divino, Rome: 318t; STA Travel Group: 368c; Superstock: Tips images 208.

Trambus Open S.p.A: 384tr, **Topham Picture Source**: 42cl.

Vivi Bistrot, Rome: 319bl.

Zefa: 228cl, 229ca; Eric Carle 60ca; Kohlhas 229tl.

Thanks also to Dottoressa Giulia De Marchi of **L'accademia Nazionale di San Luca**, Rome for 162br, Rettore Padre Libianchi of **La Chiesa di Sant'ignazio di Loyola** for 108t, **Ente Nazionale per il Turismo**, and to **La Repubblica Trovaroma**.

Front Endpapers
Alamy Images: Jozef Sedmak Lfbr, Sklifas Steven Lfbl, Wilmar Topshotes Rtl; Corbis: Ken Kaminesky Rftl; Dorling Kindersley: Courtesy of Basilica San Clemente Rfbr; Dreamstime.com: Bramble100 Rtr, Danileon Rbc, Krylon80 Rfcrb, Maui01 Lfclb; Getty Images: Visions of our land Rfcr; Superstock: Tips Images Lbr.
Map Cover
4Corners Images: Massimo Ripani
Jacket
Front main and spine top–
4Corners Images: Massimo Ripani
All other images © Dorling Kindersley.
For further information see: www.dkimages.com

Phrase Book

In an Emergency

Help!	**Aiuto!**	eye-**yoo**-toh
Stop!	**Fermate!**	fair-**mah**-teh
Call a	**Chiama un**	kee-**ah**-mah oon
doctor	**medico**	**meh**-dee-koh
Call an	**Chiama un'**	kee-**ah**-mah oon
ambulance	**ambulanza**	am-boo-**lan**-tsa
Call the	**Chiama la**	kee-**ah**-mah lah
police	**polizia**	pol-ee-**tsee**-ah
Call the fire	**Chiama i**	kee-**ah**-mah ee
department	**pompieri**	pom-pee-**air**-ee
Where is the	**Dov'è il telefono?**	dov eh**el** teh-**leh**-
telephone?		foh-noh?
The nearest	**L'ospedale**	loss-peh-**dah**-leh pee-
hospital?	**più vicino?**	oovee-**chee**-noh?

Communication Essentials

Yes/No	**Sì/No**	see/noh
Please	**Per favore**	pair fah-**vor**-eh
Thank you	**Grazie**	**grah**-tsee-eh
Excuse me	**Mi scusi**	mee **skoo**-zee
Hello	**Buon giorno**	bwon **jor**-noh
Goodbye	**Arrivederci**	ah-ree-veh-**dair**-chee
Good evening	**Buona sera**	**bwon**-ah **sair**-ah
morning	**la mattina**	lah mah-**tee**-nah
afternoon	**il pomeriggio**	eel poh-meh-**ree**-joh
evening	**la sera**	lah **sair**-ah
yesterday	**ieri**	ee-**air**-ee
today	**oggi**	**oh**-jee
tomorrow	**domani**	doh-**mah**-nee
here	**qui**	**kwee**
there	**la**	**lah**
What?	**Quale?**	**kwah**-leh?
When?	**Quando?**	**kwan**-doh?
Why?	**Perchè?**	pair-**keh**?
Where?	**Dove?**	**doh**-veh

Useful Phrases

How are you?	**Come sta?**	**koh**-meh stah?
Very well,	**Molto bene,**	**moll**-toh **beh**-neh
thank you.	**grazie.**	**grah**-tsee-eh
Pleased to	**Piacere di**	pee-ah-**chair**-eh dee
meet you.	**conoscerla.**	coh-**noh**-shair-lah
See you soon.	**A più tardi.**	ah pee-**oo** tar-dee
That's fine.	**Va bene.**	va **beh**-neh
Where is/are ...?	**Dov'è/Dove sono...?**	dov-eh/doveh **soh**-noh?
How long does	**Quanto tempo ci**	**kwan**-toh **tem**-poh
it take to get to ...?	**vuole per**	chee voo-**oh**-leh pair
	andare a ...?	an-**dar**-eh ah...?
How do I	**Come faccio per**	koh-meh **fah**-choh
get to ...?	**arrivare a ...?**	pair arri-**var**-eh ah...?
Do you speak	**Parla inglese?**	**par**-lah een-**gleh**-zeh?
English?		
I don't	**Non capisco.**	non ka-**pee**-skoh
understand.		
Could you speak	**Può parlare**	pwoh par-**lah**-reh
more slowly,	**più lentamente,**	pee-oo len-ta-**men**-teh
please?	**per favore?**	pair fah-**vor**-eh?
I'm sorry.	**Mi dispiace.**	mee dee-spee-**ah**-cheh

Useful Words

big	**grande**	**gran**-deh
small	**piccolo**	**pee**-koh-loh
hot	**caldo**	**kal**-doh
cold	**freddo**	**fred**-doh
good	**buono**	**bwoh**-noh
bad	**cattivo**	kat-**tee**-voh
enough	**basta**	**bas**-tah
well	**bene**	**beh**-neh
open	**aperto**	ah-**pair**-toh
closed	**chiuso**	kee-oo-zoh
left	**a sinistra**	ah see-**nee**-strah
right	**a destra**	ah **dess**-trah
straight ahead	**sempre dritto**	**sem**-preh **dree**-toh
near	**vicino**	vee-**chee**-noh
far	**lontano**	lon-**tah**-noh
up	**su**	**soo**
down	**giù**	**joo**
early	**presto**	**press**-toh
late	**tardi**	**tar**-dee
entrance	**entrata**	en-**trah**-tah
exit	**uscita**	oo-**shee**-ta
restroom	**il gabinetto**	eel gah-bee-**net**-toh

free, unoccupied	**libero**	**lee**-bair-oh
free, no charge	**gratuito**	grah-**too**-ee-toh

Making a Telephone Call

I'd like to place a	**Vorrei fare**	vor-**ray far**-eh oona
long-distance call.	**una interurbana.**	in-tair-oor-**bah**-nah
I'd like to make	**Vorrei fare una**	vor-**ray far**-eh oona
a collect call.	**telefonata a carico**	teh-leh-fon-**ah** ah ah
	del destinatario.	**kar**-ee-koh dell dess-
		tee-nah-**tar**-ree-oh
I'll try again later.	**Ritelefono più**	ree-teh-**leh**-foh-noh
	tardi.	pee-oo **tar**-dee
Can I leave a	**Posso lasciare**	**poss**-oh lash-**ah**-reh
message?	**un messaggio?**	oon mess-**sah**-joh?
Hold on	**Un attimo,**	oon **ah**-tee-moh,
	per favore	pair fah-**vor**-eh
Could you speak	**Può parlare più**	pwoh par-**lah**-reh
up a little, please?	**forte, per favore?**	pee-oo **for**-teh, pair
		fah-**vor**-eh?
local call	**la telefonata**	lah teh-leh-fon-**ah**-ta
	locale	loh-**kah**-leh

Shopping

How much	**Quant'è,**	kwan-**teh**
does this cost?	**per favore?**	pair fah-**vor**-eh?
I would like ...	**Vorrei ...**	vor-**ray**
Do you have ...?	**Avete ...?**	ah-**veh**-teh...?
I'm just looking.	**Sto soltanto**	stoh sol-**tan**-toh
	guardando	gwar-**dan**-doh
Do you take	**Accettate**	ah-chet-**tah**-teh **kar**-teh
credit cards?	**carte di credito?**	dee **cre**-dee-toh?
What time do	**A che ora apre/**	ah keh or-ah
you open/close?	**chiude?**	**ah**-preh/kee-oo-deh?
this one	**questo**	**kweh**-stoh
that one	**quello**	**kwell**-oh
expensive	**caro**	**kar**-oh
cheap	**a buon prezzo**	ah bwon **pret**-soh
size, clothes	**la taglia**	lah **tah**-lee-ah
size, shoes	**il numero**	eel **noo**-mair-oh
white	**bianco**	bee-**ang**-koh
black	**nero**	**neh**-roh
red	**rosso**	**ross**-oh
yellow	**giallo**	**jal**-loh
green	**verde**	**vair**-deh
blue	**blu**	bloo
brown	**marrone**	mar-**roh**-neh

Types of Shops

antique dealer	**l'antiquario**	lan-tee-**kwah**-ree-oh
bakery	**la panetteria**	lah pah-net-tair-**ree**-ah
bank	**la banca**	lah **bang**-kah
bookshop	**la libreria**	lah lee-breh-**ree**-ah
butcher shop	**la macelleria**	lah mah-chell-eh-**ree**-ah
cake shop	**la pasticceria**	lah pas-tee-chair-**ee**-ah
department store	**il grande**	eel **gran**-deh
	magazzino	mag-gad-**zee**-noh
delicatessen	**la salumeria**	lah sah-loo-meh-**ree**-ah
fishmonger	**la pescheria**	lah pess-keh-**ree**-ah
florist	**il fioraio**	eel fee-or-**eye**-oh
greengrocer	**il fruttivendolo**	eel froo-tee-**ven**-doh-loh
grocery	**alimentari**	ah-lee-men-**tah**-ree
hairdresser	**il parrucchiere**	eel par-oo-kee-**air**-eh
ice cream parlor	**la gelateria**	lah jel-lah-tair-**ree**-ah
market	**il mercato**	eel mair-**kah**-toh
newsstand	**l'edicola**	leh-**dee**-koh-lah
pharmacy	**la farmacia**	lah far-mah-**chee**-ah
post office	**l'ufficio postale**	loo-**fee**-choh pos-**tah**-leh
shoe shop	**il negozio di**	eel neh-**goh**-tsioh dee
	scarpe	**skar**-peh
supermarket	**il supermercato**	su-pair-mair-**kah**-toh
tobacconist	**il tabaccaio**	eel tah-bak-**eye**-oh
travel agency	**l'agenzia di viaggi**	lah-jen-**tsee**-ah dee
		vee-**ad**-jee

Sightseeing

art gallery	**la pinacoteca**	lah peena-koh-**teh**-kah
bus stop	**la fermata**	lah fair-**mah**-tah
	dell'autobus	dell **ow**-toh-booss
church	**la chiesa**	lah kee-**eh**-zah
	la basilica	lah bah-**seel**-i-kah
garden	**il giardino**	eel jar-**dee**-no
library	**la biblioteca**	lah beeb-lee-oh-**teh**-kah
museum	**il museo**	eel moo-**zeh**-oh
tourist	**l'ufficio**	loo-**fee**-choh
information	**turistico**	too-**ree**-stee-koh
train station	**la stazione**	lah stah-tsee-**oh**-neh

closed for the public holiday	**chiuso per la festa**	kee-**oo**-zoh pair lah **fess**-tah

Staying in a Hotel

Do you have any vacant rooms?	**Avete camere libere?**	ah-**veh**-teh **kah**-mair-eh **lee**-bair-eh?
double room	**una camera doppia**	oona **kah**-mair-ah **doh**-pee-ah
with double bed	**con letto matrimoniale**	kon **let**-toh mah-tree-moh-nee-**ah**-leh
twin room	**una camera con due letti**	oona **kah**-mair-ah kon **doo**-eh **let**-tee
single room	**una camera singola**	oona **kah**-mair-ah **sing**-goh-lah
room with a bath, shower	**una camera con bagno, con doccia**	oona **kah**-mair-ah kon **ban**-yoh, kon **dot**-chah
porter	**il facchino**	eel fah-**kee**-noh
key	**la chiave**	lah kee-**ah**-veh
I have a reservation.	**Ho fatto una prenotazione.**	oh **fat**-toh oona preh-noh-tah-tsee-**oh**-neh

Eating Out

Do you have a table for …?	**Avete una tavola per … ?**	ah-**veh**-teh oona **tah**-voh-lah pair …?
I'd like to reserve a table.	**Vorrei riservare una tavola.**	vor-**ray** ree-sair-**vah**-reh oona **tah**-voh-lah
breakfast	**colazione**	koh-lah-tsee-**oh**-neh
lunch	**pranzo**	**pran**-tsoh
dinner	**cena**	**cheh**-nah
The check, please.	**Il conto, per favore.**	eel **kon**-toh pair fah-**vor**-eh
I am a vegetarian.	**Sono vegetariano/a.**	**soh**-noh veh-jeh-tar-ee-**ah**-noh/nah
waitress	**cameriera**	kah-mair-ee-**air**-ah
waiter	**cameriere**	kah-mair-ee-**air**-eh
fixed price menu	**il menù a prezzo fisso**	eel meh-**noo** ah **pret**-soh **fee**-soh
dish of the day	**piatto del giorno**	pee-ah-toh dell **jor**-no
appetizer	**antipasto**	an-tee-**pass**-toh
first course	**il primo**	eel **pree**-moh
main course	**il secondo**	eel seh-**kon**-doh
vegetables	**il contorno**	eel kon-**tor**-noh
dessert	**il dolce**	eel **doll**-cheh
cover charge	**il coperto**	eel koh-**pair**-toh
wine list	**la lista dei vini**	lah **lee**-stah day **vee**-nee
rare	**al sangue**	al **sang**-gweh
medium	**al puntino**	al poon-**tee**-noh
well done	**ben cotto**	ben **kot**-toh
glass	**il bicchiere**	eel bee-kee-**air**-eh
bottle	**la bottiglia**	lah bot-**teel**-yah
knife	**il coltello**	eel kol-**tell**-oh
fork	**la forchetta**	lah for-**ket**-tah
spoon	**il cucchiaio**	eel koo-kee-**eye**-oh

Menu Decoder

apple	**la mela**	lah **meh**-lah
artichoke	**il carciofo**	eel kar-**choff**-oh
baked	**al forno**	al **for**-noh
beans	**i fagioli**	ee fah-**joh**-lee
beef	**il manzo**	eel **man**-tsoh
beer	**la birra**	lah **beer**-rah
boiled	**lesso**	**less**-oh
bread	**il pane**	eel **pah**-neh
broth	**il brodo**	eel **broh**-doh
butter	**il burro**	eel **boor**-oh
cake	**la torta**	lah **tor**-tah
cheese	**il formaggio**	eel for-**mad**-joh
chicken	**il pollo**	eel **poll**-oh
clams	**le vongole**	leh **von**-goh-leh
coffee	**il caffè**	eel kah-**feh**
dry	**secco**	**sek**-koh
duck	**l'anatra**	**lah**-nah-trah
egg	**l'uovo**	loo-oh-voh
eggplant	**la melanzana**	lah meh-lan-**tsah**-nah
fish	**il pesce**	eel **pesh**-eh
French fries	**patatine fritte**	pah-tah-**teen**-eh **free**-teh
fresh fruit	**frutta fresca**	**froo**-tah **fress**-kah
garlic	**l'aglio**	**lahl**-yoh
grapes	**l'uva**	**loo**-vah
grilled	**alla griglia**	ah-lah **greel**-yah
ham	**il prosciutto**	eel pro-**shoo**-toh
cooked/cured	**cotto/crudo**	**kot**-toh/**kroo**-doh
ice cream	**il gelato**	eel jel-**lah**-toh
lamb	**l'abbacchio**	lah-**back**-kee-oh
lobster	**l'aragosta**	lah-rah-**goss**-tah

meat	**la carne**	la **kar**-neh
milk	**il latte**	eel **laht**-teh
mineral water sparkling/still	**l'acqua minerale gasata/naturale**	**lah**-kwah mee-nair-**ah**-leh gah-**zah**-tah/nah-too-**rah**-leh
mushrooms	**i funghi**	ee **foon**-gee
oil	**l'olio**	**loll**-yoh
olive	**l'oliva**	loh-**lee**-vah
onion	**la cipolla**	lah chee-**poll**-ah
orange	**l'arancia**	lah-**ran**-chah
orange/lemon juice	**succo d'arancia/ di limone**	**soo**-koh dah-**ran**-chah/ dee lee-**moh**-neh
peach	**la pesca**	lah **pess**-kah
pepper	**il pepe**	eel **peh**-peh
pork	**carne di maiale**	**kar**-neh dee mah-**yah**-leh
potatoes	**le patate**	leh pah-**tah**-teh
rice	**il riso**	eel **ree**-zoh
roast	**arrosto**	ar-**ross**-toh
roll	**il panino**	eel pah-**nee**-noh
salad	**l'insalata**	leen-sah-**lah**-tah
salt	**il sale**	eel **sah**-leh
sausage	**la salsiccia**	lah sal-**see**-chah
seafood	**frutti di mare**	**froo**-tee dee **mah**-reh
shrimp	**i gamberi**	ee **gam**-bair-ee
soup	**la zuppa, la minestra**	lah **tsoo**-pah, lah mee-**ness**-trah
steak	**la bistecca**	lah bee-**stek**-kah
strawberries	**le fragole**	leh **frah**-goh-leh
sugar	**lo zucchero**	loh **zoo**-kair-oh
tea	**il tè**	eel **teh**
herbal tea	**la tisana**	lah tee-**zah**-nah
tomato	**il pomodoro**	eel poh-moh-**dor**-oh
tuna	**il tonno**	**ton**-noh
veal	**il vitello**	vee-**tell**-oh
vegetables	**i legumi**	ee leh-**goo**-mee
vinegar	**l'aceto**	lah-**cheh**-toh
water	**l'acqua**	**lah**-kwah
red wine	**vino rosso**	**vee**-noh **ross**-oh
white wine	**vino bianco**	**vee**-noh bee-**ang**-koh
zucchini	**gli zucchini**	lyee dzoo-**kee**-nee

Numbers

1	**uno**	**oo**-noh
2	**due**	**doo**-eh
3	**tre**	treh
4	**quattro**	**kwat**-roh
5	**cinque**	**ching**-kweh
6	**sei**	**say**-ee
7	**sette**	**set**-teh
8	**otto**	**ot**-toh
9	**nove**	**noh**-veh
10	**dieci**	dee-**eh**-chee
11	**undici**	**oon**-dee-chee
12	**dodici**	**doh**-dee-chee
13	**tredici**	**tray**-dee-chee
14	**quattordici**	kwat-**tor**-dee-chee
15	**quindici**	**kwin**-dee-chee
16	**sedici**	**say**-dee-chee
17	**diciassette**	dee-chah-**set**-teh
18	**diciotto**	dee-**chot**-toh
19	**diciannove**	dee-chah-**noh**-veh
20	**venti**	**ven**-tee
30	**trenta**	**tren**-tah
40	**quaranta**	kwah-**ran**-tah
50	**cinquanta**	ching-**kwan**-tah
60	**sessanta**	sess-**an**-tah
70	**settanta**	set-**tan**-tah
80	**ottanta**	ot-**tan**-tah
90	**novanta**	noh-**van**-tah
100	**cento**	**chen**-toh
1,000	**mille**	**mee**-leh
2,000	**duemila**	**doo**-eh mee-lah
5,000	**cinquemila**	**ching**-kweh **mee**-lah
1,000,000	**un milione**	oon meel-**yoh**-neh

Time

one minute	**un minuto**	oon mee-**noo**-toh
one hour	**un'ora**	oon **or**-ah
half an hour	**mezz'ora**	medz-**or**-ah
a day	**un giorno**	oon **jor**-noh
a week	**una settimana**	oona set-tee-**mah**-nah
Monday	**lunedì**	loo-neh-**dee**
Tuesday	**martedì**	mar-teh-**dee**
Wednesday	**mercoledì**	mair-koh-leh-**dee**
Thursday	**giovedì**	joh-veh-**dee**
Friday	**venerdì**	ven-air-**dee**
Saturday	**sabato**	**sah**-bah-toh
Sunday	**domenica**	doh-**meh**-nee-kah

Rome Transportation Map

Key

- 62 — Bus route
- 62 — Start/end of bus route (capolinea)
- ➤ — Direction
- 19 — Tram (streetcar) route
- 19 — Start/end of tram route (capolinea)
- Ⓜ — Metro station
- ◼ — Train station
- ◼ — Major sight

0 meters 500
0 yards 500

CRITICAL ACCLAIM FOR
BARBARA MICHAELS

"A writer so popular that the public library has to keep her books under lock and key."
—*The Washington Post*

"Miss Michaels has a fine sense of atmosphere and storytelling."
—*The New York Times*

"This author never fails to entertain."
—*Cleveland Plain Dealer*

"Michaels has a fine downright way with the supernatural."
—*San Francisco Chronicle*

"Michaels has a human touch that adds charm to the well-controlled twists and turns."
—*Virginian Pilot/Ledger Star*

"Simply the best living writer of ghost stories and thrillers."
—Marion Zimmer Bradley

MORE PRAISE FOR BARBARA MICHAELS
AND
VANISH WITH THE ROSE

"I leapt on *Vanish with the Rose* as if it were chocolate. . . . This book and this writer are addictive."

—Alexandra Ripley,
New York Times bestselling author of *Scarlett*

"High-voltage mystery . . . a witty, intricate, and ultimately surprising story, with strong characterizations that keep the sparks flying."

—*Publishers Weekly*

"Involving . . . a cleverly spun mystery."

—*Booklist*

"Barbara Michaels can always be counted on for a darned good mystery with fascinating characters and a chilling tale. . . . Magnificent!"

—*Ocala Star-Banner*

HERE I STAY

"An absolutely first-rate job of summoning up the spooky . . . takes on the added dimension besides that of a very good ghost story."

—*Publishers Weekly*

"Scary, interesting. A winner."

—*Pittsburgh Press*

INTO THE DARKNESS

"The suspense builds into a smashing final chapter that does full credit to Michaels' powers of invention."

—*Murder Ad Lib*

SHATTERED SILK

"Her most enticing yet . . . will capture any woman's fantasy."

—*Cleveland Plain Dealer*

"An utterly enchanting book."

—*Roberta Gellis*

"Superior Michaels. . . . Like the antique gowns the heroine collects, *Shattered Silk* glitters!"

—*Kirkus Reviews*

SMOKE AND MIRRORS

"The perfect curl-up-at-homer for a frosty . . . eve."

—*New Woman*

"Barbara Michaels tells her story with grace, wit, and unflagging suspense."

—*San Jose Mercury News*

BOOKS BY BARBARA MICHAELS

Be Buried in the Rain
Here I Stay
Search the Shadows
Shattered Silk
Stitches in Time
The Grey Beginning
*The Dancing Floor**

Published by HarperPaperbacks

*coming soon

ATTENTION: ORGANIZATIONS AND CORPORATIONS

Most HarperPaperbacks are available at special quantity discounts for bulk purchases for sales promotions, premiums, or fund-raising. For information, please call or write:
Special Markets Department, HarperCollins*Publishers*,
10 East 53rd Street, New York, N.Y. 10022.
Telephone: (212) 207-7528. Fax: (212) 207-7222.

be buried in
the rain

Barbara Michaels

HarperPaperbacks
A Division of HarperCollins*Publishers*

HarperPaperbacks
A Division of HarperCollins*Publishers*
10 East 53rd Street, New York, N.Y. 10022-5299

To the Delaplaines,
One and All—
Bettie and George,
Buckie and Ted,
Jim and John

be buried in
the rain

one

🌺

The old pickup hit a pothole with a bump that shook a few more flakes of faded blue paint from the rusted body. Joe Danner swore, but not aloud. He hadn't used bad language for six years, not since he found his Lord Jesus in the mesmeric eyes of a traveling evangelist. He hadn't used hard liquor nor tobacco either, nor laid a hand on his wife in anger—only when she talked back or questioned his Scripture-ordained authority as head of the family.

It would never have occurred to Joe Danner that his wife preferred their old lifestyle. Back then, an occasional beating was part of the natural order of things, and it was a small price to pay for the Saturday nights at the local tavern, both of them getting a little drunk together, talking and joking with friends, going home to couple unimaginatively but pleasurably in the old bed Joe's daddy had made with his own hands.

Since Joe found Jesus, there were no more Saturday nights at the tavern. No more kids, either. Joe Junior had left home the year before; he was up north someplace, wallowing in the sins he'd been brought up to hate . . . Only somehow the *teaching hadn't taken hold. Not with Lynne Anne, either. Married at sixteen, just in time to spare her baby the label of bastard—but not soon enough to wipe out the sin of fornication. She lived in Pikesburg, only forty miles away, but she never came home any more. Joe had thrown her out of the house the night she told them she was pregnant, and Lynne Anne had spat in his face before she set out on a four-mile walk in the traditional snowstorm, to collapse on the doorstep of her future in-laws. They had raised a real ruckus about it, too. Methodists. What else could a person expect from Methodists?*

Another pothole lifted Joe off the seat, bringing his head in painful contact with the roof of the cab and ending his sullen musings about his thankless children. Darned county gov'mint, he thought. New roads, not even a year old, and already gone to . . . heck. Why they'd built it in the first place he'd never understand. Nothing wrong with the old one. This route was shorter, maybe, but . . . Well, he just didn't like it. Especially the steep downhill slope into the hollow. Deadman's Hollow, the kids called it. Said it was haunted. Fool kids . . . He wasn't afraid of haunts or dead men, not with the power of the Lord Jesus in his heart. All the same, there was something funny about that low place in the road . . .

Joe stamped on the brake as the truck approached the downhill curve. The road was slimy-wet after the night's rain; tangled brush and twisted trees, thick with foliage, reduced the sunlight to a golden haze. The fields would be a solid sea of mud; couldn't use a cultivator till they dried. Gol-durned rain, gol-durned gov'mint . . .

Jesus Christ! The words came bursting out of the deep recesses of his mind, exploding in a high-pitched shout. His heavy boot slammed the brake pedal to the floor. The tires squawled and slid, and he fought the skid with the skill of long years of driving on bad roads in bad weather. The vehicle finally shuddered to a stop, skewed sideways across both narrow lanes; and Joe sat staring down at the thing in the road.

Had he hit it? He hadn't felt anything. He knew how it would feel. Coons and possums and groundhogs, he'd run over plenty of the varmints. A body—a human body—would make even more of a bump.

Sweat slicked his lean cheeks and trickled into his beard as he climbed down from the truck. He was already composing the excuses he would give the police. It was on the road when he saw it—still and recumbent, dead or dead-drunk—not his fault—sharp curve, wet road . . .

Not his fault. If he could back and turn, go the other way, the old way—leave it for someone else to find . . . Still, better check it out. He'd had enough trouble with the police. That fuss last year, about whipping the kids at church school—all according to the Scriptures, spare the rod and spoil the child—but some busybody had raised cain, and he was an elder.

Slowly Joe went around the front of the truck, dreading what he would see. But everything was all right. He hadn't touched it. The wheels were a good foot away. Must be dead—or dead-drunk. It hadn't stirred. It? She. Woman's dress, but a durned funny one—long, covering even the feet, a faded calico print that had once been blue. She lay facedown, the back of her head covered by a scarf or shawl. Her arms were crooked, one over her head, the other at her side. The voluminous folds of fabric were strangely flat, and as he edged closer, Joe's fears faded, to be replaced by rising anger. It was just an empty dress. Couldn't be a body under that. Some fool kids—could've caused an accident, playing a trick like that.

He lifted the scarf.

It grinned up at him, baring twin rows of earth-browned teeth. The ivory curve of the skull was pale against the black macadam of the road. A drop of water, caught on the rim of the empty eyesocket, winked in the sunlight.

Somehow he got the truck backed and turned. The last wild twist of the wheel produced the faintest crunching sound, and an echoing quiver ran through Joe's own bones. For some reason all he could think of was Lynne Anne, struggling through the winter storm. He could see her face drawn into ugliness by her hate, superimposed on that fleshless horror in the road.

He had not seen the other, smaller bundle of cloth that lay half-concealed by the full sleeve and crooked armbones, as if it had fallen from a failing grasp. A very small bundle, not of calico, but of finer stuff, stained with rust and mold in a strangely beautiful pattern of greens and browns. Once it had been white—delicate, fragile lawn, lace-trimmed, hand-tucked and embroidered, just the right size to fit a child's doll-baby. A life-sized doll-baby.

The story was macabre enough to make the national newswires. I suppose I was one of the few people in the eastern United States who didn't read it. I wasn't watching TV or reading newspapers that week. Final exams were looming, and that first year in med school is the one that separates the sheep from the goats. When I wasn't crouched over my desk rereading pages I had read a dozen times, I was pacing the floor mumbling to myself. The twelve cranial nerves, the facial nerves—optic, trigeminal, glossopharyngeal . . . Now and then I heard myself break into song. "The hip bone's connected to the thigh bone, the thigh bone's connected to the leg bone . . ." Then I would do aerobics for a few minutes or dash out to the store for another jar of instant coffee.

Actually, I have a vague recollection of seeing a headline on one of the trashy journals near the check-out stand in the grocery store. Waiting in line, one couldn't help glancing at the headlines. Princess Di's private life vied with lurid lies about Hollywood and rock stars, promises of wonder diets, cancer cures, and proof of life after death. That was the sort of headline I noticed: "Returned from the Grave! To Seek Revenge????" Just more gruesome sensationalism, and it made no lasting impression on a mind stuffed to overflowing with anatomical terms.

If I had read the story, would I have gone to Virginia? Yes, of course—all the more readily, no doubt, because of the coincidence and the intriguing aspects of the case. On the other hand, I was awfully sick of bones.

The summons came. I use that old-fashioned phrase deliberately; it was one *she* would have used. The call didn't come from her, however. It came from my mother, who informed me irascibly that she had been trying to reach me for three days.

"I told you I was in the middle of exams."

It was five o'clock on a rainy spring afternoon and I was in bed with a beer and a mystery story and a bowl of pretzels. I had not yet received the exam results, but at that moment it was enough just to be done with them. Mother's grumbles washed over me without making any impression. I had heard it all before: I had no business cutting myself off from the world; what if someone became ill? What if . . . She had a superstitious reluctance to say the words, so I said them for her.

"If somebody died I'd find out soon enough. That's not the sort of news I'm anxious to get."

Though she had lived in Pittsburgh for years, Mother had never quite lost her pretty Virginia accent. It softened her voice even when she was angry, and was, I think, partially responsible for her success as an executive secretary. "Mrs. Newcomb is so ladylike!"

She sighed gently. "Julie, I wish you wouldn't joke about such things. It makes you sound so callous."

It was a mercy the dear woman couldn't hear some of the jokes that pass around the dissecting room. She thought I was growing callous, did she? I was beginning to wonder if I would ever become callous enough.

"I was going to call you this evening," I said, sliding away from the subject of my sense of humor. "I really was. So, what's new?"

"What are you going to do this summer, Julie?"

"You know what I'm going to be doing. Same as last summer."

Another sigh trembled along the miles of wire, and I said firmly, "Now, Mother, don't give me a hard time. I know you think being a cocktail waitress is one step away from prostitution, but it's a perfectly respectable occupation, and I can make more money that way than I could at any other job. Lord knows we need it. I feel bad enough using your savings and letting you borrow from your boss . . ."

She let me run down before she spoke. "It isn't that. It's Martha. She needs you, Julie."

The idea that Martha needed anyone, much less me, was so incongruous I laughed aloud. "Don't tell me she's dying at long last."

"I wish you wouldn't talk that way!"

"Sorry. But she's ninety if she's a day."

"Eighty-five."

"Oh well, that's different."

"Julie—"

"All right, all right. But be honest, Mother. Her death can hardly come as a shock. Eighty-five isn't exactly the springtime of life, and to call our relationship tender and loving—"

"You shouldn't speak of her that way, Julie. She is your grandmother."

She was my grandmother. She was also my mother's mother. Neither of us used the familial, affectionate words. We called her Martha, when we didn't refer to her simply as "she."

Mother went on, "She wants you to spend the summer at Maidenwood."

I spilled the pretzels all over my lap. Out of respect for my poor mother, of whom I am really very fond, I did not yell. All I said was, "Why?" and I spoke in a quiet, controlled voice.

She was relieved at my calm. "It's logical, Julie, when you think about it. She was recovering rather well from the stroke until a few days ago. Then she had another. The doctor thought it would be the end, but it seems she has rallied in the most amazing way . . . What did you say?"

"Nothing."

Mother decided to let it go. "She is paralyzed. She can barely speak."

"Then how did she manage to ask for me?"

She hadn't asked for me. Mother finally admitted as much, but not until I had pressed her; she insisted Martha would have asked for me if she hadn't been—er—well— "You know, Julie, how a stroke affects a person's brain . . ."

Accustomed as I am to my mother's conversational style, it took me a while to sort through the clutter of conventional clichés that obscured the facts.

"Wait a minute, Mother, let me get this straight. Martha had another stroke? And she's at home—in that tumble-down wreck of a house—not in a hospital?"

Another shower of conventionalities rained down on me. The wishes of the dying, the last days in the old home, et cetera, et cetera. What it all came down to was that Martha wanted it that way. And what Martha wanted, Martha got.

"Yes, I understand," I said resignedly. "What I don't understand is why I've been chosen as the sacrificial lamb. It's Matt's problem. He's on the spot, he's Martha's heir, he has no family or financial responsibilities—let him deal with it."

"But, honey, he's a man."

"I figured he must be. Last time I saw him he was a boy, so—"

"Julie, your cousin is doing all he can. He has his career to think of. This is an election year and he is very busy."

From the awe in her voice you'd have thought Matt were in the running for the presidency, instead of being only a lowly state senator. The key sentence had been the first. Matt was a male and hence automatically exempt from the family tasks that are a woman's responsibility. The dirty, unpaid, boring tasks—like bedpans and cooking, scrubbing floors and carrying trays.

It would have been a waste of time and energy to try to convince my mother of the injustice of this attitude. She had grown up with it; it was engraved on her brain. So I didn't yell, "What about my career? What about my needs?" I listened in mounting depression as Mother outlined the arguments in favor of my going to Maidenwood. I felt sure she had got them from Matt; they had the glib, specious appeal of a political speech.

"You wouldn't have to do any actual nursing, Julie. No—er—no nasty things. Shirley Johnson is there— maybe you remember her? Such a fine woman, very conscientious, and Matt says she has her certificate as a practical nurse."

Mother probably did not realize that her argument affected me in a way she had not planned. I didn't remember Shirley Johnson, but I pitied her with all my heart.

Another convincing argument was that Matt had agreed to compensate me for the wages I would lose. I cheered up a little, because I was pretty sure Matt didn't know how much a good cocktail waitress can earn in three months. Of course he counted on getting the money out of Martha. I wished him luck. Maybe she'd die before the summer was over. . . .

But the argument that turned the trick was the one Mother didn't make. If I did not go, she'd have to. I knew how she felt about Martha, even if *she* didn't. She would never admit to herself or anyone else she hated and feared her own mother; she would risk her job and her health for some outmoded notion of duty. I was her surrogate, and like the paid substitutes during the Civil War, I would have to shoulder arms and march out to be killed.

I had to go. And I would have gone even if I had known that the fanciful analogy about the sacrificial lamb was more accurate than I imagined.

two

Matt met me at the bus station in Richmond. Cost was
certainly a factor in my decision to take the bus—so far I
hadn't got any money out of Matt, only promises, promises—but I must admit another reason was my suspicion
that Cousin Matt would rather be caught dead than mixing with the hoi polloi who traveled by Greyhound. I had
expected he would send one of his lackeys to pick me up,
so when I saw him standing there at the door, I almost fell
over.

He was wearing slacks and a blue denim shirt, the
sleeves rolled up and the collar open. He waved and
called out, in a voice loud enough to make heads turn,
"Cousin Julie! Good to see you, honey!"

Well, of course I should have figured it out sooner.
This was an election year. It wouldn't hurt Matt's image to
be seen mingling with the underprivileged, dressed like
one of the boys. I fully expected a flash to explode, but
there didn't seem to be a photographer in sight.

Matt gave me a big brotherly hug and held me out at

arm's length, his hands on my shoulders. "You're a sight for sore eyes, honey. Prettier than ever."

"So are you," I said. It wasn't much of a compliment. The last time I had seen Matt he had been sixteen years old, with all the normal tribulations of that age—acne, long, gangly legs and arms, and a voice that turned from soprano to bass at odd moments. He was thirty now, seven years older than I, and in spite of my sarcastic semicompliment I had to admit that he had turned into a good-looking guy. His casual clothes showed off his tan and his muscles and his flat stomach. I felt sure that all three were the products of an expensive health club, but the working-man image wasn't bad. He had the family features, the jutting nose and high, prominent cheekbones and heavy jaw. Unfortunately I had them too. One of the reasons I let my hair grow long was the hope of softening those pronounced and prominent protrusions. My best friends wouldn't call me pretty. The women of my family are seldom pretty. By the time we reach middle age we all look like tribal matriarchs. But on a man the "Carr face" is attractive; it gives a (deceptive) impression of strength and reliability—the Abe Lincoln look, only handsomer. We looked enough alike to be brother and sister, Matt and I, even to the dark chestnut-brown of our hair.

Matt noticed the resemblance too. His smile faded and he gave me another, longer inspection before he said, "No mistaking you for anybody but a Carr, Julie, even if you don't have the name."

The driver had unloaded the belly of the bus and I indicated my three suitcases. I picked up the lightest of the three, ignoring Matt's polite protest. When he had hoisted the other two he stopped protesting. An expression of mild distress crossed his face, but he carried them easily enough; the health club must be doing its job.

"What the hell have you got in here?" he asked.

"Clothes, books, the usual. If I'm going to be here all summer I can't get by with one pair of jeans."

He nodded, saving his breath. I was soon to discover what he was saving it for; as we neared the exit a man stepped into our path, hand outstretched. "Senator Ellis! Hello, Senator."

Matt dropped the right-hand suitcase—on my foot— and took the extended hand. He didn't raise his voice, but all of a sudden you could hear him all over the station. It's called projection, I believe.

"Well—Mr. Busby, isn't it? Good to see you, sir. How's the wife?"

"Much better, Senator, since she had that operation. Had to thank you, sir; hadn't been for you, we couldn't have afforded it. Just no way to tell you, Senator, how much we all think of you and the great job you're doing for us—"

"Please." Matt dropped his admirer's hand and gave him a friendly slap on the shoulder. "You good people deserve everything you get and a lot more. I'm delighted to hear that Mrs. Busby is doing well."

They played it to the hilt as a small crowd gathered. Matt introduced me—"My li'l Cousin Julie, come to nurse our granny—the dear old soul is sinking fast . . ." Finally Mr. Busby—if that was his name, which I rather doubted—backed away, bowing and scraping. Matt spread a friendly, self-deprecating smile around the watching crowd, picked up my bags and shepherded me toward the door, followed by an admiring murmur.

We were out on the street before I spoke. "Can I throw up now, or would you rather I waited until the chauffeur can clean it up?"

The fourteen-year-old Matt would have turned purple

with rage and tried to slug me. Senator Ellis smiled. "That's the way it's done, honey. And I do it well. I'll be governor in five years."

He wasn't smiling now. His voice was dead serious. I believed him.

"And then?" I asked.

"Every little boy in America envisions being President."

"And every little girl."

"I agree, darling. You can't fault me on women's rights. Look at my record."

"How do you get away with that in your district? The word 'redneck' comes to mind . . ."

"The word is one we use pridefully," said Matt, with a twist of his lip. "I get away with it because I am also great at huntin' and fishin' and man-talk. It's all image, honey."

He stopped by a nondescript vehicle—a five-year-old tan Chevy with rust stains. I took one look at it and burst out laughing.

Matt joined me. "Image, Julie. I told you—I'm good at it."

He helped me in with a burlesqued gallantry and got behind the wheel. We kept up a desultory spatter of conversation as he drove skillfully through the noonday traffic—the usual polite catching up on each other's lives. Not until we had left the city and were heading south did I break a long silence. "How is she, Matt?"

He didn't need to ask who "she" was. "Same as ever. She could be deaf, dumb, blind, and paralyzed and still rule the roost." He waited for me to comment. When I didn't he said, without looking at me, "Are you still afraid of her, Julie?"

"No. Yes. How the hell should I know? I haven't seen her for five years."

"I am," Matt said. "Afraid of her."

"You were always her favorite."

"Isn't there something in the Bible about chastening those you love?"

"Oh."

"She did favor me," Matt admitted. "I was the boy. The only boy born into the family for God knows how many generations. It's funny, how we run to girl-babies . . . Your standard male chauvinist has nothing on these tough old ladies when it comes to putting down other women. And I'm sure that when she talked about me to you, she praised me to the skies. That was a favorite trick of hers—invidious comparisons. But she never allowed me to have a very good opinion of myself."

"Matt, she's a sick old woman and you're a successful young man with your life ahead of you. Don't tell me you are suffering from some neurotic obsession—"

"No." Matt's tight grasp of the wheel relaxed. When he went on, the strained bitterness had left his voice. "No, I think I've come to grips with my neuroses. Whatever she did, she is paying for it now. There could be no worse punishment for her than lying helpless. If you could see her—"

"I will."

He took one hand off the wheel and patted my knee. "Don't think I'm not grateful, Julie. I'll try to make it up to you. If there's anything in the house you want—furniture, china, that sort of thing . . ."

The sympathy and affection I had begun to feel for him abruptly vanished. I don't know why the offer repelled me so. Heaven knows I had no reason to feel sentimental about my grim old grandmother.

He felt me stiffen and removed his hand. "That wasn't expressed too well," he said.

"No. I don't intend to prowl the house like a ghoul looking for loot. She's not dead yet."

"She can't last the summer," Matt said flatly.

We went on for another mile in silence. For all its battered appearance, the old car was in excellent condition. The engine ran smoothly and the air conditioning kept the interior comfortably cool. Under a bright hot sun the level fields of the riverbanks were green with new crops.

Finally I said, "She's a tough old lady, Matt. She might recover. I'm going to do everything I can to ensure that she does."

"Naturally."

His expression was so glum I had to laugh, though without much humor. "We're a fine pair of loving grandchildren, aren't we? You'd better start briefing me—things to do and not do, subjects to mention and to avoid, topics that might raise her blood pressure or improve her disposition—if there are any of the latter . . ."

"There aren't," Matt grunted. "But don't mention the skeleton on the road. She doesn't know about that."

"The skeleton on the . . . What on earth are you talking about?"

Matt glanced at me. "Didn't you hear about it?"

"No."

Matt touched the brake and signaled for a turn. "It's time we stopped for lunch anyway. I'd better fill you in on the local sensation before you see Martha."

The restaurant was one of those roadside types that have names like Joe's Place or Flo's Place or Harry's Place. This "place"—fake Tudor stucco and beam construction, two whiskey barrels filled with petunias flanking the entrance—belonged to Sam, whoever he was. It was obviously one of Matt's hangouts; the waitress greeted him by name and asked if he wanted the usual, which turned out to be bourbon on the rocks—a lot of bourbon on a few rocks. We were only half an hour from Maidenwood and I figured that Matt was in the habit of stopping at Sam's for a shot of Dutch courage before confronting his grandmother.

"Now," I said, sipping my gin and tonic, "about that skeleton."

There had, in fact, been two skeletons; one was that of a newborn infant. I listened with my mouth open, too astonished to question or interrupt. When the waitress came along to ask if we wanted refills on our drinks, Matt laughed at my aghast face and nodded at the girl.

"Drink up, Julie, you look as if you need another one."

"I never heard such a crazy story in my life! Come clean, Matt. You made it up. You used to tell me things—"

"I never made up one like this. It's crazy, all right, but if you read the newspapers as conscientiously as you ought, you would know that cases just as weird turn up from time to time. Unfortunately this one happened in our backyard, so to speak. The new road cuts through our land."

I finished my drink and shook my head, marveling. "I can see why you warned me not to tell Martha. She'd view it as a personal insult. Was that the motive, do you think? And where did the bones come from? I'm not as ignorant as you suppose; I've read about cemeteries being desecrated—"

"That was the first place the police looked, naturally. There are three cemeteries in and around Carrsville—the Methodist, the Episcopal, and the old Catholic cemetery. There were no signs of disturbance."

"Medical-school specimens, then."

"Use your head, Julie—and give your colleagues and the police some credit. Sheriff Jarboe called in an anthropologist from William and Mary to examine the bones."

"Oh, of course. That would be the thing to do." I pondered the matter while Matt watched me quizzically. The waitress brought our second round of drinks. Without looking at the tattered menu, Matt ordered for both of us. "Well?" he said.

"Well what?"

"You med students are supposed to know something about bones. How much can an expert tell from a skeleton?"

"I'm no expert. But I took a course in forensic medicine, and I've done some reading on my own. A pathologist can determine the age of the individual, within a few years. The sex of an adult or adolescent—sexual characteristics don't mark the bones until after the onset of puberty. Medical history, general health, sometimes cause of death . . ."

"Sometimes?"

"Only if the cause of death left a mark on the bone. A fractured hyoid bone may indicate the individual was smothered or strangled. A fractured skull suggests a fatal fall or a blunt instrument. But breaks in the bones can be post-mortem injuries, and it's hard to tell for sure whether they occurred just before or after death."

The waitress put two chef's salads in front of us. The lettuce was brown around the edges but I was too hungry to care. "You can tell a lot more from the soft tissues, if any fragments remain. I remember reading about an examination of Egyptian mummies, where the pathologists were able to perform histological sections, after rehydrating the hardened tissues with sodium carbonate. They found parasitic worms in the intestinal mass . . . Aren't you hungry?"

Matt pushed his salad away. "I'm sorry I asked. Let's change the subject."

I took a roll and buttered it. "Okay. I assume your tame anthropologist was not able to determine the cause of death. Not surprising. What did he find out?"

"Just the age, and in the case of the woman's remains, the sex. She was between sixteen and twenty years old." Matt continued to contemplate his food with faint disgust.

"Mmmm. He wouldn't have been able to determine the sex of the infant. Maybe the woman died in childbirth. When?"

"That's the question." Matt picked up his fork and looked at me dubiously. "Are you finished talking about—er—histological sections?"

"For the moment. If they could determine when the woman died, it might give some clue as to where the bones came from."

"That's what I was about to ask you. How they deduce something like that."

"It wouldn't be easy. A lot of factors affect the rate of deterioration of animal bone and tissue. The type of soil, the weather, the absence or presence of a coffin, whether the body was embalmed—"

Matt had taken a bite of salad. He stopped chewing and looked at me reproachfully. I laughed. "Okay, we'll skip the details. The truth is, archaeologists usually depend on other factors to date skeletal remains, such as the objects buried with the bodies, like scraps of clothing, buttons, coins, and so on. Without such clues, or the use of a process like carbon fourteen—"

"I've read about that. Why couldn't it be used in this case?"

"First, because it only works with specimens that are hundreds of years old. The margin of error is too great. Second, because you have to destroy the specimen in order to get results. Matt, why are you worrying about this? Surely it's obvious where the poor girl and her baby came from. There are old forgotten cemeteries all over the state. Indian, colonial, Civil War . . . We're walking on the dust of our ancestors every time we take a step."

"Very poetic," Matt said distastefully.

"Very true. It is also true that illegal digging has been going on around Maidenwood for a long time. That old lie about Blackbeard's treasure—"

"It's not so farfetched," Matt protested. "Teach, aka Blackbeard, did operate in the Tidewater area; after he was killed in a sea fight, some of his crew were hanged at Williamsburg, and he—"

"Matt, my boy, I detect a greedy gleam in your eyes. Don't tell me you dug for treasure in the pastures of Maidenwood?"

"Sure I did. What red-blooded American boy could resist a story like that?"

"You never let me help."

"You," Matt said solemnly, "were just a girl."

I couldn't help smiling. Matt grinned back at me, and I found myself liking him again. "I did most of my treasure hunting in the years after you left," he said, half-apologetically. "I didn't spend that much time at Maidenwood when you were in residence."

"I suppose I was something of a nuisance," I admitted. "Seven years is quite a gap in age when people are children. I mean, when children are—I mean—"

"I know what you mean. But Blackbeard's treasure isn't a myth, and every now and then public interest revives. Martha caught some idiot in the woods with a bulldozer a few years back—she ran him off with her shotgun. He had bought a treasure map from a con man for fifty bucks."

"There you are then. A gang of kids, looking for pieces of eight, came upon an old grave and decided to be cute. Isn't that the conclusion the police arrived at?"

"Yes . . ."

"So that's it. Are you going to eat the rest of your salad?"

He shoved it toward me and I began picking out the good parts—strips of country ham and fragments of cheese. I should have known from the way he kept glancing at me that we weren't finished with the subject.

"That's why I decided to give the archaeologists permission to excavate," he said. "Their presence will deter trespassers, and if they find the cemetery the bones came from, the police can close the case."

I speared an olive and popped it into my mouth. "Martha will have a fit," I mumbled. "She's always refused to allow . . ." Then I caught on. The pit flew out of my mouth and bounced uncouthly on the table. "Archaeologists? You wouldn't be referring to one archaeologist in particular? Not—not . . ."

"His name is Petranek," Matt said. "He claimed to be an old friend of yours."

I picked up the olive pit and put it on my plate.

I could tell by the smug set of Matt's handsome mouth that he suspected the truth. It was the same smirk the fourteen-year-old had worn when he put snakes in my bed and told me I was going to get rabies from a rooster that had pecked my legs. I was determined not to let him see the news had disturbed me. Actually, I told myself, I wasn't disturbed. It had been a long time—five years.

I was a wide-eyed innocent freshman at William and Mary, and Alan was a grad student in anthropology, earn-ing his stipend by teaching an introductory anthro course. He looked like a young Indiana Jones—lean and bronzed, his brown hair sun-bleached after a summer in the field. I practically swooned with rapturous disbelief when he picked me out of the gaggle of adoring girls who surrounded him. There was some vague talk of an engagement—mostly from my mother—before I caught on to Alan's real reason for courting my favors.

Even then he had his future career mapped out. Historic archaeology was a relatively new discipline, applying the standard techniques of excavation to recent historical sites. You might think we know all we need to know about the early settlements in America; not only were those people literate, they seemed to have spent most of their spare time writing letters, declarations, diaries, and documents. But there are gaps, especially in our knowledge of the living conditions of ordinary people, that can only be filled in by archaeology. Digs around Williamsburg, Plymouth, and other sites have proved that.

I could go on. I knew a lot more about historic archaeology than I wanted to know. I heard a lot about it that year, in coffee shops and college bars, in my room and in his apartment, in and out of bed. He even talked about it in bed. That should have told me something.

I didn't catch on, though, not even when Alan complained about the difficulty of advancement in a field so poorly funded and so competitive. He had no doubt he'd make it to the top eventually. Humility was not one of his virtues—or failings—and he had reason for vanity. He was good—intelligent, innovative, hard-working. But he didn't want to wait until he was fifty before he fought his way to a full professorship or to one of the big curatorships. He wanted instant success, and the only way he could get it was to make a really sensational, significant discovery.

He didn't lust after my maidenhood; he lusted after Maidenwood. (It shows you how young I was, that I could get a grim relish out of that poor pun.) I never really understood why he was convinced that the discovery that would make his career lay hidden under the tangled brush and weedy clay of my family's land. Like all old houses, Maidenwood had its share of legends; the buried pirate treasure was only one of them. And, as Matt had pointed out, not as farfetched as one might think.

Then there was the story of beautiful Lady Jocelyn, who had fled the dissolute court of James I to find freedom in the wilderness of the New World. This was not only farfetched, but downright ridiculous, in my opinion. Women of seventeenth-century England were not their own mistresses, they couldn't hop a boat and take off on a cruise without the permission of husband or father or guardian—especially if they were wards of the King, as Lady Jocelyn was supposed to have been. However, Alan always insisted the tale contained a germ of truth.

And there was Maydon's Hundred. Or, if you were credulous enough to believe in Lady Jocelyn, Maiden's Hundred. Duller (i.e., more sensible) scholars scoffed at the claim put forth by some of my romantic ancestors that the Carrs were descended, in a roundabout and questionable manner, from the Lady. They attributed the name to an otherwise anonymous settler named Maydon.

Maydon's or Maiden's, it had been one of the "hundreds" granted to Virginia Company emigrants in the early 1600s. There had been a settlement at Maidenwood in 1622, when the first Indian uprising almost destroyed the young colony of Virginia. Three hundred settlers massacred out of a total of twelve hundred, two of the four towns burned to the ground, many of the "hundreds" reduced to smoking rubble strewn with the corpses of the inhabitants. I didn't know why Alan believed he could make his reputation by digging up burned timbers and rotted bones, even if he could find them in Maidenwood's five hundred acres. But that is what he believed, and that is what he was after. Permission to excavate.

He met his match in Martha. She saw through him, damn her. Damn her, not because she read his mind but because she was careful to explain his motives to me.

I had taken Alan to Maidenwood that afternoon, at his request. I remember the sunlight slanting through the windows and gleaming on the silver tea service that had been in the family for two hundred years. I remember the smile on Martha's face . . .

Alan buttered her up with great skill. Not too much, only the best butter. It didn't work. She turned him down flat. She had never allowed outsiders to profane the soil of Maidenwood, and she never would allow it—not developers, nor archaeologists nor treasure hunters. She left him with no illusions of eventual success, but he took it with seeming grace. Not until after he had gone for a walk, so I could have a little time alone with dear Grandma, did Martha really get to work. With pitiless accuracy she described my failings, physical and emotional. How could I possibly imagine that a man like Alan—handsome, sophisticated, worldly—could be interested in a callow, homely girl like me? Flat-chested, with lusterless stick-straight brown hair, and the Carr features—"so unfortunate on a woman"—and, of course, no charm whatsoever.

I retreated, not in good order, before she had quite finished. The next year I transferred to the University of Pennsylvania, even though I lost the family-connected scholarship that had been my principal reason for returning to Virginia for college. Alan made a few attempts to see me, but he wasn't a man to persevere in the face of such sullen resentment, such unreasoning demands for reassurance. Oh, yes, I had been unreasonable, I could admit that now—now that it was too late. The past can't be changed. Alan probably wouldn't want to change it. He had been, and still was, all the things Martha had called him—handsome, sophisticated, worldly. There must have been countless other women in his life . . .

"You don't mind?" Matt asked, as we left the restaurant.

"Mind what? Oh—the excavations." I laughed lightly, and then caught my breath as the warm air closed over me like a sauna. "I feel sorry for the archaeologists, that's all. I had forgotten what Virginia summers are like. They'll be up to here in sweat when they aren't drowned by rainstorms."

"I felt it was the proper thing to do," Matt said. He started the engine and the air conditioning blasted out.

"How did you convince Martha?"

"Are you kidding? She doesn't know about it. If she finds out she'll probably have another stroke."

"You have her power of attorney?"

"No." Matt scowled, and swung out to pass a tractor that was chugging down the road at ten miles an hour. "I'm expecting to get it—my legal advisers are working on it. At the moment, Martha's lawyer is acting for her. You remember him?"

"No."

"He's seventy-eight. It's ridiculous, allowing a man that age to handle Martha's affairs. I'm sure the court will allow my application, but until then I have to sue for favors from Ronald Fraser McLendon, and I do mean sue—hat in hand. He had to agree with me about the excavations, though."

We were back to the excavations again. Did Matt know he was probing an old wound? I hadn't realized the spot was still so tender till he brought the subject up. Over the years the memory of Alan's features had faded into a blur. Now, suddenly, I could see him in my mind as clearly as if he stood before me—his eyes alight with enthusiasm, his brown hair tousled, his hands moving in quick, emphatic gestures as he spoke. I had heard the arguments so often . . .

"Martha should have given them permission to excavate a long time ago," I said. "The heritage of the past belongs to everyone. Treasure hunters and casual diggers can destroy a site; the light it might throw upon our history is gone, forever. The best way of preventing vandalism like that is to let the archaeologists go in first."

Matt smiled. "Is that a quote?"

"I'm sure it's been said before," I murmured. "Wasn't that Mr. McLendon's argument?"

"Well, not exactly. He was more concerned with the legal ramifications. We want to do everything we can to cooperate with the police. Until they identify those bones . . ."

I didn't want to hear any more about bones, or excavations, or archaeologists. "Where are you going?" I asked. "Wasn't that the turnoff we just passed?"

"There's a new road," Matt explained. "That's it, ahead."

He swung on to the narrow road, its entrance half-concealed by the branches of the trees that crowded close on either hand. The road surface shone with wet, and Matt slowed to a cautious twenty-five.

"Looks just like the old road," I said.

"You remember."

"It hasn't been that long."

Long enough, though, to make the contrast between

the well-traveled state highway and this unnumbered county road even more striking than before. There were new developments all along the highway, clumps of crackerbox houses, shopping centers, factories. The county road might have been in another country or another time; there was no sign of the present century except for the power lines and poles flanking the rutted macadam. Not even fences. Yet I knew it was all Maidenwood land. Cut by ravines and gulches, carved by the streams that emptied into the James River and the Bay, its tangled woodland had not changed for three hundred years. It must have looked much the same when the first settlers came to Maydon's Hundred—Jacobean cavaliers in high boots and half-armor, women in long gowns carrying their babies in their arms. Had the girl-mother and her infant been among them? It was not likely. The heavy Virginia clay would have reduced their delicate bones to dust long ago.

The car rounded a steep curve and glided down into a shadowy hollow. "Is this where she was found?" I asked.

Matt's eyebrows lifted. "How did you know?"

"It is what you might call a suitable ambience," I said.

Even as the words left my lips I realized that the casual, half-joking comment was literally, grimly accurate. Through the lichen-smeared trunks of the trees whose branches shadowed the narrow road, I could see masses of tangled green vegetation on either side, fecund and overgrown like a tropical rain forest. I could almost feel the dampness, even through the closed car windows.

"What a horrible place," I said involuntarily. "Has it got a name?"

"You don't remember it?"

"No. Should I?"

The road leveled out and straightened. We crossed a

one-lane wooden bridge, and sunlight dispelled the shadows. "Should I?" I said again.

Matt shrugged. "Probably one of the places forbidden to you, as a mere female. The local kids have some weird name for it—Deadman's Hollow, something like that."

I didn't pursue the subject. Neither of us spoke again until we reached the entrance to Maidenwood.

Five years before there had been traces of the gateposts—tumbled piles of stones intertwined with weeds. The stones had vanished now under heaps of rank greenery. Pink trumpets of bindweed raised triumphant heads over the ruin. The narrow track between them had been freshly graveled but, from the way the car bounced along it, not graded. The trees edged closer as if resenting our presence—scrub pine and dogwood seedlings and sycamore, strangled by the hangman's noose of honeysuckle. Matt's hands were tight on the wheel and I realized he was as reluctant to reach Maidenwood as I was. When we came out of the trees and saw the house ahead I felt like a stranger, viewing with detached and critical appraisal a monstrosity that had long since outlived usefulness or beauty.

The decay of the house was something they couldn't blame on the damn Yankees. It had survived the "War Between the States," as they called it in these parts, intact, thanks, family legend claimed, to a daughter of the house who had charmed the Union captain into sparing the mansion and its contents. In the 1880s the lord of the manor had had less compunction than the Yankees. An inveterate gambler, he had sold the family treasures and gutted the house, stripping off the hand-carved walnut paneling and even selling the lead off the roof. Another family legend claimed that his long-suffering wife had finally poisoned him before he could hock her jewelry and her best bed. The jewels had carried the family through the next lean half century. In 1917 fire had destroyed the east wing, and since there was no money for repairs, that part of the house had been abandoned to the ravages of wind and weather and weeds.

I saw it as a stranger, and yet I had visited often, when my parents lived in Richmond, and I had lived in the house for four endless, aching years, from the age of eight until I was twelve. Mother had had no choice but to hand me over to Martha. Left alone, untrained and unskilled, she had a long uphill struggle before she could send for me. In the intervening years I had returned only once— on that single disastrous visit with Alan—and only because he made me go. I couldn't admit to him that I would rather have paid a visit to the Fifth Circle of Hell, and I had assumed that his presence beside me would make it easier . . .

Five years ago. It was only a moment in the life of the old oak trees shading the front lawn. They looked the same. The lawn was unchanged too—not soft green grass but acres of cropped weeds.

I remembered the trees. I remembered the slope behind the house that led through pastures thick with clover to the riverbank. I remembered, only too clearly, the formal drawing room where Martha had torn my pathetic little love affair to ribbons. And that was all I remembered. It was as if a black wall shut off the rest of the house and the years I had spent there—a wall more than ten years thick.

Matt stopped the car and reached for a cigarette.

"I didn't know you smoked," I said curiously.

"I never want to smoke except at Maidenwood," Matt said wryly.

I laughed—but not loudly, and not long. We sat in

silence while Matt blew furious clouds of smoke between pursed lips and I stared at the house in a queer confusion of emotion.

The house was of bricks shaped from clay dug on the site. A flight of steps led up to the entrance door in the center of the western face. The wrought iron railings that had flanked the steps were long gone. One of the chimneys was only a stub, and the famous leaded roof had been replaced by rotting wooden shingles.

"What a mess," I said.

There was no chagrin in my voice, only a satisfaction so strong it couldn't be missed, even by Matt, who had never been sensitive to innuendo. However, he answered as if my comment had been a criticism instead of a crow of triumph. "I can't keep the place up. Martha doesn't have a bean, and I'm up to my eyeballs in debt. Politics is an expensive profession."

I didn't ask why he could not get help from his mother. I am named after my Aunt Julia, but the names are all we have in common. A pretty, frivolous creature, who had been spared the tragedy of "the Carr features in a woman," she had married a struggling young lawyer of good family—that is, poor—and had given birth to Matt before she got bored with genteel poverty. She was on her fourth husband now, and he was no more inclined than Aunt Julia herself to waste money on a decaying house in the wilds of Virginia. None of that Tara sentiment for them! It would never have occurred to anyone, least of all her son, to suggest that Julia give up her summer in Europe to care for her dying mother. That was the kind of person she was. I only wished I knew how she got away with it.

"I don't know why you care," I said. "Houses like this are anachronisms. Let it collapse."

Matt didn't reply. He sat smoking and staring at the

house with a mixture of loathing and longing, and I read his thoughts as clearly as if they had been printed on his face—which in a sense they were. He was seeing Maidenwood as it had once looked and as it might look again if he had half a million bucks to spend on it—gracious and beautiful, a perfect background for the aristocratic governor of the Old Dominion.

"So sell the land," I suggested. "I don't suppose it's worth much, but there are hundreds of acres, aren't there?"

"You know Martha would never allow that. And," he added, with a sidelong glance at me, "I wouldn't go against her wishes."

I smiled to myself. Matt was so transparent. He wouldn't make any damaging admissions for fear I would betray his nefarious plans to Martha and try to supplant him as her heir. Even supposing I were low enough to attempt such a trick, it wouldn't work. If Maidenwood were mine I would sell off every damned acre, assuming I could find a buyer stupid enough to invest in a tumble-down house and five hundred acres of weeds—and Martha must know I would. Matt would at least try to keep the house, poor romantic snob that he was; but unless Martha could tie the estate up in some sort of trust it would be broken into quarter-acre lots before she was dead a year. I felt confident it was sheer spite that had made her refuse to let Matt sell before this, but maybe she had been smart to hang on to the land. Property values had gone up, if the new subdivisions along the highway were any indication.

Matt opened the car door. "Let's go," he said, and ground the cigarette butt to scraps under his heel.

* * *

My first thought was: My God, she looks terrible. My second was: She's just the same.

She had been eighty the last time I saw her. That's old by any standards. By the standards of eighteen it's antique, ancient, older than the Pyramids. But there was an ironic truth in the seeming contradictions of my impressions. Martha had always had one of the most expressionless, rigidly controlled faces I had ever seen. Frozen by the partial paralysis of the stroke, it was no colder now than it had been.

She lay propped up by pillows in the big bed—Mary Carr's bed, the one she had saved by poisoning her husband. My third impression was that Martha looked a lot better than I had expected. Her white hair, still thick and healthy, had been cut short, and it cupped her head in a surprisingly modern, stylish look. It was a well-shaped head, sleekly rounded, elegantly curved. Though her hands lay limp on the counterpane, they were beautifully tended. She had always been proud of her hands—a Carr feature I had not inherited. The room was stiflingly warm, but she wore a pink flannel bedjacket that cast a flattering glow on her sallow, lined features.

She had been looking to one side when I entered— deliberately slighting me, I thought. Now she turned her head on the pillow, very slowly, and I understood her real motive. The stroke, one or both, had chiefly affected the left side of her body. The drooping eyelid and sagging mouth would have appeared pitiable on any other old woman. But her right eye was wide open and it blazed with intelligence and pride that defied pity. Either my mother had been mistaken about the extent of the paralysis or Martha had regained some muscular control in the past few days. She could move her head, though with difficulty, and she could speak, in a fashion. The croak that issued from her tight lips was obviously, "Come here," and it was accompanied by a flexing of the fingers of her right hand.

I had made up my mind I would call her "Grandmother," but I couldn't do it. I said, "Hello, Martha," and bent to kiss her cheek. She turned her head. A trickle of hair brushed my lips and I straightened, feeling the familiar surge of frustrated anger.

She looked me over from head to foot. One black eyeball rolled like a jet marble in its socket. She didn't speak again. Her voice had always been one of her best weapons, its soft southern cadences lending a special sting to the cutting words she used with such deadly effect. She gestured again, a gesture all the more imperious for its slowness, and I obeyed, turning to greet the woman who sat in a chair by the head of the bed.

Behind me, Matt said, "You remember Shirley Johnson. I don't know what we'd do without her."

"Mrs. Johnson." I held out my hand.

"You'd best call me Shirley." She shook my hand and released it. Her palm was slick with perspiration and the hair that had escaped her cap curled into wiry coils around her forehead. "You don't remember me, Miz Julie?"

I couldn't fit her placid, coffee-brown face into any niche of memory. She was a comfortable-looking woman, plump and sweet-lipped, with warm brown eyes. I shook my head, smiling apologetically, and she said, "It was a long time ago. You were only eight or nine. I was thinner then."

"Shirley's husband was one of Martha's tenants," Matt prompted. "They moved to Atlanta where, luckily for us, Shirley got her training as a nurse."

"Practical nurse," Shirley corrected. Her eyes shifted to

the bed. "She wants to rest now. She wants me to show you your room and tell you what you're supposed to do."

"Good idea," Matt said heartily. "You get your rest, Martha, and I'll see you this weekend—"

Martha's fingers writhed. Shirley said in the same, soft, calm voice, "She wants you should stay, Matthew. Come along, Miz Julie."

She closed the book she was holding—Tennyson's *Poems,* of all things—and rose. I followed her to the door. I should have been relieved that the interview was over, but I had an odd feeling of incompleteness. Not that I'd expected a loving welcome, but all the same . . . I said, "I'll see you soon, Martha. Have a good rest."

I got the response I might have expected—none. Matt winked at me before turning to Martha.

It wasn't until Shirley had closed the door and started down the hall ahead of me that I realized how tense the atmosphere in that steamy room had been. Was it only the heat? The temperature in the hall was almost as hot. Shirley was wearing nurses' whites and as she preceded me I saw the wet patches on the back of her dress.

"Can't you get Matt to install a window air conditioner or at least a fan?" I asked, catching up with her. "That room is like an oven."

"Old people feel the cold," Shirley said. "The blood runs thin at her age, Miz Julie."

"Skip the 'miss,' Shirley. You and I are about to become sisters in misfortune."

She didn't acknowledge the poor joke except to say sedately, "I'll be glad of someone to spell me, and that's a fact. Miz Martha takes a heap of care."

"You don't mean you've been alone with her all this time?"

"Miz Danner comes most days to clean and cook. She sits with Miz Martha afternoons."

"When do you sleep, Shirley? Or do you?"

"I'm used to sleeping with one ear open, like you might say. It's no different than in a hospital; if you're at the far end of the corridor from the nurses' station, you could fall out of the bed before anybody'd notice, and—"

"I wasn't criticizing, Shirley, I was commiserating. We'll split the shifts from now on. You tell me what you want me to do."

Shirley indicated a closed door, and I stopped short, almost in pain. The lost memories of my childhood at Maidenwood were returning, not sliding smoothly into place as I saw again the rooms and corridors I had known, but thudding into the vacant spaces in my mind with jarring force. I remembered this door and the room behind it. I had spent many hours shut in that room, as penance for my various misdeeds.

The room had changed less than Martha had. Dark and gloomy, its single pair of windows overlooking the kitchen yard, it contained a small iron bedstead, a pair of faded rag rugs, and a cheap chest of drawers. A calico curtain across one corner of the room concealed the rope on which I had once hung my clothes.

Shirley stood silent beside me, but I think she sensed my outrage. Martha had assigned me my former room, at an inconvenient distance from her own, as part of a deliberate campaign. Well, I wasn't a cowering eight-year-old now. I glanced at Shirley, but I didn't have the heart to ask her to move furniture; she had more than enough to do already. I would do it myself—strip the other bedrooms of anything that would make this one more comfortable.

"My room is next to Miz Martha's," Shirley said. "We

share the bathroom. You'll have to use the one down the hall, I guess."

"Okay. I'll be in to relieve you as soon as I change."

"No, that's all right; Miz Danner will sit with Miz Martha for a while. *She* wants you to sit with her mornings. Mostly she wants you to read to her."

"Tennyson's *Poems*?"

Shirley permitted a small smile to curve her lips. "It's better than Dickens. We tried him, but Miz Martha says I don't read good."

"I doubt that my efforts will please her any better, Shirley."

"Then she wants you should sit with her again after supper. She wants you—"

"She wants? What about you? I'm not squeamish, Shirley. I'll empty bedpans and bathe her and change sheets. I didn't come here to read Tennyson and Dickens."

"She don't want you should do those things." Shirley added, "She's the patient, Julie. It's my job. I've done worse."

I could believe that. And I thought I understood why Martha wanted my services restricted to those of a genteel lady's companion. She'd fight to keep the shreds of dignity remaining to her while there was breath in her body. Well, I could sympathize with that feeling. At least I wouldn't have to brush her poodle. Martha hated animals. She had never allowed pets at Maidenwood.

Matt came in just then, ending the discussion. Shirley gave him a smile, much warmer than any I had received, before slipping out. Matt had my suitcases. He dumped them willy-nilly onto the floor and mopped his brow.

"God, what an awful room. Why did you pick this one?"

"I didn't. It was Martha's selection."

"Take another one—the Green Room, or the Jefferson Room. She'll never know the difference."

"No, I rather like being this far away from the throne room. But I'm going to borrow some furniture."

"Go ahead. Uh—want me to help you?"

He looked so hot and rumpled and distraught I took pity on him. "That's okay. I'm sure you're busy. If I yearn for something I can't move myself I'll enlist your services next time you come."

I walked him to the front door, trying to think of things I had forgotten to ask him about. He had given me a list of phone numbers, some money for expenses, and promised me the loan of a car as soon as he could find someone to deliver it. "I'll have it here by the weekend," he promised. "That's only a couple of days. If you need to go out before that, I'm sure Shirley will let you borrow her car. Doc Green said he'd stop by tomorrow . . . Let's see—is there anything else?"

"Probably. I'll think of it after you've gone. Where is the archaeological team working?"

"The southeast pasture. I told them not to come near the house. If Martha hears sounds of activity and asks about them, the story is that I'm setting out young pines as a windbreak."

"Okay."

"You won't see anything of them unless you want to, Julie."

"I don't care one way or the other."

"Right. Well . . ."

He opened the car door and got in. The air was as clammy as a wet sheet. To the west the piled cumulus clouds had changed from white to dirty gray. We were going to have a thunderstorm—probably one of the hum-dingers common to the area. The basement would flood, the power would go out. A horrific picture flashed into my mind, a preview of the evening ahead: reading Dickens by candlelight, with the sweat running down the back of my neck and Martha's single eye fixed on me in silent mockery.

It was all I could do not to wrench open the car door and jump in.

three

The evening wasn't quite that bad. The lights flickered and dimmed periodically but the power did not go off. Thunder rattled the windowpanes and rolled among the trees. I cringed when a particularly violent crash shook the house like a cannonball dropped onto the roof, and I could have sworn Martha's watching eye brightened.

By the weekend I felt as if I had been there forever. I didn't mind the morning duty so much, but I really dreaded the evening round. The days were stretching out, but darkness had usually come by the time I settled myself for another session of Dickens. Shirley had not been kidding about Dickens. The book Martha had me reading was *Bleak House*. The plot was rather interesting, but the heroine, Esther Summerson, was so pious and goody-goody she turned my stomach.

Martha only permitted one lamp, the one by my chair, and the big, high-ceilinged room felt like a dark cave occupied by a half-visible, shapeless thing that might have been animal or human. Occasionally, when I paused for breath, I heard a faint rustle of linen—fingernails, scratching at the sheet. It sounded like dead leaves crackling as the creature crouched in its lair, shifting before it sprang.

Martha never asked me for any personal service, not even a sip of water. One evening, when the air was especially hot and sticky, I asked if she would like me to wipe her face with a damp cloth. Her response was instantaneous, and unmistakably negative.

Shirley relieved me at ten o'clock, so I really had quite a bit of free time—the rest of the evening and every afternoon from noon till about seven. At first I had no trouble filling the hours. It gave me a mean satisfaction to loot the unoccupied rooms for furniture that would give my own shabby bedroom some comfort. Not that there was much to choose from. I hadn't realized just how little was left from what had presumably been a wealthy and well-equipped home. There were no Chippendale highboys or Sheraton chairs. Great-Great-Grandpa had really screwed his descendants; the objects he had disposed of, probably for pennies, were fetching five- and six-figure prices at antique auctions these days. I suspected the late Victorian replacements had some value, since antique freaks are into Victorian these days, but they weren't of much use to me since most were too heavy to be moved. I swiped the mattress from the only bedroom, aside from Martha's, that was decently furnished. Shirley confirmed my assumption that it was the guest room, occupied by Matt when he condescended to spend the night. She seemed faintly amused by my activities, but did not ask why I just didn't move into the guest room. Maybe she knew the answer. It was directly across the hall from Martha's room. Besides, I got a childish pleasure from taking the things, late at night when Martha was deep in the drugged slumber the doctor had prescribed.

Aside from Shirley and Martha, and "Miz Danner"—of whom more later—the only human being I saw for four dreary days was Dr. Green, who came the afternoon following my arrival.

The doctor was in his late fifties. He had watchful, hooded blue eyes and a thatch of snow-white hair, and an accent that made him sound as if he were talking through a mouthful of syrup. I cracked a joke about doctors who made house calls, to which he replied with deadly seriousness. "I've practiced in this region for thirty years, Miss Julie. Anyhow, Miss Martha is a special case."

"In what way?"

We were sitting in the drawing room partaking, if you will excuse the expression, of sherry. At least the doctor partook, and with gusto; I sipped politely at the glass I had taken to keep him company. I had learned from Shirley that Maidenwood sherry was supposed to be something special, and that it was one of the doctor's perks for making house calls. I wasn't impressed, but then I've never claimed to be a connoisseur of fine wine.

He stared at me as if he thought I wasn't quite bright. "She can hardly come to my office, can she?"

"Why isn't she in hospital, or a nursing home?"

"Well, now, Miss Julie—"

"I know hospitals don't like to give space to terminally ill patients, and I also know that it is good medical practice, as well as common decency, to allow the dying to pass their last days at home, if it is at all practicable. But Martha is a long way from dying, in my humble opinion. Considering her age, she is making a remarkable recovery."

He looked surprised, as if a dog had addressed him in understandable English. "Now, Miss Julie, it may seem that way. The patient's attitude is important, and Miss

Martha hasn't made up her mind to give up. But if you could see her records—"

"I'd like to see them."

"You wouldn't . . ." He broke off. He could hardly tell me I wouldn't understand the technical terminology, but he obviously resented being questioned by a lowly student. "I can't show them to you, my dear. Medical ethics—"

"I know I've no right to see Martha's records. But I am responsible for her care and I ought to know what I should be doing for her."

His frown smoothed out. "There's nothing to worry about, child. Shirley Johnson is one of the most capable nurses in the county. She knows what to do. It's only a matter of time, Miss Julie. You must resign yourself. You are giving her what no one else can—the tender love of a woman of her own blood."

He left soon after that remarkable and exasperating statement. Still, the fact that he had burbled nonsense instead of giving me a straight diagnosis wasn't necessarily a sign of professional incompetence. A southern male of his generation would find it hard to take a woman seriously.

Competent or not, he was no specialist, only a country G.P., and I couldn't help wondering why he had not insisted that Martha be moved to a city medical facility for treatment. The problems of aging had received greater attention in recent years; a good doctor didn't shrug his shoulders and write a patient off just because she was eighty-five. Modern therapy might preserve Martha's life for several more years.

The question was—did I want it preserved?

The fact that I could even think the question horrified me so much I took another sip of sherry, reminding myself to lay in a stock of something stronger when I went shopping. The point was not what I wanted, but what decency and the ethics of the profession I hoped to enter demanded.

I replaced the decanter on the sideboard and collected the used wineglasses. Before I could pick up the tray there was a timid tap at the door, and "Miz Danner" sidled in.

"I heard the doc leave," she said. "Shall I take the tray, Miz Julie?"

I had told her to call me Julie, but she couldn't or wouldn't do it. I had met her the day before; I was in the kitchen making myself a glass of iced tea, after Matt left, when she shuffled in, her shoulders hunched as if she expected a blow or a reprimand, and I had the odd feeling of looking at a double exposure. Her scrawny body and nondescript features left so fleeting an impression on the senses that she might have been transparent. Yet, behind the woman that she was, I seemed to get a picture of the woman she once had been—heavyset and plump-cheeked, with cosmetics inexpertly but cheerfully smeared across her face.

She greeted me by name, before I could introduce myself, and her implicit assumption of previous acquaintance jogged my recalcitrant memory. Of course—that was the reason for the double image. I had known Mrs. Danner way back when; her husband was one of Martha's tenants. They lived in a ramshackle frame house a few miles away, and farmed a few acres, ran a few cows, raised a few chickens and pigs—not poor white trash, but not exactly upwardly mobile. Visiting them had been a rare treat for me. They had a daughter about my age with whom I was sometimes allowed to play; Mr. Danner used to take me for rides on the tractor, and Mrs. Danner gave me cookies.

She had been a pretty woman—pounds overweight, but rosy and smiling.

Consternation filled me as I saw what the years had done to her. Gray hair strained back into an ugly knot, gray sunken cheeks, a gray-and-black dress that covered her arms to the wrists and closed tight around her neck.

I tried to think of something to say. Even "How are you?" carried ironic overtones. I could see how she was— terrible. In my attempt to avoid a minor faux pas I committed a worse blunder. Something Matt had told me slipped into place, and I said, "How is Mr. Danner? It must have been a terrible shock, finding the—er— remains. He was the one who found them, wasn't he?"

Mrs. Danner's face froze like an ice sculpture. Without replying she turned to the cupboard and began banging pans around.

Mercifully Shirley had appeared then and I escaped, berating myself for my tactlessness. I hadn't seen Mrs. Danner since. Now she appeared to have forgiven me. She repeated the question, "Shall I take the tray?" with something approaching animation.

"No, thank you, Mrs. Danner. I'll get it. Can I do anything to help in the kitchen?"

She shook her head. "Dinner's fixed. I got to go. Mr. Danner'll be fetching me any time."

"Go on, then. I'll take care of the tray."

She looked as if she wanted to insist, but then came the insistent blast of a horn. Mrs. Danner started, her hand going to her breast. "He's here. I'm late."

"He's early," I corrected, glancing at my watch.

Mrs. Danner didn't debate the issue, but moved at a rapid shuffle toward the door. I followed, curious to see what sort of man could inspire such frenzied obedience. She hadn't called him "Mr. Danner" when I knew them. It was "Joe," then, or sometimes "Stud." I liked that name; once I called him "Mr. Stud," and he laughed so hard he almost fell off the tractor. Then he warned me not to repeat the word in front of Martha . . .

I was too late to see whether an equivalent transformation had affected Joe Danner. The pickup pulled away as I reached the front door. It rattled down the drive, emitting black fumes from its tailpipe.

Deprived of even that uninspired hope of social intercourse, I went back to the drawing room. It was an oasis of cleanliness in the general decay, and the few remaining antiques of which Maidenwood could boast were gathered there. Mrs. Danner earned her pay in the cleaning line; I wished I could give the same praise to her cooking. If the meal I had eaten the previous night was any indication of her culinary talents, I might be driven to take drastic actions—such as doing the cooking myself. The stew had been a disaster—chunks of meat and mushy vegetables swimming in a bland, tan, watery gravy. To accompany it we had been offered store-bought bread and frozen coconut pie.

I took the wineglasses to the kitchen. It was the most pleasant room in the house, which admittedly isn't saying much. The appliances were old, the linoleum was worn down to the nub, and the woodwork needed painting. An antique refrigerator chuckled and grumbled in the corner; like Martha, it couldn't last long. But there were windows on two sides and a screened-in porch beyond; the plank-bottom chairs were surprisingly comfortable, and the big table had a lovely patina from years of scrubbing. There were none of the country-chic touches one might expect in a house that age—no fireplace, or exposed beams. The kitchen wing had been added during a relatively affluent period in the late nineteenth century, when the lord of the manor got tired of food served ice-cold after it had been carried clear across the yard from the separate kitchen house. It was still a considerable distance from the dining room, at the end of a long windowless corridor with rooms on either side—pantries and storerooms and small cubicles that had housed some of the servants.

I opened the oven door and found my most dire suspicions confirmed. The casserole within consisted of noodles mixed with the remains of the stew and covered with a leathery layer of cheese.

I was contemplating this catastrophe with my hands on my hips and a sneer on my lips when Shirley came in. "Is Martha supposed to eat this?" I demanded. "I don't think I can force it down myself."

Shirley reached for a saucepan that stood on the back of the stove. It contained soup, which she ladled into a bowl. The aroma of the soup did nothing to tickle my taste buds; it was a canned variety. She added a few slices of bread to the tray.

"There's cans of soup and tuna in the pantry if you don't fancy the casserole," she said.

"How about lending me your car? I'll run into town and pick up a few things. Even fast food would be better than this."

The request caught her off guard; for the first time I saw her serenity ruffled. "I can't. I mean—didn't Matthew say he'd fetch a car for you to use?"

"Saturday. I can't wait till Saturday."

She frowned, and I burst out laughing. "Sorry. I sound like a whiny kid. I'm a good driver, Shirley, honestly. Or if you would rather, I'll give you the money and you can go shopping later."

"It's not that. Truth is, I don't have the car. I lent it to—to someone."

I almost asked to whom, but caught myself in time. It was her car, after all. She muttered, "I'm sorry." Picking up the tray she went out, moving rather more quickly than usual.

Have I mentioned that it rained every day? Not all the time, just during my hours off, so I couldn't even indulge in the dubious pleasure of a walk. By Friday I was ready to climb the walls and I'd have killed for a bacon cheeseburger. I kept myself sane by making a shopping list, to which I added daily. Not only food and drink, but basic necessities such as light bulbs; the only one-hundred-watt bulb in the house was in the reading lamp in Martha's room. In the other rooms they were forty or sixty watt, or missing altogether. Even in daylight the grey gloom was so depressing I felt as if I were walking through a tropical rain forest. My list got longer and longer. Electric fans, flashlights, paperback books, magazines, newspapers . . . Martha wouldn't have a TV in the house, she didn't take a daily paper, only the twelve-page local weekly, and I had finished the mystery I had brought with me. Stamps. I hadn't even written my mother.

On Friday after lunch I left Mrs. Danner to her criminal activities in the kitchen and went on a tour of exploration. She was making spaghetti sauce, I assumed—canned tomatoes bubbling furiously on the stove, with a chopped onion for seasoning.

There was one flashlight in the house. I took it with me when I started toward the part of the house I had not yet visited. It was pouring outside, the afternoon skies were as dark as a winter evening, and I knew the lights would be cut off or the bulbs burned out in the regions where I was headed. That wing of the house was closed. But there was, or had been, a library, and that was my destination.

Why hadn't I gone there before? It's a good question. I know the answer now; at the time I was only aware of a vague disinclination to open the door into the west wing.

The long gloomy corridor led past closed and cobwebbed doors—drawing room, dining room, music room, billiard room . . . I was glad I had brought the flashlight. I was sorry I had come. Dark and depressing, smelling of mold and mildew—even the boards of the floor felt soggy under my feet.

The library was at the end of the wing, with long windows like French doors opening onto a flagstoned terrace. I reached for the knob and then it happened again—another of those thuds of returning memory. There had been a number of them the first day I arrived, but this was the first in some time. I literally flinched, as if something had struck me, before I opened the door.

I had spent a lot of time in this room during the years I lived at Maidenwood. Reading was almost my only pleasure. I had no one to play with. Martha wouldn't permit me to invite schoolmates to the house, and I was seldom allowed to go to the Danners' place. The Danners weren't "our kind." Neither were the other families whose children attended my school.

The heavy draperies were open. Sun had rotted their linings; they hung in tatters from the gilded rods. The furniture and chandeliers were swathed in cobwebs like soft gray dustcloths.

The flashlight beam moved erratically around the room, spotlighting familiar objects. The sagging leather chair near the window, my favorite seat. The row of children's books on the bottom shelf of the bookcase to the left of the fireplace—books that dated, all of them, from my mother's youth, or from times even farther back. *Ruth Fielding at College*, *Kim*, and a lugubrious little masterpiece called *Beulah*, about a homely orphan girl who grew up to be one of the most appalling prigs in the history of literature. Remembering Beulah, I felt a positive affection for soupy Esther Summerson.

Martha did not forbid me to use the library, but she effectively censored my reading by putting the verboten volumes on shelves that were too high for me to reach. Another memory made me cringe—the night I was caught in flagrante, climbing up the steplike shelves to get a book called *The Golden Bough*. I thought it sounded like a fairy tale. When I asked about it, Martha said, no, it was not a fairy tale (she was right about that, at any rate!) and I was not under any circumstances to read it. There must have been a few smoldering embers of rebellion still burning in me, because the prohibition made me all the more determined to see for myself. I waited until late one night, when I was sure Martha must be asleep. A spring night, it must have been—the smell of blossoming, burgeoning new greenness came back to me, when I remembered . . . I had almost reached the top shelves when the French doors flew open and there she stood. She didn't speak, she just reached out, as if to grasp me, and the moonlight fell full on her outstretched hands. They were stained and streaked with black clear to the wrists, as if she had plunged them into a bucket of oil or liquid mud.

I lost my hold and fell, a good ten feet. I must have knocked myself out, because I woke up in my bed, with a bandaged head, and without the slightest notion of what had happened to put me there.

No wonder I had fought to suppress so many of those childhood memories. I couldn't have handled them then.

I wasn't sure I could handle them now. My hands shook so violently that the yellow beam of the flashlight darted up and down, and side to side, like a hysterical firefly. It would have been completely in character for Martha to lie in wait for me, let me make that painful, dangerous climb before revealing herself—suddenly, silently, shockingly, like some monster from a child's worst nightmare. But she had not followed me through the house. She had come through the French doors, out of the night. What had she been doing out there, to stain her hands with darkness? Or had I only imagined that?

I grabbed a couple of the children's books, without looking at the titles, and ran.

The clouds lightened as the day wore on, and a daring idea occurred to me, born of desperation. I had to get out of that house. Shirley had said nothing more about her car and I didn't like to ask. Either she didn't want to lend it, or the unknown borrower had not returned it. But there might be another way.

I was waiting, purse and list in hand, when Mr. Danner sounded his asthmatic horn. Mrs. Danner gave me a startled look when I followed her out, but she got in the truck without comment, and I circled around to look in the driver's window.

"Hello, Mr. Danner. Remember me? It's been a long time. You're looking—you look—uh—"

I would never have known him. He had been a tall, burly man with a red flush of health under his tan and a ready grin. The face that looked back at me was that of a well-preserved mummy, the cheeks cadaverous, the wrinkles etched as if by acid, sour-shaped and ugly. His lips parted just enough to let a few words squeeze out. "Evening, Julie. How's your mama?"

"Fine, thank you. How is . . ." I couldn't recall the girl's name, much less that of her brother, whom I hadn't known as well. "How are the children?"

"I have no children. Good-bye, Julie."

I was so taken aback I didn't respond immediately. He had shifted gears and taken his foot off the brake before I woke up. I made a desperate grab at the car door and yelled, "Wait. Wait a minute. Can you give me a ride to town? I need to get a few groceries. It won't take long . . ." He continued to regard me with stony disapproval and I added, "I'll be glad to pay for the gas, and your time."

His scowl deepened. "It ain't that. A Christian don't take money for doing a deed of charity."

"Well, then—"

"I don't have the time. Services tonight. I could take you in, but there's no way you could get back."

"I'll hitch a ride. Or—is there a taxi?"

He shook his head. Mrs. Danner squeaked, "There's Will Smith, Mr. Danner. He obliges for some of the ladies—"

"Be quiet, woman. Will's a drunk and a fornicator. No decent female would get in that car of his."

I had my head in the window, intent on winning the absurd argument. He came across the rain-softened grass, silent as a snake. I didn't know he was there until he spoke.

"Looking for a lift, Julie?"

I straightened up so fast I hit my head on the window frame. Danner promptly gunned the engine and took off. I jumped back, slipped on the wet grass, and would have fallen if Alan had not caught my arm.

"Typical Joe Danner courtesy," he remarked. "Are you okay, Julie?"

The rap on the head had brought tears to my eyes. I blinked them away, hoping Alan hadn't noticed them, or mistaken their cause. I'd known I would have to face him sooner or later. I had worked it all out in my mind—the casual smile, the cool, composed words of greeting. So much for that scenario. I did what I could to retrieve my dignity, trying to ignore the treacherous warmth that was spreading from his hand, up my arm and shoulder, into my body.

"Yes, thanks, I'm fine. I'd better get back to the house. Martha—"

"I thought you wanted a ride."

He hadn't changed. He was the only person I had seen who had not changed. Bareheaded, his hair darkened and sleeked by wet, he towered over me by almost eight inches. He was wearing jeans and a long-sleeved shirt, buttoned up to the neck—you don't wander Virginia's woods with your muscles bared, not if you have any concern about poison ivy, mosquitoes, ticks, chiggers, and brambles. But I didn't have to see the muscles to know they were there. I could still feel the pressure of the fingers that had gripped my arm. Long slender fingers, capable of an infinitely delicate touch in excavation—and elsewhere.

I reminded myself that I was a grown-up person, not a silly adolescent. That my feelings for Alan Petranek were those of polite indifference. And, most important, that he had the only set of wheels available.

"Thank you," I said. "If it's not too much trouble."

"No trouble at all."

The Jeep was parked behind the house, near the old stables that served as a garage. Instead of heading back to the front of the house, Alan turned onto a track I hadn't known existed. It had never been paved, and if there had been gravel laid, it had sunk into the mud. Two tracks filled with water led east toward the woods, curved sharply, and debouched on to the road just below the bridge.

As we rattled over the bridge I looked down. The stream was up; water the color of dried blood rushed between banks that showed the raw, new scars of flooding.

"It'll be higher before morning," Alan said, reading my thoughts with the uncanny accuracy I remembered—and resented. "Maybe over the bridge. Nothing to worry about, though. The house is on high ground."

"I'm not worried. Why are you going this way? Carrsville is back—"

"I know, to my sorrow, where Carrsville is located. The dullest town in Virginia. I thought you might prefer something more exhilarating than Millie's General Store."

"I didn't know there was anything more exhilarating."

"There's a shopping center a few miles down the highway. Compared to Carrsville, it offers a wealth of amenities."

"Oh. I—uh—I appreciate this, Alan. You needn't worry that it will take a lot of time. I have to be back by seven."

"How is Miss Martha?"

"Stable."

He nodded. "And your mother? I hope she's well."

"Fine, thank you."

The stiff, formal sentences might have been uttered by strangers who didn't like each other very much. He sounded even more ill at ease than I felt. I couldn't believe that he was; a glib tongue and charming manner were part of Alan's stock in trade; he could carry on a conversation

with a mortician and sound as if he were genuinely interested in the composition of embalming fluid.

I said, matching his polite, disinterested tone, "How is
your work progressing?"

"Do you really give a damn?"

"No, not really."

Ahead, through a break in the trees, a bar of crimson
showed where the clouds were breaking, but under the
trees twilight deepened. Alan switched on the headlights.
He seemed more relaxed; perhaps my blunt and not entirely honest reply had relieved some of the strain.

"I'll tell you anyway," he said amiably. "At the moment
my work isn't progressing. Every time we dig a hole the
rain fills it."

"Too bad."

"Your sympathy warms the cockles of my heart."

"Whatever they are."

"Are we going to go on sniping at each other all summer?"

"I don't intend . . ." I stopped, before I dug myself
into a hole of my own, a hole I might not be able to climb
out of with dignity. Unless Martha obliged me by dying, I
had a long hot summer ahead of me, with massive boredom the least of the difficulties that might ensue. Matt
obviously had no intention of spending any more time at
Maidenwood than he could possibly help, the Danners
were, to say the least, uncooperative, and Shirley . . .
Shirley had problems of her own. It was distinctly possible that I might find myself facing an emergency, the
result of bad weather, Martha's condition, or any number
of other contingencies. If I did, the proximity of a few
husky archaeologists might come in handy.

Besides, hadn't I told myself that the past was over and
done with?

"No more sniping," I said. "I am interested, naturally. What is it you're looking for? Maydon's Hundred?"

It was surprisingly difficult for me to pronounce the name. The last time I had used it to him I had hurled it like a missile, accusing him of using me to get the site he wanted. But once the words were out I felt as if I had jumped a hurdle. The barricade was behind me now.

If he remembered that occasion, he gave no sign of doing so. "That's what I'm hoping to find, yes. But there are other things."

"Such as?"

"The remains of the first manor house. Property and tax records show that there was a house here in the late seventeenth century. The present building wasn't begun until 1735, so presumably it replaced an earlier structure which was destroyed. I don't expect to find traces of that, though. It probably lay close to the present house and we're supposed to keep our distance."

"What about cemeteries?"

We had reached the highway. Alan gave the "Stop" sign a jerk of acknowledgment and turned on to the pavement. "You heard about our local scandal?"

"Not till I arrived. Matt said it was because of that that he decided to give you permission to dig."

"He didn't magnanimously yield, he was forced to give in. There was some public pressure."

"Public, hell," I said, forgetting my resolution. "The pressure came from you, I'll bet."

"I orchestrated a certain amount of it," Alan said smugly. "To refuse wouldn't have been good for the senator's image. The proud aristocrat, letting vandals flout the law . . ."

"Much you care for the law."

"I care about vandalism. There has been too much looting of archaeological sites. Especially at Maidenwood, with all that crap about pirate treasure. Here we are . . ."

I forgot about his problems as the full glory of the shopping center burst upon me. Bright lights, people, cars . . . I felt like a backwoods hick seeing the big city for the first time.

Alan pulled into a parking space. "I'll wait for you at the coffee shop. Take your time."

He strode off without a backward glance, his briefcase in hand. I hesitated, torn between the exotic offerings of Safeway and Drug Fair. There were a liquor store, a gift shop, a McDonald's . . . I would not have believed the golden arches could be so enticing. I hadn't even seen a newspaper for four days.

I bought groceries and booze and stowed them in the Jeep before heading for the drugstore. The coffee shop was part of it, and when I went in I saw Alan in one of the booths, his head bent over the papers spread on the table. He used to complain about the amount of paperwork necessary in a dig . . .

I acquired an armful of magazines and paperbacks and newspapers. When he saw me, Alan gathered his work up and shoved it into his briefcase. "Ready?"

A glance at my watch told me it was later than I had thought. I asked him to stop at the drive-in window at McDonald's and got something to eat along the way, for I knew I would not have time to prepare a meal if I was to be on duty by seven, and Mrs. Danner's spaghetti was a horror I preferred not to face.

I offered Alan a french fry. He shook his head. "That stuff is poison to your system. I'd rather starve."

"There speaks a man who has not eaten Mrs. Danner's cooking."

He chuckled. "I haven't had the privilege, but if her cuisine resembles her personality—"

"It's so bad I may be driven to take over the cooking."

I half-expected some crack about my culinary talents, or lack thereof; it had once been a standing joke between us. But Alan seemed as anxious as I to avoid unfortunate references to the past. He went on, "Do you ever get an evening off? We can do better than Mrs. Danner, or even Ronald McDonald."

It sounded like a dinner invitation—a surprisingly tentative invitation. Perhaps he had learned some humility in the past five years. His invitations always used to sound like orders.

I said I didn't know. "Shirley is the only other person there full-time, and I hate to ask her to do more than she is already doing. I sit with Martha mornings and in the evening from seven to ten."

I hadn't meant it to sound like a hint. Anyhow, he didn't take me up on it. "If you get bored in the afternoon, come out and join us. I can always use another pair of hands."

That sounded like the old Alan. Since I did expect I would be bored, I said I would think about it.

He dropped me at the front door. He didn't offer to help me carry in the groceries, but took off in a spatter of mud and gravel as soon as I had removed the bags from the Jeep. No doubt he was late for his Friday-night date, I thought.

I carried the groceries to the kitchen. Shirley had been in the room during my absence. The lights were on and the tray with the remains of Martha's dinner was on the table. The back door was open.

A trickle of uneasiness touched me. I had not been surprised to find the front door unlocked, for Shirley knew I was out. But Mrs. Danner had closed and locked the kitchen door when she left, and the only reason why it should be open now was because Shirley had gone outside—and had not returned. What could she be doing in the dusk-shrouded, empty kitchen yard?

The clouds had closed in again. It was dark outside—how dark, only those who have lived in an area without street lights and nearby houses can possibly realize. I put the groceries on the table and tiptoed to the door.

Shirley was there. Or someone was there . . . I could see a crouched darkness beyond the porch steps; it was still, but not silent. She was talking, apparently to herself, in a low crooning voice. I could not make out the words.

I crossed the porch and opened the screen door. Shirley got to her feet. I heard the rustle of leaves as something fled into the bushes. Shirley's body had concealed the object on the path—a bowl, filled with an all-too-familiar mess, the remains of last night's casserole.

"What are you doing?" I asked.

It was a stupid question. Yet I half-expected her to tell me she was feeding the local brownie—the atmosphere was that uncanny.

"I was going to throw it out anyway," she said defensively. "I knew you wouldn't want it—"

"For God's sake, Shirley, you can have all the food you want and you can do anything you want with it. Is it your pet? Dog or cat?"

"It's not mine. Just a stray—a dog, that is. It's been hanging around. I guess I shouldn't feed it, but—"

"Not that stew. It's only fit for the buzzards. I bought a couple of pounds of ground beef; let's try that."

I took the meat out of the bag and put some of it onto a plate. The plate was cracked and its design was faded, but there were traces of gold remaining around the rim, and I smiled as I put it down next to the bowl of stew. Feeding stray dogs with hamburger in a Sèvres plate—typical of Maidenwood.

"Here, doggy," I said.

The bushes rustled, but the animal didn't show itself. Shirley said, "It won't come out while you're here. Took me all week to get it to come near me."

I followed her into the house. "What about some milk?" I asked. "Or water? It must want something to drink."

"There's plenty of water around," Shirley said, straight-faced.

"True, too true." I folded the plastic wrap around the remains of the ground beef. "It can have the rest tomorrow. I'll buy dog food next time I go to the store."

"That's nice of you, Julie."

"Nice, shmice. I'm not going to let some animal starve right under my nose."

"I don't suppose it would starve. There's plenty of game around. But it's used to somebody feeding it, you can see that, even though it hasn't been treated right. Guess the owner got tired of it and dumped it here."

I muttered something, not quite under my breath, and Shirley looked at me severely. "Doesn't do no good to swear, Julie. People are . . . people."

"People are no damn good. Shirley, would you mind putting the groceries away so I can get up to Martha? Fix yourself something decent to eat—I got cheese and ham and fresh fruit—"

"That's all right, you run along. I'll take care of it."

I grabbed a banana and ate it as I ran upstairs. I left the peel on the table outside Martha's door. What the heck, she wouldn't know the difference.

I was late and Martha let me know it. If looks could

have killed, that glaring eye of hers would have turned me into a block of stone. Her hand moved with almost normal vigor as she gestured toward the chair and the book.

I wish I could say I learned to love the Victorian novelists that summer. I wish I could say it, but I can't. The sight of a volume of Dickens on the library shelf brings on an almost physical revulsion, as if the events of that incredible summer had permeated the pages, and opening the volume would set them free, like a bad-smelling fog. But, as Dickens might have said, all that was in the future. In the early days I despised Dickens for his own sake—his egregious sentimentality, his soupy, soppy heroines. God, but they revolted me—especially sweet Esther Summerson. Already I had learned to mouth the words like a tape recorder while my thoughts strayed.

Had Shirley really believed I was such a monster that I would scold her for feeding a hungry animal? Anyhow, she had warmed to me; her parting smile had been broad and friendly. I was glad. I needed friends. Even a dog. It would be nice to have a pet. I had never had one. Mother was allergic to animals . . . For the first time I wondered whether her supposed allergies might be based on other factors—her own mother's violent dislike of animals, for instance.

As I read on, page after close-printed page, the night breeze turned pleasantly cool and stars began to bloom in the night sky. I should have been in a good mood. I had a collection of munchies to eat before I went to bed, and a new mystery story to read; Shirley felt more kindly toward me; God willing, I would have wheels of my own next day. I don't know why I was depressed. Maybe it was the muffled cry I heard, just before I stopped reading to Martha. It sounded like an animal in pain or distress.

It could have been any animal. The cycle of life is a

cycle of death as well, and natural selection seems to consist mostly of things eating other things. But long after I had turned out my light I lay awake thinking of all the homeless, hungry creatures that cower in the dark; and I dreamed that something young and troubled came to my window and pressed a white drained face against the screen. Its eyes were empty holes in a framework of polished bone, and the fingers that scratched at the window, pleading for entry, had no flesh to strengthen their appeal.

four

At any rate, it was not the stray dog that had met an untimely end in the night woods. I caught a glimpse of it next morning when I replenished its empty food bowl— only a pair of worried eyes and a long muzzle poking through the bushes. When I went toward it, it vanished altogether, so I left it to its breakfast. The bowls had been licked to gleaming cleanness, as if they had been washed.

I was usually the first one down in the morning, for Shirley stayed with Martha until I relieved her and Mrs. Danner didn't come until noon. She worked for someone else in the morning. On Saturday she didn't come at all; according to Shirley, the church to which she and her husband belonged celebrated the Sabbath in the old style. No, Shirley said, she wasn't Jewish, or Adventist; it was one of those small sects—she couldn't remember the name.

Mrs. Danner's religious needs had left Shirley to carry the burden unassisted on Saturdays. Shirley said she didn't mind; it gave her a chance to run over home for a few hours on Sunday, when Mrs. Danner condescended to stay late.

I had not given much thought to Shirley's domestic arrangements. I guess I had assumed the family had imported her from Atlanta when the need arose, and that her husband and children were still in that city. When I said as much, her friendly smile froze. "I moved back here ten years ago," she said, and changed the subject.

But she wasn't reluctant to gossip about the Danners. I had been brooding about my faux pas when I asked about the children, wondering what nerve I had inadvertently struck. If the boy and girl I remembered had died, I didn't want to be guilty of arousing unhappy memories.

No, Shirley said, they weren't dead. They were alive and well and, last she'd heard, doing just fine. Lynne Anne had three kids and Joe Junior was somewhere up north, working in construction.

I listened greedily. You can laugh if you want to, but small-town gossip is the stuff of which great novels are made. Look at Jane Austen. Look, for that matter, at Dickens and Tolstoi. As I was to learn, there are few quirks of human behavior that don't exist in small towns. In fact, they show up all the more strongly for being isolated.

The bizarre transformation of the Danners from nice, amiable slobs to stern Puritans was the first such case I had encountered, and it left me aghast. "I can't believe it," I said. "I remember them—he laughed a lot and smelled of beer, and she made terrible cookies—she never was a good cook—but she handed them out lavishly, and teased the children . . . He really, literally, threw that girl out into a snowstorm?"

"It wasn't like sending her out to die," Shirley said practically. "There was some traffic on the road, and a neighbor half a mile away. It was plain spite that made her walk so far. That's how they are at that age."

"Even so . . ."

"He's got some virtues," Shirley conceded. "He don't get drunk, or fight; and he used to be a real heller with women."

"Well, I'm glad you told me, Shirley. I won't mention the children to them again."

We were standing outside Martha's room talking in whispers. She had settled down for her afternoon nap; I was on my way out, freed for a whole afternoon of mad, frivolous pleasure. I thought I might clean out the refrigerator or maybe do something really exciting, like take a walk.

I had a ham-and-cheese sandwich and a cup of coffee and washed my dishes. There was no need to clean out the refrigerator; there was nothing in the refrigerator to clean out, except one lonely chicken and some fruit and cheese. As I contemplated the bare shelves I felt like giving Matt a swift kick where it would hurt the most. I wasn't feeling as kindly toward Shirley as I had, either. How the hell was I supposed to run this house without food or the means to acquire it? The mystery of Shirley's missing car was still unsolved; obviously it had not been returned, since it wasn't there. I wished I had asked Matt precisely when he meant to arrive. Was he expecting to stay for dinner? The chicken wouldn't stretch far, especially if I gave half of it to the dog. The hamburger was gone—long gone.

I decided there was no sense in hanging around the house waiting for Matt. He might not come until evening. If he arrived at 6 P.M. with a big hungry smile on his face, expecting a meal, he was out of luck. And if he arrived without a car for me, I *would* kick him.

Having settled that point in my own mind, I went out. The food I had left for the dog was gone, but there was no sign of him, or her. I had placed a pan of water under the steps, but I couldn't tell whether it had been touched.

I suppose that first stroll around the family estate should have depressed me. The place was certainly a sad ruin, overgrown and unkempt; but I could not remember it as ever having been otherwise, and since I tend to be something of a radical in my social thinking, I wasn't cast down by what some people might describe as the decay of a once-proud old family. There was nothing left of the terraced gardens and wide lawns that had once surrounded the house, or of the outbuildings, extensive as a small village, that had served its needs. The dairies, tobacco barns, craftsmen's shops, and slave cabins had crumbled into ruin long ago. When I lived at Maidenwood I was forbidden to go near that part of the grounds, for there were abandoned wells and sunken cellars under the weeds. A few small structures had been kept up—the old smokehouse, solidly if crudely constructed of field stone, and two tiny brick buildings where garden tools and junk were stored.

The ridge of higher land on which the house stood ran roughly north and south, paralleling the river half a mile to the east. To the south, separated from the house by a belt of trees, was pastureland, uncultivated and overgrown. Another stretch of open ground sloped down from the ridge to the riverbank. In the distant past it had been the river approach to the house, from the landing on the James. Visitors sometimes came by water instead of risking the rough, muddy roads, and the tobacco from which the wealth of the plantation flowed was loaded there for shipment. Most of the area between the house and the river was thickly wooded; small streams had cut the ground into ravines and gullies.

The ground was still damp in shady places but the sun shone bright in a cloudless sky, and everything that could bloom at that season was blooming its head off. White blossoms starred the vigorous green of tangled blackberry and raspberry thickets, wild roses raised crumpled pink clusters out of the weeds.

I followed the track toward the woods. It was early in the year for mosquitoes, but the poison ivy looked very healthy, and there would be ticks in the tall grass. Snakes too. I stuck to the track so I could see where I was putting my feet. I had added "boots" to my shopping list, but all I owned at the moment were sneakers, and they don't offer much protection against snakebite.

Later in the season the woods would be almost impenetrable except in the deep secret places where heavy shade and fallen leaves restricted plant growth. Even now the edge of the forest was fenced by head-high tangles of bramble and honeysuckle, wild grape and poison ivy, like a barbed-wire barricade. The vines had been hacked away at one point, where a footpath left the track and plunged into the dusky shade.

I wandered on, keeping a watchful eye out for creatures. Wild animals are shy and wary; I knew that if I met one, even a harmless variety like a possum or a rabbit, and it just stood there glowering at me instead of running away, there was a good chance it had rabies. I armed myself with a stout branch and marched bravely onward. If I was going to get nervous about things like that, I wouldn't dare leave the house all summer.

I had another motive for exploring, other than boredom and the need for some exercise. I was curious about what Alan and his crew were doing. This seemed like a good chance to have a look around. I didn't expect to understand what I saw, assuming I saw anything; in the old days, Alan had dragged me out to a couple of digs, and without a program or his comments I couldn't have distinguished an archaeological site from a hole in the ground—which some sites decidedly resemble.

I didn't meet any snakes or rabid possums, but I found an archaeologist. The first thing I saw was his rear end. The rest of him was head down in a hole between two pine trees. A broad patch of brown mud stretched across the seat of his jeans, but I had no difficulty in recognizing him.

The opportunity was too good to pass up. No, I was not tempted to employ my stick. That would have been childish and uncouth.

At least I wasn't much tempted.

"Hi, there," I said loudly.

The results were even better than I had hoped. His foot slipped on the mud at the edge of the hole and he fell flat. When he wiggled to a sitting position, there was mud on his face to match the mud on the other end.

"Did I startle you?" I inquired.

Alan spat out a chunk of dirt. "My God, but you're a petty woman. Feel better now?"

"Much." I squatted. "Are you finding anything interesting?"

"Four beer cans, five Big Mac wrappers, and a random sampling of contraceptives. Plus some bones."

"Human?"

He handed me a sample. It was a long bone, stained by the red clay and ominously splintered.

"What is this, a test?" I asked. "No, it's not human, as you know perfectly well. Equine?"

"What would you say to a deer?"

"Very little." I tossed the specimen aside. "Looks to me as if you've come upon a local trysting place. Not my idea of an ideal location for lovemaking."

"Oh, I don't know." He leaned back, supporting himself on his elbows, and lifted his face to the sky. "It's private and peaceful; and at night, you can see the stars."

I decided not to pursue the matter; he had spoken with the air of a man who knows firsthand what he's talking about.

"Well, it was nice seeing you," I said.

"Wait a minute." He scrambled to his feet.

"Well?"

He hesitated. Then he said bluntly, "Five years ago we parted on bad terms. I never knew why—"

"Didn't you?"

Alan's eyes narrowed. "Maybe I was to blame. Maybe you had a few hang-ups of your own. I don't really give a damn who was responsible. I've never believed in the popular modern fallacy that people can solve all their problems by talking them out. The procedure usually results in a new exchange of old accusations. So far as I'm concerned, the past is dead and buried. I had hoped you felt the same."

"It's okay with me," I said. "I stopped caring a long time ago."

"Good," he said coolly. "Because I meant it last night when I said I could use some help. I'm damned short-handed."

"What do you want me to do, dig?"

"No. I've got a couple of muscular jocks to do the heavy work. But I need practically everything else— record-keeping, surveying, photography. I'm running this dig on a shoestring."

"What, no grants from the university or the *National Enquirer*?"

He didn't smile. Where his work was concerned he had very little sense of humor. "The national rag has already been here. I had to run one persistent reporter off with a club. But that is an area in which you can be most useful—getting rid of unwelcome visitors. As a member of the family, you can threaten trespassers with the full force of the law."

"I'd do that in any case. You talk as if you were expecting an invasion."

"It could happen, now that the weather has cleared. The sheriff tells me these woods are popular with local hunters and trappers and lovers." A sweep of his hand reminded me of the evidence littering the ground. "It's the only large undeveloped tract of land in the area. The publicity stirred up the old pirate-treasure rumor, and I don't want a gang of louts wrecking a potentially valuable site."

"You still haven't found out where the skeletons came from?"

"For God's sake, there are over five hundred acres to search, most of them overgrown. I can't even be certain the bones came from Maidenwood, though it certainly is the likeliest possibility."

I grimaced. Alan looked at me curiously. "Don't tell me you're superstitious. If the bare idea of a skeleton gives you the shivers, maybe you've chosen the wrong profession."

"Don't be insulting. It isn't the skeleton, it's the sickies who put it on the road that bother me. How could anyone do a thing like that?"

"I've no answer except the one you suggested. There are a lot of sick people in the world. But looting graves isn't necessarily a sign of sociopathic behavior; there are good practical reasons for the exercise, including my own. Even our culture inters valuables with the dead."

"Like wedding rings," I said. "Was she wearing one?"

"Not when she was found. Which doesn't mean she never had one."

"Why haven't the police been able to track down the people who did it?"

"They don't have much to work on, Julie. No fingerprints, no footprints, no tire tracks. And the clothes it—she—they were wearing—"

"Clothes! What clothes?"

"I thought you knew."

"All I heard from Matt was the word skeleton. I never read the story. Can't you date the remains from the clothing?"

"The dress and the baby's gown couldn't have been the clothes they were buried in, Julie. The cloth was too well preserved. It was cumpled and musty, as if it had been packed away in a trunk, but not rotted."

"You mean someone dressed those pathetic bones in clothes he found in his granny's attic? That really is sick, Alan."

"Weird, but not necessarily sick," Alan said, sounding so pompous I wanted to shake him. "Kids have a peculiar sense of humor; some of the fraternity hazing procedures are just as bizarre, believe me. The clothes obviously came out of someone's attic, as you suggested. So we haven't a clue as to the origin of the bones. That's why I get so incensed at this kind of vandalism. If we had found the skeletons in situ, there would have been evidence with them—buttons, scraps of fabric—"

"How old?"

"Huh?"

"How old were the dresses? Were they made by hand

or by machine? What kind of fabric? You could get a rough idea of their age by the style."

Alan looked blank. "I don't know."

"Neither would any other man." I sniffed. "I don't suppose it occurred to any of you experts to have a woman examine them?"

"What difference does it make?" Alan demanded irritably. "I told you, they weren't the original grave clothes."

"It might give a clue as to whose attic had been raided. If the police could locate the jokers, they could persuade them to tell where they found the skeletons. Then you wouldn't have to dig up five hundred acres of dirt."

The suggestion was so eminently reasonable it infuriated Alan—because he hadn't suggested it first. His face reddened. "Why don't you talk to the sheriff? I'm sure he'd love to have your advice."

"I may do that."

It was clear that he was not interested in the subject; with a preoccupied frown he was squeezing the damp lumps of clay between his fingers, as if he expected to find gems hidden in them.

"Look here, Alan," I said. "I'm not superstitious or anything . . ." No, not me—but I dream of fleshless faces wailing at my window.

"Bones are bones," I went on firmly. "Objects. Things. I'm not concerned about the dead; it's the live bastards that worry me, as somebody once said. The ones that may be prowling around the house."

"I see your point," Alan said agreeably.

"Damn it, Alan, where did they come from?"

"The skeletons?" Alan wiped his muddy hands on his pants. "I've no idea. Possibly from your family cemetery."

He saw how the suggestion jolted me, but he didn't understand why. Relenting, he said in a more friendly voice, "I feel sure the police have looked there, Julie. Though these local clods wouldn't notice an open grave unless they fell into it."

"Why don't you look?"

"My dear, we low archaeological types aren't allowed near the house. Your stupid cousin insisted on that; every goddamn crook in Virginia strolls in and out, but we can't. Look at this." He indicated the hole at his feet. "It's recent—within the past week. I do try to patrol the area from time to time and this wasn't here last weekend."

"You don't think this was—"

"Her grave? Couldn't have been. The skeletons turned up two weeks ago. No, I think the treasure hunters are with us again."

"Why doesn't somebody do something?" I demanded angrily.

"Who? It would be impossible to guard this area twenty-four hours a day." He was silent for a moment. Then he said awkwardly, "I didn't mean to yell at you, Julie. It's just that this kind of destruction makes me so damn mad—"

"I know."

"Still interested in helping me out?"

"Sure. When do you want me to report for work? Tomorrow?"

"I don't work on Sunday. Not," he added, scowling, "because I have any qualms about the Sabbath, but because I've already had trouble with some of the local religious nuts about profaning the Lord's day. They can't seem to make up their minds whether he favors Saturday or Sunday, so they ban both. How about Monday?"

"Okay. Where?"

"I'll show you."

"I had better get back. Matt said he'd come today and I don't want to miss him."

"This won't take long. It's on the way."

He picked up a shovel that was propped against a tree and started forward. Before long we came out of the trees into a meadow high with grass and wild flowers. Several hundred yards away the river sparkled in the sunlight. To the left were the roofs and chimneys of the house. The air was thick with insects. A couple of bees floated inquisitively around my face, and I began flailing at them.

"Ignore them and they won't bother you," said Alan, striding manfully forward.

They didn't bother him, but something about me was irresistible—my shampoo, maybe; I wasn't wearing perfume. When we left the meadow my admirers turned back, presumably because they had decided that although I smelled delicious, I was disappointingly devoid of nectar.

The neighboring field had been mowed but not plowed. The surface underfoot was soggy; we were on low ground, not far from the river. Big sheets of black plastic were spread here and there. Pools of water shimmered in their folds. Alan's Jeep stood next to another vehicle, a small van whose back doors were open. He tossed the shovel in, where it clattered onto an assortment of other tools, and then closed the doors.

"How did you get the van in here?" I asked, looking in vain for any sign of a road.

"With great difficulty," Alan said sourly. "And I won't be getting it out until the ground dries. This is not exactly the most convenient dig I've ever run."

The memories that stirred as I surveyed the field were devoid of emotional overtones or jarring shocks—just your ordinary conventional memories of past experience.

The plastic sheets covered test holes and trenches; they were not as random as they appeared, but formed a pattern, part of a grid overlaying the mowed area. I reached for a loose corner of the nearest piece of plastic, which was weighted down with stones. Alan struck my hand away, hard enough to sting the skin.

"Never put your bare hand near anything you can't see," he said. "I found a six-foot copperhead sheltering under a flap of plastic once."

"Oh."

"There's nothing to see anyway," Alan went on. "This area appears never to have been occupied; it's sterile. We'll dig a few more holes just to make sure and then move to another spot."

"It sounds absolutely thrilling. I can hardly wait."

"Don't blame me if it's dull, blame your cousin. If I could dig nearer the house, I'd find foundations and rubbish pits and . . ." A speculative gleam warmed his eyes. "Did you say he was coming this afternoon? What time?"

"He didn't say. If you're thinking of hanging around in the hope of seeing him, forget it. Martha would have another stroke if she knew you were on the premises."

"She wouldn't know."

"Forget it, I said. I don't know when, if ever, Matt will turn up."

He didn't say yes, no, or maybe, just stood smiling at me with his lids half-veiling his eyes. I had seen that look before. "Till Monday," I said, and turned away.

He yelled at me when I had gone a short distance, to point out I was heading in the wrong direction. I waved— it was a "Mind your own business, get lost" flap of the hand rather than a friendly gesture—and went on.

Something about the excavation bothered me, and it was not the prospect of being bored out of my skull. I could see why Matt didn't want an archaeological team working near the house. Martha's hearing had always been abnormally acute—at times I thought she wasn't hearing, but reading people's minds at a distance. But that restriction left Alan with a lot of territory at his disposal, and if he was supposed to be looking for an abandoned cemetery, from which the girl's skeleton had been taken, he wasn't going about it in the right way. Nobody would dig a grave in a low-lying spot near a river that flooded frequently, and if he had, there would be nothing left of the contents of the grave by now. I remembered one flood when that whole stretch of pasture had been under water.

I was walking uphill as I headed away from the river. The slope was gradual, but it meant that the house stood well above the flood plain, and so did the old family cemetery, half a mile north of Maidenwood. The higher ground was the only sensible site for a house, or a cemetery—unless you didn't care whether your relatives' remains got washed away every few years.

I climbed a rotting wooden fence and cut across the corner of another field, chest-high with weeds. Alan had, not surprisingly, misinterpreted my reaction when he mentioned the cemetery. Another memory had thudded into place. Without hesitation I turned away from the house along a brick walkway enclosed by appropriately funereal cypresses.

The cemetery was surrounded by a brick wall and by more of the cypresses, so dark their foliage looked black, so tall they cast a perennial shadow over the graves. Family tradition claimed the trees had been brought from England, seedlings of venerable giants carried home from the Holy Land by a crusading ancestor. (When it comes to inventing romantic legends, nobody beats the Carrs.) In the center of the plot was a red brick mausoleum. Its roof was a startling, brilliant green, the slate shingles completely coated with moss.

The wrought iron gates were closed with a brand-new shiny padlock. A case of locking the barn door after the horse has been stolen? It was impossible for me to tell from outside the gate, but the padlock was evidence that someone had checked the place out recently. There was no sign of regular upkeep or renovation; the weeds were knee-high and some of the stones leaned drunkenly, their inscriptions blurred by smears of lichen.

Ah, the nostalgic memories of childhood! The last time I had stood peering through the bars with the pitted metal biting into my palms I had been eight years old—and I had stood *inside* the gate, with night drawing in and a wind rustling the long grass over the graves. Matt had locked me in and run away. I was hoarse with crying by the time the grown-ups finally found me. I still had a scar on the ball of my thumb, where rust had ground into a bleeding cut.

Dear Cousin Matt. If he didn't show up pretty soon with that car, I would kill him.

He had not arrived when I got back to the house, nor was Alan anywhere in evidence. I hoped Alan had taken my warning to heart. Martha might not realize he was there, but I didn't want him around. One male menace from the past was enough.

Without stopping to change or wash my hands, I went to Martha's room. Shirley was changing the bed. I didn't offer to help; I had tried that once before and had been refused in no uncertain terms, by both parties. I suppose it was easier for Shirley to do it herself, without my un-skilled assistance. It was a job for an expert or a weightlifter; Martha was a tall, big-boned woman, and she had not lost any weight to speak of.

"I'm about to start supper," I said. "It's chicken—is there any special way you'd like it prepared, Martha?"

Martha had got over her self-consciousness about talking to me, but I couldn't understand her very well. Shirley translated the harsh gabble. "She wants to know where you've been."

I suspected that wasn't all she had said. The inimical eye fixed on my untidy person spoke volumes, and she had never been reticent about criticizing my personal appearance. I said, "I went for a walk. Don't worry, Martha, I'll shower and change before I handle the food. I'm not much of a cook, but I can't do worse than Mrs. Danner."

"Better stew the chicken," Shirley said. "She shouldn't have fried food or anything with a lot of seasoning."

Martha's eyes rolled in Shirley's direction and the movable half of her mouth drooped. I felt an unwilling tug of sympathy for her; she had always had a hearty appetite, and when you're lying in bed, helpless and bored, food means a great deal.

"I'll think of something," I said. "Will Matt be here for dinner? When will he be here?"

I didn't need Shirley to translate the reply; the gist of it was that Matt was a law unto himself; he came, and went, when he felt like it. I caught another word. "Doctor? He is coming today?"

"He called up when you were out," Shirley said. "Miz Martha wants to know if there's enough wine."

"Wine? I don't know."

Martha mumbled at Shirley, who nodded reassuringly. "I'd best go and show her. I'll only be a minute."

As we descended the stairs, Shirley explained. "Miz Martha's daddy was noted for his wine cellar. There's still

a few bottles left, and she likes to offer it when the gentlemen come. I'll show you where, then you can make sure
the decanters are kept filled. But you aren't to give the
doctor more than two glasses of the amontillado."

"If amontillado is what I think it is, he got three last
time," I said.

"Miz Martha figured he'd take advantage. He likes his
wine, does the doctor."

No jarring shock of memory struck me when Shirley
opened the cellar door. Evidently Matt had never shut me
in the cellar. I wondered why he hadn't thought of that
one, and then remembered that the cellar door always
used to be locked. We weren't supposed to play there; the
stairs were unsafe, there might be rats or snakes, and the
lower regions had never been electrified.

Conditions underground had not improved in the last
ten years. Creatures scuttled away from the beam of the
flashlight as we cautiously descended stairs that sagged
ominously under our feet. Shirley made quick work of
extracting the bottles from their cobwebby bin, and we
beat a hasty but equally cautious retreat.

I really needed a shower after hugging those filthy
bottles. Clean and refreshed, I went to the kitchen. Matt
still hadn't appeared, and it was after four o'clock.

There wasn't much sherry left in the decanter. I
splashed it recklessly onto the chicken. I needed sour
cream and fresh mushrooms and wild rice, and a lot of
other things without which the dish would not amount to
much, but it was the best I could do. I put the back and
neck on to simmer for soup. Then I sat down at the
kitchen table with the bottle of vodka. I seldom drink
alone, but I was mad at Matt. If he didn't show up pretty
soon, I would not have time to go to the grocery store,

and there was nothing in the house, not even eggs for breakfast.

A clinking sound sent me to the kitchen door just in time to see the dog head for the bushes. He had been licking his empty bowl; the noise I made had sent him flying. He made pretty good time, considering he only used three legs. There was something wrong with one of his paws, the back left.

I stood by the screen door, biting my lip. There went my dinner. I didn't mind that so much—there aren't many women who think they are thin enough. What bothered me was the injury. It would nag at the back of my mind until I did something about it. Don't get me wrong. I am not noble—you must have realized that, after reading some of the admissions in these pages. I just can't stand seeing misery without wanting—no, needing—to do something about it.

I didn't find out until after that you aren't supposed to feed dogs chicken bones. I kept the breasts for Shirley and Martha, and gave the rest to the dog, including the quondam soup. He was hiding in the bushes when I went out. He didn't emerge, but he didn't retreat, either; I decided we were making progress. He didn't belong to any breed I recognized. He was brown and white and medium-sized—that was all I could tell. A mutt.

I sat down on the step. The dog stayed where he was, but I could hear him sniffing hungrily. I wasn't trying to tease him; I thought maybe if I stayed still and didn't move or speak, hunger might overcome his fear of people. Once he knew me, he was sure to love me.

I didn't hear the car until it came to a crunching halt out in front. I abandoned the dog to his—my—dinner and went flying to the door. But it wasn't Matt; it was the doctor, already inside the house. Since he didn't apologize for intruding, I deduced that in this neck of the woods it was correct social conduct to walk in without knocking.

He said he'd go right upstairs. I was about to accompany him, uninvited, when I saw another car approaching. This time it *was* Matt. Strain my eyes as I might, I saw no sign of another vehicle, and I went out with my sleeves rolled up, metaphorically speaking.

"Where's my car?" I demanded.

Matt's broad smile faded. "Is that any way to greet your favorite cousin?"

"Unless you have brought me a car you are not my favorite cousin."

Matt extracted himself and stretched. He was dressed formally on this occasion, in a lightweight summer suit and a tie. "I brought you a present," he said winningly.

"I don't want flowers or candy. I want a car."

"It's coming, it's coming. Not quite as fast as a speeding bullet, but it is coming. I had to ask one of my aides to drive it down. He left half an hour after I did."

"Oh. Well, that's all right, then."

"Hi, Julie."

"Hi, Matt. What did you bring me?"

Matt started to laugh. I gave him points for that; lots of people wouldn't have considered my rude behavior amusing. I didn't consider it amusing myself. So I apologized. "Sorry, Matt. I'm out of my head with loneliness and a sense of abandonment. If I had to face another week without some means of escape from this place, I'd run amuck."

"Don't whine to me. I spent vacations with Martha for years before I got a driver's license. Here's your present for being a good girl."

He handed me a brown paper bag. I sat right down on the steps and investigated it. Pâté, French bread, smoked baby clams, anchovies . . . He must have visited one of the gourmet delis in Richmond. I flung my arms around him and gave him a resounding smack on the cheek.

"You *are* my favorite cousin. I even forgive you for locking me in the graveyard."

"What on earth are you talking about?"

He helped me return the goodies to the bag, while I told him what I was talking about. "You're kidding," he said incredulously. "I never did a thing like that."

"I said I forgive you."

"I can't believe it! I was a rotten kid, but that was . . . Well, if you say so, I must have done it. You're sure it wasn't an accident?"

"Don't worry, I won't tell the press. Smoked clams compensate for a lot of sins. The doctor's here."

"I know."

"Are you going up?"

"I am going to get a head start on the sherry," Matt said. "And the clams."

He carried the food to the kitchen and made himself useful with openers and glasses. I glanced out the back door. The dog was gone and so was the chicken. I decided not to mention the animal to Matt. It was my problem. Anyhow, it wasn't important.

Dr. Green couldn't have been upstairs more than five minutes. He greeted Matt deferentially, addressing him as "Senator," and accepted a glass of wine.

"How is she?" Matt asked gravely.

Green shook his head. "You know it is only a matter of time, Senator."

"How much time?" I asked.

Green's solemn expression changed. He shot me a disapproving look. "You are a student of medicine, I believe. Would you care to hazard a guess? That's all it can be—a guess."

"Since she is eighty-five, I wouldn't be guessing too wildly if I said her chances of making ninety weren't high," I said. "But her condition has improved markedly even in the few days I've been here. Her muscular coordination is visibly better, her vital signs are good—"

"You carried out an examination?" Green demanded.

He sounded as if he were about to have me arrested for practicing medicine without a license. "She asked me to," I snapped. "Obviously I'm not going to prescribe for her, or carry out any procedures for which I'm not qualified. I'm not stupid! But there's no law against taking someone's blood pressure or using a stethoscope—people do it for themselves all the time, you can buy the instruments at any medical supply house. If you are accusing me—"

"No one is accusing you of anything, Julie," Matt said smoothly. "We're all grateful to you for giving up your vacation to watch over Martha, all the more so because your training makes you better qualified to act quickly in an emergency, should one arise. Isn't that right, Doctor?"

"Yes, yes," Green muttered. "But I know Miss Martha; she is a very—er—determined woman. It is hard to resist her when she demands something she should not have."

"She won't overrule me," I said. "I'm pretty determined too, Doctor. And she is completely helpless right now."

It was an idle boast, born of resentment, but as the words left my lips I realized it was the literal truth. Martha had dominated me and frightened me all my life. Now I had the upper hand.

The doctor did not linger after his second glass of sherry. As he rose to go, I heard the sound for which I had been listening. Matt caught my eye and grinned. "That must be Joel. He made better time than I expected."

The man at the door was not the unknown Joel, however. It was Alan.

"What the hell are you doing here?" I demanded in a furious whisper.

He didn't answer me. Instead he spoke to Matt, who was behind me. "I saw your car, Senator. I've been trying to reach you all week. There are one or two things we have to talk about."

"Come in." Matt opened the door, adding, dismissively, "I'll see you next week, Doctor. Thank you."

Green went out, Alan came in. He paid no more attention to me than if I had been a sofa or a potted plant. Matt gestured him into the drawing room. They left me to close the door, which I did.

"I thought I would give you a progress report," Alan said.

"*I* thought you weren't supposed to come to the house," I said.

"Relax, Julie," Matt said. "Even if Martha hears voices, which is unlikely, there's no way she could tell who the visitor is. How are things going, Dr. Petranek?"

"No luck so far. I'm planning two more days on the site. If nothing turns up, we'll try somewhere else."

"Where?" I inquired.

"I haven't decided yet."

"So long as it isn't near the house," Matt reminded him.

"I am well aware of the restrictions," Alan said coldly. "Have you any objection to my making a few trial digs around the smokehouse?"

"Well . . ."

"Look, Senator . . ." When Alan used the title it sounded like an insult. "I can't do a proper survey of the site if you are going to keep me away from the one area where habitation was most likely. I'm not proposing to bring in my crew, I just want to do some solitary prospecting. You can tell the old lady I'm fixing the cesspool."

"All right. But if she asks too many questions you'll have to quit." Matt's voice was slick as oil, but it was obvious he didn't care much for Alan. I didn't blame him. That hectoring manner would annoy anyone. "Is that all you want to talk about?" he added.

"No. You're still having trouble with trespassers. I found signs of recent digging this morning. I want you to post some new signs, and insert a notice in the local paper warning people off."

"Good God, man, that's the wrong approach entirely," Matt exclaimed. "Why draw attention to the problem?"

"Is that the way a politician solves a problem?" asked Alan, with his usual tact. "Ignore it, and hope it will go away? I've received a dozen crank letters in the past week." He took a manila envelope from his pocket and dumped the contents onto the table. "Look at these."

Matt eyed the untidy pile distastefully, but made no move to follow Alan's suggestion. "I've had my share of such things. These people are all crazy."

I picked up the letter atop the pile. It was written on cheap lined paper torn from a dime-store tablet. The letters were round and unformed, the writing of someone who did not often indulge in the art of correspondence. "Dear Mr. Arkeologist," it read. "You are sinning against God's Holy Word when you dig up dead bodies. If you dont stop you will be struck by His Rath."

"Crazy? Of course they're crazy," Alan said. "Who do you think commits crimes, sane people? There ought to be a guard here at night—"

"The sheriff doesn't have enough manpower for that," Matt interrupted. "How many men would it take to patrol all this territory?"

Alan brushed this minor tactical problem aside with a wave of his hand. "You may not care about your property

rights but you ought to give some thought to the three
women who are here alone—one of them bedridden. If
anything happened—"

Fortunately, at that moment I heard the long-awaited
sound. I ran out, without saying good-bye. If I had spoken a word, it would not have been printable.

I can't tell you what Joel looked like. He was a man
with a set of car keys, that was all I cared about, and if he
had not been Joel, but an insurance salesman or a cop, I
would have done exactly what I did—snatch the keys,
mumble, "Go on in, the room to your right," and leap into
the driver's seat like a romance hero vaulting into the
saddle of his mighty stallion. I was off, in a cloud of dust
and a roar of the exhaust . . . No wonder I had heard
Joel approaching; that engine hadn't been tuned in years
and there was something funny about the muffler. I did
not care. The thing moved.

If I had not left the house I would have said something
rude to Alan. Curse the man! It had never occurred to me
to be nervous. Now I'd lie awake starting at every creak of
a branch or squeak of a mouse. I knew I was safer here
than I would be in a city apartment. I did not doubt that
drug abuse, vandalism, and burglary had invaded Carrsville's rural innocence; but the random, sick violence that
occurs in cities was not likely to happen here.

Yet in a way, Alan had done me a favor. I now had an
excuse to acquire a dog.

When I got back, there were no cars in the driveway. Matt
had decamped, without even waiting to say good-bye to
me. He had also not waited to give me any money.

By the time I had carried in the groceries and put away
the perishables and filled the Sèvres saucer with a heaping

pile of dog food, I was starved. Shirley had served herself and Martha; she had taken exactly half the chicken, dividing it as punctiliously as if she had used a ruler. I made myself a sandwich and headed upstairs, munching. One of these days I would get a decent meal, but this wasn't the day. It was after seven, and Shirley had been on duty all afternoon.

Martha's door was open. Shirley was reading—Milton, this time. I don't think Martha was listening. Her eye was fixed on the doorway, and the moment I appeared she began gabbling.

"I know, I know," I said thickly, through my sandwich. "I'm sorry I'm late. This has been a wildly exciting afternoon. I'm not sure I can stand such a whirlwind of social activities. How was the chicken?"

Martha said, "Grmph." Shirley said, "She enjoyed it very much, Julie."

I offered to go on with Milton, but Martha said no. I never did figure out why she kept poor Shirley reading poetry—and the dullest, most pompous poetry in the language at that. Maybe she enjoyed hearing Shirley struggle with the long words and the sedate, difficult meter, just as she enjoyed my loathing of sweet Esther Summerson. Esther was recovering from smallpox, which she had caught through nursing an abandoned waif. Her face scarred, her lover lost to her forever, she was so revoltingly noble any sane woman would want to murder her. She talked to herself all the time too. "Once more duty, duty, Esther! And if you are not overjoyed to do it, more than cheerfully and contentedly . . . you ought to be. That's all I have to say to you, my dear!"

I exchanged a few words with Shirley when she came up to take over for the night. She said Matt had paid his usual fifteen-minute duty call on Martha. He had left no message for me.

When I went downstairs I found Shirley had cleaned the kitchen and put away the rest of the groceries. The dog had come and gone. Whatever else was wrong with him, his appetite was excellent.

five

It was after midnight when I turned out my light and settled down. The night was cool and dry. The night was also very dark. What the hell had happened to the moon, I wondered? As I lay there listening for bumps in the night I cursed Alan again.

I finally fell asleep, to be awakened minutes later—at least it felt like only a few minutes—by an outrageous noise. A human voice raised in pain and anger mingled with the howls of a dog.

I was out the door, my shins aching from a couple of encounters with the furniture, before I realized I had moved. At least my professional instincts were working; my first thought had been for Martha, shocked out of sleep by the racket.

The door of her room opened as I ran into the hall, shedding some welcome light on the scene. One look inside reassured me as to Martha's condition; she was wide awake, alert and staring, and the expression on her face was not of fear but of indignant interest. She raised a wobbly hand and jabbered to me. I said, "Right, I'm going."

"Wait—Julie—" Shirley made a grab at me.

"Call the police," I told her and took off again.

She knew how to reach the cops; I would waste time looking up numbers and arguing with the operator. Besides, I was twenty years younger and twice that number of pounds lighter. I went down the stairs, flicking on the lights as I ran, and snatching up a bronze statuette from the hall table as I passed.

The noise had subsided to a duet of growls, one animal, the other a monotonous undercurrent of profanity. Shirley's notion of locking up was perfunctory, to say the least. There wasn't a bolt or a chain on the door, and the key protruded from the lock, a flimsy old-fashioned affair I could have picked with a bobby pin. I turned the key and opened the door.

At least Shirley had turned on the outside lights. The sixty-watt bulbs shone on a recumbent form sprawled at the foot of the steps. If he was a burglar he was either stupid or very confident; he had parked his car, a vintage sixties' Olds, smack in front of the house. He was a young black man wearing a sleeveless T-shirt that displayed muscular arms and shoulders, and blue jeans so tight it was a wonder he could move at all. He wasn't moving, but he was swearing, with admirable inventiveness. The least obscene term he used was "son of a bitch," and I had to admit it was appropriate. Attached firmly to his left leg was the dog—my dog—the mutt.

I went down the steps. A suspicion of the truth had dawned; I let the bronze swing carelessly from my hand. The man turned his head to glower at me. "I didn't know you had a damn dog!"

I sat down on the bottom step. "I don't. Who are you?"

"Ron Johnson. Tell him to let me go."

"I don't know how. You're Shirley's son?" He nodded, grimacing. "What the devil are you doing here at this hour?"

"Bringing her car back."

"At four in the morning?"

"She wants it to go to church," Ron said sullenly.

I started to laugh, but turned the sound into a cough. His dignity had already taken a beating. It appeared to be the only part of him that had really suffered.

I said, "I'm Julie."

"I know." After a moment he added, "I'm sorry I woke you up."

"That's okay, I wasn't doing anything except sleeping. How are you planning to get home—assuming, that is, that I can persuade the dog to let go?"

"Buddy of mine's waiting for me." A movement of his head indicated the end of the driveway.

"Fine buddy. Why didn't he come to your rescue?"

Ron's expression strongly indicated that he thought we were wandering off the subject. He was younger than I had thought at first—eighteen or nineteen, at a guess. The drooping pirate's mustache made him look older—no doubt that was why he had grown it—but his cheeks and forehead were as smooth as a baby's. The night air was strongly scented with the smell of beer, though he didn't appear to be incapacitated. His remarks had been more to the point than mine.

I turned my attention to the dog. It had stopped growling as soon as I spoke. Now, sensing my eye upon it, it raised its tail and flopped it up and down in a tentative wag. I said experimentally, "Good dog. Three cheers for the dog. You can let go now."

The tail wagged more confidently but the dog did not let go.

"I told you it wasn't my dog," I said. "What do we do now?"

"Don't ask him, tell him," Ron said in an exasperated voice.

"Oh. Let go, dog! Drop it!"

It worked. I felt as amazed and pleased as Aladdin must have been when he said, "Open Sesame," and the magic door responded.

It took a while to get Martha settled down. I told enough lies to get me a couple of hundred years in Purgatory—a stray dog, a lost, drunken coon hunter. . . . Shirley was no help. She remained silent, avoiding my eyes. I figured it was safe to assume she had not called the police.

I checked Martha's pulse and blood pressure. She was in fine shape. That was probably just what she needed, a little rumpus now and then to maintain her interest in life.

I was in the kitchen watching the dog polish off a bowl of food when Shirley came in. "He's not hurt," I said. "Ron. The dog didn't lay a tooth on him, just tore his pants."

"His new Calvins!" Shirley's anguished tone echoed the outrage that had colored Ron's voice when he examined the damage. I had not laughed then, and I didn't laugh now. I'd have howled myself if I had ruined a new pair of designer jeans.

Shirley dropped heavily into a chair. "I'm sorry, Julie. I don't know what I'm going to do with that boy. But he's a good boy—he's never been in any real trouble. . . ."

"He has very nice manners." The amusement I had been repressing for the past half hour would not be restrained any longer. I added, through my laughter, "Under the circumstances, very nice manners indeed. Honestly, Shirley, it was funny. You'd have laughed too."

"No, I wouldn't," Shirley said grimly.

"He brought your car back."

"He should've had it back last night. Told me he needed it to look for a job. Don't suppose he found one, or he wouldn't have snuck in here in the dead of night."

"I don't imagine it's easy for him to find work," I said, sobering.

"Not here."

"Teen-age black unemployment is high everywhere. But he might have a better chance in a big city."

The dog had finished his food. I got down on the floor beside him and lifted his foot.

"I know I'm selfish to keep him here," Shirley said with a sigh. "There's three others at home and he's a real help to me. But it's not just that. I'm scared of what he'll get into if he's away from home. There's so many temptations."

"I don't blame you. Steady there, boy," I added, as the dog winced and turned his head. "I'm just taking a look."

"What's the matter with him?"

"I can't tell for sure. There's a great deal of swelling and some infection, maybe a couple of bones broken. He could have been struck a glancing blow by a car, or been caught in a trap."

"Can you fix him up?"

"I'm no surgeon." I got up and filled a bowl with warm water. "I'll try soaking it, but I suspect he needs a vet. I'll take him in tomorrow—no, I guess it will have to be Monday."

"You're going to keep him?"

"I wouldn't turn a dog . . . I mean, I wouldn't turn

any injured creature away. To be honest, I'd feel better
with a dog on the premises. Weren't you nervous here
alone with Martha?"

Shirley shook her head. Her eyes were fixed on the dog
but it was obvious she wasn't thinking about him, or
about my argument for keeping him. I suspected it was
not physical fatigue—though heaven knows she had good
cause—but worry that made her mouth droop and her
eyelids sag.

"He'll be all right," I said awkwardly. "All kids go
through periods like this."

"I know. But it's hard, raising a boy without a man in
the house."

"It's hard raising any child with only one parent to do
the work of two," I said. "You're divorced?"

"No. I never—I guess he never, either . . . He walked
out, Ron's daddy—there was some woman . . . Haven't
heard from him in ten years."

"So did mine."

"What?" She raised her drooping head.

"So did my daddy. Walk out. It's been almost fifteen
years."

"But I thought . . ."

"Sure. So did everybody else in Carrsville and vicinity.
Martha told people my mother was widowed." The water
in the bowl was an ugly reddish-brown. I rose, rinsed and
refilled the bowl, and found a cloth before resuming my
place. "I don't understand," I said, half to myself. "Why
did it matter so much to her? Why did she care?"

"Miz Martha? No, you wouldn't understand. Small
town, old family, pride . . . She was born in 1900, Julie.
Appearances were everything when she was growing up.
Some people adjust to change, but she's not that kind. To

her, divorce is still a shame just next to murder. Maybe worse."

"And for my mother. Can you believe I didn't find out until two years ago that my father was still alive?"

"I can believe it. I guess—I guess I feel that way too."

"You've got better sense," I said curtly. "You feel betrayed and angry and humiliated. Those feelings are bad enough without adding a gratuitous load of guilt."

Shirley's smile was wry. "Thanks for the advice, Julie. I'll bet your mama really took it to heart, didn't she?"

"She told me to mind my own business." I grinned at Shirley. She laughed softly. I said, "Look, I know you can't change your feelings by pushing a button. I'm telling you how I feel, that's all. And you can tell me to mind my own business whenever you want."

"I will." She laughed again. "That looks better."

"Huh?" I realized she was referring to the injured paw. The other subject was closed. That was okay by me. I didn't particularly relish discussing it; can't imagine why I had done so. People say funny things when they are awake in the dead dark hours before dawn.

"Actually," I said, inspecting the paw, "it looks worse than I thought. Do you think one of the local vets would see him on Sunday? He needs antibiotics, the sooner the better."

"I'll call my doctor in the morning," Shirley said. "She's a nice lady. I think she'd make a special case."

"Do you have a dog, Shirley?"

"Cats." Shirley rose heavily to her feet.

"How many?"

Shirley hesitated. "Five. No, six. There was another stray dropped off last week. They do that, you know—city people—bring them out and dump them in the country, think they'll make out all right. Most of them get killed by cars or wild animals, or starve, or get sick . . ." Her voice trailed off.

I said, "I think I love you, Shirley. Go to bed."

"You too."

She left the room. I wondered whether she had meant that I should go to bed too, or . . . The dog licked my hands.

Later, I lay awake watching the curtains blow in the pre-dawn breeze. I wasn't nervous any longer. The thought of the dog, sleeping on the back porch on the old carpet I had found for him, was that little extra touch of reassurance I needed. I only hoped he would not feel duty-bound to bark at every moth that blundered into the screen.

Shirley was some woman. I didn't know what Matt was paying her, but knowing Matt, I felt sure it was no more than he could get away with. She had held that family together for ten years—four kids, she had said. Three younger than Ron, who was about nineteen. And she still managed to squeeze out enough money to take in abandoned animals and pay a vet to care for them.

I got out of bed and set my alarm. I didn't want Shirley to be late for church. If she didn't have clout Up There, nobody did, and you never know when you may need a friend in high places.

Shirley came downstairs next morning with a spring in her step and a light in her eyes and a handsome flower-bedecked hat on her grizzled head. She looked marvelous.

After some bullying on my part, she had agreed to take the whole day off, providing I let her make it up to me during the week. Maybe it was the prospect of spending the whole afternoon with her kids that brought that light to her eyes. Mothers are peculiar.

"Get going," I said, propelling her toward the door. "And stop worrying. A whole day with Martha isn't going to kill me. It may reduce me to babbling idiocy, but it won't kill me . . . Just kidding, Shirley. Go, leave, vamoose."

She lingered, pulling on her gloves. White gloves! "Miz Danner will sit with Miz Martha while she naps . . ."

"I know. Run along. Depart. Take your leave."

"And the Judge will be here this evening. It's his day."

"Who's the Judge?"

"I knew I forgot to tell you something. That's Miz Martha's lawyer. He's a very old friend of hers and always spends Sunday evening with her. They like to be private, so you can sneak off and have a little time to yourself."

I meditated a ribald remark, but decided it would be tasteless. "I suppose I bring out the sherry."

"She'll tell you what to do."

"I'm sure she will."

"You can't go wrong with the Judge," Shirley assured me. "He's a real gentleman. You'll like him. Everybody likes Mr. McLendon."

She finally left. I squared my shoulders and gritted my teeth and went up to Martha.

She seemed brighter that morning. There was no doubt in my mind that she was getting better. Old fussbudget Green was right, sooner or later she would have another stroke; nothing can prevent the inevitable when the patient is eighty-five. But I was beginning to think that it would be later rather than sooner. Or was Green giving Matt, not a medical diagnosis, but what he thought Matt wanted to hear? If Matt shed tears at Martha's funeral, they would be crocodile tears. He could hardly wait to get his hands on the property.

With Martha, feeling livelier was synonymous with feeling meaner. She kept nodding off, but every time I stopped reading her eyes would snap open and a growl would remind me to continue.

The fourth time she woke from a pleasant doze to demand that I go on reading, I rebelled. I had been at it for two solid hours and Esther was more revolting than ever. She had just welcomed her former lover back to England and was rejoicing over the fact that he seemed to be very sorry for her.

When Martha croaked, "Go on," I shut the book. "You've been struggling to keep awake for half an hour," I said. "I'm going to see about lunch."

Martha snarled at me, and I went on, firmly, "If I don't do something before Mrs. Danner gets here, she'll dish up some revolting mess. How would you like a nice juicy hamburger with cheese, and a tossed salad?"

A gleam of greed replaced the gleam of outraged malice in Martha's eyes. (It's a subtle difference, but I could tell.)

"Good," I said. "I'll be back in fifteen minutes."

I had the salad made by the time Mrs. Danner arrived. I was very tactful; I told her I was taking over the cooking because I thought she had too much to do, even though she was a better cook than I . . . It was wasted effort. She didn't care. She didn't appear to care about much.

I took Martha's lunch up and fed it to her. She grumbled at my awkwardness. She had cause—I wasn't very good at it; but she would have grumbled anyway, so I didn't take her criticism to heart. Her appetite was excellent; she ate every scrap. I hoped the food had mellowed her, but when I started to assist with the more intimate needs her helplessness demanded, she began thrashing around and sputtering.

"I told Shirley to take the afternoon off," I said, interpreting the gist of her complaints without difficulty.

Martha never used profanity, not even a teeny damn or hell. She didn't have to. I got the idea: I was an officious, interfering brat, and I had no right to decide what Shirley's duties should be.

I interrupted the tirade, principally because I was afraid she was hurting herself. "Might is right, Martha. I'm in charge now. When you get back on your feet, you can kick me down the stairs and out the door. My advice to you is to conserve your strength so that that happy day is quick to arrive. Now. I'll just lift you up and slip this in . . . Oh, sorry. I'll improve with practice."

It was not a pleasant time for either of us, but I finally got her washed up and tucked in and settled down. She looked exhausted. I felt guilty about my clumsiness, and about bullying the poor old witch, so I offered to read her to sleep.

"How about some Milton?" I offered. "God in him for her, and that sort of thing."

She shook her head. "Talk," she mumbled. "Mother?"

It was the first time she had indicated any interest in my maternal parent—her daughter. I sat down on the side of the bed and started talking. Told her about Mother's job and her recent promotion, about her apartment, about her friends and her arthritis and so on. Martha seemed to enjoy it—at least she didn't stop me—so I went on, and told her about me. Med school was rough but I thought I was keeping up; my grades were good, and I had had a half-hearted compliment from one of the professors.

After a while she interrupted. "Bows?"

I couldn't figure out what she meant at first. My failure

to comprehend brought a faint flush of rage to her cheeks. It wasn't until she fumbled for my hand and jabbed at the third finger that the light dawned. "Beaux?" I repeated. "Boyfriends? One or two. I'm not engaged, no. Nothing serious. I don't intend to tie myself down until I finish school."

Martha stared at me without blinking. The drooping eyelid and the slight twist of her mouth turned her expression into a cynical leer.

She said, quite clearly, "Judge coming."

"I know, Shirley told me. I'll break out the sherry. And shall I make some hors d'oeuvres?"

"Bring here."

"Okay."

"Change . . . dress. Look decent."

I glanced at my faded shirt and jeans. "All right."

"Some respect . . . Manners . . ."

"I said, all right."

"Sleep now." She closed her eyes.

She had outscored me again. She wasn't interested in Mother's life, or in mine; it had all been designed to lead up to the humiliating admission that I was still unsought and undesired—not a beau to my string. Then the curt orders, the kind she'd have given a servant . . . It was such a petty way of getting back at me, not so much for my clumsiness in helping her as for the fact that she needed help. I should have pitied her. I didn't. But I did not feel humiliated. She had lost the power to hurt me.

I had left part of the salad for Mrs. Danner, but she hadn't touched it. When I went to the kitchen she was finishing a thick sandwich made of cheese and bread—no lettuce, no tomato, no nothing. She started guiltily to her feet when I entered.

"Take your time," I said.

"I was goin' to clean the parlor."

"I'll clean the parlor. If you've finished, go up and sit with Miss Martha."

She began gathering up the luncheon dishes. "I'll do that," I said impatiently. "Go on upstairs. I have to go out for half an hour or so, but I won't be long."

She turned, alarm written plainly across her drab features. "I don' like to be alone with her. What if somethin' happens?"

"Then you pick up the phone and call the doctor. Nothing is going to happen, Mrs. Danner. I'll be back in half an hour—an hour at the most."

"But I don' like—"

"Don't be silly. The doctor's phone number is on the pad by the telephone. So is Shirley's. She's home today. Run along."

I could hardly blame her for her reluctance. I too would rather have scrubbed floors or cleaned privies than sit with Martha. Did she insist that Mrs. Danner read aloud to her—T. S. Eliot, perhaps, or Dostoevski?

After I had rinsed the dishes, I went to the back door. The dog was nowhere in sight. I realized I should have had sense enough to tie him up or confine him when he came for his breakfast. Shirley's veterinarian had agreed to meet me at her office at one. There was no point in my going unless I had the dog with me. I couldn't even call him. I didn't know what to call him.

Finally I got one of my brighter ideas. I put some of his dry food in a dish and went out on the back step and rattled it, calling softly. It was, perforce, an anonymous call. "Here, dog—come on, dog."

It was probably the sound and smell of the food, rather than my voice, that attracted him. In daylight he had lost the confidence he had demonstrated the night before. He came skulking, tail low, eyes wary.

I didn't know much about dogs. I couldn't tell one breed from another. He had long drooping ears and a low-slung body that ought to have been heavier than it was. He was brown and white. He was either very nearsighted or very absentminded, because after a few feet of slow forward progress he finally recognized me; then his tail started flapping and he advanced more quickly. While he gulped the food I tied a scarf around his neck. He came with me readily and climbed into the front seat of the car as if he knew what was going on.

It was my first visit to Carrsville in years. The town had not changed much. A sign on the outskirts reminded me that the population was 1350. The houses on the main street—the only street—looked as if they hadn't been painted since I left. There was one block of commercial establishments—two gas stations, a grocery store, a drugstore, a five-and-ten. The visit convinced me of one thing—except for the vet, there was absolutely no reason for me to return to Carrsville.

I had wondered how a woman veterinarian could establish a practice in an area like this, where macho traditions prevailed and most of a vet's practice involved farm animals. When I saw May Rubin I understood. She was about six feet tall and must have weighed a hundred and ninety pounds, most of it muscle. Those brawny arms could easily hobble a cow or throw a sheep—if that's what you're supposed to do with cows and sheep. Her graying hair was cropped short, and she had not bothered with makeup. Her eyes were gray too; they appraised me, without prejudice, from behind her horn-rimmed glasses.

I started to tell her how much I appreciated her coming in to work on Sunday. She shrugged the speech away with the air of a person who has no time and little sympathy for meaningless courtesies. "Let's see what you've got here," she said.

I drove back to Maidenwood half an hour later and sixty dollars poorer. Rabies shot, distemper shot, parvo shot, penicillin shot, bottles of pills, ointment, flea shampoo . . . I had the feeling that I was in much deeper than I had expected. The dog thought so too. He sat bolt upright on the seat beside me, with a distinctly proprietorial air.

I also had a little book called "How to Care for Your Dog."

When May realized I was as ignorant about the canine species as I claimed, her contempt turned to pity. She even presented me with an old collar one of her clients had left behind.

My brain was reeling with new information. The dog was a mixed breed—part hound, part shepherd, part God-knew-what. He would always limp; several of the small bones in his paw had been broken and they had already started to knit, badly. It would require a painful and expensive operation to put them right, and May saw no point in doing so. She supposed I didn't care whether he ever won any prizes catching rabbits? I assured her that was not one of my aspirations. So, she said, all we had to worry about was the infection. Make sure he had his pills twice a day, use the ointment four times a day, keep him from licking it off, bathe him, de-flea him, worm him . . .

I groaned aloud. The dog glanced at me and flapped his tail sympathetically, but he didn't appear at all embarrassed at putting me to so much trouble. I don't know how he knew, but he did; anybody who has spent sixty hard-earned bucks on a dog *owns* that dog.

I drove around to the back and left the car in the yard. The dog curled up on his rug and prepared for a well-deserved nap. He had yelped once or twice while May was cleaning and disinfecting his foot, but he had not snapped at her. I told him he was a good dog. I'd have to think of a name for him. Couldn't keep calling him "dog."

The trip had taken longer than I anticipated, but I figured I had another half hour before Martha woke up. I browned the roast, poured a generous dollop of wine over it, and set the burner to simmer. Martha still had all her own teeth, but I thought pot roast would be easier to chew than oven roast. That only took ten minutes. I was about to sit down for a rest when I remembered I had promised Mrs. Danner I would tidy the parlor. It shouldn't take long; no one had been in the room since Friday, and I had carried the used wineglasses to the kitchen that evening.

As I approached the room I saw the door was open. Mrs. Danner must have been a little deaf. I stood in the doorway for several seconds before she realized I was there. She started and turned. Her hands were empty, but there was a can of furniture polish and a dustcloth on the table.

"I thought I told you to stay with Miss Martha," I said.

"She's asleep. I was gonna—"

"Please go back upstairs."

"I was—"

"I said I'd clean this room. Go on, please. Tell me when she wakes."

She obeyed without further argument, ducking her head as she passed me like someone expecting a blow. She was so damned humble and Uriah-Heepish she made me feel guilty; but what the devil was she there for, if not to relieve Shirley and me in watching over Martha? Not

that the house couldn't have used a full-time housemaid;
in its heyday, it must have had a large staff. But there had
been no attempt to maintain the old standards, just keep a
few rooms habitable.

And why, if the idea of being in the same room with
Martha terrified her so, had she accepted the job?

I knew the answer, of course. She had accepted it because she needed the money. I ought to know; I had done
a lot of things I detested for the same reason.

The table on which she had been about to operate was
mahogany, with the soft reddish patina of age. I picked up
the can of polish. It was one of those spray jobs, and even
I knew you aren't supposed to use it on fine old wood.
Mother used a special polish on hers, together with a lot
of elbow grease. Actually, the furniture didn't need polish-
ing, only dusting.

I rather doubted that Mrs. Danner had intended to
polish anything. She had been looking at some object, and
it wasn't hard to figure out what that object was. It lay on
the table, where she had dropped it when she heard me at
the door—one of the letters Alan had brought to show
Matt, in order to make his point about the need for protection from trespassers. The rest of the letters were there
too. I could see Matt stubbornly refusing to look at them,
and Alan stubbornly refusing to take them back. I hadn't
noticed them when I cleared away the wineglasses.

I was a little surprised that Mrs. Danner would be curious enough to examine the peculiar documents. I gathered the papers and took them to a chair by the window.

The one she had been inspecting was the letter I had
read—the difficult, childish handwriting, threatening Mr.
Arkeologist with the Rath of God. There were half a dozen
others. They had nothing in common except the craziness
of their contents. One, on scented pink notepaper with

fancy gold initials, offered the services of the writer to
"Professor Alan" in terms that left the extent of those services wide open. She had seen his picture in the newspaper and she just knew they would have an awful lot in
common. Another, neatly typed on business stationery
with a printed letterhead, was from an organization
named The Research Center for Psychic Archaeology. It
requested—perhaps demanded would be more accurate—
permission to excavate at Maidenwood, at a location that
had been revealed to the writer during a séance. A third
offered to sell Alan a map showing the exact spot where
Blackbeard had buried his treasure. The price was a mere
ten thousand dollars—no personal checks, please, only
cash or certified check.

The others were even more exotic. If these were a sample of Alan's mail, I wondered what kind of trash Matt had
received. I also wondered whether any of the letter writers
and their ilk were given to prowling the fields and forests
of Maidenwood by night. Someone had done so—someone with a very unpleasant sense of humor. I lavished a
few silent but passionate adjectives upon my cousin Matt.
He might have had the decency to warn me about this
feature of the job. However, to give him his due, he probably never thought of it as constituting a potential danger.
He had very little imagination. I, on the other hand, probably had too much.

I picked up the letters and went in search of Mrs. Danner. She was in the kitchen, motionless as a monolith,
staring at the door. The dog stared back at her, eyes
pleading, nose pressed against the screen.

I poked her. "Mrs. Danner—"

She pointed. "It's a dog."

"I know."

"I'll run him off."

"You'll do nothing of the kind. It's my dog."

"It's the Beekins' dog. Beekins run him off a while back."

"Beekins must be a real charmer," I said. Mrs. Danner transferred her glazed stare to me. "Anyhow, he's my dog now," I said firmly. "You needn't have anything to do with him. Just leave him alone."

"Miz Martha won't have no animals around the place."

"Miss Martha won't know unless you tell her. And," I added, "if you do, it will be your fault if she has another stroke. Clear?"

Mrs. Danner stared.

"Okay," I said. "If you get bored you can—you can dust the parlor. Don't use that polish, just a dustcloth. Got it?"

Mrs. Danner stared.

Martha was too dignified to yell for me; had that not been the case, I'd have heard her at the bottom of the stairs. She had plenty to say once I had made my appearance. She started by complaining about being left alone.

"I've been thinking about that," I said. "You're so much better, I don't believe you need constant attendance. You must be sick of people around all the time. Oh, I don't mean you would be left alone in the house; but if I could get Matt to install a bell, like they have in a hospital . . . Wouldn't you like that?"

She indicated she would think about it. I smothered a smile as I went about my nursing duties, because I knew she was considering pros and cons I had not mentioned. The idea of pressing a buzzer to bring her slaves running, panting and puffing, from far corners of the house, had its appeal.

I flattered myself that I was rather deft in tidying her up that time, but she wasn't satisfied. She wanted her hair

brushed and arranged, she wanted her new bedjacket—
not that one, the other one—no, not that one . . . she
wanted her nose powdered and her nails buffed, and a
touch of cologne. Her vanity was a little pathetic and more
than a little grotesque. It is hard to believe when you are
still firm-fleshed and unwrinkled that you will ever be
old; yet I think the pathos would have outweighed the
grotesque with anyone except Martha.

When I had finished the job she glowered at me. I
knew what she was going to say. My only defense was to
beat her to the punch. "I'll run and change now," I said. "I
didn't have time before."

She nodded grudgingly.

The Judge was early. I was on my way upstairs with the
plate of "hors d'oeuvres"—crackers and cheese—when I
heard his car; but it wasn't that sound that made me drop
the plate onto the nearest piece of furniture, and bolt for
the door. It was the sound of a dog barking.

However, the dog was easily seduced. When I went
out, he was sprawled on the ground, squirming with pleasure because his belly was being scratched by the tip of a
gold-headed cane.

The Judge was a handsome old man. He had probably
not been handsome when he was young; sagging muscles
and loosened skin had blurred and softened features that
might have appeared too bold, even coarse, thirty years
earlier. He had a beautiful mop of snow-white hair,
brushed back from a high forehead, and he looked as if he
had dressed for a wedding—dark grey three-piece suit,
white shirt, silk tie.

When he saw me, his eyes widened. "Julie?"

There was a questioning note in his voice. I said, smiling, "I suppose I've changed."

"Yes. Yes, I thought for a moment . . . The family resemblance is very strong."

I decided not to pursue that subject. I definitely did not want to be told that I reminded him of Martha.

He had to make a wide circle around the dog, who was staring admiringly at him. "A fine animal," he said politely.

The dog wound itself into a pretzel and began biting furiously at its flank. By now I knew what that meant. "I'm afraid he has fleas," I said.

"A fine hound," the Judge repeated. "What is his name?"

It must have been the word "hound" that put the idea into my head. Normally I am more inventive.

"Elvis," I said.

"Elvis?"

"Elvis."

The stupid dog stared off into space, paying no attention. "Elvis," I repeated loudly. "Good dog, Elvis. You can go and—er—do whatever dogs do . . ."

Elvis continued to gaze raptly into the infinite, so I gave up. "Do come in," I said, opening the door. "Martha is looking forward to seeing you."

"And I her. But first, may I have a word with you?"

I led the way into the parlor. He waited for me to take a chair before seating himself.

"How is your mother?" he began.

I should have known he would have to go through the formalities first. If the house had been ablaze he would have asked after Mother before he yelled "Fire." We established that Mother was fine and I was fine before he got down to business.

"I fear you found Martha sadly changed."

"Actually, I think she's doing remarkably well."

"Do you?" A glow of pleasure warmed his sallow cheeks. "I am delighted to hear it. Dr. Green has not been encouraging."

"He's the doctor," I said quickly. "I mean, don't take my word for anything. I wouldn't want to raise false hopes, since I don't know what I'm talking about. I was just giving you an inexpert opinion."

"You are being modest." He smiled approvingly; modesty was a proper attribute for nice young women. "I did not want an expert opinion, I wanted encouragement. Green is a good man, but . . ."

"I'm sure he is. However, I can't help wondering why Martha is not in a hospital—a city or university medical center, with up-to-date facilities. I'm in a difficult position. Dr. Green hasn't volunteered any information, and I can hardly ask questions without sounding like some smart . . . like some smart-aleck med student."

"You have the right to ask any questions you like. But it isn't Dr. Green's fault that Martha is here. He recommended the University of Virginia Hospital. Martha refused."

"I can understand her feelings," I began.

"You can't really understand," the Judge said gently. "You are too young. Old age is, above all else, ignominious. One by one our strengths are stripped away. Arthritis and rheumatism cripple our limbs, hearing and vision diminish, beauty fades . . . Martha is clinging to the only shred of dignity remaining to her—the right to die in her own home. Here she is an individual, not one of many bodies in many sterile rooms—addressed as 'mother' by impertinent interns who can't be bothered to remember her name, and as 'dear' by nurses young enough to be her grandchildren . . ."

"I do understand. I'm sure I'll feel the same way when my turn comes. But you must admit the situation places a considerable responsibility on my shoulders. Shirley is first-rate, one couldn't ask for a better nurse; but she is not a young woman, and we are so far away from help if an emergency should arise—"

"Yes, I see. You must be nervous here alone, especially at night."

"I am not nervous. I am understandably concerned. We are isolated, and some peculiar things have happened."

"Is that why you got the dog?"

"I didn't get the dog, he got me. But I do feel better with him here. I know Martha hates animals—"

"You are quite mistaken."

"She never let me have a pet," I said. I had not meant to say it. It made me sound sullen and childish.

"Martha doesn't hate dogs. She had a dog, long ago—a beautiful hound named Jason. Her father gave him to her on her twelfth birthday, and she had him for over ten years. She found him dead—shot—one morning, and it almost broke her heart. She vowed then that she would never own another pet."

Moisture sparkled in the corners of his eyes. Poor dear old man, he found the story touching. But I couldn't agree with the idea of cutting oneself off from love because of the fear of losing it.

"I didn't know that," I said gently, but noncommittally. "Martha doesn't know about the dog—Elvis—and I don't intend to tell her unless I have to. But if she refuses to go to a hospital she must accept the consequences. Don't you agree that it would be irresponsible of me not to take security measures?"

The Judge began, "A gun—"

I laughed. "I'd probably shoot myself in the foot, Judge. Besides, I don't want to kill some harmless screwball, just scare him away."

It was the second reference I had made to the neighborhood sensation. Again Judge McLendon tiptoed delicately away from the subject.

"You are a very persuasive young woman, Julie. And a very sensible one. I am much more at ease about Martha's safety now that I have talked with you, and I am in complete agreement with your arguments. I had better go upstairs now, if you will excuse me." He pushed himself to his feet, with the help of the cane. Then he winked. "I won't mention—er—Elvis," he whispered.

I got to the kitchen in time to prevent Mrs. Danner from dumping a quart of water onto the roast. I splashed in more wine; as I turned to reach for a fork I caught her staring, not at me, but at the bottle, with an expression I could not mistake.

The only thing that surprised me was my own obtuseness. I should have known, the day she had been so eager to take the wineglasses, one of which was more than half full.

Well, I didn't begrudge her an occasional nip. If I were married to born-again Joe Danner, I'd have taken to the bottle myself.

"You can run along if you like," I said.

"Mr. Danner's not here yet."

"Suit yourself. But I can't think of anything else for you to do. Unless you'd like to read the rest of those letters."

In detective stories a sudden, unexpected accusation

produces a guilty start, or a guilty blush, or a guilty some-thing. Mrs. Danner just stared blankly.

I elaborated. "The crank letters. The letters on the table in the parlor."

"I wasn't reading nothing. I was dusting the table."

"I'm not blaming you. I suppose a phrase in one of them caught your eye. They were peculiar letters."

"I wasn't reading nothing."

I shrugged. "Go on, then. Sit on the step and wait for Mr. Danner, if you can't think of anything else to do."

She couldn't.

Elvis was at the back door, ears up and tail flapping. I had not had time to read my manual on dog care, but I had a feeling I wasn't supposed to feed him four times a day. I decided the hell with it. He was too thin anyway.

I slipped a pill in his food and rubbed ointment on his foot while he gobbled his dinner. The fleas hopped mer-rily up and down on his back. I thought I'd bathe him in the morning, after I had studied the manual. No need to be precipitate about such things.

Mr. Danner duly arrived, just as the grandfather clock in the hall struck five. I watched the truck drive off; the Danners sat side by side staring straight ahead, not speak-ing. American Gothic on wheels.

I wondered if they ever spoke to one another, beyond the basic remarks dictated by common needs; and if they did, what they talked about. Not their children. Perhaps they read aloud to one another from the Bible, with particular attention to doomsday prophecies.

How much of a fanatic was Joe Danner? He was fanati-cal enough to disown his daughter and alienate his son. A man like that might feel duty-bound to write threatening letters to blasphemers and heretics. It wouldn't have sur-prised me to learn that Joe had penned the letter his wife had been examining; but was he crazy enough to fall upon the heretics with fire and the sword? I certainly hoped not. But I found myself unwillingly remembering a movie I had been fool enough to see with a friend who was an aficionado of horror films, the bloodier the better. This film had featured an insane handyman who did in a dozen people with various tools—hammer, saw, chisel. Moviemakers do amazing things with special effects these days. Blood spouted, heads fell off, arms and legs littered the terrain. I could see Joe Danner, in his faded dungarees, coming up the stairs at Maidenwood, brandishing an ax . . .

Nonsense. If Joe decided to exterminate anyone, it would be Alan, who was planning to desecrate graves. Comforted by this reasoning, I went back to the kitchen and had a drink.

I was waiting in the parlor when I heard Martha's door open and Judge McLendon descend.

"I hope I haven't tired her," he said, as soon as he saw me. "She'd like you to come up now."

"I'm sure it did her good to see you."

"I'll run along now. Please telephone me at any time, day or night, if there is anything at all I can do."

The visit had certainly not pepped him up. He looked ten years older than he had when he arrived—and that is very old. To me, Martha might appear to have improved, but her condition must seem pitiable to an old friend who remembered her in her vigorous youth—especially a friend who knows that only good luck or the Grace of God has preserved him from a similar fate.

Martha hadn't much to say that evening, but she never took her eyes off me. She didn't scare me—not any longer—but that bright, unwinking glare would have affected anyone's nerves. I handed her over to Shirley with enormous relief.

Another neglected duty was nagging at me, and I decided to get it over with. I had forgotten to buy stamps, and I owed Mother a call. She had written once, a conventional note hoping I was not finding my duties too onerous, but I knew she wouldn't use the phone unless she was desperate. Long distance, to her, was not a convenience but a last resort.

She said she had been hoping I would call. "Such a long time, Julie. I always worry—"

"You could have called me, you know."

"Oh, honey, I've just been so busy. Work is frantic, you've no idea."

I laughed at the complacent enjoyment in her voice. She loved the frantic schedule and the compliments that followed her achievements. "I don't know how you keep so calm, Mrs. Newcomb. I don't know what we'd do without you."

"I wish I could say the same, Mother. I had anticipated being driven crazy by Martha, but I didn't realize it would be so damn boring."

"How is she getting on?"

"I am sorry to report that the patient is recovering nicely," I said.

Mother had a way of responding to particularly outrageous remarks with pained silence. It was much more effective than a scolding, and usually ended with me scolding myself.

"That was a terrible thing to say," I offered.

"Yes, honey, it was."

"So I apologize. But she is so . . . Why does she hate me so much, Mother?"

Mother's ladylike laugh was a little strained. "Now, Julie, you know she doesn't like anyone, not even her own daughters. You mustn't take it personally."

"It's more than dislike. It's active, malevolent . . . When she looks at me I feel as if she isn't seeing me, but someone else—the child I used to be, perhaps. Was I that bad? Lord knows I hated every second I spent in this house—"

"Julie, I took you away the instant I could. It was impossible for me to have you with me at first."

The child I had been didn't believe that. As an adult, I could understand her reasons. She had had a desperate struggle at first, working at minimum wages during the day and going to secretarial school at night. Not impossible with a young child, but close to impossible, and there were other major disadvantages—inner-city schools, a cheap room in a bad neighborhood, drugs, child molesters . . . I understood, yes, but I also wondered, with my grown-up wisdom, whether there had not been another factor, a kind of social snobbery, sometimes called pride, that made Mother refuse to have anyone, even me, see her until she had attained the goals she considered minimal— a nice garden apartment in a pleasant suburb, a car, a good school for her daughter.

I had never voiced any of my doubts to her, and God willing I never would. She went on protesting, excusing, anxiously demanding my acknowledgment that she had acted for the best.

I cut her short. "Sure, Mother, I know. How's the weather up there?"

Hot. The weather was hot. I said it had been raining here. Finally she said, "So Martha is better. Still bedridden, though? Well, we can't expect miracles, can we?"

"No," I said. "At least I hope not."

I made my farewells and hung up before she had that comment figured out, and before I had to admit it was a terrible thing to say.

six

I reported for work the following afternoon, to be received with something less than enthusiasm. I didn't take it personally; the weather was hot and muggy, and the open field swarmed with insects of all varieties. I couldn't blame Alan for being in a glum mood, particularly since it was apparent that his new trial trenches had yielded nothing. (I deduced this because a big young man was filling them in.)

"I came to tell you I can't come today," I told Alan.

Through the cloud of gnats that hovered around his nose he said, "Why not?"

"I have to wash my dog."

"Your dog," Alan repeated. His lips barely parted; whether he was controlling passionate emotion or trying to keep a bug from flying into his mouth I was not certain.

"And see the sheriff."

"The sheriff?" This time, voice and expression indicated rising interest. "Has something else happened?"

"Sorry to disappoint you. It's about that other matter."

"Ah. Any new information?"

"I don't know why it's any of your business, but since there is no new information, I have no hesitation in informing you that such is the case." After a moment, during which I decided there really was no reason for keeping the facts from him, I added, "He wants to know what to do with them. The bones."

"That is my business."

"Since when have you been the residuary legatee of all the miscellaneous bones found in this county?"

"Let me rephrase my remark. I have an interest in those bones." He tossed his clipboard and pen onto a card table that had been set up to serve as an extremely temporary and portable office. "I'll come with you."

I lied. "Sheriff Jarboe specifically requested that you not attend."

"But—"

"I don't want you either."

"But—"

"I can't stand around here arguing with you. I'm late. See you tomorrow."

I didn't look back. The big young man with the shovel stopped shoveling and gave me a hopeful "Hello" as I passed him. I smiled and went on.

I had a drive of almost forty miles ahead of me, so I wasn't lying when I said I was short on time. On back roads encumbered by slow-moving farm machinery, it took an hour—ample time to think over what the sheriff had told me.

I had been in the kitchen when the telephone rang. It was eight-thirty, and breakfast cooled on the stove as the sheriff rambled on. He had called me by my first name. That didn't mean anything; everybody in these parts called everybody by first names, unless prefixed by "Mr."

or "Miz" if the person addressed possessed the dignity of age or social position. Yet there had been an underlying assumption, in the way he talked to me, that he knew me and expected me to remember him. I didn't. It was beginning to worry me, how little I did remember from those years with Martha. It had not worried me before this visit because there was no reason for me to remember—no reason to think about that time. I had blotted out four years of my life with a thoroughness that was rather unnerving.

At any rate, he knew me, if I didn't know him, and he granted me a status I had not realized I possessed—that of resident relative-in-charge.

"I been tryin' to reach Matt," he said aggrievedly. "That boy is never in his office."

"It's an election year."

"Yeah, well, it's damn early to start campaignin'. When I vote for a man I want him there workin', not ridin' the roads lookin' for more votes."

I didn't care whether the sheriff voted for Matt or not, so I had no reason to placate him. "I haven't seen Matt since Saturday evening, and he didn't tell me what his plans were. Is there anything I can do?"

"Well, yeah, sure—that's why I called. I got to do somethin' with those damn bones, Julie. They can't lie around here forever."

"Oh. Those bones."

"You know the ones I mean. The ones that was found—"

"I know the ones you mean. What do you want me to do about them?"

"It's rightly Miz Martha's responsibility. But I don't want to bother her when she's so poorly. I can't find Matt.

So I figured you'd be the one to speak for the family, or at least get them to make up their damn minds."

I could have told him it was not my responsibility, or my right, to decide anything. I don't know why I didn't simply refer him back to Matt. Yes, I do. I was flattered at being asked to participate in a decision, instead of obeying orders, like hired help.

With one eye on my congealed eggs, I said, "I'll come to your office and talk to you about it. Would this afternoon suit you?"

He allowed as how it would, always providing he was not called away by a murder or an accident. I said I'd take my chances; we agreed on two o'clock.

Apparently it was a quiet day for crime in the county. The sheriff was in his office, feet on the desk and cigar in his mouth, in approved county-sheriff style. He swung his feet off the desk when I appeared and rose, stubbing out the cigar.

He was a little man. From the rumbling, grumbling voice that had vibrated over the telephone I had expected someone taller and heavier, with a beer belly hanging over his belt, like the caricature sheriffs in the television programs. If I had met him on the street I'd have taken him for a barber or bank clerk. Thinning hair that had once been blond and was now an indeterminate shade halfway to gray framed a narrow, almost ascetic face, with lined cheeks and wide ingenuous blue eyes.

"Well, now, it sure is good to see you again, Julie," he said. "You sure have growed up to be a pretty girl."

He *had* known me back then. I hadn't the faintest recollection of ever having seen him. I didn't say so; I shook his hand and took the chair he indicated. He asked after my mother and I asked after his family—a photograph on the desk, of a little woman and three hulking children, gave me the clue.

"I really don't know what I can tell you," I began. "I tried to reach Matt this morning; his secretary said he was in Washington and wouldn't be back till the end of the week. Surely he has talked to you about this business?"

"Not for a couple of weeks. See . . ." He paused, studying me, and I realized that the baby-blue eyes were not as naive as they appeared. "How much do you know about this? Did Matt talk to you? Was it in the northern papers?"

"I don't know much," I admitted. "Only the bare facts and the reasonable assumptions one might draw from them."

"Reasonable assumptions." Sheriff Jarboe looked as if he wanted to spit. "I'm gonna tell you what the law says, not what some professor *assumes*. Human remains turn up, then the law's gotta be notified. They turn up oftener than you might think—sewer lines, new roads, building sites—not to mention the damn archaeologists. Now if they turn up in the course of digging, whether it's construction or something else, the professors can tell us how long they've been in the ground. If they're what you might call real antiques, then we don't worry about how they died; but we do have to worry about what's done with them. There are laws about disturbing Christian burials, and lately the Indian groups have stirred up a fuss about their people. So that's one problem. Everybody raisin' hell about what to do with the remains."

He reached for his cigar, then glanced at me. "Go ahead," I said.

"I think better with the damn thing in my mouth," he said apologetically.

"You haven't done badly without it, Sheriff. I see what

you're getting at. There is a problem of jurisdiction even with skeletons found in situ. But in this case you can't even be sure whether they are—antiques, as you put it— or remains that might demand a criminal investigation. Right?"

Jarboe's blue eyes narrowed. "There was a crime committed, no question about that. Those bones didn't walk out onto the road and lay down. I want to find the kids who played that little joke. But near as I can tell, that was the only crime committed. There was no evidence of violence. I've gone through the missing-persons files for thirty years back, and nobody fits the description. I don't understand why the damn-fool professors can't tell me how old those bones are, but they say they can't."

"That's the way it is, though. Soil conditions, type of burial—"

"Yeah, well, I've heard all that stuff. Point is, she must have been dead a long time or we'd have some record in our missing-persons file. Without evidence of identity or criminal violence, I've got no reason to keep the case open. I want to get her out of the morgue and back into the ground. The question is, where?"

"Why ask me?"

"Because—" He stabbed the air with his cigar. "Because that reasonable assumption you talked about suggests that she came from Maidenwood. The road cuts through your land; I can't think of any reason why the jokers would carry those bones very far. If they'd been left on somebody's porch I'd figure the comedians had a grudge against that person, but they couldn't predict who would be the first one to drive that road. The doc says she was white—not Indian or nigra—so it's possible she was an ancestor of yours."

"Are you suggesting the family cemetery at Maidenwood?"

"Any objections?"

"It's okay with me. I can't imagine why Matt would object, but I'll ask him. What do you need—some kind of legal document?"

"I'm not sure what I need," Jarboe mumbled, scratching his head. "But I can't move without the family's permission."

"You have mine, for what it's worth. I can't understand what all the fuss is about, to be honest."

"Yeah, well, most of the fuss came from that big-mouthed young prof who's digging at Maidenwood."

"Alan?" I leaned back in my chair. "What does he want you to do?"

"Wants me to give him the skeletons so he can study them. He acts like they were—you know—pieces of wood."

"Sounds like him. He hasn't actually seen the remains?"

"No. He barreled in here and pounded on the desk and . . . I maybe would have let him if he hadn't been so damned high-handed," Jarboe added, with a sheepish grin.

"I know what you mean."

"Hell, he's not even an anthropologist," Jarboe said rather defensively. "We had a prof out here from UVA; I did all the right things. You can see 'em if you want."

"Who, me?" I said, startled. "I'm not an anthropologist either. I couldn't tell you anything you don't already know."

"You are a member of the family," Jarboe said. "Seems as if somebody ought to go through the formalities. Course if it would upset you—"

"It would not upset me. I just don't know . . . Oh, well, why not?"

You have to be fairly hardened in the handling and viewing of cadavers to find yourself at ease in a morgue. More hardened than I was, at any rate. There's a smell about such places, and a cold, hard, white look. I certainly was not upset, however. In fact, I had been annoyed by Jarboe's assumption that I would come all over queer with faint feminine flutterings at the sight of a harmless old skeleton. I was not prepared for the emotion that seized me when Jarboe yanked out the drawer in which the bones had been placed.

Never before had I been quite so conscious of the frailty of the inner structure that holds us upright. She had been a small woman. The soft ivory bones had a sculptural delicacy.

I hadn't been completely honest with the sheriff when I disclaimed any knowledge of bones. I was no expert, but I had attended a couple of seminars given by Kaufman, the "bone man" at Pennsylvania. He was a popular lecturer because he had served as consultant to the state police, and he had a repertoire of gruesome case histories. So I knew enough to observe some technical details. Such as the teeth. They were in excellent condition—no sign of caries or abscesses. No fillings, either. The absence of dental work would have made positive identification difficult, even if the missing-person files had come up with a possible candidate.

The baby's skeleton lay next to that of its presumed mother. Whether by design, or because the space was limited, it huddled close to her latticed rib cage. The bones were not so undamaged as hers; the frail shell of the skull had not withstood the weight of earth. I assumed the pathologist had determined that the injuries were postmortem. I assumed it because I had no intention of handling those softly curved scraps.

I don't think I exhibited any sign of distress, but Jarboe was determined I should react like a lady. He put a fatherly arm around me. "I shouldn't have let you look."

I shrugged off his support. "I'm all right," I said curtly.

Jarboe closed the drawer. "I shouldn't have let you. Let's go back to the office. I just might be able to scare up a little bourbon, strictly for medicinal purposes."

"The clothes," I said, remembering my comments to Alan. "Could I see the clothes they were—er—wearing?"

"Yeah, sure."

The clothes had been wrapped in brown paper. Jarboe cleared his desk, pushing the accumulated debris to one side, and opened the package.

Psychologists say the sense of smell is more evocative than any other sense. I don't know why, or even whether it is true. But the faint aura surrounding those faded garments evoked images, and vivid ones at that—attics of old houses, sunbeams stretching across worn floorboards, hot closed-in air, dust tickling my nose, and a strong, distinctive odor . . .

"Mothballs," I said faintly.

Jarboe nodded. "Yep. Stored away someplace, these were. I showed them around, nobody recognized them. Thought maybe they came from Maidenwood."

"I wouldn't know. There's a lot of junk in our attic; I used to poke around up there . . ." Another shuddering jolt of recollection—but this one didn't drop neatly into place, it streaked through my mind and vanished. I didn't realize I was swaying gently to-and-fro, like a windblown weed, until Jarboe's arm guided me to a chair.

"There, now," he said, not without satisfaction. "I knew

I shouldn't have let you. Here, this'll make you feel better."

I took the glass he pressed into my hand. The momentary faintness was gone, but I couldn't deny him his amiable revenge. Served me right for being so smug.

I assured him the liquor had indeed restored me, and brushed away his apologies. "I'm only sorry I can't help you, Sheriff. I don't remember . . ."

"Pity I can't ask Miz Martha."

"It's not likely that they came from our attic, is it? We've had trouble with trespassers, but I can't believe thieves could get into the house without leaving signs of forced entry. Shirley Johnson has been on duty ever since Martha became ill, and if anyone had broken in before that, Martha would have raised Cain. She was always a light sleeper, and she had ears like a hawk."

Jarboe nodded agreement. "Not to mention a double-barreled shotgun. I guess you're right, Julie. If Martha had caught a burglar on the premises, she'd have peppered him good."

"Martha has a gun?"

"Well, sure; she always did, didn't she?"

"Oh, yes. I—uh—I'd forgotten. I haven't seen it since I arrived."

"Better find it and keep it handy." I stared at him in consternation and he added hastily, "In case of trespassers, and there's rabid animals around . . . You don't need to worry about anyone getting into the house, you were one hundred percent right about that. Carrsville is a nice quiet little place, not like Pittsburgh."

A nice quiet little place inhabited by people who got a kick out of playing with human bones. The expression on my face convinced Jarboe he had better drop that argument.

"Nothing familiar about the clothes, then?" he asked.

I picked up the dress. The calico was a drab print, small white figures on dark grey-blue ground. It looked as if it had been made at home, and by an unskilled seamstress; the sleeves were unshaped tubes, the neck was high, unadorned by collar or frill, and the body of the dress fell straight and full from a narrow yoke.

"I'll tell you one thing," I said. "This was never made for *her*. It's miles too big."

"That fits our reasonable assumption," Jarboe said. "Somebody took this out of his mama's attic."

"It's maddening," I muttered, examining the dress more closely. "I mean, there is absolutely nothing distinctive about this dress. It was made on a sewing machine, but women have been using them for—at least a hundred years, I suppose. The fabric doesn't look like a synthetic and the print is old-fashioned, but these old prints are popular for quilts and country clothes. The style doesn't tell me anything because the dress hasn't any style to speak of."

"Some old ladies in the country still wear dresses like this," Jarboe agreed. "We thought of all that, Julie."

"It's a hideous dress," I said vehemently. "No girl that age would be caught dead in it . . . Sorry. That wasn't intentional."

Jarboe grunted.

"Now this," I went on, touching the folded white garment with my fingertip, "is altogether different. Handmade and probably old."

"Pick it up if you want," Jarboe said, watching me. "Can't hurt it."

I didn't want to pick it up. The stains were probably rust but they looked like dried blood. I told myself I was acting like a fool and lifted the garment from the table.

"Hand embroidery," I said. "Every inch of it, all along the ruffles and frills. I think it's what they call *broderie anglaise*. The fabric is lawn or batiste—I'm not up on such things. All handmade." I dropped the stained small dress onto the table. "No clue there either. Both boys and girls wore dresses like this years ago. If that matters . . ."

"Well, no, it doesn't. Except people save things like this, handmade, family heirlooms like. The woman's dress is no heirloom."

"You can say that again." I realized I was unconsciously wiping my fingers on my skirt. I put my hands in my pockets. "Sorry I can't be more help."

"You sure you won't have another nip?"

I had another nip. I needed it. I had not been able to conceal from Jarboe that I was "upset," as he tactfully put it, but he didn't know how upset I had been—or why. It wasn't good old-fashioned female squeamishness at the sight of a few bones. The skeletons hadn't frightened or repelled me. They had only made me feel sad. But the clothes . . . Why couldn't I pin down that flash of memory, as I had so many others once lost and unwanted? My arguments as to why the clothes could not have come from Maidenwood were convincing, so far as they went. And I certainly didn't relish the idea that unknown persons were prowling freely around the house . . .

I said good-bye to Jarboe and left the building, but I still couldn't get those pitiful garments out of my head. That baby's dress, so lovingly and exquisitely made—and such a contrast to the woman's dress. Well, but that didn't mean anything. Both garments must have been picked at random from a trunk of old clothes; the mother who had fashioned that dainty gown would never have worn such a homely dress.

As I drove out of the parking lot, I thought of something I should have realized earlier. The dress would not have been too big for a woman in the last months of pregnancy.

After a quick stop at a supermarket to lay in more dog food (my estimate of Elvis's appetite had been wildly wide of the mark), I started back to Maidenwood. I was annoyed with myself for a number of reasons, and it did not improve my disposition to find that Mrs. Danner had made soup out of the stew-meat I had intended for supper. It had obviously been boiling for a long time. The package of frozen vegetables she had added to the pale gray broth had been reduced to mush, and the kitchen felt like a steam bath.

I would have dashed upstairs to yell at her, but the sight of a flea-infested muzzle and two hopeful brown eyes peering in at the door reminded me of another duty. Why do dogs have such soulful eyes? According to approved theology they have no souls. I took a dim view of approved theology—or I had always believed I did. So why was I so perturbed at the thought of the pitiful bones lying in a cold metal drawer? Why were images of chanting priests and neat gravestones with "Here lies . . ." pressing at my mind?

I turned off the burner under the soup and filled a bowl with dog food. Elvis started whining at the sight of it, but before I took it out onto the porch I surreptitiously gathered my equipment, whisking around the kitchen with my back turned to the door so he wouldn't see what I was doing. I waited until he was deeply immersed in his food before I carried the big washbasin and the brush and the flea shampoo and the towel and the kettle of hot water outside. Elvis didn't look up. Maybe he had never had a bath. He certainly looked as if he'd never had a bath. I sat down on the step and rechecked the pertinent pages of

"How to Care for Your Dog." It didn't sound formidable: Put the water in the basin and the dog in the water.

Five minutes later I was drenched from hair to sneakers. The only damp parts of Elvis were his paws. He stood a few feet away, grinning and wagging. Obviously he considered this a new and fascinating game—you pick me up and put me in the basin, then I jump out. The wetter you get, the more points for me.

I was about to try again when Elvis turned and dashed off, rounding the corner of the house at a good clip. He was back before I had time to swear, escorting Alan and acting as if they had known one another all their lives. He hadn't even barked.

I said bitterly, "How sharper than a serpent's tooth to have a faithless dog."

Alan acknowledged the witticism with a polite smile. "We met earlier."

"Oh?"

"Your cousin *said* I could investigate the smokehouse area."

"Oh."

"I think I've located a rubbish dump."

"Gee, that's wonderful."

"If your cousin would let us work there—"

"Oh, come off it, Alan, you aren't really interested in the first manor house. You're only interested in harassing Matt. I suppose," I added, as Elvis squirmed unbecomingly at Alan's feet, "you found some eighteenth-century steak bones in the trash. Or did you bring the wherewithal with which to bribe my dog?"

"He didn't need bribing. He's a smart dog; he recognized my charm and sterling character immediately."

I sighed. "What do you want, Alan?"

"I came to help you give the dog a bath," Alan said.

"Oh, to coin a phrase, yeah?"

"I figured you might have a little trouble." Alan surveyed me from dripping hair to soggy sneakers, and grinned offensively. "You used to be terrified of dogs."

"I was not terrified of dogs. My mother was terrified of dogs."

"Anything you say. Come here, dog."

"His name is Elvis," I said, in a more amiable tone. I am not too proud to accept help, and besides, I hoped Elvis would saturate Alan too.

"Elvis? Good God." Alan grabbed the dog and popped him into the tub. The damned animal stood like a rock, with his tongue hanging idiotically out of his mouth.

Alan got pretty wet, which soothed my ego somewhat. I decided it is not possible to bathe a dog without getting wet. "The tricky part is to keep him from rolling in the dirt the instant he gets out of the tub," Alan explained, taking a firm grip on Elvis's collar. "Give me that towel . . . Damn!"

I backed away out of the shower Elvis produced by vigorously shaking himself. "Oh, sorry, Alan. I'm new to this."

"To coin a phrase," Alan began.

He showed me how to brush out the dead hair and dead fleas. Elvis loved that part of the process and I was able to return to a more pertinent topic of conversation.

"You really came to find out what the sheriff said," I remarked, watching with mild revulsion as Alan disposed of a few fleas whose stronger constitutions had resisted the shampoo.

"What did he say?"

"He wants to get rid of the bones. Not," I added, "give them to you. He pointed out that there are laws governing the disposal of human remains."

"Don't I know. I suppose he wants you to plant them in the family plot."

"I can't think of any reason why not."

"Neither can I," Alan said agreeably.

Elvis, lying on his side in blissful abandon, stiffened and started to squirm. "Hold on, I'm not finished," Alan said. "What's the matter with him?"

"Now and then he remembers he's supposed to be a watchdog. That sounds like Mr. Danner's pickup. Damn it; I thought Mrs. Danner would come to the kitchen before she left. I wanted to read her the riot act for making mush out of my dinner."

I realized after I had said it that it sounded suspiciously like a hint. Alan didn't take it up. He went on brushing, and I said, "Why aren't you looking for burial sites?"

"What makes you think I'm not?"

"In the middle of a pasture that's under water a good part of the year?"

Alan cocked a quizzical eyebrow in my direction. "Have you been taking archaeology courses, or can it be that the pearls of wisdom I dropped all those years ago—"

"It's just common sense. You're looking for evidence of occupation, not for vandalized graves."

"The two are not incompatible."

"In this case they are. The settlement at Maydon's Hundred dates from the first quarter of the seventeenth century. I saw the skeletons. They are too clean and well preserved to be that old."

"I know."

"How do you know? You haven't seen the skeletons."

"Perkins, the pathologist, is a friend of mine. Anyway, I knew as soon as I read the story in the newspaper that the bones couldn't be three hundred and fifty years old. Unless . . ."

"Unless what?"

Alan might not have heard me. He released the dog, who promptly flung himself into the nearest patch of dirt, and rolled. Sitting cross-legged, hands resting lightly on his knees, Alan stared dreamily into space as if he were visualizing the scenes he described.

"It's hard to imagine what it was like for them. Tangled wilderness as far as the eye could see, none of the comforts, even the necessities, they had always taken for granted. Elizabeth the First had been dead only a few years. James was king—that sour-faced Scot who amused himself with handsome young men and solemn researches into witchcraft. The men who landed at Jamestown wore ruffs and swords; they boasted of being 'gentlemen,' too good to dirty their hands clearing land or building houses. The settlement almost died because of their gentility . . .

"But it survived. Towns grew up; the Hundreds sent representatives to the Assembly at Jamestown. There were seventy-eight people at Maydon's Hundred in 1622. They had built homes, and a church, all clustered around the fort they believed would intimidate the 'savages.' The Indians weren't intimidated. The uprising of 1622 wiped out one third of the Virginia colonists. Maydon's was the hardest hit. The slaughter was so terrible, the destruction so complete, that no attempt at resettlement was ever made. For years afterward, hunters camping near the site swore that the spirits of the dead crowded around them in the darkness, baring their bloody wounds and wailing for vengeance in thin, high voices. The spot was shunned, its very location forgotten. Maydon's became 'the lost Hundred.' "

I had heard it before, but the spell of his voice was as strong as ever. Even the dog lay still, his head on his paws, his liquid brown eyes fixed on the speaker.

"But they say she still lingers in the green shadows of the forest," Alan went on softly. "Not as a mutilated victim but in all her youthful beauty. Raven-haired and blue-eyed, gems at her throat and in her hair, long velvet skirts rustling the dead leaves—"

The spell was broken. I sat up as if I had been stung. "You're wasting your talents in archaeology," I said rudely. "You ought to write romantic novels. That story *is* a romantic novel. I read it, *To Have and to Hold,* by Mary Johnston. One of those fatuous, sentimental, old-fashioned—"

"Sure it is," Alan said. "Pure fiction. The high-born Lady, fleeing a hated marriage with the king's favorite, disguising herself as one of the servant girls the Virginia Company had recruited as wives for the settlers. But there's a germ of fact behind that story; there was a Lady Jocelyn Cartwright among the residents of Maydon's Hundred—"

"You told me that five years ago. Alan, I understand why Maydon's is important. So little has survived from those first settlements—only a few have been located, much less excavated. But your fantasy about the Lady was what ruined your article. Every scholar in the field ridiculed it; it almost wrecked your career. She never existed."

"She wrote to the king. There was a letter."

"Then where is it? The only person who claimed to have seen it, in a collection of family papers, was one of those dilettante nineteenth-century historians. He probably made it up."

Alan refused to be provoked. He gave me a sweet, lazy smile and said cheerfully, "You've seen the portrait."

I had not seen the original. It was in the National Portrait Gallery in London—an exquisite miniature on ivory, attributed to one of Holbein's students, and done with almost the master's genius. I had seen copies. They were all over the place, including Maidenwood. One of my crazier ancestors had claimed we were descended in a roundabout way from Lady Jocelyn. Very roundabout, considering that if she wasn't a figment of someone's imagination, she had died in 1622 without issue.

"The attribution is questionable," I said, in my nastiest pseudo-scholar voice.

"But just suppose," Alan persisted. "Suppose it did happen, in the way the lost letter described it. When King James realized she was in earnest, he relented. He granted her a vast estate here in Virginia—so long as she never married. If the husband he chose for her wasn't good enough, she could damn well live and die a virgin. Doesn't that fit his peculiar personality, the blend of cruelty and sentiment that distinguished his actions?"

This time the magic of his voice failed to entrance me. I suppose, in an odd way, I had always been jealous of the Lady. Jealous, not even of a ghost—the ghost of a fantasy! But the miniature was so beautiful. The raven hair, the wide blue eyes . . .

"And then the massacre," Alan went on. "One version of the story claims she was captured and carried away by the Indians; that she fell in love with her stalwart brave and bore him children. Another version suggests that she killed herself rather than be taken alive. When the rescue expedition arrived, too late, they found the dead lying where they had fallen, decomposed and torn by wild animals. The bodies were tumbled into hastily dug, unmarked graves. But just suppose . . . suppose they thought her worthy of more respectful treatment. A well-made coffin, a leaden shroud—some method that would preserve her bones through three and a half centuries."

"Alan," I said, half convinced, "you are just—just romanticizing—aren't you? You don't really believe—"

"Hell, no." He looked directly at me. His eyes were no longer dreamy; they sparkled with devilish amusement. "But doesn't it make a great publicity story? You haven't heard the rest of it—the infant, born in defiance of the king's command—"

"You son of a gun," I exclaimed. "Are you really going to print that yarn? Your colleagues will crucify you."

"Oh, I'll hedge it around with all the proper scholarly reservations. But if all else fails—sure, I'll publish it. I have to do something to get funding, Julie. I've waited too long to let a little thing like money stop me."

"I have never heard anything so immoral, dishonest, unprincipled, shameful—"

"I said it was just a story." Alan grinned. "But Maydon's Hundred isn't. It's here, damn it, and I'm going to find it."

"So that's where you got to," said Shirley, at the porch door. "Is this mess on the stove supposed to be supper?"

We ate soup for supper, because that's all there was. I promised Shirley something exotic next day—crab, lobster, whatever she wanted.

Martha grumbled over the meal, which I took as a compliment to my cooking. After supper we settled down to *Bleak House,* and for once I found Esther's hideous optimism almost soothing. Every time I thought of Alan's underhanded scheme for raising the money to carry out his heart's desire, I couldn't decide whether to laugh or swear.

After Martha dismissed me I was too restless to sleep. What I needed was exercise—a long brisk walk, attended by my faithful dog. But the darkness intimidated me, not only because there was a chance I'd fall over something and sprain an ankle, but because the night teemed with dangers—ancient phantoms and crazy live people. I made sure everything was locked and bolted, and then I went to the library.

It was a grisly promenade at night, with only the sallow light of a single flashlight to push the dark away. I didn't prolong my visit, but went straight to the shelves containing volumes on history. I had not been much interested in those books in the past, but I vaguely remembered having seen a book about Maidenwood. The shelf was shrouded in cobwebs, but the book was there; my memory was working admirably now that it had been jogged so often. I took the Maidenwood book and a few others on Virginia history, and left the room, almost running. There were ghosts haunting Maidenwood all right, and the most terrifying of them was the shade of the angry, unhappy child that I had been.

I woke next morning with a bad taste in my mind, like a mental hangover. The window was opaque with soft white mist. The air felt close and hot; it was going to be a warm day once the fog burned off, which it inevitably would. A super day for digging in an open field full of bugs.

I heard Martha's voice raised in protest as I stumped grumpily past her door. I was not moved to stop and inquire what she was complaining about. I put the kettle on; then a scratching at the back door reminded me of my new responsibilities. The sight of Elvis, clean and eager-eyed, and unashamedly delighted to see me, wiped away some of my evil humor. I was beginning to understand why people own dogs. It's nice to have someone adore you uncritically, even if your position as a source of food is a large part of that adoration.

He didn't want to eat out on the step all by himself. He wanted to come in. My mind was so muzzy I had to concentrate before I figured out the solution: close the kitchen door. Elvis had polished off his breakfast by the time the kettle boiled. He settled down at my feet while I drank my coffee, his tail making a soft rhythmic sound.

I knew why I was in a bad mood, and it was not lack of sleep, though I had sat up late reading. It was the content of what I had read that bugged me.

The little book about Maidenwood, written at the turn of the century by one of my dippier distant relatives, was an uncritical hodgepodge of fact and fancy, legend and history, served up with a generous dollop of self-esteem. Anything that augmented the pride and glory of the Carrs was fact, to him. Not only did he believe in the Lady, he referred to her as "my ancestress."

The other books reduced Lady Jocelyn to her proper position—"a pretty legend," as one historian condescendingly put it. Maydon's Hundred had a more solid foundation. There had been such a settlement, the authorities agreed on that. They did not agree on its location. Nobody had ever mounted an expedition to look for the remains of Maydon's Hundred, and for very good reasons. The biggest reason was lack of money. Archaeology is an expensive activity, and there were dozens of other sites that attracted greater interest. The author of the book on Maidenwood, who (erroneously) fancied himself a scholar, had done some casual digging. He was convinced that the lost Hundred had been located at Maidenwood, and he offered, as proof, a rusty piece of metal he claimed was part of a suit of armor dating to the reign of James the First. There was a photograph of this artifact in the book; it looked like a fragment of a fender from a Model-T. I could see why it had not impressed the historians. Some of them agreed that Maidenwood was one possible site, but only one of several, and nobody really cared enough to find out.

I guess I had hoped to discover that Alan was as far off-base with regard to Maydon's Hundred as he was about the Lady—for I still was not convinced he had wholly abandoned his "pretty legend." No such luck.

The kitchen door opened. "How come you closed—" Shirley began. "Oh, I see. Now, Elvis, don't do that—you get me distracted . . . Julie, there's a woman at the front door and she—"

The woman wasn't at the front door, she was at the kitchen door, right behind Shirley. Elvis, who had greeted Shirley with lickings and waggings, began to growl. I caught his collar in time to keep him from launching himself at the newcomer.

"Who—" I began.

"Restrain your dog, please," the woman said in clipped tones. "If he attacks I shall be forced to take legal action. My card."

Keeping a safe distance from the dog, she flipped the card at me. I let it fall on the floor. With some effort I got my wits together—Elvis out, Shirley back to Martha, a cup of coffee in her deserving hand, the kitchen door closed. Then I turned my attention to the intruder, who had stood her ground, immovable as a granite statue.

She looked like someone's secretary, stocky and shrewd-eyed, wearing a grey pinstripe suit and sensible shoes. Horn-rimmed glasses dominated her face; her features were otherwise unremarkable except for those knowing eyes. She had retrieved her card. When she thrust it at me a second time, I took it.

"Pauline A. Hornbeak, P.A., B.A., M.B.A. . . ." I looked up. "P.A.?"

"Psychic Archaeologist."

"Oh, damn," I exclaimed.

Pauline A. Hornbeak raised her eyebrows. "I beg your pardon?"

"You should. What's the idea of barging into a private home without an invitation—and at this ungodly hour?"

"I apologize for the earliness of my arrival," said Pauline, sounding as insincere as a politician explaining what he was doing with that fan dancer. "I have written Senator Matthew Ellis without having received the courtesy of a reply. My letters to Professor Alan Petranek have also gone unanswered. Their unaccountable rudeness left me with no alternative but to come to you."

My adrenaline had begun to flow, tardily but strongly. I shouted at her. "No alternative? You had the obvious, reasonable alternative of staying away. What the hell is the matter with you people?"

From outside the door Elvis let out a sharp, agitated bark, and I moderated my voice. "I can't believe you, lady. Go away before I call a cop."

Pauline gave me a pitying smile. "Your lack of courtesy does not touch me, Miss Newcomb. I am in tune with my Masters. I am insulated by a blanket of karmic invulnerability. Are you going to ask me to sit down?"

"No."

"A cup of coffee, perhaps. Normally I do not indulge in stimulants, they are rank poison to the system and cloud the psychic senses. But as a symbol of good feeling—"

"I am not going to offer you a cup of coffee. A cup of rank poison, if I had it . . . See here, Miss—Mrs.—"

"Call me Pauline."

"Thank you, no." I straightened the card, which I had squashed between my clenched fingers. "The Research

Center for Psychic Archaeology. I read one of your letters."

"Then you understand my purpose in coming. Let me explain further. I know where—"

"If you run, you can probably get into your car before the dog catches up with you. He's a little lame."

I had to lead her to the door and shove her into her car. She kept talking every step of the way. Only the advent of Elvis, limping but full of zeal, prevented her from continuing her lecture. I held him, stroking and praising him, to keep him from chasing the car down the driveway, and from barking. Either he was sensitive to atmosphere or he had been trained not to bark unnecessarily. He certainly paid no attention to most of my other orders.

I went back in the house. Shirley was waiting at the top of the stairs. "Miz Martha—" she began.

"Right. I'm coming."

Shirley always left the lying to me. I told Martha the visitor was a Jehovah's Witness, hoping that group was as prevalent and as pushy here as it was in my neighborhood. Apparently it was, for Martha didn't question my story.

It was an inauspicious beginning to a day that held little promise of anything better. I asked Shirley's indulgence while I made a quick trip to the grocery store. When Mrs. Danner arrived, I dashed downstairs to threaten her with a painful death if she laid a hand on the pots and pans. I had changed to jeans and a long-sleeved shirt; they clung like molten lead, it was so hot, and when I went out the back door and saw Elvis sprawled lazily in the shade, I had a strong inclination to join him.

He was bored, though. When I started along the path

to the pasture, he went with me. We found Alan folding his tents. A few patches of raw earth were the only remnants of his unsuccessful excavations, and he was loading his card table into the van.

"Where are you off to today?" he inquired.

"Whither thou goest," I replied.

He gave me a dirty look. "Come and meet the others."

There were only four of them—a skeleton staff, to use a not-too-nice pun. The hulking young man was a football player—third-string tackle, he proudly informed me. His name was Willkie. He would have told me more, but Alan whisked me away and introduced me to the girls. They really were girls, not more than eighteen, and obviously infected with the same virus that had blinded me to Alan's character defects when I was the same age. One was blond and one was brunet; both looked at him with wet-lipped adoration and at me with identical expressions of hostility.

The fourth member of the team was Alan's protégé, a graduate archaeology student from the University of Virginia. He was even bigger than Willkie—very handsome, very black, very muscular. He could have been a football player, but, as he informed me, he had never really enjoyed being mauled by other big muscular males. He was obviously intelligent as well as handsome. Alan treated him with a courtesy he did not accord the others; he ordered them around like galley slaves, but he occasionally said "please" and "thanks" to Jono.

Alan left Jono to supervise the packing up, and offered me a seat in his Jeep. We went bouncing off across the pasture toward a belt of trees on a ridge to the northwest. I expected Alan would stop when we got to the trees; instead he drove over a mound of rubble that had once been part of a fence and headed straight for a pine tree two feet in diameter.

He didn't hit it, or the tree behind it, but he didn't miss either by much. After I had opened my eyes I saw that a rough trail had been hacked through the woods. It ended in a clearing—not a natural glade, but a man-made opening. The uprooted trees and brush had been pushed to one side, where they stood like a wall.

"You had a bulldozer in here," I said, as Alan stopped the Jeep next to the brush pile. "Did Matt give you permission?"

"I didn't ask him. Watch out, that's poison ivy."

It was, and there were equally unpleasant plants among the debris that loomed at my shoulder. Instead of getting out, Alan rummaged under the seat, emerging with a paper bag, from which he took a sandwich and a bottle of beer.

"Want some?"

"No, thanks."

He applied himself to his lunch with the same single-minded concentration he applied to his work. After a while I said, "Aren't bulldozers frowned on in your profession?"

"I'm not crazy about using them myself. In this case I had no choice."

"I assume you had a reason for picking this particular spot? It doesn't look promising to me."

"That's because you don't know anything about it," Alan said. "This is probably where your Great-Great-Uncle Albert found the piece of armor. You do remember my talking to you about Albert?"

I didn't tell him my memory was as leaky as a sieve. There was some excuse for its inadequacy in this case, since at the time he had lectured me about his pet theories I had been intent on the cadences of his voice and the way his lips shaped the words, instead of paying attention to what he was saying. I saw no reason to go into this, in view of the fact that I was freshly informed about Great-Great Uncle.

"Where did you find that book?" I asked suspiciously.

Alan crumpled the bag and tossed it and the bottle into the back of the Jeep. "Not in your library, my dear. I was never admitted to that holy of holies, if you recall."

"I thought we agreed not to call up the past."

"We did. Sorry. Your ancestor presented copies of that inane book to every library in the state. I don't suppose he actually sold more than ten. They were received with proper gratitude and promptly filed away in the farthest possible storeroom. A few are still in existence, forgotten but not beyond reach."

"And this is where he found the—whatever it was?"

"I can't be certain. He was no surveyor, and his measurements are vague in the extreme. The pasture was one possible site. I started there, partly because it was more accessible, and partly because many of the early settlements were close to the river. This is farther away, but in a healthier situation, not so susceptible to the malarial mosquitoes that wiped out so many of the settlers at Jamestown. This was an open field ninety years ago. If you look at the vegetation you can see it has grown up in the last half century."

The fallen trees looked older than that to me, but what did I know? Before I could comment Alan said, "Here they come," and got out of the Jeep.

In spite of my grounding in archaeological technique I still harbored a few fantasies—plunging my spade into the earth and turning up a golden necklace glittering with gems, or a chest of pieces of eight. Nobody plunged a spade or anything else into the earth that afternoon. The entire time was spent in what Alan called plotting the site.

I would have called it plain ordinary manual labor. The bulldozer had left the ground littered with broken branches and twigs, tangled vines and roots. So our first job was to finish clearing the ground. We used rakes—plain ordinary garden rakes—and Alan yelled at us every time we disturbed a clod of dirt.

He had already surveyed the site. He and Jono brooded over the papers for a while, muttering about things like base lines and datum points, and then we all got to help lay out the grid. The area was divided into equal squares approximately eight feet on a side, and stakes were driven into the corners at the intersections of the grid squares and the balks.

I asked what a balk was, and everybody looked at me with varying degrees of contempt and pity. Everybody except Willkie—he didn't know what a balk was either, and I suspected he didn't care. (It is an earth partition left between squares, so the digger doesn't have to walk on the area he has dug. By keeping the edge of the balk perfectly straight, he can also check the stratification and chart the precise depth of any objects that are found.)

I was prepared to pound in a stake or two, but that wasn't good enough. They had to be set in concrete and then surveyed so that their precise elevations could be scratched into the concrete before it hardened.

It struck me as an awfully complicated procedure, in view of the minuscule staff and the limited time at Alan's disposal, but I didn't want to ask any more idiotic questions. Everyone was visibly wilted by the end of the day, and I was relieved to throw down my tools and announce my imminent departure. Willkie and the girls looked as if they would have been glad to join me.

Alan looked up from some abstruse calculations he was

scribbling on a yellow pad. "Are you leaving already?" he demanded.

"It's after five. I have to get supper. Are you going to drive me to the house?"

"I can't quit yet."

Glowering, I started toward the track by which we had come. Jono intercepted me. "My scooter is over there. Want a ride? It's the long way around, but easier than walking."

I accepted with alacrity. "How come you get off early?" I asked. "Clout or blackmail?"

Jono grinned. "I work nights. Short-order chef. It drives Alan up the wall to have me leave at five, but he can't afford to pay me and I can't afford not to work, so he has to put up with it."

"You work all night and dig all day?"

"So I'm crazy. It's an occupational hazard for archaeologists."

"Is Alan that hard up? I thought the university funded operations like this."

"Some. Not this one. It's strictly a one-man show."

The scooter was leaning up against a tree. I got on. "That's why he's so uptight," I said thoughtfully. "So meticulous about the procedure."

"You got it. If he can find something—anything—that is incontrovertibly early seventeenth century, he can apply for funding to several places and stand a good chance of getting it."

"If I were in his place, I'd be tempted to salt the site."

Jono had mounted. Foot poised over the pedal, he glanced at me. "He wouldn't do that!"

"Just kidding."

"Oh. Right."

I wrapped my arms around his narrow waist and we

were off. As we bounded over ruts and boulders I shook with silent laughter, imagining what Martha would say if she could see me.

Mrs. Danner had left when I got back. There was a note on the table, a short list of cleaning items she needed. The writing was nothing like the penmanship of the crank letter; though just as laborious, it was stiff and spiky rather than rounded.

After I had dinner started, I went to the library to return the books I had taken. I put them back and looked to see if I could find anything fit to read. The place had lost its terror for me now; it was just a dusty, abandoned room.

When I examined the set of shelves devoted to classics and belles-lettres, I remembered something else I had forgotten. It was almost the only happy memory connected with those years—the summer I had discovered poetry. Martha had censored the poetry section too, but she couldn't find much to complain of in Keats and Tennyson. (I didn't find out about Lord Byron until later; he led, you know, a most dissolute life.) And there was one book Martha had overlooked. Squeezed in behind *The Collected English Poets,* leather-bound and gilt-edged, was a slim volume of verse by Edna St. Vincent Millay. After Milton and the rest, her poems hit me like a fresh wind blowing off the sea.

The book was still there. I picked it up and blew the dust off the spine.

> Love has gone and left me and the days are all alike;
> Eat I must, and sleep I will,—and would that night
>   were here!

But ah!—to lie awake and hear the slow hours
    strike!
Would that it were day again!—with twilight near!

I smiled as I read the lines, but I felt my eyes filling. It
is so awful to be almost thirteen years old. All those burgeoning hormones and romantic dreams, all those pim-
ples and long, bony legs . . . There was no acceptable
vent for such emotions, certainly not for me, with Martha
hovering over me like a Puritan witch-hunter searching
for sin. What was that boy's name? Ragged and sun-
burned, the child of one of the nearby farmers. He liked
me too. He brought me daffodils from his mother's garden, and dusty field flowers that withered in a day. When
Martha found out, she hit the ceiling. There had been
nothing but innocence in those shy encounters until she
started calling me names, calling me . . .

I groped toward the nearest chair and sat down,
my head on my knees, until the spots stopped dancing in
the air. When I left the room, I took Edna St. Vincent
with me.

seven

As the days passed, the neat excavated squares in the clearing sank lower and lower. We found some fascinating items. A Coca-Cola bottle, circa 1956. (Willkie collected bottles; he became inarticulate with pleasure when Alan grimly presented him with this specimen.) A rusted sickle blade, circa nobody knew when. A few scraps of coarse white pottery, Sears Roebuck, circa 1946. Alan's face got longer and longer. The only one unaffected by the general atmosphere of gloom and despair was Willkie. His oars weren't always in the water, but I found his good cheer very soothing. Even the "girls" got gloomier as Alan's temper wound tighter and tighter. The temperature rose another couple of degrees every day. I got into the habit of accepting a ride home from Jono every afternoon. He understood why he couldn't drop me at the house; once, when he had a few minutes to spare we sat on the crumbled gateposts and had a cigarette and talked. I liked him, even if he did view Alan as a cross between Heinrich Schliemann and Saint Peter.

I kept trying to reach Matt, without success. His secretary coyly refused to tell me where he was. She admitted he telephoned twice a day to get his messages; yes, she had told him I wanted to speak to him. Of course, if it was an emergency . . .

"His grandmother isn't dying, if that's what you mean," I said crudely. "Where the devil is he—making a deal with organized crime?"

Shocked noises came from the other end of the line. The woman had no sense of humor. (Or maybe she was shocked because the accusation was true.) In fact, I figured Matt was probably taking a few days off with a girlfriend.

It was not until Thursday that he condescended to get in touch with me. After I had explained what I wanted, he let out a loud, exasperated sigh. "Is that all! You said it was important. I thought Martha was worse."

"You did not. You thought I was going to quit and leave you stranded. And I may yet."

"Now, Julie, honey—"

"We have to talk, Matt."

"Sure, honey."

"And don't call me honey. These fifteen-minute visits of yours are a pain in the butt. I need at least two hours to tell you what is bugging me."

"Okay. When?"

His capitulation left me speechless. I had been braced for an argument. Finally I said, "I want to get this other business settled first. Have you any objection to my telling the sheriff he can go ahead with the burial?"

"I guess not. Though I don't see why he has to foist this on to us."

"Because we're the lords of the manor," I said. "The Big Cheeses. A little moldy, and full of holes, but still the best they've got. Hell's bells, Matt, I'd give grave space to a dog! It's only a hole in the ground; what's the problem?"

"None." The uncertainty had left his voice. "You're right, Julie. I'll call Jarboe right now and tell him to make the arrangements. Call you back."

He did call back, an hour later. "I'll take you to dinner Friday evening," he announced. "Seven o'clock. I'll be spending the night. Shall I bring my own sheets?"

He sounded pleased with himself. I assured him that sleeping accommodations were available, and waited for the next announcement. "The services are set for eleven Saturday morning," he said. "I have to leave immediately afterward, since I have a political dinner in Richmond. Can you—"

"Services?" I bleated. "What services? I assumed they would just dig a grave and—"

"If we're going to do this, we're going to do it right," Matt interrupted. "Now don't you worry about a thing. I have it all arranged."

He rang off before I could ask any more questions. I almost called him back, but decided there was no need; I had a premonition of what Matt intended, and since there was no way of stopping him, there was no sense in worrying about it.

I'm not sure why I decided to take Elvis with me to the dig that day. Mrs. Pauline Hornbeak, P.A., et cetera, would undoubtedly have claimed I had received a message from the Infinite Whatever. The message came, I think, from my nasty suspicious subconscious, which found something a trifle peculiar in Mrs. Danner's behavior. The first thing I noticed was that she was carrying a purse—a "pockabook" as she called it. I had never seen her carry one; not surprising, since she didn't use cosmetics, or smoke, and it was a good bet that Joe Danner didn't trust her with cash or credit cards. She handled this one as if it contained the family savings; when I picked it up to move it out of my way she bleated like a nervous sheep.

It also seemed odd to me that she made a timid attempt to ingratiate herself with Elvis. She had never paid the least attention to him before; he had learned to tolerate her but he showed her none of the affection he showered on me and Shirley. Now, when she stooped to give him a gingerly pat on the head, he didn't respond at all, not with a growl nor with a wag. I can't honestly say I was suspicious, though, not even when she offered to feed him before she left that afternoon. I told her not to bother; but when Elvis proposed to escort me I let him come along.

Willkie was delighted to see him. Willkie was bored. Alan wasn't so enthusiastic, especially after Elvis started to help dig. Elvis ended up tied to a tree, at a safe distance. He didn't seem to mind; sometimes he watched what was going on, sometimes he slept, and sometimes he carried out his own excavation. He was hurt when I wouldn't let him ride home on the scooter with me and Jono, but he enjoyed running after us.

He had fallen behind when Jono and I reached the gate in time to observe the Danners' pickup turn on to the highway. They were going in the opposite direction, but they saw us; Danner stared so fixedly he almost ran into a tree.

I waited for Elvis to catch up and then, since he was with me, I went around to the back door. The first thing I saw was his food dish, filled to the brim with a noxious blend of dry dog food and what appeared to be Mrs. Danner's famous stew. Fearing the worst, I left Elvis to it and dashed into the kitchen, but she had not been cooking; my supplies were undiminished, and there was no ghastly mess on the stove.

I was chopping onions and tomatoes and peppers for the western omelet I planned for supper when a series of horrible sounds from Elvis sent me flying to the door. He had eaten about half the mess in the bowl. It hadn't stayed with him long.

In retrospect I can't believe I was so stupid. But at the time I had no grounds for doubt. Mrs. Danner's cooking was enough to make anyone throw up. I assumed she had brought something from home in an attempt to win over the dog—something that had been around a little too long. I abominated her cooking, but I had no reason to question her motives.

Elvis, looking as green around the gills as a brown-and-white dog can look, had gone to his water dish and was lapping furiously. Cursing Mrs. Danner, I dumped out the rest of the stew, and rinsed and refilled the bowl. Then I decided I had better do something with the remains; I didn't want a pile of garbage right outside the porch. It would attract flies, if nothing else. Cursing Mrs. Danner some more, I looked for a shovel. There must be tools in one of the sheds.

I had not explored the outbuildings. The second one I looked into had the tools, rusted spades and rakes. But it was the contents of the first shed that puzzled me; I kept wondering about them as I dug a shallow hole and scooped the detritus into it.

The things in the first shed had not been rusty discards. Wooden packing crates were neatly lined up along one wall. The floor had been swept and the place smelled faintly of bug spray. Rolled up in a corner was a down sleeping bag.

The explanation was not long in coming. Alan had admitted he had done some test digging near the smokehouse. He had probably stored some of his supplies in the shed; he had nerve enough to do something like that, without bothering to ask permission.

I gave the incident no more thought. I had lost time, and Martha would be yelling for her supper. I went back to my innocent omelet without the slightest suspicion of what was to come.

Yet deep in the distant recesses of my mind some taint of trouble ahead must have persisted. I found Martha more than usually infuriating that night; it seemed to me that her half-smile was more pronounced, as if something amused her, and from time to time she let out a hoarse little sound that might have been a cough—or a chuckle. When I asked if she was catching cold, the smile turned to a glare. Lord knows there was no excuse for her to catch cold; the weather was stifling, and I was sticky with perspiration by the time I left the room.

Heat lightning flickered in the sky when I looked out the back door before locking up. If only it would rain! Elvis looked as if the heat was getting him down too. Sprawled on his rug, he wagged his tail but did not rise to greet me.

He was so limp and depressed I knelt to feel his nose. It was warm. According to the book, that didn't mean anything. My nose was warm too. His lethargic air made me a little uneasy, though. Perhaps the food had been tainted. It would seem logical to Mrs. Danner to feed something that was not fit for human consumption to an animal. His tongue rasped the skin of my hand as I examined him. He had got rid of the stuff almost immediately; and surely, if he had been afflicted with food poisoning he'd be worse by now . . .

"Come on, old boy," I said. "You can sleep inside tonight. I wish I could take you to my room, but the kitchen will be more comfortable than the porch, especially if we have a storm, which I hope we will."

He followed me in. I offered him a dog biscuit; the relish with which he crunched it reassured me as to the state of his stomach. Then I said good night and closed the kitchen door.

It may have been the heat that kept me awake, or it may have been my worry about Elvis. I dozed and woke and dozed again, before falling into a sticky, heavy slumber.

A sound woke me. Struggling back to awareness after a nightmare of Elvis writhing in fatal convulsions, I thought at first I had heard him bark. Then I realized I couldn't have heard him, not from the kitchen. The horrible vividness of the dream got me out of bed, however. I knew I wouldn't rest until I made certain he was all right.

I had bought half a dozen flashlights and distributed them around the house. I took mine from the bedside table and went out, moving quietly to avoid waking Martha or Shirley. We left a light burning in the hall, near her door; I didn't need the flashlight.

I had almost reached the head of the stairs before I heard something. Not the same sound that had wakened me, but softer and less distinct; not a distant crash or thud, that might have had any number of innocent explanations—but nearer at hand and familiar, and all the more frightening because I knew exactly what it was: the creak of the sagging boards of the floor in the downstairs hall.

Someone was there. Old houses moan and mumble in response to changes in humidity and temperature, but this was not such a sound. I had heard it too often to be mistaken—whenever my feet crossed that spot.

I wanted to believe it was a paw, and not a human foot, on that creaking board, that Elvis had escaped from the kitchen and come in search of me. I wanted to believe it, but I couldn't. There was no way Elvis could push the door open. I had tested it to make sure.

Another, softer crack as the unseen foot shifted position. It wasn't courage that forced me to fumble for the switch of the flashlight, it was fear—fear of the dark and of the unknown. Surely no visible horror could be as bad as the monsters created by my own imagination.

The light caught him and froze him like a germ on a slide. Joe Danner, in his faded dungarees and work shirt, a long glittering knife in his hand.

I don't know why I didn't drop dead on the spot. I suppose I was in a state of shock, but sheer incredulity was a factor too. I do remember thinking, My God, you're so brave! when I heard a voice that didn't even *sound* like mine say sharply, "What are you doing there?"

His face turned livid. The knife fell from his hand. "Who is it?" he gasped. "Oh, Lord—who is it?"

"Julie." I started down the stairs, keeping the light in his eyes.

The nightmare had faded. Instead of the maniacal handyman from that horror movie, it was just disgusting old Joe Danner, caught in the act, and more afraid of me than I was of him. At least I hoped he was. At any rate, it was too late to retreat, and on the assumption that a good offense is the best defense, I continued in the same aggressive voice, "Stay right where you are, don't move. How did you get in the house and what do you want? You're not leaving until I get an explanation."

He backed slowly away as I descended, as if I were the homicidal maniac. That was reassuring, as was the fact that he had not tried to retrieve his weapon. However, I stopped a safe distance from him.

"All right, Mr. Danner, what's your excuse?"

He was not a quick thinker. He licked his lips and looked away. "I—uh—I came in the front door. I got a key. We's always had a key. In case somethin' happened to Miz Martha."

"Nothing has happened to her. What were you after? You were going to steal something."

"No, ma'am." The firm denial sounded sincere. But I had a feeling Joe Danner's definition of theft might not be the same as mine. He went on, "I was—uh—I seen somebody prowling around the house. I thought he come in."

Though I had tried to keep my voice down, our conversation had been heard. A door opened upstairs and Shirley called out. "Julie? Is that you? Miz Martha heard voices—"

"It's all right," I called back. "At least I think so. . . . Now see what you've done, Mr. Danner. You scared the liver and lights out of an old woman who is in poor health—"

"No, ma'am!" Disconcertingly, the mention of Martha put him more at ease. "You ask her. She'll tell you it's all right for me to be here. Keeping watch over Miz Martha, that's my job."

"I will ask her. Stay where you are."

Martha was sitting upright in bed. She started yammering at me. I cut her short. "It's Joe Danner. He says he's here with your knowledge and permission, but I don't believe him. I'm calling the sheriff."

"No!" The word came clear and strong. The rest of her speech was not so articulate, but the meaning was clear.

"You told him it was all right?" I demanded. "You knew he had a key?"

Martha nodded.

I reached for her wrist. She flung my hand away. The only word I caught in the next tirade was "faithful."

"You might have told me," I said angrily. "I'm supposed to be responsible for you."

Martha's wide-open eye shone with unholy amusement. "Now you know," she mumbled. "Go to bed. Sleepy." And with that, the old witch closed her eyes and lay back.

I left her to Shirley—I was afraid if I stayed any longer I'd throttle her. Danner was waiting for me, his expression little short of insolent. "You want I should look around the house?" he asked.

"No. What I want is your key." I held out my hand.

"But Miz Martha—"

"Give it to me."

He had a key, all right. I took it, knowing my gesture was no more than a meaningless assertion of authority. If the Danners had one key, they might have a dozen. But it reinforced the lecture I delivered, in my most belligerent voice.

"Don't ever do this again, Mr. Danner. I'm in charge here now, not Miss Martha, and if I find you inside the house, or prowling around outside without permission from me, I'll charge you with trespass. Is that clear?"

He didn't argue, but he didn't apologize, either, and the look he gave me just before I slammed the door on him told me that I had not made a friend.

Before I went back to bed I checked on Elvis. He was his old self; I had to grab his collar to keep him from bolting out of the room to see what had happened. His look was one of reproach: If you hadn't locked me in here, I'd have warned you.

Right, Elvis, I thought. But if you hadn't thrown up the

food Mrs. Danner put out for you, you might not have been in any condition to warn me.

I couldn't complain to the police about Danner without Martha to back me up. But I could, and would, complain to Matt. It was a good thing he planned to stay the night on Friday. I had lots to say.

I was almost asleep before I figured out something else that had been nagging at my mind—the weapon Danner had been holding. He had picked it up and put it in his pocket while I was upstairs talking to Martha, but I had got a good look at it before that—and it wasn't a knife. It was a pair of scissors.

What on earth was Joe Danner planning to do with a pair of ordinary household scissors? I mean, if you have a chain saw, why use scissors?

My indignation had not lessened the following morning. I held forth at some length on the subject of the Danners to Shirley when she came to fetch Martha's breakfast. Her only reaction was a resigned shrug and a comment to the effect that Miz Martha was a law unto herself. But when I told her about Elvis getting sick her expression turned to one of shock and surprise.

"I been wondering . . ." she began.

"What?" She didn't answer. "Do you think it could have been deliberate?" I persisted.

"I wouldn't want to say that. But why don't you just run Elvis in to the vet's and make sure he's all right? It's Dr. Rubin's day in Carrsville."

Actually, I had planned to do just that. I had even scooped up a sample of the revolting meal to take with me.

Elvis didn't look like a dog who required medical attention. He loved riding in the car; it was not until we actually got into the office that he remembered what had happened to him the last time, and it took both Dr. Rubin and me to drag him out from under my chair.

She gave him a checkup and pronounced me a qualified dog owner. The foot had healed well, and the flea population had decreased. When I told her he had thrown up his dinner she smiled. "That happens sometimes. They aren't fussy about what they eat. Dead birds or rodents—"

"I know that," I said indignantly. "It says so in the book. It also says in the book that if there is any question, take the dog to the vet."

"Is there any question?" She gestured at Elvis, who was struggling to get off the table. "He's fine. Did he eat this morning?"

"Yes. But I wondered . . . Is there any chance he could have been poisoned?"

Her smile faded. "You mean deliberately?"

"I'm not sure. Someone gave him some scraps. They could have been contaminated . . ."

"There's no way I can tell now," she said slowly. "Whatever it was, it's out of his system."

"I know. That's why I brought this."

I produced my sample. Her heavy brows lifted. "You're taking this seriously, aren't you?"

"Yes."

"Okay. I'll let you know when I get the results. It may take a few days."

I thanked her. She nodded brusquely, but as Elvis and I started for the door she said, "Talk to you soon, Julie," and, for the first time since I had met her she patted me on the back. It felt like an accolade.

* * *

I hadn't intended to tell Alan about the latest developments; if I had wished to unburden myself I'd have been
disappointed, because he was in no mood to sympathize
with other people's troubles. His temper had been visibly
worsening all week. Later that afternoon he finally
cracked. Willkie presented his glorious leader with a new
find—two rusty arrowheads and the jawbone of a deer.
Alan placed them in the box devoted to finds from that
square—otherwise empty—and gravely recorded the information in his work book. Then, as we all stared in
fascinated horror, he ripped half a dozen pages from the
book, tore them into confetti-sized scraps, and flung them
into the air.

"Go home," he said in an ominously quiet voice. "That's
it. No more."

"That's it?" Willkie was being paid—minimum wage,
but he *was* being paid. He looked horrified. "You mean
you don't want me to come no more?"

"What are you talking about?" Alan demanded. "Be
here Monday as usual."

"Oh, right. Sure."

"Before you go, put the tarps over the squares."

"It's not gonna rain," Willkie said innocently. "Weather
man said more of the same till—"

Alan cleared his throat. The crew scattered, quaking.

After the tarpaulins had been spread, Willkie and the
girls piled into the Jeep. I was about to follow Jono when
a roar from Alan stopped me. "I want to talk to you, Julie."

I gestured. "I was going—"

Alan moderated his voice—not in deference to me, but
out of respect for Jono, who was watching him inter-
estedly. "I'll take Julie home, Jono. You go ahead."

"Right, boss." Jono's expression was so preternaturally

solemn I knew he was struggling to keep from smiling. I could not imagine what he thought was so funny.

Alan waited till the others had left. "Are we going to walk, or what?" I asked.

He yanked open the door of the van. "Get in."

"You can't drive that out of here. Not unless you squash your precious excavations. There isn't room to turn."

"I said, *please* get in."

He backed the van out—all the way out, through the trees. I was not capable of watching. When I felt the vehicle reverse in a wild swing, I opened my eyes.

"I'm sorry the site is turning out to be a bust," I said.

"That's life." The insane ride had rid Alan of some of his bad humor. "I'll check my calculations over the weekend. Looks as if we are in the wrong place again."

"Looks as if," I agreed. "Alan, don't you have any leads except the ones you got from that crazy book of my crazy ancestor's?"

"I wish I did. The terrain is a factor, of course; some areas are more suitable to occupation than others. Local legends can be useful—even place names. That's something I had hoped you might help me with. Any old tales of Maidenwood you never told me?"

"A couple of hundred, I should think. The one about the gal who poisoned her husband to keep him from gambling away the estate—"

Alan grinned. "I've heard that one. I'm not interested in modern scandal, but in stories you would probably dismiss as myths or fairy tales. Buried treasure, ghost stories—"

"Ghost stories?" I repeated incredulously.

"Most of them are standard fiction, of course. But you'd be surprised how long the memory of a startling or tragic event can survive, passed down from father to son. Distorted and misinterpreted in the transmission, of course, but often retaining a grain of truth among the chaff. A massacre like the one at Maydon's would be such an event. As I think I mentioned, stories about wailing ghosts sprang up soon afterward, and the ghost stories might survive after the initial cause was forgotten. A certain room or a certain spot, reputed to be haunted—shunned by those whose fathers had warned them about it, and who warned their children in turn . . . Names that linger on centuries afterward, like Gallows Hill or Deadman's Dyke or—What is it?"

"That's the name!" I exclaimed. "Deadman's Hollow. It was one of the places on Maidenwood land that was strictly off limits for me when I was young. Martha said the ground was boggy, crawling with poisonous snakes and insects . . . The boys went there sometimes, though; they would dare one another to spend the night, especially at Halloween. A boy I—a boy I knew, back in sixth or seventh grade, told me about it. You don't suppose . . ."

Alan shook his head, smiling. "Sorry. I've heard that one too. I even checked the place out. Next to the new road, at the bottom of that steep curving hill?"

I nodded. "That's where she was found."

"She?" It took him a few seconds to figure out what I was talking about. "Oh, the skeleton. That doesn't mean anything, Julie. The comedians who found it could have carried it some distance in order to put the fear of God into good old Joe Danner. Or were you thinking she crawled up on to the road by herself?"

His smile vanished abruptly when he saw the look on my face. "Julie! I didn't mean—I'm sorry! It was a stupid thing to say."

I pressed my hands to my cheeks. Hands and cheeks were icy cold, as if all the blood had drained out of them. Gradually feeling and warmth returned, and I summoned a sheepish smile. "It's all right. I don't know what came over me. It was such a gruesome idea . . ."

"Gruesome, sick, black humor," Alan agreed quickly. "And not very humorous."

I really couldn't imagine what had come over me. I felt like a fool. "So," I said, to prove that I wasn't a fool, "Deadman's Hollow is a washout."

"In every sense of the word." Alan acknowledged the horrible pun with a polite smile. "Even the reputation of the place seems to be fairly modern. I haven't come across any reference to it in the older records."

"Oh. Well, I'll give it some thought. Maybe I can come up with something."

"How about dinner tonight?"

I was so surprised I lost my grip on the window frame and hit my head on the roof as the van bounced over a ridge.

"I can't," I said.

"Aren't you entitled to an evening out occasionally? You've been on duty for almost two weeks."

Two weeks . . . The phrase triggered a flood of memory. Our "two week anniversary . . ." I had been so anxious to impress him with my culinary skills; but I forgot to turn the heat down after the veal had browned, and then we got a little distracted . . . I had paid eight dollars a pound for that veal. The stench of charring meat finally tore me from his arms, screaming like a Victorian virgin as I rushed to the kitchen. Too late . . . Alan had laughed so hard I thought he'd choke—and insisted on eating every blackened, leathery scrap of that wretched meat.

I glanced at him out of the corner of my eye. He was

staring straight ahead, his profile impassive, but a muscle at the corner of his mouth twitched, as if he were remembering that arduous exercise in mastication. I almost said something—but I got cold feet.

"I can't," I repeated. "Matt is coming to take me to dinner, and there are some things I want to discuss with him."

"Oh, yeah? Why the change in routine? I thought Saturday was his usual day."

His cool, calm tone hit me like a slap in the face. The memories that had softened me hadn't touched him at all. I hated myself for succumbing to sentimentality, and I hated him for making me succumb.

"How did you find out?" I demanded.

"Find out what?"

"Don't be clever. You knew Matt was coming this evening and you knew why. Who told you the burial service was tomorrow morning?"

"You did." A slow satisfied smile curved the corner of his mouth. "I knew it was on the agenda, but I didn't know when."

"You really are a bastard."

"For asking you to dinner? When are you going to overcome that stupid . . ." He stopped. Then he said quietly, "I didn't know Matt was coming out this evening. The invitation was made in good faith. It still stands."

"Thanks, but I'd hate you to waste precious cash that could be spent digging holes."

Alan shrugged. "Do you mind if I attend the obsequies?"

"Yes, I do mind. But short of an injunction, which I couldn't get in time, and a shotgun, which I disapprove of on principle, I can't think of any way of preventing you from coming."

Alan stopped in front of the gates. "See you tomorrow, then. Er—what time did you say?"

"I didn't say. Eleven o'clock."

As I started down the long road to the house I saw Elvis coming—a brown-and-white blur enclosed in a cloud of dust. He always seemed to know when I was due back. I hastily sat down. Once he had knocked me off my feet with the exuberance of his greeting. Now he flung himself into my lap and we exchanged pleasantries— licks, hugs, compliments, excited whines. He was too big to be a lap dog, but he didn't know that.

I had had a few words with Mrs. Danner about Elvis before I left the house. Quite a few words. I would have said even more if she had not taken the wind out of my sails by starting to cry.

It was awful. I wouldn't have felt quite so bad if she had burst into loud lamentations, but she didn't utter a sound. It was not until the first tear oozed down along one of the deep lines in her cheek and twinkled in the sunlight that I realized what was happening.

So what could I do but tell her I was sorry? I *was* sorry for her. Poor woman, she was caught between a rock and a hard place, with me on one hand and her husband on the other. If there had been an attempt to poison Elvis, Joe Danner was behind it; his wife wouldn't have had the gumption to take such a step on her own, nor would she dare resist his orders. All the same, I repeated my warning before I left. Shirley had promised to keep an eye on Elvis, but the most reassuring fact, to me, was that Mrs. Danner didn't have her "pockabook."

I was in no hurry to get to the house, so I continued to sit, with Elvis sprawled across my legs drooling onto my jeans. Martha's supper was prepared—tuna salad, for the second time that week. I was running out of ideas. No wonder women hated cooking. Three meals a day, year after year after deadly year . . . Chicken and beef and pork and fish, chicken and beef and pork and fish . . . If Matt tried to take me to that local hangout of his, I'd have hysterics. I wanted tripe or brains or sweetbread—anything but chicken or beef or pork or fish.

I decided I would not tell Matt that Alan planned to attend the funeral. He'd find out soon enough—and probably blame me. I condemned both Alan and Matt to an even hotter climate than the one that prevails in Tidewater Virginia in the summer.

I had planned to dress in my best, in the hope that my gorgeousness would inspire Matt to take me someplace fancy for dinner. The heat defeated me. I settled for bare legs and sandals and the coolest sundress I owned. My hair got bushy and unmanageable when the humidity was high; I yanked it back from my face and bundled it into a knot at the back of my neck.

Martha had been in a snit of excitement all afternoon, running Shirley ragged with orders. Matt's room had to be cleaned and garnished with flowers. (Little did she know I had swiped his mattress; the one on the bed now was the musty, hard object that had been allotted to me, and I sincerely hoped he would sleep well on it.) I had been summoned to the presence three times, to get *my* orders. I had also been told to come in before I left, to say good night. After I was dressed I decided I might as well get it over with, so I knocked on her door.

Her movable eye surveyed me from top to bottom and stayed fixed on my bare calves.

"It's too hot to wear stockings," I said, anticipating the

criticism. "We're not going to the Ritz-Swank-Carlton, Martha; I'll be lucky if I get a Big Mac and fries."

The next complaint was about my hair. She waxed so vehement on the subject that I couldn't understand what she wanted me to do about it, but she obviously disapproved of the style. "It's too late now," I said ambiguously.

Matt was on time, I'll say that for him. I suppose punctuality is a political necessity; he had never exhibited that trait as a child.

I was ready for him. "Get me out of here," I hissed, as he came in.

Matt laughed with professional heartiness. "Can you hang on for ten more minutes? I ought to spend a little time with Martha."

I knew it would take longer than ten minutes. Martha was lying in wait, bedecked in pink and smelling of cologne. As I had hoped she would, Shirley took advantage of Matt's presence to slip downstairs for her supper. I had it ready—tuna salad and sliced tomatoes, rolls, and iced tea.

"That's nice, Julie," she said appreciatively. "Looks pretty, too."

"I feel guilty enough walking out on you. Are you sure you don't mind?"

"Goodness, honey, I did it for two weeks before you came. Anyhow, I owe you an evening out."

"You look awfully tired."

"It's the heat. Gets to you when you're my size."

"Gets to you, period." I sat down across the table from her and sipped my tea. "I'd forgotten how awful summers can be down here."

"You get used to it."

"I don't plan on getting used to it."

She smiled but said nothing, and for a while we sat in

silence. She was a comfortable person to be with; I felt my frazzled nerve endings smooth out and wondered why the hell I was letting myself get uptight about petty things. Compared to Shirley, I had little to complain about.

"How is Ron?" I asked.

"He's got a job." Shirley beamed.

"Really? That's great! Why didn't you tell me?"

"Just got it today. Night shift at the chicken-and-chips place on the highway. It's only six hours a day, but it's a help."

"What about the other kids?"

"The neighbors will keep an eye on them. Frannie is sixteen, big enough to watch the little ones."

A suggestive whine at the back door interrupted the conversation. "I'm sorry," I told him. "You can't come in. Believe me, Elvis, it is just as hot inside as it is out."

Elvis looked as if he had more to say on the subject, but the arrival of Matt prevented further discussion. Matt's eyes widened at the sight of the furry face pressed pensively against the screen, but another aggravation was uppermost in his mind. "Let's get out of here, Julie," he grumbled, mopping his brow. "This house feels like an oven."

"That's one of the subjects I wanted to discuss."

"I offered Martha a window air conditioner. She said no."

"Try forcing one on me and you won't hear any objections. Shirley too."

"Of course she can have an air conditioner if she wants one," Matt exclaimed. "Why didn't you say something, Shirley?"

"Now, Matthew, it's been quite comfortable until the past few days. Julie's not used to it, she feels it more."

Matt put his hands on her shoulders. "You don't complain enough," he said affectionately. "You know, Shirley, that all you have to do is ask. How am I supposed to know what you want if you don't tell me?"

It seemed to me that only a minimal degree of intelligence was required to note that the temperature was sizzling; but Shirley, like so many women, was easily seduced by a sweet smile and a pat on the shoulder. She told Matt not to worry, everything was fine. "Run along now and have a nice time."

Matt helped me into the car and closed the door. "Where do you want to go for dinner?" he asked, starting the engine and flicking on the air conditioning.

"I don't care." The rush of cool air dispelled a great deal of the aimless animosity I had felt. In our controlled environment many of us have forgotten how excessive heat affects the emotions; there's a definite correlation between temperature and violent crime, and I can understand why.

"I don't suppose," I added wistfully, "that there is such a thing as a taco or a piece of moussaka anywhere around? I'm so sick of chicken and hamburgers."

"Spoiled, effete city girl," Matt said. "But you have it coming. I'll find you a taco if we have to drive to Washington. What else do you want?"

There were so many things, I hardly knew where to begin. I started with the worry uppermost in my mind. "More help—or better help. Surely there's someone better than Mrs. Danner."

"I can't fire her," Matt said indignantly. "The Danners have been with the family for thirty years."

"What is this, the Old South? I don't care if the Danners have been around since Sherman ravaged the old plantation. She's incompetent, and her husband is crazy. He broke into the house last night."

I expected a cry of outrage or an exclamation of disbelief—something. Matt didn't even look at me. "Why would he break in? He has a key."

I was the one who emitted the cry of outrage. "Is that all you can say? I tell you the man was wandering around the house at three A.M., and you calmly inform me he has a key. He scared the hell out of me!"

"I suppose it was a shock," Matt said broad-mindedly. "I'll have a word with him."

"I already had a word with him. But I suppose he'd pay more attention to you. I'm just a weak-minded female who gets all het-up about finding strange men in her house."

"You don't understand the local customs—"

"If you give me that crap about faithful family retainers I'll scream. Danner scares me. He isn't right in the head."

"He's perfectly harmless, Julie. Martha wasn't upset about it, was she?"

"Well—no. But she isn't right in the head either."

Matt laughed tolerantly. "She knows and trusts Joe. He has a rather feudal attitude toward Martha—unusual in this day and age, I admit, but no less admirable for all that. I admit he's a little peculiar, and he hasn't fully recovered from the shock of his discovery that morning a few weeks ago. That's probably why he was wandering around last night—he's hoping to lay hands on the pranksters who played that gruesome trick on him."

The explanation was so glibly reasonable it cut the ground out from under my protest. I knew there was no hope of persuading Matt to get rid of the Danners; secretly he adored the idea of having a faithful serf to protect the manor. I gave it one more try.

"At least let me fire Mrs. Danner. There has to be someone better—if something happened to Martha while she was on duty she'd just stand there wringing her hands. It's not fair to Shirley. She has the brunt of it, even with me there."

"Shirley's quite a gal, isn't she," Matt said fondly.

I'm sure Matt honestly believed he was paying Shirley the highest tribute in his power. I saw through the evasion, but instead of telling him that Shirley didn't need compliments, she needed help, I heard myself ask him a question that had nagged me for some time.

"How long have you known her, Matt?"

"Years—I hate to think how many. She helped raise me, you know."

"I didn't know."

Matt glanced at me in surprise. I said, "I don't remember. I've forgotten her. I have almost no memories of the years I lived at Maidenwood."

"You remember my sins," Matt said lightly.

"I had forgotten about you shutting me in the graveyard until I went there the other day. Oh, I don't mean those four years are an absolute blank, but I should remember more than I do."

"Have you talked to anyone about it?"

"A shrink, you mean?"

"Anyone. A friend, your mother . . . Why not a shrink? I didn't expect ignorant prejudice about psychiatry from you."

"I didn't talk to anyone because I didn't know I had a problem," I said, my voice rising. "How often would you reminisce about the good old days when you were ten, if you were miles away from where you had lived and nothing happened to remind you? Mother hardly ever talked about Martha—"

"That's a clue for you," Matt said dryly. "Face it, Julie. Martha is a mean old devil. She used to be a mean younger devil. She isn't the person I'd pick to look after a child."

"You mean she beat me?"

Matt burst out laughing, and I blushed for my brief descent into melodrama. "Martha handed out a few spankings and slaps," he said. "But she didn't have to resort to physical violence. She could cut you to pieces with a look and a few words. I don't know much about psychiatry, but I suspect we both have reason to blot out many of our childhood memories."

We didn't have to go as far as Washington to find tacos. Matt knew a good Mexican restaurant in Petersburg. Though he advised me not to take my missing memories seriously, he told a lot of "Do you remember?" stories that evening, without ever asking a direct question. As he talked, the incidents and people and places he mentioned began to come back to me. It was a gentle, sensitive probing into the past, without pressure and without risk.

We were on our way home when I told him I knew what he had been doing and thanked him for it. "You've reassured me, Matt. I remember a lot more than I thought I did. Maybe I am playing with a full deck after all."

"You're no crazier than any of us—if that's any consolation. To tell you the truth, Julie, I enjoyed talking about it. The memories weren't all bad, were they? It's nice having kin who share a common heritage. The tie of the blood, and all that stuff."

"The old blood is running thin, Matt. There aren't many of us left."

"Only two of us, in the direct line of descent. It's a pattern that has repeated itself for a long time—your mother and mine in the generation before ours, Martha and her sister before that."

"Didn't Martha's sister have children?"

Matt chuckled. "She may have. Didn't your mother tell you about her? She ran away from home with a totally unsuitable man, as Martha put it. That's another pattern that seems to run in the family—unsuitable marriages. Martha hasn't spoken to my mother since she divorced Dad, and she has never referred to her sister. The poor woman wrote several times after she fled the nest, but Martha never answered. Finally Melissa gave up, and no one has heard from her in years."

"If Martha never talks about her, how did you hear all that?"

"From the Judge. He warned me not to mention Melissa to Martha."

"You mean Martha has never forgiven her, after all those years? We aren't a very nice family, Matt."

"We're okay; it's Martha who isn't. In my opinion, her marriage was a worse sin than any divorce. You know she married a cousin in order to keep the family name. Did you ever see a picture of our grandfather?"

"I think Mother has one somewhere. Didn't he have a mustache?"

"Not just a mustache—big, black, sweeping mustachios, like a pirate's. And under them, the softest pursed lips . . . The poor devil died young. Martha kept him around just long enough to breed two children off him."

Chilled by the contempt in his voice, I said, "And I thought I had a grudge against her! What did she do to *you*, Matt?"

I expected him to reply with an equivocation, but the form it took surprised me.

"Here lieth one who would resign
Gladly his lot, to shoulder thine.
Give me thy coat; get into mine."

"Matt! Poetry?"

"I'm not a barbarian, Julie. But don't tell my constituents."

"What's wrong with quoting poetry?"

"Nothing, if it comes from Lincoln or the Bible. If it were known that I read lyric poems, it could lose me the election." His voice was back to normal—light, amused, concealing emotion.

Shirley had left the outside lights burning. When we got out of the car I lifted my face to the breeze. "It's cooler," I said. "Maybe we can sleep tonight after all."

"Rain by morning," Matt said.

"It is not going to rain."

"Sure it is. Look at those clouds." As if in affirmation a red light flared in the belly of the clouds, followed by a mutter of thunder.

"Heat lightning," I said firmly.

I heard the first drops patter on the roof after I had got into bed. Alan had been right—he was always right, even about the weather.

It was a lovely morning for a funeral. Fog clung to the trees like bolls of dirty gray cotton; water dripped from the leaves. As we walked down the path toward the cemetery I was still in a state of shock. When Matt had mentioned services I had expected some inappropriate demonstration, but I had not imagined he would go this far.

His suit wasn't black, but the charcoal gray cast a suitably somber note. The umbrella he held over my uncovered head was black. Ahead of us, another of the same hue shielded the minister. Ahead of *him,* six stalwart men, recruited by the undertaker, carried the coffin—a pine box so ostentatiously simple it almost ranked as a valuable antique.

Matt had my hand firmly imprisoned in the crook of his arm. My canvas sandals and yellow cotton dress were the only incongruous details in the decorous scene. Dire suspicions began to take shape in my mind. They were soon confirmed by a bright light that blinded me and left spots dancing in front of my eyes. Behind the spots I saw the photographer, camera at the ready.

Matt stopped. "Please," he said reproachfully.

Another photographer advanced from the left flank. Matt repeated his plea for privacy, but he was careful to give the second man a good profile. I put my tongue out and grimaced. Matt didn't notice what I was doing until the photographer started to giggle; then he jabbed me in the ribs.

"Don't make a farce of this, Julie."

"I can't do any worse than you. Damn it, Matt—"

"Not now," the future governor muttered, sotto voce. "Let's get on with it."

Accompanied by reporters, we wended our damp way onward. At the gate of the cemetery Matt stopped and faced the press. "Keep a straight face, or no air conditioner," he told me, out of the corner of his mouth. Aloud, he said, "Ladies and gentlemen, I understand that this is your job and I respect the public's right to know. But I beg you won't follow us into this sacred enclosure. I'll answer any questions you may have afterward. Fair enough?"

He closed the gates, leaving the pack outside. I noticed that the grave had been dug in a spot not far from the gates, and that the open grille did not impede the photographers.

I was furious with Matt, but I knew that making a scene would only prolong the discomfort. At first I didn't see Alan, and hoped he had had the sense to stay away. Then I found him, kneeling by one of the stones near the east corner. He rose to his feet when the procession entered, but kept at a distance. He was wearing tan slacks and a white shirt instead of his working garb of jeans and blue shirt—respectable but not theatrical.

He was not the only spectator. Also at a respectful distance from Alan, and from the grave, was Sheriff Jarboe. Catching my eye, he nodded, without smiling or speaking. I had expected he might be there; I had not expected the Danners. They stood apart from the others, and neither of them looked at me. Mrs. Danner's head was bowed. Her husband never took his eyes off the open grave.

The pallbearers went about their business, supervised by the undertaker, a plump man in black. He had full cheeks and a couple of chins, but years of looking solemn had trained his face in lines that made it look longer and thinner than it really was. The minister took his place at the head of the grave and opened the book.

"I am the Resurrection and the Life . . ."

Traditionally the Carrs were Episcopalians, when they went to church at all. I assumed Matt had chosen an Episcopal minister for that reason; but the formal service had its advantages, leaving the pastor no awkward problems of how to eulogize an unknown. I hoped she didn't mind, whoever she was. Joe Danner would have minded. He had transferred his inimical stare to the minister, and I had the distinct impression that if someone had read the wrong service over his bones, those bones would have risen in protest.

The service was quickly concluded. The minister looked up from the book. "Would you care to say a few words?"

Though I felt sure Matt had planned that last, outrageous gesture, he seemed for once at a loss for words. I was as surprised as anyone when I heard my own voice break the stillness; and although, like another well-known person, I can quote Scripture for my own evil purposes, the phrases I repeated did not come from the Bible.

"Down down, down into the darkness of the grave
   Gently they go, the beautiful, the tender, the kind;
   Quietly they go, the intelligent, the witty, the brave.
   I know. But I do not approve. And I am not re-
      signed."

A frown furrowed the pastoral brow at this pagan sentiment, but I didn't care; that was how I felt. And the quotation seemed to strike a responsive cord in Matt. Like an antiphony his words echoed:

"The sun that warmed our stooping backs and
      withered the weed uprooted—
   We shall not feel it again.
   We shall die in darkness, and be buried in the rain."

"Where did you get that?" I whispered, surprised but impressed.

"Your fault." He was as good as a ventriloquist; his lips

scarcely moved. "I had a Biblical quote ready, but you got me off the track . . ." He took my arm to lead me away, but I shook off his grasp. Alan was coming toward us and I didn't want him to think I had been an active participant in the proceedings.

The cameras flashed as Matt and Alan confronted one another.

"I don't recall inviting you to be present, Professor," Matt said. "This was supposed to be a private family service—"

"I suppose they're all cousins," Alan said, indicating the reporters. "I wouldn't have missed this for the world, Senator. Particularly the last act."

"Last act? What—what—" Matt's voice failed him, a phenomenon I had never expected to see once, let alone twice, in a day.

Alan pointed. "She's been there behind the mausoleum the whole time."

She emerged, trying to look as if she had been planning to make her appearance at that point. She wore the same pinstriped suit, but she had tied a transparent rain bonnet over her head. Ignoring the rest of us, she minced through the rain-soaked grass till she stood by the grave.

"Hail to you, sister. Hail, Lady Jocelyn! Not to your mortal remains, which lie here, but to your immortal spirit, with which I spoke last night. Your wishes have been followed, Jocelyn; you lie in holy ground at last."

This speech wiped the grin off Alan's face. He started for Mrs. Hornbeak, who skipped nimbly aside without interrupting her cozy chat with the ghost of Lady Jocelyn. "Fear not, sister, I will impart to these skeptics the tidings you gave me. Rejoice in the sunshine and love of the hereafter with your wee babe—awk!"

She slipped but recovered herself, and I went in pursuit of Alan, who really looked as if he wanted to strangle the woman. The photographers were having a field day. Flashes exploded like fireworks.

It was Sheriff Jarboe who halted the farcical pursuit. Darting forward, he took Mrs. Hornbeak by the arm and stood between her and Alan. "Shame on the both of you," he said sternly. "Don't you know better than to act up at a time like this?"

"I came on an errand of love and mercy," Mrs. Hornbeak cried. "My messages have been unanswered, my offers of help ignored—"

"I don't care what you came for, lady; the fact is, you're guilty of trespass. Want I should arrest her, Senator?"

"No, no, of course not. I'm sure Mrs. Er-um's motives were of the best. If she will leave quietly I'll forget the whole thing."

"But I know where she once rested," Mrs. Hornbeak insisted. "I can show you the place—she wants you to know, you who are her descendants."

"If you don't shut that woman up, I will," Alan said, trying to get at Mrs. Hornbeak.

"You shut your own face, Professor, or I'll arrest you for creating a disturbance. Everybody out of here."

The undertaker wrung his hands. "But, Sheriff—"

"I don't mean you, Sam. Get on with it."

Alan shrugged. Thrusting his hands into his pockets he strode angrily toward the gate. One of the reporters hesitated, and then took off after him.

The others converged on Matt. "Please follow me to the house," he instructed. "I'll talk to you there. Julie . . ."

"Go on," I said. "I'll be there in a minute."

Mrs. Hornbeak was led away by Jarboe. The minister had made his escape somehow; I didn't blame him for wanting to distance himself from the proceedings. The

Danners had gone too. Mopping his brow, the undertaker followed the others. His assistants began to fill in the grave.

I stood watching them. The mist had thickened; drifting clouds of soft white veiled the ugly scene. The hollow thud of damp earth on the coffin was the only sound that broke the silence.

I wondered if she had been laid to rest in that ugly, ill-fitting dress. I hadn't thought about it before. Perhaps if I had, I would have done something, found a more becoming gown . . . Becoming to bleached bones and grinning skull? Cheap modern polyester trimmed with machine-made lace at so much a yard? But I might have searched the old trunks in the attic . . . Why hadn't I done that?

Because—the answer came swift and clear—because I didn't want to go there. Because I was afraid to climb the narrow, dusty stairs, afraid of awakening hurting memories—afraid of what I might, or might not, find.

"Whoever you were," I whispered, "I'm sorry . . . But none of this really matters, does it?"

I was beginning to sound just like Mrs. Hornbeak. I groped for a more formal epitaph, but nothing came to me. Rest in peace? I had no reason to suppose she did not. Matt's strange quotation came back to me. "Be buried in the rain . . ." At least it was appropriate. Rain is kinder than sunlight on the bowed heads of the mourners.

I went to the back of the house and sat on the porch communing with Elvis. He had better manners and better sense than most of the people I had seen that morning. I had heard voices, even laughter, from out in front, where Matt was entertaining the press and getting his picture taken on the steps of the family mansion. He'd make sure the photos didn't show the broken windowpanes and overgrown boxwood. It would be so easy to despise Matt, if it weren't for those occasional moments of communication. I liked him so much, when I didn't want to murder him.

Eventually the tumult and the shouting died. I continued to sit on the steps. I ought to do something about lunch. This was Mrs. Danner's day off and I owed Shirley some Martha-sitting time. I felt as shapeless and forlorn as the fog that hung over the trees. No wonder Matt had given in to the sheriff's request. He had seen a chance to get his name in the papers; for the ending to the bizarre story was bound to attract media attention. Alan was just as bad. He had sneered at Matt, but he had not avoided the photographers.

Shirley found me still sitting, with Elvis's head on my lap. "Here's where you're hiding. Miz Martha's having a fit. She wants to know what all the racket was about."

"Tell her to ask Matt."

"He left already."

"Damn him." I scrambled to my feet, pushing poor Elvis out of the way. "As usual, he's left me holding the bag. What are we going to tell Martha?"

"I don't know," Shirley said helpfully.

I went to the kitchen and started taking things out of the refrigerator. "I'm tempted to tell Martha the whole story. All this tender concern for her sensibilities—she doesn't have any, she's tough as steel."

"You want to take the responsibility, you go right ahead," Shirley said. "It's not my place to do it."

"Nor mine, I guess. Oh hell. Go home for a few hours, why don't you? I'll give Martha her lunch, such as it is, and tuck her in. I've nothing better to do anyway."

* * *

I told Martha part of the truth—that the people she had heard had been reporters and photographers, interviewing Matt about something to do with his campaign. She was more restless and agitated than usual, and when I started to tuck her in for her nap she shook her head in vigorous refusal.

"Do you want me to read?" I asked resignedly.

Another shake of the head. She wanted something from the shelves next to the fireplace.

I guess I've forgotten to mention that Martha's bedroom was as crowded as a pack rat's nest. It was spotlessly clean—Shirley and Mrs. Danner saw to that—but every drawer and shelf was crammed with odds and ends. Photograph albums, scrapbooks, boxes filled with clippings, other boxes filled with God-knows-what. Several of the scrapbooks were devoted to Matt's career. Until she had had her first stroke, Martha had kept them up to date.

She didn't want the scrapbooks. She didn't want this box or that one. I finally found the one she had in mind, an antique cookie tin, and handed it to her. Her nails scratched ineffectually at the lid.

I said, "Here, let me—" and reached for the box. Martha's claws closed over it. "No!"

"Okay, okay."

"Read."

When I looked up from the book a little later she was asleep, hands resting protectively on the tin box.

I dozed off too, lulled by the dripping rain and gloomy skies. Waking from a dream of fire—one of my recurrent worries in that old barn of a house—I realized that the siren ringing was that of the telephone. By the time I reached it, Martha was awake and cursing—or maybe not, her mumbles usually sounded as if she were swearing.

It was Matt. "Hi, Julie."

"You son of a—" I began, and broke off, seeing Martha's beady eye fixed on me.

"What's the matter?"

"What's the . . . We were sorry not to see you before you left. You and your buddies made a lot of noise. Martha was disturbed."

"What did you tell her?"

"The truth."

A gurgling noise at the other end of the wire made me feel better. I waited a few seconds before relieving his anxiety. "I couldn't tell her what it was all about. Your political machinations leave me baffled."

"Oh." He let out a sigh of relief. "I knew I could count on you, Julie."

Martha was waving her hands and mumbling. I said, "Martha wants to talk to you."

"Holy God, Julie!"

"Here." I handed Martha the phone and settled back to enjoy the proceedings.

Matt did most of the talking. I don't know what he said—I'm sure ninety percent of it was cover-up and the rest was a lie. When I retrieved the phone, Matt's first remark was, "I owe you one for that, Julie."

"I haven't begun to even the score, Matt."

"Why don't you buy a couple of air conditioners tomorrow? Tell them to send me the bill."

"Tell who? I think you're trying to bribe me, Matt."

"Me? Now, Julie, you know—"

"Forget it. What's on your mind?"

"Has that woman shown up?"

"You mean Mrs.—"

"Ssss!" The sound blasted my ear. He went on, "You're with Martha still, aren't you?"

"Yes."

"We don't want her to find out about Hornbeak."

I said, "Let me call you back. Where are you?"

"You can't call me back. I'm—er—at a friend's."

"You little devil," I said.

Matt ignored the comment. "She was very persistent. If she bothers you, call the sheriff. I wouldn't put it past her to break into the house—"

"Thanks. That makes me feel great."

"She's not dangerous, she's just a bloody nuisance. I don't want her bugging Martha, that's all."

"Well, I don't want her bugging me either. What do you suggest I do with her while I'm waiting for the sheriff to arrive?"

"Damn it, Julie, if you can't watch what you're saying in front of Martha, I can't talk to you. Just keep your eyes open, that's all."

He hung up before I could think of an appropriately withering response.

I turned to find Martha staring at me with a face like stone. She might have died between one breath and the next. Cursing my temper and my big mouth, I reached for her limp wrist.

Her fingers writhed like worms, clamping over my hand. "Who?" she mouthed. "Woman—who?"

The unexpected, painful strength of her grasp was another shock. I can lie with reasonable facility when I have time to concoct a story, but I'm not good at spontaneous invention.

"Uh," I said brilliantly. "Uh—er—nobody important. She calls herself a psychic or something like—"

Martha cackled. Her grasp relaxed and she pushed my hand away. "Hornbeak. Institute."

"Yes, right."

I should have expected Mrs. Hornbeak would have been in touch with Martha. Maidenwood had been the object of interest to a lot of people and institutions, from land developers to treasure hunters. Martha enjoyed running them off, threatening them with lawsuits. Since she knew so much, I couldn't see any harm in telling her the rest.

Her reaction was typical of her. "Gun," she said emphatically. "Shoot."

"Gun," I repeated. "That reminds me. What became of that shotgun you had?"

Martha's open eye narrowed suspiciously, so that it matched the other eye. I said guilefully, "I can't shoot her if I don't have a gun, can I?"

She hesitated, almost believing me. Then she muttered, "Gone. Not here. Get one."

I was half tempted to tell her about the dog, but decided to follow the path of least resistance. Elvis's presence might reassure her, or it might make her furious.

She kept muttering about shooting, and guns, and buckshot. Vindictive old witch . . . Didn't she realize that if I peppered a trespasser I could be sued—and I'd probably lose the case?

Suddenly she said something that brought my train of thought up short, like crashing into a boulder on the track.

"Bones. What did you do . . . bones?"

eight

I stopped breathing. Martha's fingers crooked and twitched. She looked as if she wanted to slap me, but lacked the strength. Her other hand fumbled at the box that now lay open on the bed beside her. It was filled with an untidy tangle of objects, mostly sewing materials—spools of thread, scraps of cloth. And newspaper clippings.

The clipping she indicated had not been neatly cut out. It was ripped and crumpled. She must have done it herself, struggling to overcome the handicap that had paralyzed one arm.

"You've known all along," I gasped. "Matt was so worried about your finding out . . . Why didn't you say something before this?"

Martha's lip curled. She never explained her actions or her failure to act. "Bones," she repeated insistently. "Where?"

I didn't know what to say so I sought refuge in the

truth. "We buried them in our cemetery," I said. "Nobody knew who they were or where they came from, so . . ."

The sounds coming from her parted lips froze my voice and sent chills coursing through my body. They resembled the screeching of rusty hinges, but after a while I realized she was laughing.

For once I was glad to return to Bleak House. It had been, to say the least, an unnerving ten minutes. Martha had been, for her, absolutely garrulous; she had asked questions and even answered a few. What had happened to shake her out of her customary close-mouthed habits? Could it have been something I said? She had only heard my side of the conversation with Matt, and I couldn't recall having made any startling pronouncements. Something about a woman coming to the house, causing trouble . . . When Martha found out it was Hornbeak I was talking about, she had appeared relieved. Was there some other woman she feared, as she did not fear the psychic? Then the sudden change of subject, from shotguns to skeletons, and her horrible, eerie laughter . . .

I didn't ask any more questions. I wasn't sure I wanted to know the answers.

That night I did not dream of skeletons. I dreamed I was six years old and Mother had taken me to a revival of *Snow White.* When the Wicked Queen turned into the Wicked Witch and cackled over the poisoned apple, her laughter sounded just like Martha's.

Sunday dawned dreary and wet. Shirley eschewed her flowery hat in favor of a raincoat with a pointed hood, in which she looked like a benevolent gnome.

"I hate to leave you alone all day," she said anxiously. "Are you sure—"

"I'm sure. Mrs. Danner will be here, and I haven't anything to do anyway. Run along. And, Shirley—"

"Yes?"

"Say a prayer for me. That I won't lose my cool and smother my grandmother."

Under the shadow of the hood her eyes shone like sunken stars. "I will."

She must have prayed. Mrs. Danner never showed up, and by late afternoon I was sorely tempted, not to smother Martha, but to run howling out into the fog. Only Shirley's arrival, late in the afternoon, saved me from self-destruction.

"You're back early," I said, restraining myself with difficulty from embracing her.

"Figured I should get here before dark. It's a miserable day—foggy and dark."

"I'll start dinner." I rose. Martha flapped her fingers.

"Sherry," she said, quite clearly. "Late. Coming soon . . ."

"She means the Judge," Shirley said. "It's his day."

I had forgotten. I hurried downstairs. Everything in the house was soggy with damp, except for a single box of crackers I'd had the foresight to put in the refrigerator. I smeared cheese on a few of them and arranged them on a plate. Four o'clock struck, but there was no sign of Judge McLendon. I began to think he wouldn't come. The weather was miserable. The fog had thickened as the day wore on; it pressed against the windows like white sheets hung out to dry. Even Elvis was depressed. He sat by the door moaning until I opened it, and then he slithered into the kitchen, crawled under the table, and lay down, his head on his paws. I didn't blame him for wanting company.

I had almost given the lawyer up when I heard the

sound of a car, and I went quickly to the door. The fog came in with him like a cloud of ectoplasm; the pallor of his face, his snow-white hair and white suit completed the ghostly image. I took his hand, not so much as a gesture of courtesy as to reassure myself that he was actually there, in the flesh. His hand was as cold and damp as that of the specter he resembled.

"You shouldn't have come," I said.

"Come now." He smiled. "Surely I don't look that bad."

"Oh no. I meant—the fog is so thick—driving must be hazardous."

"My eyes are as good as ever," he said firmly. A sudden fit of coughing spoiled the picture of good health; his shoulders shook, and he reached for a handkerchief. "I beg your pardon, Julie. A touch of bronchitis. Damp weather always brings it on, but it's nothing to worry about."

"I'll get the sherry."

"Thank you, my dear. Just what I need to clear my chest."

When I returned from the kitchen with the tray he was only halfway up the stairs, leaning heavily on the balustrade and pulling himself from step to step. I backed up and stayed out of sight until he had reached the landing, knowing he would be humiliated if I followed his difficult progress and bitterly offended if I offered an arm.

After I had arranged the wine and crackers on a table, Shirley accompanied me back downstairs. "He looks terrible," I said.

"Well, he's not a young man," Shirley said reasonably. She glanced at the shrouded window and shivered. "It sure isn't a fit night for man nor beast. Fit for . . . for other things . . ."

"For God's sake, Shirley, give me a break! I'm ready to

howl like a banshee already." Shirley smiled faintly, but did not reply. After a moment I said, "Do you believe in . . . other things, Shirley?"

"I don't believe in them," Shirley said. "I don't *not* believe in them, either. Especially on a night like this."

"Let's have a drink."

"You go ahead. Coffee's what I need; I'm so sleepy with this weather, I can't hardly keep my eyes open."

I put together a rather slapdash meal while she sat yawning over her coffee. Neither of us spoke; I couldn't think of a cheerful topic of conversation, and I certainly didn't want to discuss "other things" or the Judge's fragility. I had forgotten about Elvis, who was keeping very quiet under the table. Like all canny canines, he knew he could stay where he was, in the nice lighted, friendly kitchen, if he didn't remind anyone of his presence. Shirley had not seen him. When he rose to his feet, growling softly, she let out a shriek and I dropped the plate I was about to give her. The hamburger slid off onto the table and a shower of french fries flew into the air.

Close upon the dog's signal came a sound that echoed down the hall and through the kitchen door, which neither of us had remembered to close. A series of muffled thuds, followed by a final, louder thud . . . Shirley struggled to get out of her chair and I bolted for the door.

I knew what had happened before I reached the scene—that slow, painful ascent of the stairs should have warned me. I fully expected to see the old man sprawled lifeless on the floor, but when I got to him he was struggling to sit up.

"Lie still," I begged. "Don't move, let me—"

"I assure you—no damage done . . ." His smile was like the bared teeth of a death's head. "Clumsy of me. Lost my footing . . ."

Shirley knelt beside him. Her firm brown hands moved capably up his legs and over his chest. "Don't seem like anything's broken . . ."

"No, no. Just bruised." In a sudden, frightening burst of strength he escaped our hands and staggered to his feet. "You see? Fully recovered. So sorry to have worried you."

His color was so ghastly I would not have been surprised to see him drop at my feet. "You can't drive home after a shock like that," I exclaimed. "I had intended to ask you to stay anyway. Matt's bed is all made up—"

"No. No, thank you, child—I must go. I can't stay. I must . . . There are matters I must attend to tonight—at once."

Short of physically restraining him there was nothing I could do except continue to plead, which I did as I followed him to the door. He walked steadily, but I had a feeling—professional instinct or feminine intuition—that he was making an enormous effort to keep from collapsing. When he reached the door he turned and put his hand on my shoulder.

"You're a good girl, Julie," he said gently. "I hope—I am certain—that all will be well with you. Go upstairs now. Reassure Martha. Tell her . . . Tell her not to worry."

The door closed right in my face. By the time I opened it the car was already in motion.

I turned to Shirley. "I'm tempted to call the sheriff."

"He's driving all right."

The taillights were red blurs in the fog, but they held a steady course. They flared brighter as the car reached the road, and then disappeared.

"We shouldn't have let him go."

"Child, there wasn't nothing you could do to stop him. Now stop fretting. You're in a state of nerves tonight, and no wonder. I'd better get up to Miz Martha. She'll be thinking he broke his neck or something. You get on out to the kitchen and eat that hamburger—unless Elvis already ate it."

Elvis was under the table, looking angelically innocent. The hamburger was gone. I preferred to assume he had eaten it rather than blame its absence on . . . other things.

Come to think of it, his performance had been a bit on the uncanny side. He had moved and growled a moment before the Judge fell.

I told myself not to be absurd. The dog's keener ears had caught a sound mine had missed, a scuffle or a stifled cry of alarm.

I didn't feel like eating. I put another hamburger on to broil for Shirley and sat down at the table to finish my wine. Elvis put his head on my feet. The warm prickly weight felt good. I wished I could take him to my room. If I were awakened during the night, to hear howling in the woods and see fog shifting at the window like hollow-eyed, white faces looking in, it would be comforting to know he was there.

Out of the question, of course. But it gave me an idea. I got up and went into the hallway.

I had never had reason to investigate any of the closed rooms along the kitchen corridor. The first one turned out to be a pantry, the shelves empty of everything except spiders. The second and third were low-ceilinged and small; rain had beat through the broken windowpanes and rotted the floor boards.

I worked my way along the opposite side of the hall, back toward the kitchen. Another miserable little cubby hole—a servant's room, perhaps. The last room on that side was a small bathroom, antiquated but functional.

There was only one other door I had not opened, and for a while I thought I wasn't going to be able to open it. The door was not locked, though; it was only stuck. When I threw my weight against it, it suddenly gave way and I staggered a few steps forward before I could get my balance.

At first glance it was no different from the other rooms except that it was a little larger. In the foggy twilight, I could make out few details; there seemed to be something obscuring the window, like shutters or draperies, that cut off even the misty evening light.

I went back to the kitchen and got a flashlight. With its assistance I found the light switch. When I pressed it, nothing happened. I hoped the only problem was a dead or missing bulb, for if the wiring was faulty I wouldn't be able to use the room.

I don't know why I wanted to use it. If someone had asked me, I could have produced glib, rational reasons. I could keep Elvis with me at night. This room adjoined the bathroom. It was in no worse shape than the others . . . Perhaps this reasoning influenced my decision, but I don't think so. I simply knew, without hesitation or reservation, that this was where I had to be.

I'd have moved in that very night if the room had been habitable, but it really wasn't, not even by my relaxed standards of housekeeping. I decided I'd favor Mrs. Danner with the job of cleaning it. If I couldn't get rid of her, she might as well earn her keep.

I carried Martha's tray upstairs and sent Shirley down to have her supper. I was definitely out of sorts with Martha, and she did everything she could to push my temper to the breaking point. I had to cut her food for her, but she insisted on feeding herself, and a sloppy mess she made of it. After I had cleaned up, she ordered me to read.

The tin box she had been inspecting earlier was back on the shelf. That news clipping had been taken from the local paper, the weekly that came to us in the mail. The skeleton episode had occurred after Martha's first stroke, so someone must have brought the paper to her. It had been naive of me, and of Matt, to believe she would submit to being cosseted and coddled and kept in ignorance of what was going on in the world—especially in her own immediate world, where she ruled like a despot. And it was just like her to let us go on thinking we were getting away with our plan to protect her. No wonder she had howled with laughter—mocking my stupidity, proving that, though physically helpless, she was still in command. She had known all along. What else did she know? Had Matt's decision to allow excavation at Maidenwood been reported in the local paper?

I read on and on. Mr. Bucket, the great detective, drove the erring Lady Dedlock toward her doom. Esther wrung her hands and bleated platitudes. Martha drowsed and woke and drowsed again. " 'Miss Summerson,' said Mr. Woodcourt, 'if without intruding myself on your confidence I may remain near you, pray let me do so.' " Men didn't talk that way nowadays. And a damn good thing too, I thought. Or was it a good thing? A little kindness, a little courtesy . . . " 'Twas brillig, and the slithy toves/ Did gyre and gimble in the wabe . . .' "

Martha lay still. I finished the first couple of verses of "Jabberwocky" without arousing a protest. She was asleep. I tiptoed to the bed and bent over her.

Sound asleep and snoring—the harsh, difficult breathing of old age. Her eyes weren't quite closed. Between her folded lids shone narrow slivers of shining white eyeball.

The slits were not quite symmetrical; one was wider than the other. I thought, irrelevantly and cruelly, that she looked like a vampire—one of the undead, in her coffin, waiting for sunset before she rose to suck the blood of the living. She had derived pleasure from the pain of others. She was still doing it. Perhaps that was why the stroke that would have killed a weaker woman had left her with strength enough to fight back.

Shirley wasn't in her room. I went downstairs, stumbling with fatigue but too wakeful to sleep. For two cents I'd have dragged a mattress into the kitchen and sacked out there, with Elvis's wet muzzle in my face.

I expected Shirley would be in the kitchen, and she was; but she was not alone. Elvis was under the table and across the table from Shirley, slurping coffee like an old friend of the family, was Alan.

Shirley started guiltily when she saw me. "Oh Lord, Julie, I'm sorry. I didn't realize it was so late."

"You're not late, I'm early. Martha must have been tired. She conked out a few minutes ago."

"I'll go right up."

"Take your time. She's dead to the world. If you'll pardon the expression." I got a cup out of the cupboard.

Shirley murmured something unintelligible and made her escape. Smart woman, Shirley. Never explain, just walk out. She must have picked that up from Martha.

The kettle was still hot. I made a cup of coffee and pulled out a chair. Alan didn't move. Elvis twitched and whimpered in his sleep.

"Aren't you going to demand to know what I'm doing here?" Alan asked.

"No." I drank my coffee.

"Shirley and I are buddies."

"That doesn't surprise me."

"It doesn't?"

"You're good at making friends with people who can be useful to you." A gigantic yawn interrupted me before I could develop the insult. It hardly seemed worth the effort.

"My so-called charm didn't win Shirley," Alan said. "What won her heart was my offer of a commodity nobody else has bothered to provide—protection. I usually spend the night out there." He waved vaguely in the direction of the great outdoors, but I knew he had a more specific location in mind.

"The gardener's shed?"

"Oh, you found my lair, did you?"

"Mmmm."

"Unlike some people, I take my responsibilities seriously."

"So where were you the other night when I was confronting a maniacal handyman?"

The dramatic question fell flat. Apparently Shirley had spilled the beans.

"Sorry about that," Alan said calmly. "It was one of my nights off."

"Mmmm."

"I'll do better from now on."

"I wondered if it was you Danner saw. Assuming he was telling the truth about following a prowler."

"It wasn't me. Did you check the house to see if there were any signs of unlawful entry?"

I might have resented his hectoring tone if I hadn't been so tired—and if I hadn't been so grateful for his efforts. He must care a little, or he wouldn't spend his nights in that comfortless shed . . . Then, wearily, I told myself I was jumping to conclusions. He did take his responsibilities seriously. His actions meant no more than that.

"Alan, this house is such a wreck I couldn't tell if someone had broken in. Actually, I had the impression Danner was lying about seeing a prowler. Another funny thing—he was carrying a pair of scissors."

"Nasty weapon."

"Your sense of humor is as sick as Martha's." I didn't feel like explaining that slip of the tongue; before he could ask what I meant, I hurried on. "What would he want with scissors?"

"The logical conclusion is that he wanted to cut something."

"Oh, clever."

"Were they heavy scissors, like tin shears or metal clippers?"

"I don't think so. Just ordinary household scissors."

"Hmph," Alan said.

"Never mind about the scissors. Danner's mind works in ways incomprehensible to the normal world. Did you have any luck with your research? Any ideas as to where to excavate next?"

"A few," Alan said coyly.

"So don't tell me. I don't care. I think I'll go to bed."

"Not yet. I've had a few ideas about another subject that is of more immediate concern to you."

I sighed ostentatiously and propped my chin on my hand. "Proceed. There's no way of stopping you when you decide to deliver a lecture."

A lecture was just what I got.

"Maydon's Hundred was founded in 1619," Alan said. "And totally destroyed in 1622. The other towns and hundreds were resettled after the massacre. Not Maydon's.

The site was abandoned until your ancestor began the first manor house, a century later. In spite of your entertaining family legends, there was no connection between the inhabitants of Maydon's Hundred and the first Carr—except for the name Maidenwood, indicating a lingering tradition. Hey—wake up, I'm talking to you."

He jogged my elbow. Lulled by the familiar academic tone, I had fallen into a semidoze.

"I'm listening."

"The first manor house was destroyed in 1735. The present house was built on or near the foundations of the first one. I'm not much interested in either of the houses. What does concern me—and it should concern you and your dim-witted cousin—is where the original Carr burial ground was located. The earliest graves in the present cemetery date from the middle of the eighteenth century—contemporary with the second manor house. There must have been an earlier graveyard with burials dating from the building of the first house."

I was wide awake now. "You think that's where the skeletons came from?"

"The connection is unproved, but logically seductive. A lost cemetery and bones from a lost grave. What I don't understand is why the earlier cemetery was abandoned."

"It's a good question . . . Oh my God!" I started upright, kicking Elvis, who woke with a yelp. "Under the house! It's the only explanation, Alan; they couldn't go on using the old graveyard because they put the house—"

Alan burst out laughing. "You've been seeing too many horror films. Get it out of your head, Julie. There was no break in occupation between the destruction of the first house and the building of the second. The location of the cemetery would not be forgotten, and people weren't that callous about the remains of their kin. Besides, how could the jokers who found the skeletons get to them if they were under the house? Your grandmother is old, but she would have noticed if people were digging in the basement night after night."

"Oh." I wiped perspiration off my forehead. "It's getting hot in here."

"It's cooler, if anything. You're the one who is uptight. Shirley is spooked tonight too. What's the matter?"

"Nothing's the matter. I've had a tedious day. And there are . . . things out there."

"You're drunk," Alan said.

"Not yet. But I'm considering it. This weather isn't exactly soothing. Was that an owl I just heard or a vampire?"

"Owl. Good hunting weather."

"There *are* things out there," I said. "Cute characters who think it's funny to dress up dry bones and leave them littering the road. Crazy people like Mrs. Hornbeak. I wouldn't put it past her to want to dig in the basement."

"I ran her and her crew off the property not long ago."

"You what?"

Alan grinned reluctantly. "The stupidity of the woman is only equaled by her effrontery. They drove right in along the track we've been using. Flashlights and lanterns all over the place, pickaxes and shovels . . ."

"I didn't hear anything." I leaned down and stared at Elvis, who yawned. "What were you doing while all this was going on, noble dog?"

"It happened before you adopted him," Alan said. "Acquiring that dog is the smartest move you've made. Why don't you put the old lady in a nursing home and get the hell out of here?"

"You know how she is."

"Yes, I have good cause to know how she is. What I have never understood is why the rest of you let her bully you. For Christ's sake, Julie, she's eighty-five years old and she has never been quite sane. Matt has considerable influence; why can't he have her declared incompetent and get her into a hospital?"

"I don't think that's any of your business."

"I guess not," Alan said.

"You just want her out of the way so you can have a free hand. You and your Lady Jocelyn—"

"I don't know why you want to drag her into this."

"Neither do I." I put my head between my hands. Elvis, sensing my mood, began to lick my ankles. "I'm sick and tired of virginity," I mumbled.

Alan's smothered gasp of laughter made me realize what I had said. I felt my cheeks burn. When I looked at him he had his face under control, except for his eyes, which shone with amusement.

"I didn't mean that the way it sounded," I explained haughtily.

"What did you mean?"

"The motif—the—the theme. Isn't that one definition of the very word 'maiden'—a woman who hasn't lost that oh-so-precious commodity men make such a fuss about?"

"Well, I wouldn't say—"

"They *used* to make a fuss about it, anyway. Brand the Scarlet Woman, drive the erring daughter out into the snowstorm . . . Look at your Lady Jocelyn. One of the main fascinations of that story is the virginity angle. If she had been a widow with five children, nobody would give a damn about her. Including Mrs. Hornbeak."

"I don't know what you're so excited about," Alan said mildly. "I agree with you on every point, from the absurdity of the virginity fetish to the stupidity of Polly H. The skeletons can't possibly be those of Jocelyn Cartwright and her baby; they aren't that old. They may have come from the original cemetery of Maidenwood. Though I am only peripherally interested in the remains of that period, I am willing to turn my complete attention to the location of the cemetery, if only to prevent other people from looting it and possibly threatening you and Shirley."

"And Martha."

"She doesn't need me," Alan snapped. "She's got you and Shirley ready to die in her defense. I can't do the job, though. Matt has thrown too many barriers in my way."

"I'll talk to Matt."

"Good luck. I tried that."

"I said I'd talk to him." Far off in the dark night a faint cry rose and fell. I shivered. "Damn owls."

"That wasn't an owl."

Alan got to his feet. The dog was already at the door, whining and scratching. Alan said, "Quiet, Elvis." He took a piece of rope from his pocket and attached it to the dog's collar.

I followed the pair, man and dog, on to the porch. Elvis tugged at the leash but obeyed Alan's low-voiced command to refrain from barking.

The weather was clearing. Fog lay along the river meadows like a pale carpet, but in the black reaches of the sky, stars shone incandescently. Lower down, there were other lights—half blurred by the mist that lingered among the trees on the ridge north of the house, fluttering like will-o'-the-wisps—the dead man's lanterns.

"Son of a bitch," Alan muttered, and trotted off, towed by Elvis.

I stopped to close the porch door before I followed. I had to run like crazy to catch up with Alan, which I did at the start of the path leading to the cemetery. The lights were east of the path, between the ridge and the river.

Alan didn't order me back to the house; he only mut-

tered, "Don't make any more noise than you can help."
After that he ignored me, letting me climb over a rotten
section of fence and snag my pants on rusty barbed wire
without offering a helping hand.

The owls were hooting and the mist swirled along the
ground, but I felt a hundred percent better than I had all
day. In spite of the eerie appearance of the drifting lights, I
knew they were human in origin. The only thing that
puzzled me was the boldness of the invaders; they didn't
seem to be concerned about their lights being seen, and as
we came closer I heard voices. Surely trespassers wouldn't
be so open. Could it be a search party, looking for a
missing child?

I should have known. Alan knew; restraining the eager
dog, he marched into the clearing where the group was
assembled, and though his voice was not raised above its
normal speaking level, it stopped conversation. "I warned
you once, Mrs. Hornbeak. This time I'm calling the police."

Mrs. Hornbeak had changed from her pinstripe suit
into riding breeches and knee boots. She must have copied the outfit from an old lithograph showing turn-of-the-
century archaeologists; she even wore a pith helmet. Her
glasses flashed as she greeted Alan, brandishing a shovel
with an enthusiasm that made him retreat a few steps.

"Just in time to share the great moment," she exclaimed. "I bear no malice, Professor; those of us on the
path are above petty revenge, and I invite you to join
me—"

"You're trespassing," Alan said.

Mrs. Hornbeak leaned picturesquely on her spade.
"You have no authority to evict me, Professor."

"She does." Alan pushed me forward.

"Ah, Miss Newcomb." Mrs. Hornbeak nodded familiarly. "I intended to call on you in the morning. How much more fitting that you should be present when we disinter the remains of your ancestors!"

She indicated the muddy hole beside her. Two of her cohorts stood nearby; one held a trowel, the other a shovel. A flash went off in my face as I stepped forward.

I knelt by the hole. One of the cohorts obligingly turned his flashlight into the depths. Odd shapes made lumps and bulges under a thin layer of dirt. Other shapes protruded, pale against the surrounding soil.

I couldn't bring myself to look at Alan. "It's a grave, all right," I said. "Those are human ribs."

Another flash blinded me. Mrs. Hornbeak had brought several assistants to do the actual digging, but at least some of the people in the clearing were newspapermen. The fat was in the fire and sizzling merrily.

nine

❧

Mrs. Hornbeak wasn't intimidated by Alan or by me,
but she was afraid of dogs. Alan used Elvis, who was more
pleased to oblige, to run the woman and her crew off the
property. The reporters were not so easy to disperse, but
after a rain of "No comments" from Alan, they decided to
follow the more cooperative interviewee. They didn't even
get "No comment" out of me, only muffled, inarticulate
grunts. I didn't dare open my mouth for fear I'd laugh.
The situation was so horribly, comically grotesque I almost felt sorry for Alan. All his scientific study and intelligent research had come up empty, while Mrs. Hornbeak's
dippy excursions into the infinite had led her straight to
the gold. Even a nonexpert like me could tell that the
grave she had found was old. The bones were fragile and
discolored, and there was no trace of a coffin. So maybe
Mrs. Hornbeak wasn't that dippy after all.

Alan sent me back to the house with Elvis. He stayed,
brooding over the grave like a vulture. Before I went to
bed I called the number he had given me and asked for

Jono. I explained what had happened; Jono said incredulously, "You're kidding."

"I'm not kidding. She found something, Jono. Alan is
out there now, and he wants—"

"I'll be there in half an hour."

I passed on the rest of Alan's instructions. Jono could
hardly wait to get off the phone and get going. The last
thing I heard from him was a rapturous "Hot damn! This
could be it!"

Alan had also suggested—by which I mean ordered—
that I telephone the police. I decided that call could wait
until morning. I was in no mood to explain the situation
to a sleepy cop, and I doubted Mrs. Hornbeak would
return that same night. She'd be too busy talking to reporters.

I should have done what Alan told me. I was awakened
by Shirley shaking my shoulder. "There's some people
down there, Julie. Reporters."

I sat upright. Sunlight blinded me. "What time is it?"

"Eight o'clock. One of 'em's been there since six. I tried
to let you sleep, but—"

"I'll get up. Give me a minute."

"I brought you some coffee."

I grabbed the cup. "You're a saint, Shirley. Call the
sheriff and tell him we're under siege. I'll go down as soon
as I put on some clothes."

"Did something happen last night? Don't tell me there
was more—"

"No, nothing like that. I'll explain later—just make that
call, will you please?"

I scrambled into pants and shirt and sneakers, and trotted downstairs. The front door was closed. I opened it. "I
just called the police," I said.

The invasion consisted of one balding middle-aged

man. Apparently the others had given up or gone after Alan.

"How did you feel—" he began.

"Is that the only question you people can ask? Look, there's an old lady upstairs recuperating from a stroke. She needs peace and quiet. Why don't you give her a break?"

The reporter looked thoughtful. I made sure he understood the implications. "What paper did you say you were from? I mean, I want to know whom to sue if she has another stroke."

I closed the door before he could think of a counterargument. Looking through the window, I was pleased to see him retreat to the end of the drive. There was nothing I could do about that; the road was public property.

I was dying to get out to the site and see what Mrs. Hornbeak's discovery looked like in daylight. Maybe I had been misled by the general air of rapture; maybe she had only uncovered the carcass of a horse or a deer. I doubted it, though.

Shirley didn't respond to my suggestion that she go and see what was happening. She had no interest in archaeology. "I don't care about bones so long as they stay where they're supposed to be," was her summary of the situation, and I had to admit she had a point.

The law didn't appear until almost midday. I was in the kitchen making Martha a sandwich when I heard the knock at the front door. I greeted Jarboe with reproaches.

"What kind of service is this? I called almost four hours ago."

"They been bothering you?"

"Well, no, not lately. But no thanks to you and your men."

"That's not what I come about."

"What did you come about, then?"

"Judge McLendon. He's dead."

"No," I said. "He can't be. I saw him last night."

"Well, he is." The sheriff scratched his head. "Can I come in the house?"

I said dazedly, "Sure. I'm sorry. I can't believe it. Damn, damn, damn! I should have made him stay here. He wasn't fit to drive in the fog, after that fall—"

"Fall?" The sheriff followed me to the kitchen and sat down at the table.

"He tumbled down the stairs in the front hall. I tried to persuade him to stay all night—"

"That accounts for the bruises, then. Got a cup of coffee, Julie?"

"Sure." Then I realized what he had said. "Bruises . . . Wasn't it a car accident?"

"No, he got home all right. Don't blame yourself on that account. It was a heart attack. He lives alone; it was his first client that found him this morning, slumped over his desk."

"That doesn't make me feel any better." I filled two cups and joined him at the table.

"Maybe this will." Jarboe took a folded sheet of paper from his jacket pocket. "He was writing you a letter."

The handwriting was quite firm, with none of the tremulousness one associates with old age. "My dear Julie," it began. "I must apologize for startling you as I did this evening by my clumsiness. As I assured you, there was no damage done except to my pride. Please tell Martha I will see that her wishes are carried out to the best of my . . ."

The final "y" trailed off and ended in a ragged gouge. It was surrounded by ink spatters, like flecks of blood around a wound.

"He was always writing people notes," the sheriff said, averting his eyes from my stricken face. "Old-fashioned habit of his."

"I see."

"His heart was bad. He knew it; told me once the doc was after him to retire, but he wanted to die in harness, not rotting away in a nursing home. He got his wish. You could say he was lucky."

"You could say that." I folded the letter. "I'm sorry, Sheriff, I didn't mean to get teary, but—well, I liked him. He was a good man, and a kind man. I don't know how I'm going to break it to Martha. She'll be devastated."

"I wouldn't be too sure of that. Old people are peculiar about friends dying. Oh, they're grieved, sure, but there's a kind of funny satisfaction too—like they won another round by surviving."

If that was true of old people in general, it would be particularly true of Martha. She'd be annoyed, though. McLendon had handled all her legal affairs.

"Have you notified Matt?" I asked. "I suppose he'll have to find another lawyer."

"Called him a couple of hours ago. He said to tell you not to worry about the business end, he'd deal with that. He'll call you this evening to find out how Miz Martha took the news."

I thought of several replies to this cool announcement but decided I would save them for Matt. "Is there anything I can do?" I asked.

"No, thanks. Just thought you ought to know, seeing as I was coming out this way anyhow. Don't worry about reporters, this story will die in a day or two. It's pretty small potatoes."

"What you're telling me is that you can't spare a man to patrol the place."

" 'Fraid not. What I can do is put up a barricade at the entrance."

"How am I supposed to get out?"

"Oh, it'll be something you can move—a sawhorse, like, with a 'No Trespassing' sign. There's no way you can wall this place off, Julie; all you can do is create a moral effect. Your pal the archaeologist has things under control in his work area—ropes, signs, and a couple of husky kids with spades standing around looking aggressive."

I had hoped for more but I knew I wasn't going to get it. He was probably right about the news being a purely overnight sensation. So I thanked him and showed him out, and then went up to tell Martha her old friend was dead.

I held her hand when I told her. The pulse under my fingers didn't skip a beat or change tempo. There was a cry of surprise and distress, but it didn't come from Martha. Turning, I saw Shirley in the doorway of the bathroom that connected her room with Martha's. I said, "I'm sorry," and it was to her I spoke.

She shook her head dumbly. Tears filled her eyes.

Martha twitched her hand from my grasp. "Note," she said. "Note?"

"It was a heart attack, not suicide," I said. "People don't leave . . . Oh." She of all people would know of the old man's note-writing habit. Perhaps he had told her he would write her that evening.

"He was writing to me," I said, taking the paper from my shirt pocket. "But there is a message for you."

She read it without the slightest sign of emotion. Perhaps the corner of her mouth lifted a fraction of an inch, but that was all. The sheriff was right. Under her grief was a kind of satisfaction.

"Matt," she said. "Get him here."

"He said he'd call this evening. It's hopeless trying to reach him during the day, Martha. I know; I've tried."

"Hmph," said Martha, quite emphatically, and for once I agreed with her.

When I went downstairs to retrieve a somewhat wilted sandwich, Mrs. Danner was there. "What happened to you yesterday?" I demanded.

"Truck broke down."

No apology, no expression of regret. I said, "If you had called, I'd have picked you up."

"Weather was bad."

"Not that bad."

Mrs. Danner stared.

I abandoned the inquisition, wishing I could decide whether Mrs. Danner was abysmally stupid, or smart enough to know how to defend herself against such assaults. "I've got a job for you," I said. "I want the room next to the kitchen cleaned. Here, I'll show you."

The room was hardly brighter by daylight than it had been the night before. The windowpanes were opaque with dirt. Mrs. Danner stood watching as I struggled to raise the window. Finally it shuddered up; I propped it with the stick lying in the sill, and then I saw something the dirty glass had obscured. There were bars on the window—thick iron bars, set in a grilled frame that had been nailed or screwed onto the outside of the frame.

The sight of them made me feel easier about sleeping downstairs. Nobody would get in that window, at any rate. Perhaps the other rooms on the remote ground floor corridor also had barred windows. I hadn't looked.

I turned to Mrs. Danner. "You had better start by sweeping the floor. I want it and the walls scrubbed—get off as much of the old wallpaper as you can, half of it's hanging in strips anyway. The windows and woodwork need washing too."

Mrs. Danner put one foot forward, and then pulled it back, as if she had stepped on something slimy. She shook her head.

"What's the matter?" I asked impatiently. "You don't do windows?"

Her head kept moving mechanically from side to side. "I do windows real good. But I don't like . . ."

I didn't interrupt; her voice just trailed off into echoing silence.

I was in no mood to be patient with Mrs. Danner's vagaries. "I know it's a filthy mess, but the longer you stand there gaping, the longer it will take to get the job done. Where's the broom?"

I practically had to push her into the room. She kept glancing from side to side like a nervous animal who scents a hunter hidden in ambush. Once inside, she seemed to resign herself to the inevitable. She began sweeping while I carried in a ladder from the shed and replaced the light bulb in the ceiling fixture. It worked. That was a relief, though I had been prepared to make do with flashlights and electric lanterns if necessary.

I left Mrs. Danner to get on with it, hoping she wouldn't turn tail the minute I walked out of the house. She was obviously not a happy woman, but I couldn't figure out what was bugging her. Nor, to be honest, did I really care.

I changed into work clothes and reminded myself again to buy some boots. When I went out the back door, Elvis rose from his rug and ran to greet me.

The sound of voices led Elvis and me to the site. There was no path from the direction of the house, and it took a

long time for me to get through the underbrush, since I
had to untangle the dog's leash every few steps. When I
emerged into the clearing I was immediately accosted by a
large young man, Willkie-type, who politely but firmly
asked me to go away.

"It's okay," Jono called. "She's one of us. Over here,
Julie."

The opened grave had been refilled. Only a square of
blank dirt indicated its presence. "I thought you'd have
the bones out by now," I said.

"Good Lord, no. There's a week's work here before we
can start digging. Actually, Julie, there's nothing for you to
do unless you want to help clear the brush. Alan didn't
say anything about you . . ."

"Where is he?"

"In Richmond, getting some more equipment and starting the paperwork. The Commonwealth has laws about
disturbing human remains; it'll take several days to get a
court order. We've got to clear the site and survey it, lay
out a grid, sink some test holes . . ."

"It seems to me you're going to a lot of trouble without
being certain you have something to take trouble for.
Wouldn't it be smarter to sink your test holes first?"

Jono shook his head. His eyes were shining. "I saw it,
Julie—last night, before we filled it in. We've found it. It's
the right period."

"You're sure?"

"I can't show it to you; Alan took it with him. A tinned
brass hook, the kind used on clothing around 1600–
1650."

"Then this is it. Maydon's Hundred."

A veil dulled Jono's sparkling eyes as professional caution moved in to cool his excitement. "Well, we can't be
sure, not until we find some evidence of occupation. But

the grave is definitely of the right period, and he wouldn't have been stuck out in the woods, miles from the settlement."

"He?"

"The hook was used to hold men's pants to their doublets."

"I see. Well, if manual labor is all you have to offer, I can find plenty of that elsewhere. I'll drop in again tomorrow."

"One of us will be here all the time from now on," Jono said. "So don't worry about trespassers."

"What about your job?"

"I haven't quit yet. But I hope to soon."

"I see," I repeated.

Alan's big problem, aside from Martha's intransigence, had been money. It was a classic dilemma for archaeologists; without results there was no funding, without funding the chance of getting results was lessened. Alan was the world's fastest talker, but even he couldn't build a convincing case out of nothing. With a grave and a seventeenth-century gizmo, he could probably con some foundation or university into backing the dig. Once he got the money, he could afford to pay his staff and hire others.

I wished him well. If he got a big grant, I would demand wages too.

So I spent the afternoon scrubbing dirt off walls and floors instead of digging it out of a grave. Prodded and assited by me, Mrs. Danner accomplished wonders.

The end result was still not very attractive. The woodwork was blistered and cracked, and the dingy old wallpaper had peeled off in long strips, except where it refused to come off at all. At least the room was habitable.

I left Mrs. Danner washing the window and went upstairs to reconnoiter for a bed. When I reached the head of the stairs Martha's door opened and Shirley came out.

"Goodness, what have you been up to?" she asked. "You never got that kind of dirt on you out in the woods."

I explained what I had been up to. Shirley looked dubious. "I don't know what Miz Martha will say."

"I don't intend to tell her. We can rig up some kind of signal system—a cowbell, if I can't find anything better—so you can summon me in case of an emergency. Never mind that now; what the hell am I going to make for supper, Shirley? I'm completely out of ideas."

"That's what I was going to tell you. *He* called a while back. Said to tell you he was coming about six, and he'd bring some fried chicken."

"Matt?" The suggestion didn't sound like him, so I was not surprised when Shirley shook her head.

"Alan. He's a devil, that boy. Didn't give me a chance to say yes, no, or maybe, just told me."

Beware of archaeologists bearing gifts. But when the gift is edible and you are extremely sick of domesticity . . . "Sounds great," I said. "I had better clean myself up. Is she all right?"

"Kind of restless. Been looking at old pictures and papers this afternoon. She keeps nagging at me to call Matthew again. Well, I tried, and left a message, and they told me the same thing. He'll telephone tonight."

"I suppose he has a lot to do," I admitted. "The Judge was handling all Martha's affairs. But I still think Matt ought to come out here."

Shirley wisely refused to comment.

After I had cleaned up, I scouted the bedrooms. All I really needed was a bed and a table and chair, and maybe a lamp. I found a small table and took it down. Mrs. Danner was still washing the window. I pried her away from it and set her to scrubbing the table. The outside of the window was still dirty. There was no way of getting at it through the bars, but enough light came in to convince me that I couldn't stand those scabby walls after all. There was just enough time to run to the shopping center and buy a couple of gallons of paint. Yellow, I thought. The room was dark, with only one narrow window.

When I looked in my purse I found I only had about twenty dollars. I'd have to tap Matt for more money for expenses. And had there not been some vague talk of a salary? I added another damn to the pile I was heaping on my cousin, and informed Mrs. Danner I was going out.

Elvis decided to come along. I wasn't keen on leaving him with Mrs. Danner, though I believed my lecture had had the desired effect—and, perhaps more significantly, the "pockabook" had not reappeared. As we drove along, with Elvis's ears flapping in the breeze, I wondered how I had existed so long without a dog.

The man in the hardware store was willing to take my credit card, so that still left me with twenty dollars. I ducked into the grocery store. Elvis ate dog munchies and I ate cookies all the way home, crunching in chorus.

My nice big cans of paint made me itch to start on the walls, but I controlled myself; it was almost six, and I knew from past experience that painting is fun for the first hour. After that, it isn't. Anyhow, the best time would be in the morning, so that the paint smell would have a chance to dissipate before I went to bed.

The table I had brought downstairs was standing in the middle of the kitchen, where Mrs. Danner had left it. A cheap rickety affair of painted green pine, it was still damp from her scrubbing. I carried it into my new room. The place looked even emptier with that single piece of furniture in it.

I was scraping wallpaper when Alan arrived. Scraping wallpaper has a bizarre, hypnotic fascination; once you get started it's hard to stop. Alan walked right in the back door without knocking; only Elvis's rapturous whines warned me of his arrival.

There were two brown paper bags on the table, and Alan was taking out cartons of food. "Put this in the oven to keep warm," he ordered.

"Don't you ever say please?"

"Please put this in the oven."

I put it in the oven. "Want a drink?"

"You talked me into it. What are you doing with that?"

The scraper was covered with flakes of white plaster and scraps of wallpaper. I decided not to put it on the kitchen table.

"Scraping wallpaper, obviously. I'm going to move into that room next to the kitchen."

"Any particular reason?"

"To make it more convenient for burglars and rapists to get at me, of course."

"Mmmm," Alan said absently. "Not a bad idea."

"What, making it easier for burglars and—"

"Moving downstairs. You'll hear the dog if he barks, and you'll be closer to me if you need help. I won't be sleeping in the shed tonight, though."

"What are you going to do, camp by the grave?"

"Right."

"Nice cheerful place."

"It's no worse than any other place. I didn't expect you of all people to be so spooky about a few bones."

"Me, spooky? Listen, buster, I just finished anatomy. There isn't a bone in the human body I don't know by its first name."

"That's what I meant. Where do you keep the liquor?"

"Under there. No, there."

Alan took out my two bottles. "What, no fine vintage wines? Never mind, they'd be wasted on me. But you'll have to hide the liquor if you want to keep Mrs. Danner from tippling."

"She does drink on the sly, then. I wondered."

"If you were married to Joe, you'd drink on the sly too. I hear she used to be the toast of the town, the belle of the bars. Big, cheerful, laughing woman, with a vocabulary like a truck driver."

"I remember her. She sure has changed." I took the glass he handed me.

"She didn't change, he changed her. And himself. Finding Jesus can have a revolting effect on some people."

"That's an awful thing to say."

"I'm not blaming it on Jesus," said Alan, compounding the blasphemy. "Danner scares me. He's one of the reasons why I've been sleeping in the shed."

"Thanks for cheering me up, Alan."

"Oh, I don't think he'll bother you." I didn't care for the faint emphasis on "think"; before I could protest, Alan went on, "Danner is a bigot and a sadist, and religious mania takes peculiar forms."

"Like writing crank letters?"

"Yes, like that. After he kicked his daughter out of the house he apparently made a bonfire of everything she owned—which wasn't much, poor kid—and almost set the barn on fire. He's stupid as well as sadistic, and that combination can be dangerous."

"How do you know all this?"

"I frequent the local taverns," Alan said with a grin. "You think women are the only ones who gossip? To revert to the original topic—"

"I don't remember what it was."

"Bones," Alan said. "Anatomy. Why didn't you tell me you had studied with Kaufman?"

"Because the subject never came up. Because it's none of your business. And," I said, warming to my theme, "because I might have known you'd find out anyway. What the hell is the idea of checking my credentials?"

Alan ignored the question. "You're not qualified, of course. But at the moment I can't afford an anthropologist. I have a job for you."

"Paid or volunteer?"

Alan blinked. "I might be able to scrape up a few bucks."

Honesty forced me to admit the truth. "Alan, if you're talking about the skeleton you found last night, you were right the first time; I am definitely not qualified to tackle something like that. Those bones are so fragile they'll crumble if you try to lift them. I don't know how—"

"Oh, I can deal with that," Alan said confidently. "That's a simple matter of preservation. I had something else in mind for you."

"What?"

Instead of answering he reached into one of the paper bags. He used both hands; his long, blunt fingers and broad palms half covered the object he drew out, and since I was thinking in terms of food, for one wild moment I thought he was holding a cauliflower. A distorted, peculiarly shaped cauliflower . . .

Fortunately for me—not so fortunately for her—Shirley chose that moment to walk into the room. Her shriek drowned my gasp of surprise. Alan started. "Damn it," he exploded, juggling the skull.

Finally he got a firm grip on the thing. With a reproachful look at Shirley he said, "You shouldn't have startled me. It's fragile; would have shattered if I had dropped it."

"Don't put it on the table," I said squeamishly.

"Why not? It's nice clean plaster."

He propped the skull against one of the grocery bags. It grinned whitely at Shirley, who retreated a step. "Perfect copy," Alan said, regarding the grisly object affectionately. "I've still got the mold, but making another one would be a devil of a job. It's not really plaster, but one of those new synthetics."

"I don't care what it's made out of," Shirley said. "Just you take it with you when you go. I come down to get Miz Martha's supper and see you waving that thing around . . . Good thing I come, too. What's wrong with you, child, putting that paper in the oven? I could smell burned cardboard all the way upstairs."

She whisked the charred container out of the oven.

"I hadn't forgotten about it," Alan said in injured tones. "That's the way I always heat it. The chicken isn't burned."

"Hmph. I think I'll take my supper with Miz Martha tonight. No, you stay sitting, Julie—I'll just get a couple of plates and then you two can enjoy your meal. You got company already, so you don't need mine."

"Ouch," Alan said. "Here, Shirley, I got biscuits and cole slaw and potato salad."

Shirley watched him warily when he reached into the bag, but all he took out were a few plastic containers. She filled the plates and left.

Alan pushed the container of potato salad toward me and picked up a chicken leg. "That's the job," he said, waving the leg at the skull. "Reconstruction. You know the technique, don't you?"

"I watched Kaufman do it. Would you mind putting that out of sight while I eat?"

"I thought you might like to study it while you chewed."

I informed him he was mistaken. With a shrug he returned the cast to its bag. "Can you do it?" he asked.

"I'd need the reference tables."

"I can get them for you."

"Materials—"

"Those too. What have you got to lose, Julie? It's just an experiment. Good experience for you."

He knew I was tempted. Reconstruction is one of the most evocative techniques of anthropology—the restoration of musculature and flesh to dry bones, the re-creation of a face from its underlying structure. Two German scholars were the first to approach the problem scientifically, back in 1898; their paper included a series of tables that gave the average thickness of soft tissue at various points on the human face. The results could only be approximations; the measurements varied according to age and sex and a number of other factors. But some of the results had been astonishing; in one case Kaufman had mentioned, reconstruction had enabled a murder victim to be recognized and identified.

I remembered how Kaufman had gone about it. He had worked on molds too. Measuring out from the established points, setting his markers—he had used pencil erasers—then building up layers of clay, following the curves of the bones to the limits designated by his markers. He had completed the process by painting the plaster, adding false eyelashes and glass eyes, a wig. Building a person. I had always thought it must make you feel like Dr. Frankenstein.

"I could try," I said.

"Good." Alan took another piece of chicken.

"Why?"

"What do you mean, why?"

I touched the paper bag. "This is from the skeleton Joe Danner found, isn't it?"

"Right."

"You and your pathologist friend talked Jarboe into having a cast made before the bones were buried. No reason why he shouldn't agree to a request like that. But why reconstruction? That's your idea, not Jarboe's. And don't give me that bull about knowledge for its own sake. What you're proposing is time-consuming and complex. Why are you so curious about what she looked like?"

For a moment Alan concentrated on his chicken. Then he said, "I don't suppose you have seen today's paper."

"No. We only get the local weekly."

Alan reached into one of the bags and produced another item—the *Pikesville Bulletin,* dated that morning. It took me a few minutes to find the story. The headlines concerned the latest disasters in Africa and South America, and the latest presidential lies about the deficit. In a box at the bottom of the page was a smaller headline. "Grave of Virginia legend found by psychic investigator. Lady Jocelyn was real! See page C-1."

I turned the pages. The story was featured in the Style section, first page, and the first thing I saw was a photo of myself, glaring at the camera. My hair stood out in a frizzly bush and my eyeballs reflected the flash. The caption under the picture read, "Julia Newcomb, Lady Jocelyn's descendant, at her ancestress's grave."

"Oh, hell," I said.

"Read on," Alan said.

There were photographs of Alan, and of Mrs. Hornbeak, shovel in hand. Elvis was in one of them. He photographed better than any of us. Mrs. Hornbeak had had her revenge. The discovery was (correctly, I must admit) attributed to her. She claimed to have been in touch with Lady Jocelyn, "the aristocratic beauty who fled the lust of a royal favorite to find love and freedom in the New World." But the grave Mrs. H. had uncovered was not that of the Lady. Jocelyn's violated sepulcher was nearby; from it she had been wrenched by impious hands, and although she had found rest among her descendants, she wanted the world to know the truth and save her friends who rested near her from a like fate . . .

The real kicker was in the final paragraph. Even Mrs. Hornbeak's purple prose paled by comparison to the revelation contained therein. The newspaper fell from my hand. "She's offering to finance the dig?" I exclaimed.

"You got it."

"But she—you—where does she get her money?"

Alan wiped his greasy fingers carefully on a napkin. His neatness was an ominous sign, but he had his temper well in hand. "The organization she heads is loaded. There are a lot of rich nuts in the world."

"But she—you . . . You aren't going to accept the offer, surely."

"I'm trying to get funding. So far this is the only offer."

"You can't. It would ruin you."

"Not if I found Maydon's Hundred."

The depth of his obsession was greater than I had realized. But for once I was right and he was wrong. If he found the remains of Lost Atlantis or the Fountain of Youth, it would still be the end of his career. In the eyes of the academic world, the results would be hopelessly flawed by the nature of the expedition's funding.

"You can't do it," I said.

"Do you want to help me avoid it?"

"Well—yes."

"Then do that reconstruction for me."

I thought I understood what he had in mind. The basis of Mrs. Hornbeak's claim was Lady Jocelyn. Anyone with an ounce of sense knew the forlorn skeleton could not be hers, but bare bones have no identity. Put the reconstructed face on view, next to the famous miniature of the Lady, and Mrs. Hornbeak's error would be demonstrated by a display worth more than a thousand words. And if the reconstruction was clever enough, it might attract the attention and the funding Alan wanted. Most people, even learned foundations, are more attracted to pretty copies than ruined originals.

"You're on," I said. "The works—false eyelashes and all."

Alan nodded. He had known all along he had me hooked. "Are you going to eat any more?" he asked, reaching for the last piece of chicken.

"I haven't had any of it yet," I said, grabbing the piece from him. My appetite and my good humor were restored. He thought he was using me, but I had a few axes to grind as well. If the reconstruction was good, it wouldn't do me any harm to get my name in the papers. Besides, this was a chance to do something requiring skill and intelligence—something I needed, after two weeks of bedpans and *Bleak House*.

And it would put Lady Jocelyn to rest forever.

Alan insisted on leaving the cast with me. He also insisted on knowing where I intended to keep it; he didn't want to risk damage or loss. At first I couldn't think what to do with the damned thing. The kitchen was out of the question; Shirley had already indicated she hoped never to see the cast again, and if Mrs. Danner came upon it in the course of her quest for dirt and liquor, she'd probably have a fit. We finally decided to stow it away in my new sleeping quarters, since that room would be my workshop. Alan pointed out that the light was poor. I pointed out that I'd be working under artificial light in any case, and that it was up to him to supply me with proper lamps. Part of the equipment.

"Equipment? You don't even have a decent table," he complained, rocking the rickety object I had brought downstairs.

"I don't have a bed, either, but all that will come. Let's put it in the closet for the time being."

Mrs. Danner and I had not done much about the closet, since I did not intend to transfer my clothes from upstairs. We had swept up the fallen plaster and removed the cobwebs, but that was about all. The closet had been wallpapered—they had an excess of cheap labor in the old days. I had ripped off the loose, hanging strips and left it at that.

"First thing you need in here is a light," Alan said, squinting into the dark corners. "And a few shelves. You could store your materials in here."

"The first thing I need is bug spray," I said, shying back as a big fat black spider swung toward me, like Tarzan. "But right now I have to get up to Martha. I'm overdue."

"Go ahead." He whipped a folding rule from his pocket and, bravely ignoring the insect life, began measuring the dimensions of the closet.

"If you start hammering and banging things around—"

"With this door and the one into the hall closed, your grandmother couldn't hear me if I set off a charge of dynamite."

I couldn't argue with that, so I left him to it.

The evening had never seemed so long. Now that I had something I wanted to do, I begrudged the boring hours with Martha. She insisted I read, though I doubt that she paid attention. She had an enameled box on her lap, and she kept fumbling through the papers it contained.

Matt finally called at a little after nine. I tried not to watch the clock, but I couldn't help it. The bell roused Martha from a doze and she began grunting demands even as I lifted the phone.

"She wants to talk to you," I said, after I had exchanged greetings with Matt. "And so do I, dear favorite Cousin."

"Put her on," Matt said wearily. "Might as well get it over with. Then I'll talk to you."

I haven't reproduced Martha's speech patterns precisely. To do so I would have to eliminate about half the consonants. She couldn't articulate clearly; understanding her was partly a matter of knowing what the subject was, and partly watching her lips and her expression. She started by asking Matt when he was coming to see her, but this is what the sentence sounded like: "We'e' 'oo cuh?"

Matt figured that one out; he was expecting some such inquiry. But as she rambled on he appeared to comprehend less and less, and every time he asked her to repeat a phrase she got madder and less intelligible. Finally she tried to throw the telephone at me—it fell on the bed—and collapsed against her pillow, glowering.

"It's me again," I told Matt.

"Thank God. How do you cope with that?"

"In my usual inimitable fashion. When are you coming?"

"Saturday, I guess. I have a lot to do."

"Saturday," I repeated.

Martha gibbered at me, her eyes bright with rage. Watching her, I said, "She wants you to come before that."

Martha nodded. " 'A-morrah," she said.

"Tomorrow," I repeated.

"I can't. I had a full schedule before this last disaster happened. You have no idea how much extra work the Judge's death has caused."

"She's quite emphatic," I said, as Martha continued to flap her hands and lecture. "I have a few points to raise with you too. I presume a rising young politico reads the newspapers every day?"

He was quick to catch on. "Son of a bitch," he exclaimed. "There wasn't anything in the *Post* or the *Times* or . . . The *Pikesville Bulletin*?"

"That's it."

"I'll check it out. Is it that important?"

"I think so."

"Oh, all right. Tell her I'll be out tomorrow evening. Maybe we can have a quick dinner somewhere."

I relayed the message to Martha. Another half hour's reading put her to sleep and I decided I had done my duty for the evening.

Alan was gone when I got downstairs. There was a light in the closet and several shelves were in place; it smelled of fresh lumber and bug spray. Inefficiency was not one of Alan's failings.

After Shirley had gone to roost for the night I dragged my mattress downstairs and put it on the floor of the empty room. A few other things followed, all small and portable—a lamp, bedding, a chair. I would need help with the heavier things, and anyway I didn't want to crowd the room with objects that would have to be moved when I painted. I sat in the kitchen reading for a while, and then went to bed. If I had expected raptures from Elvis when I invited him to share my quarters I was disappointed; he settled down on his rug with the air of a dog who has finally established his right and proper place, even if it did take a while to get the idea through to his dull-witted human. We both slept through the night in perfect contentment. I didn't hear the owls wailing in the dark or remember the proximity of the thing in the closet, staring into the blackness with hollow eye sockets.

ten

We slept so soundly that I, at least, didn't wake until Shirley opened the door and Elvis ran to greet her.

"This looks like one of those pads I used to hear about," she said disapprovingly. "I don't know how you can stand being in this room, Julie. It's so dark and gloomy."

"Mrs. Danner doesn't like it either." I sat up, yawning and rubbing my eyes. "The way she acted yesterday you'd have thought I had asked her to clean a medieval torture chamber, complete with mutilated bodies."

Shirley looked around the room. Her expression was not one of fear or disgust, but of increasing puzzlement. "It's not that I feel scared, or anything like that . . . I don't know what it is. Gloomy. Sad . . ."

"It suits me just fine." I followed her to the kitchen. "Sorry I overslept, Shirley. We're out of bacon; how about scrambled eggs for breakfast?"

"Miz Martha has a fancy for hot cakes," Shirley said,

taking milk and eggs from the fridge. "Sit down, Julie, till you wake up."

"I don't know how to make hot cakes. I didn't buy a mix—"

"You kids and your mixes. Don't take offense, child; you're a heap better cook than Miz Danner, but—"

"But that's not saying much. I'm not offended, Shirley, I humbly admit the truth."

"It's not your fault," Shirley said. She mixed the ingredients and began beating them briskly. "Didn't your mama teach you?"

"According to Mother, she never lifted a ladylike finger to manual labor. The servants did everything."

"Servants my foot."

"No servants?"

"Oh, they had girls come in to help out—my own mama worked here for a while. But there hasn't been any money in the family for a long time. And at that, things was better when your mama was growing up than when Miz Martha was a girl."

"I suppose you heard about those days from your grandma," I said, amused.

"You know how it is in a small town. Everybody knows everybody else's business. And the Carrs were always important people, whether they had money or not."

"Why were things better when Mother was growing up?"

"Well, you know Miz Martha married a cousin—same last name. He was an insurance man over at Pikesville, and made a good living. Not enough to keep up this old barn of a house, but they got along all right. Miz Martha's daddy was something else. Never could keep a job. Guess he thought a Carr wasn't supposed to work for a living. An' if you think Miz Martha is hard to get on with, you should have known her mama. A real tartar, she was. Kept those girls close to home. They had to do all the housework, and they had hardly any beaux, 'cause nobody was good enough for one of the Carr girls. It's no wonder the youngest run off the minute she got a chance."

"But Martha stayed." I was fascinated by this glimpse into my family history—a far cry from the hints Mother had dropped of gracious living in the antebellum style. It was easier for me to believe in Shirley's version, and the image of Martha scrubbing and cooking and never going out on dates satisfied my mean streak.

"That kind of treatment takes children different ways," Shirley said philosophically. "Some rebel and break away. Some just fall into the same pattern as their folks, and that's what Miz Martha did. My granny said it was scary to see her turn into the spitting image of her own mama—same way of talking, dressing, doing her hair. Mr. Carr died when the girls were in their teens, so there was just the three of them here. Granny felt real sorry for Miz Melissa—she was the youngest—alone with those two sticks. Now, Julie, you watch what I do. The trick to good hot cakes isn't in the mixing, it's in the cooking."

It looked easy when she did it and the results were divine—I ate three. I had a feeling they wouldn't turn out the same way when I did it. I had never been able to make pancakes, even from a mix. They always stuck to the frying pan.

I offered to give Martha her breakfast so Shirley could eat. "She won't like it if you show up in your nightie," Shirley said dubiously.

"Then she'll have to lump it." Martha scrubbing, on her hands and knees . . . She couldn't intimidate me. I added, "Eat. Even I know there's nothing worse than cold pancakes."

One advantage to Martha's difficult speech was that you had to concentrate in order to understand her and so, if you didn't concentrate, you couldn't understand her. I felt sure her comments had to do with my state of undress and my generally rotten attitude toward life, but I didn't concentrate, and when she saw what was on the menu she stopped bitching and devoted her attention to eating.

"I'll take the tray down," I said, when she had finished. "Back in a minute."

Shirley was washing the dishes. I told her I had a proposition for her.

"You want me to set with Miz Martha this morning? Glad to. If you're going out you can fetch some more eggs."

"I'll get eggs, sure. But what I was going to do was paint."

"That room? Honey, what do you want to do that for?"

"Because I'm going to sleep there. I can keep Elvis with me and—"

"Yes, I know, you told me all that. Well, you suit your-self. How would you like to have Ron paint for you? It's not that I mind setting with Miz Martha, but you shouldn't be doing work like that."

"I'm a damned good painter," I said, wounded. "As for Ron, I'd be glad to have him do it, but—well, to tell you the truth, I don't have the money to pay him. I'm broke."

"Can't you get some from Matthew?"

"That is my intention. But I don't know how much I can wangle out of him."

Shirley snorted. "He's just like all the men—stuff their faces with food and ask for more, then yell when you tell 'em you need money for groceries. Ron don't have to be paid right this minute. You want me to ask him? Might be he could do it this morning."

"Can you call him?"

"He'll be here pretty soon, with my car. I let him have it yesterday. Promised he'd bring it back last night, but . . ."

"After what happened the last time, I don't blame him for not wanting to come around at night," I said, smiling.

"Anyhow, I'll ask him."

"Okay. If he can do it this morning and if he doesn't mind waiting for the money . . . Matt is supposed to come this evening. I'll hit him up for the cash then."

"This evening?" Shirley sounded surprised. "Oh, I suppose it's to do with the Judge's death."

I was ashamed that I had forgotten about the lawyer. So ephemeral is our presence in this world, so soon forgotten . . . When one is old there are few to remember or to care.

However, I reminded myself, it's no better when one is young.

I should have been finished with *Bleak House,* but for the past couple of days I had been cheating. Whenever Martha dozed off, I slid my paperback mystery out from under my shirt and read it until she roused herself and asked why I had stopped. That morning she finally caught me. I was so absorbed in the mystery that when she mumbled, "Read," I did.

"The body lay in a pool of blood on the library rug. Its lovely Bokhara pattern was stained a more deadly crimson. The girl's white bosom . . ." I stopped and looked up to meet Martha's black stare. "Whoops," I said.

She asked, if I understood her correctly, "What is that trash?" I showed her the cover. The victim's white bosom was conspicuous and there was blood all over the place.

"Hmph," said Martha.

"Now, Martha, admit it—you're as sick of *Bleak House* as I am. I'll bet you know it by heart. How about a nice murder for a change?"

I could have sworn she was amused. Such was the distortion of her features that the gleam of humor didn't improve her looks appreciably, but it made me feel more kindly toward her. Maybe I had done her an injustice; maybe there was warmth and kindness buried under the layers of frigid rectitude that were not entirely her fault. At any rate, she allowed as how she wouldn't mind listening to *Murder on the Hearthrug,* so long as I started back at the beginning.

The only disadvantage to the new book was that it kept her awake. I finally excused myself on the grounds that I ought to start lunch. I found that Shirley had been to the store and had put together a ham pie crowned with cheese biscuits.

"I'll pay you back," I said guiltily. "In money and time. It's not fair for you to do the cooking."

"I cook better than you," said Shirley.

"I can't deny that. Well . . ." The smell of the pie overcame my scruples. "We'll take turns. Where is Elvis? I'd have expected to find him drooling at the door."

"Ron took him along to the store. He ran out of paint."

Ron and Elvis returned in time for lunch. The young man greeted me with a sheepish grin, and neither of us marred the occasion by the slightest reference to our first meeting. Nor did I comment on the fact that he and Elvis were now on first-name terms.

Shirley took Martha's lunch up, and Ron and Elvis and I finished the ham pie. Ron also polished off a pint of chocolate ice cream and a box of cookies, assisted by Elvis, and then we went to inspect his painting.

He was my kind of painter—slapdash but fast. I noticed that the closet door was slightly ajar. I had warned
Shirley about the cast, and asked her to tell Ron not to
touch it for fear of an accident. Evidently his curiosity had
gotten the better of him. I couldn't blame him, but I
thought I had better reinforce the warning.

"Don't bother painting the closet, Ron. There are
shelves up, and some fragile objects inside. If it—if anything got broken, I'd be in trouble."

"Sure, right." He avoided looking at me.

I left the dishes for Mrs. Danner and started for the dig.
I left Elvis too; with Ron and Shirley at hand, I figured it
was safe. I had warned Ron not to let him eat anything;
from the quick, oblique look Ron gave me I knew Shirley
must have told him about Mrs. Danner's dog stew, but he
didn't say anything except that he would keep an eye on
Elvis.

I felt sure I could trust him, and I didn't blame him for
sneaking a peek at the skull; but as I picked my way
through the tall grass I wondered whether he might not
know more about the original of that skull than he cared
to admit.

I could understand Jarboe's reasons for believing that
local juveniles were responsible for the placement of the
skeletons. A gang of kids could have gone into the woods
to get drunk or smoke pot or dig for treasure—or all of
the above. If they had discovered the skeletons they might
have thought it would be funny to scare someone, especially if they knew Joe Danner would probably be the first
person along that road. Joe was obviously not the most
popular man in the county. Ron could have been one of
the gang. At the least, he must know or suspect who was
involved.

I wished I dared ask Ron to come clean. It would have

relieved my mind considerably to know there was nothing more sinister involved than the weird sense of humor of some pie-eyed teenagers.

This time there was no guard blocking the entrance to the dig, and I was received with flattering enthusiasm by all concerned. "Just in time," Jono said, smiling. "We're going to sink our first trial trench."

The cleared area was divided into squares, with the now familiar stakes marking the intersections of squares and balks. They must have worked their collective butts off to get so much done. The trial hole was six feet from the grave Mrs. Hornbeak had found. The diggers were not using shovels; squatting, they removed the earth with trowels, inspecting every clod of dirt as if it might contain gold.

Sidling up to Alan I murmured, "I'm ready to start as soon as you get the stuff."

I didn't realize how ambiguous the statement sounded until one of the female acolytes turned from her digging to give me a long, hard stare. Alan said abstractedly, "I've got it. What's that, Willkie?"

The large young man stared stupidly at the clump of dirt he held. From it Alan deftly picked a square of dull metal. Then he shoved Willkie out of the way and took over the digging. The hole was only a foot deep when he stopped. He handed the trowel to Jono, who was beside him; like an operating nurse attending a surgeon, Jono replaced the trowel with a brush. Finally Alan said in tones of deep disgust, "Damn. Another grave."

"What's wrong with that?" I asked.

One of the girls laughed in a sneering way. Alan returned to his careful scraping without comment. It was Jono who explained. "I told you, Julie, we can't disturb burials until we have legal permission. Besides, we know there were burials in this area. What we want now is evidence of occupation. Foundations, rubbish pits—"

"Get started on the second test hole," Alan said, without looking up. "You know where."

Jono left reluctantly. He might pretend to be professionally blasé about graves, but he was as curious as the rest of us. He began digging at the far end of the cleared area, on a direct line with the first hole but fifty feet away.

Alan sat back on his heels and beckoned me. "Have a look."

It was not a pretty sight. The skull lay bedded in the dark soil. The mandible had dropped, so that the mouth was wide open, as if the person had died screaming.

"Well?"

"Well, what?" I pointed. "It's a human skull."

"Male or female?"

"How the hell should I . . ." I leaned over for a closer look. "Sizable brow ridges . . . I'd guess male, but it's impossible to be sure without examining the pelvic and long bones. The incisors aren't shovel-shaped, so it's probably not an Indian. The damage to the skull—"

"Don't touch it," Alan said sharply. "We'll have to undercut the soil and lift it out in a block. It's too fragile to be moved otherwise. Well? What were you going to say about the damage?"

I tried to remember old lectures. "It's broken on the left side. Pressure from earth heaped on the body wouldn't result in lateral damage, but . . . This is ridiculous. I can't tell anything from half a skull."

"Hmmm," Alan said. He began trickling dirt back into the hole. "No point in excavating any further until we're ready to take it out. Jono?"

"Pottery." Jono's voice shook with controlled excitement. "Practically on the surface, Alan. Looks as if there was an old animal burrow here—groundhog, maybe."

"Okay. It may be a rubbish dump. Be careful."

The unskilled help—which, to my chagrin, included me—was put to work enlarging the cleared area. Later in the afternoon I was promoted to sifting dirt. Every square inch that came out of the hole had to be put through a wire sieve so that tiny objects like beads and pins wouldn't be lost.

From the tense silence, broken only by muffled exclamations of pleasure, that reigned over the actual excavation, I could tell that Alan and Jono were delighted with the results, but I found the whole business as boring as I had always expected I would. By the end of the afternoon we had a handful of pottery fragments and a few scraps of rusty metal. The hands of my watch reached five o'clock and moved on. Alan showed no signs of stopping work. Finally I announced I had to go.

"My materials," I said, poking Alan in the back to get his attention.

"In the Jeep."

"And where is the Jeep?"

"There." One arm flapped briefly.

They had not been able to bring the vehicles to the site, since a deep gully intervened. It had been bridged by a couple of planks, over which I crossed with some trepidation. The Jeep was there, and Alan's van. I rummaged in the Jeep and found the charts I had asked for, plus a shopping bag that contained modeling clay and a gross of yellow pencils. I picked up the bag and started for the house.

Elvis was lying by the back steps. He informed me he had not been fed, so I did that first, then took the supplies into my room. Ron had finished. The place looked nice, if

you didn't examine the woodwork too closely; neither
Ron nor I had thought it worthwhile to scrape off all the
old paint. The closet door was closed, as I had left it.

I assumed Mrs. Danner had come and gone, though
there were no signs of her presence. The pot of chicken
and vegetables simmering on the stove smelled like Shirley's work, thank goodness.

I went upstairs to tell Shirley I was back. She put down
the book from which she had been reading; I was amused
to note that it was not Milton or Tennyson, but my murder mystery. Martha asked where I had been.

"Walking in the woods," I admitted. There was no
point in denying it; I was covered with dirt and leaf mold
and bits of vegetation.

I had expected Martha to express disapproval, but her
reaction was a good deal more vehement. Her hand
moved with something close to normal quickness, the fingers crooked like claws. "Told you," she spat. "Years ago
. . . stay away . . . filthy, dirty . . ."

"Take it easy, Martha. I know I'm a bit grubby, but I
fully intend to wash."

We had finished eating before Matt showed up. I was
reading *Murder on the Hearthrug,* but without pleasure; the
section Shirley had read contained several vital clues, so I
had no idea what was going on. I had left Martha's door
open, and when I heard the car I closed the book.

"I want to talk to Matt for a few minutes," I informed
Martha. "About expenses and things like that. I'll send
him up shortly."

Martha objected, of course. She wanted Matt right
now. I smiled sweetly and closed the door as I left. I must
be mellowing, I thought; I almost felt sorry for her, sputtering and helpless and unable to enforce her dictates.

Matt's first remark was not "Hello" but "I can't stay

long. This is damned inconvenient. What does she want me for?"

"She doesn't confide in me, Cousin dear. I suppose it has to do with legal complications following the Judge's death."

"Well, I can't do anything yet," Matt grumbled, following me into the parlor. "He won't even be buried until tomorrow—"

"The funeral is tomorrow? Where?"

"Carrsville, the Episcopal church. Why? You aren't thinking of going, are you?"

"One of us ought to be there. Martha can't go. Besides, he was a lovely man."

"Naturally I ordered a floral tribute," Matt said.

"What time?"

"Ten. Actually, it would be a nice gesture. If you don't mind representing the family—"

"I will even wear a dress instead of jeans."

"Wow. Are you sure that isn't asking too much?"

His smile disappeared when I went on to the next subject. "Money? How much?"

"My God, you sound like a husband," I said disgustedly. "Here, have a glass of sherry."

Matt produced a feebler edition of his original smile. "You don't have to get me drunk, Julie. I know it costs money to run this place, and God knows I owe you. I'm just not sure I can draw on Martha's account right now. The Judge and I were co-guardians, and until the court decides who is to succeed him, or whether to grant my petition to act as sole—"

"For crying out loud, what are people in Martha's position supposed to do while the law sorts these things out? Live on air?"

"The law," Matt said sourly, "doesn't give a damn.

However, I'll see what I can do to expedite matters. In the meantime—will you take a check?"

I was about to say no, when I decided I might get more out of him than if I insisted on cash. After I had the check in my hot little hand I graciously dismissed him and watched him head for the stairs like the schoolboy in Whittier's poem, dragging his reluctant self to school.

I figured I had at least half an hour, maybe more, if Martha was in a garrulous mood. I settled down in the kitchen and looked through the reference material Alan had given me. He had photocopied not only the tables but the entire German monograph. My German isn't too good, but since most of the vocabulary was technical I was able to make it out. The tables were still a basic source, though they were almost ninety years old. Alan had also copied a few articles describing recent reconstructions, including one of a settler from Martin's Hundred, a site excavated by the Colonial Williamsburg people. I wondered if it was this example that had given Alan the idea.

I took the papers to my new room. Ron had piled the odds and ends of furniture on top of the mattress and covered the whole lumpy pile with a drop cloth. It was lavishly spattered with yellow and white paint, like bird droppings. The table was covered with newspapers. I cleared them off and took the cast from its shelf in the closet. Reading the material had fired me up; I was anxious to get started. With a soft pencil I began marking the places where the depth markers would be set. Heel of the mandible . . .

I was so absorbed I didn't hear him coming. His exclamation startled me; I let go of the cast and bumped the table, setting it rocking. I managed to grab the skull as it rolled toward the edge, and turned, cradling it in both hands.

We both spoke at once. I said, "Damn it, Matt, don't do that! If this had been smashed—" And he said, "What the hell is that?"

We stared at one another in mutual indignation. "A present from your boyfriend?" Matt inquired sarcastically.

"In a way." I relaxed; after all, no damage had been done. "I suppose it did look weird, but if this had broken . . . I'm doing a reconstruction of that skeleton—the one Danner found in the road."

The room and the corridor beyond lay deep in shadow, except for the bright circle of light from my lamp. Matt's features were indistinct. I saw a gleam of white as his lips parted, but he didn't speak for a while. Then he repeated, "Reconstruction?"

"It's a process of restoring the person's original appearance. Clay is molded over the bone, following tables of average tissue depths on the human head. Very scientific."

"It can't be accurate," Matt said. "You don't know about skin color or eye color or whether the person was skinny or fat—"

"It's only an approximation. But you'd be surprised what an accurate likeness can be achieved."

"Is that right?" Matt came closer and looked curiously at the cast. "Are you going to do it now?"

"No, I was just fooling around, getting some ideas. It'll take days." I put the cast in its bag and returned it to the closet. "First I have to measure and cut the depth markers, then glue them to the skull, then—"

"Each to his own taste," Matt said, stepping back to let me pass out of the room. "Is this where you'll be working? I'd forgotten this room was here."

"It's convenient," I said, somewhat vaguely. I had no intention of telling Matt I meant to sleep in the room;

Shirley had already given me a hard time about it and I was afraid Matt would lecture me too.

Matt followed me to the kitchen. "Where is your boy-friend?"

"Don't keep calling him that."

"Sorry. I was under the impression that you two had picked up where you left off."

"Well, we haven't. I'm doing some work for him, that's all."

"I'll have to have a talk with him."

"What about?"

"Stopping work. Martha's got wind of what he's doing, Julie. I don't know how she knows, but she does, and she's furious. Your . . . Petranek will have to leave."

"Matt, you can't do that! He's just made a big find—something really important."

"I don't care if he's located Blackbeard's treasure. I'm kicking him out."

I was surprised at the extent of my distress. A few days earlier I'd have said I didn't give a damn whether Alan was allowed to work at Maidenwood or not. In fact, I'd have been happy to have him off the premises. Now I was involved. With the work—and what else? I searched for an argument that would carry weight with Matt.

"It won't look good for your image if you shut down the dig just as they are finding something significant, Matt. Who are you to stand in the way of scientific achievement?"

"Damn." Matt dropped into a chair. For the first time he looked older than his true age. "I'm going crazy with all these unreasonable demands and conflicts. I don't know what to do."

"It's not that difficult, Matt. Just tell Martha—"

"She's crazy," Matt muttered. "Senile. She's talking the

most insane garbage . . . Sometimes I think she does have supernatural powers. How does she know everything that goes on?"

"You really are in a state. Did Martha give you a hard time?"

Matt laughed—a mirthless rattle of sound. "You'll never know, Julie."

"I do know." I patted his hunched shoulder. "Don't let her get to you, Matt. There's a simple explanation for her seeming clairvoyance, and I think I know what it is. Mrs. Danner."

"Rosie?"

What an inappropriate name for that poor frozen wraith of a woman! "Rosie," I repeated. "She hasn't a brain cell she can call her own, Matt. She's scared to death of Martha. I'll bet she's been getting the newspapers for her, and answering all her questions."

The more I thought about it, the more I was convinced I had found the explanation. I only wondered why I hadn't figured it out before.

Matt did not appear cheered by the theory. "That could be," he said listlessly. "It doesn't really make any difference. Look, Julie, I have to go. I'll keep in touch."

I had to sympathize with him. No one knew better than I the power Martha had wielded over her unlucky descendants.

Shirley was disappointed she couldn't go to the Judge's funeral. I hated to take advantage of her, but there was no way we could both go, and Shirley agreed with Matt that someone ought to represent the family. I preferred not to think of it in such formal terms; "representing the family" implied white gloves and a hat, neither of which I owned. Still, I wanted to go.

I was late, since I didn't know where the church was. The service was underway when I slipped breathlessly into a back pew. I was surprised to see the place was almost full. I should not have been surprised; he had been a public figure known to three generations.

I didn't spot Matt until we rose to sing a hymn. He was one of the first on his feet—right up in front, as I might have expected. When the service was concluded I stayed in my seat until he saw me, then joined him.

"Late as usual," he said out of the corner of his mouth, his head decorously bowed.

"I thought you weren't coming."

"Changed my mind."

"Are you going to the cemetery?"

"No. Let's have lunch. I want to talk to you."

That had an ominous sound, but I saw no reason to turn down a meal. One of the reasons why I had been late was that I had stopped to cash Matt's check. I had an argument with the teller, and it was not until one of the bank officials recognized me as Martha's granddaughter that I was able to get the money.

We came out of the dimness of the church into bright sunlight. Matt had taken my arm and I stopped when he did, blinded by the light. When my vision came back I saw the inevitable photographer. Matt always seemed to have one or two following him around; I wondered if he hired them himself.

I refrained from making a face at the camera, out of respect for the Judge, and let Matt lead me to his car. His idea of a restaurant turned out to be a drive-in on the highway, and I grumpily accepted a cheeseburger and shake, which we ate in the car.

"Why can't we go inside?" I complained. "It's hot as hell out here."

"I want to talk privately, that's why," Matt said. "Take a look at this."

He unfolded the newspaper that lay on the seat between us and thrust it at me.

Alan must have gone straight from the dig to his office and called every newspaper in the state. He had even rated a minor front-page headline in the *Washington Post*. "A New Light on Virginia's Dark Ages. Spectacular New Discovery at Maidenwood Plantation."

"Plantation, yet," I said admiringly. "That's pretty fancy."

"The son of a bitch has cut the ground right out from under me," Matt said through his teeth. "Read the last paragraph."

After some fulsome and only mildly inaccurate predictions as to what the new discoveries would mean to historians, the reporter had quoted Alan. " 'Virginia owes a special debt of gratitude to Mrs. Martha Carr and her grandson, the distinguished senator, Matthew Ellis. Without their gracious permission and unfailing support, this magnificent contribution to the cultural and historical traditions of the Old Dominion could never have been made.' "

Through my peals of laughter Matt exclaimed, "You see what he's done? I can't make him leave now."

"No, you can't. His next interview would deplore your strange indifference to tradition, history, and the Old Dominion. He'd probably have the president of the university and the Governor backing him up."

Matt growled and bit savagely into his hamburger.

"So what are you going to do?" I asked.

Matt swallowed. "What can I do?"

"Lie to Martha."

"That, certainly. Listen, Julie, if you're right about Rosie Danner, I'll have to get rid of her. I can't have her blabbing everything she knows to Martha."

"There's a theory in espionage circles that you don't dispose of a spy, you feed him false information."

"Oh, come on, Julie, don't be cute. You can't tell Rosie your buddies have gone when everyone in the neighborhood knows different. Rosie and her husband have always been under Martha's thumb. If she told Joe to shoot a trespasser he'd blast away."

"She's not very bright," I said, reluctant to abandon my idea. "If we told her . . ." Then, belatedly, the implications of his last sentence sank in. "Rosie . . . Joe Danner . . . She's already told Martha. She . . . Start the car, Matt, hurry, I've got to get back."

"Why the rush?"

"Elvis," I said, gulping. "Martha must know about Elvis."

eleven

❧

I forced myself to drive at the speed limit. Though my first impulse had been to make for Maidenwood as fast as the old car would go. I couldn't believe I had been so stupid. Martha had known about the dog for some time—probably from the first. I had suspected the Danners of trying to poison him, but I should have known neither Joe nor Rose would take such a step without being prompted. Martha wouldn't give up after one attempt. She'd tell Joe to try again—another method this time, a rifle or a car. Shirley couldn't protect him from that sort of thing; she assumed, as I had, that the first attempt had been the result of idle malice, and that the Danners wouldn't dare try the same trick twice.

I could have cried with relief when I turned into the drive and saw Elvis lumbering to meet me. He would always limp, although he could cover ground at amazing speed. I brought the car to a stop and opened the door for him. He was surprised but quite pleased when I threw both arms around him and hugged him until he wheezed.

Shirley was in the kitchen, her feet up on a chair, reading *Murder on the Hearthrug*. "I finished it this morning," she explained a little guiltily. "Got me kind of curious; I figured I'd read the beginning and find out how it all happened. Was there a good crowd at the service?"

I sat down and told her all about it—the eulogy, the hymns, the size of the crowd, the number of "floral tributes." She asked if I had seen hers—"Lilies, in a nice pot, with a purple ribbon"—and I improvised. "It was right in front of the casket, Shirley."

"Was Matthew there?"

"Yes, we had lunch afterward. That's why I'm late. I owe you, Shirley."

"Honey, we're not keeping track, we're just trying to get by. It's been a lot easier since you got here, I can tell you."

"That reminds me." I lowered my voice. "Mrs. Danner is upstairs with Martha, isn't she? Then I can tell you . . ."

Shirley wasn't interested in Matt's dilemma with regard to the dig—the archaeological activities had always seemed more than a little absurd to her—but her eyes widened when I explained that Mrs. Danner must be the source of Martha's uncanny knowledgeability.

"That old devil," she exclaimed. "I did wonder, now and then, when she'd let something slip . . . It wasn't me that told her, and it wasn't you, so who else could it have been?"

"Matt and the Judge are the only other possibilities. But I don't believe either of them would play informer. Matt doesn't want her to know he has gone against her wishes, and the Judge didn't want her to be upset."

"Upset?" Shirley sniffed. "It hasn't hurt her one bit. She enjoys having her little secrets."

"You're right about that. As I see it, we've got three choices. We can get rid of Mrs. Danner. At first I was in favor of that, but now I'm not so sure. She's not worth much, but she does give you a break from Martha now and then. The second possibility is to let Mrs. Danner stay and stop playing games with Martha. She knows everything we're doing anyway, so why bother lying?"

"Hmmm," said Shirley, impressed by my logic. "What's the third choice?"

"To go on the way we've been going. Let Martha think she's fooling us. So long as we know Mrs. Danner is blabbing to her, we can take precautions."

"Maybe that's the best way. Miz Martha can fuss all she wants about the archaeologists, but there's nothing she can do to stop them. The only thing is . . ."

Her troubled dark eyes moved to Elvis, whose head was resting on her feet.

"Yes," I said. "For two cents I'd confess to Martha and tell her that if anything happens to Elvis—"

"You'd do what?" Shirley shook her head. "The way I see it, Julie, it doesn't make any difference whether you tell her or not. Only thing we can do is never let that dog out of our sight."

Elvis knew the word "dog." His tail thumped in acknowledgment. Shirley went on, "It's a good thing you decided to stay downstairs at night, I guess. You can keep him with you. I don't like to think Miz Martha would stoop so low as to order somebody to feed him poison, but . . ."

"You're right as always, Shirley. That reminds me—I want to make a phone call."

May Rubin was in her office. "I was going to call you," she said.

I knew from the tone in her voice that it was bad news, and my heart sank. I had hoped I was wrong.

I didn't recognize the name of the chemical. May translated. "It's a weed killer—not the standard commercial variety, but stronger. A lot of farmers use it. Do you have any idea—"

"A lot of ideas. No proof."

"Is there anything I can do?"

"Thanks, May. I'll let you know."

When I told Shirley she didn't look surprised, only grimly determined. "That won't happen again," she said.

Even though I had half expected it, the confirmation of my suspicions made me furious. "I'm going to kick that woman out of here right now!"

"That won't do any good. It isn't Miz Danner so much as her husband."

"A man who would beat children and throw his own daughter out of the house wouldn't think twice about shooting a dog," I agreed. "Well, we'll just have to cope. Which reminds me—I got some money out of Matt. How much did you spend on groceries the other day, and what do you think I should pay Ron for the paint job?"

We agreed on a figure that sounded uncommonly low to my city-accustomed ears, and then I started for the dig. I took Elvis with me.

Apparently Alan had got his court order. He and Jono were at work on the first grave, the one Mrs. Hornbeak had found. The bones had been exposed and they were undercutting the entire mass of soil, preparatory to lifting it out. Watching the work was a newcomer, inappropriately dressed in a tweed jacket and neatly pressed slacks.

Alan hoisted himself to his feet and advanced to meet me, smiling. This demonstration took me so by surprise that I gaped at him. "Here she is," he said. "Our physical anthropologist. Julie, this is Mr. Barton Wilkes—from the National Geographic Society."

Oho, I thought, and also, aha! No wonder I'm getting all the sweetness and charm and professional courtesy. Physical anthropologist yet.

Mr. Wilkes stepped carefully around the open grave, his hand extended. He wore glasses, from which the sunlight twinkled, and there were streaks of gray in his brown hair. "It's a pleasure, Miss Newcomb. Alan is fortunate to have assistance from a lady who is not only qualified, but who is also a member of one of Virginia's old respected families."

"No, not at all," I mumbled, trying to restrain Elvis, who couldn't make up his mind whether to help with the digging or greet my new friend.

"What a handsome dog," said Wilkes.

"Tie him to a tree, will you?" Alan said, trying to keep the irritation out of his voice. "I'd like your advice before we try to lift this."

He knew that I knew that I didn't know a damned thing about the procedure, but I realized this was all part of the plan to impress a potential donor with our dedication and our expertise. If my cooperation could get Alan the grant he wanted, I was willing to do what I could. I handed Elvis's leash to Jono and knelt by the grave.

"Fascinating," I said.

"I know you can't make a proper examination under these conditions," Wilkes said. "But I would be most interested in any preliminary comments you might feel justified in making."

The preliminary comment that leaped to mind was a simple "yuck." This skeleton was even more battered than the other one Alan had found. Many of the bones were disarticulated; the mandible stuck up at right angles. All the remains were darkly stained.

"You understand I would hate to commit myself to anything at this stage," I began.

Wilkes and Alan made encouraging noises. I went on, "The skeletal material appears to be that of a male." That seemed safe enough, judging from the length of the long bones of the legs, and the fact that the hook found in this grave had come from male clothing. The upper teeth were in fairly good condition; all were present, none were worn, and the wisdom teeth had erupted. "He was probably between eighteen and thirty years old," I said. "Laboratory study can narrow it down, but right now . . ."

"Yes, I see." Wilkes sounded impressed. "I don't suppose there is any clue as to how he died?"

Alan didn't nudge me, he just got very, very quiet. I knew what he wanted me to say. Most of the settlers at Maydon's Hundred were killed during the Indian Massacre of 1622. If I said that one of the breaks in the battered skull appeared to have been made by a tomahawk, or that there was evidence the man had been scalped, Alan would be a giant step forward toward the confirmation of his theory and the funding he needed.

I had nothing to lose. I had already qualified my comments to the point of meaninglessness, and as for risking my reputation—how can you risk what you don't have? Something held me back. I would like to think it was integrity.

"No," I said. "I couldn't say, at this point. But you'll notice that the mandible—the jawbone—has been displaced. Pressure from the earth might be responsible for a certain degree of displacement, but this is extreme. It suggests that the mandible had been broken before the body was buried—perhaps that the body was in an advanced stage of decomposition before burial took place."

"Most interesting," Wilkes breathed. "Well. I have a long drive ahead, and I must be on my way. I hadn't planned to spend so much time here, but it has all been most—er—interesting!"

Wilkes and Alan went off together, and I heard Wilkes say, "You will hear from us in a few days, Dr. Petranek. Of course I can't guarantee how the committee will respond, but I can assure you that insofar as I am concerned . . ."

The rest of his words were lost as the two men moved along the track. Jono's lips parted in a wide grin and he gave me a thumbs-up signal.

"You think he's got it?" I whispered.

"Looking good. You were a big help, Julie. Good work."

When Alan returned, his assessment was more cautious. "I've learned not to uncork the champagne until the check is in my hands. But if it does work out, Julie, I owe you a glass or three. Thanks." I was beginning to preen myself when he added critically, "Did you have to bring that damned dog?"

"Yes, I did have to. Can you take a break? I have a couple of things I want to discuss with you."

"I suppose so. Come on, we'll sit in the van."

Thunderheads were piling up on the horizon. Alan gave them a worried look. "Make it snappy, will you? I want to get that skeleton out this afternoon. Rain would ruin it."

"Well, excuse me," I said. Alan stared at me. Then he gave himself a little shake, and I realized he was so tired he barely knew what he was saying. No wonder, if he spent his nights watching out for burglars . . . I was about to apologize when he beat me to it.

"Sorry. I'm a little preoccupied these days. What's on your mind?"

"Well . . . First, congratulations for foiling Matt. Or was that newspaper story a case of coincidental timing?"

"I figured he'd be getting cold feet about letting me excavate," Alan said coolly. "The old lady is bound to know what's going in, with Rose Danner under her spell."

"If you're so clever, why didn't you warn me about Elvis?"

"What do you mean?"

"Well, Mrs. Danner must have told Martha about him too."

"So?"

"So Martha hates animals. Someone gave me a kitten once—from a litter his barn cat had—and she . . ." To my horror I felt my throat close up. I hadn't thought about that incident for fifteen years.

"I didn't know that," Alan said.

I turned away from him, struggling to get myself under control. That's the trouble with amnesia; when memory does return, it is as fresh and painful as if the event had just occurred. For a moment I thought I felt something brush my bowed head; but when I turned, Alan wasn't even looking at me.

He said quietly, "I'll keep the dog with me during the day. He won't like being tied, but he'll have to put up with it. Shut him in your room at night. I'll also have a word with Danner."

Arbitrary, arrogant, bossy man . . . "Thank you. Maybe I had better talk to Mr. Danner. I'm one of the elite to him, and he doesn't think much of you."

"As you like. I have to get back to work. Are you going to stick around?"

"I thought I'd start the reconstruction, unless you need me for anything in particular."

"Oh, that. Sure, go ahead."

His ardor for that project had obviously dimmed. Now that he had a genuine find to show the men with the money, the reconstruction didn't interest him any longer.

"I'll leave Elvis with you, then," I said, getting out of the van.

"Okay. Oh—one more thing—you'd better put that barricade back up at your gate."

"Reporters?"

"Could be. But I was thinking of Mrs. Hornbeak. Her nose may be a trifle out of joint and she may approach you."

"Thanks. That gives me something to look forward to."

I don't think Alan heard me. He was heading away as fast as he could go, back to his rotten bones.

I went the long way around, down the track to where it joined the road, and so to the gates. The sawhorse, with its warning sign, stood where I had left it when I drove out that morning. I dragged it back into place. It was not much of a barrier. And I doubted that the moral effect the sheriff had mentioned would move Mrs. Hornbeak, who appeared to be sadly lacking in rudimentary manners, much less morals. It was the best I could do, however.

I still hadn't made up my mind what to do about Mrs. Danner. We had to have someone. Shirley was working for wages, Matt could impose on her to the extent she allowed—and she obviously had a soft spot for him, heaven knows why. But I was damned if I would let him make a slave out of me. Firing Mrs. Danner wouldn't eliminate the danger to Elvis.

I checked the mailbox to see if the mail had come. It had. Most of it was circulars, but there was a letter from

Mother and a postcard from a friend who was vacationing in Europe, blast her. And one other item addressed to me—a five-by-seven manila envelope thick enough to contain a booklet or brochure. But the address was hand-written, and I recognized the writing.

To receive a letter from the dead gives you an uncanny sensation. I stood turning it over in my hands, noting that the postmark bore Monday's date. Either someone had found it on his desk and put it in the mail, or else the old lawyer had posted it himself, late Sunday evening. The latter seemed the most likely alternative; if he had meant to wait until Monday before mailing it, surely he would have left it unsealed until he had finished the note he had been writing to me at the moment of his death.

I sat down on the grass and opened the envelope. There was another, slightly smaller envelope inside, criss-crossed by heavy tape. A letter had been attached, in such a way that it covered the flap of the inner envelope.

The letter was brief. "My dear Julie. Enclosed is a small memento I think you should have. I know I can trust your honor not to open the envelope until after your grand-mother is gone. With most sincere regards, et cetera."

Curiouser and curiouser, I thought. I wasn't tempted to peek, partly because I felt sentimental about honoring the old gentleman's final request, but mostly because I suspected what the "memento" was. He hadn't asked me not to feel the envelope; my fingers traced the outline of what could be a cardboard photo frame, one of the old-fash-ioned variety with fancy, curved edges. Perhaps it was a picture of me in my misspent youth, or of me and my parents. I could think of a number of reasons why he might not want Martha to know he had given it to me—none of them to her credit.

Mrs. Danner was in the kitchen. She wasn't doing anything, just sitting, staring blankly into space. When I entered she got clumsily to her feet.

"You didn't say what I was to do. I don't know—"

"That's all right, Mrs. Danner." I wished I could dislike the woman wholeheartedly and completely, without any weakening touch of pity. But it wasn't possible to hate someone that miserable. No wonder she was reluctant to sit with Martha. She could no more resist Martha's demands than a gourmand can turn away from a chocolate éclair. She was in trouble whatever she did.

"You want I should start supper?"

My sympathy vanished. She couldn't be that stupid or forgetful. She had her own little ways of hitting back at the people who hassled her. I wondered how she got back at her husband.

I put her to work washing lettuce and vegetables for a salad and went to inspect my room. Though I had told Alan I meant to start working on the cast, there was a lot to do before I could begin the actual reconstruction. I needed a large, sturdy table, and some arrangement to hold the cast steady. And a bed. I was not keen on sleeping on the floor. There were mice in the house and snakes outside the house and I was afraid one of them might decide to go for a stroll across my stomach.

There was a big oak table in the library. I couldn't move it alone, so I enlisted Mrs. Danner. The ease with which she hoisted her end gave me an odd feeling. I had not realized she was so strong.

I also stole a rug from the library—a beautiful old Persian rug, so worn it wasn't worth selling—which is probably why it was still there. Its faded gorgeousness improved the look of the room so much I threw caution to the winds and hauled in all sorts of things, including a brass bed from one of the upstairs rooms.

Any normal person would have asked why I was furnishing the room. Mrs. Danner didn't ask a question or make a comment. She was about as much company as a robot, but she had a machine-like utility, and by the time we finished I had made up my mind what to do about her. I didn't really care what she told Martha. The only thing I was concerned about was Elvis, and Martha already knew about him.

When five o'clock rolled around and Danner's truck rolled up, I was lying in wait. I think he had been expecting a confrontation, and was only surprised it had not come earlier. Not that he appeared embarrassed or apologetic. He didn't even turn off the motor and I had to yell over the untuned rattle-and-chug. I didn't mind yelling.

"You know I've adopted a dog," I began.

I had to wait some time for a reply. Finally his lips parted. "Miz Martha don't want animals around."

"That's between me and Miss Martha. It's not your affair. There are too many unauthorized people wandering around here at night—"

"Miz Martha said I could—"

"Miss Martha isn't in charge here now, I am. She's old and ill and she won't be around much longer. Senator Ellis will own Maidenwood after she dies, and I'm acting by his authority. If I catch you anywhere on the premises after dark, or if anything happens to my dog, I'll swear out a warrant. Is that clear?"

He gave me a long baleful look before lowering his eyes and grunting a reluctant acknowledgment. Mrs. Danner didn't speak or move, but she enjoyed his humiliation. I could almost feel her glee; it puffed her cheeks with laughter she did not dare express. I knew she would pay later—not for her disloyalty, but for my tirade. Joe Danner would vent his rage on an object that could not fight back.

Feeling a little sick, I stepped aside and waved them on.

Before the old blue truck reached the road, another vehicle turned into the drive. Joe Danner had not replaced the sawhorse. I couldn't blame him for that, but I swore under my breath when I saw that the driver of the car was the middle-aged reporter.

I went down the drive at a run and waved him to a stop some distance from the house. "Don't bother to get out," I said. "Just turn around and leave."

I guess journalists have to develop hides like coats of mail. Smiling and unperturbed, he offered me a folded newspaper. "I thought you might not have seen the evening edition, Ms. Newcomb."

I took the paper. "Thanks. Now go away."

"What do you think of the discovery of—"

"I never think. See here, Mr.—"

"Miller. Chris Miller."

"You're wasting your time with me, Mr. Miller. My cousin, Senator Ellis, is Mrs. Carr's representative, and Dr. Petranek is in charge of the dig. Go heckle them. Even if I wanted to admit you to the grounds, which I don't, I couldn't, and I don't know anything except what I read in the paper."

He asked me more questions—all beginning with "What do you think"—but I stood my ground, smiling and shaking my head. Finally he gave up. I followed the car to the end of the drive and dragged the sawhorse back in place.

When Shirley came downstairs I was drinking bourbon and reading the paper. I had had a hard day, and what I read didn't improve my disposition.

The paper was the latest edition, the ink damp enough to stain my hands. Matt must have called a reporter as soon as he left me, and hopped onto the archaeological

bandwagon driven by Alan. He had even used some of the
phrases I had quoted ironically that morning. "Magnificent contribution—historical tradition—the Old Dominion . . ."

As I read on, amusement replaced my annoyance. Matt
had had no choice but to accept a fait accompli with as
much grace as possible. He was a smooth talker, all right;
platitudes rolled from his tongue like water off a greased
pig. The only time he came close to losing his temper was
when he was asked about the astonishing psychic discovery of Mrs. Hornbeak. " 'Pure coincidence,' the Senator
snapped." Lady Jocelyn was dismissed as a charming legend. " 'She is part of the traditions of Maidenwood, but
historians have assured me that there is no factual evidence for her existence, much less her presence at
Maidenwood. Mrs. Hornbeak has let her overheated
imagination run away with her.' "

I was chortling over this when Shirley came in. I
showed her the newspaper, but she refused to read it. "It's
all a pack of nonsense. I just hope Matthew can keep
those reporters away from here. They get on my nerves."

"One of them was here a little while ago." I folded the
newspaper and rose. "I got rid of him. But I'm surprised
we haven't heard from Mrs. Hornbeak. She is not going to
appreciate Matt's comments."

Perhaps our barricade did deter Mrs. Hornbeak. She
called instead of coming in person. At first she was gently
reproachful.

"We are accustomed to being ridiculed; but you, Ms.
Newcomb, must realize that coincidence cannot explain
my success. I would like you to tell the reporters . . ."

She went on in the same vein for some time, despite
my denials and interruptions; toward the end of the discussion her voice became shrill and her manner very close

to abusive. I had just hung up the phone when something hurled itself against the screen door and I saw Elvis.

We had an enthusiastic reunion on the steps. He obviously shared my feeling that we had been parted too long.

Alan sat down on the steps. "How about offering me a drink, if you can stop slobbering over that mutt?"

I decided to overlook the pejorative comment in view of his contribution to Elvis's continued survival. "Let me feed him first."

I brought Alan's glass of bourbon along with mine outside. The sun hung low over the wooded slope to the west, and a ruffle of rainbow-colored clouds framed its orb. There was the faintest trace of a breeze.

"Have you seen the paper?" I asked, offering it.

Alan smiled sardonically as he scanned the story. "Your cousin is a smart politician. Stupid man, smart politician. Have you had the press here?"

"One. I'm getting pretty good at running them off. Mrs. Hornbeak wasn't as easy to put off."

"She was here too?"

"No, she telephoned. I wish you and Matt would deal with your own enemies and stop foisting them off on me."

Alan smiled wickedly. Leaning back, he braced his elbows and lifted his face to the breeze. His hair clung damply to his forehead.

"She said something, though, that got me to thinking," I went on. "That her discovery was too accurate to be dismissed as coincidence. She's right, Alan. Out of all those acres of wilderness, how could she pinpoint the spot so neatly?"

"No doubt you've thought of an answer too," Alan said peaceably. "Spirit guides?"

"Bah, humbug."

"My sentiments exactly."

"Don't you . . . Do you believe in any kind of . . . well, of survival?"

I was afraid he might laugh at me. Instead he said seriously, "There's no easy answer to that one, Julie. I am willing to accept the possibility that the spirits of the dead might try to communicate with the living, if there was an urgent need, or a strong commitment. What I can't believe is that they would waste their time swapping clichés with a horse's ass like Polly Hornbeak."

"Nicely put."

"Thank you. So what's the explanation for her success?"

"Obviously she has access to information you don't have."

"I wouldn't say obviously. It is one possibility."

"You're a pompous bastard," I said, without malice. "Where could she have found it?"

"Again, there are several possibilities. They have a rather impressive library at the Institute."

"Yes, but it's another possibility that worries me. What if she found her information here?"

"Where here?"

"Huh? Oh. Alan, this house is full of junk that hasn't been sorted for decades. There could be material in the library, in the attic . . . I don't think anyone has broken in since I arrived, but who knows what went on before that?"

"Oddly enough, that possibility had also occurred to me."

"Well, you're damned cool about it, I must say! Weren't you the one who read Matt the lecture about leaving three defenseless women unprotected?"

"I doubt that anyone will bother you now that you

have the dog," Alan said, with maddening calm. "How are you getting on with the reconstruction?"

The change of subject caught me by surprise. "I haven't started it yet," I muttered. "I had to get the room arranged."

"Let's see." He rose.

I displayed my interior decoration, and Alan was kind enough to approve. He was amused by my makeshift stand for the cast: a porcelain cachepot, which cradled the rounded cranium.

"Not bad," he admitted. "That will do for a start, but I'll get you a proper stand."

He seemed disposed to linger, but I showed him to the door, explaining that I had to relieve Shirley. "You're not really nervous about burglars, are you?" he asked.

"I am not nervous! I possess a reasonable degree of logical concern about the subject. Mrs. Hornbeak was really furious. Suppose she decides to come back and have another look for secret documents?"

"I would suggest something if I didn't think you'd bite my head off."

"What?"

"Never mind."

"You mean let you look first?" I hesitated only briefly. "I wouldn't mind, Alan, but the only place I can let you explore is the library. Martha would hear you if you moved around in the attic."

His lip curled, but he said only, "You had better check with the senator first. I don't want to get arrested now that I'm on the verge of something big."

Martha gave me a hard time that evening. She acted like a child who is trying to postpone the moment of bedtime.

She wanted a glass of ice water and a cup of tea and she wanted me to have a cup with her and she wanted toast and the first piece was too dark and the second piece was too cold . . . The final demand was for her sleeping pills, but I balked at that; I had agreed with Shirley that she should be solely responsible for administering Martha's medication.

When Shirley finally relieved me I collected my nightgown and slippers and went downstairs. It was still early, so I decided to work on the cast.

I had already marked the measurement points and begun cutting the markers. The latter was a finicky job, because they had to be accurate to a millimeter. Gluing them in place didn't take long, but it was close to midnight before I finished, and I knew I ought to get to bed. Yet I hated to stop. It would be a good many hours before I could get any sense of what the woman had looked like, but I was beginning to feel quite possessive about her. I took out the modeling clay and started the next stage—connecting the markers with strips of clay, laying a foundation on which the final modeling would be made.

The skull looked really weird by the time I finished. The bands of interconnecting clay resembled the helmet of a Viking warrior or a futuristic Star Wars fighter. It wasn't until I stopped that I realized how tired I was, and I decided to leave the cast in its cradle for the night. If Elvis had been a cat instead of a dog, I wouldn't have risked it, but he was not in the habit of jumping onto tables unless there was food on them.

I let him out for a moment, and as I waited in the doorway I saw a light—not a flickering, distant warning of trespassers, but the square of a lighted window. Alan had not said he planned to sleep in the shed, but I knew the light must be his. It shone steady and unconcealed, and I will candidly admit I was glad to see it.

Elvis finally came back in. I gave him his dog biscuit; he crunched it appreciatively while I locked the door. We were both asleep within five minutes.

I woke with a start, every muscle taut and quivering with the urgency of the dream that had broken my slumber. The dream had been shattered too; nothing remained of it except that sense of desperate need, and a lingering sound—a soft, weak wailing, the lament of something small and helpless, worn out with long weeping.

I knew I was awake, but it seemed to me I could hear it still—the saddest, most heartbreaking sound I had ever heard. Tears filled my eyes and trickled down my cheeks. And then at last—or so I thought—I came fully awake. The sound was not that of a baby crying. It was the dog.

My cheeks were still wet with tears as I fumbled across the tangled bedding in search of Elvis. A dog growling in the night doesn't do a lot for a person's nerves, but it was better—anything would have been better—than that forlorn weeping. Finally I found Elvis's collar. He hushed at my whispered command, but I could feel his entire body quivering.

The night was still. There was no breeze to rustle the branches of the shrubs outside the window, not even a cricket or a tree frog chirping. I had no doubt that Elvis had heard something, and after a moment I heard it too. It didn't come from inside the house. The door of my room was solid oak, an inch thick, and it fit tightly into the frame. The sound came from outside—a metallic scraping at the back door.

Still holding the dog's collar, I slid out of bed. The shrubs outside the window screened off the moonlight and for a moment I was completely disoriented. I couldn't find my flashlight or my shoes. It's funny how defenseless you feel in your bare feet. I couldn't have located the door if the dog had not pulled me in the right direction.

He was practically choking, he wanted so badly to bark. His presence calmed my nerves. He was a combined burglar alarm and defensive weapon, but I didn't want to use him in either capacity. If the burglar entered the house, he or she would have to pass the door of my room on the way to the front hall. I had no intention of going on the offensive, with or without Elvis, but I was determined to find out who the midnight visitor was.

I reached for the doorknob. My fingers had just closed over it when I felt it turn.

It had never occurred to me that the intruder would come into my room, and it scared me so badly that I retreated as far as I could go, and huddled at the foot of the bed, clutching Elvis in my arms. The door opened. A beam of light, slender as a sword blade, invaded the room. It fell full on the skull, with its grotesque tracery of clay. I almost screamed myself at the sight. The person in the doorway let out a soft hiss of breath and started forward.

Elvis had obeyed my orders like a lamb up till then, though it obviously went against all his instincts. This was too much. His barking exploded in my ear and he squirmed free. I sat down ignominiously on my bottom. I don't doubt that the person with the flashlight said something as the dog launched itself at him, but his comment was lost in Elvis's howls. The flashlight wobbled and fell and went out. I heard a sharp cracking sound that I took for a shot, and a yelp from Elvis. That brought me to my feet. I plunged forward, straight into the footboard of the bed.

The top of the post crunched into my diaphragm and my big toe connected with the bottom of the post. It hurt more than I would have believed possible. My yell of pain was drowned in the general uproar—smashes and crashes and the frantic barks of Elvis. He was still alive, at any rate. As I nursed my aching toe I heard footsteps beat a rapid path toward the door. He—she—it—whatever—was getting away. Elvis went after him. The rapidity with which the volume of his barking diminished suggested that pursuer and pursued were setting a good pace. I started to follow. My foot came down on a sharp object that seemed to pierce it to the bone.

Complicated as it sounds, the whole business couldn't have lasted for more than thirty seconds. It seemed to take a lot longer. As I hopped toward the door and the light switch, I couldn't understand why no one had come to my rescue. The racket should have aroused everyone for miles around.

I had just switched on the light when I heard running footsteps returning. If I had been able to lay my hands on a heavy object I'd have brained the newcomer, but luckily I couldn't find a weapon, because the newcomer was Alan.

He was fully dressed, including his heavy work shoes. He held a rusty crowbar. I swayed toward him; he dropped the crowbar and lifted me clean off my feet, holding me so tightly his arms seemed to restrain rather than support me.

"Julie—what . . . Are you—"

"Never mind," I yelled. "I'm all right—go get him!"

The arms that held me relaxed. I couldn't see Alan's face, since his chin was pressing down on my head, but I heard his breath come out in a ragged gasp that might have betokened relief . . . or exasperated laughter, or . . .

"There can't be much wrong with you. Quit kicking, will you? There's blood all over the place. Did he—"

"He didn't touch me. I stepped on something sharp . . . Oh, damn! The cast—it's smashed to smithereens. And Elvis is gone, he chased him out, he'll get shot—"

Alan lowered me onto the bed and knelt, taking my bleeding foot into his hand. My lament over Elvis ended in a bleat of pain as his fingers gently probed and squeezed.

"I want to make sure there are no fragments of glass in the wound, Julie. You must have stepped on the broken glass from the flashlight; the edges of the cast aren't sharp enough to make such clean cuts. His flashlight, I presume?"

"Or hers. Ouch! Alan, stop fussing over me and go look for Elvis."

"The dog is all right, Julie. We'd have heard shots or yells or barks, or something, if Elvis had caught up with the guy. Where do you keep your first aid stuff?"

Fortunately for my blood pressure, Elvis came back before Alan had finished bandaging my foot. At my shriek of joy he leaped onto the bed and allowed me to embrace him. He looked awfully pleased with himself—the Heroic Dog in person. Though he was covered with dirt and dry grass, there was not a mark on him, nor, to my regret, was there a convenient fragment of cloth caught in his teeth.

"Hold him till I get this glass cleaned up," Alan said, and proceeded to sweep the floor while I watched.

"I'm sorry about the cast, Alan," I said. "I should have put it in the closet, but I was so sleepy—"

"I'll have another one made," Alan said curtly. "I've got the mold."

"You may not have caught him, old boy," I told Elvis, "but you sure helped him make one hell of a mess."

As soon as Alan had finished sweeping, I got up. "Where are you going now?" he demanded.

"I'm going to shut Elvis in the kitchen and then check on Martha."

The first thing I saw when I opened Martha's door was the horrid gleam of a white eyeball. She appeared to be sound asleep; but the sound of the door opening, soft as it was, roused Shirley in the next room. She appeared in the open doorway, her wide eyes reflecting the glow of the night light.

"Miz Martha—"

"She's all right. I just looked in to—ah—just looked in. Sorry I woke you."

Shirley padded to the bed and bent over Martha. "Yes, she's sleeping." She straightened and looked at me; though she spoke in a whisper, the hurt dignity in her voice was unmistakable. "You don't need to worry, Julie. I'd wake if I heard her."

"I wasn't checking up on you, Shirley—honest. I just . . . Look, I'll explain in the morning. Go back to sleep now—please."

I retreated, feeling like a worm. I'd apologize and set things straight in the morning; there was no need to ruin what was left of Shirley's repose. I had heard that nurses can train themselves to sleep undisturbed by extraneous noises, and to rouse instantly at the slightest sound from their patients. Mother claimed she had done the same thing when I was little.

When I got downstairs Alan was making coffee. He offered me a cup. I shook my head. Reaction had set in; I felt myself shaking all over and I was afraid I'd drop the cup if I tried to hold it.

Alan gave me a sharp glance and placed the cup on the table. "Drink it. It's half sugar—you need a stimulant."

What I needed was someone to hold me and hug me and tell me there was nothing to be afraid of. But I'd rather have died than say so. I had only imagined that Alan's first spontaneous embrace held anything more than normal concern. Maybe if I had blubbered and clung to him . . . Well, it was too late now. Besides—I assured myself—I wouldn't resort to that kind of emotional entrapment.

Alan was watching me. I sat down and drew the cup toward me, slowly, so it wouldn't spill.

"Are you feeling better?" Alan asked. His voice was cool and disinterested.

"I'm all right."

"He won't be back tonight," Alan said. "It will be light in a few hours. Why don't you go back to bed?"

"I couldn't sleep."

"Do you want me to stay?"

Did I want him to stay! "I'm sure you have other things you'd rather be doing," I said.

Alan got up. "As soon as the sun rises I'll take the dog and try to track your burglar. No sense blundering around in the dark."

"Who do you think it was?"

Alan shrugged. "It could have been one of several people."

After he had gone I sat staring at the closed door. A core of icy cold had settled around me. One of several people . . . including Alan himself. It would be a perfect cover-up for an intruder—to turn on his tracks and return as the heroic rescuer.

twelve

Daylight revived my nerve a little—but not much.
What bothered me most was the unavoidable conclusion
that the intruder had been after me. There was no other
reason why he should have entered that room.

Alan found me huddled over the kitchen table staring
at my cold coffee when he returned shortly after six
o'clock.

"No luck," he announced. "There are broken branches
in the boxwood, where he forced his way through. But the
ground is too dry to take footprints and Elvis copped out
when we got to the road. He must have left his car there."

"You keep saying 'he.' How do you know it wasn't a
woman?"

"I don't. When will the sheriff be here?"

"Huh?" I looked blearily at him.

"Didn't you call him?" Alan snatched at the telephone.
"For God's sake, do I have to tell you to do everything?"

"I hated to wake him up," I said yawning.

"Someone would have been awake. You think the cops close down at five and don't reopen until . . . Hello?"

When he hung up he was scowling. "They bawled me out for not reporting the incident earlier. Go get dressed."

"Are they coming?"

"Of course they're coming. Breaking and entering is a crime, hadn't you heard?"

I got the impression that Sheriff Jarboe was getting a little tired of the Carrs and their problems, but he was very nice. He didn't even blame me for not notifying him immediately; he blamed Alan.

Feeling somewhat ashamed of my cowardice, I pulled myself together and started breakfast. When Shirley came down Jarboe and his deputy had joined Alan at the kitchen table and I was serving toast, scrambled eggs, and coffee.

"There was nothing you could have done," I said, cutting short Shirley's broken exclamations of guilt and distress. "It was all over in a few minutes."

"Yes, but I should have woken up. I don't usually sleep that hard."

The sheriff interrupted. "She's right, Shirley. Quit calling yourself names and get back up to Miz Martha. You better not tell her about this."

"No, I sure won't. I just don't know what's going on. We never had things like this happen before. . . ."

She went off with Martha's tray and the rest of us finished the scrambled eggs. "We'll have another look around before we go," Jarboe said, crunching into his third piece of toast. "But I didn't see a damned thing. Must have been the same gang, though."

"Gang?" Alan repeated, raising his eyebrows. "Julie said there was only one person."

"She only saw one. The others were probably outside, waiting for the scout to give them the all clear."

Jarboe was sticking to his theory. Alan didn't reply, but his sardonic smile told me he was as skeptical as I of Jarboe's facile explanation.

Before Jarboe left he examined the debris Alan had swept from the floor of my room. "Smart of you to keep it, Professor," he said grudgingly. "Nothing here, though."

Nothing there *now*. It would be smart to sweep the floor if you weren't sure whether you had left some evidence of your presence. But why would Alan break into the house? He had managed to work his way into my confidence, and Shirley's; he could come and go as he pleased during the day.

Jarboe picked up his hat. "I'll increase the number of rounds the patrol car makes," he promised. "And I'll tell the boys to drive up to the house instead of passing on the road. Don't be worried if you hear a car at night."

"I don't suppose I could talk you into leaving a man here at night," I said.

Jarboe repeated the familiar litany. "Not enough manpower. Uh—Julie—you aren't going to sleep in that room again, I hope."

I said I hadn't thought about it.

"Better not. You're safer upstairs. Not," Jarboe added quickly, "not that I think they were looking for you in particular. But there's no telling what they might do if they found a woman alone . . . I mean, why take chances?"

Having said all the wrong things, he beat a hasty retreat. I turned to Alan. "I feel worse now than I did before he showed up."

"Get a few hours' sleep and you'll be fine." Alan stood up. "Want me to leave the dog?"

"Yes. No . . . I don't know."

"I'll leave him. I have a few errands to run. Stop looking like a wounded doe, nobody is going to bother you in
broad daylight. I'll be back about noon."

Shirley also suggested I take a nap, which confirmed
my suspicion that I looked as haggard as I felt. I snapped
at her and then repented, for she was clearly still blaming
herself for my misadventure. "I don't need any more
sleep," I assured her. "I get by on a lot less than five hours
a night when I'm in school. Why don't you run home for
a while?"

"You sure you aren't scared here alone?"

I laughed heartily.

"Maybe I will run over home and do some cleaning,"
Shirley said. "I need to do something to wake myself up. I
must be getting old to sleep so sound."

We were standing outside Martha's door, I on my way
in, Shirley on her way down with the tray. "She must have
slept good too," Shirley said. "Bright as a new penny this
morning. She didn't even ask me what was going on down
there, with the police and all. She just lies there and sort
of smiles. I hope it's not a sign . . ."

I stifled another laugh—my first genuine laugh of the
morning—at the picture of Martha beaming beatifically at
the angels who were gliding in to carry her away to the
Golden Gates. "It's more likely that she's planning some
dirty trick to play on one of us," I said. "Run along, and
don't worry about me."

Martha was no more gracious than usual, but I thought
I understood the reason for her smiles. When I went in
the room I caught her in the act of lowering herself back
against the pillow. She had been sitting up—and she must
have raised herself, because Shirley wouldn't have left her
in that position. The dear old wretch was flexing her mus-

cles on the sly. It was just like her to carry out her own version of exercise, after refusing the help of a trained therapist.

I had not been reading long before the telephone rang. When I heard Matt's voice I realized I should have notified him of the events of the past night. He was concerned, reproachful, and angry in turn.

"How did you find out?" I asked, watching Martha. For once she had the courtesy to pretend she wasn't listening, but her good eye was cocked in my direction.

"Jarboe called me. You ought to have let me know, Julie. It's a hell of a note when I have to find out about my cousin being attacked from the police—"

"I wasn't attacked."

"You're sure you're all right?"

"Yes."

"What the devil were you doing down there anyway?"

The anger in his voice didn't annoy me; I took it as a sign of cousinly concern and was rather more pleased than otherwise. "Do you really want me to explain?"

"Oh—you're with Martha. Never mind, then. I'm going to try to get out there this evening. Let me talk to her for a minute, okay?"

I handed Martha the phone, observing the increased strength with which her hand closed over the instrument. Her speech was the only thing that hadn't improved. She let Matt do most of the talking. Her eyes sparkled as she listened; I assumed he was telling her of his intention of seeing her soon.

The morning wore away in the usual fashion. When twelve o'clock came around, Shirley had not returned, so I closed the book and told Martha I was going to get lunch.

Elvis was under the kitchen table, looking bored and forlorn. I let him out for a run and investigated the food situation. I was stirring an unattractive blend of noodles and peas and cheese when Shirley came in, breathless and apologetic.

"I'm sorry I'm late," she began.

"You'll be even sorrier when you taste this." I waved a spoon over the pan on the stove.

"Ron's lost his job." She dropped heavily into a chair.

"Oh, Shirley, I'm sorry! What happened?"

"He says he got kicked out because a friend of the manager's wanted the job. But I wouldn't be surprised if he smart-mouthed somebody."

"That's a shame, Shirley. Maybe I can find some more work for him around here. Or Alan might need another worker."

"I'd sure appreciate that. Goodness, child, what have you got in that pan?"

She went to work on the noodles. I let the subject drop; I too had heard Mrs. Danner's shuffling approach and I didn't blame Shirley for not wanting to discuss Ron's situation in front of Martha's stooge—especially that aspect of Ron's situation that worried his mother most. She must be well aware of how Jarboe's suspicions were running. That was why she had rushed home, to make sure Ron had an alibi for last night. Obviously he had none, and the loss of his job gave him an even stronger motive for turning, or returning, to burglary.

Shirley took Martha's tray upstairs, and Mrs. Danner and I sat down to finish the noodles, which weren't half bad, thanks to Shirley's intervention. Mrs. Danner ate in silence, her eyes on her plate. I thought I'd try a little detective work of my own, so I said abruptly, "Somebody broke into the house last night."

The even tempo of her chewing and swallowing didn't alter. The element of surprise having failed, I asked point-blank whether her husband had left their house during the night.

"No, ma'am. He didn't. You want I should clean the parlor?"

"What is this strange obsession you have with the parlor?" I asked.

Sarcasm was wasted on Mrs. Danner. She gave me a blank stare. I knew the answer to the question: the wine decanter was in the parlor. I said slowly, "No, Mrs. Danner, I don't want you to clean the parlor. Go and relieve Shirley." I couldn't resist a last shot, mean person that I am; as she trudged toward the door I added, "If Miss Martha asks what went on here last night, go ahead and tell her."

Mrs. Danner's stooped shoulder twitched, the way a cow's does when a fly is biting it, but that was her only response.

I was sitting at the table scribbling a shopping list when Elvis's whines alerted me to Alan's arrival. He was loaded down with parcels, so I opened the door for him.

"I see you're still alive," was his greeting. "No more burglars?"

"Thanks for noticing. What have you got?"

"Presents for you."

"Oh, no. Not another . . . How did you get it done so fast?"

Alan looked smug. "I had an extra on hand."

"In case I screwed up?"

"It's a good thing I did, isn't it?"

I couldn't deny it. "I don't know that I'm in the mood any longer."

"You had better get in the mood." Alan began unloading the bags. "Speed is of the essence. I want this yesterday. I'd like you to start on it right away." After a moment he added, "Please."

"Why? No, don't tell me, let me guess. National Geographic is hesitating."

"I need all the ammunition I can get," Alan said.

"Don't you want me to help you dig?"

"The dig is closed down temporarily until I find out where I stand financially. N.G. isn't my only lead. I should hear from someone by the end of the week, and then I can set up a proper excavation."

It seemed to me that there was some inconsistency in his statement. If he needed the reconstruction to impress potential donors, further evidence from the dig would serve the same purpose. I was distracted, however, by the objects he had removed from the bags. Another cast of the skull—that broad white smile was becoming as familiar as the face of an old friend—a proper stand, modeling clay and erasers, and several new items. I gulped when he took the lid from a box and I saw a pair of eyeballs staring at me.

"Might as well do it right this time," he said. "I got false eyelashes too, and a wig."

"They're brown," I said, staring back at the eyeballs.

"Indubitably."

"But hers were . . ."

Alan pretended he hadn't heard. "Brown is the most common eye color."

"Like mine."

"Yours aren't brown. They're hazel. Anyhow," Alan said, before I could comment, "let's get it set up."

I followed him to my room and watched him lay out the supplies. "What's that?" I asked, as he removed the final object from the bag.

"Lock for the door. I'll install it while you get started."

He had brought the necessary tools. As he set to work drilling I remarked casually, "I am not sleeping here to-night."

"Suit yourself. But I want it kept locked, whether you're in or out of it."

By the time he had installed the lock I was well under way. I had gone through the same process so recently that it was easier the second time. Alan leaned over me, breathing on the back of my neck, until I said irritably, "Will you stop that? I can't concentrate."

"Are you almost finished with the markers?"

"Six more."

"Hurry up, will you?"

I did not reply. When I had set the final, twenty-sixth marker in place, I turned on him. "What do you want?"

"Want? A lot of things." Alan's eyes were veiled, opaque. "But I'll settle for an hour or two in the attic."

"Alan, I told you, I can't—"

"Why not?"

"Martha might hear you. She—"

"She'd do what?" His voice was even, his pose relaxed, but I felt the anger that seethed under the thin surface of his apparent calm. "Call you bad names? Threaten to cut you out of her will? When are you going to get it through your head that she can't hurt you any more? You're not a child, you're a healthy, independent adult—and she's a sick old woman. I swear to God, when I see what she's done to you I could almost believe in witchcraft!"

I stared at him, silent and shaken. It may have been my look of blank helplessness that shattered his self-control; his anger boiled over into quick, hot words. "What the hell is the matter with you and your precious cousin? Don't you care whether uninvited visitors stroll around the house at all hours of the night? I could put locks on every door and window—which is more than the honorable Senator has bothered to do—but that still wouldn't guarantee your safety. Something peculiar is going on here, and I want to know what it is. Are you going to take me upstairs, or do I go alone—stopping on the way to spit in Martha's eye and tell her what I think of her?"

Anger can be a sign of caring. Instead of resenting his outrage, I felt strengthened by it. I even summoned up a shaky smile. "That would be the end of Martha; she'd have a fatal stroke at the mere sight of you. I'll take you. But what do you hope to find?"

Alan relaxed. He could afford to; he had won the argument. "It's more a question of what I hope *not* to find— signs that someone has been up there recently. Polly Hornbeak found a lead somewhere; good old Joe Danner is looking for God knows what—and don't forget the clothes the skeletons were wearing. Nobody in the neighborhood recognized them. They had to come from somewhere." He didn't give me time to reconsider, but reached for my hand and pulled me to my feet. "Come on."

Neither of us spoke again until we stood before the door that concealed the stairs leading to the attic. Martha's door had been closed when we tiptoed past—I tiptoed, at any rate; Alan made no effort to moderate the sound of his footsteps. The attic stairs were at the far end of a wing that had been closed off ever since I could remember. At first the door refused to open, and I felt a cowardly sense of relief, remembering that during my childhood it had always been locked. It wasn't locked now. Alan gave the handle a mighty tug, and the door creaked and yielded.

The smell of stale, musty air triggered the memory flash I had known would come. Sunlight stretching long fingers across dusty floorboards, the shrill buzzing of a fly trapped by the sticky strands of a spiderweb high under the rafters, splinters scraping my bare knees as I knelt to look inside . . .

Inside . . . something. I couldn't see it. It was gone. Alan was gone too—up the stairs, into the attic. I heard the boards groan under his feet.

My hands were sticky with sweat. It would be hot as the hinges of Hades up there; the big circular window under the eaves had probably not been opened in years. Part of me—the coward child—wanted to run away. But another, wiser part knew I had passed the point of no return, that I would never be free of Martha, or of the past, until I saw what was waiting for me at the top of the stairs.

It seemed to take an eternity to climb up there. There was no door at the top, only an opening in the floor. I kept my eyes fixed on the steps until my reluctant feet had reached the last of them.

Dim sunlight, starred by dancing dust motes, lay in remembered pathways across the uncarpeted floor. The center of the big room was bare; discarded furniture, boxes, barrels, crates had been arranged around the perimeter, against the walls. The only footprints that had scuffed the dust were Alan's; he stood with his back to me, head tipped to one side as if he were listening.

I saw it all in a single glance, saw and discarded everything except one object—the humpbacked trunk in the corner farthest from the stairs. I don't remember crying out, but I must have done so, for Alan turned with a lithe, startled quickness. "Julie? What—"

My voice was no more than a whisper. "The trunk. I was looking inside. I forced the lock—I don't know why—it was the only thing that was locked, I thought there must be something special in it . . . She found me. She always found me—she always knew. Alan . . ."

Wordlessly he held out his hands. I caught at them as if they were a lifeline. The next moment I was in his arms, cradled, sheltered; his lips met mine with an urgency no less than my own.

We had made love in some peculiar places before that. Under the table in Alan's office—the only space that wasn't filled with books and desks and filing cabinets; in a muddy pasture outside Williamsburg, with three puzzled cows for an audience. Never could there have been such a wildly inappropriate spot as that filthy, steaming attic— the splintered boards hard under our bodies, the dust tickling our throats and our nostrils.

And never before had our loving been as it was that day—a dizzying, dazzling achievement of oneness that wiped out the last shreds of doubt as a clean flame cuts through clinging cobwebs. I had not known the barrier was there until it went down and I knew I was free of it now forever.

We lay side by side on the floor. Idly, with my finger, I traced a heart in the dust; Alan laughed, and drew an arrow through it.

"She came here regularly—every few weeks. Always alone. She never carried anything up, she never brought anything down. I became curious. Lord knows I didn't have much to occupy my mind in those days. She kept the door locked, but that didn't stop me; I found a key, in one of the other doors, that fit the simple lock. I was scared to death the first time I ventured up those stairs; but in a way, that made the whole thing more exciting. It was an adventure, a small but important act of defiance.

"I must have been up here three or four times before I got nerve enough to attack the trunk. Nothing else was locked; I decided there must be treasures inside, jewels, Blackbeard's gold . . . I didn't really expect I'd be able to open it. The hasp must have been worn with rust; it gave way, with a horrible crack, the first time I tugged at it. I lifted the lid . . . I had been squatting on the floor, you see; I got to my knees and leaned forward to look in . . ."

Alan reached for my hand. "Get it out," he said gently. "What did she do? Hit you, or—"

"No. Oh, no. She . . . I don't know how she crept up on me without my hearing her. One of the boards creaked, but not until she was right beside me. I looked up and there she was, still as a statue . . . She seemed to be ten feet tall. When she stooped down it was like a boulder falling on me. I couldn't move. I heard her say something about satisfying my curiosity . . . She put me in the trunk and closed the lid. I don't remember anything more . . . Alan, you're hurting my hand."

He put his arms around me and held me close. He didn't speak at first; then he said in a stifled voice, "I knew something was wrong, but I never suspected it was that bad. Why didn't you tell me?"

"I had forgotten. I wiped out practically every memory of those years. They're coming back to me now, suddenly and shockingly at times. Now I know why I hate my bedroom upstairs. She'd lock me in there for punishment—usually on stormy days or late in the evening—and take away the lamp. There was one particularly gruesome story connected with that room—it was supposed to be haunted by a girl, a visitor, whose hair had caught fire while she was getting ready to meet her lover. She leaned too close to the candle by the mirror, to admire her pretty face . . . Martha said I'd never suffer from the sin of vanity, at any rate."

"I'd like to kill the old witch," Alan muttered.

"I did—in fantasies—over and over. But my favorite idea of revenge was to have Martha repent. I'd picture myself dressed for a ball, in long skirts and ruffles, with jewels in my hair—and Martha kneeling at my feet, suing humbly for pardon. I've wondered, since, whether Martha made up that story about the girl who was burned to death. She told me a lot of moral tales about 'light women' who were struck down by the righteous wrath of God. I knew words like 'harlot' and 'fornication' before I could spell 'Mississippi.' "

Alan grimaced. "And I wondered why you carried on so vehemently about virginity! Martha made up a lot of garbage, Julie—including your homeliness and lack of sex appeal. I knew you had a low opinion of yourself— though how you could hang on to it, with me falling over my own feet every time I looked at you—"

" 'The Carr features are too strong for a woman's face. I took after my mother's people, but you, poor child . . .' "

"That's a quote, isn't it?"

"Straight from the horse's mouth. Wasn't it a Jesuit who said, 'Give me a child before he is seven and he is mine for the rest of his life'? I was eight when Martha got her hands on me, but she did a thorough job in four years. She had no trouble convincing me that you were using me to get permission to dig at Maidenwood."

"I can't criticize you," Alan said wryly. "She did a number on me too. I don't suppose it ever occurred to you that I had a few insecurities of my own."

"You? I always thought of you as utterly self-confident."

"You don't remember what I told you about my background—my family?"

"You come from Brooklyn or someplace," I said lazily. Alan leaned over and kissed me thoroughly. "That," he said, "is for remembering only the important things. It never mattered to you, did it—that my father was illiterate and my mother scrubbed offices at night, and my uncle . . . Well, the less said about my uncle, the better."

"I don't care what he was."

"But I cared," Alan said. "I was such a damned snob—all children are, I guess. You know, that is something people who have it take for granted—a sense of self-worth that stems from decent living conditions and family stability. I buried the slum kid under a pile of college degrees, but he was still there, with a chip on his shoulder as big as a house, looking for insults where none were intended. Nobody put my back up worse than these soft-spoken, smug aristocrats. I don't know how your grandmother spotted my weakness, but she sure as hell knew how to exploit it."

I sat up with a start. "Alan! You mean she told you I looked down on you because . . . Surely you didn't believe that?"

"The professor didn't; but Al Petranek fell for it."

"Five years," I murmured. "We lost five years that we can never get back. When I think what she did to you—"

"To me? What she did to *you* was child abuse, pure and simple. The sheer malevolence of the woman . . . Are you sure that trunk didn't contain black candles and unholy devices, and a copy of the contract she signed with Satan?"

He spoke lightly, but his face was anxious as he rose on one elbow and looked at me. Smiling, I shook my head. "I'm not suppressing that memory, Alan. I never got a good look inside the trunk. Something white and crumpled—fabric, from the feel of it; but whatever it was, it was at the very bottom of the trunk. There was plenty of room inside for me."

Alan sat up and reached for his clothes. "Let's get out of this filthy place. I'll never forgive myself for dragging you up here."

"It was the best thing you could have done. You've exorcised the last of my ghosts, Alan. I'll never be afraid to come here again."

"Well . . . Maybe it wasn't such a bad idea, at that." Alan tossed his shirt aside and reached out for me.

Some time later I left him rummaging happily among the books in the library and went back to my reconstruction. I was so dizzy with happiness I felt drunk.

At first the strips of modeling clay went in all directions. But they were easy to peel off, and after a while I got myself under control. Gradually the work cast its own spell. My fingers moved with a skill I hadn't known I possessed.

Alan's low whistle of surprise woke me from a daze of concentration. Hands resting lightly on my shoulders, he studied the cast in silence for a time. Then he said, "That's good, Julie. That's damned good. I didn't know you were such an expert."

"I'm not. This is just a matter of filling in the blank spaces, following the contours of the bone."

"Speaking of bones, yours aren't bad." His fingertips traced them—temples to cheekbones, the angles of the lower jaw; then they curved and tightened, tipping my head back. The kiss had barely begun when we both heard footsteps, and Alan swore.

"Close the door," I suggested brazenly.

"I have to go."

"Oh. Well, of course, if you're in a hurry—"

Careless of Mrs. Danner's proximity, he lifted me out of

the chair and convinced me that he was as reluctant to leave as I was to have him go.

"I'm already an hour late for a meeting," he said.

"With someone who might give you money?"

I smiled, but Alan didn't. "I wouldn't go if it weren't important. Are you sure you'll be all right?"

"Of course."

"I may not be back till late. I hope you aren't going to sleep downstairs."

"Not me. Once was enough."

"Be sure you lock up."

"I will."

Mrs. Danner had passed the door and gone into the kitchen. Alan kissed me again. "I think I'll call and tell them I broke a leg," he murmured.

"Get going. We need that money."

"What a beautiful word."

"Money?"

"We."

After an interval—a long interval—we went to the kitchen. Mrs. Danner was wiping the sink. Alan greeted her; she mumbled something and went on wiping. Alan said casually to me, "Someone has been in the library, no question about that. I couldn't tell whether anything was missing, the place is in such chaos, but I made sure no one will get in that door without setting off an alarm."

"How could—"

Alan cut me off with a shake of the head and a meaningful glance at Mrs. Danner. "Oh," I said. "Thanks."

I followed him into the yard. When we were out of earshot of Mrs. Danner he said, "There's no way those doors can be made secure. But at least the word will get back to one of the possible suspects."

"Do you think it was Joe Danner?"

"I think Danner was interested in the library. The only reason I can think of why he would carry a pair of scissors was to cut something out—a map, for instance."

"A map!"

"He may have been bit by the treasure bug," Alan explained. "Think how pleased his God would be if he were given Blackbeard's loot. Joe is smart enough to know that libraries contain old books with old maps; not smart enough to know that none of them would be of any use to him." He glanced at his watch. "Damn. I wish I didn't have to leave."

"There's nothing to worry about. Things are no different now than they have been all along."

"That's what worries me."

Romantic novelists gush about a thing called the inner glow of happiness. There may or may not be such a thing, but happiness does show on the outside. Martha noticed it. I guess that had always been her secret—not clairvoyance or a pact with the Devil, but the same skill possessed by successful fortune tellers—the ability to detect and interpret small involuntary muscular movements. Not that it took much insight to see the change in me. I couldn't seem to stop smiling.

Her comment was a sarcastic "You look very pleased with yourself."

"I'm in a good mood. Since when is that a crime?"

"Why?"

"Why not?" I riposted brilliantly.

Martha's lips twisted in the movement that always preceded a particularly withering comment. She glanced significantly at my left hand, and I laughed. "Martha, you have a one-track mind. If and when I get engaged, you will be duly informed. Now what would you like me to read? We finished *Death on the Hearthrug* yesterday."

Martha was still wide awake and staring when Shirley came. Earlier, I had heard the sound of a car leaving. It had not returned, so I gathered Ron had borrowed it again. Shirley's worn expression also suggested she had had an encounter with her eldest child, but I didn't want to raise a subject that obviously upset her, and she did not volunteer anything.

The kitchen door was locked. I also locked the door of my room before I went back to work.

Dark pressed in at the windows and the trees muttered softly as the breeze moved their branches. I had expected to be nervous, despite the locks and bars, but I wasn't; the presence of Elvis, sprawled on the rug, twitching and whining in his sleep, was as good as a tranquilizer.

It was well after midnight before I realized that my hands had lost the delicacy of touch so essential in this final stage. I had roughly blocked in the facial planes indicated by the markers and the connecting strips of clay; now came the part that was almost pure guesswork, for some of the structures of the living face leave no imprint on the bone. Had her lips been full and red, or narrow and pale? Her nose retroussé or aquiline?

When I leaned back and looked at what I had done, I had a flash of something like déjà vu. It came and went so quickly I couldn't pin it down. I had begun with the easiest part, the forehead. People don't have fat foreheads, and a young woman's brow would be smooth and unmarked. The setting of the eyes presented problems, but I had blocked them in too. Enclosed in the modeling medium, the glass reflected the lamplight as living eyes might have done.

Tentatively I smoothed away a slight bulge in the clay

over one temple. The fleeting impression was gone. I only
hoped I had not yielded to the temptation to reproduce a
face with which I was familiar.

I put the cast on a shelf in the closet, unlocked my
door, and peeked out. Elvis rose and stretched. He appeared unperturbed. I counted on his instincts more than
on my own. I let him out for his last run. There was no
comforting square of light visible tonight. Alan must not
have returned. I wished now that I had decided to sleep
downstairs. The room was as secure as human effort could
make it, and Alan could have come to me there, no matter
how late he returned. Tomorrow night we would make
better arrangements. My body tingled at the thought.

Elvis was pleasantly surprised when I attached his
leash and led him up the stairs. He had to inspect the new
room, sniffing in every corner, before he jumped onto the
bed. His eyes were bright and his tongue lolled out, as if
he were laughing.

"Enjoy it while you can," I told him. "You're excellent
company and I'm glad to have you, but I rather wish you
were someone else."

People do silly things when they are feeling sentimental. I talked to Elvis; if he hadn't been there I would have
talked to myself. I studied my features in the mirror, and
for the first time my face pleased me; it looked almost
pretty. Instead of braiding my hair I let it fall to my shoulders, and I spent a ridiculous amount of time brushing it.
I put on my best nightgown, an imitation Victorian garment of white cotton, with lots of lace and ruffles. I pos-
tured and smirked at my reflection. After I got into
bed . . . Well, never mind what I thought about.

Tired as I was, I didn't sleep at once. I was too happy. I
had just begun to drift off when the dog shifted his weight
and sat up.

Approaching sleep had dulled my senses; at first I thought I must be dreaming, reliving the experience of the night before. It was against all reason that lightning could strike twice—and not even in the same place. How could Elvis hear sounds from the floor below, through closed doors and miles of corridor?

He had heard or sensed something. This time he didn't growl. I touched him and felt the stiffened hair on the back of his neck, over rigid muscles.

I had not locked my door. I didn't even have a key for it. I did have a light, and as my fingers found the switch of the bedside lamp I blessed Edison and all the other scientists, from the first discoverer of fire, who had freed mankind from the terrors of the dark.

I wasn't especially afraid. The sounds of this part of the house were new to the dog; perhaps he had heard an animal in the bushes under the window, or a night bird. I said softly, "What is it, Elvis?"

He turned his head and looked at me, in a gesture so human it was rather startling. Then he jumped off the bed. Stiff-legged, he crept toward the door.

Then I was afraid. I had never seen him behave like that. His movements were dragging and reluctant, as if he were forcing himself to face a danger that terrified him.

It cost me a considerable effort to turn out the light. But to open the door without doing so meant exposing myself to whatever walked in the darkened house. I heard the dog whimper low in his throat as I passed him. I wanted to whimper back.

The hall outside my door was pitch-black. Something was wrong. There should have been light to the left, where the sconce outside Martha's door was always left burning.

Then I heard the sounds the dog's keener senses had

caught. Not footsteps, but the creak of the aged boards of the floor under the pressure of feet. The dog had not moved. I heard him panting heavily, as if he had been racing for his life.

I opened the door wider and stepped out. Another creak of sound and another, closer . . . Someone was moving along the hall—toward my room. It had to be my burglar. But how had he made his way into the house and got all the way upstairs? And why wasn't the dog sounding the alarm, as he had the night before?

I didn't dare think about the answers to those questions. If I had, I would have jumped back in bed and pulled the covers over my head. Instead, I turned on my flashlight and directed it straight at the end of the corridor.

The beam caught her full-on, in a frame of brightness. I saw the long gown and the heavy stick, and the face frozen by shock into a plastic monster mask. I saw the shotgun she carried.

Elvis had crept unnoticed to my side. He let out a long wavering howl, a cry of pure terror. Martha's lips parted. She croaked, "You came back. Again. You . . ."

Her hands lost their hold on gun and cane and she toppled forward. The whole house seemed to shake with the force of her fall.

thirteen

❧

The amazing thing was that she was still alive. My body went into automatic overdrive, performing the necessary actions with machinelike efficiency. I had to slap Shirley to waken her; my mind noted, "drugged," even as I ran back to kneel by Martha.

By the time the ambulance arrived, we had done all we could. It wasn't much; but the harsh breath still rattled in and out of Martha's open mouth and she was still alive when the medics carried her out.

They left the front door wide open. I knew I ought to go down and close it, but I didn't have the strength to move. Shirley and I sat side by side on the top step, like two survivors of a tornado. Elvis tried to crawl onto my lap. His head lay heavy across my knees. We were still sitting in exhausted silence when a car came roaring down the driveway and screeched to a halt in front of the house.

Alan's headlong advance halted briefly when he saw us. Then he ran up the stairs and dropped down beside me. "You're all right! I passed the ambulance, and I was afraid. . . ."

I crawled onto his lap, in the same manner and for the same reason Elvis had tried to crawl onto mine. "It's good to see you," I said inadequately.

My account of the night's proceedings left even Alan at a loss for words momentarily. Only momentarily, though.

"It's a wonder you didn't have a stroke yourself. To see her there like that, when you thought she was incapable of getting out of bed, much less walking—"

"I knew she was trying to strengthen her muscles, but I had no idea she had been so successful. She must be senile! Why would she sneak and deceive us? Giving Shirley her own sleeping pills so she wouldn't know—"

"It's not senility, it's pure meanness," Alan said. "I know I shouldn't speak ill of the dead, but . . ."

"She isn't dead yet." I started to rise. "I had better call Matt, and get dressed, and go to the hospital."

Alan's arms closed around me. "You aren't going anyplace except to bed." He rose in one smooth movement, lifting me like a child. Then he turned to Shirley, who was staring at us, her eyes still heavy with sleep. "Alone," he added, smiling. "She's too pooped for hanky-panky tonight."

Shirley produced a weak answering smile. "I'm pretty pooped myself; I wouldn't know what anybody else was up to. I'll telephone Matthew. It's up to him if he wants to go to the hospital, but there's nothing any of you can do for her."

I clung to Alan after he had lowered me gently onto my bed, but he stepped back, shaking his head and smiling. "Shameless woman! You look like a demure, old-fashioned girl with your hair loose on the pillow; try to act like one. Until tomorrow, anyway."

"What happens tomorrow?"

"Anything you want. Don't you understand—you are free now. This is the end. Whether she lives or dies, you'll never have to live in this house again."

Relief spread through me like a wave of sunlight. I had not had time to consider the consequences of the night's terror.

"Do you want one of those sleeping pills?" Alan asked.

"No, I don't need one. I feel . . . It's as if some dark cloud that had hung over me were gone."

"A hurricane named Martha," Alan said rudely. "Sleep well, my dearest. I'll go and tuck Shirley in too, she looks exhausted. She won't get this, though . . ."

"Poor Shirley," I murmured.

I was awakened next day by Shirley's voice raised in protest. But it was not Shirley's face I saw when I opened my eyes.

"Matt," I said. "Go away, Matt."

"I told him not to wake you," Shirley said. "Here's that coffee, Matthew, but you hadn't ought to—"

"It's after noon." Matt sat down on the edge of the bed. I groaned in protest and tried to pull the sheet over my head. He removed it and tickled my chin. Another trick from the good old days.

"I'm sorry, honey, I really am." But his broad smile belied his considerate speech. "You had a hell of a night, I know," he went on. "But there are things that need to be done. Have some coffee."

"Matthew, you just come on out of here," Shirley insisted.

"It's all right." I dug both fists into my eyes and yawned

till I thought my jaws would split. Matt plumped the pillow behind me and helped me sit up.

"Keep your hands to yourself, buster," I said half-jokingly.

Matt grinned. "I'm only human. You look good in the morning, Julie. A lot better than—"

"Please don't recite the list. Just give me that cup of coffee."

A snort of disapproval from Shirley indicated her opinion of Matt's behavior. She stomped out.

Matt sat beside me, watching me. There was something different in his expression—a new speculation, curiosity, interest. It made me uncomfortable.

"You're very cheerful this morning," I said. "Is she dead?"

Matt didn't pretend to be shocked. "No," he said gloomily. "But my God, she can't go on like this forever."

"What did the doctor say?" Shirley's coffee, like everything she made, was excellent. I felt more kindly toward Matt; not every man would have thought of bringing coffee to mitigate the pain of waking. And I surely didn't blame him for refusing to play the hypocrite about Martha. She had never wanted or earned love. It had been her choice, not ours, that she was dying with no one to mourn her.

"You know how those damned doctors hedge and quibble," Matt said. "She'll have another stroke eventually—maybe today, maybe a year from now—it will be the last—maybe it won't . . . How can they be so vague?"

"You, a politician, complain about vagueness? Really, Matt, how can they commit themselves? The odds are against her living much longer, but individuals sometimes beat the odds. And her heart is in good shape."

"Well, I've made up my mind about one thing," Matt

said. "She isn't coming back here. Now that the Judge isn't around to back her up, I can put her in a nursing home, which is where she should have been all along. I should never have asked you to take this on in the first place. I hope it's not too late for you to get another job?"

The question took me by surprise. My new freedom had not sunk in yet; I had not had time to think about the future. "I won't be going home," I said. And then, before he could react, because I had to tell someone—"Alan and I are—well, we're back together. We haven't made any plans yet, but unless he throws me out, I'll be around. There's a good chance he may get funding for the excavation, and I can help him with that."

"So that's what Shirley was hinting at," Matt said. He looked not so much disapproving as thunderstruck. "I didn't realize . . ."

"I hope you aren't going to object. Not that it would make the slightest difference if you did."

"Object," Matt repeated. His face cleared as if by magic, but there was a wistful quality in his smile. "Honey, if that's what you want, I'm delighted. You're sure?"

"Yes. Oh yes."

"Just as well. I was beginning to get some mildly incestuous feelings about you." He saw my face change and added, laughing, "I'm kidding—I think. . . . What a prude you are! Our grandmother married her first cousin."

"She made a big mistake," I said.

"Forget it. I only wish you luck."

He kissed me, with fraternal chasteness, on the brow.

"Well, to business," he said briskly. "I'm going back to the hospital in a little while. Want to come along?"

"No, I think not. I ought to call Mother, though."

"I was going to, but I thought you'd prefer to talk to her yourself."

"How about Aunt Julia?"

Matt laughed shortly. "She said to let her know if there was any change."

Mother had a summer virus. I'm sure she really believed she had. I told her there was no need to rush to her mother's bedside, since the doctors were equivocating about Martha's condition. "You will let me know if there is any change," she said. That euphemism again.

It was a wonderful day, the sort of summer day that is a feature of books about Old Virginny, and that seldom ever occurs. The only thing that kept me from going out to lie in the sun with a soft breeze caressing my body was the fact that I knew I would be eaten alive by ticks, chiggers, and mosquitoes. And the only fly in the ointment was the knowledge that I wouldn't see Alan that day. He had called earlier, while I was still asleep, to say that he had had to go to Washington, but that he would call again that evening. It looked as if the funding he wanted might be coming through. He had told Shirley not to wake me, but I wished I could have heard his voice.

Matt was scrounging around in Martha's room. I didn't know what he was looking for. He had invited me to join him, but I had refused; I couldn't pretend to be fond of Martha, but there was something unseemly about going through her most private possessions while she still clung to life.

So I went to work on the cast. At least it reminded me of Alan. But I had to admit ours was a peculiar romance if the fondest memento I could find of my beloved was a human skull.

I was smoothing clay over the cheekbones when I heard Matt calling. Just like Matt, I thought irritably—standing perfectly still at the far end of the house and yelling for what he wanted. I yelled back and went on working. He came clattering down the stairs, continuing to call out. "Where the hell are you?"

"I'm in here," I shouted.

I heard his footsteps falter and halt in the doorway. I didn't turn around. "What is it?" I asked.

"I thought . . . Shirley told me that god-awful thing got broken," Matt said.

"It was just a copy—a cast. This is another of the same. You didn't suppose the sheriff would hand over the original, did you? There are laws. You've heard about laws—passed by the legislature."

He came slowly toward the table with the fastidious delicacy of a cat edging toward a suspicious object. "I don't make a specialty of human skeletons. How can you stand to—to caress that gruesome thing?"

"*Chacun à son goût,* as the French say. Did you find anything interesting in Martha's room?"

" 'Fraid not." Matt leaned against the closet door, his eyes fixed in unwilling fascination on the half-completed face. "I thought maybe she had squirreled away some cash. You read all the time about little old ladies who tuck hundred-dollar bills in copies of Dickens and Sir Walter Scott, or in their corset drawers."

I had to admire his candor, even if I didn't admire his ethics. "Are you going to the hospital now?" I asked.

Matt pried himself off the closet door. "I can take a hint. Look here, Julie, why don't you send Shirley home and go to a motel tonight?"

It was a kindly thought that I had not expected. But I had already considered, and dismissed, the idea. "It wouldn't be wise to leave the house empty, Matt. It's no different now than it was before; it was always me and Shirley, and she's agreed to stay on until . . . until something happens."

Another euphemism. It was a hard habit to break.

Matt nodded. "Okay. Is Alan spending the night?"

"No, he is not."

"Don't be so defensive. I had hoped he would be here; I'd feel better."

"He's in Washington," I said, relenting. "It's okay, Matt, really. Let me know if anything . . . Let me know."

Shirley and I celebrated by going out to supper. Of course I didn't use that word when I invited her; I felt ashamed even thinking it. But it was like a celebration, to get out of the house, and she seemed to enjoy herself. She consented to join me in a drink; the liquor loosened her tongue and we had a good, confidential chat. She wasn't worried about finding another job. There was plenty of demand for a woman with her skills. I said I'd ask Alan if he could find a place for Ron among the football players, and Shirley's face lit up.

The sun had set and twilight was thickening in the trees when we got back. At Shirley's suggestion we had left a few lights burning to discourage unwelcome callers, but they looked lonesome and isolated in that looming dark pile. The chimneys brooded over the house like giant figures of gods or demons, remote and detached from human passions.

The telephone was ringing when I opened the front door. It continued to peal insistently while I ran to the kitchen. As I had hoped, it was Alan. "Where have you been?" he asked.

"Shirley and I went out to dinner."

"The funeral baked meats?"

"I'm afraid it was rather like that, if a bit premature. How did things go?"

There was a pause, and my heart started to sink. Then Alan said, in a strangely quiet voice, "I'm on a roll. First you, and then this . . . I'm almost afraid to believe it. I didn't dream it, did I—yesterday, in the attic?"

"If you did, we dreamed the same thing. Oh, Alan, I'm so glad. You got it?"

"The works. Funding for the rest of the season—six months, unless the weather takes a weird turn—full staff, complete publication costs . . ."

"Tell me more."

"Not over the phone. I can't wait to see you. I'm starting back in half an hour."

"Be careful."

We exchanged a few more remarks, none of which are pertinent, and I went galloping upstairs to tell Shirley.

"All the way from Washington tonight? The man must be crazy."

Her sympathetic smile made it a joke. I threw my arms around her. "Why don't you go home, Shirley? He'll be here in a few hours, and I know you miss your kids."

"No, ma'am." She shook her head decisively. "I'm not leaving you all alone here, not for five minutes. I think I will go to bed, though. It's been a tiring day. I'll sleep like the . . . I'll sure sleep sound tonight."

"Tactful woman." I hugged her again. "You go on. I think I ought to call the hospital."

The word was "no change." I asked if the senator was there, and was told he had left, but would probably look in later. Having heard the news, or the lack thereof, Shirley went to her room with one of my mystery stories, and I went downstairs.

It felt strange to wander the house without worrying about Martha's prohibitions and complaints—leaving all the doors open, letting Elvis explore as he pleased. He knew things had changed; there was confidence in the way he held his head, and his tail never stopped moving.

Alan would be hungry and tired if he drove straight through. I hoped he would have sense enough to stop for coffee occasionally—and I hoped he wouldn't, that he would come as quickly as he could. I explored the refrigerator, thinking he might like a sandwich, or soup, or something. I got out the cherished sherry and polished two of the precious crystal glasses. This night would be our celebration—the first chance we had had to linger over loving, to plan ahead and toast the future.

I was glad I had furnished the little room near the kitchen. Private and distant from the rest of the house, it was a perfect trysting place for illicit lovers . . . I wondered why that adjective had come to my mind. A touch of ESP from Shirley, perhaps? Or from Martha. She was miles away, lying in the dim borderline between life and death, but a shadow of her presence still permeated the house, and it always would, for those of us who had known her domineering presence. Perhaps that was the true kind of haunting—the memory of the dead in the minds of the living. In the same way, memory was the only certain form of immortality. Like the old couple in *The Blue Bird,* who woke from the dreamless sleep of death only when their children and grandchildren remembered them.

I stirred uneasily. Morbid thoughts, from a woman eagerly awaiting her lover. I was anxious, perhaps. It was pure superstition to think that something might happen now, just when we were on the verge of the happiness denied us for five long years. Yet I had an odd sense of urgency—of something vitally important I had forgotten to do.

Forcing myself to a brisk, purposeful walk, I went to my room and switched on the light. It didn't take long to straighten the spread and sweep the floor. I had five hours to fill—four, if Alan risked a citation and his precious neck, and drove as fast as he probably would.

I took the cast out of the closet and set to work. I was killing time, not trying to finish—though it would have been fun to have a completed piece of work to show Alan. I hoped, though, that he would have other things on his mind.

I was vaguely aware of Elvis padding into the room and collapsing onto the rug with a comfortable thud. The air felt heavy and thick; the clouds we had seen gathering as we drove back after dinner would be denser now, raising the humidity, threatening rain. Outside the window, a soft gray mist softened the outlines of the shrubbery. The crickets were practicing for a concert. Peaceful, familiar sounds—and under it all was that rising demand, peremptory and undefined.

My fingers went on moving in automatic precision as my thoughts ran down a list of duties I might have neglected. Telephone calls made, doors and windows locked, stove and appliances turned off . . . The door of my room was open. Though it was hours too early, I was listening for the sound of a car. There was no cause for concern, not with Elvis snoring on the rug. He would hear a suspicious noise long before I did; I'd have time to reach the telephone or lock myself in, whichever seemed best.

Had it been Martha who had entered this room the night before last? No, surely not. She had proved herself capable of moving around unaided; heaven only knew how often she had prowled the dark halls on nameless and unsuspected errands—but she could never have mustered the physical strength to fend off the dog and run at full speed around the house and back in an open door or window.

Mrs. Danner? Shirley's first act that morning had been to call and tell her she was no longer needed. Was she as lumpishly void of feeling as she appeared, or did her phlegmatic manner conceal rage and frustration that sometimes boiled over into violence?

Joe Danner? I had no doubt he was capable of violence, and equally capable of justifying his acts in terms of his own narrow religious creed. Had his discovery of the displaced skeletons been accidental, or was there some connection I did not fathom? What were his real feelings toward the old woman who had ruled him all his life— blind devotion, or bitter resentment?

The names repeated themselves over and over in my mind. Rose Danner and her husband, Mrs. Hornbeak, Ron, the "crazy kids" of Jarboe's theory; Rose Danner, Joe, Mrs. Hornbeak . . . Which of them? Or an unknown, driven by motives as yet unsuspected?

It seemed to me that I had only been working for a few minutes when my hands stopped moving; but my muscles ached with stiffness, as if I had been sitting in the same hunched position for hours. Tendrils of white mist plucked at the bars of the window like boneless fingers. The clock on the bedside table said twenty minutes after one. And on the table, facing me, was the completed cast, finished even to the wig, which my hands had just put in place.

I had set false eyelashes to frame the wide brown eyes and sketched eyebrows with brown paint. The parted lips were tinted pink, and a wash of paler pink covered the heavy cheekbones. The hair was thick and brown; it fell in heavy masses to where the shoulders should have been. And the features that confronted me, like an image in a mirror, were my own.

fourteen

I had lost three hours—hours in which my hands had moved independently of my mind, with a skill and precision that verged on the miraculous.

I sat back in the chair, my stiffened muscles creaking in protest, and let my hands fall into my lap. I could see the pulse beating frantically in my wrists. The only thing that kept me from fleeing the dreadful reflection of my living features was the peaceful breathing of the dog.

Gradually my own breathing slowed, and sick disappointment replaced superstitious terror. Absorbed in egotistical meditation, I had unconsciously reproduced the features I knew best—mine. The fact that the wig resembled my thick straight hair was pure coincidence; naturally Alan had selected a neutral style that could be dressed in a number of different coiffures.

I had, in short, screwed up. It wasn't a catastrophe; Alan had the mold, we could make other casts. But I hated to have him see how badly I had failed. My hand went out, fingers clawed, to tear off the damp clay.

Something stopped me, like an invisible hand closing gently but inexorably over mine. Not the sound—that came a few seconds later, as I struggled to complete the act of destruction I had contemplated. The sound was that of a soft footstep.

I was afraid to turn around. I could feel the presence, like a block of ice in the open doorway, exuding waves of cold air that brought goosebumps out on my bare arms. The dog had not barked. He had not barked the night before, when he sensed a living power of evil in the hall outside my door.

The paralysis that held me snapped, as if someone had cut ropes binding my body. I turned.

She wore the long gray flannel robe I had last seen hanging on a hook inside the wardrobe in her room. One hand held a heavy cane. I had seen that before too. A scarf or shawl, thrown over her head, shadowed her features— the bony, protruding nose, the wrinkled skin, and sagging cheeks.

The figure came rushing toward me. I managed to get out of the chair, though my knees felt like rusty hinges. I stumbled back, raising my arms to shield my face. The cane crashed down on my head.

I couldn't have been out for more than a minute. When I woke up I was huddled on the floor under the window. The hands of the clock said one twenty-five. The door was closed and the key was gone from the lock. On the floor, between me and the door, were a hundred fragments of plaster and clay and paint, mixed with the tangled hair of the wig.

The bump on the head had knocked the cobwebs out of my brain. In the initial shock I had half believed in the incredible; but I knew I had not seen Martha's ghost, sent speeding out into the night at the moment of her death.

Strong, living muscles had brought the heavy stick down on my head. And a living mind had made one fatal mistake.

The cast was the second one to be demolished. The cast, not my worthless person, had been the object of the invasion of my room. That fact could be the key to the puzzle. I felt as if the answer were almost in my hands—that I could see it hanging in the air over my head, that if I reached up I could touch it.

Finding the answer was all I could do. I couldn't get out of the room, nor should I have had any desire to do so. The mysterious figure didn't want to hurt me, it wanted me to stay locked up until it had finished its task. It had hidden its face behind a Halloween mask so I couldn't identify it. So long as I stayed where I was, I was safe. I wasn't concerned about Elvis either, though he had vanished, without making a sound. I knew why he had not barked.

I reached for the bars to pull myself to my feet. As my fingers closed over the rusted, pitted metal, a horrible feeling of claustrophobia clamped down on me. I had never suffered from any such thing, so the sensation was all the more terrifying. Part of my mind clung to the knowledge that my safety depended on remaining in the room, but another part moaned, "I can't get out—I can't get out . . ." and shook the bars with bleeding fingers.

Then all at once there was a great quiet, in my mind and in the room.

White mist lay along the ground, but high overhead the moon rode bright and perfect, dominating a blazing tapestry of stars. Blurred by the fog and by the branches of the shrubs, another light moved like a fallen moon, rolling down the slope behind the house, in the direction of the cemetery. And in my hand I held a rusted iron bar. It had not been wrenched away by the superhuman strength of desperation; it had been loosened over fifty years ago.

"All right," I said. I wasn't talking to myself. "All right."

I went to the closet and opened the door. Alan had used a hammer and drill and screwdriver when he installed the lock; being lazy, I had put them in the closet instead of carrying them back to the shed. I hoped I wouldn't need a weapon, but one never knows. I took the hammer.

Then, almost as if some other mind were moving my body, I got down on my knees and lit a match. I held it low, so that it illumined the narrow strip of wall inside the closet door. The letters would have been invisible in direct light; only the infinitesimal shadow cast by the flame made them stand out. A name and a date, and two scrawled words: "Remember me."

With the bar removed, I was able to get out the window. It was a tight squeeze. It had been tight for her too . . .

I walked through a fallen cloud that softened nearby objects as in a Japanese painting. Far above, the moon shone and the stars were alight.

The wrought iron gate of the graveyard was open. The worn gray stones showed dark in the shrouding fog. A shadowy form stooped and rose, stooped and rose again in its ghoulish task. I could hear him breathing heavily. Each shovelful of earth thudded as he tossed it onto the rising heap. How long would it take him? They had laid her six feet deep, but the earth over her was soft, unpressed by time or weather.

A vagrant gust of wind set the mist swirling and left him exposed. He had thrown off the long robe in order to work more easily. The mask was gone too—no more need for it—but if I hadn't known who he was I would not have recognized him. Dirt and perspiration streaked a face distorted by emotion into a caricature of the one I had known.

I saw something else in that parting of the fog that brought a brief touch of low comedy to the scene, like the gravedigger in *Hamlet*. No wonder Elvis hadn't warned me of the intruder. Elvis knew a pal when he saw one, and Elvis knew which side his dog biscuits were buttered on. The digger paused for a moment, panting for breath. His hand went to his pocket, and Elvis, poised and ready, caught the thrown tidbit as it dropped toward him. He crunched it and sat back, waiting for another.

The intensity of his cupboard love had kept him from noticing me. Then the wind swirled again, coming from behind me, and my faithful dog bounded toward me, barking rapturously.

I couldn't let the gravedigger complete the task he had begun. Once the object he wanted was destroyed, there was no legal proof of what I had discovered. A court of law wouldn't accept a plaster cast as evidence without the original from which it was made. I couldn't explain even to myself why it was so important that I prevent him; it was a given, like an axiom in geometry. I had not considered how I could stop him without risking another knock on the head, from a weapon much heavier than the cane. I might have had a bright idea, though, if Elvis had not betrayed me.

I knelt to embrace him. "I'm glad you're all right, you idiot," I said softly. "Hell of a watchdog you turned out to be."

"Don't run away, Julie." The voice echoed oddly in the heavy air. "I can run faster. How did you get out?"

"One of the bars was loose."

"Oh. You should have stayed where you were. I don't want to hurt you."

"Good, because I don't want you to. Why are you doing this, Matt? What possible difference can it make to anyone now?"

He lifted his lantern and set it atop one of the gravestones, adjusting it so that the light struck straight into my eyes. I shielded them with my hand.

"Why does it matter to you?" he asked reasonably. "You ought to be helping me, Julie. It's your family too—your shame, your disgrace."

"The only disgrace is hiding the truth. The crime itself—if it was a crime, and not simply a brutal, selfish piece of stupidity—wasn't yours or mine. But if we conceal a crime, we are committing an immoral act, and that is our responsibility."

"Very noble," Matt sneered. "But very impractical. If this came out, it could ruin my career."

I felt sure he was wrong. But my opinion didn't count. He believed it and he was willing to break the law to prevent disclosure. Nor could I deny that there was something in his point of view. Why drag out an old tragedy, when the perpetrator could never be punished and only the innocent might suffer?

I had no answer. I only knew what must be done.

"Tell you what," I said, with false heartiness, "let's go back to the house and talk about it."

"Fine. As soon as I finish here."

I started impulsively forward, and Matt laughed. "Trying to trick me, weren't you? No dice, dear Cousin. Once I've disposed of this—" the shovel lifted and pointed—"there's not a damned thing you can do."

From Elvis, crouched at my feet, came a muffled whimper. He was confused. The tones of our voices, perhaps the scent from our bodies, warned him that his friends weren't friendly any longer. He didn't know what to do.

I didn't know either. The hammer was no damned good to me; he could knock me flat, with the shovel or his fists, before I got close enough to use it.

I turned and ran.

He was after me like a flash. The mist was clearing on the higher ground; it offered no shelter, and the moon was too high, too bright. Elvis kept pace with me. He had completely lost his head and was baying like the hound he basically was. In the brief intervals between howls I heard Matt's feet thudding in pursuit. He was right; he could run faster than me.

I couldn't leave the path, the brush on either side was sticky with brambles and twined with wild grapevines, tight as a fence. Ahead, at the top of the rise, I saw the end of the path, where it opened on to the weedy lawn. It looked like a bright cloth woven of mist and moonlight. I don't know why it should have seemed a haven, for there was no safety and no shelter on the open ground, but it was a goal and I hurtled toward it, hearing the following footsteps come closer and closer. I broke out into the light—and fell over Elvis, who had finally got it through his thick skull that I was running away from someone who wanted to hurt me. Turning, with a mighty howl, he flung himself at my pursuer.

Flat on the ground, expecting at any second to feel the edge of the spade shatter my skull, I heard a hollow thud, and a squawl from Elvis. I raised myself on my elbows and rolled over. He loomed above me, a dark shape against the moonlit sky. He stooped, hands extended. I grabbed his leg with both arms, and pulled.

He toppled backward. I got to my feet. He sat up. The moonlight fell full on his face.

"Jesus Christ," he yelled. "What the bloody hell is going on here?"

Matt lay sprawled in the grass, his arms outflung, the shovel across his legs. Elvis doubtfully contemplated the thoughtless person who had stepped on his tail; should he resent the injury or forgive it, in view of past favors?

"My hero," I said, between tears and laughter. "How did you get here so fast?"

"I flew," Alan said.

"Angels do that," I agreed.

It wasn't the welcome I had planned. We drank the sherry, since it was at hand, and all the while Matt sat huddled on the bed in my room, with his hands over his face. Both of us talked about him as if he weren't there, which in a sense he wasn't.

"I'm sure he never meant to hurt me," I said.

"Yeah? I suppose he was brandishing that shovel for the exercise. Thank God for the dog; it was his barking that led me to the cemetery, after I had pounded on the door and then looked in your window. What I saw didn't exactly reassure me."

He claimed that he had suspected from the first that the burglar's aim was the destruction of the cast, but he couldn't understand why anyone would care.

"If you had seen the finished reconstruction you would have understood," I said grimly. "I thought at first I had goofed—copied my own face. Then I realized it wasn't mine. It was Melissa's."

The family features were distinctive; how many times had I been told that? If she had lived, if there had been those who remembered her, they'd have told me I was the spitting image of Melissa as a girl. Martha remembered. No wonder she loathed me! The Judge remembered too.

How much of the truth had he known? At the end, I felt sure he had known the whole story. Martha must have told him on the last night of his life, and the shock of it had killed him—one way or another. His dying message was for her, not for me: a promise of silence. And before his failing heart—or some other means—had freed him from the burden of guilty knowledge, he had sent me a remembrance. He never meant to betray Martha, but it had seemed right to him, as it did to me, that someone should remember Melissa.

I opened the envelope he had sent me. The message was a single photograph—the only picture of Melissa that had survived. Martha must have destroyed all the others.

I handed it to Alan. The two sisters stood side by side, one on either side of the lawn chair on which their mother was enthroned. She reminded me of Martha, not because their features were so similar, but because of their matching expressions. Martha stared unsmiling at the camera. The straight, unfitted clothes she wore did not flatter her stocky figure.

Melissa must have been about sixteen. She too wore a plain, old-fashioned dress, but the camera had captured her vibrant youth, her smile and shining eyes.

"I don't see it," Alan said. "There is a resemblance, but—"

How much of that mirror identity had been real and how much a product of—well, call it sympathetic imagination? Call it what you would, I had felt her presence that night—her desperation, her fear, her short-lived flight.

"It was strong enough to enable her to be identified," I said. "Once the family resemblance was noted, people would have started asking questions. They have long memories in this region; they pass stories down from parent to child. Shirley knew about Melissa. Run off with a traveling man, that was what Martha told everyone. No one heard of her, or from her, again. Martha lied about receiving letters and postcards from her."

"But it was an outside chance," Alan argued. He glanced contemptuously at the hunched, silent figure on the bed. "He risked so much for so little. Even if the story did come out, what harm could it do him?"

"Not enough to matter to anyone but him. Martha's influence over him was as strong as hers over me, but it took a wildly different form. He jeers at old traditions and drinks beer with blue-collar voters, but he dreamed of being lord of the manor again, an aristocrat with an honored name. You could say that Martha infected him with her own warped sense of pride; and hers weren't even the standards of her own time, they were those of her parents—Victorian prudery at its worst. She couldn't admit to anyone that her own sister had borne an illegitimate child to a low-down stranger who bedded her and deserted her.

"There wasn't enough money to send Melissa away, as was the custom for young ladies of good family who had committed a small error of that sort. I wonder, though, whether Martha would have done it even if she had had the money. I think she enjoyed keeping Melissa shut up here, a virtual prisoner. Delivering the child herself, under conditions that . . ."

I stopped, shivering. Even the wine couldn't warm me when I thought of that. Alan took my hand. "Julie," he said gently, "there's no evidence that Martha did anything worse. No signs of violence. Maybe Melissa died in childbirth and the baby with her."

"I wish I could believe that. I don't believe Martha planned to—to kill her. She hoped the baby wouldn't live. A lot of them died back then. If it did survive, there were ways of getting rid of it . . . Melissa wouldn't go along with the plan. Once she had seen her child, held it, she wouldn't give it up. Martha kept her locked in here—in this room. There were no servants, and this room was miles from the rest of the house; visitors wouldn't suspect anyone was here. Melissa managed to loosen one of the bars on the window. She was desperately afraid by then, for the child if not for herself. She got out. But she didn't get far."

"It's only a theory, Julie," Alan argued. "There is nothing to contradict the other version. It doesn't let Martha off the hook entirely, but once the girl was dead . . . Martha buried her secretly, somewhere in the woods?"

"And shot her own dog so it wouldn't go looking for Melissa," I said, shuddering. "That's why she wouldn't have another dog on the premises. Even after all these years she was afraid . . ."

Matt raised his head. "It was an accident. The baby died. She—Melissa—lost her mind. She was running wild in the woods, carrying her dead child, and Martha went after her to stop her, help her."

"She told you that?" Alan asked skeptically.

"Yes, a few days ago. She's been sick with remorse and regret all these years; she had to unburden herself before she died." Matt's face was serene under the streaks of dirt. His eyes were dry; they met Alan's with the apparent candor the practitioners of his profession learn how to simulate. He went on glibly, "Naturally I assumed Martha was wandering in her wits, that the story couldn't be true. Then I started to wonder. That's why I decided to disinter the remains."

"That's your story, is it?"

"I think it will play, don't you?" Matt smiled insolently. He rose, keeping a cautious eye on Alan. "I'll run along now. Perhaps I'll see you at the hospital tomorrow, Julie."

"Just a goddamn minute, you hypocritical bastard," Alan shouted, jumping up. "If you think you're going to walk away clean after what you did—"

"What precisely have I done? My intention was to return the bones to the sheriff's office so that he could re-open the investigation. Julie misunderstood. When she tore off into the dark, I went after her, to keep her from hurting herself."

"And it's your word against hers," Alan muttered.

"Correct."

"Breaking and entering—"

"A man can't be charged with breaking into his own house. Anyway," Matt added, "you can't prove it was me. Can you?"

Alan's fists clenched. "How I would love to smash that supercilious smirk down your throat," he said longingly.

"Let him go," I said. "He's too slippery for the likes of us. Next thing you know he'll be charging you with assault."

Matt sidled toward the door. Alan took a step toward him; Matt broke into a trot and disappeared.

Alan dropped onto the bed and pounded the mattress with his fist. "I hated letting him get away like that. I really hated it."

I sat down beside him. "I know, darling. What does it matter? We can always vote against him."

"Small consolation. He lied, didn't he? Martha told him—"

"The truth. He wouldn't have been so desperate to cover the story up if Melissa's death had been an accident.

He's known for a long time. Martha probably told him as soon as she could speak after the stroke. She felt it necessary to warn him, in case the police investigation turned up damaging evidence. She didn't know what they could deduce from the skeletal evidence, and neither did Matt— until I, of all people, told him!

"He had agreed to let you excavate because he hoped that would get people thinking in terms of old cemeteries instead of more recent missing persons. He made so many mistakes, I ought to have suspected him much earlier."

"I did," Alan said modestly.

"Maybe you were a trifle prejudiced."

"Who, me? You know I never allow personal opinion to color an academic judgment. No, honestly, I did suspect some kind of local scandal. I knew the skeletons couldn't be very old because I've seen what prolonged inhumation in this region does to bones. I even wondered whether Joe Danner's daughter . . ."

"I wondered too. But Shirley assured me Lynne Anne is alive and well."

"I know she is. I looked her up. But it could have been some other unfortunate girl in the same situation. Even in this so-called civilized society there are people who follow the old savage rules about women and fornication, and the curse of bastardy. I got that far in my reasoning, but the destruction of the cast baffled me. It was a futile gesture, since the cast could easily be replaced."

"You knew that, but Matt didn't, until I spilled the beans. When he found out, he realized he would have to destroy the skull itself. Without it to back up our reconstruction, the identification would be questionable."

Alan put his arm around me. "You're sure, Julie?"

"Very sure." I couldn't tell him all the reasons. That

eerie moment of identification was my secret, and my burden.

"Okay. But the other thing—how she died . . . Maybe you'd rather not talk about it."

"No, I have to get it out of my system. You're trying to help me, Alan, but it won't work. Martha killed her sister and she told Matt she had done it; the reason I'm sure is a little thing, a few words that no court would ever accept as evidence.

"Matt quoted part of a poem the day we buried Melissa and her child, in their rightful place at last. It took me a while to identify it, but I finally did, in a book that might have belonged to Melissa herself.

Let us go home, and sit in the sitting-room.
Not in our day
Shall the cloud go over and the sun rise as before . . .
The sun that warmed our stooping back and withered the weed uprooted—
We shall not feel it again.
We shall die in darkness, and be buried in the rain.

"It's a poem by Edna St. Vincent Millay, about the Sacco-Vanzetti trial. The title is 'Justice Denied in Massachusetts.'

"That's what it's all about, Alan. That's why I couldn't let him destroy her poor bones, the only evidence that she had lived and had died too soon. It's about justice denied."

Do you want to know what happened "afterward"? I wish I could tell you Matt lost his bid for reelection. Alas, he did not, and I may yet have to vote against him for governor. I doubt that Melissa's story would have damaged his chances, nor should it have done so, but in fact, the story was never made public. The district attorney's office refused to take up the case. From a practical point of view, they were quite right. The identification was questionable, there was no evidence of homicide, and every possible suspect was dead. Why waste time, when they were overburdened with contemporary crimes?

Matt continues to flourish like the green bay tree, but Joe Danner is no longer with us. A load of hay fell on him and he smothered before Mrs. Danner could dig him out. Yes, she was on the spot, helping . . . I hear she's gained forty pounds and is once again Rosie, the belle of the bars.

We finally figured out how Pauline Hornbeak located the graveyard of Maydon's Hundred. It wasn't a message from Beyond, but a combination of luck and the triumph of stupidity over scholarly subtlety. My ancestor's little book gave confused directions as to where he had found the piece of armor; in interpreting them, Alan had made too many corrections. Polly H., whose mental processes were on the same low level as Albert's, had taken him literally—and hit the jackpot. But she's never admitted it.

The case of the transported skeleton has never been officially closed, but Sheriff Jarboe admits he has no hope of solving it. "Kids grow up," he says broad-mindedly. "They won't try it again, especially with you and the prof digging all over the property."

He's satisfied he was right. I'm not. There are too many things his theory doesn't explain.

The shotgun, for example. I can easily believe Martha had kept it hidden, even from Shirley; but why was she carrying it that night? The gun was loaded. Did she plan to use it—and on whom? She hated me as she had hated the dead girl I resembled; and there were moments, toward the end, when she wasn't sure which of us she was seeing.

Had I caught a glimpse of a baby's gown, lovingly hand-sewn and embroidered, in the trunk in Maidenwood's attic? There is no tiny white garment there now. The trunk is empty. But there was something in it once—something that drew Martha up the attic stairs, month after month for unnumbered years. I wonder what she saw when she lifted the lid of the humpbacked trunk. Why didn't she destroy the clothes—or bury them with the bodies? And isn't it a little too much of a coincidence that the boys who found the skeleton—according to Jarboe's theory—should also happen upon the very garments they had worn when they died?

Too many questions . . . But there is another reason why I reject the sheriff's comfortable explanation in favor of another so bizarre and so unthinkable I don't dare express it, even to Alan.

I saw Melissa that night. No—more than that—I *was* Melissa. Her terror set my heart pounding; her fear for her child shivered through my brain. I ran with her in desperate flight, through rough pastureland and tangled woods, down into Deadman's Hollow.

That was where Martha caught up with her. That was where Martha buried her and the baby. We're certain of that now. Alan found the evidence—only a few pitiful scraps of mortality and certain stains in the boggy soil . . . Never mind the details, you wouldn't want to hear them.

I remember the night I saw Martha come into the library, her hands black with the wet, muddy loam found only in low-lying places—hollows . . . It was a spring night. The same time of year Melissa died—the same day of the year—I wonder? The very hour of the same day?

I can't forget the last words Martha spoke. I can't help believing, against all common sense and all reason, that they were not the delirious mutterings of the dying, but a literal statement of fact. You see, Martha died a few days after the events I have described. She was conscious at the end, and she asked for me. But I don't think she knew who I was. I alone heard her last words. As I bent over the bed, her eyes opened and focused with the same dark hatred that was all I had ever known from her. Her lips parted.

"Again, Melissa. Every year you come back . . . the same day, the same place . . . I burn your clothes. Not once, but every year. Every year I dig the grave . . . *Why won't you and your bastard brat stay where I put you?*"